To Julie,
with warmest regards,

Stéphane

My Odyssey

Southampton, June 16, 2003

My Odyssey

Stephane Groueff

Writers Advantage
New York Lincoln Shanghai

My Odyssey

Writers Advantage
an imprint of iUniverse, Inc.

For information address:
iUniverse
2021 Pine Lake Road, Suite 100
Lincoln, NE 68512
www.iuniverse.com

ISBN: 0-595-25709-7

Printed in the United States of America

I dedicate this book to the memory of my brother Simeon ("Boubi"), who chose the much harder road.

Table of Contents

viii   MY ODYSSEY

PREFACE TO "MY ODYSSEY"

Ever since he was a child, my son Paul loved to ask questions about my past. "Dad, being a Bulgarian and an American citizen, how come you became a *French* journalist?…Tell me about Bulgaria, why did you leave and why don't you go there any more?…Is it true that Grandpa was tried and executed?…When and how did you and Mom meet?…Is it true that before that you had a fiancee in Ireland?" He was a boy with great curiosity and over the years the questions multiplied. "And poor Uncle Boubi, why doesn't he come and live here, instead of suffering the misery and the labor camps there?…What did *you* have to do with the atom bomb?…Show me your photos from the South Pole again!"…He loved hearing about my expeditions with oceanographers in the Pacific, about the American gangsters I had done research on, about movie stars that I knew, about my visits to scientific laboratories and giant telescopes. "How?…When?…Why?"

I thought that one day my grandchildren might ask similar questions, but there might be no one to answer, so I sat down to write. And before I knew it, I became so involved in my memories and in rereading the hundreds—nay, thousands!—of old letters, pictures and notes, which I kept for 55 years, that this supposedly private and amusing family project turned into a voluminous memoir.

My wife Lil teases me that she warns friends never to ask me, just out of politeness, "How are you?" or "How do you do?" unless they dispose with considerable time and patience. "Because Stephane just waits for that to start really telling you in detail how he is and exactly what he's doing"…Like many wives, she exaggerates, of course, but maybe my reputation for being long-winded isn't entirely without foundation, when you think that it took me 650 full pages to answer my son's simplest question: "Dad, where did you come from and how did you end up here, in New York?"

Writing an autobiography is a very special task, a literary genre new to me. It requires considerable courage and has its own rules, motivation, risks and rewards. One of the difficulties for me was overcoming my reluctance to undress in public, my hesitations about sharing very personal experiences and reveal intimate thoughts and feelings. But without them, any memoir would be incomplete, insincere, and, let's face it, boring for the reader. However, what are the limits an author should observe? This, of course, is a matter of personal judgment, a question of discretion, self-respect, upbringing, and consideration of other people's private lives. There are no objective standards for this kind of thing and in the end it all boils down to one's own sense of decency and good taste. Many times my doubts and scruples were so overwhelming that I stopped writing, feeling neither the desire nor the moral justification to continue. Most painful for me was describing the personal drama and psychological disquietude of my beloved brother, which, alas, had always been a dark cloud in my otherwise happy life. When I reached these poignant, extremely personal episodes, I had no heart to continue and for a year or two I stopped writing altogether, although Boubi, after reading the drafts I had sent to him, had given me his full approval to publish them. I had to wait for the sad end of his life, before I took up my pen again.

Some readers may be surprised that in memoirs, telling about the suffering of my family and friends, about my career as a journalist and writer, about my political activity in exile and similar "serious" themes, such a large place has been devoted to frivolous happenings, romantic stories, and anecdotes. I had my doubts myself about the propriety of recounting such intimate and sometimes superficial experiences. But those who have the patience to keep on reading will discover that my odyssey is a good illustration of the old truth that, for better or worse, each and every step in our lives has some influence on the next one and that nothing happens entirely by chance, but follows some laws of cause-and-effect. Would I have, for instance, ever met Lil if I hadn't been such a passionate skier? Isn't my first journalistic success described in Chapter 17 related to the romantic fantasies of a new Bulgarian refugee in Paris nightclubs 8 chapters, and 6 years, earlier? Would I become a Paris-Match reporter if an Irish teenager, Neelia, hadn't appeared in chapter 11? But I'll let you read the details and convince yourselves that even the most insignificant and shallow pages may to some degree shape the events in the chapters that follow.

With so many reservations and need for delicate decisions, what makes people write autobiographies? A desire to tell the "true" version of facts from the past? A need for self-analysis of one's own life, like reviewing a home movie projected when the end is approaching? A good opportunity for self-justification? Could it be pure vanity and ego? Or looking for a catharsis, as one does in the confessional or on the psychoanalyst's couch? I think it's a little of all these things.

I tried to be as objective as possible, but fully conscious of the relativity of everything in this world. Not only the interpretations, but also the very perception of the so-called "objective facts." No memoirs can claim total impartiality, or a monopoly on "absolute truth." I wouldn't be surprised if other witnesses of events described by me at times contradict their accuracy. Some people might disagree with my impressions of certain characters and it's very possible that I have not always been right: the facts are often the same, but each one of us sees them from a different point of view and puts the accent on different place. Therefore, let's not read these memoirs as an infallible testimony of the ways things really were, but rather as a subjective recalling of how I saw the world, the events, and the people, with my eyes at that time.

STEPHANE GROUEFF

PROLOGUE.

Trouville, August 1946.

The printed sheet that nearly reduced me to tears at the hotel's desk that day in Trouville was certainly no great piece of lyric poetry, nor some nostalgic sunset picture which could have reminded me of my pitiable condition. If this were the case, emotions would be understandable for a rather sensitive young man of 24, especially one with my history, a man no stranger to occasional bouts of exaggerated sentimentality. (At Geneva University, the girls used to tease us, we Bulgarian students, about our *"ame slave,"* the Slav soul…) No, the piece of paper that burst the dam where tons of self-pity had been accumulating during the last two years, was nothing more than a dull registration form, poorly printed on cheap, wartime-ration paper. "Name and surname," asked the first line, as I dipped the pen into the old-fashioned inkwell. And then…

Then, I was stuck. "Permanent address," was the second question. What should I write?—I had no address, no home any place. The questions continued: "Nationality, Number of Passport." Yes, by the way, what nationality was I? I had arrived in Paris three days ago with my old Bulgarian passport, but it was now not valid, and, after the horrors that happened at home, I certainly was not about to apply for a new, Communist passport! The next line read "Profession." How should I answer that one? My friend Christo G. had promised to take me as a trainee at the new company he said he was forming in Paris, and that's was why I had come to France. But that company was not yet formed.

The only line I was able to fill in was the one asking for "Date and Place of Birth." But no sooner had I written the words "Sofia, Bulgaria," and the old haunting vision reappeared. It had followed me relentlessly from Geneva, and through Paris, and all the way to this sea resort, always the same, cruelly vivid and upsetting: the distressed faces of my family, their frightened eyes begging me: "Help us, Stefcho, please, please help!" Where were they right now? Were they alright, were they free or under arrest, did they have a place to sleep and something to eat?

Maybe one of them—mama, Radka, Simeon—was dying at this minute, or had already died? Had anyone buried my father after the execution? And what could I do for them? The guilt was matching the pain and the sense of helplessness.

It was at that precise instant that the realization of having become nobody, of being all alone in the world, a refugee not belonging anywhere, struck me full face. Now, away from the friends I left in Switzerland and who had helped me to survive by softening the blows, the whole truth of my situation appeared to me for the first time in all its upsetting clarity. I had no family, no home, no citizenship, no country, and, of course, not a penny. Suddenly, I felt sorry for myself, pathetically sorry. I was desperately lonely. I was lost.

It occurred to me that at this moment not a soul in the world knew where I was: I had come to Trouville on a sudden impulse, simply because my hosts in Paris were still vacationing on the Cote-d'Azur, and Paris in late August is very hot and empty, especially when one doesn't know anyone there. I had read some ads about the charms of nearby Deauville beaches. I had nothing else to do and I hadn't seen the sea for such a long time, so it sounded like a dream. But it was too expensive for me. Trouville was cheaper, I learned, and the next morning, after a rather lonely night in Paris, I found myself at the railroad station.

It's a peculiar, dizzy sensation, this feeling of being totally incognito, being unmoored and on your own, becoming an anonymous flotsam that no one will notice and, as a matter of fact, would care about. Sad, in my case, and quite frightening. I was ashamed, a young man with a law diploma in his pocket, to be overcome by tears at a hotel reception desk! But I shouldn't have been. Now that I know better, I actually feel sorry for those who cannot cry in private. Self-pity is not a cure, but it definitely has a soothing effect, similar to the consolation a crying child finds on his mother's shoulder. I wouldn't knock self-pity, I think it's God's charitable gift to those, motherless in life, who suffer. And it has, no doubt, its little satisfaction. Some people have a tendency to overdo it: Russians, for example, as Dostoyevski tells us, elevated self-pity to an art form. But applied in small doses, it does relieve pain.

But as I was pitying myself over the registration form, I was surprised to realize that, at the same time, another, and quite different, feeling was unexpectedly getting hold of me. It may sound absurd, but I felt a sort of liberation, almost exhilaration that, from now on, everything in life was becoming possible; that exciting things, or disasters, marvelous adventures, or painful ordeals—everything—could happen to me. Now I was free to act any way I would choose, without anybody watching me, judging me, supervising me; with no one to give account to, explain to, or apologize to, whether I choose to be a saint or a criminal, a hard-working man or a loafer. The total freedom! The thought that anything, the most unexpected things, can and will happen tomorrow, next month, next year, cheered me up and gave me great stimulation. Nothing in life is more exciting than expectations. Alas, the thrill of contemplating a future on the verge of unfolding is the exclusive privilege of youth. One can never experience it later in life, and that's probably the one thing I mostly envy the young for.

I was lucky to be so young then, and in spite of all my sadness, I started to fantasize about exciting happy days and also, being on the immature side, about all sorts of exotic adventures—for instance, signing on as deck hand on a ship, or becoming a ski-bum, or, if I were braver, joining the French Foreign Legion. Totally ridiculous, of course, but the very thought that nobody could stop me from trying whatever I wanted, and nobody even knowing or caring, some-how excited me and made me forget my self-pitying.

I unpacked my suitcase and ran to the beach.

Curiously enough, I found something rather familiar about it. I'd never been in France before, let alone in Trouville, and yet the beach was not foreign to me. Maybe the sound of all seas—our Black Sea, and La Manche here, and the rest of the oceans—is one and the same, going uninterrupted around the globe, as the waves chase each other endlessly, since the beginning of time? The salty air smelled the same, and I recalled the familiar sensation of sizzling sand burning the soles of my bare feet, of the hot sun caressing my shoulders, of the taste of seawater in my mouth. Happy children were splashing each other noisily; ladies in bathing suits were applying cream to their suntanned skins. As in my childhood in Sozopol.

Looking closer, the differences were obvious between this beach scene out of some exquisite Boudin painting, and the more primitive beauty of a romantic

Black Sea fishing port. But for me, the feeling was similar, a feeling I had almost forgotten in the last few years. And as I lay on the hot sand, scenes from the past reappeared behind my closed eyes, memories from another life. I remembered a particular summer day in Sozopol, long time ago, and the thought of it warmed my heart.

*   *   *   *   *

Chapter 1

Sozopol, first love affair.

I still don't know why I didn't drown that day in Sozopol. Because when she suddenly switched from breaststroke to backstroke and pulled me to her, all sense of reality, including the self-preservation instinct, abandoned me and the reassuring Archimedes laws regulating the floating of solid bodies in water lost their relevance.

Solid bodies?—At that moment, my skinny, 16-year-old frame was more like a limp, heavy-breathing mess of paralyzing shyness and irresistible desire.

The water under us was deep and, in the distance, the sunbathers under the multicolored beach umbrellas were barely visible. Mesmerized, I was only seeing one thing: the eyes, into which I'd had never before the courage to stare, and the full, sensuous lips I knew so well from my feverish fantasies.

Oh, how much had I dreamed of that lady, ever since I arrived with my family for our summer vacation on the Black Sea! When I first saw her on the beach, I remember that I stopped talking in the middle of a sentence and blushed violently, as if the people with whom I was lying on the sand could see what went in my mind. Those were not very pure, avowable thoughts, and I was shocked myself by the power of their unholy fascination. Shapely girls and sex appeal have, let's face it, always been the main topic in high school conversations, as well as in the private daydreaming of most Bulgarian adolescents. But except for a fleeting glimpse in some foreign movie or the tantalizing pictures of scantily dressed sexy girls in high heels, shown in color on the pages of the *Esquire Calendar*, a highly coveted publication then, I had never seen anything resembling a boy's sex-dream-girl in the flesh. And, one should better believe it; the erotic fantasies of a red-blooded teenager are unbeatable in their creativity.

And yet, here she was, the ideal "older woman" (she must have been 25 or so), strutting down Sozopol's magnificent beach, long legs, blond hair, beautiful curves, copper suntan and all. What I found particularly thrilling was her unusually highly placed buttocks, which, added to the prancing posture of the ankles, made the lengthy legs look as if permanently wearing very high heels, even when barefooted.

For the rest of my vacation, I never found my peace of mind again. The innocent joys that the picturesque fishermen's town had been offering us every summer—the carefree mornings with friends on the hot beach, the excursions with donkeys to remote, desert beaches, the picnics at vineyards overloaded with grapes and melons, the tours in small rowboats, the fishing, the dinners at outside cafes—all this no longer seemed to satisfy me. In the morning, I couldn't wait to go to the beach, hoping to see her. There I was an absent-minded listener, a nervous wreck until she would appear with her group of "grown-ups." Then I would spend hours staring languidly at her, like a pathetic hungry puppy, torn by insecurity and desire. I had painful complexes at that age: while most of my classmates were beginning to look like men, strong and athletic, my delicate, white-skinned body was still childlike. No girl would even look at me in bathing suit, I thought, finding pretexts for keeping on my shirt whenever in mixed group on the beach. Nothing made me feel so inferior and miserable that summer as the sight of the handsome, muscular young men flocking around this enticing lady. (I'll be discreet and call her "Diana.")

It wasn't long before Diana and her group were introduced to my family and friends, casually, as we were all lying on the sand. I was, of course, petrified with timidity and all I could utter, blushing to the roots of my hair, was an awkward "Hi!" For several nights thereafter I tortured myself with bitter regrets about the missed opportunity to say all the marvelous things I had intended to say to her if we ever talked, things well rehearsed in my mind, and which would, I hoped, reveal the depth of my soul and the beauty of my feelings.

The hopeless, eager staring continued in silence. But after a few more days, I began to believe—to imagine, to hope?—that she had noticed it. Was it really at me that she looked from time to time, or was it in the general direction of my group?

Was it a coincidence when sometimes she changed her place on the sand in order to face me, or was it wishful thinking on my part? Did I see a smile on her face when I devoured her with my eyes?—I didn't know; I was too shy to meet her eyes. Until that day…

She was passing by our chaise-longues, chatting with some friends, when she suddenly stopped, greeted us and said loudly: "The water is fabulous today. We should all swim!" Then reaching for my hand: "Aren't you coming with me?" I sprung to my feet and followed her into the water. Without exchanging a word, we swam for a long time, slowly, further and further from the shore, getting nearer and nearer to each other. Until she took me into her arms. Then the impossible teenager's dream, accumulated for weeks and growing crescendo with every passing day, came true. She clasped her hand around my neck and kissed avidly my lips. Did I faint?—I'm not sure what the medical definition of fainting is, but if I did, I can say that it was a fantastically pleasant state to be in. All I remember is a Nirvana-like sensation, and an unforgettable taste of salt water combined with lipstick and sun cream. When I came to, or rather when Nature forced me to grasp for air, my heart had moved from the chest into my mouth, pulsating in an incredibly fast and loud throb. And while swimming under such conditions was rapidly turning into a disastrously perilous exercise for me, my beautiful siren didn't seem to be affected in the least, gracefully progressing toward the shore and smiling seductively to her half-drowning suitor. But the gods obviously loved a lover and the Black Sea spared my young life.

———

Unfortunately, my romance took place at the very end of our stay in Sozopol, only two or three days before we had to leave for Sofia. I saw Diana the next morning at the beach and we went out swimming again, to less deep waters this time, but we couldn't manage to be alone: her friends, as well as mine, seemed to follow us everywhere. It took me some maneuvering to approach her enough in order to touch her without being noticed, to which she reacted with an accomplice's smile and a sexy underwater hand squeeze. This was all for that day, but I was in seventh heaven in my new role of conqueror of ladies' hearts.

My ego however was deflated that afternoon during the group promenade to the windmills, when Diana walked ahead, with the "adults," courted by all those

30-and 40-year-old guys, while I strode behind with the kids, barely standing their childish talk and immature jokes. Was this my first exposure to jealousy? To top the humiliation, my mother continued calling from the "grown-ups" eche-lon: "Put on your sweaters, children, it's getting windy!" I would've been totally mortified that evening, had Diana not managed to whisper in my ear, before parting, that she would meet me alone on the beach the following afternoon.

The night was half-torment, half-ecstasy, but I suppose the satisfaction of joining the category of the heroes of *Romeo and Juliet* and *The Sufferings of Young Werter*, books which had left deep impression on me, must not have been negli-gible. Alas, the romanticism of our date the next afternoon was somehow impaired by the unexpected appearance on the empty beach of our devoted housemaid Elenka, who chose to sit, fully dressed, right next to me on the sand. I had to resort to some clumsy stratagems in order to get rid of her and join Diana, who was approaching, strutting seductively along the water. I don't think the slightest suspicion of a possible romance between the sophisticated lady and the shrimp-like boy ever crossed the mind of the virtuous Elenka.

Romantic literature hardly suffered from the lack of a recording of that day's dialogue between Diana and me. Conversation was obviously not her principal talent and as for myself, shyness had made me swallow my tongue. Trying to break the painful silence, I ventured some pathetic remarks on today's weather as compared to yesterday's, but all I received in return was a pale smile. We contin-ued walking along he water.

"We're leaving tomorrow," I finally managed to say.

"Yes, I heard your mother say so..." Silence again. "Where do you go to school?"

"The First Sofia Gymnasium." I was afraid that she would ask in what grade and changed the subject. "And where do you live?"

"In Varna." Long pause. I didn't know what to say, I felt so stupid and awk-ward, and yet hundred questions were burning my lips: who was she, what was her life, her interests, her past, was there any man in her life? And there were so many things I wanted to tell her about myself. Nothing came out. We were pac-ing the beach. Finally she took my hand. I hadn't dared even that much.

"Tell me," she whispered, half-closing her eyes. "Why do you stare at me like that on the beach? Nobody else looks at me that way." I was totally confused. She insisted: "Why? Even before we met."

"Because…" I stuttered, "Because you're so beautiful." It was hardly a very original answer, but for the first time she laughed and squeezed happily my hand

"Naughty boy!" she said teasingly in mock reproach, as she continued laughing.

At that moment Elenka stood up from her beach chair and started waiving to us.

"They're calling you. So, goodbye, if I don't see you tomorrow!"

That's how we parted, without me learning anything about her. And during the year that followed, I didn't hear anything from or about the woman who disturbed my innocent summer vacation.

Call it chance, call it predestination or fate, but why such utterly improbable things always happened to me, all my life? Granted that Bulgaria is a small country and only has a dozen of Black Sea resorts, and that eight million inhabitants is not an astronomical figure in terms of the theories of probabilities, but still…You must agree that when one arrives in Varna and on the very first day, barely having had time to change into a swimsuit at the Saint-Konstantin beach, one bumps "by chance" into the woman about whom one had fantasized during the entire year, well, one has some right to doubt about "coincidences"…

"Look who's here! I can't believe it, what a surprise! I didn't know you were in Saint-Konstantin!" She sounded happy.

"Just arrived…this morning."

"The whole family?"

"No. As a matter of fact, I'm visiting with friends. They rented rooms here in the hotel."

I was obviously extremely perturbed, but her unconcealed joy of seeing me again put me ay ease. I found her gorgeous in her bathing suit, even more attractive that I had remembered her, and the heat I felt coming from the sun-baked skin of her shoulders made me dizzy. While we were talking, her companions started calling her and as she took leave, she only asked: "What's your room's number?" Hardly believing my ears, I gave it to her. "Wait for me at 4 o'clock!" she whispered.

————————

Stage fright, I suppose, has nipped in the bud more opportunities and marvelous adventures that we can ever suspect, and we'll never know about the millions of timid souls who miss the best chances of their life by backing out just one minute before time. The look for any plausible, not too dishonoring way out, such as feigning sudden sickness before the first public speaking, or pretending that a string broke just when the long-awaited opportunity to play before an audience finally presents itself.

I was lucky that, short of a most ignominious capitulation, no retreat was possible on that gorgeous hot summer day. All my masculinity was at stake, forbidding me to surrender to the overwhelming fear of being ridiculous and showing my inadequacy that had taken hold of my virginal, totally inexperienced self. In addition, all bridges behind me were definitively burnt when I asked my friend and roommate Sava to stay away that afternoon, a request to which he reacted with unhidden admiration and envy. For the better or the worse, "the die was cast," as the cliché goes.

The excitement, as the hours passed, was unbearable and so was my apprehension. Long before 4 o'clock, I went to the room to straighten it up, to brush my teeth and comb my schoolboy's short hair, the mirror only adding to my sense of insecurity. Although ashamed to admit it to myself, I knew that nothing could've made me happier at that moment than if, for some reason, she didn't come. I usually don't have a good memory for rooms and interiors. But that simple white-walled room in the Saint-Konstantin hotel overlooking the sea remained engraved in my mind to the minutest details. I can still hear the seagulls and the sound of the waves coming through the open window, and the flapping of the curtains. I can feel the summer heat, even smell the Black Sea water in the afternoon breeze. Children's voices were heard outside and from time to time a door would slam in the corridors, but otherwise the hotel was plunged in the hot torpor of the siesta hour.

Then, the knock on the door. I let her in and greet her awkwardly, not knowing what o say, what to do. Luckily, she seems at ease and acts normally, although she doesn't say anything, just examines the room briefly with an amused eye before sitting on the edge of the bed. She's silent but her stare, suggestive to the point of indecency, makes me blush. The short, sleeveless dress is appetizingly bursting in all right places, like a tight wrapping over a luscious peach, the whitish shantung material accentuating the copper suntan of the forearms and the high-heeled legs. Standing up helplessly, I'm dizzy with excitement and desire, but at the same time paralyzed by the fear and complexes of the novice, overwhelmed by shyness.

She motions me to sit next to her. We embrace and at the first touch we are in fire, the shyness is gone. Or almost gone, luckily, some dose of shyness being an irreplaceable ingredient of the erotic. The shantung dress is removed impatiently and, like a curtain rising to a dazzling scene, the revelation strikes me in its entire splendor.

Now, I pause in the middle of this rather naughty tale to ask myself why I am relating this frivolous, although delightful, incident, when my intention was to seriously try to understand my own biography. Indeed, I hoped that recapitulating the significant episodes of my life would unable me to grasp the sense of it all, to decipher the cause-to-effect sequence (if there is really such a thing), to uncover the mechanism of the "whys," to place correctly each piece of the jigsaw puzzle. Diana with all her charms would, no doubt, be a shapely piece in anyone's jigsaw-puzzle, but when I search for the keys to the big enigma, is she, should she be, anything more than a simple vignette? By now I know that she is, and very much so, and that's why I'm talking about her. I know that something crucial happened to me that day in the Black Sea hotel. It wasn't simply the loss of virginity, which is a pretty important event in itself. Maybe it was the way it happened? I haven't checked with Dr. Freud, but I'm convinced that we are all marked for life by the circumstances of our sexual debut. Recalling this brief hot summer affair, I see the beginning of a lifelong trend, which no honest self-analysis can ignore. Trying to understand my attitude in many cases in the years to come, I often find the key in the sunny Varna hotel room.

Talking about debuts: in my case it was exultation, a taste of Nirvana that instantly made me an addict for life. Many young men were less lucky. Few of my schoolmates would admit it, but I know that their first experience was disastrous. Some more daring and precocious boys in our high school received their initiation in the shabby apartment of two whores, Nadia and Michon, who lived in the vicinity. I was too timid to try it myself, but I heard enough about the two ladies to have a good idea of the proceedings in their boudoir.

To say that they were attractive would be an overly generous exaggeration. But they were capable of offering the much coveted forbidden fruit that none of us boys had tasted. None, with the enviable exceptions such as our friend D. who, the rumor went, was regularly being awakened, since the age of 13, by the nanny of his baby-sister. The thoughtful servant would join him in bed and devote her matronly body to his sex education. Leaving out such fabulous luck, Nadia and Michon seemed to be the only available door to the dreamland every by was talking about. And the price was affordable: the ladies offered discount for students. Not so much, I guess, because of some sense of civic mission or as contribution to Bulgaria's youth, the nation's best hope for a bright future, but rather in accordance with the marketing principles of higher business volume and word-of-mouth promotion. And also because experience had taught them that the average durability of a scared schoolboy was rabbit-like, seldom exceeding two to five minutes, counted after disrobing.

The boys arrived usually in small groups. While still in the street, they tried to look tough and experienced, boasting loudly and talking dirty, to give themselves courage. Once inside the house and greeted by the hostesses in immodest negligee, they looked more like lambs headed for sacrificial ritual. "Who's first?" the lady would ask in businesslike manner. Then: "Give the money and come in!" The décor of the room is hardly aphrodisiac—the stained wall, the filthy threadbare rug, the soiled bed sheets, the rusty sink in the corner with the still wet towel, the room reeking of kitchen and perspiration. I bet that even Rubirosa or any of the proverbial studs would suffer temporary impotence there.

"What are you waiting for? Get your pants off!" The voice is decidedly not romantic. And as the robe is shed matter-of-factly and the faded forbidden fruit is within reach, the petrified boy hears the next command, cold, scornful, humiliating: "Haven't you seen a naked woman before? Hurry up, show me your little worm!" The action that follows will remain an alcove secret, and it's better to be so. But after the gallant adventure many schoolboys rush home to encyclopedias and medical books to read the chapters "Impotence" or "Premature Ejaculation," according to the case. For some of them, the self-doubt and inferiority complex caused by the experience will last for years. But you wouldn't guess it if you saw them leaving the bedroom, trying to look cool and manly. "How was it?" the waiting classmates would ask excitedly. "Faan-tas-tic! Terri-fic!" Some went overboard: "Three times, man! She finally begged me to stop. And what tits, what a lay!" After such boasting, it would be unthinkable for the boy next in line not to rave in his turn about the delights of sex, no matter how the séance with Nadia and Michon turned out to be.

But to return to my own initiation, to the moment when the last veil fell. There are few thrills in life comparable to the very first close vision and touch of a desired body, and I envy anyone who's about to experience it. A similar excitement is, thank God, relived again and again in subsequent encounters, but it will never be quite as overwhelming as the ecstasy of the original revelation. That day in Saint-Konstantin I experienced a momentary passage into another level of consciousness and discovered a new, breathtaking reality in which, for a few moments, the world became totally understandable and felt that I knew everything about Diana and about existence.

Regaining slowly consciousness, I looked around. The room became recognizable again. The sea waves resumed their roar, the curtains started flapping anew, the Earth, I suppose, resumed its rotation. Everything was the same as before, only the silk underwear on the floor, next to the hastily discarded dress, witnessed that I had not dreamed And the burning body asleep in my arms.

To her, this was probably nothing more than a whimsy, a little adventure among many others. (Although I'll never understand what attraction could a lady in the full bloom of her beauty find in a skinny, shy, and clumsy boy...) But to me, the tenderness, the avidity, and maybe some love, with which she performed the initiation ritual, determined forever my attitude to sex, God's marvelous gift.

Ever since, I believe that the ultimate, the truest, way to really know another human being is through this kind of intimacy. Maybe it's not a coincidence that the Old Testament euphemistically uses the verb "to know" when talking about making love. "Adam *knew* Eve, his wife, and she conceived and bare Cain...And Cain *knew* his wife and she conceived and bare Ednoch..."

Chapter 2

Childhood in Sofia

My very first recollection is of an explosion, a sort of a huge thunder that shook the house and terrified me. I was almost three-year-old, and from the alarm I saw in my mother's and grandmother's eyes, I sensed that something very bad had occurred. The grownups in the building rushed to the windows or to the street, looking extremely worried and asking each other "What happened? What happened?" Minutes later, my mother was crying, repeating frantically "Oh, God! Pavel is there!" Pavel was my father's name.

Something terrible had happened indeed. That day, April 16, 1925, Sofia's cathedral "Sveta-Nedelia" was blown up by a powerful explosive device, killing 160 people and maiming or wounding over 320 others. Most casualties were from the ruling circles and from the capital's elite, attending the state funeral of a prominent army general. Perpetrated by the Bulgarian Communist party and directed from the Kremlin, the monstrous crime had the sad distinction of being the first act of mass terrorism in Europe. Peacetime political terrorism became, as we now know, a common phenomenon in the 20-th century, but by its scale and its planning in cold blood the "Sveta-Nedelia" outrage remained unmatched.

These were turbulent times in Bulgaria. The country, near collapse after World War I in which it had fought on the losing side in the hope to recover territories lost in the 1913 Balkan War, was still licking its wounds. In the 6-and-a-half years of his reign, young King Boris had already experienced one soldiers' mutiny, one hostile government under the peasants' leader Alexander Stamboliyski, one coup d'etat which ended with Stamboliyski's assassination, and an aborted attempt for uprising against the new strongman, Professor Alexander Tzankov. Then, just a few days before the "Sveta-Nedelia" explosion, an ambush of the king's car in a mountain pass, in which Boris miraculously escaped the assassins' bullets but two of his companions were shot dead.

Another miracle happened on the day of the explosion in the church: delayed at the burial services for those two men, the King headed too late for the state funeral at the cathedral, thus spoiling the meticulously staged Communist plot and escaping death for a second time in a week. My father, who usually accompanied King Boris everywhere, would've probably been among the casualties. But being just a three-year old, I was, of course, unaware of all this.

****

It was only late in my childhood that I learned that many people in this world were <u>not</u> born in Bulgaria and that many didn't even speak Bulgarian. In fact, the opposite turned out to be true: the overwhelming majority of the Earth's population was <u>not</u> Bulgarian. At first, this bit of information struck me as rather odd, but with the age the Bulgarocentric perception of the Universe gradually disappeared, or at least was considerably mitigated. (This, I'm afraid, did not happen to all my compatriots…) I suppose children in all countries feel the same way, whether they first popped up on the surface of our globe at the latitude and longitude of France or Zanzibar. (In England, of course, the distinction between "us" and "the foreigners" remains forever.)

As my own appearance on this Earth happened to take place in the city of Sofia, Bulgaria became, as zoologists would say, my "habitat." So, during all my childhood and teen-age years, my universe, the center of the world, was Bulgaria, a womb 42.000-square-mile-wide and 13-century-old, which formed and nourished me biologically, psychologically, and culturally. I don't know whether to say "luckily" or "unfortunately." I can only describe the way I saw this habitat and what it meant to me. I could've been, of course, born elsewhere and in another century. It's an amusing, but totally futile, mental exercise to speculate what I would have been then. For one thing, it wouldn't have been <u>me</u> and I wouldn't be telling <u>this</u> story, which is basically a story of a chain of causes and effects. Why precisely in Bulgaria and between the two World Wars? Who knows! I hesitate to say "by pure chance," because I believe that the existing Universe, the way it is now, was the only possible one. If different versions were possible, we won't and can't ever know about them. But let's go back to the "habitat" of my formative years!

It's difficult to be totally objective about one's own homeland, especially when one is Bulgarian. Describing the Bulgarians' extraordinary, almost mystical attachment to their country, I wrote, several years later, in my book "Crown of Thorns:" "…It comes partly from the physical beauty of the land. True, Bulgarians are rather chauvinistic and absolutely convinced that their country is the most beautiful in the world. But, quite objectively, there is no foreigner who would not agree that its mountains remind him of the Swiss Alps, that the lush valleys and fairy-tale forests are among the loveliest in Europe, and that the unspoiled golden Black Sea beaches have no rival on the Riviera." But there is something else, something intangible and yet unmistakably Bulgarian, that inspires a unique fascination with the country…Maybe it is the air, an incredibly fresh and invigorating air that one never forgets and one never finds elsewhere. Maybe it is the colors, or the way the sun shines and the wind blows. Poets and romantics speak of the brooks and the wild flowers, of the fragrance of "zdravetz," the exclusively Bulgarian wild geranium that covers acres of meadows and woodland. They speak of the hundred-mile-long Valley of Roses, another unique phenomenon, or the smell of freshly cur hay. They insist that they would recognize the sound of native cowbells out of thousands in foreign pastures. The skies in Bulgaria have a different color, they like to say, and the water tastes different. They describe the cry of roosters at sunrise in the villages and become nostalgic over the sound of dogs barking somewhere far away in the darkness of the night, as if roosters and dogs are different in other countries…It is, doubtless, a biased and romantic outlook. But, who knows, Bulgarians may be, objectively speaking, right. Maybe it is a special country, or in any case, a different one? Less sentimental words—latitude and longitude, soil, climate, altitudes, oxygen in the air, chemistry of the water, geological history—could perhaps explain the same reality in another, non-subjective way. Be this as it may, the undeniable attraction of nature in Bulgaria is there, and countless men have succumbed to it."

The central figure in my universe was an extraordinarily gentle and quiet blue-eyed man with a graying beard, who never raised his voice in anger, but whose soft-spoken words were taken for gospel in our home. Pavel Groueff, my father, held the high functions of Chief of King Boris III's personal cabinet and was one of the monarch's closest confidants, probably because of his culture, disarming modesty, and proverbial discretion. In 1918, when the 24-year-old king succeeded his father Ferdinand on the Bulgarian throne, he found secretary Groueff among the few familiar faces who had remained in the palace. Twenty-five years later, five days before the king died, it was in my father's office that Boris was working in the late afternoon when he collapsed, never to recover full consciousness again.

As it was the case with most high functionaries and states-men in the poor Balkan country, my father's financial condition did not correspond at all to the prominence, notoriety and honors that went with his rank. We lived in a small, unassuming apartment on Moskovska Street, in a house where the royal accounting services were located and I remember that my parents had to exercise great caution to make ends meet. The children—my brother Simeon ("Boubi"), my sister Radka and myself—had never had allowances for pocket money until we finished high school; we were not allowed to buy any cookies or soft drinks; we brought to school our home-made sandwiches; the sweaters we wore were all knitted by my mother. She was a very resourceful lady and I know that it took her a lot of ingenuity to manage, on an extreme economy budget, to maintain an adequate wardrobe for the frequent diplomatic functions she and my father had to attend. Somehow, she was always dressed nicely, although never fancily, and her svelte figure, plus her smiling, youthful face with her sparkling teeth and pure white hair, certainly helped. My parents never entertained: they had neither the means nor the proper home to do it.

But in our eyes, this relatively modest life-style was thousands times compensated by the prestige and glamour of my father's official position. Having to represent the king at many public occasions—inaugurations, arrivals and departures of important foreign guests, openings of exhibitions and concerts, commemorative ceremonies, etc.—there was seldom a week in which, to our enormous pride, his picture, or at least his name, did not appear in the newspapers. On the most solemn occasions, such as the yearly ceremonial opening of the Parliament, my father stood on the left side of the king during his Speech of the Throne, while the Prime Minister and the members of the Cabinet stood on the king's right side. I must admit that seeing the photographs in the next day's press used to make me feel incredibly proud of my father, whom we children worshiped anyhow. The most exciting moments however I used to savor every few months on the side-walks of Sofia's main boulevard, when some new foreign ambassador would be presenting his credentials to the king, or an old one would be taking leave of him. On such occasions, my father accompanied the diplomat and the pageant was quite spectacular. The cortege consisted of two or three open carriages, escorted by a squadron of trotting horse guards in their splendid scarlet uniforms with silver braiding and gray astrakhan bonnets with a tall eagle's plume. In the first carriage sat the ambassador and my father, both in full diplomatic regalia—gold-embroidered jackets, decorations and medals, bicorn hat with white ostrich feathers, ornamental gilt sword. How handsome my father looked in his uniform! This ceremonial suit used to fascinate me as a child, especially the sword with its embossed steel blade and its mother-of-pearl handle. We could admire and "touch" the uniform, the sword and father's numerous decorations very seldom, only when we visited him occasionally at his office in the palace, where they were kept. Nevertheless, I learned to distinguish a dozen or two Bulgarian and foreign decorations and became quite knowledgeable about grades, classes, cordons and stars of medals and orders, a knowledge which, I'm afraid, didn't prove of particular practical value in later years.

When the sound of the approaching cavalcade was heard on the boulevard, I felt like children of stars and celebrities probably feel when watching anonymously a performance of their famous parents. I was thrilled to hear by-standers talk to each other: "Is that the French ambassador? Or the British? And who's the man with the feather hat next to him?" "Don't you know? That's Pavel Groueff, the king's counselor." In such moments I was dying to tell everybody: "He's my Dad! My Dad!" But I simply blushed, overwhelmed with pride and love for my hero.

Yes, there was a certain dose of vanity in my love for him. I remember a climax that surpassed even the thrill of the gilt horse carriages. I was 14 or 15 when my father took me to the soccer finals for the Royal Cup. I couldn't believe my ears, because he didn't have the slightest interest in any sport, but my incredible luck was that he, of all people, was assigned to present, on behalf of the king, the trophy to the winning team. He didn't, of course, have a clue what this meant to a schoolboy like me: to talk personally to, even to shake hands, with the idols of my childhood, legends like Lozanov, and Peshev, and Mishtalov, and Rafailov, guys whom every Bulgarian boy dreamt of touching while they emerge from the dressing room into the stadium. And now, at the end of the game, they all come to us, sweaty and covered with mud, and stand at attention in the Royal box as my father mumbles a few words and awkwardly presents the cup. (He had a great talent for writing, but couldn't speak in public.) Photographers take pictures. The great Anguelov and Panchev talk to us! Wait until I tell my schoolmates tomorrow!, I think, drunk with happiness and pride. If I ever had the slightest doubt that Dad was the greatest, the apotheosis at the stadium dissipated it forever.

This mythological figure, who not only rode with horse guards in regalia and commanded the respect of national-team goalies, but also appeared to me, the child, as being omniscient, was in reality simply human. But this I discovered only later, when adolescence began. In fact, I believe that the end of childhood, for everybody, is the moment when we discover the human nature of our parents and when their omnipotence disappears in our eyes. Instead of Mount Olympus, my father was born in Koprivshtitza, a picturesque small town in Bulgaria, famous for its old wooden houses with overhanging eaves, red-tile roofs, and beautifully carved or painted ceilings. Also for the 1876 rebellion against the Ottoman domination, which erupted there and led, two years later, to the Russo-Turkish war and the liberation of Bulgaria. Although both his parents came from old Koprivshtitza families, they lived in the city of Plovdiv, the ancient Philippopolis, where my father grew up. After finishing the local gymnasium (high school), young Pavel was sent to study in Lyon and Grenoble, from where he returned four years later with a law degree and perfect command of the French language. His career of young diplomat at Sofia's Foreign ministry ended by the end of World War I, when he was transferred to the Royal palace as a junior secretary. King Ferdinand abdicated soon after, and Pavel Groueff continued under his son, King Boris III.

*   *   *   *

We children adored our father. His returning home from work, just before dinnertime, was for us the brightest moment of the day. As soon as we heard him coming, we rushed to meet him at the door, each of us eager to be the first to hug him, to tell him about school or the relatives my mother took us to visit. We fought for the newspapers and magazines he brought home every evening and devoured the cartoons and the photographs, asking hundred questions, which he answered patiently, while Mama and Granny were calling us for dinner. After dinner, my father would sit in his armchair and start the interminable ritual of cleaning his pipe and stuffing it with deliciously aromatic "Prince Albert" tobacco. While he smoked and read some French novel, we read our books or played for awhile in a corner (activities permitted only after my mother assured herself that all homework for the next-day classes had been done), then we said goodnight and went to bed.

As in most Bulgarian families of the period, my father didn't lift a finger in the house. Being the family breadwinner and working long hours (he usually lunched in the palace, with the aide-de-camp on duty and often stayed in his office until 8 PM, including Saturdays), it had been accepted that he had no role in the running of the household. In addition, he was pathetically unhandy: I've never seen him attempting to change a light bulb or, God forbid, hammer a nail. I'm sure he didn't know how to boil water or cut a loaf of bread, and if he tried, it would be taken as a critical hint directed to my mother or my grandmother for job not well done by them; not to mention our live-in maid, who would've died of shame. I don't even speak of helping with the dirty dishes, setting or clearing the table, or other "women's jobs:" it was something totally unconceivable.

The children's behavior, schools, clothes, and vacations were entirely of my mother's jurisdiction. Dad's domain was limited to loving us and talking to us. Talking about current events and history, about books and music (his hobby), about foreign countries, stamps collecting, and also about his childhood in Plovdiv, the relatives and funny things that happened to people. We loved listening to his stories and I felt extremely close to him.

But close as we were, there were subjects I would never discuss with him. As teenager, I wouldn't dare talk about girls I was interested in, about romantic feelings and, of course, anything connected with sex. He would be the last person I would confide in in these matters, or ask for advice. He would've been so surprised and embarrassed, that he wouldn't have known what to say. Even for a puritanical society like the one in which I grew up, my father was particularly prudish, the kind of person in whose presence people feel uneasy to use four-letter words or discuss their sex lives. Any insinuation of sex was taboo in our home, and people's love affairs were not to be mentioned "in front of the children."

Compared to today's mores, Bulgarian attitudes were Victorian and tinted with machismo. A respectful, gallant machismo, I should say, because nowhere were women more admired, courted, loved, desired and idealized, than in old-time Bulgaria. As my friend Boris N. used to say in English, imitating heavy Balkan accent: "In our country, vee beat dee veemen, but aftervords vee play guitarillos oonder der balconys…" Ladies were very much respected, but were considered different from men. There were definitely double standards: kissing hands and sending flowers, but no right to vote; opening the door for her, but of course, no question, of equal jobs; ready to die defending her honor, but never taking seriously her opinion on "important things," like politics. But the girls, like their mothers and grandmothers before them, didn't seem to mind. On the contrary, they seemed to enjoy beeing treated as delicate, helpless, desirable creatures, relying on the protection of strong, passionate Bulgarian "machos." The double standard was most obvious in people's attitude toward the love lives of young men and women. While a male's amorous exploits were a source of amused admiration and a certain family pride, the mere suspicion that a girl may have slept with someone would bring deep shame and disgrace to the same family.

We wouldn't discuss such subjects with my mother either, but for different reasons. We were afraid of her. We loved her dearly, but we also feared her. She was the disciplinarian at home, and a very strict one who wasn't above punishing and some spanking when we were children. She would never hit us on the face, but would ask, with a chilling expression on her face, for the culprit's belt—the worst, petrifying part of the ritual—and then give him half-a-dozen lashes on the fanny. It must have been very effective, because I feared her until I finished high school.

But we felt that she was a devoted, fulltime mother and we appreciated the things she was doing for us. In contrast to her laid-back, slow, conservative husband, who hated any change, Dafina Groueva was an impatient, active woman, who took all sorts of initiatives to improve the life and education of her children. It was on her insistence that we had a French teacher coming home regularly. It was also she who sent Boubi and me to study violin with a great teacher, Christo Petkov, a patient man who endured our screeching during three or four years despite his early realization that the Groueff boys were no Paganini material. We never went beyond Boccherini's menuet, and it says a lot about Maestro Petkov's integrity when he himself advised my parents to let us quit. But in the process we at least learned something about scales, arpeggios and the G-clef. Without my mother's initiative, I wouldn't have started skiing, the sport which became a passion for the rest of my life. I was twelve or so when she enlisted a friend-skier to take us to the Marko Kosturkov sports shop and outfit us with wooden skis (with no metal edges), leather bindings, bamboo poles, boots and anoraks, and start our first lessons on the slopes of Lyulin, outside of Sofia, where we traveled by the streetcar to Kniazhevo and then walked about one mile. She came skiing with three of us, a highly unusual venture in those days for a lady in her forties, and of course she was carrying the heaviest rucksack with the sandwiches, the hard-boiled eggs and the first-aid kit. After opposing the whole idea as being extravagant, crazy, and expensive, my father reluctantly surrendered, but his skepticism about these "break-a-leg" activities never left him. Later, my mother had to wage a long campaign to convince him to inscribe Boubi and me in the rather exclusive Tennis Club in Sofia's Boris Park, where many of our friends played. As a teen-ager, I spent many of my happiest hours on the club's red courts and I'll be always grateful to my mother for making me discover the delights of tennis.

Nothing in her background presaged her desire to expose her children to experiences of this kind. She came from a modest family in the town of Stara-Zagora, where she finished high school, before moving to Sofia to look for a job. She worked as a secretary at the foreign ministry, where she met my father. What caught the eyes of the bashful bachelor was her erect carriage and the agility of her walk, I learned later. As for her, she could hardly believe that such a cultured, refined and sophisticated diplomat would pay attention to a simple provincial girl like her. She was 25 and he was 40 when they married.

My mother also made the arrangements concerning our vacations. Bulgarian schools allowed three months in summer, ten days for Christmas-New Year, and a week for Easter. Father had to stay in hot Sofia in summer, and he used to join us only now and then for a few days. Easter we usually spent in Plovdiv, where my aunt Minka still lived in our grandfather's house, with her superb Alsatian dog Leda, the main attraction for us children. Summers we split between the mountain (Koprivshtitza, Tcham-Koria in the Rila mountains, twice in Biala-Cherkva, in the Rhodopes), and Sozopol, on the Black Sea, our favorite resort. We stayed in Sofia during the Christmas holidays, until my teenage years, when the Panitza family began to invite Boubi and me regularly to their beautiful Tcham-Koria villa, for ten days of winter sports, days of paradise for me. When my friendship with the Panitzas grew to a point that I became practically a member of the family, I started spending part of my summers in Tcham-Koria (now Borovetz) as well. This extraordinary friendship marked deeply the rest of my life. But before telling that story, I'll return to my own family and the other important person in our home, my maternal grandmother, "Baba."

*   *   *   *

My grandmother, a saintly old lady dressed invariably in black, lived with us and, as our parents were going out several times a week, she was the person with whom we spent most of the evenings during our early childhood. I never knew the exact age of this tiny, frail woman, but to me she was the oldest creature on earth, with her wrinkled face, the thick eyeglasses she used in her constant reading of the Bible, the black turban hiding her hair, the cane which supported her bent body when walking slowly to the church across the street.

Her constant wearing of the turban was especially intriguing to me: in some unguarded moments when she was changing it, I had noticed a strange growth on her scalp, the size of a walnut, protruding through her sparse white hair, and it had fascinated and mystified me for years. Grandma (or "Baba," as we called her) never discussed it, but the family legend, repeated by cousins and servants, held that the odd-looking bump was the result of some great shock, caused by things seen (or experienced?) during "the Turkish atrocities" which had followed the national uprisings in the last century.

Like most old Bulgarians who had lived before the Liberation of 1878, Baba used many Turkish words and colloquial expressions, which often puzzled us and made us giggle. But to the child's mind, the Turkish words, combined with Baba's mysterious lump on the head and her unfathomable age, represented a personal, almost tangible link between my world and the 500-year Ottoman domination in the Balkans, about which we were beginning to learn in school. Because of Baba, the Turkish rule, although ended some 45 years before I was born, still had a ring of reality, while most other events of the past seemed simply abstract and fictional.

Baba's incredibly old age also credited her in my eyes with some "personal" witnessing of another series of events, much older than the time of the Sultans. She seemed to be an authentic link between my early Sofia childhood and the time of Christ.

The reality of Christ's story came to me at least once a year. Each spring, during the Holy Week services, I saw Baba, the most believing Christian I've ever met, crying and sobbing unabashedly as the Gospels, read by our parish priests, related the sufferings of the Savior. The Holy Week evening masses at "Sveta Sofia" church was a most exciting event in our early childhood, not only because of the solemnity of the Orthodox rite, but also because it was a rare occasion when children were allowed to go out by night. And what exciting evenings they were! The sound of church bells in the dark, the crowds of people packed in the old church, including family friends with their neatly dressed children, the smell of incense, the holding of candles, lit and blown out twelve times on Thursday night as the twelve Gospels were read (this was the children's favorite mass), Christ's funeral on Good Friday, with the procession led by priests in funereal cassocks, magnificent choir, crosses and banners on the square around the church, and finally, the climax on Saturday midnight, after the long, solemn mass, the explosion of joy in the crisp spring night at the announcement of Christ's resurrection, the thousands of festive faces assembled in front of the church, the bells and songs of glory, the traditional breaking of the multicolored eggs that we carried with us, impatient to hear the jubilant "Christos Voskresse!"—Christ is risen—before we proceed to knock them against our friends' Easter eggs.

It was the week when the metamorphosis of Baba's face became progressively noticeable. As the drama was unfolding in the Gethsemane gardens, at the Last Supper and the Calvary of Golgotha, the weak eyes of the old woman filled with tears, her trembling lips whispered passionate prayers and words of compassion, her infirm knees bent in genuflexion of infinite adoration. I must have been 7 or 8 years old when I already knew the story by heart, and, touching as it was, the Passion contained hardly any element of suspense for me. But what fascinated me each year was the intense concentration with which grandma followed every word of the Gospel, each time surprised by Pilate's cowardice, shocked by the hypocrisy of the Pharisees, indignant of the cruelty of the crowds, and, above all, hoping, sincerely, desperately, hoping that the end won't be so tragic, as if the story she had devoutly heard for 70 or 80 consecutive years, could somehow change this year…As the monotonous voice of the priest described the last prayer in the Gethsemane gardens, ("He fell with the face to the ground and prayed 'My Father, if it is possible, may this cup be taken from me…") Baba's lips were repeating the heartbreaking plea. Alas…Inexorably, Jesus' destiny was headed toward the ultimate drama. By Wednesday night Baba (who, of course, had fasted for the last 40 days, as she had done ever since she could remember), was already a wreck, a pitiful, sad, and deeply distressed old lady. By Thursday, after Judas' betrayal, after the arrest of Christ, the beatings and the humiliations, she was crying softly, already inconsolable. By Good Friday, an especially sad day for her, she had stopped eating and drinking at all, for the three days before Easter.

Grandma's suffering from the agony of beloved Jesus used to touch me deeply, as I stood at her side, the well-behaved little boy I was. At the paroxysm of the drama, when Jesus on the cross cries loudly: "My God, my God, why have you forsaken me?" and the Gospel goes on: "One man ran, filled a sponge with vine-gar, put it on a stick and offered it to Jesus to drink," the pity used to overwhelm the old woman and her frail body shook in incontrollable sobbing. "Poor Jesus," she whispered, "please, God, help Him! Save Him, I beg you!"

How much the little boy loved his grandma in these moments! How much I wanted to be able to console her, to tell her not to worry, because He will arise the next day! But I was just a child, as powerless as she was. These are the first recollections I have of experiencing limitless compassion—an overwhelming feeling that I knew on a few occasions later in my life, and I always associate it with Baba.

Probably it was also because of her that humility has always appealed to me. Even as a child, I could notice that she was a person without much authority or importance. She was totally self-effacing, gentle and humble to a fault, an uneducated old lady with no ambition or ability to ever impose her opinions or will. Except in religious matters. She firmly believed, for instance, that "it's easier for a camel to pass through a needle's eye, than for a rich man to enter the kingdom of heaven," and, accordingly, she sincerely pitied the wealthy. I remember how sorry she felt for the neighbor who owned the opulent house next door, a Mr. Stefanov, about whom she had heard nice things. "He seems to be a nice man," she would tell me during the long evening conversations we had, with me curled at the foot of her couch. "It's too bad that he has to be so rich!…"

Her position in the family was always in the background. While my mother (who was Baba's daughter) was the strong personality running the household, and my father was universally respected because of his culture and official position, grandma was liked by everybody but had little authority, both with servants and with us children, when we passed the very tender age. To our relatives and friends, she wasn't very interesting and few people paid much attention to her. In a word, she was an unimportant person. Yet her humility and gentleness were so total and sincere, that she left a deep and lasting mark on me.

I still remember distinct occasions when she praised me for some "good deeds" she thought I had done. Patting me tenderly on the head, her eyes full of love, she would say softly: "Stefcho, you're a good child!" Those are very treasured memories of being appreciated and loved, moments of genuine pride and comforting certitude of being "right." Later in life, when doubts about right and wrong tortured me frequently, I met few people among the brilliant, erudite and important in this world, whose approval could give me better reassurance or worse sense of guilt that my humble, unimportant grandma.

$$*\qquad\qquad *\qquad\qquad *$$

If I believed in horoscopes (which I definitely don't), I would probably make a case of the curious coincidence that Sava Panitza, the closest friend of my youth, had been born, like a twin, on the same May day ("Gemini") of the same year as I, in the same city, just across from the great "Alexander Nevsky" cathedral. Our mothers thought that we were both born at about the same hour of the evening, which information may be astrologically quite meaningful, but is hardly verifiable, given the fact that they both had three children each and that in those days babies were delivered at home, by a midwife, rather than in hospitals, where records are kept of such details.

Whether predestined by the stars or not, we became inseparable from the age of 14, and this unusual friendship oriented my life in a different direction. We had seen each other before, but only occasionally, during summer vacations in Tcham-Koria, the beautiful pine-forest resort in the Rila Mountains, where Sava's family owned a big villa. In Sofia too, I had noticed this handsome, tall boy, always smartly dressed in foreign-looking clothes, on his shiny, rich-kid bicycle, or riding next to an uniformed chauffeur in an American limousine. We attended different grade schools, but met a few times at children's parties, where Sava (or "Pouffy," as they called him when he was little), seemed always to be the star. Because of this personal quality of his, and because of his family's prominence, we, other boys, expected him to be spoiled and haughty. But one summer, my brother and I were pleasantly surprised to discover how friendly he was and what fun it was to play with him.

He was less "bookish" than we were, less good a student. But he was far more enterprising and daring, a bigger, stronger boy than we were, and better in sports. My brother Boubi and I used to have a few comedy routines which "Pouffy" found irresistibly funny, while we were fascinated by his skills in fist-fights with other boys and also by what we considered his "expertise" in girls: he had already kissed a girl ("on the mouth!") and seen naked women (spying on maids while they were taking a shower).

We liked each other almost immediately, and Sava's parents encouraged the new friendship, probably because "the Groueff children" had a reputation of polite, obedient boys and good students; in other words, not a bad influence. We were invited more and more often to their villa, and at the end of summer, when Sava and I entered the same high school, the First Gymnasium for Men, we were already each other's "best friend," and I had become an almost daily visitor to his home.

There was, by Constitution, no titled nobility in Bulgaria. The half-century of national independence after the long Ottoman domination had been too short a period for the creation of a real aristocracy. Elites, of course, existed, but they were based on cultural, political, or financial criteria. That last category was rather limited in number and the few dozen wealthy families, whose fortunes were made mostly in tobacco, rose oil, or banking, could not be compared to the famous rich families in the rest of Europe.

Among Sofia's rich however, some families were known as "the high-life" (so designated even when spelled in Cyrillic letters). The term was used in all seriousness and even in awe, only by those who didn't belong, and was an embarrassment and taboo for those who did belong.

The distinctive characteristics of this class were good manners and education (in that order), foreign languages, a certain savoir-vivre and Western sophistication, and, essential, participation in Sofia's social life. The small Balkan capital offered a limited but select choice of more-or-less elegant social events, and they were usually connected with the foreign diplomatic corps, a few charity balls, bridge games at certain private homes, tennis at the BTK Club or the Diplomatic Club (there was no golf in Bulgaria), dinner-parties and cocktails at the top Bulgarian homes or week-ends at villas in Tcham-Koria or Varna, on the Black Sea. No family represented better this class of wealthy, cosmopolitan, and social Bulgarians than the Gueshoff-Yablansky-Panitza clan.

Sava's maternal grandmother, Mrs. Haritina Yablansky, was a daughter of the great statesman Ivan Evstatiev Gueshov, the Prime Minister during the Balkan

War and wealthy head of banks and insurance companies. Gueshov, a highly educated man who had graduated from Istanbul's Robert College and then London, was related to the philanthropists Evlogui and Dimitri Gheorghiev, the brothers who founded the University of Sofia. Haritina's husband, Dimitri Yablansky, a vigorous self-made man who had built his own fortune and had briefly held the post of cabinet minister, died when I was a child, so I knew Mrs. Yablansky mostly as a widow. An energetic, bright and opinionated matriarch, she ran her family and large household with undisputed authority. Even after her daughter Mika and son-in-law Stati Panitza had their three children, the formidable "O'mama" continued to treat the couple as beloved live-in children, not yet ready to be fully emancipated.

The elegant three-story French-style house on "Tsar Osvoboditel," Sofia's central boulevard, was one of the capital's most distinguished homes. Mrs. Yablansky kept a permanent staff of eight: Petar and Assen, the valets in yellow-and-navy-striped vests; two uniformed chamber maids, Nadia and Nona; the chef Nikola and his kitchen help Kiro; the chauffeur Leonid, who drove the huge Chrysler in black uniform, cap, and gloves; plus a seamstress-laundress. Also Manny, the governess of Sava's baby-brother Dimi. Occasionally, when we boys played volleyball in the back yard, we enlisted Assen and Kiro to complete the teams.

I had great respect for Mrs. Yablansky and was flattered that, in spite of her authoritarian ways with other people, she was attentive and warm to me, and liked to talk with me. This dynamic, short lady, always dressed in black and wearing no make-up, was bursting with energy and never minced her words, whether she was fighting over the menu with her obstinate, moody chef, or playing her regular bridge game with the Sofia top players, such as Prime Ministers Kiosseivanov and Filov, and financier Bourov, or else commenting angrily about the radio news bulletin. Politics and international affairs were her hobby. But her strongly expressed opinions could sometimes exasperate even the gentlest and most deferent opponent she could have—her own son-in-law. Then, around the formally set dining table, we witnessed the rare spectacle of someone contradicting openly the formidable old lady. As the international conflict was deepening in the West, the arguments became more animated between the urbane Mr.

Panitza, an inveterate Francophile, who saw the future with black pessimism, and his outspoken, nationalistic mother-in-law, who refused to believe that better, even great, days were not in store for her beloved Bulgaria. The heated debate always ended with the smiling, but resolute, intervention of Mika Panitza, who charmingly managed to appease their passions and change the subject, to the delight of the antagonists, who both had an unlimited adoration for her.

Although a pure Bulgarian by blood, Evstati Panitza, Sava's father, was the quintessential Westerner who never completely blended into the Balkan scene, where he stood apart, almost an outsider. Born and raised in Vienna in a prosperous merchants' family, he had studied in the prestigious Theresianum school, then had lived the elegant life of a well-to-do bachelor in pre-WW1 Paris—garconniere, a personal valet, a motor roadster, and all. As the family had shares in the insurance company 'Balkan," young Stati started attending board meetings in Sofia since 1907. When the Vienna Panitzas joined in the general Bulgarian enthusiasm for the 1912 Balkan War, donating motorized ambulances for the front, Stati drove them to Bulgaria and his visits became more frequent. Later, he met Mika Yablansky, Sofia's best catch, married her in 1918, and moved into the Yablansky's mansion. A banker by training, he became a director at "Balkan" and a few banks, a distinguished citizen and a model husband and father. "Stati" Panitza spoke Bulgarian well, but his first languages were Austrian and French, which he mastered to perfection and which he spoke at home with his wife, also trilingual since childhood.

But language was only a part of his distinctly non-Bulgarian personality. His tastes and habits had remained those of a gentleman from Vienna and Paris. He and Mika traveled frequently abroad, where they ordered their clothes; he read *Le Temps* and *Neue Zurcher Zeitung*, appreciated vintage Bordeaux, and enjoyed Viennese operettas. Extremely gentle and polite, he was totally lost and helpless in any situation involving the slightest rudeness or vulgarity. He would simply not have a clue of what a four-letter word in Bulgarian meant. Good manners was a religion with him, together with dignity and self-respect, which began, he used to tell us, with the gentleman's duty to appear always properly attired, impeccably clean and tidy, composed and courteous, no matter what the circumstances are.

Mika Panitza told me, many years later, that she had never seen her husband unshaven or disheveled, not once in their long married life. Even when sick, he would make the effort to shave, wash, and comb his thick hair carefully, and, yes, polish his shoes. He had a fetish about shiny shoes and tried, unsuccessfully, to teach Sava and me how to use a large bone when polishing a pair of shoes. To appear with unpolished shoes or soiled shirt, he used to tell us, was an inexcusable way of showing lack of respect for the other person.

During the years I lived around the Panitza family, I received hundreds of similar lessons and tips on proper manners, etiquette, and dress from "Uncle" Stati, a man for whom I developed a filial affection. Some of the "dos" and "don'ts" I learned from him dated from the Old World's code and were really obsolete, before becoming totally impractical in the modern age. He was, for instance, appalled by suit-sleeves with false buttonholes that didn't open; or a false boutonniere slit on the lapel. No decent tailor would make such an abomination, he thought, forgetting that ready-to-wear clothes were replacing custommade suits. The very notion of a gentleman wearing suits from the rack filled uncle Stati with sincere sadness. Or going out on the street without a hat and without gloves! While considering some of uncle Stati's standards as anachronistic, Sava and I were amused by his sincere respect for the code. He was one of the last practitioners of a disappearing savoir-faire, which demanded, for instance, to let the waistcoat's last button unbuttoned, not to wear sports wristwatch with a dinner jacket, or shirt cuffs with buttons instead of cuff links. For them to wear a ready-made bowtie with the tuxedo was as offensive as to go out in a suit without a necktie. The same went for rayon shirts, plastic flowers, and paper napkins at dinner table…the lack of taste knows no limits! No wonder that people like that eat fish with a knife and tell you how much money they make and how much their possessions cost! At parties, such parvenus would speak loud, kiss the hand of young girls, and, when introducing guests, present the lady to the man and the elder person to the younger, instead of the opposite. They would wear flamboyant neckties or keep an extra-long nail on the pinky. *Quelle horreur!*, Stati would say. But he was too goodhearted to ridicule or have contempt for such people. He simply felt sorry for them, sincerely sorry that they either didn't know better, or couldn't afford it.

But among the "grown-ups" of the family, the closest to me was Sava's mother. As a boy, I was an admiring fan of the glamorous Mrs. Panitza; as adolescent, I began to confide in "Aunt Mika," a most understanding listener to young people's "secrets" and a comforting, sometimes mischievous, adviser on the affairs of the heart; as a young man, I was already a devoted friend, vastly amused by the playful side of her personality and trusting her judgment and taste. Being around her was always great fun, more entertaining than being with most friends of my own age, and I enjoyed the moments this very much-in-demand grownup would spare for us youngsters.

No doubt, her name, looks, family fortune, and proper upbringing as a "jeune fille de bonne famille" made Mika Panitza a star of Sofia's social life. But the success and popularity she enjoyed couldn't have been explained without her lively personality and convivial charm. Her looks corresponded to the 1920s and 1930s standards of attractive femininity. It was an era that admired delicate, white skins, roundness in the forms, careful make-up and red lipstick on heart-shaped mouths, Garboesque profiles with pronounced noses. None of those skinny, boyish figures; no bronze tans, no hard, muscular limbs. It was a satin-and-lace femininity of soft flesh and rich fragrances, of high heels, authentic jewelry and fur coats. Showy outfits and sexy dresses were, of course, unbecoming for a real lady, they were left for the *demimondaines*. Gallant men were expected to kiss hands and send flowers, to open doors and pull chairs for the ladies, and, of course, to inundate them with flowery compliments.

Sociable, talkative, and enjoying a good gossip, interested in fashion, Mika excelled in the beau monde. But behind her perennial smile, one felt the strong personality of an intelligent woman used to have it her way. Always ladylike, she commanded respect and discouraged any familiarity. I've seen many times her friendly dark eyes turn icy when a word out of place or in bad taste displeased her.

She was an affectionate and demanding mother and the three children, who adored her, knew better than to disobey her. She insisted on good manners and was very strict about things like children not standing up when a grown-up person entered the room, or leaving the dining table without asking permission. She was much less strict, during their adolescence, about romantic weaknesses: Sava's continuous crushes on girls, ever since he was twelve, amused her thoroughly, and later, when his infatuations became more serious, she participated wholeheartedly in his love and languish. For one thing, because she was herself as sentimental and emotional as he was, and nothing interested her more than romantic stories—in movies, in books, and mostly, in real life. No matter what the story plot was, she always fervently rooted for the lovers. And secondly, because when it came to the people she loved, she was not only fully "engagee," but she was also unabashedly and fiercely partial. It mattered less whether the person involved was right or wrong; what counted for her was that it concerned her child or husband or mother or friend, and she stood by them like a tigress, ready to scratch the eyes of whoever did them wrong. In later years, I had many opportunities to realize that her unqualified loyalty also applied to me: she wouldn't forgive anyone who had said something unpleasant about me, even when I had deserved it and long after I had forgotten it myself.

Even a child can feel this kind of things, and there is no wonder that as early as in my Sofia days, I knew that "Aunt Mika" would play a key role in my life.

****

Chapter 3

First attempts at writing.

I must have been 15 or 16 when I first learned about Sisyphus and his tragic fate, and he made an unusually strong impression on me. I loved many of the classic legends we read in the mythology class, but the story of the Corinthian king fascinated me particularly. That poor man had a really terrible problem, I felt: the gods condemned him to roll a huge rock up a very steep hill, and each time he was about to reach the summit, the rock rolled down to the bottom and Sisyphus had to start all over again. This, to perpetuity.

I was in the age when I was already tormented by a painful need to understand the enigma of the human condition, and it occurred to me that Sisyphus's story was the perfect allegory of life's tragedy. But the myth became a true revelation when I read the rest of it and discovered the reason why the king was given such a cruel punishment: he had dared to challenge the god Thanatos and had almost defeated him. Thanatos was the god of Death. In other words, Sisyphus had tried to escape death, to vanquish it! Now the myth became even more beautiful, its symbolism more grandiose. I was thrilled, for days and weeks my thoughts were preoccupied with the story and, somewhat childishly, I felt as if I had discovered a great secret.

Escaping death. I don't remember since what early age the thought of death started disturbing my childhood universe. I suppose all children go through those chilling moments of panic after they realize that all life has to end one day—the parents,' grannys' and grandpa's, the pet dog's, everyone's life. As for the child's own mortality, it seems to be different: even though everybody else is sure to die, I myself, I feel, I sort of know, that somehow—don't ask me how—but somehow an exception will be made for me. It's not possible that I'll cease to exist; the idea of nothingness is, in my case, simple inconceivable.

Maybe Death will be vanquished one day? Hopefully, before my turn comes. There MUST be a solution, I know it, I know it! Sisyphus...Thanatos...What a titanic duel! Something to make you proud of belonging to the human race. Although frequent, these attacks of fear of death and nothingness did not occupy my child's mind constantly. But they would strike suddenly, without warning, in the middle of playing in our Moskovska Street courtyard, or while walking to school, or in bed before falling asleep. Most often, when my parents went out in the evening and we were left with my grandmother. Was it the fear that they may not return that triggered the horrible thought that one day, in a few years (but in how many years?), they'll die and we'll be left without them? Or was the loneliness conducive to such morbid thoughts? To me, even today, loneliness is always a reminder of the inevitable end, a foretaste of the great, permanent silence. Or was it perhaps Grandma's tales of the Hereafter, of the Last Judgment, Resurrection, and Paradise, her self-styled compilation of Dante, the and Old and New Testaments, and folklore superstition? For me as a child, Grandma (we called her "Baba") represented the unimpeachable authority in those matters, and her rather fundamentalist cosmology, even if not entirely reliable, had the advantage of reassuring me that there was life after death, thus pushing aside the much more terrifying thought of nothingness. And having said my prayers and crossed myself before going to sleep, I managed to chase the disturbing thoughts out of my head. With adolescence though, Baba's version ceased to give me comfort, and I joined the angst-ridden legions of those billions, past, present, and future, who remain haunted by the greatest of all questions.

In the days when I was reading the myth of Sisyphus, I was nursing a secret dream, which I was too shy and afraid of ridicule to share with anyone: I wanted fervently, "when I grow up," to be a playwright. This desire had two sources: a genuine intellectual interest, and vanity. My parents were assiduous theatergoers and they used to take us often to the National Theater, where plays and operas were shown on alternate days. As the King's Chief of cabinet, my father was entitled to the use of the box adjacent to the large royal box. The two boxes shared a private salon and a private entrance from the street. With a telephone call in advance, the families of the senior palace officials could reserve the box, when not used by the royal family, and the Groueffs were the most frequent users. As teenagers, we were allowed to go to matinees by ourselves, without our parents, which permitted us to see almost all productions and we developed a real passion for the theater and the opera. Bulgarian singers had excellent international reputation and we were lucky to hear many times the best operas of Puccini, Verdi, Rossini, Bizet, Gounod, Tchaikovski, Wagner, and Mussorgski. On the lighter side, we loved particularly Strauss's *Fledermaus* and *Gypsy Baron* (saw them 4 or 5 times each) and Offenbach's *La Belle Helene*, our favorite, which we knew by heart, for having seen it seven times.

Opera was entertaining. For intellectual thrills, nothing affected me more than the theater. I listened to the words of Shakespeare and Ibsen and Tchekov, as though I was receiving the scroll's wisdom from the Mountain, and my hungry, innocent soul seemed to have then more affinity with the stage than I had in my later years. To me, playwrights were the most enviable people in the world, and their profession—the most rewarding. Especially after seeing a few local authors taking a bow at the end of the show, with the public standing up and shouting "Author! Author!" What an apotheosis, what a supreme gratification! To see myself one day in this role became my most cherished secret dream.

Fascinated by Sisyphus, and dreaming of "Author! Author!" I decided, with all the inexperience of a 16-year-old, but also with the presumptuousness of that age, to write a drama—no, a masterpiece!

It had to be in verse, of course: the classical tragedies we studied in school were all written in verse. During several weeks, I even had the nerve (or self-delusion?) to try to put it in rhyme, but it didn't take more than four or five pages in the school notebook, bought especially for this ambitious project, to realize that the Homeric task was far beyond my capacities: the awkward verses were pathetically contrived. Never mind, I rationalized, some of the best contemporary poetry is in free verse. And in free verse I continued, eagerly, writing every moment I could steal from homework time, pretending to be studying for the next day classes. Although very close to my family and friends, I would've died of embarrassment had anyone found out that I was writing a play. It wasn't before long that I had full reasons to congratulate myself for my discretion: indeed, when I reread the 30 or 40 pages in diligent schoolboy calligraphy, I had to blush and feel grateful that nobody had seen my naive prose. Anyway, I never went further with my project. After the flowery, melodramatic start, I didn't know how to end it, abandoning poor Sisyphus to his tragic lot, halfway up the hill.

But this didn't end my playwright dreams. In the meantime, in addition to my "cosmic" preoccupation, I had become fascinated by ethical problems to which I was incapable of finding satisfactory answers. One wouldn't expect a conformist, God-fearing boy like me, so obedient and respectful of authority, religion, and tradition, to become obsessed with moral challenges and conflicts, but that's exactly what was happening to me. The problems were, of course, only theoretical, because I don't think I had had the guts, or mischief, rebelliousness, or whatever it takes to question, defy or break any rules. Although brought up to always act as a "good boy" and do the "right" things, I nevertheless had felt acute, sometimes painful, doubts about what is right or wrong, and these questions haunted me with increasing intensity as I was growing up.

Among them was the question of forbidden love. Why would an 18-year-old worry about it, and what could he possible know about love, fidelity, and marriage? Except for my Black Sea experience with 'forbidden fruit," all my knowledge about problems related to Original Sin was second-hand information—books, movies, friends' indiscretions. And yet I took these problems very seriously, as if somebody had asked me to be the judge. In matters concerning sex, adultery, and divorce, we were living in a puritanical, Victorian society, where a mere discussion of such subjects was considered inappropriate. In all my childhood years, for instance, I had known only two divorced ladies— a niece of my mother's, and a dignified Russian matron, whose eyes seemed constantly filled with tears, ten years after an important Bulgarian general had divorced her. We felt sorry for both women, because "divorced" was synonym of being abandoned, repudiated, and had a stigma about it. I don't think I ever had a classmate—child of divorced parents.

But what does one do, I asked myself, if one falls in love with a married person? What does a decent spouse do if (or when?) the original passion subsides and he or she falls in love with another person? Can love be eternal, and if not, should one remain faithful forever and renounce romance for the rest of the life? (And life seems so long when one is 18!...) Are they good answers, what's right and what's wrong, what should a decent person do? What should one do?—I'll tell you what one should do! Here young Stephane, age 18, buys another school notebook, takes his newly-acquired fountain pen (no more inkwells and old fashioned pen-holders, we go with modern progress, don't we!), and starts writing his second play. The plot is simple; the perennial "love triangle." An irresistibly attractive young lady of irreproachable virtue and two sophisticated, equally admirable gentlemen, who have deep respect for each other. The problem is that one of the men is married to the dream girl when the other one meets her, not knowing who she is. Coup de foudre on both sides. Then the bitter truth, the moral conflict, the drama.

Sounds familiar? We've seen similar plots in countless films and novels, I admit it. Many authors have written about the same old conflict. But have they found the right solution? Of course not, not to my knowledge. And this is where I come with my play. Let ME tell you how such conflicts should be resolved! Righteousness sustained my zeal during the long months I wrote and rewrote, hiding the precious manuscript at the bottom of my desk drawer, under the geometry and Latin textbooks. I suffered together with the couple in love, shared their platonic ecstasies, felt guilty for the unsuspecting husband. Above all, I was very proud of my heroes, because they were each one nobler than the other and succeeded in finding the right, moral solution. The only possible solution for noble, morally superior, self-respecting human beings. I don't deny that I was also proud of myself as author who didn't permit his *dramatis personae* to succumb to the flesh and led them towards this admirable triumph of decency over human weakness.

Everything was so clear, so pure, in my universe then! Confronted with the option of adultery and betrayal, the two noble souls did find the moral strength and, out of respect and affection for the third noble soul, decided heroically never to see each other again. Tragic, yes, but also what a sublime moral satisfaction! Goodbye, forever! Moved to tears myself, I wrote "Curtain" and went to bed, relieved that the painful conflict is finally solved and will no more disturb my peace of mind.

The play, of course, never left the drawer's bottom, and frankly, I don't think the Bulgarian public was deprived of a great masterpiece. But later in life, I've been more than once envious of its bravely naive author and the gratifying nobility of his solution. Finding myself a few times in the role of that marvelous, self-sacrificing hero of the play, I've been, I'm sorry to confess it, less admirable than him. The 18-year-old author would've been disappointed, had he known then that he would behave like everyone else, not worse, but not better either. But I'm sure that he would've judged me with more indulgence if he had an idea of what a cruel price guilt is. So, virtue triumphed over the weakness of the flesh. Or rather that was the way I wanted it in my play. In reality, I needed badly to reassure myself about right and wrong in general, and in writing the play, I was fooling myself that I had found this certitude. But deep in myself, I knew that it wasn't true, that I was more insecure and mixed-up about ethical standards than ever.

It's hard for a very young person interested in problems in ethics not to have firm beliefs and strong opinions, and often I had difficulties in handing this deficiency in my character. Young people are usually opinionated, sure of their likes and dislikes, seeing things in black and white. Lucky guys! I often thought when listening to their passionate arguments and being incapable of taking sides. "Am I not right? Tell him, Stephane!" some angry kid would summon me, just before throwing a punch at his opponent's face. I wished I could join the quarrel, but I simply was not convinced in either side's arguments.

Most disputes seemed ridiculous and pointless, they reminded me of two excited men facing each other, pointing to the same object and arguing:

"It's on the left side!"

"No, that's the right side, idiot!" Of course, they both are saying what is true to them, but it wouldn't stop them from screaming at each other until their faces turn red. Obviously they are BOTH right! I must have been a child when this simple truth occurred to me. Isn't it amusing, I had thought, that people in California would point West when showing where the Far East is?

It sounds easy now, but just try to grow up in a macho society without taking sides vehemently, "like a real man," in all confrontations which constantly erupt around you! Some kids considered me a weakling without firm opinions on anything, and that bothered me terribly. Sometimes I thought myself that something might be wrong with me, that maybe I lacked courage and virility. Look at my best friend Sava, with his quick temper, brave, strong, enjoying a good fistfight, in other words a normal, red-blooded boy. Even skinny, bantamweight Jivko, my other close friend, he wouldn't let anyone tease him without instantly retaliating with his sharp, witty tongue, and often with his fists. Why only I had to be the perennial conciliator, appeaser, and mediator?

My problem was not in my inability of being FOR something or somebody— I had enough admiration for many causes and personalities. The deficiency was in my inability to be fully AGAINST, to be really furious, to hate. I've been born with the talent (or the affliction?) of seeing the many sides in the same person, the different aspects of the same situation. In a mature person, it may be an advantage not to see things in black-and-white; but it's hell for a youngster struggling to understand himself and the world around him. I've been through this hell, so I know. There have been moments when I thought that I would see clearer and be less confused if only I could experience the natural, human, feelings of anger and hate. But the sincere hatred, wanting to punch and smash and destroy. Or to believe that somebody or something is totally evil, with no imaginable excuse, with no redeeming possibility whatsoever. Then I would be able to say, like everybody else, things like "I hate him!" and "This is 100-percent wrong and I'm unconditionally against!" With all my heart, without an iota of doubt. Like "normal" people.

Doubting constantly, always finding an excuse or at least an explanation, for the opponent, was often too painful. How comfortable I used to feel with the old Westerns, where the good guys—the Gary Coopers and John Waynes—were really good, and the outlaws and Indians really bad, so evil that you couldn't wait to see them get what they deserved! No tolerance, no pity for the sons-of-bitches! Everything used to be so clear and uncomplicated. Later, the new, "psychological" Westerns spoiled my pleasure, with their explanations that the horrible rascal wasn't that bad after all, he simply had to support a sick mother and ten hungry orphans and that's why he was so mean…And Sitting Bull reveals, between two scalpings, how brutally Jimmy Stewart and his otherwise gorgeous cavalry men had abused the defenseless tribe he had to protect. How could you, after that, hate really the villains?

The early discovery that most "bad" people were in fact not so bad, and that many "wrong" things may be explained differently, shook my universe in a probably more disturbing way than if I had come to the opposite conclusion, i.e. the conventional stereotype that "people are mean." It was disconcerting for an adolescent brought up with the Ten Commandments and the accepted ethical values of the period, while his critical mind searched in vain for more rational criteria.

Just as I was getting more entangled in my private labyrinth of "rights" and "wrongs" and "true" and "false," I saw a couple of Pirandello plays, which touched a very sensitive chord in me. The Italian playwright seemed to have put in words things, which I had only vaguely sensed, without being able to articulate. A similar experience occurred to me later, when I first saw the film and read *Rashomon*. What if Truth did not exist objectively? What if "right" was not an absolute notion? The very thought gave me shivers, as if the entire edifice of my internal peace had cracked. The heart was tremendously upset, but the brain, curiously, was excited and stimulated.

I was 19 and about to enter my military service when I embarked on my third, and last, play. I called it *Colored Eyeglasses*, suggesting that we are all looking at the same reality but wearing glasses of different color. It had four acts and I managed to complete it before I finished the service.

Believing that no matter how different or odd people and lifestyles are, they all make some sense if we look from their point of view, I attempted to assemble on stage half-a-dozen widely disparate people and let them share an identical situation. The plot I devised was rather gimmicky, but I thought it served my purpose and, after all, we were talking about theater, weren't we? The lawyer-executor of an eccentric wealthy man's will undertakes a discreet search for the beneficiary, a person the dead man had only seen once but who had impressed him so deeply as to change entirely his lifestyle and vision of the world. The will only gives the address of the unsuspecting heir and mentions that he's somebody people consider a little odd, if not crazy. But no name is given. So the lawyer contacts the building's residents under some pretext, keeping secret the purpose of his investigation. There we find the following cast: a starving, longhaired poet who lives in the clouds; a rational, materialistic physicist; a nonconformist who has his own bizarre ideas about everything; a cheerful, elegant playboy, committed to hedonistic pursuit of pleasure; a serious, reputable neurologist; and finally, the physicist's fiancee, an average girl who only dreams of love and the simple joys of home life.

Showing them in consecutive meetings with the lawyer and then among themselves, I tried to make each one look more or less insane to the others. Unaware that a huge inheritance is at stake, everyone points to some of the others as being crazy, while doing his best to explain and rationalize his own behavior. Even the lawyer is not above suspicion.

The end?—Everyone in the cast, when given the opportunity to explain his behavior, makes some sense. The least "normal" appears to be the person who sees insanity in the others. Or, in this case, the late millionaire.

Chapter 4

Bulgaria 1936-1944

Of the three Groueff children, Boubi, my older brother, was the best student and the most avid reader of books. Also, the most introvert. At school, he was always the best in his class, from the first grade to the last, without any particular effort. Each term, his marks were invariably "6" (the maximum), and the rare "fives" he ever brought home were either in gymnastics, or math and chemistry, subjects in which he wasn't particularly interested. Literature, history and philosophy, on the other hand, were his passion and he was reading so much on his own, that he did his required homework in a matter of minutes.

He must have been 15 when he read Dostoyevski; not just read, but also was deeply impressed by some of the writer's heroes, such as *Idiot's* Prince Mishkin. As a teenager, he plunged into the philosophy of Kant, Nietzsche, and Hegel with the engrossment of today's kids for rock music. With his best friends Mitika and Tosho, they debated heatedly the problems of Man's role in the Universe, the purpose of life and, above all, the ways to reform Mankind and improve its lot, with the concentration and assurance of people just about to solve them. I'm not quite sure how close they were to finding the answers, but there was something touching in the naive but passionate dedication they, as well as countless other youngsters of that period, were putting into their lofty discussions. Intellectually, Boubi and his friends looked a little down upon young men like Sava and myself who, in their eyes, were too preoccupied with the superficial pleasures of life, such as leisure, sports, and chasing girls. Not that Boubi was not interested in girls, quite the contrary! But Love to him was always spelt with a capital L and the Beloved One was immediately put on a pedestal of virtues and eternal fidelity, often to the embarrassed surprise of the lady herself. A dreamer, he had disappointments in finding the ideal purity, understanding, and nobility of soul among Sofia's teenage Dulcineas. Most of them, attracted by his good looks and interesting personality, had nothing more in mind than having a nice time with him and became scared of the platonic depths into which he insisted to bring their romance. He was badly hurt a couple of times and suffered a lot, becoming depressed and uncommunicative for weeks. But he wouldn't compromise and the search for the perfect woman resumed.

We never talked about his feelings, to him they were something too personal to discuss. I knew that he disapproved of light flirtations and casual affairs, such as Sava and I wouldn't mind to engage in, and this made me uncomfortable to talk to him about my romantic experiences. I felt that he would judge them frivolous, if not rather "immoral" and that's why, although we were close in other matters, I didn't tell him about my Sozopol affair. What's more, I never used four-letter words in his presence, so intimidating, idealistic and prudish he appeared to me.

We were both very interested in political and international news, and totally indifferent and ignorant about economics. We read regularly the newspapers my father brought home every day and had even invented our own "political" game which we played with 2x3" portraits of statesmen cut out from newspapers. Using our collections of heads of Prime ministers, presidents, and party leaders, and a lot of imagination, we were creating and solving international conflicts and cabinet crises, holding conferences and negotiating treaties. Thus, the facial features of Chamberlain and Mussolini, of Hoover, Stalin, the Negus, Hitler, Franco and the pre-war local and Balkan leaders remained forever familiar to me.

As for my very private feelings, romantic experiences and little sins, my main confidant was Sava. This kind of confidential revelation—mutual, made in total trust and with most intimate details, shamefully indiscreet,—were at the basis of our "best-friend" relationship, an institution quite current among Bulgarian youths. The nearest analogy I can think of is the father confessor or maybe the psychoanalyst, if only they could be as humorous, enjoyable and, let's face it, juvenile. I never found anything quite equivalent in the West—maybe it was the different mores, or maybe such intimacy isn't possible once one leaves school or military service?—and it is a pity, because it is a marvelously rewarding catharsis.

So I lived through all Sava's romances, and he through mine, but nothing unusual or particularly interesting happened while we were still in high school. Nothing, until our senior year, when he met Lucy. Then all Sofia gasped and watched. Because Lucy, a good-looking, provocative brunette, was the premier jazz-singer and the most talked-about young woman in town. Tall, willowy, with a sensuous mouth and naughty black eyes, she was a few years older than us and was already a sort of a pop star with a large following of fans, a totally liberated woman who smoked and drank in public and exchanged dirty jokes with the fellows.

Through films, records and radio stations, my generation was just discovering American jazz music and we loved going to the concerts and *thes-dansants* of the local Ovcharov band, which played Louis Armstrong, Ellington and Count Basie tunes. When Lucy, the star of the band, sang languorously *Mood Indigo*, trying the inflexions of Ella Fitzgerald and Lena Horn, we were all melting, before her vigorous *Dinah* and *Alexander's Ragtime Band* brought us back to swing. We had an older friend, a college student called Zhoro Markov, who played the trombone with the band and for whose *Stardust* solo a la Tommy Dorsey I envied him more than I ever envied any friend. It was Zhoro who introduced Sava to the jazz diva. The moment they shook hands, an almost visible spark passed between them: my best friend was in love! So much so, that he didn't care about the perils and the scandal he was letting himself in for.

Like in any good B-movie, the star had to be the girlfriend of a dangerous guy. In this case, he was a good-looking heavyweight prizefighter, Boyan Gavrilov, whose numerous fans would never believe that any dame in her right mind would prefer a high-school student to their glamorous champ. But unpredictable are the vagaries of a lady's heart, and Lucy became Sava's girl, "body and soul," as the songwriter would say. The body part was less surprising, because chastity was not one of her cardinal virtues, and Sava, at 18, had the appetite and potency of a ravenous bull. What was far more unexpected was the sincerity and depth of the feelings this experienced, naughty young lady developed for the preppy scion of a conservative family who had still to ask permission each time he wanted to be late for dinner. The romance blossomed rapidly, to the delight of Sofia's gossips and to the envy of all of us students. Luckily for Sava, the boxing champion peacefully conceded "the end of an affair" (his), and let Lucy alone, without using the rich kid for punching bag. Sava began to be seen more and more often at the back door of *Bulgaria* hall, where she performed, and in front of her apartment house, and Sava's tiny green *Topolino*, (he was the only student in town who owned a car), with Lucy on the seat next to the driver, became a familiar sight on the boulevards. When my mother heard the rumor, she was alarmed. Sincerely upset, she summoned me for a serious talk. "I couldn't sleep the whole night," she said, and forbade me to see "this loose woman," warning me about the perils such "adventurers" represent for credulous, decent youngsters like Sava and me. Later, when "the affair" became public knowledge, many friends of Mika Panitza's, including my mother, discussed the terrible problem with her, commiserating and offering advice. Mika was also disturbed by Lucy's reputation, (was it true that she'd been married and divorced, had an illegitimate child, had lived with several men?...) but being always sympathetic to lovers, any lovers, she didn't panic and didn't really try to restrict or punish Sava. In a way, she became a reluctant accomplice: worried, not very happy about the romance and hoping that it will end soon, but hiding the news from the real head of the family, her mother. For Mrs. Yablansky would never understand such an affair and wouldn't hesitate to put her foot down and forbid it.

I grew to like Lucy very much. She was a happy soul, warm and funny, marvelously free and extraordinarily generous, ready to do anything for a friend. And she really loved Sava. Her lifestyle, lack of inhibition and racy language were, of course, totally different from our ways, but that only made her more fascinating to us. As for her, she became really attached to us, the "square kids," to whose bourgeois attitudes she reacted with a mixture of curiosity, humor, and tenderness, probably wishing sometimes to be like us. In spite of the general disapproval, her romance with Sava—passionate, stormy, rich in fights and sentimentality, jealousy scenes and reconciliation—lasted for about two years, well after we had gone to the barracks for our military service.

*   *   *   *   *

Those were happy days. Life in Sofia in the late 30's was quite pleasant, especially when one was a healthy, optimistic teenager with a loving, close-knitted
family and many friends in and out of school. In class, we were pretty disciplined
students; in the old system, teachers were formal and rather feared, demanding
and getting respect, some of them very strict and exacting. During the recess
periods, we were as boisterous as kids are everywhere else, teasing and pushing
each other, calling classmates by funny, often cruel nicknames, using slang and
dirty words. Then the bell would ring and the boys in their high-collared, black
uniforms and hair cut short to the roots, would obediently take their seats in the
crowded classrooms. Sofia's First Men's Gymnasium, as my high school was
called, an excellent public school attended by boys from all social backgrounds,
where, apart from receiving a rather solid basic education, I found some of my
most interesting and amusing friendships.

The friendships outside of school, equally rewarding, bloomed during vacation time, on the beaches of Sozopol and Varna or in the villas of Tcham-Koria,
favorite places for swimming, and skiing, and hiking in our carefree years. Back
in Sofia, we couldn't wait for the weekends to resume the new friendships and
flirtations on the courts of the Tennis Club in the Boris-Park, or at the public
beach of "Diana-Bad," or at the first dancing-parties we were allowed to attend.
How clumsy and how thrilled we were, leading equally shy teenage girls through
the "foxtrot" or the "English waltz," and hoping, if the partner was attractive, for
a tango or any kind of "slow," so we could attempt a cheek-to-cheek! A thrill of a
different sort were the skiing weekends with friends on nearby Mount Vitosha,
in spite of the exhausting 4 or 5-hour climb of foot on Friday nights (there were
no lifts in those days), carrying skis and heavy rucksacks, arriving dead-tired at
the primitive, smelly lodge "Aleko," and trying to sleep on the hard wooden
bunks and ignore the noisy banter and bawdy skiers songs, which lasted all night.
We would get up at dawn, dress up, prepare our equipment—wooden skis with
steel edges and leather-and-metal-spring bindings, and leave, in bright sun or in
snowstorm, for Cherny-Vruh, Vitosha's highest peak, another rough climb. The
downhill run from there was fast, very steep and challenging at places. On
Sunday afternoon, supreme reward!, we would ski all the way from Cherny-Vruh

down to the village of Kniazhevo, where we would take the tramway to Sofia, the weather-beaten faces swollen and every muscle aching, but elated and already planning the next excursion.

By the time of my senior high school year, the perspective of entering soon what I fancied then as "the free life" appeared extremely appealing. I could hardly wait to graduate, and not only because I'll be allowed to let my hair grow, wear "civilian" clothes, and be admitted to bars and movies "for adults only." The promises of the so-called "real world," no doubt naively romanticized by me, stimulated my imagination, and each discovery I was making during my late teenager years—a great novel, sex, symphonic music, the joys of skiing, jazz, first-hand reports of how people lived in Western Europe and America, the thrill of holding a pretty girl very close on the dancing floor, tales of great adventures, even the first tipsiness I experienced after two vermouths at "Maxim's," a cabaret off-limits for minors,—was to me a mere preview of fascinating things to come. I felt like an impatient spectator just lifting a small corner of the curtain and having a glance of the exciting stage behind it—the "real world" of great stories enacted by exceptional men and ravishing ladies. Oh, how much I would like to experience again, be it just for a moment, this intoxicating tingle of anticipation, the physical sensation of being alive and healthy and young, at the threshold of the great adventure!

World War II was not directly felt in Bulgaria before 1941. The policy of King Boris III and his governments was to keep the country out of the titanic confrontation which was ravaging Europe since 1939, and this position of neutrality seemed to be succeeding, in spite of tremendous pressure applied by the two belligerent sides. Life was not only normal, but also the remarkable recovery from the disastrous World War I had accelerated and the nation was beginning to enjoy considerably improved living standards. The country was peaceful, orderly, and, according to the unanimous opinion of foreign diplomats, businessmen, and visitors, quite pleasant to live in. People of course talked incessantly about the war and worried very much about it, but the war was still far away and the daily life was hardly affected by it.

All this began to change during the first months of 1941. Italy imprudently undertook a military adventure in Albania and Greece and was suffering humiliating defeats at the hands of the Greeks. Thus, the perspective of the British opening a second front in the Balkans became real. Germany, secretly preparing the invasion of Russia, could not afford such danger at its flank and felt compelled to go to the aid of its ally, Italy. Hitler had massed a formidable army in Rumania, and for him to go south and crush the Greeks was child's play. But there was a problem there: between the German divisions and Greece, across the Danube, stood Bulgaria and Yugoslavia. Hitler asked them to join the Tri-Partite Pact (Germany, Italy, Japan), and let his troops go through, "peacefully," without participating in his campaign against Greece.

For the Bulgarians, this was a tremendous dilemma. At the apogee of the Third Reich's might, with most of Europe already conquered and half of it destroyed, with the United States still neutral and the Soviet Union an ally of Hitler, with the victorious, best-equipped 680,000-men army in the history of the world waiting across the Danube for its orders to attack, with only England, badly wounded, relentlessly bombed and in desperate need of supplies, still resisting,—to say "no" would amount to a suicide. If France and Great-Britain couldn't stop the advancing panzers, and neither could Belgium, Holland, Poland, Czechoslovakia and Denmark, how could anybody expect little Bulgaria to do it? There was another factor: ever since the foolish, baneful Treaties of Versailles, Neuilly, and Trianon, whose vindictiveness only matched their authors' ignorance, had been imposed on the WWI losers, there was, for twenty years, not one Bulgarian heart indifferent to the dream of revising the treaties. Revision had also become a national goal for the Austrians, Hungarians, and Germans. Bulgaria had been so cruelly punished, amputated, and humiliated, that I myself, and a few generations before and after mine, grew up with deep indignation of an enormous historic injustice and ardent desire to see it corrected. As students, our modest contribution to the just Bulgarian cause was to demonstrate each year on November 27th (the anniversary of the 1919 Treaty) in front of the Yugoslav, Greek, and Rumanian legations and scream "Down with Neuilly!" as the mounted police dispersed the unruly crowds with truncheons. I was barely 14 (and looking like a ten-year-old altar boy), when my patriotism overcame my fear of police and my mother, and I joined the anti-Neuilly demonstration for the first time. My act of civil disobedience was short-lived. The first policemen arriving on the scene picked me up rather brutally and brought me, with scores of other demonstrators, into the cobble-stoned yard of the IV-th Precinct. There I was subjected to one of the worst humiliations in my life: As the tough chief of the Mounted police rebuked the demonstrators and ordered them detained for the rest of the night, he suddenly saw me, in my short pants, and burst into laughter: "And what is this child doing here?" he asked. "Get out of here, boy, and go home before I get angry!" Everybody laughed as I was leaving the precinct, red-faced and with tears in the eyes.

But to return to the mood in Bulgaria at the beginning of WWII. It's an axiom that the policies and alliances of small nations are determined far more by regional issues than by universal ideologies and Great-Power rivalries. This has always been the case with the Balkans nations. Revision of the post-Versailles status quo was a most important issue for Bulgaria. Preserving the status-quo, on the other hand, was a central goal for the beneficiaries of the Versailles treaties: Yugoslavia, Greece, and Rumania. The global confrontation between Fascism, Nazism, and democracies was, of course, of interest for the Balkan countries too, but in a more abstract way, not yet directly. They were more concerned in the regional conflicts—Macedonia, Thrace, Dobrudzha, the status quo.

Of the Great Powers, the only one openly crusading for revision of the Peace treaties was Germany, and this revisionism had a favorable echo in countries like Bulgaria, Hungary, and Austria. It had absolutely nothing to do with the ideological struggle between Democracy and Nazism. The Allies, for their part, were staunch supporters of the status quo in Central and Eastern Europe. In addition, in the fall of 1940 Germany had pressed Rumania to return Southern Dobrudzha peacefully to Bulgaria, a bloodless reunification that made the Bulgarians ecstatically happy. And grateful. Thus, Hitler's request to pass through Bulgaria came veiled as a sincere friend's invitation to the Tri-Partite Pact. King Boris, an exceptionally intelligent man and adroit manipulator with no sympathies for the Nazis, was not fooled. But he didn't fail to realize the tragic reality of the impasse: with his consent, it would take the Wehrmacht two days to cross Bulgaria and reach Greece; with his refusal, it would take it five or six days, and Bulgaria would be devastated. In both cases, the Germans will invade Greece. Boris tried to delay, to postpone. When he didn't succeed, he asked for and obtained assurances than no Bulgarian soldier would be asked to fight on the Greek front. Then, reluctantly, he signed the Pact. The same day, the German troops entered in Bulgaria, as allies. The country remained intact.

Yugoslavia also signed, but reversed itself a few days later and refused passage. The German troops crossed it anyhow, but as enemies, and the country was devastated.

*   *   *   *   *

This happened during my last year in the Gymnasium. In June I received my high school diploma, "cum laude," at a ceremony that meant a lot to me, because my father, who never came to school meetings, attended the event and looked very pleased and proud. All my life he had been my beloved hero and I was always looking for his approval and affection. That day he gave them to me in public and almost made me cry with happiness.

Finally a "free man," I spent a most delightful summer between Sofia, the Black Sea and the Yablansky villa in Tcham-Koria. I gladly discarded the hideous black uniform and my father took Boubi and me to his tailor to order two new suits for each of us. It was quite a notable event for me, used to wear his altered old suits, and also a strain for the tight family budget. For the first time since early childhood I was able to let my hair grow and started using, with dubious result, various hair lotions and creams to control undesirable curls. I had however a big problem, which gave me a terrible complex: at 19, I still had a child's face and was the only one in my class who not only didn't shave, but had nothing to shave. This may not sound like a problem, but at that age and in a society that prized virility so highly, being beardless amounted to a true infirmity, and I was ashamed of it. The other kids didn't let me forget it. I was teased cruelly, and each time a word like "shaving," "razor," or "mustache" was mentioned in class, forty mocking heads turned in my direction, in a chorus of bad jokes, while I blushed pathetically, wishing to disappear from the face of the earth. The worst was on occasions like when we went in a group one evening to a Varna nightclub and the bouncer at the door let everybody in, except for me. "No children!" he said, in front of the girl I was courting.

Because of my complex, I tried smoking in public, as a trick to look more manly, awkwardly holding the cigarette I really disliked, puffing and coughing at each drag. I still failed to look like Humphrey Bogart. But, this problem apart, I was having a marvelous time. Not knowing Paris or London, to me Sofia was a marvelously stimulating and enjoyable place. We saw a lot of German military around, mainly Austrian alpine troops, but in that early period they were considerate and discreet, and we had no personal contact with them. The German and Italian envoys were old, polite aristocrats, Baron von Richthofen and Count Magistratti. After the arrival of the German troops, the British and the Americans left, but the French and the other Western legations remained in Sofia. So did the Russians, in spite of the German presence. The war still seemed far away.

And just when I was enjoying my new freedom, the time came for my military service.

****

Military service was obligatory and lasted two years. For a young man in good health, to evade it was not only quasi-impossible, but also carried the stigma of being a sissy or unpatriotic, or both. "A woman who hasn't given birth and a man who hasn't done his military service, know nothing about life," a proverb said. The age was 19, but high school graduates used to have the choice of going to college first and serving afterwards. My brother Simeon, for instance, had done just that when he entered Sofia's University the previous year, and such was my intention too.

Unfortunately, that very year the law was changed: university or not, everybody had to do his service first. "Unfortunately?" That's what we thought then, myself, and Sava, and Jivko, and all friends of our grade, impatient to savor the joys and freedom of college life. We were very disappointed. But, as it often happens with presumed misfortunes, this turned out to be a blessing in disguise. Indeed, this seemingly trivial technicality allowed me, two years later, to go and study abroad. No young man was permitted to leave the country before serving his military duty. So, looking back, shouldn't I say "fortunately" instead of "unfortunately?"

The above-mentioned blessing was in fact more than well disguised. Sympathy should not be wasted too much on 19-year-olds in good health, for their resilience is miraculous, but it wouldn't be unfair to state that the living conditions of raw recruits in the otherwise glorious Bulgarian army were brutally primitive.

****

It's still dark outside and the vast dormitory of the Fourth Battery is totally silent, if one doesn't count the pacing of the soldier on night duty, some heavy snoring and sporadic salvos of uninhibited, spontaneous farts. The latter scarcely affect the general quality of the air, the staleness of which is anyhow taken care of by the 110 sleeping bodies, and even more so by the 110 pairs of old, deformed, but polished to regulation, military boots, neatly arranged at the foot of each bed, complete with the "partenkis," the pieces of cotton cloth to wrap the foot, which privates use instead of socks. In cold weather, the burning stove and the partenkis hanging around it to dry, add supplementary dimensions to the nocturnal odor, well preserved by the hermetically closed windows.

It's exactly 5:30 when the bugle sounds the reveille. One-hundred-and-ten groggy men jump out of bed and frantically start straightening sheets and blankets with one hand, while trying to dress with the other. Every second counts: Sergeant Branko, an imposingly built young giant, is already at the door, slowly undoing his leather belt and thundering: "Move your asses, you lazy bums! Faster, faster! Don't dilly-dally like old grannies! I'll start counting and God help you if you're not out when I say 'ten'! One…two…three…" Most of the men are already rushing through the door, half-dressed, hobbling with one boot on and the other not quite, clutching their towels, soap and toothbrush. At "ten," Branko gleefully starts hitting the fleeing men right-and-left with his belt. He does it almost in jest, but the blows sting. The punishment for the slowest two men is worse: one of them will empty the spittoon, an essential and liberally used piece of furnishing in every dormitory; the other one will clean the toilets that day.

Outside, as the sun rises, long lines form in front of the overcrowded lavatories. The quick "washing" with cold water is merely a symbolic ritual, not easy to perform when dressed in high-collared jacket, heavy overcoat and with visor cap on the head. As there are not enough indoor sinks, long lead pipes are installed horizontally outdoors, with faucets to serve several men simultaneously. But the real problem are the latrines. Just entering this filthy, malodorous establishment, where rows of bare-assed men squat, in uninhibited communal camaraderie, over stained cement orifices, requires considerable callousness and absence of squeamishness; to use it without dire effects, acrobatic skills and strong leg muscles are necessary, plus a private supply of news-papers, which the more intellectual among us tried to scan for news, before tearing into manageable squares of toilet paper.

For most of us, city boys, it took several days to overcome revulsion and adjust to the new conditions. But as my Uncle Mitcho would note so correctly, "Necessity Is the Best Teacher," or some proverb to that effect, we got used to it, and the hygienic imperfections became soon the least of our worries. We became used to the coarse daily soup (white beans one day, cabbage the next) with chunks of tough meat or lard, a food we sneered at for a few days, only to await it with eagerness and devour with animal voracity later on. The harsh daily routine and physical exhaustion made us so hungry, that the half loaf of bread each man received with the meals seemed barely sufficient and we were ready to fight or cheat to get more. As for fussiness, we totally forgot what the word meant. Nobody minded if a film of grease from last night's meal floated on the surface of the morning tea, served in the same aluminum containers in which we ate lunch and dinner and cleaned rather summarily with the last piece of bread; or if an overlooked bean or speck of lard enriched today's compote. Who cares! In fact, the promise of breakfast was the only bright note in the morning reveille, the only thing worth waking up for at the start of another dreary, exhausting day. The "holiday specials," usually roast pork or lamb with rice and a mug of cheap red wine, became most coveted events. The parcels with food brought at the periodic family reunions at the gates of the barracks, turned into most cherished treasures, to be shared with the closest friends and consumed parsimoniously.

Military discipline was more difficult to get accustomed to. Since the very first day of service, it was made clear to the new conscripts that officers and noncommissioned officers meant business and wouldn't tolerate any lax, "civilian" attitudes. To begin with, speaking to a superior in a normal conversational voice was not acceptable, one had to shout at the top of one's lungs. "What's your name?" was the sergeant's first question. When I answered, he said angrily that he couldn't hear. I repeated my name in a louder voice, but again he said "I can't hear you." This was repeated three or four times, until I was screaming like a madman: "Private Stephane Pavlov Groueff, of the First Army Artillery Regiment of His Royal Highness Prince Simeon of Turnovo." Those who didn't shout loud enough received a humiliating punishment: they had, during the lunch break, to face a tree in the middle of the barracks' yard and scream their name for a half-an-hour.

The sergeants had their own logic, peculiar maybe, but final and irrevocable for sure. "Sir, this cap is too narrow for me, Sir!" some new soldier would venture during the initial outfitting session. "Nothing wrong with the cap, stupid! It's your head that is too big!" I remember how shocked we all were during the first formal lining-up of the battery. Standing at attention, the 110 yesterday's civilians, still awkward in their ill-fitted uniforms, waited for a long moment for the arrival of the "feldwebel," as the sergeant majors were called. Tzeno Nikolov, an experienced and wise professional, was in fact our direct chief, the real "mother of the battery," the man in full charge of our daily life. Walking slowly from one end of the line to the other, he examined each rookie's appearance, stopping occasionally to point at an unbuttoned button or to put a finger under a soldier's belt, indicating that the belt wasn't tight enough. To judge by the patronizing smile on his lips, Feldwebel Tzeno was more amused by our *unsoldierly* looks than sarcastic or shocked. Then, after lecturing us on duty to the Fatherland, regimental rules, and our daily routine and chores, he asked how many of us were from the city, how many had finished high school, and a few similar statistical questions, including how many had never slept with bed sheets (there were quite a few, all from the villages). As he was about to dismiss us, Tzeno suddenly asked: "Is there a house painter here?"

A short fellow with a big grin stepped forward. "Where are you from, lad?" "From the village of Rila," the grinning guy replied, not very loudly. "I didn't hear you." This time the man shouted: "Village of Rila, Mr. Feldwebel." "What a combination!" Tzeno exclaimed, "Not only a painter, but also from Rila!" With that, the feldfebel walked to the new recruit and, to our utter surprise, slapped him across the face. "Everybody dismissed!" was Tzeno's last command, as he walked away. We were absolutely shocked. What injustice, what an arbitrary, inhuman gesture! I was profoundly disturbed and for a long time I held this incident against Tzeno, although I grew to like him and developed great respect for his wisdom, devotion to duty, and, strangely, his fairness in promoting iron discipline in our unit. A couple of times he punished me too for some minor infraction, but each time I had to admit he was right.

We didn't go on home leave for three months, and when the first permission came, we were ecstatic. We were free to leave the barracks on a Saturday by noon, spend the night at home—supreme happiness!,—then the whole day of Sunday in town, until 7 PM. But seven it meant, and not a minute later, and we knew that punishment for the slightest tardiness was draconian. Accordingly, heavy-hearted but obedient, we were all back to the regiment before the deadline, sighing, comparing notes with our buddies, and boasting about true or imagined romantic conquests. A few minutes later, the bugle sounded for the night line-up and the sergeants began reading loud the names. One-hundred-and-nine men answered with "Present!" One man was missing. The painter from Rila. "We'll wait for him," the feldwebel announced calmly.

The wait seemed interminable. All the other batteries went to bed, while we remained lined-up, tired and freezing in the dark, cold December night. Finally, a staggering silhouette appeared at the gates. His cap askew, his jacket unbuttoned, the drunk Rila boy zigzagged toward us, giggling and happily humming some barroom song. "He'll be court martialed!", somebody whispered behind me. "Tzeno will kill him now!", another predicted. In the ominous silence, as the painter reached the line, Tzeno walked to him and said softly, almost fatherly:

"Now you go to sleep, boy! You need it. And don't you ever do that again!" Then, to the startled battery: "I know what you thought of me when I slapped him. But he already had his punishment in advance. Believe me, I know my men! I've never met a house painter whom you can trust, or a man from Rila who's not a rascal. Battery, dismissed!"

*   *   *   *   *

We had the bad luck to be serving during the coldest winter of the century, when temperatures fell to minus 40 degrees. There were days when being out-doors for even a few minutes was an ordeal. This was the winter that stopped the German offensive on the Eastern front: it was so brutally cold, that engine fuel froze, totally paralyzing aircraft, Panzers, and motorized divisions, just about to enter Moscow. If unaware then that the unforeseen cold was changing the course of History, we knew enough to dread any moment spent out of the dormitory. Alas, not an all-outdoor routine was canceled during the sub-zero days: the Army wanted its warriors prepared for all seasons and believed in the didactic value of "toughening" exercises. Some pushed it to the extreme of considering the wear-ing of gloves as a show of weakness, which was particularly painful for me, as my hands freeze easily. The worst however during the periods of extreme cold was the sentinel duty. Although it was reduced, because of the severe temperature, from two to only one hour at a time, this hour was barely supportable by the human body, especially when there was wind: there were cases when soldiers had to be relieved before the hour and, half-frozen, to be revived. Each evening, as the sergeant read the names of the next day's sentinels, I said prayers in myself that the bitter cup would pass me this time. When it didn't—twice, if I remem-ber correctly,—I spent the night dreading the morning when the atrocious round of one-hour-watches would begin.

That was the worst I suffered as a recruit. That, and being home sick. I had never realized before how much I would miss my family. But there were many moments when, in the privacy of my bunk, I felt ashamed of myself, of the 19-year-old soldier who was just longing to go home, to Mom and Dad…

Most of the basic training was sheer tedium. Every day, hundreds of times, we dismantled and reassembled again our antiquated "Manliher" rifles, until we could do it even in our sleep. Twice a day, we cleaned each part thoroughly, whether the rifle had been used or not, and then greased it again. To find a trace of dirt on a weapon was a very serious offense; and if rust was found, the culprit could be court martialed. The country was too poor to afford new rifles. That's how our *Manlihers*, pampered and venerated as quasi-cult objects, had lasted since the 1885 Serbo-Bulgarian war...The cannons were a different matter. We were very proud of our 105 mm. Krupp guns, the most modern "heavy" pieces in Bulgarian artillery. So modern that we looked down upon our colleagues from the horse-drawn artillery. Loading and unloading cannons was a boring daily drill and the ballistics lessons were not more exciting. But in those days, belonging to a fully motorized regiment made us feel as being part of a most advanced military technology.

✶✶✶✶✶✶✶✶✶✶✶✶✶

I was at the regiment when I heard the news, very busy preparing the automobiles and trucks of my battery for the maneuvers. At that time I had the rank of sergeant-cadet and commanded the drivers' platoon of the 4-th Battery. Sava had the same rank and function in the 3-rd Battery. In order to reach this position in the glorious artillery of His Majesty, a number of privates with high school education were selected after the basic training at the regiment and sent for nine months to the School for Reserve Officers. There, we had classes on military subjects, drills with rifles, handguns, and artillery pieces, and countless hours of marching and goose-stepping. During the summer, we spent one month or two in camp, on a muddy field outside the village of Bankia, near Sofia, where we slept, eight or ten men to a tent. The leaking canvas tents, mounted by ourselves, were so narrow, that one could lie only in profile, and the ground was hard, in spite of the thin layer of straw we spread under the rough blankets. But with the long, exhausting hours of drills and marching, insomnia was the least problem.

I'm not sure how well I mastered the skills of an artillery officer, but I'm grateful to God that I never saw war and was spared the opportunity to prove it. Later in life, ill-intended wits insinuated that with fighters like me there was no wonder that Bulgaria lost the war. That's nonsense: not only was I a very diligent Reserve Officers School cadet, but also on graduation day, when we were promoted sergeants and bestowed officer's sabres, I ranked second of the entire school! (I was a little chagrined to overhear a rumor that "he got it because he's is Pavel Groueff's son," but chose to attribute it to pure jealousy.)

Those sabres! How proud we were of these long, slightly curved, nickel-plated status symbols! Feeling the sabre dangling along the left thigh, the gloved hand holding casually the sculpted brass haft as we walked and graciously accepted the stern salute of passing soldiers, gave us, at age 20, a delightful sense of self-confidence, elegance and authority. We were assigned to different regiments and, wearing better-fitted uniforms with sergeant's epaulet and snappy, custom-made knee-high boots, we were put in command of 20-25 men platoons, outranking the professional non-commissioned officers. So I returned, for one year, to my old First Army Artillery Regiment and to the same 4th Battery, where I found my old buddies and same good old sergeants Tzeno, Libren, Mihal, and Branko. The only differences were that now they all had to salute and call me "Mr. Feldwebel-Shkolnik" (Sergeant-Cadet), and that I had a new immediate superior, Kleo Daskalov, a handsome Second-lieutenant, whose father was the Minister of Defense. Kleo was a charming, romantic man whom I liked immediately, but there was a problem for me: he was crazy in love, and the object of his passion was, of all people, our friend Lucy. Sava was serving in the battery next to ours, just across the courtyard. His romance with the jazz star was supposedly over, mainly because of the prolonged separation, but the two rivals couldn't' t stand each other. This created a conflict of loyalties for me, especially since Lucy was not the kind of girl who is fanatic when it comes to drawing a clear line between ending an old romance and beginning a new one. In this gray zone she managed to accommodate both admirers for several months, until Kleo's perseverance and unconditional devotion won Lucy over. Her old absentee lover had cooled anyhow.

Commanding is not my forte, but I must admit it's better than being commanded, and I sort of enjoyed it. Discipline and strictly structured hierarchy in the army were such that the mere rank conferred enough authority to even the greenest and least imposing youngster to give orders and be obeyed. It was easier to command new recruits, but at the beginning I was very self-conscious when ordering the second-year soldiers, my former buddies. It was hard the first time I had to punish some of them. I had led the battery, in marching formation and singing in the streets, on the weekly visit to the public bath. While undressing, a few soldiers had sneaked out and spent one hour in town, but were seen by the colonel who happened to be passing by. The next morning he asked me to identify the culprits. It was a serious violation and I had to give them the worst punishment: I cancelled their weekend permission. They were crushed when I announced it, as the battery stood at attention. Two of them were my friends and at that moment I hated my job.

But being in charge of men had also its rewards. Teaching the new recruits to drive gave me great pleasure. I was myself at the age when cars are still very exciting objects, and not merely means of transportation. Not many Bulgarians owned cars and driving any motor vehicle was a thrill. Even the huge *MAN* trucks and caterpillar *Buessing* tractors, which pulled the heavy artillery. To get at the wheel of a commander's light *Fenomen*, another German-built car, or a powerful *BMW* motorcycle, was a real treat. Explaining carburetors and gearshift to novices, mostly peasant boys, and giving them lessons in elementary history and geography, proved unexpectedly rewarding. That was the time I discovered how much I like to teach and explain, a weakness that never left me. A captive audience is great for the ego, a dream for long-winded talkers. In civilian life, alas, one impatient look in a listener's eyes in the middle of some of my long stories is enough to make me wonder whether my soldiers have been really that interested and amused…

*   *   *   *   *   *

I was already counting the days to the end of my service—another 25 days only, according to the rumors circulating in the barracks!,—when we heard the terrible news: the King was dangerously ill! My regiment was getting ready to leave for the big autumn maneuvers, but orders came to cancel the departure. The entire country went into a state of shock and rushed to their radio sets to listen to the bulletins, and to the churches to pray. A cloud of pessimism enveloped the land, old fears of impending disaster were revived.

For Boris was not an ordinary king, and we didn't live in ordinary times. A proverbially democratic ruler, King Boris was adored by the people. He had kept his vow never to send Bulgarian soldiers to the fronts, and Bulgaria, although a member of the Axis, was still intact, sovereign, and enjoying peace as "non-belligerent ally," a curious and privileged status obtained uniquely thanks to the his unusual diplomatic skills and conciliatory attitudes. But alarming signs were increasing in the summer of 1943. The war surrounded us. After our neighbors Yugoslavia and Greece had been crushed and occupied by the Wehrmacht, Bulgarian troops were administering the former Bulgarian provinces of Macedonia and Thrace. Our northern neighbor Rumania was fighting on the Russian front, while Allied airplanes, on their way to bombing its oil fields, flew more and more frequently over Bulgaria. The German armies were retreating in Russia and, in spite of the Nazi pep talk we were listening to daily and exclusively (the only available source for Allied news in Bulgarian was *BBC*), the German victory seemed less and less possible. And what would happen to us, the Axis allies?, people worried. Oh, the King would do something! The King knows. Look, he managed to turn down Hitler's demand for Bulgarian troops for Russia, and while Hungarians, Rumanians, Italians, even French and Belgian volunteers, are fighting on the Eastern front, we still have Russian legation in Sofia and Bulgarian legation in Moscow. And didn't he succeed in getting back South Dobrudzha without a drop of blood? And not delivering Bulgarian Jews to the Nazis? Rumors that King Boris was considering leaving the Axis and was secretly negotiating with the Western Powers grew persistently. Both pro-German and pro-Western Bulgarians counted on the king to prevent a new national catastrophe.

At this moment, the 49-year-old king fell gravely ill. Suddenly and with no warning.

*   *   *   *   *

King Boris died on the 28-th of August 1943. The official communiqué spoke of coronary thrombosis, but the death of the healthy, 49-year-old ruler was so unexpected, that few people believed that it was "natural." The suspicion of foul play was widespread. The Germans poisoned him, because the King was secretly preparing to switch to the Allies' side, said one version. But as Communist terrorists had, very recently, assassinated a number of prominent anti-Communist leaders, many people were sure that King Boris was their latest and most logical target. Others were convinced that the Kremlin had most to gain from creating instability in the heart of the Balkans. Another rumor implicated the British, quoting Churchill's current anger at Bulgaria and his ruthlessness. Some Nazi circles even suggested a bizarre plot involving the Italians…The mystery persisted. But there was no doubt about one thing: the extraordinary attachment of Bulgarians to their king and the depth of the popular grief.

The entire country was shaken. Also myself, I felt very sad about the loss of a man I liked and respected so much. I knew how terribly upset my father was, so I asked the regiment's commander for a few hours leave and went to see him at the palace. He was alone in his office, and seeing his grief broke my heart. My father looked aged, ashen, with heavy circles under his eyes. Immersed in thought, he barely said a few words and seemed strangely remote and listless. He told me that the King had worked with him only five days before his death, in the evening of August 23rd, when he suddenly felt sick and left the room. A few moments later, my father learned that he had collapsed on the way to his private quarters, never to regain consciousness again. "Here he signed his last decrees and letters," my father said, pointing to the blotting paper atop the desk, where one could still see distinctly several imprints of the intricate *"BORIS III"* handwritten signature.

When I walked in, my father was reading some papers spread atop his second desk. My curiosity was piqued when I realized that they were coded telegrams. The fact that my father worked with codes and cyphers had fascinated me since childhood, so I stole a glance, and to my surprise, my father didn't react. He was so dejected, that, very uncharacteristically, he didn't seem to mind my reading the confidential mail, as he was looking absent-mindedly out of the windows.

The telegram on top of the pile was a coded message from King Boris, sent from Germany and describing a tense conversation he had had with Hitler.

Mixing humor with high drama, referring to world leaders by nicknames (the Fuehrer was, I don't know why, "Vurban;" Mussolini was "Firmen;" the King of Italy—"Father-in-Law," etc.), Boris wrote how hard it was for him to parry Hitler's insistent demands for Bulgarian troops on the Eastern front and expelling the Soviet legation and consulates from Bulgaria, in other words, to enter the war actively. He listed the arguments, little stratagems and ruses he used to convince an increasingly irritated Fuehrer that it was in Germany's best interest if Bulgaria remained neutral toward Russia and kept the Bulgarian army intact. The meeting had obviously been quite stormy, but Boris had managed once more to postpone an involvement he wanted to avoid at any cost. "Dad, who's the 'Pendarliya'?" I asked at one place, mesmerized. "That's what the King called Goering" he said, smiling faintly. "You know, all these medals he wears…" (*Pendar* is Turkish for large gold coin or medallion.)

I was fascinated to read that the King wanted my father to communicate certain parts to Prime Minister Filov, or to the Foreign minister, while other passages were not to be shared with them. He also instructed my father to send him open telegrams, pretending that he was needed urgently back to Sofia, thus giving him an excuse to decline some unwanted invitations. In his exceptional state of emotions, my father answered me when I asked about this code: yes, it was a special personal code the King used only with him and his old confidant Parvan Draganov, and it was different from the foreign ministry cypher. It served to transmit confidential messages when the King traveled, and also to keep a record of his conversations abroad; my father was on the receiving side in Sofia.

As we were talking, the King's brother, Prince Kyril, entered the room. I jumped to my feet and gave him a military salute. He smiled in a friendly way and asked me a few polite questions, then he left. I noticed that my father had abruptly closed the file and had pushed it into the drawer, as if to hide it. It made me feel as if we, he and I, were sharing some great secret, a State secret. "I shouldn't have shown you that!" my father said in a self-reproaching manner. I promised not to tell anybody, and at that moment I felt very important, and also very proud of my father's trust.

I saw my father again a few days later, at King Boris's funeral at Rila monastery. Cannons from Sava's and my batteries were selected for the last gun salute in honor of the late monarch. The previous day we drove up to the majestic ancient monastery (I found the 40 miles journey on winding mountain roads on the wheel of a tractor towing a huge Krupp cannon quite a harrowing experience), and took position near the pine forest outside the walls. In the evening I went inside the large cobble-stoned courtyard, packed with officials, church dignitaries and pious crowds converging for the funeral. In the approaching night, the dark contours of the overhanging mountain peaks, the dim lights in the cloisters and the bells' mourning toll rising above the muffled voices, gave a surrealistic touch to the solemn scene. The King's body and the royal party, traveling on the funereal train to the nearest station and then by cars through the gorgeous Rila mountain woods, had arrived and my father had come with them. He was surprised and very happy to see me, and so was I. It was a happy coincidence (I thought "symbolic"), father and son meeting on this extraordinary occasion, both doing their duty: I, in full battle dress, taking part in Army's last homage to its Commander-in-Chief; he, the King's faithful companion, getting ready to stand by the Queen as the casket is lowered in the grave, inside the church, in front of the side altar.

It was a very emotional encounter, but we both tried to control our feelings and just hugged each other in silence. He had had an enormously trying day, both physically and emotionally, and it was showing. That morning in Sofia, at the religious service at "Alexander Nevsky," he had stood up for hours, just behind the royal family. Then, as the solemn cortege proceeded along the streets of Sofia, he had walked on foot on the side of the gun carriage with the King's casket. It's a long way, from the cathedral to the railroad station, a couple of miles, and it must have been a Calvary for my phlebitis-afflicted father. Hundreds of photographs of the funereal procession show the indescribable outpour of popular grief that day: a city draped in black, with thousands of people sobbing inconsolably in the streets as the cortege passes, at the sound of funeral marches. When I saw the newsreel, nothing touched me more than the sight of the frail, white-bearded man in black, pathetically stooped and sad, walking with difficulty next to the coffin. My father.

*   *   *   *   *   *

I wasn't the only one who had this weird sensation: as in a dream in which one attends one's own funeral, the nation, heartbroken and helpless, celebrated its own last rites. Sensing an imminent tragedy, crying for King Boris was in a way crying for us. The general lamentation could be summed up in one sentence: "To whom are you leaving us now?"

This anxiety hit me full force later in winter, during the aerial bombardments of Sofia. I had finished military service and had started my first semester in Law at the University, just one year behind my brother Boubi. Neither of us was particularly interested in the legal profession, but a Law diploma was required for joining the Foreign ministry, and we both intended to follow in our father's steps in the diplomatic service. In fact, my real interest was in journalism and an old dream came true when the director of the best daily paper "Zora," Danail Krapchev, my schoolmate Jivko's father, agreed to take Jivko and myself as part-time trainees at his newspaper.

But I was also dreaming of something else. Since October, Sava had left for Switzerland, to study at the University of Geneva. It was difficult to travel through war-torn Europe, but as Bulgaria remained calm and orderly, it was still possible, if the neutral Swiss granted the visa and if one had finished the military service. Sava's sister Harri had already been in Geneva for a year or two, and had just announced her engagement to a young Genevois, Bertrand Cheneviere. My childhood friends Tania and Lilliana Danev, Anni Tchaprachikoff, and others were also studying in Switzerland and I was dying to go too. But my father was not keen of the idea. By nature, he hated any change and risk, and to him going abroad in wartime was an "adventure." I couldn't insist too much, because I knew that sending me to Switzerland would be a financial sacrifice for him, but my mother was on my side. And my best ally was Mika Panitza who encouraged me to leave and tried to influence my father.

When Sava was leaving for Switzerland, his parents invited me to accompany him as far as Bucharest, where the family kept an office with a small apartment. Thus I finally had my first trip abroad. To me, the Rumanian capital looked as glamorous as Paris and we spent a marvelous week drooling after the local ladies and eating caviar by the ladle, which Rumanians still did at amazingly affordable prices. Then the time came for saying good-bye. At the railroad station, he boarded the train to Geneva, and I, to Sofia. With the war all around, we didn't know when, or whether, we were going to see each other again.

By November and December, the situation changed considerably. American and British airplanes attacked four or five time Sofia, putting an end to the illusion that Bulgaria was non-belligerent and the war, foolishly declared on the two Anglo-Saxon powers two years ago, was merely "symbolic." The first bombings were relatively not too severe, as WW2 bombings go—a few dozens victims each time. But the psychological effect was tremendous: the sinister howling of the sirens was enough to disrupt life for several hours and make the citizens' blood curdle in terror. We had had air alerts before, but usually without, or with just a few, bombs. I was still in the regiment during the first attack and happened to be the officer of the day. I remember my heart beating wildly when the anti-aircraft fire erupted; I was really frightened. But having to give orders and lead the alarmed soldiers out of the barracks and to the nearby trenches, I completely forgot my own fear and even managed to laugh about it. Later, as civilian, when not responsible for other people and not forced to be a model, the sound of sirens, flak and bombs seemed much more frightening.

Nevertheless, when my family moved before Christmas to Tcham-Koria, I continued to go regularly to Sofia, for two reasons: not to interrupt my apprenticeship at *Zora*, and to apply for Swiss visa. The latter I did with the knowledge of my mother and the help of "Aunt Mika," but without publicizing it too much to my father; I simply mentioned to him that I might, "just in case," ask for a visa, which doesn't commit me to anything and won't probably be granted for several months…

That's why I was in Sofia, alone in our apartment, on that terrible morning of January 10th. It was about 10 AM when the sirens started screaming. Almost simultaneously, the staccato, hysterical flak was heard and a tremendous roar of engines shook the city. When I looked up, I could hardly believe my eyes: the sky was black with low-flying aircraft, literally blanketed with hundreds of American "Flying Fortresses." It looked as if all the bombers in the world were converging in dense formations, carrying Armageddon over Sofia. The sight was breathtaking, the sound terrifying. I rushed down to the cellar, already filled with tense, haggard neighbors. Two other cities had been bombed heavily that week and everybody was frightened. When the bombs started falling, we all withdrew into ourselves, stunned, counting the hits, praying silently, and hoping. In the dark, someone was weeping quietly. The hell lasted for half-an-hour, maybe more. When the even tone of the "all-clear" of the sirens was finally heard, I thought it the most divine sound in the world.

Many buildings were demolished that day, but ours was not hit. On our street, there was not one single window unbroken. The apartment was a mess, but not damaged. I packed a small bag and went out, determined not to spend the night in town: the American daytime raids were usually followed by repeat performance by British night bombers. I had no transportation to Tcham-Koria and decided to go to the villa of family friends, Goldstein, in Kniajevo, a half-hour trip by tram. By tram? How naive of me! Several neighborhoods were in ruins, many streets were made impassable, the streetcars didn't run, and half of the population was trying to leave town. I walked to Sveta-Nedelia square, then joined the crowds of heavily laden pedestrians trying like them to get a ride in a passing vehicle. After a couple of miles on foot, I was picked up by a military truck and finally reached Kniajevo.

The Emperor Nero would've enjoyed the nocturnal sight from the Goldstein villa that night. No fireworks could possibly match the fantastic pyrotechnics of thousands of British incendiary bombs, anti-aircraft searchlights and luminous-trace bullets, criss-crossing Sofia's sky. The city was aglow with raging fires and the glare of slowly descending Bengal lights. Horrified, we watched in awe, thinking of the friends who were there.

The damages were heavy and several hundreds civilians were killed, as is always the case with terror bombings of open cities. This time, R.A.F. and U.S.

Air Force had used the infamous tactics of "bomb carpet," the systematic and indiscriminate bombardment of populated areas with the sole purpose of breaking an enemy's morale. They hadn't invented the tactics, the Germans also had done it in England and all over Europe. But "bomb carpets" are not only inhuman and barbaric—they're, I'm convinced, counter-productive. True, they temporarily knocked out the administrative services on January 10th and forced the evacuation of the government. True, the citizens were terror-stricken. But the overwhelming feeling on the morning of the 11th was not one of capitulation and self-recrimination; it was anger and indignation. The terror bombing played into the hands of the die-hards, and upset and disconcerted those who were hoping of negotiating with the Western Powers.

There was little use for me to stay in Sofia. Our apartment had no heating and no windows, and the University classes were disrupted. I joined the family in Tcham-Koria, but checked regularly with the Swiss legation about my visa. My father stayed with us, since the Queen, as well as the government, were spending part of their time there. He went often to work at the royal residence in Vrana or, just for the day, to Sofia, and sometimes I went with him. But there was not a word about my visa, and I began to lose hope. Winter was ending, Sofia was recovering slowly, and in spite of the constant fear of new air raids, I took the courage to spend some nights in town, cam-ping in the cold apartment and helping at *Zora* editorial offices.

I was just leaving the newspaper building in the morning of March 29th, when the sirens announced the raid. With a lady-colleague we ran to the nearby new building of the Second Gymnasium for Girls, a massive, unfinished construction of concrete and stone, whose basement offered the most solid shelter in the neighborhood. We had barely reached the entrance, when we heard the rapid cracks of the anti-aircraft guns and the thunderous rumble of the approaching American bombers. As in January, they came again by the hundreds—200?, 400?, more?—and proceeded to laying their deadly carpet.

Hundreds of people were taking refuge in the damp basement, between unpainted cement columns and stone walls under construction. We realized immediately that bombs were falling very close. Each hit was preceded by a whistle, faint first, then increasing in pitch, and finally followed by the explosion. Holding our breath, we listened and counted. As each plane dropped bombs in series, the diminishing or increasing loudness of the consecutive blasts told us whether the hits were getting nearer or away from us. When the bomb-carpet approached, the noise became horrendous, the walls shook, dust filled the basement. Now it was our turn, it was a matter of seconds. The last bomb had fallen next door, we felt it. The next one is already released, I thought, and started counting: eight, seven…four, three…It's amazing how rich the emotional kaleidoscope was during those seconds! The thought of The End came to me, but without interrupting my meticulous countdown; and also the hope that, after having hit the house next door, the deadly path would perhaps deviate to a different direction. Simultaneously, I wondered whether a device could be invented to make bombs explode in the air before hitting the target. I found time to look around for shovels, in case we survived but were buried alive; there was none. Then I realized that the last blast had thrown my colleague and me into each other's arms and we were hugging—trembling, scared, out of breath; strange, I had time to find it comforting, even pleasant, and it occurred to me that I hardly knew her. Her name was Radka, like my sister…

Then, the ominous whistle again, nearer, nearer, and the deafening, blinding Big Bang. So, that's what Death was!, I thought. Slowly I opened my eyes, but we were in a cloud of thick dust, coughing violently, our eyes burning. The building had suffered a direct hit and it was difficult to breathe. When we came to, I was still hugging my stunned co-survivor. Staggering and coughing, we ran through the debris and looked for the exit Everybody was fleeing frantically. Outside, the streets were burning.

I never imagined that fire could make such tremendous noise and cause gusts of such violence…That day, the planes had dropped enormous amounts of incendiary bombs, transforming many streets into a blazing inferno. On both sides of "Dondukov" boulevard and "Stara-Planina" street, houses were flaming like torchlights, and the smoke and overheated air forced me to change routes several times. Out of breath, I continued running in the general direction of the "Eagles' Bridge," where I hoped to find some transportation to Tcham-Koria.

When I reached "Moskovska" street, the "all-clear" had already sounded and, feeling less frantic, the idea occurred to me to check our building. I made a slight detour, saw that the house was still there and not burning, and as I was about to continue, I suddenly had a second thought. I returned to the building, entered the hall strewn with litter and broken glass, and checked the mailbox. There was an envelop with letterhead "Legation de la Confederation Suisse." My visa had arrived.

When several hours later I arrived in Tcham-Koria (hitch-hiking all the way, changing cars and trucks), my family welcomed me as if I were re-turning from the other world. They'd been worrying to death and mama, not given to demonstrate affection, hugged me and cried on my shoulder for a longtime, while my father couldn't conceal his delight. It was only in the evening that my mother, who used to fuss about a broken glass or a stain on the carpet, suddenly remembered to ask: "By the way, what happened to our apartment?" I loved them so much that day that I felt sort of guilty about receiving my long-coveted visa.

*   *   *   *

Chapter 5

Student in Geneva

I had so many lucky breaks in leaving Bulgaria that spring, that one could think God really wanted me to go to Geneva and had, for this purpose, generously improvised a scenario of highly unlikely coincidences. In the chaotic weeks following the big bombardments, with government offices and foreign consulates scattered in different villages around Sofia and working only rare, irregular hours, I seemed to have no difficulty in getting my passport, visas, and tickets, although I came down from Tcham-Koria only when I could find transportation and avoided staying in town for more than a few hours at a time. But as though by enchantment, the persons I needed to see at each office somehow happened to be there at just the right moment, with the right seals and documents ready for me. The fact, of course, that at ministries and consulates I introduced myself as Pavel Groueff's son, didn't hurt, although I never asked my father to intervene. Not only because he disapproved of any form of nepotism, but also because I knew how unenthusiastic he felt about my leaving, and was afraid that he would not support my application persuasively enough.

It was my luck that my ticket to Vienna, via Belgrade, was for May 1st: soon after I bought it, the airline announced that all flights were to be discontinued on the 2nd of May. Luck was on my side again on the early morning in Tcham-Koria when, after kissing my parents, Boubi and Radka goodbye, I stood with my suitcase in the middle of the road, nervously waiting for some vehicle to pass and give me a ride to Sofia. Indeed, an open truck stopped and drove me to Samokov, where I found another truck going to Sofia. That's where I thought I ran out of luck.

Dropped in the center of town, in front of the Parliament, I spent what seemed to be hours looking in vain for a taxi to take me to the Bojourishte airport. It was hopeless. The air raids had reduced the capital's traffic to near zero and no cab was in sight on the deserted boulevard. As noon approached, I began to panic: the plane was leaving in a couple of hours, and it was the *last* flight to Belgrade! Desperate, I tried stopping some of the rare cars that passed, pleading, offering money; nobody was interested. As I looked at my watch, I began to realize that I was missing the flight and it made me sick to think that this meant the end of my dreams of Switzerland.

Then suddenly I thought I was seeing a mirage: an empty cab was speeding toward me. Gesticulating frantically, I almost threw myself under its wheels. Reluctantly, the driver stopped. "I'm not working!" he barked at me. I begged him, I insisted, I almost cried. But to no avail. The man refused categorically. "I just can't, young man, don't you understand? I don't have enough gas, and I must go home, all he way to Bojourishte." I couldn't believe my ears. Bojourishte? But that was exactly where I wanted to go! Talk about coincidences!…I was so happy when I jumped into the cab that I could've kissed him. But then I looked at my watch: it was past the departure hour. My heart sunk, but nevertheless I went on with the ride.

It turned out that the heart had sunk somewhat prematurely. It seems that at that point, whoever was writing this episode had recourse to the old, well-tried trick authors use when they don't know how to get out of an impasse: *Deus ex machina*. My departure had already benefited from so many strokes of luck, that a few other improbable happenings wouldn't affect the script's credibility too much. And indeed, it happened again: the flight had been delayed considerably, allowing me plenty of time before take-off. It was my first flight in an airplane.

Traveling across war-torn Europe was a hazardous venture and it took me a few days to reach Switzerland. In Belgrade, arriving at an unheated hotel with windows broken from previous bombardments, the sirens sounded air alert and we had to rush down the pitch-black stairs to the shelter. The alerts continued on and off during the night, and each time we had to feel our way up and down in total darkness. We heard a lot of shooting and explosions that night, but I never found out what was hit or where. It wouldn't have made a difference, because hadn't the slightest idea where I was.

The next day, unwashed and dusty, with dark rings under my eyes, but nevertheless excited, I continued the flight, to Budapest first, then, after a long delay at the airport, to Vienna. The only person I knew in Vienna was a Sofia and Tcham-Koria friend, Sava Riaskoff, who was studying there. Luckily, he was at home when, with some difficulties, I located his address and he invited me to stay with him. He took me to a cafe where Bulgarian students used to meet and before long a small crowd of them surrounded me, all eager to hear news from home and anxious to find out whether I was bringing Bulgarian cigarettes. Indeed, I was. I had been told in Sofia, where foreign currency was extremely hard to get, to carry as many packs of cigarettes as I could, and I had in my suitcase a few cartons of hundred *"de luxe."* I knew that many compatriots in Austria and Germany relied on the black market for a living, and I knew that cigarette prices were very high, but what I was offered that day seemed astronomical. Not only the Deutsch marks I received covered largely the price of my train ticket to Geneva, but also other students told me the next day that I had been shamelessly "cheated." But I was extremely relieved to find the money for the train, and totally satisfied with my first (and last) transaction on the European black market.

As far as sightseeing is concerned, my two-day stay in fabulous Vienna was hardly a success: there was so much destruction everywhere, and also frequent air alerts. Of the famous nightlife, I only saw the shelter under my friend's building where we rushed each time the sirens sounded…But I was lucky that there were no bombings those nights. The sirens had become an obsession with me. The moment I heard them howling, my heart started racing, my nerves tensed to a near cracking point, and I was unable to concentrate on anything else. The sirens followed me even during the train ride to Switzerland, which lasted the entire day, with the train stopping a few times in the middle of nowhere and re-starting again. Once, the passengers were ordered to leave the cars and disperse in the fields. Some planes passed high above us, but nothing happened. In the evening, we finally reached the Swiss border at Feldkirchen, and after the customs control, we found ourselves in peaceful, neutral Switzerland.

The place was called Buchs, and as long as I live I won't forget the newfound tranquility and marvelous sense of being sheltered that I felt that night. I won't forget the warm coziness of the small inn's room, the cheerful flower-pattern wallpaper, crispy clean bed sheets and puffed eiderdown, the welcoming smile of the red -cheeked maid serving hot chocolate and croissants, luxuries I had almost forgotten. So this kind of world still existed!, I thought with delight while taking a hot bath and going to bed. Sirens and noise of airplanes gave me a jolt during the night, just the time to realize that they came from the other side of the frontier. They were not for us. The war was far from here, we were safe. Relieved, I closed my eyes and slept my first relaxed, happy sleep in a longtime.

The next day Sava Panitza met my train at the station in Lausanne and we traveled together to Geneva. It was the happiest of reunions, laughing, joking, and trying to catch up with each other's news and impressions. He brought me to the pension where he and his sister Harri were staying and where he had reserved a room for me. Madame Masset's pension on Route de Florissant was a modest old house where she lived with her aging husband, a daughter of our age, Gaby, two older sons, Albert and Hugues, and a spinster niece, Rita. Apart from us, M-me Masset had two or three other young boarders and provided three rather frugal meals a day, which we had to take at strictly fixed hours, all together in the dining room. She insisted on punctuality and good table manners, would not tolerate noise, and frowned upon people asking for second helpings or taking too much jam at breakfast. Butter, milk, meat and other products were available but rationed in Switzerland, and each boarder had to give Madame Masset part of his or her ration coupons. But the price she charged was reasonable and students on very limited budget, as it was my case, could afford it.(My monthly allowance which my father was sending through the Bulgarian National bank was 360 Swiss francs, barely enough to pay for room, food, and school.) The rooms were rather worn-out but decent, the overgrown garden was restful, and the family atmosphere of the quiet, old-fashioned pension suited me perfectly.

My first task was to register at Geneva University, which presented some problems as the school year had begun in September, and we were already in May. But the authorities accepted my proof of having attended one semester in Sofia's Law school and having been unable to continue because of the bombing of the University, and I was admitted directly to second semester, with Sava. The exams for the first year I had to pass in the fall. Thus, after being born on the same day as Sava, after finishing the same high school, served in the same battery in the same regiment and attended the same School for Reserve Officers, we were now students in the same class and sharing the same address in Geneva. Our biographies were becoming more and more similar.

Geneva in the spring is a delightful place to live. But during the war, it was more than that, it was an oasis of normalcy and civility, miraculously preserved and protected from the horrors and devastations that had engulfed the rest of Europe. I was very conscious of my good fortune and fully appreciated every moment of my new life. The group of old friends who had arrived there before me couldn't be more attractive: in addition to Sava and Harri, Tania Daneva and Anni Tchaprachikoff were in Geneva; Louli Daneva, Ilko Riaskoff, and Vladi Balabanov studied in Lausanne, less than an hour away from us. I quickly befriended Harri's fiancé, Bertrand Cheneviere, and Tania's and Louli's boyfriends- Jean-Pierre Cellerier and Michael Brisby, as well as Anni's friend Jurek Byczkowski. We made some new friends at the University, and for a few months I tasted of the wondrously pleasant and carefree life of a student in prosperous, cosmopolitan Geneva.

Apart from the courses, given by some internationally known professors, and which I attended regularly, we enjoyed bicycling in the well-paved, clean streets or along the quays, meeting friends at *La Clemence* on the Bourg-du-Four, a students' hang-out in the Old Town, or ogling the mannequins on the terrace of cafe *Canonica*, on Lake Leman, just next to the Mont-Blanc bridge. I had a crush on a blond model with the cutest buckteeth, whom I designated with the Bulgarian word of *"Zubi"* (teeth), but to whom I never gathered enough courage to speak. Shyness used to be s serious problem with me, especially when I was interested in a girl. I would just sit at a table facing "Zubi," stare, and blush, until she and her friends leave, promising myself that the next time I'll go and say "hello." It never happened. She looked very shy herself and I'll never know whether she was pleased or annoyed by my staring at her.

By night, when we could afford it, we went to a little club in the Old Town, where students and 'bobby-sockers' danced wildly the jitterbug, the rage of that period, terribly amusing to watch but too uninhibited and acrobatic for self-conscious young men like Sava and myself to even try. The place for our kind of dancing was *Moulin Rouge*, a helvetized version of the Montmartre cabaret, where they played numbers such as *Sentimental Journey* and *Amor, amor*, and where we could stay for hours without ordering a secong "gin-fizz." A more elegant place was *Amphitryon*, the piano-bar of Hotel des Bergues, the hotel of the rich. It was much too expensive for us and we went there rarely, only when taken for an after-dinner drink by some Swiss friend, or by Anni, who had more money than we did.

We joined the University tennis class and started playing on the courts of the Parc des Eaux-Vives. When the public beach opened, we went swimming in the lake. Incidentally, it was there that I tasted Coca-Cola for the first time. "What's so great about it?", I wondered after the first sip, not knowing that I would acquire the taste very rapidly. It may sound curious today that a 22-year-old had never tasted Coca-Cola before. But other "firsts" were even more indicative of the isolated world in which I had grown up. It was in Geneva, for example, that I met for the first time a black man. He was the saxophonist of *Moulin Rouge*, a dapper American Negro, who was a sort of a star to us, the jazz fans. I don't think I had ever seen a black person in Bulgaria, if we don't count a very dark-skinned boy in school, whose Negroid features the nasty gossip attributed to the brief occupation of the country by French colonial troops at the end of World War I...

In a different vein, a "first" for me was the talk heard in Geneva about attrocities on a scale hard to be believed, being allegedly perpetrated in Nazi concentration camps. Coming from Bulgaria, I was shocked to hear rumors of systematic, premeditated extermination of thousands, reports of organized genocide. Back home, where the radio and most of the press were pro-German, we hadn't heard such reports. German camps for prisoners and enemies, yes; deportation to forced labor camps, yes; harsh, often cruel, treatment of inmates, yes, all this had been rumored, and Nazis' hateful, inhuman anti-Jewish measures were no secret and provoked general revulsion among Bulgarians. But one hadn't heard of *organized mass extermination*, of what later became known as the Holocaust. And for good reason: the Nazi "Final Solution" plan, adopted at the secret conference at Wansee

Strasse in 1942, insisted on total secrecy and stipulated that the Axis governments be assured that the Jews would be deported as laborers to their "new homeland," Poland. No mention of death camps had to be made.

In my ignorance, my first reaction was that the rumors were rather clumsy exaggerations of the Allied propaganda; indeed, they were too monstrous to be believable. But my friends, having been exposed to more objective information sources, seemed to think otherwise. Since my arrival, I was surprised to see that, contrary to most young people in Sofia, my friends in Switzerland were all pro-Western and anti-German. Among them, there were a few young Bulgarian diplomats whom I knew from Sofia, and they made no secret of their hostility to Germany. After a few weeks in Geneva, I learned many facts that I hadn't known and which disturbed me profoundly. Among the people who opened my eyes to many aspects of the war was Evgueni Silianoff, a bright and worldly diplomat with a reputation of a Casanova, who was *en poste* in Bern and Paris. He had been a favorite of my father's and a man I looked up to since my high school days, when many of our girlfriends used to have a crush on this "experienced older man." An admirer of France and French culture, Silianoff hated the Nazis as much as did the young vice-consul, Sveto Radeff, and almost as much as another diplomat, Ivan Radeff, who also joined us in Geneva. The two Radeffs, both highly cultured and sophisticated, were not related but were friends and came from well-known families whom I knew in Sofia. "Ivantcho," an extremely polite but hyper-emotional gentleman, used to go into tantrums when listening Hitler's speeches on the radio, crying with tears and shouting insults, as if the Fuehrer were in the room.

Once a week, Sava and I were invited to lunch at "Aunt" Antche's, a close friend of our families and the wife of a wealthy tobacco merchant, Takvor Takvorian. A chic and beautiful lady, who treated us with all the warmth and attention of a real aunt, Antche Takvorian used to prepare delicious meals and pretended not to notice the voracious appetite with which we served ourselves with copious second and third helpings. Meanwhile, "Uncle" Takvor lectured us on world affairs, pontificating with the self-assurance of the pasha he was to his family and his associates. Takvor was quite a colorful character, a hugely successful businessman with a reputation for integrity, a kind and warm man, but a braggart and an egocentric, a big gambler at the European casinos in the style of the flamboyant Greek ship-owners. Although speaking French with a very heavy accent and atrocious grammar, he was extremely proud of being a French citizen and always spoke of "we, the French." To a skeptical customs officer he had said once: "What do you mean I'm not French? I'm more French than you are. You're French by birth, just by accident. I'm French by merit: I elected to become French!"

In a way, it was true. An Armenian who grew up in Bulgaria, in Plovdiv, where his friendship with my father began, he had worked in Greece and in Turkey, and spoke those languages. He had made a big fortune in Balkan (Oriental) tobacco, to become one of the most important exporters (my friend Anni's father, Krum Tchaprachikoff, before he died long before the war, was another tobacco baron, probably the biggest). During the war, Takvor moved to Geneva. As I knew the Takvorians since I was a child, it was comforting to find them a few blocks away from my pension Masset.

Happy as I was in Geneva, I couldn't forget that the world was at war and I worried continuously about my family and Bulgaria. The events were unfolding rapidly and it was clear that Germany was losing the war. In June, the Americans landed in Normandy, and the Russians were advancing on the Eastern front. What was going to happen to my country? True, Bulgaria was trying discreetly to extricate itself from the Axis and looked to the Western powers for help, but the British and the Americans were refusing to negotiate without the their allies, the Soviets. We couldn't understand how they didn't see that the greatest peril to us was namely the Soviet Union and communism, and we were tremendously frustrated and alarmed. I realized that our ignorance about Nazi atrocities was no worse than the Western ignorance about the monstrosity of Stalinist terror and the scale of Soviet genocide, facts of which everybody at home was fully aware.

I had been barely two months in Geneva when the disturbing reality of the situation hit me full force. My father sent me a telegram asking me to return. I was crushed, but I knew that he must have had good reasons to do it, and I wouldn't think of disobeying him. Later I learned that a remark made by the Regent, Prince Kyril, the late King Boris's brother, that high State officials whose sons and daughters were studying abroad in those critical days were not giving a good example, had hurt my father's feelings and prompted his decision. Very upset, I packed my suitcase, bought my ticket, and started a round of farewell visits to all compatriots in Geneva. They all had letters and parcels for back home and nobody traveled to Bulgaria any more. So I was dined and wined lavishly for several days and by mid-July I was ready to leave, carrying large quantities of clothes, shoes, chocolate, watches and Swiss cheese in my luggage, which had increased to several suitcases. One gentleman, whom I knew only vaguely, asked me to carry several gold coins, a real fortune. "They won't search you," he assured me, offering me a generous percentage. I don't know whether it was honesty or fear that made me turn him down, to his great disappointment and surprise.

I'm often amused to observe how insignificant, trivial occurrences may influence the course of one's life. The fact, for instance, that Mr. Koutzouglou's brother in Plovdiv suffered from rheumatism and needed to wear warm long johns, difficult to find in Bulgaria, considerably affected my destiny. Vassil Koutzouglou was a wealthy Bulgarian (tobacco export again), a pedantic, cranky old man who lived in Zurich and whose sister-in-law was a close friend of my mother's. Informed that I was returning to Bulgaria, he called to ask me whether I would bring some underwear ("Jaeger" pants, he specified) to his brother. "Since you pass through Zurich, be my guest for one night!" he proposed. "I know your parents and I'll be glad to meet you. Come to the *Baur-au-Lac!*"

Baur-au-Lac, gee! I had heard so much about this hotel, one of the best palaces in Europe. King Boris used to stay there, as did many royalties and celebrities. I certainly wouldn't miss such an opportunity. After an emotional goodbye to Sava, Harri and the friends who came to the station, I boarded the morning train to Zurich, on my way back to Sofia. The day with Koutzouglou and his gentle, obedient wife, couldn't have been pleasanter. After I passed an exam on Bulgarian history and world politics, to which he subjected me with abrupt, inquisitorial questions, he relaxed and became a charming host, treating me to a gourmet lunch, taking me up on the funicular to the superb hotel Dolder for tea, showing me around town. After an exquisite dinner, I retired to my luxurious Baur-au-Lac room, grateful that my last night in Switzerland was spent in splendor.

I was awakened in the morning by an ecstatic phone call of Sava from Geneva. "Stefo, great news!" he screamed, overjoyed. "A telegram just arrived from your father. He tells you that if you haven't already left, you should stay! I'm arriving by the first train to celebrate it in Zurich." At first, I didn't believe him. Sava was not above this kind of jokes. But he read and reread the telegram, down to the "letter follows," until I realized that the miraculous news was true. By lunchtime, Sava was in my room, the telegram in his hand. I canceled my seat on the train to Vienna, which was leaving in a few hours. Koutzouglou, slightly disappointed that his brother had to do without the Jaeger long johns, kindly invited both of us for another night at the *Baur-au-Lac*. When we returned the next day, I was the happiest man in Geneva. Another week of lunch invitations followed, this time to return the watches, shoes, and chocolates which never reached the unlucky Bulgarian relatives. All this because I had stopped, by chance, for just one day in Zurich. I still keep my father's telegram, and each time I look at the date (July 14), I can't help asking myself what would've happened if I had left one day earlier, as planned.

The summer passed in studying for the first exams and worrying about our families. The situation was rapidly deteriorating. In the first days of September, Bulgaria decided to break with the Axis and ask the German troops to leave. But it was too late. The Red Army was already next door, in Romania. In order to prevent a Bulgarian surrender to the Anglo-Americans only and to gain the status of co-belligerent, the Soviet Union, although keeping full diplomatic relations with Sofia during the entire war, suddenly declared war and invaded the country. On the 9th of September, a coup overthrew the government and installed a leftist regime, dominated by the Communists. Anguished, we were devouring the scant newspaper reports, fearing the worst but hoping that the presence in the new government of several well-known leftist, but non-communist, politicians represented some guaranty against possible excesses. Alas! As letters from home became very sparse and were extremely cautious, we didn't realize at first that a bloody period of terror, retaliations, and summary executions had begun in Bulgaria, unmatched in savagery in any other Soviet-invaded Eastern European country. I was especially worried: the anti-royal campaign was particularly vicious, and with his 25 years in the King's service, my father could now go through some unpleasant moments. Nothing really bad would happen to him, all my friends agreed—he wasn't, after all, a political figure, and his reputation for kindness and for helping people was notorious,—but still, the very possibility that this gentle, delicate man could be submitted to rudeness and humiliation, bothered me tremendously.

In this state of mind, Sava and I prepared the exams for the first year and passed them in October rather adequately. A serious problem was Sava's pathological panic of exams. Fearless in sports and fist fighting, calm in situations of physical danger, he used to become literally petrified at exams, vomiting and unable to think or speak. I had to spend hours to cajole and threaten and insult him, before dragging him by force to the classroom, a difficult task, as he was bigger and stronger than me. But we both knew that in Sofia his father was anxiously waiting for the results, and there were few things in the world that could pain more the sweet, traditionalistic Stati Panitza than his son failing his exams.

In the fall, we left our pension and moved to a studio apartment with a small kitchen, where we could cook our own meals. *Cooking* is a big word for heating of can food and soups, boiling spaghetti or frankfurters, and frying eggs, which we, equally incompetent and untalented, practiced at 7, avenue Weber. For variety, we made *"croutes-au-fromage,"* i.e. slices of gruyere cheese that we let melt in the oven on a piece of bread. But this lean diet was supplemented with the weekly lunch at the Takvorians, occasional meals at homes of new friends, and the kindness of gifted girlfriends, lured to come and cook *chez nous.* Incidentally, the decision to leave our pension had been partly motivated by a desire for privacy: lady visitors were strictly *verboten* at Madame Masset's.

Not that we had such great need of love nest: our romantic life in those days was rather modest and mostly platonic, although Sava, more enterprising and having been in Geneva for a longer time, had had a couple of amorous adventures (in fact, the influential father of a local maiden had caught him in the act with her and was threatening to have him thrown out of Switzerland). As for me, my few flirtations were limited to holding hands on park benches and stealing a kiss in the darkness of the movie theater. Nevertheless, having a *garconniere* opened the way to new opportunities, and we were quick to explore them. In afternoons when one of us expected a visitor, the other discreetly went out for a walk, which could be too long and not particularly enjoyable during the cold, rainy season. Luckily, our generous friend Anni's studio was in the same building, and as she traveled frequently, we used it as a pleasant waiting room.

But the carefree days were numbered. Late in October I received the news that my father had been arrested, along with most of his colleagues of the palace. A great number of former ministers, members of the Parliament, generals, and political leaders were already in jail, and the new regime was talking of starting court trials against them. We were receiving no Bulgarian newspapers, but Sava's small set could catch, although with a lot of static, Radio Sofia. The venom, distortions, and vindictiveness of the furious propaganda I had to listen to every evening frightened me. My friends were trying to comfort me, but they too worried about their families. Takvor and his wife began to invite me more often, showing great understanding, and so did another old friend of my father's, former Prime Minister Georgi Kiosseivanov, who was the last Bulgarian minister in Bern and had moved now to Geneva. Before long, other Bulgarian diplomats who happened to be abroad and refused to return, began to arrive and join the families already in Switzerland—the Stancioffs, the Petroff-Tchomakoffs, the Belinoffs, all friends of my family's. Like after a shipwreck, a spirit of solidarity, anxiety, and need of human warmth pushed the survivors close together.

I needed it more than ever. Suddenly I noticed the low, gray winter skies of Geneva, the penetrating "Bise Noire" blowing over the Mont-Blanc bridge, the depressing warm and humid *foehn*, which, the saying went, drove people to suicide. What happened to the smiling, beautiful city we loved so much in sunny days? Nothing is as melancholy as a lake under a late-autumn rain. It was that kind of November day when I heard on Radio Sofia that a so-called "People's Tribunal" had been constituted in Sofia and my father was going to be among the accused. The weather never changed for the rest of that winter, or so it seemed to me.

Suddenly, everything appeared sad, alarming, difficult. My monthly allowance stopped, the bills were piling up. For a while, Sava had to pay the entire rent. I had no overcoat and to buy one was out of the question. Madame Masset's son Albert kindly offered his old coat, a charcoal color one, so threadbare that I had to have it turned inside out. I was very grateful to have something warm to wear, although the altered coat buttoned the wrong way, like a lady's garment, and the mending above the former chest pocket slit was quite visible. Aware of my predicament, a few well-to-do compatriots chipped in and tactfully offered to help me financially "until things get better…" Thus, between "Uncle" Takvor, a young businessman, Christo Gheneff, who enjoyed being with our group, and another businessman, Luben Stoykoff, who barely knew me, my monthly 360 francs were guaranteed. Without me asking for it, without the remotest chance of repaying. Ever since, when I hear that people are basically mean and help only when they see some advantage, I simply don't believe it.

The first "People's Tribunal," an outrageous kangaroo court against one hundred high officials—Prince Kyril and his two co-regents, all cabinet ministers since 1941, the King's advisers and palace high-rank staff, and most anti-Communist members of Parliament,—opened in December, in an atmosphere of noisy *agitprop* rally. For several weeks, Sofia's Palace of Justice looked like a modern version of the arenas where Roman emperors threw slaves to hungry lions, to the delight of bloodthirsty crowds. Militant Communist women in black babushkas were brought daily in army trucks in front of the huge marble building, where ugly mobs shouted hysterically "Death to the Criminals!" and "Kill the Fascist traitors!" Similar "People's Courts" were constituted elsewhere to punish Army officers, politicians, policemen, journalists and intellectuals, industrialists and wealthy people, clergymen, and other "enemies of the people." Official records show 11,122 people thousand persons tried by these courts, (in many cases dead people already killed without sentence), a monstrous figure for a small country which never sent one single soldier against the Soviet Union or the Allies, when compared to the Nuremberg trials, where only 22 Germans were brought to trial. In Bulgaria, the Communists didn't even try to give an appearance of legality: only a few among the "judges" were jurists; the overwhelming majority were listed as "workers," "agriculturers," "housewives," or at best, "former teachers."

My father was the first to take the stand. It was extremely painful for me to listen on the radio the daily summaries of his deposition, the bias and sarcasm in the questioning, the hateful distortions and insults of the commentators. The other accused that followed him were treated in the same manner. They were all well known figures, most of them decent, respected men. Many were friends of my family's or fathers of classmates of mine. The elite of Bulgaria's public life. Similar "people's tribunals" were set elsewhere to punish Army officers, politicians, policemen and judges, clergymen, journalists and intellectuals, rich people, industrialists, and other "public enemies."

I couldn't sleep, suffered anxiety attacks, and my nerves, tied up in knot, felt like a permanent, heavy stone in my stomach. With the days getting shorter, colder and darker, my depression became quite serious. Christmas was approaching and just as I was dreading the idea of staying alone in gloomy Geneva, a kind Bulgarian couple, Zheko and Lyuba Metcheff, (he was also fired from his job at the legation), invited Sava and me to the modest apartment they had rented in Davos. The change of air, the skiing, and the company of the Metcheffs and their niece Svilena, helped me to get temporarily out of my depression. But the recovery was superficial. Back in Geneva, I had to cope again with reality, and too young and vulnerable as I was, I just didn't know how.

January was a month of nightmares and fear. And a tremendous sadness. Having always had a happy, optimistic nature—in my family, I was the light-hearted one, the joker,—this was something new to me, something out of character. Usually the comforter to my friends, now I was the one in need to be comforted. And they all tried their best. As tension mounted before the "People's prosecutor's" final speech when he was expected to ask for the death penalty for all, my friends surrounded me with unusual care and sympathy. Conscious of the gravity of the situation, Sava, who was again "madly in love" and couldn't wait to visit his paramour in Davos, cancelled his trip in order to stay with me.

Then one day at the end of January the telephone started ringing in our studio and, one after the other, several friends called to congratulate me. "Even the Prosecutor doesn't ask for death sentence for your father! So you can relax, he's safe!" announced Sveto, and Tania, and Ilko, and many others after them. The

State Prosecutor had indeed spoken, he had demanded the death penalty for almost everyone, but he had abstained when it came to Groueff and his colleague Pomenov. The news made the tour of the Bulgarian colony in the matter of minutes. Soon afterwards, Kiosseivanov called me to confirm it. "Don't worry, Stefcho," the wise ex-Premier said. "In days of upheaval like now, the crucial thing is to survive. In prison, in exile, in hiding—it doesn't matter how. But to survive, that's what counts! After the storm, they'll be released."

I'd never thought that I could feel happy with my Dad in jail, but that day I cried for joy. And Sava rushed to Davos to join his lady.

*   *   *   *   *

Chapter 6

Tragic news from home, end of 1944

It was on a day early in December that my family received the first word from father. He had been arrested on October 6th in Sofia, when the ranking Palace officials were summoned to the Regency building on Moskovska street, while Mama and Radka were still in Tcham-Koria, and Boubi had started his military service. Since then, not only they hadn't heard from him, but they had been unable to find out in which prison or militia station he was held, or whether he had not been sent to the Soviet Union, as rumors ran that Prince Kyril, the regents, and a few high officials had been secretly delivered to the Russians. Worried to death, Mama had knocked at every door that she could think of, in order to find some information, but nobody could or would give an answer. "Don't you worry," told her the rare officials of the new regime who agreed to receive her, "he'll be released as soon as he's interrogated." She had gone to the Queen, still tolerated by the new government as mother of the child-king Simeon, in whose name it pretended to rule, pending the Communist decision on the monarchy. But Queen Giovanna was receiving the same answers each time she inquired about the fate of her brother-in-law Kyril and the arrested Royal court officials. Mama had even taken the step of paying a visit to the Soviet ambassador, who had always pretended to respect my father, and even like him for his knowledge of Russian literature. The diplomat finally received her, only to say that he knew nothing about the arrests and that, as a foreigner, he couldn't intervene in Bulgaria's internal affairs…

There was a moment of hope when a mysterious young man arrived at the door, introducing himself as a monk from Bachkovo monastery that knew where my father was and had ways of transmitting messages and parcels. "I had met your husband and your son Stephane when the visited the monastery last year," he said, giving pretty accurate personal details about them. Drowning persons clutch at straws, so Mama trusted him and gave his clothes and money to bring to my father; then, a few days later, more clothes and money to "bribe the guards;" then money and my clothes that I'd left in Sofia, for himself. The monk once brought as proof a bag with laundry from prison. It was dirty and torn beyond recognition, so she had no other choice but to believe that it was my father's. The visits continued for a month, until the monk brought a message from my father, saying that he was returning home that coming Sunday. Indescribably excited, the family spent the day waiting at the window, from dawn to midnight. He never came. After that, the monk vanished. When Mama and Radka bumped into him by chance in the church, he tried to escape, then confessed shamelessly that his whole story had been a hoax and warned them not to talk about it.

It was a most cruel disappointment in a long series of ordeals they were going through since leaving Tcham-Koria. They had returned to a hostile, unrecognizable Sofia, a city invaded by ugly crowds, jubilant "partisans" brandishing semi-automatic "Schmeizers," Gestapo-type militiamen, coarse women in army boots, and barbarous Soviet troops. A Sofia blazing with Communist slogans and Party posters, where countless people were being arrested every night and stories of atrocities and torture were circulating clandestinely. A city living under curfew, in fear and hatred.

With father under arrest, my family was told to evacuate the apartment we rented. Having no place to go, they were lucky to accept the hospitality of Boubi's best friend "Mitika" Nikolov, whose family, wealthy fish merchants, was at that time in Istanbul. The Nikolovs feared that if empty, their apartment would be requisitioned. It was one of Sofia's better cooperative buildings, situated centrally at the corner of "Moskovska" and "Rakovski" streets facing the Russian embassy.

Through the palace services still functioning, a truck was provided for one single trip. Mama, Boubi and Radka packed hastily whatever they could, loaded a few beds, chairs, and trunks, and moved them to their new dwelling, just three blocks away. They left all the rest behind them, hoping to recover it one day. The long evenings were spent gloomily in the apartment, as the curfew was strict. But even without it, it was unpleasant and risky for women to walk alone in the streets: there were too many stories about rape by unruly Soviet soldiers, and Boubi, living in the barracks, was seldom home to protect his sister. Luckily, he happened to be with her the day drunken Russian soldiers crossed them in the stairway of the building. "You shouldn't keep your wife for you alone, let her with us!," they said as they tried to grab Radka. Terrified, but knowing that any resistance would be useless, they had the sang-froid to convince the Russians to let them go take a bath and change, and then come to fetch her in one hour. Once inside, Radka hid in a closet, and when the soldiers returned, Boubi and Mama told them that she had gone with a Soviet officer, and they left them alone. Such was the advice given a few days before by a Russian wife in the building, when Radka had asked her for help and protection. "Look, lady," she had said, "nobody can help you when our men want a woman. The only authority they fear is the officers'. So say that you're already with an officer. And even if you have to go with an officer, it's much better, believe me, they're at least cleaner and more civilized!"

After this incident, Radka spent most of the time at home, with the doors barricaded with pieces of furniture, as in most apartments in the building.

*   *   *   *   *

Then, the postcard arrived. A laconic card, sent from Sofia's Central prison through the official mail and asking them to come to the prisoners' visiting hour, a couple of days later. Although the family no longer lived at the old address, the convocation had been sent correctly to the Mitika's building: obviously, every move of the family had been carefully watched. The postcard caused great excitement in the crowded apartment, harboring, apart from Mama, Radka, Boubi, and a Mitika's aunt and uncle, also my old Grandmother and my father's sister, Lemi, just arrived from Plovdiv. Warm clothes and clean underwear were packed, cakes were baked, and the scarce cash was spent on the black market to buy food and fill a basket with "things that Pavel likes to eat…"

Sofia was still totally dark on the wintry morning when Mama and Radka, well wrapped for the cold, and Boubi, in his shabby army uniform, took the city streetcar at 6 AM in the direction of the prison. A faithful friend, Katia Saraivanova, good-looking and chic as ever, had insisted to accompany them and was carrying her own basket with food and pastry. It was still very early when they arrived at the prison, but a crowd of about 80 was already waiting in front of the sinister, fortress-like edifice, mostly women and children, all nicely dressed. There were many familiar faces in the group.

The prison gates were opened at 8 AM and the meticulous search of the parcels began. After every basket was inspected most thoroughly, handbags opened rudely, linings of suits examined, the visitors were ushered into a large waiting room, where militiamen divided them into small groups and asked them to wait for their names to be called. "No more than three visitors per prisoner!" shouted a sergeant. "Please let me too, I'm a very close friend!" Katia pleaded with him. "Out of the question!" the guard snapped, and that was that.

After an interminable wait, which lasted for about two hours, the visitors were ordered to leave overcoats, hats, and umbrellas in the waiting room and to follow the guards in a long corridor protected by iron bars, then another corridor with bars, where the guards collected all parcels and baskets and disappeared. The corridor began to be filled with people. "This is Mrs. Sevova," Mama whispered, pointing at the solitary figure standing silently in the corner. Then, "Good morning, Mrs. Handjieva! Good morning, Mrs. Morfova!" All wives of father's colleagues. Mrs. Pomenova arrived, with her children Lilliana and Kossio, and after her, Mrs. Guencheva and daughter Elena. Another long wait, maybe an hour. It was already afternoon, when the militiaman appeared. "No more talking!" he shouted as he positioned himself with his back to the group, facing the bars. In the silence that followed, one began to hear metal doors being opened on the other side of the bars, and one saw guards slowly bringing forward prisoners, one by one. The first figure they were helping walk, looked familiar, but much too old and feeble to be recognized, especially that his white head was completely shaven. It was only when Mrs. Handjieva let out a scream that Mama, Radka, and Boubi realized that it was her husband, the 49-year-old Chief of Protocol of the palace.

"Gheorghi, is this you? she said in disbelief, as their conversation began across the two rows of bars and the guard's back half obstructing her view. Then two more militiamen appeared, dragging some human figure so near the floor that the wall below the bars made it difficult to be seen. Kossio Pomenov, taller than the others, craned his neck and screamed: "Daddy! Daddy!" His mother and sister started crying, and one heard faintly, from somewhere down below, the voice of the Chief of the Royal Chancery. He was in a terrible shape, obviously beaten badly during his interrogations. The next man, the Inspector of the Palaces and alleged political adviser to the King, Dimitri Guenchev, was in even worse shape: his head was blue and swollen from beatings, the eyes half-closed, the hands covered with wounds. He spoke with great difficulty.

In contrast, my father didn't show any external signs of violence. When his turn came, he walked in without being assisted, calm and even trying to smile. It was a shock to see his head shaven, but his white beard was almost the same as before. He wore the trousers of a gray suit, no tie, and was in shirtsleeves under his gray overcoat. "How are you?" he said in a quiet but clear voice. He was visibly moved, happy to see his family. "Boubi, you look great in this uniform. What news do you have from Stefcho? It's so good that he's there, I'm glad that we wrote him to stay there! And you, Radentze, (his pet name for Radka), how are you? How wrong I was to be against Giorgio, I should've let you marry him!" (Giorgio was a flirt of Radka's, the nephew of the Italian ambassador.)

Conversing at distance, across the bars, wasn't easy, especially that all visitors were talking at the same time. But father managed to inquire about his sister Minka, about Baba and other relatives and friends.. Mama and Radka, fighting back the tears, were making efforts to sound cheerful. "And you, Pavel, how are you?" "I'm alright now. After the 'monastery', now it's better, I'm O.K." (They never understood what he meant by "the monastery;" was it a place where he had been interrogated before the prison? Or had he been, in the meantime, sent to Russia?) "Do you know what I'm missing a lot?" he continued. "I miss Jerry (our dog), to sit in my lap. Good old Jerry!" (Did he want to tell them that he was cold in his cell? they wondered.)

There were other coded messages, they thought. For instance, "Are you seeing Bakish?" The industrialist Bakish, a Bulgarian Jew, was a close friend of father's, and now many Jews had become very influential with the new regime, or so one said...But he didn't seem to believe that anyone could help him now. So, when his visitors, to cheer him up, talked about "When you come home..." he interrupted them calmly, with a sad smile: "No, no, no..." He didn't act frightened, he was not a desperate man. But there was some tragic certitude in his wistful "No, no, no..."

The ten minutes allowed for the visit were over and the guards readied themselves to lead away the prisoners. Mama couldn't hold it any more and burst into tears. Father waved with his hand as he was led out, and said gently: "And forgive me! Forgive me that I didn't think enough about you! But maybe I couldn't do otherwise..."

*   *   *   *   *   *   *

"I was in bed and sound asleep," Radka remembered, "when I felt that someone was shaking me by the shoulders, trying to wake me up. I opened my eyes with great difficulty and, through the glass door of the bedroom, I saw that the lights in the contiguous room, the one Mama and Granny slept in, were lit and a man in an overcoat and hat, and carrying a sub-machine gun, was standing at the door. Another man, also all dressed up, was leaning over me and shouting 'Get up! Get up and put your clothes!' Startled, I looked around. It was in the dead of night—probably 2 or 3 AM—and Mama was already up, pale and shivering, packing hastily in the next room, under the watchful eyes of a couple of men. Baba was next to her, weeping and crossing herself. In a minute, Boubi appeared from the living room, where he used to sleep on a couch when on leave from his regiment, followed by aunt Lemi, who looked frightened. 'Take blankets, warm clothes, and food for three days! And hurry up!', the order came. Still in my nightgown, I rushed to the bathroom, but the militiamen didn't permit me to close the door while I was changing. In the hurry I put a pair of thin stockings, high-heel shoes, and nothing really warm, but, for no reason, pinned on myself the brooch with a doe, that I had received as a birthday present. Luckily, at the last minute I remembered to pack my pair of boots, the kind we used to wear in town when it snowed. Mama did much better: she wore her old ski pants, heavy sweaters, and a large woolen shawl, in which, in anticipation of emergencies, she had sewn a few antique gold coins. She wrapped some food, a big loaf of bread and a kitchen knife, and before we were pushed out of the apartment, she stripped two eider-downs from the beds and handed them to us to carry down the staircase."

*   *   *   *   *

This was the night of December 22nd, 1944. Only two days before, the sinister "People's Tribunal" had opened its sessions, with my father the first to be interrogated.

By its composition (most "judges" were listed as "workers," "agriculturers," and "retired teachers," with only a few Communist jurists), and its arbitrary procedure, the kangaroo court was reminiscent of French revolutionary tribunals during the time of the Terror. The staged rallies of crowds shouting "Death to the Criminals!" in front of the Palace of Justice, as well as the furious propaganda campaign against the accused, only stressed the analogy.

To listen to the radio was an ordeal for the family, aggravated by the marked change in the attitude of relatives and friends, frightened by the brutal repression that followed the September Soviet invasion. Mother and Radka had spent the two weeks since the prison visit looking for a trusted lawyer to defend my father in court. Most lawyers were afraid to touch anything connected with the "People's Tribunals." Finally, they succeeded in persuading a prominent attorney, an old acquaintance, to accept the defense. But just days before the trial, the attorney's son came to the apartment with a message that `it was "impossible" for his father to take the case. The young man, a friend from childhood, didn't elaborate, he just repeated, "My father regrets, but he cannot do it, he just can't…" He was pale and trembling, visibly shaken.

*   *   *   *   *

"Moskovska" street was deserted and dark when the militiamen escorted the family out of the apartment. An empty military truck was waiting in front of the building. "Get in!" the militiamen yelled, pointing to the open platform behind the driver's cabin. Boubi was ordered to return immediately to his unit and he left, heavy-hearted. Mama tried to climb on the truck, but the step was too high. Granny and old Lemi couldn't even try. The militiamen impatiently lifted them up and flung them inside. "Where are you taking us?" Mama asked, but the stone-faced men remained silent. She turned to Lemi and whispered in her ear: "They're taking us to shoot us."

In the silence of the sleeping city, the truck rumbled down "Rakovski" street, turned on "Vrabcha" and stopped in front of the Savov home. A few militiamen jumped off the car and entered the house. Lights appeared in several windows. Funny, but the idea that friends like the Savovs were going to join them, brought some courage to Mama and Radka, made them feel less forlorn. After several minutes, they saw Stefan, Siyche, and their mother being escorted out, the spunky Mrs. Savova not about to let the militiamen intimidate her, giving them hell and treating them with utter contempt. The next stop was for Mrs. Pomenova and Lilly, and after them, the wives of Handjiev and Morfov, then Mrs. Valeva and her son Vasko—all wives and children of imprisoned cabinet ministers, deputies, and palace officials, many of them friends. Pale, disheveled, the heads wrapped in heavy scarves, they smiled faintly to each other, trying not to show how frightened they were. The truck filled up quickly and by the time it turned to "Tsar Osvoboditel" boulevard to pick up Regent Filov's wife Kitta and her sister, it was packed to a point of suffocation.

It was still pitch black and freezing when they reached the railroad station. As they were unloaded on the platform, they saw several other army trucks arriving and disgorging scores of women and children. Radka recognized the Krapchev family—Jivko, Vena, Rouzha and their mother,—and rushed to greet them. Still cocky and keeping his sense of humor, Jivko was making funny remarks, in spite of the very unfunny situation. But one could see how badly stricken the family had been: only three months ago, on the very first day of the Communist takeover, their father, a prominent journalist, was killed savagely in the street.

After an hour or so on the stone platform, people began to relax a little, form-ing small groups, greeting each other, talking, and smoking. Mama went to an officer, explaining that grandma was over 90-years-old and Lemi, "an old relative," had just happened to be in the apartment that night, by chance. A few mothers of small children also pleaded with him, and after some hesitation, he separated them from the rest and led them out to set them free. Soon after, a train rolled into the station, screeching and filling it with steam, and the militiamen ordered everybody to board it. The crowd rushed into the windowless cargo cars, the kind used for cattle and horses, as families and friends were trying to remain together. Inside the overcrowded car, there was no room to sit down, and everybody stood up, leaning on each other's backs. The door shut, leaving the car in total darkness. One heard the noise of iron bars securing it from outside and the click of the padlock. Minutes later, the train took off for an unknown destination.

As the hours passed, legs got tired and people became hungry. At the beginning it was very cold, but with so many bodies packed together, the air became soon warm and fetid. A baby started crying—nobody knew why his young mother, the wife of a member of the Parliament, carried an infant with her. Through a crack between the wall boards one could see that it was already daytime. The women started searching their bags for food, bending proving difficult without disturbing the next person. Mama brought out the bread, Mrs. Savova produced hardboiled eggs, the Krapchevs had a cheese, and all was shared in a most friendly way. Thirst became soon a problem: few people had thought of bringing water. But the resourceful Mrs. Savova carried a demijohn of water, and after giving some to the crying baby, she offered a few sips to the most thirsty around her.

It wasn't before long that a child's voice announced: "Mommy, I have to go to the bathroom!" As there was no solution to that problem, the child became silent after a moment and everybody in the cattle car knew exactly what he was doing. In fact, many of the grownups had already gone through this most humiliating experience, and, wet and ashamed as they were, preferred not to notice anything and not to discuss it. Near to Radka, Vasko Valev was smoking continuously and nobody objected: frankly, the smoke was less malodorous than the air they were breathing. But when Radka asked him for a cigarette, Mama was profoundly shocked: she didn't know that her 19-year-old daughter smoked!

The train stopped for the first time around 4 o'clock in the afternoon. The door was unbolted and the human cargo was let out. It was a tiny station, totally deserted and covered with deep new snow. Under different circumstances, the snow-covered trees around the station would have looked absolutely enchanting, like on a Christmas card. But the multitude of thirsty women, children, and a few men, who came out of the other cars of the train and ran toward the trees to eat the immaculate snow, could hardly think now that tomorrow was Christmas Eve. They all looked terrible: unwashed, uncombed, with black circles under the eyes, with stained, rumpled clothes, the stiffened legs freezing under the wet, soiled pants.

"Everybody eats now!" the militiamen ordered. They brought several pails filled with foul drinking water and handed them to the prisoners who sat on the cold, wet platform and unpacked their meager provisions. Meanwhile, trays loaded with hot, grilled "kefte" (local hamburgers) were being carried to the militiamen, spreading the most appetizing odors as they passed by their starving wards.

The prisoners were allowed to go to the outhouse, but only in groups of five or six, and accompanied by a guard, who kept the door open and peeked indiscreetly at will. When the militiamen finished their meal, the doors of the cars were open and everybody boarded the train. Only the baby remained at the station: exhausted and desperate, the young mother pleaded with an officer to send the infant back to her mother in Sofia. He agreed and she took her place with the other prisoners, sobbing inconsolably for the rest of the trip. The night had fallen when the train pulled out of the unknown station, going to some other unknown destination. In the darkness of the cattle car, overtired and fighting the worst fears, the wives and children of the imprisoned leaders in Sofia were trying to have some sleep and forget. Suddenly, everybody was silent. One could only hear the deputy's young wife, crying softly for her baby.

"I wonder what Stefo is doing right now?" Jivko whispered to Radka. "Wouldn't it be wonderful if we were all there, with him?, she said.

*   *   *   *   *   *

Chapter 7

Geneva II, death of Father

Everybody was heavyhearted and very tense that evening at Takvorian's apartment on avenue Bertrand, a quiet street off Geneva's residential Route de Florissant. "Aunt" Antche Takvorian had invited me with half-a-dozen older Bulgarian friends to listen to the news of Radio Sofia and we were all waiting nervously for the hour of the evening bulletin. It was the 1st of February, the day the first "People's Tribunal" was to announce its verdict, and everyone in the room had close relatives or friends whose life was being decided at that moment.

While waiting, we had surrounded former Premier George Kiosseivanov, who commented on the latest international and political developments with his characteristic calm eloquence. The portly, soft-spoken diplomat was our most respected statesman in exile and we listened attentively to his intelligent analyses and words of wisdom. This evening he was markedly pessimistic and I saw sadness and worry in his gentle blue eyes. Most of the accused men were his former colleagues or collaborators and he would've no doubt been among them today, had he returned to Sofia. Kiosseivanov gave me a few words of encouragement, repeating that as long as life is spared (and nobody, not even the prosecutor, had asked for death sentence for my father), there was hope that he would be freed soon after the trial.

Somebody called from the adjoining room and we rushed to the corner where the radio was kept. The news bulletin had begun and in the total silence that followed, we strained our ears to hear the faint voice above the static. After a brief preface, the announcer began to read the court's verdict, starting with the three former regents. "Prince Kyril Preslavsky Saxe-Coburg-Gotha, 49-year-old," we heard the name of the first accused, the late King Boris's brother, followed by the names of Professor Bogdan Filov and general Nikola Mihov. "Guilty...sentenced to death," he said. Horrified, the small group around the radio gasped in disbelief.

The announcer went on reading. It was the turn of the cabinet ministers. Twenty-six guilty, twenty-two of them sentenced to death! General Daskalov…my God, that's my friend Kleo's father!…Dr. Yotzov, Dr. Staliyski…did one mean the fathers of the kids I knew?…Professor Stanishev, my friend Vlado's dad! My eyes filled with tears. Then Parvan Draganov, my father's friend whose daughter, Didi, we knew since childhood. And others, many others…Listening to the long list, we were all stunned. Aunt Antche and Natalia Kiosseivanov were sobbing, the men were ashen faced. The King's advisors were next. I could hardly bare the tension, I felt that everybody was looking at me. First I heard the names of two alleged "secret advisors" of the late King, Sevov and Lultchev, whom I didn't know, followed by a few familiar names—Pomenov, Handjiev, Kostov…Then, clearly…GROUEFF! Yes, "Pavel Simeonov Groueff, born in Koprivchtitza, age 65," said the announcer as he continued with the list of palace officials. All guilty. And the sentence is…Did I hear correctly? No, no, no, it's impossible! Death, said the radio, DEATH! "There must be a mistake," I thought as I started shaking uncontrollably and my heart felt as it was about to burst,—a monstrous mistake! "It cannot be, it cannot be!…Didn't the prosecutor say…" I was repeating to the others in the room, my tearful eyes begging them to help, as if they could do anything, my pleading voice conjuring them to say that it wasn't true. Aunt Antche took me in her arms and we cried together.

Strange, but at that moment I wasn't yet comprehending that I had just lost my father forever, lost the person I loved more than anybody, more than anything in the world. I was devastated by the news, but somehow I failed to grasp the finality it contained. Maybe because my father was still alive, as far as I knew? Suffering, going through atrocious ordeals, but still not dead, still existing in the same world with me. Or was I so naive as to assume that tribunals don't punish innocent people, especially when they are as kind and compassionate as my father was? It would be absurd, wouldn't it, a flagrant, immensurable injustice! Whatever the pitiful sources of hope, the delusion that some recourse was sill possible kept me charitably at the rim of the precipice of despair. "Something has to be done! I must do something!" my febrile mind was screaming, as I turned, as soon as I recovered from the first shock, to Mr. Kiosseivanov and to "Uncle"

Takvor. They have so many connections, they know important people…Please do something! Naive, fantastic, childish ideas and schemes were coming hectically out of my mouth, one more unrealistic than the other. Maybe the Vatican can intervene? Dad knew Monsignor Roncalli well, when he was papal nuncio in Sofia…Or, what about the French? Wasn't my father a well-known Francophile, decorated with the "Legion d'Honneur"?…And let's tell people about all the Jewish friends he helped! They may have a say now…But there was not much hope in the eyes of my elder compatriots, as they listened pityingly to the incoherent, tearful youth and tried to console him.

The hosts didn't want to let me sleep alone in my studio, and kept me in their apartment overnight. Aunt Antche gave me sleeping pills, and a merciful, intermittent grogginess gave me some relief between horrible nightmares and quiet weeping, until the bleak February morning.

*   *   *

The predominant feeling, at each of the hundred feverish awakenings during that night, was a wish, an ardent prayer that the previous evening had been nothing but a bad dream. Each time, I would keep my eyes closed for an extra moment, hoping that when I open them, the nightmare would vanish and I would find that nothing had changed. And each time the sight of the unfamiliar room, the wet pillow, the light under the door, left by my considerate hostess, brought me back to the unbearable new reality. Gradually and cruelly, the meaning of what had happened was sinking in, and I wanted to scream like a wounded beast.

In the morning, emotionally emptied, I went through the motions like an automat, dressing, having breakfast, going home, while incessantly hoping for something—I didn't know myself what—to happen. A miracle, perhaps. Sava called from Davos, very upset by the news, to tell me that he was taking the first train to Geneva. Tania Daneva came to pick me up for a long walk along the quays. I cannot think of a more soothing presence for that occasion. There wasn't much that she could say to relieve my grief, but I was grateful that she was at my side. I didn't talk much either, but with Tania I didn't have to, she knew now

I felt. We have been friends since childhood and have always had affection for each other; it helped now not to have to make any efforts and yet not be alone. The lake had never looked so desolate as on that day, its gray surface ruffled by a chilling wind. We walked for a longtime, absorbed in our thoughts, as I tried to suppress a sob, and she—to find a word of solace.

That day, I received many telephone calls from friends, a few visits, many warm hugs. But no words of hope, although I kept hoping. Sava and Harri never left my side. By the following day, we heard the tragic news: the condemned men were executed right after the sentence had been read. Ninety men in the first trial.* My father was killed, was dead. He didn't exist anymore. I wasn't going to see him again, ever. I would have to live without him in this world. For me, it was impossible to think of such a life, I loved him so much; I wasn't even sure that I wanted to live in the frightening emptiness of such a world. Totally devastated, I sank into a despair such as I'd never known before.

*   *   *

My father was executed on February 2. I hadn't had news from my family for a couple of months, and during the tragic days of the trial I had no idea where mother, Boubi, and Radka were and whether they were free. Left on my own, with no home or family to go to, I didn't have other choice but stay in Geneva and continue my studies. As Takvorian, Gheneff, and Stoykoff had pledged to help me financially until I get my diploma, I felt it my duty to try to take my exams in the shortest possible time. The next session being around February 20th, I had gone into high gear since December (except for the week in Davos at New Year's time), working intensively on the second year's courses of law and trying not to be distracted too much by

---

*A shocking comparison: 11 Nazi leaders were sentenced to death in Nuremberg. Japan executed 7 leaders, and Rumania, which fought against the Soviet Union, only 4. The "People's Tribunals" in small, non- belligerent Bulgaria issued 2730 death sentences!

worries about the trial. Now, after the horrible news of my father's killing, to continue work at the same tempo, or even increase it by pushing myself to the limit, became the only possible remedy. The shock left me so disoriented, I dreaded so much the black void that had opened before me, that the exams were the only peg I could cling to in order to keep my sanity. Making funeral arrangements has similar merciful effect on grieving families, forcing them temporarily to be busy and keeping them from thinking.

For three weeks, I buried myself in working for the exams. I didn't leave our 7, Avenue Weber studio, except to go to the University, or to study at the home of a friend, such as Tania's fiancé, Jean-Pierre Cellerier, who was preparing some of the same exams. At night, I worked until three or four o'clock. I didn't sleep much, but that was O.K., because dreams were hard to face. From time to time, I let go and cried, thinking of my father, finding it difficult to accept that he was alive no more. Then forced myself again back to the books. I went to exams exhausted, my head a jungle of half-assimilated legal definitions, dizzy from lack of sleep. Somehow I passed them—three written and four oral exams—very well, receiving 38 1/2 points out of a maximum of 42. Now, having "jumped" one semester, I needed only one more year for my diploma.

It was a time of slow healing, the despair turning to a chronic sorrow, interspersed with occasional distractions and even small joys. Gradually, the thick shroud of apathy was evaporating, pierced somewhat reluctantly but more and more frequently, by familiar tingles of curiosity and desire for company. The zest for life hadn't been extinguished after all, and I was surprised to recognize the thrills of vitality running though the veins again. Never underestimate the resilience of youth!

Thus, when the Universities of Geneva and Lausanne went on Easter ski vacations to Zermatt, it didn't take too much effort on the part of Sava, Tania, and Jean-Pierre to persuade me to leave my morose seclusion and join them on the sunny Alpine slopes. The change of scenery did miracles for me, especially with my love for the mountains. In Zermatt we found our friends from Lausanne— Ilko, Louli with Michael, Vladi with Peggy, and many others, including George Revay, a Hungarian-born student we had befriended not long before. George, a bright and handsome loner, was remarkably knowledgeable of nobility titles and a stickler for etiquette and form.

I had seldom seen a more attractive group of people. Skiing from early morning till dusk on the Gornergratt long runs, picnicking together and flirting on the sunny terrace of the Riffleberg hotel, dancing every evening at the Zermatterhof, all bursting with energy, this suntanned youth couldn't look happier. I had moments of joy too, for the first time since my mourning. But often, in the middle of a joyful ski-run or an amusing conversation, the pain would grab me, physically, and the demons would take me away with them, to unspeakably sad and horrid thoughts. Then I would ask myself for the thousandth time why all this had to happen, why our young people couldn't enjoy life like this, and I would feel very guilty for enjoying myself. Certain mountain winds had, I don't know why, a particular effect on me. Once I was skiing alone down the Gornergratt. It was one of those fantastic days when one feels happy just to be alive—the perfect spring snow, the sun so bright that one squints even with the darkest goggles, and so hot that one wants to take off gloves and shirt. The skis were turning well, the speed was exhilarating, and as I reached the railroad tunnel, I was in a mood for yodeling.

It was at the exit of the tunnel that this unexpected whiff of wind struck me like a revelation. It smelt and felt so familiar, that I was suddenly transported into another world. It was the spring breeze of the Bulgarian mountains, the early April air of Vitosha and Rila of my childhood. The nostalgia it brought was unbearable. I sat on the snow and sobbed unabashedly. Passing-by skiers stopped, thinking there was an accident. "Are you badly hurt?" a lady asked as I sat there.

But most of the time I enjoyed the vacation with my friends. One who didn't always act happy was George Revay. He wasn't sad, he was in love. Or, more exactly, going through the agonies of an impossible infatuation. The object of his passion was a blond divorcee, a few years older and incomparably richer than us, whom we considered as the most *chic* and most sophisticated lady in Geneva. Countess Daria Mercati, the daughter of a former marshal of the Greek royal court, was a cosmopolite who had married a wealthy Swiss perfumery tycoon.

Divorced, she lived during the war at the Hotel des Bergues, the most expensive in Geneva, and was spending her winters in St. Moritz, Gstaad, or Zermatt.

Daria was, of course, moving in different circles, but being an outstanding skier, we couldn't fail noticing her slim, graceful figure on the slopes, her elegant ski-pants and sweaters always matching the color of her many pairs of skis, which she changed every day. Skiing faster and better than most of us, she never fell, and if she did, she would spend hours fixing her hair, rearranging her scarf and redoing her elaborate makeup. Sometimes we saw her "apres-ski," having tea or dinner with her affluent friends, always ladylike and impeccably dressed, fussing with her handbag mirror, continuously powdering her minuscule, almost non-existing, nose. When we met formally, we found her intriguing and friendly, and liked her with all the respect due to a well-established, interesting lady. We skied a few times together, with her waiting for me patiently at the bottom of every difficult run. Daria was amused to learn that my father had held similar position with King Boris as her father had in the Greek royal court, and showed interest and sympathy for my case. Our casual acquaintance turned out to be the beginning of a long friendship, which was to play, much later, an important role in my life.

In Geneva and Lausanne, and Zermatt and elsewhere, Sava and I made several other friendships among the large number of foreigners who had found asylum in Switzerland during the war. Some of them were penniless refugees, like us, but others belonged to wealthy families accustomed for decades to the luxury of the Swiss palaces. The members of this international set—usually Italian, South-American, Greek, or Belgian expatriates,—spoke several languages, dressed well and had *savoir-faire*, played good bridge, and had never worked seriously. Among the scions of this privileged group we met a few amusing young men and women who often included us in pleasant parties. Among these were the popular Stagni brothers, charming Italian playboys who lived at the Lausanne Palace, when not visiting their parents at the Montreux Palace. The grandfather had made a fortune in lumber in Egypt, allowing two generations of Stagnis to enjoy the European spas, winter resorts, and the Riviera on a full-time basis. While Giovanni, the eldest brother, moved in the circle of exiled royalty, our contemporaries Ernesto and Sandro, as well as Carlo, a bonvivant a few years older, thoroughly enjoyed the company of less prosperous refugees like us. When new friends like them or a few aristocratic Spaniards and attractive French and Italian girls called us to join them at a restaurant, we pretended to be busy for dinner and joined them just for coffee or a after-supper drink. At bars, we were very careful to make the only drink last for the whole evening. At cocktail parties, we somehow happened to get involved into conversations always next to the buffet table, the one hand absent-mindedly reaching for hors-d'oeuvres as we were making a point. But such techniques were superfluous with friends: they knew we were broke, and there was no shame in it.

Indeed, I lived extremely economically. Most Bulgarians worried about expenses. Thus, the families of two diplomats who refused to return to Sofia, the Belinoffs and the Petroff-Tchomakoffs, rented jointly a large apartment on rue de Beaumont, with Mrs. Belinoff's brother, Ivantcho Radeff, and their mother, Anna Radeff. They did their cooking together, and as "Tante Anna" was Sava's grand-mother's sister, they kindly invited us to take our meals with them and share the expenses. I couldn't hope for a better arrangement. Not only did I start eating very well, but in rue de Beaumont's "commune," with families I liked and respected, with the presence of four children—Belinoff's two daughters, Petroff-Tchomakoff's Sonia, and Milava Gueshoff's, a niece of Mrs. Radeff's,—I found a home, the thing I needed most at that time. I felt very close to Mrs. Radeff, a wonderfully warm, cultured old lady (she was the prominent Bulgarian states-man Ivan E. Gueshoff's daughter) with a good sense of humor, who treated me as her own grandson. In spite of the tragic events which had hit me that year, my luck in receiving and giving affection had not abandoned me.

This was the period when I found soothing distraction in a new hobby: the jazz clarinet. Why jazz, and why clarinet? In both cases, it was for want of some-thing better. Music had always been revered in my family and playing an instru-ment was an old dream of mine. When my childhood bout with the violin lessons ended ingloriously, I didn't miss it a bit, I was relieved. But later, as my adolescent mind was overflowing with new quests and exciting ideas, and my heart bursting with love, desires, and fears, the need for expressing myself became increasingly poignant. Words didn't seem to offer the perfect outlet, even though I tried to write. There is something basically unsatisfactory with words. They are so limited, so imprecise and contrived, offering only a poor approximation when trying to describe subtleties in sensations and feelings. Music, on the other hand, gave me the feeling of being able to cover the entire gamut of human emotions so fully and so truly. Often, while listening to classical music, I suddenly had a sensation of "understanding" all—the mood, the feelings, the "*it*"—without any effort of the brain and with no need of explanations. "How lucky musicians are," I thought with envy, "to be able to express *that*, to pour out all they feel!"

With my world disintegrating, this envy became a need. But it was obviously too late, and materially impossible, for me to learn to play classical music. But what about jazz, as a second best? I already loved jazz and thought it might be easier to learn. It also appeared to serve my need for an outlet better: unlike classical musicians, who usually play somebody else's compositions, jazzmen, especially in Dixieland jazz, the style I liked, have full freedom to improvise and play directly "from the heart," even without knowing how to read music. My first choice would be trumpet or saxophone. But trumpets being too noisy for our quiet building, and saxophones—rather expensive, I rented an old beat up clarinet for the sum of eight francs a month. A colleague from the University showed me the positions of the fingers, and I started patiently to teach myself to play by ear, to the despair of Sava. To be honest, sharing a room with someone learning to play clarinet is an exasperating experience that can destroy the best of friendships. The squeak was atrocious and it took me weeks to produce a decent tone and learn the scale. But our friendship survived, and I must say that my new hobby gave me immense satisfaction and joy.

With my financial situation worsening alarmingly, I started looking for a summer job. The Stancioff family recommended me as gardener to a small pension in the canton of Unterwalden, where they were spending the summer. The gesture was as charitable as it was irresponsible: I didn't have a clue about gardening. But when I arrived in Flueli, a picturesque spot lost in the remote mountains, it was too late for *Fraulein* Lang, the pious landlady, to change her mind: not only did she have a generous heart, but she wanted to please her good tenants. Indeed, the pension was fully occupied by the huge Stancioff clan (twelve of them), five of their friends, and Sava, who came to study in seclusion for his exams.

The Stancioffs were the most colorful and cosmopolitan Bulgarian family I knew. Ivan Stancioff, a career diplomat in his early fifties, had been *en poste* in Turkey when the Red Army occupied Bulgaria, and he defected to Switzerland, where his American wife Marion and their seven children were already waiting for him. In Fribourg, his mother, *nee* Comtesse Anna de Grenaud, and his unmarried sister Feodora, a very distinguished lady who had been a childhood friend to King Boris and Princess Evdokia of Bulgaria, also joined them. A second sister, "Shoo-Shoo" Guepin, married in London to the chairman of Shell Oil Company, also arrived from London for the vacations in Flueli. (A third sister, lady Nadejda Muir, married to a Scottish aristocrat, resided at Blair Drummond castle in Scotland. There she used to write impassioned articles and "letters to the editor" each time some anti-Bulgarian editorial appeared in the British press, which unfortunately happened quite often.)

I knew few Bulgarian families more patriotic than this Franco-Anglo-Bulgarophonic clan, although most of its members had lived abroad much longer than they had in Bulgaria, and that impressed me very much. That included the old French countess, who had come to Sofia as a young girl with her father, the first Court Chamberlain of King Ferdinand, and had married the king's dashing aide-de-camp, Dimitri Stancioff. It also included Marion, the American heiress-turned-liberal-activist and intellectual, who married Ivan and fell in love with the country. I admired the closeness between the members of this large, Catholic family, and the cult they had for the late family head, Dimitri Stancioff, who had distinguished himself as diplomat and minister of Foreign Affairs. But the Stancioffs' most remarkable characteristic was their unaffected ease with people of every walk of life: they were equally charming, relaxed, and humorous with royalty and peasants, with millionaires, ambassadors, and destitute refugees, at home in any situation, in any country and language, always amusing and amused, gently teasing anyone and themselves, and genuinely interested in people. Exceptional polyglot and quite a ham, Ivan would entertain us with hilarious imitations of accents, switching from Marseillais to Belgian, from affected Oxford to vulgar cockney, and Italian spoken by American tourists. How much I would've loved to do his "*To-Be-or-Not-to-Be*" Hamlet monologue in

Schwitzer-Deutsch! Meanwhile, Marion, who was usually busy writing her memoirs, would quote her friend Ezra Pound or what the Pope said at her last audience in the Vatican. In Flueli, we became great friends with the older Stancioff children, Dimitri, Anne, and Johnny, while the younger ones, who knew a lot about plants, were of great help to me, the so-called gardener. Gathered around me while I worked, and listening to my tall stories, they saved me many a time the embarrassment of ignorantly weeding out some perfectly good vegetable, or wasting water on a weed. The physical work was very beneficial to my morale. I would get up before sunrise in order to water the vegetable garden, then work hard the rest of the day, weeding, pruning, digging potatoes, carting the trash. The evenings with the Stancioffs, Sava, and the other guests at the pension, were delightful. The intelligent conversation of the spry, still coquettish octogenarian Anna Stancioff, looking very feminine in her high lace collars and soignée bluish-white hair, and her sophisticated daughters and daughter-in-law, conferred an atmosphere of a worldly salon to the rustic living room. Ivan would comment on the latest news, such as that week's dropping of a fantastic weapon over Hiroshima, which, the radio said, had been developed in utmost secrecy somewhere in New Mexico. Everybody was showing me extreme consideration and sympathy (they all had known my father well), and the children were laughing heartily to my old, rather stupid, high school jokes. The nights were another story: in spite of the physical fatigue, the nightmares were refusing to let go off me.

Back in Geneva, I had to think about my finances again. The money my benefactors were giving me so generously, was insufficient to meet my minimal expenses, so I had the idea of a bulletin for the Bulgarian colony, so hungry for news from home in those turbulent times. Every night I listened to the news of Radio-Sofia, took notes, and typed a summary. Once a week I brought my bulletin to a mimeo-graph service to make several copies, which I mailed to my subscribers. I charged them 5 francs per month, but many people paid me ten or more. They seemed to like it, because before long, I had about 80 subscribers, mostly in Switzerland and some in France. Thus, after paying for paper, copying and postage, a made a monthly profit of about 400 fr., which, added to the 360 fr. received from my friends, permitted me to make ends meet until I took my final exams.

The future appeared totally uncertain, except for one thing: as a foreigner, I couldn't work in Switzerland, even if I stayed for another two years to go through the mandatory apprenticeship at a law firm. In addition, although I grew to love that country, it's definitely not a place for foreigners without money. I hoped that an University diploma would help me find a job elsewhere, but I didn't have the vaguest idea where. So, aiming at the July session, I went back to my studies with utmost concentration. Not that I didn't have some distractions—my bulletin was taking me a couple of hours every day,—or didn't allow time for practicing the clarinet, seeing my friends, and even skiing.

(The following March, Sava and I went again to Zermatt for Easter vacation, organized by the University, with the same friends and the same success as the year before. There, I was particularly happy to interview one of my idols, French and world ski-champion Emile Allais. I sent the article to my brother and sister, with whom I had re-established contact, and it was published in the Sofia's opposition newspaper "Free People," signed "Stefan Pavlov." Immensely proud, I sent a couple of other *reportages* that year. But the pretense of allowing a "legal opposition" was short-lived: by 1947, the Communists brutally suppressed any open dissent and all non-Communist publications were banned. Thus ended my "Letters from Switzerland." But not before I had received a witty letter from my friend Jivko Krapchev, asking "How long are you going to bore the Bulgarian readers? Wasn't it enough that you used to put them to sleep with your scribblings in *Zora* when you were here? We hoped that we had gotten rid of you!"

A more serious was a distraction of romantic nature. I had met a lady, a few years older than me, whom I admired, desired, respected, and needed more than any other woman before. The interest we showed for each other turned soon to flirtation, then to an affair, then to passion. This unexpected involvement wasn't very time-consuming, because the lady was married and we could meet only rarely and secretly. But it occupied much of my thoughts, and my concentration, in the afternoons when waiting for the doorbell ring, was hardly geared to academic matters. On the other hand, the affection and passion I received and gave were the best balm to my slowly healing wounds. Except that it added new problems to my already confused state: the guilt of adultery, the remorse of taking advantage of a genuine love without being sure of reciprocating equally, the impasse of the situation. Ironically, the problems of illicit love, which had preoccupied me, in theory, when writing my adolescent "drama" about an adulterous affair between people who wanted to remain decent, had revisited me, this time in real life. This romance—and I prefer not to discuss it any further, as I never did with anyone, except for Sava—gave me a lot of joy, in a period when I really needed it, but also much soul-searching and remorse. She was a beautiful person, romantic and loving, but I wasn't ready for anything that serious.

In July, I took my final exams and started making my suitcases. Christo Ghenev, who still had some money left from his Bulgarian tobacco and was now talking big about starting an international import-export business, had kindly offered me a job in his future London company. "But go first to Paris, as an apprentice in my office, and learn English!" he told me when I had my *Licence en Droit* in my pocket. (I only knew a few words in English.) I was overwhelmed, of course, and grabbed the offer. I was sad to be separated from Sava, who had one more semester to go. I was sad to leave my secret, tender lover. I was sad to say goodbye to Geneva and all the friends I knew out of my country, and start everything all over again, alone, in an unknown city. But did I have a choice? At least, I was lucky to have a job, and a place to stay for the first weeks: my recent friends, Guy and Mary Bancel (she was Takvorian's daughter), offered me a room in Paris. I left my news-bulletin service to a fellow-refugee, Antony Nikolov, who had been editor-in-chief of a Sofia daily paper, and on a hot August evening, escorted to the Cornavin station by a dozen of friends, I boarded a second-class car of the night train to Paris.

*   *   *   *

Chapter 8

Mama and Radka in concentration camp

It was probably not later than 5 or 6 o'clock in the afternoon, but with the short days by the end of December, it was already dark when the train reached its final destination, a small station on the shore of the Danube. Dark and very cold. The hatches of the freight cars were unlocked and the prisoners, eager to ease the numbness of their legs, rushed to the embankment. "A ferryboat will come soon to pick you up," the convoy boss said, without more explanation. Everybody flinched. The announcement seemed to confirm the worst fears: they were on the way to be deported to Russia! Or simply to be shot somewhere in Rumania, on the other side of the Danube.

They sat silently on the ground, wrapped in blankets, shawls over frozen faces, their eyes fixed on the slow, wide river. An hour passed, then another interminable, depressing hour. Around them, the impassive militiamen, an ugly lot dressed partly in civilian clothes and ragged uniforms of the old police stripped of epaulets and cockades, eyed them with hostility, brandishing their semi-automatics. Finally the officer reappeared. "Get up!" he shouted, "We'll take you to sleep. The ferry's not coming." The prisoners were led on foot through the deserted small town to the school building. There was not a soul in the streets, it was as though someone had ordered the inhabitants to stay behind the darkened walls.

The school gym had a podium on one side, with lectern, a few chairs and a theater-like curtain. The officer and part of his unkempt militiamen sat there, while the rest of the armed men took places menacingly along the walls. The prisoners were told to spread their blankets on the floor, where they were going to sleep. Undaunted, Mrs. Savova confronted the officer: "We are all hungry and we have none of our food left. There are children here. You must give us something to eat!" she said bravely. The man didn't like this at all. "We have no order to feed you, we have no food for you," he barked. The only concession he was willing to make was to permit visits to the toilets, but only one person at a time, and escorted by a guard. When mama's turn came, Kitta Filova was just returning from the bathroom, looking terrible, visibly shaken. "It's very bad, Dafina, the situation is very bad!" she managed to whisper. Mrs. Filova, the wife of the deposed regent and ex-Prime Minister, had been in terrible shape since the beginning of the trip and one didn't know what treatment she had suffered since the arrest of her husband, but everyone was concerned about her.

A few minutes later, the officer stood up and asked for attention. In his hands he was brandishing a couple of small glass vials. "Filova, come up to the dais!" he ordered the trembling woman. "How do you want us to treat you humanely," he asked rhetorically, "when the comrade-militiaman who escorted Filova to the toilet just caught her when she was about to break these vials and drink them! Do you know what they contain?" He paused for dramatic effect, then announced triumphantly: "That's medicine for syphilis! Yes, syphilis! Because this immoral woman had slept with many young men and has probably infected a lot of people. Therefore, protect your children! Don't let them drink from the same glass with her! We just found other pills on her, and we'll check whether it's not poison, whether she didn't plan to poison the drinking water of the population."

The accusation was so ludicrous, that many people in the room couldn't help bursting into laughter, which enraged the young officer. Not only were the prisoners showing no respect for him, but also for a moment the absurdity of his words had the effect of liberating them from their fear. "O.K., you wise people!" he shouted, his face distorted with hatred. "Tomorrow other authorities will take over, and I won't have to see you any more. But don't think that you came here to have a nice life! You've been sent away to die!"

A few women started crying. But, on the whole, people were more stunned than frightened; the terror had been replaced by exhaustion and apathy; no one was paying attention to the guards, no one was talking to them. Their thoughts were with their husbands and fathers who were in the Sofia prison or had just "disappeared." Mama worried that my father would think it strange that nobody was bringing him parcels or even writing to him. And, in spite of the freezing room temperature (there was a single stove on the stage, but it was for the militiamen), and the fear of being deported to Russia, the pitiful group of wives and children managed to get a few hours of sleep.

It was equally cold in the morning, and the hunger was worse. Mrs. Savova had just succeeded, after an argument, to convince the ill-humored officer to have some bread and sausages brought in, when he ordered everybody to get ready for leaving. Lugging their baggage (mama and Radka carried all their possessions in one suitcase), the prisoners walked back to the bleak railroad station on the shore. Where were they exactly? Nobody knew. Some of them speculated that they were in Dobrudja, the Bulgarian-populated territory South of the Danube and near its estuary, which Rumania returned to Bulgaria in 1940. But one wasn't sure. Not before long, they discerned, far away in the river, a dark dot moving slowly from the Rumanian side of the Danube in the direction of the Bulgarian shore. The ferryboat! The faces paled, panic grabbed the throats. As the dot approached, the contours of the boat became more and more distinct in the fog; but it still moved incredibly, unbearably slowly, Radka thought, as if it was going to take a whole year to reach the pier. It was as cruel, she felt, as though one were watching the advent of Death with eyes wide open, praying that it would never arrive, and at the same time wishing it to hurry up, so the torture would be over once and forever.

When the ferry arrived, several Soviet soldiers and Rumanian passengers disembarked, and the militia officer went aboard. Holding their breath, the prisoners watched him discuss animatedly with the captain, then return to the pier with a disgusted expression on his face. "There was a mistake. The ferry isn't for you," he announced.

"There'll be carriages to take you to your destination." The city ladies had never been happier to board the uncomfortable two-horse carriages, driven by a taciturn peasant, with a militiaman next to him. After a two or three hour drive, the convoy arrived in a small narrow-track train station, where the prisoners were loaded into tiny railway cars used to transport pigs. The stench was atrocious and they spent the entire night standing up in the overcrowded car and without food, as the very slow train advanced at snail's pace through the flat, infinite plains.

The wagon's ceiling was so low, that taller passenger, like Vasco Vulev, were unable to stand up without bending their head.

The nondescript village where they arrived the next morning did not have much to show, outside of the school and the tavern. After the prisoners were given something to eat and escorted, one by one, to the filthy outhouse whose door was kept wide open, they were led through the streets, preceded by the village crier and his drum. The passers-by showed little interest and went their way without looking or commenting. On the main square, the convoy stopped to give the militia officer the opportunity to harangue the few peasants attracted by the crier's drum. "These are wives and children of criminals," the officer proclaimed. "Their husbands and fathers are now being judged by the People's Tribunal, to answer for their crimes, for the thousands victims they killed, for the monarcho-fascist conspiracy which delivered our country to their master Hitler! Spit on them! Show them the hatred of our people!" Unsmiling, the peasants listened and then dispersed in silence.

At the school, the militiamen handed over the prisoners to a local crew and left. As the new guards spoke a different dialect among themselves, mixing Bulgarian with Rumanian words, one of the ladies took her courage and asked a young man where he was from. "Why, I'm from right here, from Dobrudja," he answered, surprised. That's how they finally learned where they were.

After a roll call, the guards asked everyone to declare what money they were carrying and to deposit it with them, "against receipt." Hearing mama's name, a young guard exclaimed joyfully: "So, you're from the palace, Granny? And now you'll be a peasant, ha-ha! Tell me, how much money did you bring?" Mama had a few gold coins sewn on her waist belt, but she also had a small sum in her wallet. She left it with the guards, who dutifully scribbled a totally illegible receipt. Then each family was asked to name the close friends with whom it would like to share living quarters. That was the first good news in this nightmarish week, and everybody felt encouraged and relieved. Eagerly, the Groueffs, Savovs, Krapchevs, Vulevs, Pomenovs, Mrs. Riaskova, and a few others signed up to remain together. When the horse carriages arrived, however, the Krapchevs, the Vulevs, and other families of friends were separated and sent with other groups.

It was a painful, tearful parting, as close friends embraced and bid farewell, not knowing whether they'll see each other again. The long caravan left the village in single file, but as the horses started trotting off on the snow-covered plain, a carriage would turn left at the first crossroad, its occupants waving for goodbye, another carriage would take off to the right at the next intersection, and so on, until no more than a couple of carriages remained on the desolate, deserted trail. It was bitterly cold on the frozen steppe, with no hill or forest in sight to break the piercing wind or at least the scenery's bleak uniformity. Although wrapped in all the blankets and eiderdowns they possessed, the prisoners suffered badly from frozen feet, hands, and ears and the carriage had to stop from time to time to rub them vigorously with snow. The peasant-driver and the armed guard sitting next to him didn't fare much better, nor did the others of the escort, in their fur bonnets and earmuffs, riding along on their blanket-covered horses. But in contrast with the vicious "partisans" and punks, who escorted the convoy since Sofia, the guards in Dobrudja were decent young soldiers who treated the prisoners humanely, ready to share their food with them or snow-friction the frostbitten face of a crying child. For four days they rode through this Siberian landscape, stopping by night to sleep on the floor in some godforsaken village, sometimes unable to advance for hours in a blinding snowstorm. Finally, they reached destination: a wretched hamlet of mud houses with mostly Turkish population, called Bosna.

The sly mayor, a tiny blond man in his late twenties, informed the prisoners that they would be consigned to a house, which they were not allowed to leave except under guard. The friendly escort took leave and an unit of unpleasant militiamen led the group to their new living quarters. After a two mile walk out the village, they reached a snow-covered field fenced by barbed wire, with a small elevation on one side, where they saw a miserable wooden structure, something like an outhouse or a tools shed. "Here it is," the militiamen said as they left. "And don't you try to go out, we'll shoot!"

The prisoners thought that it was some bad joke, that it couldn't be true. The minuscule hut consisted of a vestibule and two dilapidated "rooms" with mud floor. All windows were missing and the icy wind was blowing snow inside. There was no stove, no running water and, of course, no electricity, and it seemed unimaginable that fifteen human beings could possibly fit in such restricted quarters. Something had to be done, or at least tried. Everybody realized that they would never survive the bitter winter night if they had to spend it in the shanty with the gaping windows. After a brief conclave, Stefan Savov, the only man present, was elected to represent the group in all dealings with the authorities, and, in spite of the militia's threads, he was sent back to the village to ask for the mayor's assistance. Mrs. Savova volunteered to accompany her son.

The returned with the mayor and two militiamen, in a horse carriage filled with hay and bringing a kerosene lamp and a few candles, shovels, large cardboard panels, and an empty barrel. They also brought, paying for it, some bread, onions, and sausage. Then the new colony went to work. The windows were blocked and bed sheets were tacked over the panels, for better insulation. The barrel, mounted on two bricks, was installed in the vestibule and had to serve as stove. Some wood was discovered in the adjacent shed. That shed, although open on three of its sides, became the kitchen, when a discarded stove plate was found under the snow the following morning. Hay was spread on the floor and blankets laid on top of it. Then, donning every piece of cloth available, they lay, squeezed against each other without any possibility to move—ten people in the larger room, five in the smaller—and spent their first night in the flimsy shack they were going to share for the next several months.

It took a few days and a lot of improvisation to get organized for a minimal subsistence. There was no table for eating, for instance. So the only door around was dismantled (it happened to be the door of the outhouse...) and mounted on two carpenter's horses found miraculously in the tool shed. After the meals, it was carried back to the outhouse, to give some privacy to the users. There were no chairs. So at the next visit to the village (Stefan and Liliana were assigned to go once every few weeks to collect the mail) a bench was "borrowed" from the mayor's office. While working in the fields, the prisoners noticed the ruins of a demolished house. They went there during the night and carried out a couple of old doors, which were installed inside their shanty. For drinking water, Stefan and my sister Radka had to walk more than an hour every day to the village well, wait for their turn, and carry back the heavy buckets, balanced over the shoulder on a long wooded cane. It took several days of practice before they were able to reach home without half of the water being spilt on the way. For food, the militia supplied one loaf a bread per person daily, one basket with leeks, one with potatoes, and occasionally some onions. From time to time they could buy milk, some salted pork meat, olive oil and salt, at prices determined by the mayor who collected the money and did the shopping. All expenses were shared among the prisoners, with Stefan Savov keeping the accounting. The money was in short supply (mama's money didn't last long), but after the first couple of months Suzy Savova and Radka Riaskova, who were better off, started discreetly helping the others. The mayor, who made a profit from his shopping for them, didn't ask questions.

The women took turns with the cooking, while the rest of the group was working outside. The mandatory daily work, done under the surveillance of armed, silent militiamen who avoided speaking to their wards, consisted in clearing the field of cut wood, broken twigs, branches, old roots, and other debris, scattered on the frozen ground and covered by snow. It started early in the morning and lasted the whole day, in the bitter cold, with bare hands, as the gloves were quickly reduced to shreds. When the terrain near the house was cleared, the wives and children of the former dignitaries were marched in groups to work further and further, collecting with frozen fingers snow-covered pieces of firewood, which the militiamen carted away. And when the firewood was finished, they had to clear the thorn fences in the area. During the entire winter, everybody's hands were constantly swollen, bleeding with splinters and thorns. But there was a dividend in that: by night, the respectable ladies were stealing old fences to bring home for the meager fire in the makeshift stove.

They had to accept many other painful and degrading things. With time, lack of privacy ceased to bother them and the militiamen's stare while they were changing or washing themselves became less offensive. Hygienic conditions were harder to take, but they ended by getting used to the improvised bathing—the pail with hot water in the shed-kitchen, with two other ladies holding a sheet over the open wall to hide the bather from the men's eyes. The laundry was sent weekly to a Turkish woman in the village, until it came back full of lice and they realized that the entire population was infested. It was not only an acutely stinging, but also a particularly humiliating experience, which made Radka cry and feel ashamed. From then on, the women started boiling their clothes in a pail, in the yard, which, in winter, created a serious problem of getting them dried. Another unpleasant chore was added when the ladies were periodically ordered to wash the mayor's floors or cook for him. But they ended by accepting everything with resignation, everything except the torture of living without any news from their husbands and fathers.

They were allowed one letter a month, the mail arriving at the mayor's office and being censored by him. Mama and Radka wrote a few times to my brother in Sofia, asking for news about my father, but never received an answer. In the other prisoners' mail, the mayor carefully censured any mention of the "People's Tribunal" trial, and, of course, no newspapers were allowed to arrive. As a result, the families lived in total ignorance of the fate of their beloved, and this was their most cruel ordeal.

They didn't know that two among them, their "representatives" Stefan Savov and Liliana Pomenova, had surreptitiously read the newspapers in the mayor's office during one of their regular visit to collect the mail. Although shattered by the news (Liliana's father had been sentenced to death and executed), they decided to keep the horrible secret for themselves and spare momentarily the already suffering families. For several weeks, they managed to do it, and the tearful Liliana had to invent some illness to explain her crying. She didn't tell her mother, neither Radka nor the other close friends. Stefan finally shared the secret with his mother and with Mrs. Riaskova, for their husbands had "only" been sentenced to prison and not to death.

Thus, desolate days slowly followed other bleak days of cold, hardship, and humiliations. January came and went, then an interminable February, then the relentless Dobrudja winter continued with a freezing, windy March. It was at the end of March or beginning of April when one day the mayor came unexpectedly to the house, accompanied by several militiamen. After cheerfully announcing some new regulations, he pulled out a bunch of letters and said: "By the way, today it's me who brings you the mail; no need for you to come to the village." Radka immediately recognized Boubi's orderly handwriting on a postcard and grabbed it impatiently. It was a very short message: my brother couldn't understand why mama and Radka never answered his many letters, *especially after father's death...*

The expression on my sister's face said it all. Liliana rushed to her, hugging her and sobbing. "My father too, Radka! And many other of the husbands here..." Realizing slowly what had happened, other unsuspecting widows and orphans surrounded the militia officer, frantically asking questions. Radka, usually calm and composed, jumped to the officer and started screaming hysterically in his face: "Assassins! You're all murderers! You killed my father, you, dirty criminals!" The mayor tried to calm her, but she turned her rage to him and kicked him. "You, coward!" she shouted, continuing to hit and kick. "You liar! You've known it all this time and you continued talking to us and smiling!" Totally out of control, she had to be subdued by the guards, who began to drag her out of the house, while Stefan was trying to stop them and Mrs. Riaskova was gently pleading with the officer. In the pandemonium, one heard the commanding voice of Suzy Savova: "Get out of here!" she ordered the mayor and the militiamen. "All of you! Leave us alone! Get out!" Surprisingly enough, they left.

Mama's reaction was the opposite. From the moment she guessed the terrible news on the face of Radka, she stood like petrified in the middle of the room, motionless, expressionless, without uttering any sound. Even after the militiamen left, she remained in the same position, stunned, not saying a word, not a tear in her vacant eyes. The few friends who were not crying for their own dead embraced her, tried to talk to her, shook her by the shoulders. To no avail, she did not respond. When Radka calmed down a bit, she tried too, begging her to say something, crying, kissing her. But there was no reaction, mama acted like being hypnotized. Late that night, when the grieving, sobbing group went to bed finally and mama mechanically let herself do the same, she lay silently, her eyes wide open, staring at the ceiling. The entire night she didn't close her eyes, unblinking, like a dead person.

She remained in this state for several days, speechless, barely accepting a piece of bread or a sip of water, causing serious concern to everyone. She would leave the house and walk aimlessly in the field, not answering to anyone talking to her, then return and lie immobile, with open eyes and her hands crossed over her chest, like a dead body in an open coffin. Finally one evening she responded when Radka implored her for the hundredth time to pull herself together and go on living, for the sake of her children who need her, if not for herself. "Think of us, mama! You make it so difficult for us. Please help us!" With that, mama burst into tears, hugged Radka, and for the first time mother and daughter cried together.

On the morning after Radka had screamed at the officer and kicked the mayor, a unit of 20 or 30 militiamen surrounded the house. "Who's the one who insulted the authorities?" they asked. Radka explained what had happened and that she had been beside herself for grief, not knowing what she was saying and doing. The officer listened without saying anything. By that time, my sister had reached a state of total indifference to anything that could happen to her or to the world and nothing could frighten her any more. What could they do to me?, she thought. Kill me? Torture me? Put me in jail? So what?—After her idol, her father, the person she adored more than anything in the world, was dead, nothing seemed to matter.

The officer didn't punish her. But his men ransacked the place, opening every bag, looking under every blanket, frisking unceremoniously the frightened ladies and children. They collected all watches, pulled wedding rings off the fingers and earrings off the ears, and took away any piece of clothing that still looked half decent.

Life continued to grow harsher, sadder, with no hope left. When spring came, the prisoners were escorted daily to far away fields to help the peasants till the soil. They were forbidden to talk to the villagers while working; most peasants spoke Turkish anyhow and the contacts were very limited, although a sincere sympathy and readiness to help could be read on the villagers' faces.

One night in April, militiamen burst into the house (they always came by night). "Get dressed and come out!" they shouted rudely. "Which one is Radka Riaskova," they asked, when the women, half-asleep, lined up in the yard. The frail wife of the former Finance Minister and mother of three sons, all good friends of mine, was shaking with fear. "In spite of his crimes against the people, your husband has not been punished by death," the sergeant told her. "The magnanimous government lets you free now. Tell us where you want to go from here?" "We live in Sofia," she whispered, still trembling. "Sofia's off limits. All big towns are off limits. Choose some other place!" the man said, enjoying thoroughly his power. After some hesitation, she mentioned Pancharevo, a village near Sofia. The sergeant issued her a permit for this destination (no one could travel without a special permit) and instructed a militiaman to escort her to the railroad station. Moved, the prisoners surrounded their gentle, well-liked companion to bid farewell and wish her much luck. "Whom am I going to?" she said sadly. "My husband's is in jail, I don't know where my sons are, or whether there are still alive: Ilko used to be in Switzerland, Sava—in Vienna, and Kolio on the front..."

Other families were released, one at a time, in May and June, each one sent to reside in some smaller town or village. For weeks mama and Radka wondered where they should go when—and if—they are set free. Almost all their relatives lived in Sofia or Plovdiv, two forbidden cities, and Boubi was doing his military service. And what were they going to do, alone and with no money, in a new, unknown place?—"That's your business!" was the militia's cold answer to inquiries of this kind. As usual, the resourceful Suzy Savova came up with an idea. "We'll go to Vratza (a town in North-West Bulgaria), where we have a house and many friends and relatives. You'll come with us!" she offered generously and gave them an address to call in case they leave at different times.

The Savovs left before the Groueffs. When the order for mama and Radka finally came in the beginning of July, there were only two other ladies left with them in Bosna, and the four women were still working hard with the peasants in the field. Mama and Radka paid a horse carriage for the long ride to the railroad station of Dobritch (Mrs. Savova had luckily left them some money), where they received travel permits and tickets to Vratza, a town they had never seen before. With their clothes in rags, carrying their shabby suitcase and the old, soiled silk eiderdowns, they apprehensively boarded the train, headed for an unknown destination.

*   *   *   *   *

Chapter 9

Princess Faiza

In the loneliness of my new life in Paris, I missed the daily companionship of Sava, who had stayed in Geneva to pass his last exams. The company for which I was supposed to work had still not started its activities, but I was getting a small pay and was conscientiously going to its Champs-Elysees offices on short daily visits, waiting for the boss's word. Luckily for me, Sava managed to come on short trips to Paris and each of his visits brought refreshing variety into my monotonous days. He was far more gregarious and enterprising than me, especially when there was question of going out with friends, social life, and flirting.

At one of his visits, Sava told me that he had bumped into Hugues de Jouvencourt, an acquaintance of ours from Geneva, a painter who was quite popular socially. This tall, handsome and amusing Frenchman had suggested to bring us that evening to a cocktail party at the apartment of the sister of the Egyptian King Farouk and her husband, who were in Paris on a honeymoon. Terrific people and great fun, Hugues had said, and good friends of his. Thus, we were invited indirectly to the King's sisters.

In those days, everybody in Paris had read about the fabulously beautiful and rich Egyptian princess. At the same time, the papers were full of stories about the arrogant Farouk, a detested absolute monarch who used to shock the world with his gross womanizing and his astronomical losses at the casinos on the Riviera. The slender and handsome crown prince of yesteryear had become a fat, revolting satrap, sunken into corruption and terrorizing his subjects. His family, however, had the reputation of being quite attractive. The eldest of his four sisters, Fawzia, considered one of the most beautiful women in the world, was married to the young Shah of Iran. The second sister, Faiza, recently married to a well-born Turk, was now the toast of Paris. It was amusing to notice that the same journalists who couldn't find a single kind word about King Farouk, were raving about the charm, elegance, and gracious manner of Princess Faiza.

That evening when Sava and I arrived at the exquisite apartment in the Ritz, overlooking Place Vendome, four or five guests were already having drinks with the host. Bulent Rauf, or "Ali" to his friends, the Princess's husband, was a large, fleshy Turkish aristocrat in his late thirties, impeccably tailored, sporting a carefully trimmed blond mustache. His intelligent blue eyes sparkled with humor. In addition to his English, spoken with the accent of the upper classes, his French was faultless, and a brief conversation with him was enough to reveal his familiarity with literature, history, and the arts.

Hugues introduced us, adding some little joke about our Bulgarian origin, to which Ali, the worldly gentleman par excellence, replied with some witty but friendly remark about our common Bulgaro-Turkish past. "What a pleasant man!" was my first impression, as I observed the ease with which the host was entertaining his cosmopolitan guests, offering more champagne and caviar, and commenting on up-to-date Parisian gossip. His refined taste, the exquisite silk shirt, the white handkerchief sprinkled with cologne "Jean-Marie Farina" with which he was constantly refreshing the delicate skin of his face, as well as certain effeminate gestures, seemed to fit well with the preconceived I had had about the decadent refinement that must have reigned in the palaces of the last Sultans.

I was a little shy when I came, a little insecure among the socialites whom I didn't know, but Ali's friendliness, plus the champagne, helped me to relax and feel quite happy in the elegant surroundings. But during the entire evening I had the feeling that behind Ali's smile and superficial chatter, his wise eyes observed and analyzed everybody and me constantly.

A half-hour passed, and the princess had still not appeared. Then another half-hour, and more champagne, foie-gras and caviar. Sava and I were burning with curiosity, we had read and heard so much about King Farouk's sister, that fairy-tale princess from "Arabian Nights," whose beauty and incredible prodigality had conquered the fashion world and nightlife in Paris in a few weeks. The other guests didn't seem to be at all impatient: they were used to Faiza proverbial lateness.

They were people from most diverse nationalities, ages, and positions. The sarcastic Arthur Forbes, a millionaire and future Lord Granard, was the owner of a splendid *hotel particulier* in Paris. He had served in World War II with the Royal Air Force (or Intelligence Service?) and had accomplished missions in Rumania. The cosmopolitan Mexican beauty Gloria Rubio, (the future wife of billionaire-banker Loel Guinness), famous for her numerous romantic adventures, was in those days divorced from a German aristocrat, Count Furstenberg, and was engaged to a young Egyptian, Fakri. The cozy, rotund painter Don, a witty Rumanian-born cartoonist who amused *Le Tout Paris* with his anecdotes and aphorisms and who knew all actors, writers, and artists. The moody Michel Bibikoff was a young Russian emigre from a noble family. I knew him since my student years in Switzerland, although he didn't like me particularly: he had been jealous of me because of his then-girlfriend, which was, alas, without reason. He was even more broke than I was, if that was possible, and was making a living by training dogs for blind people. Other members of Faiza and Ali's Parisian group were the wealthy Portuguese playboy, Duke Jimmy de Cadaval; the artist Hugues de Jouvencourt; a stocky, bespectacled employee at the Egyptian embassy, Fayed; a blond, good-looking English lady, Ann (I don't remember her name, but I think her husband was a member of the Parliament); a lady from the French aristocracy, Madou de Faucigny-Lucinge; and a few other Frenchmen, British, and Egyptians passing through Paris.

Finally, long after dinnertime had come and gone and I was asking myself, disappointed, whether we hadn't overstayed, the door to the bedroom opened and the princess made her entrance, radiant as a child at her birthday party. At her appearance, even the most chaste eye would find it impossible to overlook the slender, willowy waist, or the generosity with which the Creator had filled her stylish blouse; a vision which, I must admit, caused my heart to accelerate its beat. She was really beautiful. Her burning dark eyes and superb black hair gave her just the right touch of exoticism to fit a princess out of the Scheherazade's tales. As I had expected, she was dressed according to the latest Parisian *haute couture* and her jewels were breathtaking. But, unlike the blasé facial expression of the fashion magazines' cover-girls, her 20-year-old face reflected the unabashed joy of the young bride honey-mooning in the City of Lights, liberated at last from protocol and family control. Her cheeked burned with excitement and her vivacious, doe-like eyes flirted with the entire world she had just discovered.

As soon as we were introduced, Princess Faiza engaged in a most cordial conversation with Sava and me, making us feel that everything we said interested and amused her tremendously. Her voice was switching between sensuous alto and childish tinkling laughter, while her provocative eyes flashed teasingly. Useless to say that we both were immediately and totally enchanted, and when the hosts suggested that everybody stay for dinner and silver trays with oysters and smoked salmon were passed around, we didn't raise any objection.

Ali was extremely attentive toward his young bride, with the patronizing tenderness of a veteran bonvivant to a fresh young debutante. The dinner lasted until late in the night, the company was amusing, and for a few hours I found myself transported into a world which I thought had disappeared with the war. As we were leaving, Faiza stretched our her both hands to us and, looking straight into our eyes, said almost imploringly: "Tomorrow we are dining in town. Would you please join us? We'll be expecting you here." I don't think it was solely because the alternative for us was a modest sandwich in our hotel room or the usual cheap soup at the neighborhood bistro "Chez Doucet," but we both accepted with alacrity." Do promise that you'll come!" she insisted, with one of these coaxing smiles which had for centuries pushed countless knights on the road to exploits and glory.

Walking back from place Vendome to avenue Montaigne where we lived (taking a taxi was, of course, unthinkable luxury), Sava and I reviewed animatedly the evening and raved about the charming hostess. Our heads were slightly dizzy from the champagne and the fine Bordeaux. That night we both dreamt of the same pair of eyes, and the same voice rang for a long time in our ears. When I woke up the next morning, the depressing, gray December Paris had become more beautiful and life didn't seem, after all, to be that joyless. The urgent worry that day was whether the second of my only two white shirts could be laundered and pressed in time for the evening.

Thus began the whirlpool of my fantastic and unmatched Parisian nights. Fantastic, because they contrasted so totally with my daily routine of poor apprentice clerk and stateless refugee, whose wounds were still not healed. Not to be ever matched, because of their incredible extravagance and lack of any kind of financial restraint or social scruples. The prodigal stream of money, flowing from the Ritz apartment toward the Parisian fashion houses, jewelers, and night establishments was fabulous. It represented the last spasms of a piquant and still tolerated anachronism, the swan song of a class on its way of disappearing. From that evening on, I was invited by Faiza and Ali several times a week, and it was the beginning of anew friendship. Unsuspectingly, I found myself involved in a life of international jet set, such as I had only read about in glossy magazines. To say that I had looked for it would be inaccurate. It just happened, I had just wanted to be in the company of a very attractive person. But to say that I made particular efforts to resist, would be hypocritical. For a few months, I did enjoy it. People had done worse things when following a pair of enticing eyes, so let's not be too apologetic!

In these months, I saw Faiza very seldom during the day. She slept until lunchtime, then a procession of suppliers and trades-people marched through her apartment. Directresses from Balenciaga and Jacques Fath, from Balmain and Chanel arrived with huge de-luxe boxes packed with dresses, and interminable fittings began in front of the mirrors. Sometimes the princess attended the fashion shows, in company of Ali, and received at the door by the designer in person. Some couturiers, such as Marcel and Helene Rochas, counted among the friends who sometimes joined the couple for dinner. Jewelers, hairdressers, perfumers and manicurists, each one waiting patiently for his or her turn to be ushered into the Ritz apartment, occupied the rest of the day. A good number of the boxes with exclusive models, made to order with several fittings and paid outrageous prices, remained unopened, because the month had not enough days and nights for all the dresses to be worn at least once.

Almost every evening our group met at the Ritz and when Faiza was ready after her countless fittings and changes of dresses, we headed for the restaurant selected for that night, in the rented chauffeured limousines kept at our disposal.

If no one had suggested some new or original eating place, we went routinely to Maxim's, where a half-dozen maitres-ds, wine stewards, waiters, and checkroom girls greeted us at the entrance, bowing deeply and smiling compliantly. Faiza used to recognize a few among them and never failed to greet them by name and inquire how they were doing that night. The world-famous Monsieur Albert, who presided masterfully and without appeal over the distribution of the tables in that most coveted establishment in Europe, rushed to meet us and seat us at one of the prestigious tables, usually the one under the mirrors, on the left of the entrance of the main room. Albert, the imposing, paunchy super-maitre-d', was a living legend because of his proverbial insight and memory for faces and names of the French and international society, and his diplomatic handling of hierarchy of desired guest, as well as for the way he could dismiss the ones he judged not good enough for Maxim's.

Frequently, at Faiza's and Ali's entrance the orchestra interrupted the music and the violins stroke up some of the princess's favorite tunes, such as the romantic Vienna song *Drunnt in der Lobau*, or *La Vie en Rose*, very much en vogue then. From the tables all around, curious eyes stared at us and on the faces one could read the commentaries: "She's wearing a Balenciaga from the current collection. Have you ever seen such diamond! And look at the rubies necklace!" "Who's the man next to her?…And the lady in Chanel opposite her?"

Ali was quite an epicure and at his table even I, a man with no particular culinary interests, learned a few things about refined food and wines. As for Faiza, it was a real pleasure to watch her healthy, unconcealed appetite. She ate with the same enthusiasm with which she greeted friends and with which she danced. Dancing!…It was a real passion for her. She danced during dinner at Maxim's, she continued dancing in the nightclubs that we considered mandatory to go to after dinner, she greeted the dawn while dancing on Montmartre. And she didn't do it the way Sava and I, and most young men from my Bulgarian and European years, used to do: to us, dancing was little more than a pretext for flirting, hypocritical "macho" tactics for approaching and better examining the target. No, true aficionados (usually women) love dancing for the sake of dancing; they draw an immense pleasure from it, no matter who the partner is, provided he dances well. That was the case with Faiza, who was genuinely happy on the dancing floor.

Soon after I had met Ali and Faiza, they invited me to one of the most brilliant balls of the season, which was to take place the following week. Unfortunately, I didn't possess a dinner jacket. This technical problem was solved by my fellow-emigre Milko Tzankoff who, I don't know how, had brought to Paris his old "smoking," as dinner-jackets are called in Europe. As his financial status was even worse than mine, he proposed to sell me this suit, and complicated bargaining was initiated between us, the two "hungry chickens," as Milko used to call the new refugees. Pointing out, not without considerable pride, that the dinner-jacket had been cut personally by Sofia's "top tailor," Mr. Moksa, ("supplier, by appointment, to the Royal Court," Milko insisted. "There is no better men's tailor in all Europe!"), my friend tried to convince me that the smoking fitted me "as if made to order." Unfortunately, my physique and Milko's had remarkably few similarities and just one look in the mirror was enough for me to see that in Moksa's suit I really looked like a clown. But the ball was approaching and after we reached agreement on the monthly payments of the long-term credit, and after a neighborhood dry-cleaner did some alterations on the shoulders and the length, the dinner jacket became an essential part of my scant wardrobe. As for the satin bow tie and the patent-leather black shoes, Milko generously gave them to me, "slightly used," in the name of emigre solidarity. I reminded myself that no really well-dressed gentleman would wear a brand-new suit, fresh from the tailor; he would first let his valet wear it for a couple of days, to break it in. So, with my second-hand smoking, I didn't at least run the risk of being taken for a nouveau-riche parvenu by some discerning connoisseur.

That fall and winter I became familiar with tens of Paris night establishments, from *Jimmy's Club* in Montparnasse, to the cabarets in Montmartre, where chanteuses sang ribald songs and Patachou cut customers' neckties with a pair of scissors; from the nude dancers at *Les Naturistes* on Pigalle, to the clubs on the Champs-Elysees. Often we went at dawn to Les Halles to eat onion soup, surrounded by tough teamsters unloading trucks of vegetables, warn out prostitutes with faded make-up, and festive tourists. Walking back to my Hotel-des-Theatres as the sun was rising, my ears were still ringing with Aime Barelli's trumpet from *Chez Carrere*, or Bernard Hilda's band from *Club des Champs-Elysees*. And how many times the alcohol and the gypsy violins moved me to tears at *Scheherazade*, *Dinarzade*, and *Monsignor*! The Russian and gypsy musicians would surround the table and play sentimental romances at our ears, while we sang along, out of tune but with much feeling, *Serdtze* and *Two Guitars*. After which Ali would generously stick large bills of francs under the strings, tips equal to my weekly salary.

But our favorite nightclub, the place we "checked in" regularly during our night tours, was *Florence* on rue Blanche, near Place Pigalle. There, the proprietors Monsieur Jean and Monsieur Pelletier, kept reserved for us the same table every night, whether we came that night or not, and made us feel at home. The bottles of champagne and whisky kept arriving incessantly, without anyone keeping count, the band played tunes requested by us, and Ali generously offered drinks to anyone who smiled at us from another table. And Faiza dance without a break, while we took our turns with her. Only when rumbas and sambas were played, Ali interrupted us to dance with his bride: she reserved Latin dances exclusively for him.

During these frenzied Parisian nights Faiza was in her element and I couldn't take my eyes off her, trying to understand her bewitchment power over all of us. I knew that any other person behaving like her would've shocked me with such excesses, and yet I was incapable of resenting the spontaneous, childlike joy she showed when having a good time. I felt that any condemnation of her behavior would be as inappropriate as it is irrelevant to pass judgments on a phenomenon of Nature. She gave me the impression that Nature, in a frivolous mood and as a challenge to every day's grayness of worries and responsibilities, had indulged itself in producing a concentrate of unadulterated vitality, youth, and carefree delight; then, had packaged it in the appetizing form of this blossoming young woman, and served it to post-war Paris with an exhortation: "Forget all problems for a moment! Here is the quintessence of femininity and *joie-de-vivre*! Just enjoy my gift and be grateful!"

Sava had returned to Geneva, but I continued going out with Faiza and Ali's group. The initial mutual sympathy had become true friendship. In the beginning,

I often thought: "God, haven't these people heard that there was a Second World War?" But I realized soon that Faiza was far from being the superficial, frivolous princess who only thought of dresses and nightclubs. Both she and Ali showed sincere interest and understanding for my family's drama, and Faiza began to tell me stories about her childhood, her sisters and family. She confided into me how her relationship with her brother had deteriorated lately and what a despot he had become. I was impressed by her attachment to Egypt and her knowledge of her country and its history. Behind the hedonistic facade, I was discovering the warmth of a pure, sentimental soul and a deep, but carefully concealed, sensibility. Behind the smile, I noticed a sadness in the eyes, which in the beginning I thought was fleeting or accidental, but which I realized with time was in the very essence of her nature. All this intrigued me a lot and made her even more attractive in my eyes. I think that the French term "*amitié amoureuse*" would describe well my feelings—a mixture of affectionate friendship, romantic interest, and un-avowable desire.

Chapter 10

First years in Paris

1946 came to an end and with it ended the fabulous but brief Arabian-Nights interlude in my new life in exile. Faiza and Ali were recalled back to Egypt by her angry brother, the king, highly annoyed by the reports of their extravagant spending spree in Europe, and were put in a sort of confinement at home. They kindly sent me messages through friends saying that they would not be able to travel in the foreseeable future and inviting me to visit them. I applied for Egyptian visa repeatedly, encouraged by telegrams such as the one in April, asking "When are you arriving? Answer 55 Rue Pyramides, Ghiza. Signed Rauf, Faiza." But in May the consulate informed me that "The competent authorities did not approve your application for entry visa" and I gave up. (Little did I know then that other circumstances would send me there five years later.)

Meanwhile in Paris, I had fully returned into the harsh realities of money-less exile. Luckily, my caviar-and-champagne whirl around Faiza had not in the least made me lose my common sense; playboyhood was definitely not going to be my career, therefore I soberly concentrated on the more prosaic business of mere survival.

It wasn't the lack of money that was spoiling much of the joy and the enormous luck to live in Paris. At the age of 24 and 25, even being broke can be fun in this exhilarating city, with which I had fallen in love. The dark cloud over my days was nostalgia, homesickness for Bulgaria and worries about my family; it followed me everywhere, in the boulevards and the parks and along La Seine and at every corner I never tired of admiring. It found me mostly in lonely evenings in my room, the many rooms I was constantly changing "for economic reasons"—be it at the *Franklin Roosevelt* hotel on Rue Clement-Marot, or Avenue Montaigne's *Hotel des Theatres*, or the modest sublets around Etoile or Trocadero. I didn't have Sava to share an apartment, as we did in Switzerland—he stayed in

Geneva for another year to complete take his final exams—and the solitude affected me badly.

Not that I didn't have friends in Paris. I saw a lot of Guy and Mary Bancel, Takvorian's daughter; Evgueni Silianoff and the Boris Naslednikoffs had moved there from Switzerland and couldn't have been nicer to me; among the new refugees I found friends from Sofia—Nina Nenova, Milko Tsankoff, Dobcho Palaveev, Matey Hroussanoff and Nikolay Toshkov were terrific company and despite our disastrous financial state, we had very good time together and shared many laughs. I was also keeping a very active correspondence with most friends abroad and, cautiously, with Bulgaria, mostly with my family and the Panitzas.

When the royal family was expelled from Bulgaria, after the fake "referendum" of September 1946, I wrote to Queen Giovanna in Egypt, where she went in exile. She answered from Alexandria with a long, warm letter, talking about my family and the last days of my father.

"*I always thought of you during these sad years,*" she wrote.

"*I saw Simeon* (my brother) *often and now that I know him well and could appreciate his intelligence, his tact, and his heart, it makes me happy to tell you that he reminds me very much of your poor father… I saw him* (my father) *very often after Sept.9, and the last time it was on the 4th of October. On October 6th, General Mantchev summoned the entire royal suite at 4 o'clock to the Palace intendance building. By 5:30 I was told that this general wanted to talk to me right away and that he was on his way to Vrana palace. When he arrived, he informed me that all these gentlemen of the suite had been arrested by order of the government, but no one had been harmed…Soon after, our intendant Razsukanov and aide-de-camps Bardarov were freed. I was assured that the others were all right, in some suburb of Sofia. During the trial, I had direct news about them from Balan* (her secretary) *who brought it to me every evening, until February 1st. Poor men, they looked tired of the interminable and humiliating sessions. They sent me their greetings and I did the same. We also sent them some food to the Court building. Many times I requested news about them; it seems that they were first in some monastery, then in the Central prison, but nobody knew anything definite; everybody was hiding everything from everybody.*"

"On the First of February at 4 o'clock I was in my room in Vrana listening to the radio about their fate. I can't, nor would I try, to tell you what that moment was to me...In the evening I summoned General Mantchev to Vrana and asked him to arrange for me to go and greet our men, as I knew that none of their families was in town. Your poor mother and Radka had been already deported longtime before. I wanted to see them all and show them my affection and my gratitude. I wanted them to feel that someone was near them in their last moment. I waited until midnight, but all the big-wigs found pretexts to refuse to respond to my demand. It's sad to say, but no one wanted to take the responsibility to show compassion...The next morning general M. came at 11 o'clock and informed me that it was all over...Nobody had been allowed to see them or say one word to them. It appears that they were shot the same evening.

"There were many rumors...I was told that your father fell ill after the sentence was read and died peacefully one or two hours later in a room in the Court building. I went a few times to the place where they rest, these dear, unforgettable people. Before our departure, I went again to bring flowers and light candles for a last time—I didn't want to leave our dear country without thanking them once again for their fidelity and noble behavior. Believe me, Stefcho, that I went through so much, that sometimes I'm asking myself whether all this is possible or is just a nigh-mare; but alas, it's all true."

"Before I left, I didn't have time to see your mother—on a Saturday we were told that there was a ship in Istanbul, and we had to leave on Monday, in 48 hours!,—and I didn't want to cause them trouble by seeing them." Then Queen Giovanna wrote that my father often talked to her about me and that he loved me very much and was proud of me. I always kept this letter. It started a regular and most rewarding correspondence with this remarkable woman, whom I had wor-shipped since my childhood and who now gave me much affection just when I needed it the most.

The news from Bulgaria was continuously depressing. Mama and Boubi had moved to the village of Robertovo, at 40 minutes by train from Sofia, where Boubi worked at a refinery. From their miserable room ("but we were lucky," he boasted in a black humor letter, "because we have a wooden floor, not just dirt, and electricity! And also a well-aired outhouse, just 100 yards away"), he had to walk to work, two muddy miles each way. Mama, in addition of the cleaning, cooking and washing, knitted sweaters, which she bartered against eggs, butter and meet. Radka had a secretarial job in Sofia, where she shared a room with another woman, and was also giving French lessons. "Baba," my dear grandmother who lived in the suburb of Gorna-Bania with her other daughter, aunt Mara, was getting older and more and more feeble and spent all her time in bed. When my father was arrested, she was already ailing and could barely walk or see. She moved to my aunt's modest apartment where she spent her long, lonely days and nights on her couch, worrying and praying in silence. Later I learned that during my father's trial, with Mama and Radka in a camp, Boubi in the army and myself in Switzerland, the old, infirm lady waited every evening for my aunt and cousin to come home from work and asked "How's Pavel?" From the expression on their faces, she guessed the ordeal her beloved son-in-law was going through and tears ran down her cheeks. Day after day, in the gloomy winter months of Sofia, she was praying and crying. "God, please, may this cup pass from him! He's such a good man, so kind and gentle!"...

When it happened, they tried to hide the news. But she knew. Perched on her couch, silent, lonely, she cried for days and weeks.

She asked very often about me, I was told. When I learned these details, I felt a tremendous sadness, mixed with compassion, and tenderness, and guilt. I knew how she felt. I imagined how Baba's trembling lips were mumbling prayers and tears were running behind her thick glasses, exactly like in my childhood, during the Passions of Christ in Sveta-Sofia church, when her sobbing used to touch me and slightly embarrass me. But this time the boy in short pants was not there to hold her hands, and I felt very badly about it. Now my cousin Verka wrote me: "Baba aged very much, she's in bed all the time. Jerry (our white poodle, who was also taken by my aunt) is getting old too; now he's missing two front teeth. When your mother, Radka and Boubi come to visit us, it's the greatest jubilation for Jerry..." I read and reread Verka's letter. Wasn't it enough to miss Mama, Radka and Boubi so much? Now I think of Baba, I think of Jerry, cute old Jerry...

And I shed a few tears for them too.

The news from most people who were close to me was disturbing. Since the terror started in September 1944, I was hearing about tragedies in practically every family I knew, but now, two and three years later, even the survivors weren't safe. The diplomats who remained abroad received stiff official warning to return immediately, or else...None of those I knew did, and they were deprived of Bulgarian nationality. Many friends in Bulgaria were in immediate danger. I learned that my former platoon commander and close friend of the Panitzas, lieutenant Yordan Peyev, had been caught while trying to cross the Greek border, put in jail and tortured. In June 1947 he sent me a letter through his aunt, who was married to an influential French doctor. "I suppose you know about the hard test I've been put through during five months. Unfortunately now, when I'm freed, I cannot enjoy the fresh air nor the sun of which I dreamt continually in my cell, be-cause I'm sick in bed for already four months. Anyhow, I hope to heal, although my recovery seems to go extremely slowly..." Peyev was just one example among thousands. Sveto Radeff, the young diplomat who remained in exile in Rome, wrote me about a new wave of forced internments of former non-Communist politicians. He was a nephew of an eminent statesman, the aging leader of the Democratic party, Nikola Moushanov. "My uncle and aunt are sent to Tirnovo. My aunt barely survived the terrible blow to be ordered to pack in a couple of hours and leave the house they loved so much forever. The Bouroffs (another old statesman) are in Drianovo, Gotcho Gueshoff in Troyan, Roumen Konstantinov in Doupnitza, the Goubidelnikovs...I forgot where, and the Stoicho Moshanovs in Eski-Djoumaya." An endless list of prominent Bulgarians, each one of whom I knew personally, a list to which new names were added each time I sat to have a beer with a fellow refugee at some Champs-Elysees terrace, or opened a letter in my hotel room. I wish I knew Paris without this kind of news and worries; how marvelous this magnificent city must be! But for me, they have become part of *my* Paris.

*   *   *   *   *

The firm where I worked during my first year as a refugee in Paris was called *Intraco*, which stood for "International Trade Company," quite an impressive name. The address was equally impressive—the offices occupied a spacious apartment on the Champs-Elysees, not far from Etoile, with a balcony on the avenue. The only thing that turned out to be less impressive was the firm's trading activities. In fact, I'm using the term "activity" very loosely, since it was hardly a proper description for the few hours we, the personnel, spent there every day in taking care of our personal mail, reading *Le Figaro* and *Le Monde*, and exchanging news and gossip with visiting Bulgarian friends.

To run the office, the founder Christo Ghenev had hired his good friend Dianko Sotirov, a young Sofia lawyer turned diplomat, who had recently broken with the Communist-dominated government and remained in Paris as a refugee. The other members of the staff were Sotirov's father-in-law, a mild-mannered Bulgarian Jew with some business experience and a few connections in Israel, and myself, the apprentice, groomed to take over the still-inexistent *Intraco* London office. After registering the company in Paris, Christo, more ebullient than ever and still talking big about Intraco's fabulous opportunities in the postwar world markets, left for Paris and Zurich and let us waiting for the good news. Waiting for Christo was actually our main occupation. The intervals between his telegrams and long-distance calls and his infrequent, short visits to Paris, were often disturbingly long, but each of his communications to Dianko was like a shot in the arm to us, dispelling our doubts and concern. He was a master in boosting hopes. Indeed, it wasn't only his Clark-Gablian size, mustache and vitality, which suggested some kind of a Rhett Butler character: Christo was a bold, attractive adventurer, a gambler going for the big stakes, or at least talking hyperbolically about it. Ever since he had succeeded a few coups in some tobacco deals, he delighted in acting as a grand-seigneur, a big spender in three-star restaurants and hotels, who skied in St. Moritz, dressed at expensive tailors and drank only special blends of Scotch. And plotted daring, multimillion franc deals. Not everybody saw his ambitious projects as anything more than wishful thinking. Boasting with little substance, just a charming hustler, some people thought. A few friends warned me not to count too much on his promises. But Christo had always been very kind to me, he had even contributed to my university tuition when my father was executed and I found myself with no money in Geneva. And did I have another choice? Hiring me was an extremely generous gesture, as I had no business experience whatsoever. Even worse: in the few deals that Dianko

Sotirov attempted during the existence of *Intraco* and tried to involve me, I showed a noticeable lack of commercial acumen, which, after a few months, began to be frankly disturbing. Knowing one's own shortcomings is a form of intelligence, which, for the better or the worse, I do possess. It's sometimes painful, but in this case my lack of talent was so obvious that, being grateful to Christo and conscientious by nature, I began to secretly worry about my inadequacy to fulfill his expectations for London. Luckily, my abilities were never put to test, as no London office was ever opened, no more than the highly heralded Barcelona one and the rest of the worldwide Intraco network. After a year or so of disappointing inactivity, the Paris *Intraco* office folded, as Christo, undaunted, continued crisscrossing Europe, scheming new, exciting deals.

Meanwhile, I was getting closer to my direct boss, Dianko, a quiet, intelligent man whose sober logic, objective judgment and slight bashfulness compensated well for Christo's flamboyance. The reason for Sotirov's favorable attitude toward me was certainly not to be found in my professional qualities, which, I must admit, were less than impressive. Our friendship started with a common interest we shared: Bulgarian affairs. Although a believer in the republican form of government and more "liberal" than me, the monarchist with right-of-the-center ideas, his anti-communism and desire to see freedom restored in Bulgaria were not less strong than mine. It didn't take us long to confide in each other that he contemplated some resistance activity and that I had already been in touch with a few politically minded émigrés. One didn't have to be a particularly good psychologist to judge Dianko's sincerity and integrity: they were written on his face. As for me, the communists' crimes against my family were a sufficient guaranty for my commitment. Dianko and I trusted each other immediately. It didn't take long before the elegant Intraco offices at 146, avenue des Champs-Elysees became the meeting place of a small group of Bulgarian political refugees.

An outspoken anti-communist who was ready for action had already approached me. Bontcho Dimitrov, a brother-in-law of former Defense minister general Christo Loukov, assassinated in Sofia by communist terrorists, had been chancellor at the Bulgarian royal legation in Paris who had asked for political asylum when the Red Army occupied the country. A right-wing patriot, a man of action rather than an intellectual, his credo was simple: every decent Bulgarian owed unconditional allegiance to the Crown and had the duty to fight "all Marxists and other traitors" until the Fatherland was liberated. Although older than me, he showed a sincere, older-brother affection for me soon after we met and started inviting me for lunch or drinks at the cafes around Champs-Elysees or Chatelet, where he worked. After a few meetings, he confided that he planned to start printing a Bulgarian anti-communist newspaper in French. He knew the news bulletin I used to publish in Geneva and asked me to help with the editing of the projected paper, the first Bulgarian printed publication abroad. He had also asked a Bulgarian professional journalist, Milka Ghenadieva-Boeuf, who worked at Agence France-Presse in Paris, and she had accepted to collaborate. As for the cost, Bontcho assured me that "friends" had provided the money for a few issues and that funding was going to be his responsibility.

The offer created a serious conflict for me. Since 1947, I'd had cautious "political" contacts with many Bulgarians living abroad and we were all discreetly approaching each other with the same question: shouldn't we "do something" about Bulgaria, how and what? Before leaving Switzerland, I had discussed it in more concrete terms with a few former diplomats, especially with veteran minister plenipotentiary Nicolas Balabanov in Lausanne and Ivan Zlatin in Geneva, and we had started exchanging confidential information among us. Christo Boyadjieff, a young diplomat I had always admired, had resigned his post in Budapest and immigrated to South America with his colleague Dimitri "Boubi" Racho-Petroff, and we started "conspiring" by letters. Ideas about possible anti-communist activity in emigration I had also shared with other friends-former diplomats, such as Evgueni Silianoff, Ivan Radeff, Sveto Radeff, Stoyan Petroff-Tchomakoff, Ilia Belinoff, Ivan Stancioff and his sisters, and even former Premier Kiosseivanoff, not to mention the friends of my own generation, all of them staunch anti-communists. I was therefore very excited by the idea of a Bulgarian resistance newspaper in France, and flattered to be asked, at the age of 24, to become one of its editors. But I couldn't ignore the possible consequences for my family of such involvement on my part. Did I have the right to expose them to new dangers, after all they had suffered at the hands of the Communists? It was an agonizing decision, which took several days to take. At the end, the thought of my duty as a Bulgarian who had the luck to be free, as well as my bitter indignation of the atrocities and lies of the usurpers who terrorized my country, prevailed, and I accepted Bontcho's invitation. To mitigate a little my fears and my guilt, I resorted to much rationalizing, trying to convince myself that my participation would be kept secret, that my family was on the black list anyway and, to my knowledge, no one was receiving extra punishment for actions committed by relatives abroad, and that, after all, my family should not be held responsible for my actions. Naive reasoning, of course, but when in the pangs of conscience, who doesn't look for justifications, however flimsy they are? It only half-worked. I wasn't convinced, but nevertheless I did it, and it was only a beginning. The doubts, self-reproach and remorse tortured me all my life, and I still don't know whether, in the many similar involvements which followed, I have acted correctly.

Thus, that's s how "*Le Peuple Bulgare*" was born in Paris, in the summer of 1947. The two-page leaflet, which represented the first issue, dated June 15th, could hardly be called a newspaper. It contained a long and emotional "Appeal by the Bulgarian resistance to the Free democratic world" and a shorter "Appeal to the Bulgarian people," both written in decent French by Bontcho and Milka Ghenadieva. It read as an urgent cry for help. Seven million Bulgarians are in peril of being enslaved by the Soviet empire, the manifesto declared. Bands of armed criminals are ruling now our country. "Komintern hordes," preceded by a fifth column of local communists and other traitors "have already massacred 100,000 Bulgarians," including the elite of the nation. Matching the worst Nazi atrocities, "400,000 other Bulgarians are perishing in concentration camps, comparable to those of Dachau and Siberia. Retracing briefly the 14-century-long history of the Kingdom and explaining the reasons it joined the German side in WW2 without a Bulgarian bullet being shot against the Allies!), the Bulgarian resistance pleaded with the free world to come to its aid, in the name of freedom, democracy and peace. Simultaneously, the Resistance center appealed to all Bulgarians to do their duty and declare war on the nation's two enemies: USSR and the Bulgarian communists

It was signed "The Movements for Bulgarian national and democratic resistance." The plural, suggesting the existence of several organizations, was an idea of Bontcho, who signed the manifesto with the names of five groups ("Bulgarian Militants Abroad," "Diplomats and State Officials Abroad," "Bulgarian Intellectuals," "Free Bulgarians in Europe" and "Committes of Bulgarian Resistance in the US and South America"), all, alas, non-existent. Bontcho believed that such tricks would keep the Communists worried. (In later issues, he printed coded commands by an anonymous "General Assen" to his "Liberation forces:" "Execute my order # 6!" it read, imitating Radio BBC's war-time cryptic messages.) In reality, we were only a handful of refugees, the "Committee" that met weekly at the *Intraco* offices. It was a disparate group. The highly cultured, worldly diplomat Evgueni Silianoff, the down-to-earth doer Bontcho Dimitrov, and myself, the Benjamin of the group, were firm defenders of the traditional, legitimate King-dom. The levelheaded Dianko Sotirov, a Republican, was more of a liberal. The combative Milka Ghenadieva-Boeuf, a left-wing intellectual with somewhat mannish demeanor, was actively involved with the leftist Agrarian party and its leader in exile, Dr. G.M. Dimitrov, and so was Christos Sarbov, a splendid specimen of robust Southeast Bulgaria peasant's son, an engaging man with not much formal education but plenty of common sense and integrity. There was also an unassuming, older immigrant, Dr. Rindoff, a sort of benevolent advocate for Bulgarian refugees in distress. There are, in every exiles' community, charismatic leaders, ideologues who inspire the resistance, and political brains who formulate its program; they're the heroes of the cause, but rarely the ones who help the refugees' welfare. Rindoff was the opposite; there was nothing of the resistance hero in his humble manner and proletarian looks. He had instead dedicated himself to doing, so to speak, the plumbers' jobs, and had become the Bulgarian exiles' self-appointed social worker. While the rest of us discussed lofty subjects such as Kremlin's policies or the forthcoming liberation, the limping, inarticulate Rindoff would find beds and food for newly-arrived refugees, obtain documents for them, or go to the police station to bail out some compatriot in trouble.

"The Committee" met regularly through the summer and fall of 1947 and we published three more issues of *"Le Peuple Bulgare."* Printed on four large-format pages filled with articles and information, it looked now more like a newspaper. Milka did most of the editing, I was the other editor, and when we all agreed on the material, Bontcho brought it to the printer and acted as publisher. With all committee members' collaboration, the quality improved notably and we were able to offer interesting information from inside Bulgaria and other satellite countries, as well as relevant Western news and commentaries. The execution of the opposition leader Nikola Petkov became, of course, a major subject. Our Agrarian-party colleagues Tsenko Barev and Sarbov had contacts with friends inside the country or just escaped and living in refugee camps, and were our main sources of information about events in Bulgaria. Balabanoff became a fervent and profuse collaborator, writing to me almost weekly from Lausanne.

Of all the senior diplomats in exile, this liberal, sometimes caustic, old intellectual was the most active and committed to the cause. Christo Boyadjieff and Boubi Petroff scanned the Latin-American press and sent materials through me. I was also the channel for my Bulgarian friends in Switzerland, everybody contributing anonymously and often not aware of the participation of the others. An important event in the life of *"Le Peuple Bulgare"* was the publication of the full text of Dr. G. M. Dimitrov's memorandum to the General assembly of the United nations, a lengthy document in which the Agrarian leader described in detail the events in Bulgaria since 1944 and the inside story of the Communist take-over.

The list of the people and offices to which we mailed the paper grew with each issue. In addition to the common list, each of us sent packages with several copies to trusted friends all over Europe, asking them to diffuse them, without revealing the origin. Most recipients didn't know who exactly was behind this publication, the first newspaper in exile. Many people used to guess, but we insisted on confidentiality: we all had families in Bulgaria. An exiled journalist, Antoni Nikolov, for instance, used to send me press clippings about Bulgaria from Geneva. "I'm enclosing addresses of friends abroad" he wrote to me. *"If by chance you have contacts with some of the people around the resistance newspaper, please ask them to send it to these addresses."*

The reactions varied, but in general were positive. Balabanoff insisted that our publication was of vital importance and urged me to continue. Coming from a personality of his stature, it had on us the uplifting effect we needed badly. From Brazil, Boyadjieff and Petroff sent me very encouraging words. "The 15 copies of the second issue were distributed promptly. They were more than useful, providing material to Brazilian newsmen and politicians for the many protests against Petkov's assassination. The reaction here was very strong. The Municipal council paid homage to Petkov, vigorous speeches against the red tyranny were delivered in Parliament and in the Senate. Pet-kov's name has become a symbol and the prestige of tiny Bulgaria has increased immensely. *"Le Peuple Bulgare"* was a great success. Many people call me to ask for it. Please send more copies the next time!" From Geneva, Ivan Zlatin wrote me that he fed our material to Swiss journalists and *Le Courrier de Geneve* made good use of it, especially in the Petkov case. The G.M.'s memorandum was very useful, he said. He gave me, in strict confidence, the answer to a mystery Bulgarian official services were trying in vain to solve: who had organized the well-publicized Te-Deum services in Geneva on the 40th day of Petkov's execution? It was Zlatin himself, but nobody found out.

But Sveto Radeff was skeptical. "Dear *Heruvim,*" he wrote me (using this name to tease me, after some old homosexual friend of his had told him that I looked like a "cherub," which, by the way, used to infuriate me), "you know that I'm ready to serve the cause, but I don't believe that anything worthwhile would be achieved by newspapers which don't interest anyone. The paper is better edited than the first manifesto, but there are still too many "komitadji"-like (*Balkan revolutionaries)* exclamation marks, which to West-Europeans doesn't sound serious…What is more, it doesn't add anything new, interesting enough to catch the readers' attention. Its information has already been known much earlier and in greater detail, to the people in charge of these matters, and I can assure you that there are such people in the Foreign Office, and State Department, and other services." Sveto's advice was instead of wasting efforts and money for a paper, to create contacts with important foreign journalists and try to place articles by prominent personalities published in major Western newspapers. He was maybe more realistic than we when he quoted a friend of his, a senior Western diplomat stationed during the war in a neutral country: "Frankly, all the information bulletins and brochures we used to receive from Polish émigrés, and Czechs, and Yugoslavs, etc., we simply threw into the wastepaper basket, without reading them…"

From Lausanne, my good friend Ilko Riaskov was diligently dispatching the paper to many Bulgarian legations in Europe, but counted on me not to reveal his identity to anyone. His father, an eminent financier, was also being persecuted in Bulgaria. While approving of the paper, Ilko made valid constructive criticisms. "Many labels are cut off crookedly, with incomplete addresses or written illiterately. It's inexcusable to write just "M. Petitpierre, Political Departement, Bern," or "General Guisan, Lausanne," or "Monsieur Clifford Norton, US Legation, Bern." Don't your friends know about full names, streets and number, and when to write "His Excellency?" More important, Ilko warned us about partisan tendencies in some articles. "G.M.'s memorandum is very good, but since when does the Agrarian party represent 80percent of the Bulgarian population? Try to keep the national cause above partisan interests!"

In fact, that began to worry me too. At the beginning, there was little disagreement among the Committee's members. But with time, the ideological differences began to show. Our sincere commitment to the overthrow of the communist regime was above any doubt. But we had different, often opposite, views on other subjects. Our attitude toward the fatal date of 9th of September 1944—the takeover by the Soviet-backed "Patriotic Front"—was a major point of discord. Was that coup a betrayal of independent Bulgaria and the starting point of the monstrous red terror (as Bontcho, Evgueni and I saw it), or was it an inevitable "anti-fascist" development in which sincere democrats were cynically cheated and then eliminated by their Communist allies (according to Milka, Sarbov and Sotirov)? Things became further confused when the Communists started persecuting former partners in the fictitious "Patriotic Front." Thus, Agrarian leader Petkov was jailed as a "traitor," tortured and hanged after a shameful farce of a trial, while his successor Dr. Georgi M. Dimitrov was spirited abroad with American help. Dr. Dimitrov (known simply as "G.M.," to differentiate him from the other Georgi Dimitrov, the big Communist boss) formed a "Bulgarian National committee" in Washington. Our Parisian group congratulated him on his escape and offered to coordinate our activities. By that time, out of refugee camps in Greece, Italy, Yugoslavia and Turkey, other Agrarian-party members arrived in Paris, among them a young firebrand eager for action, Tsenko Barev, who called himself "Chief of the Agrarian Youth in Bulgaria." Passionate, uncompromising and inspired, Barev was fanatically devoted to "G.M." He joined our group, became very close to Milka and, before long, the two took over most of the activities, veering them toward "G.M." and his committee. Articles began to appear in *"Le Peuple Bulgare"* before the rest of us could see them. "A misunderstanding," was Milka's answer. Deletions and corrections, agreed upon, were omitted. (For example, Barev's attacks against the late King Boris, our hero.) "Printer's fault," was the excuse. Correspondence with Washington went behind our back. "We simply forgot to tell you…" Some of us objected—Bontcho angrily, Sotirov, Silianoff and I—politely and inefficiently. In December 1947, with the fifth issue of *"Le Peuple Bulgare,"* the title of the paper changed to *"La Bulgarie Libre et Independante,"* with more and more quotations and statements by GM and his portraits. By 1948, the paper became de-facto a French organ of his "National committee," edited by Milka and Tsenko. The Paris group passed entirely under the command of the G.M.'s people. Many émigrés saw advantages in having only one and unique center of Bulgarian resistance abroad, especially when it became clear that the Americans had chosen to back G.M.'s "National Committee." But most people with centrist, conservative, or right-wing ideas disliked Dr. Dimitrov and his left-wing Agrarians and contested their pretense to be the exclusive spokesman for the nation.

Maybe I should've left, as Bontcho did, when we realized that we, the non-Agrarian members of our committee, were stripped from any decision power? But to me, the main enemy was the barbarian regime, not the left-wing refugees, whom I considered as anti-Communist as myself, and probably much more efficient than me. After all, many of them had suffered in Bulgaria, had risked their lives to cross borders, had lived in misery in refugee camps in Italy or on Greek islands; they had remained resolute resistant, ready to fight, and I couldn't not admire them for that. The political ideas of some of them disturbed me, of course. But I was honestly trying to contribute to what we still believed, naively perhaps, to be a "struggle for the liberation of Bulgaria." Thus, it wasn't without qualms that I spent a few nights clandestinely pasting posters on the walls of Paris in company of my colleague, Christos Sarbov. The posters were in protest against the legal assassination in Bulgaria of Nikola Petkov. Friends reminded me that Petkov was a minister in the "Patriotic front" government when my father was executed by the so-called "People's tribunal…" True, I said, he was guilty by association, but he atoned for his mistake tenfold by his heroic stand in Parliament, in prison, in the mock trial, and when bravely facing death in the name of an idea. When Sarbov, a Petkov's admirer who cried when he was executed, asked me to join him, I didn't hesitate. Past midnight, in the deserted streets around the Bulgarian legation, Christos carried the glue buckets and I carried the rolls of posters; furtively, we looked out for policemen, then glued on the walls as many posters as we could, before moving to another street. By the next day, most of them were torn off, and we had to repeat the operation again and again.

The conflict between "old" and "new" enemies of the regime was inevitable. I still hoped that when "The Doctor," as many Agrarians called "G.M." Dimitrov, comes to Paris, most of our disagreements would be ironed out, in the name of the common cause.

But "G.M." came, and the couple of meetings we had with him only confirmed to me that what separated me from his followers was not only ideas, but entirely different mentalities, methods and ethics. The charismatic "G.M.," a tall, handsome man, was very civil when he wanted, but behind his seductive eloquence one felt a certain toughness, a single-minded determination, if not ruthlessness, which my friends, the diplomats of the old regime, did not have. He was a fighter, most of them were not. He was a very skilful politician, which they were not. His troops were ready to fight fire with fire and "GM" condoned it. In order to defeat a hated dictatorship, be it communist or fascist, they wouldn't hesitate to use all sorts of methods that I would have scruples to even contemplate.

The disagreements with our Agrarian colleagues multiplied. During Dr. Dimitrov's stay in Paris, he was constantly with Milka Boeuf and Tsenko Barev, almost completely ignoring the rest of us. When I complained that this "triumvirate" was replacing the committee, Milka and Tsenko denied it indignantly. Finally, on the 24th of November 1948, we all met with GM. All, except for Bontcho, whom they refused to invite, without consulting the rest of us. In the course of the tense, turbulent meeting, unpleasant words and accusations were exchanged in a partisan atmosphere that upset me deeply. When our Agrarian colleagues launched an ugly and unjustified attack against Dianko Sotirov, I couldn't stand it any longer. "I was one of the founders of this committee," I said, "and am probably the only one still in good personal terms with every one of its members. Tonight Dr. Dimitrov spoke candidly and put things clearly: the time has come, he said, for each of us to decide whether or not he or she joins his organization. But once accepting his committee, there is no way back; one becomes a disciplined and obedient member. Personally, I must say frankly that the way the struggle is led now, doesn't correspond to my concept of united national struggle for liberation. Therefore, in order to be true to you and to myself, I'll remain no longer a member of the committee's Parisian group ." With that, in the stunned silence that followed, I shook hands with GM. "Goodbye, Dr. Dimitrov, and I wish you good luck! I hope that, under different circumstances, we'll meet again for the common cause." Trying to control my emotions, I said goodbye to my other colleagues, assuring them that they'll always can count on me when there is question of Bulgaria. As I was leaving, Sarbov rushed after me in the corridor and hugged me. "You're making a mistake, Groueff!" he said, visibly moved. I hadn't realized be-fore how close I had become to this colleague of mine, the fervent Agrarian-party member.

   After this rather dramatic evening, I never worked again with Dr. G.M. Dimitrov or his *National Committee.*

*　　　　*　　　　*　　　　*

   Meanwhile, I had looked for another job, as Christo informed me that Intraco was "temporarily" having difficulties and had to cut expenses. Modest as it was, my salary was my only income, and losing it threatened me with a disaster. Indeed, although I lived very penuriously, I had to worry about paying my rent, my laundry and bus fare, even about eating. How was I going to survive?, I often asked myself, turning and tossing in my bed as sleep was difficult to come. Small debts were quickly piling up. In fact, most my friends were also broke and often the few francs I would borrow in an emergency from Tosh, Milko or Dobtcho, were the same that they had borrowed from me only a few days earlier. Never did I accept with such alacrity any invitation to lunch or dinner than during those month, and never did I stuff myself more with second and third helpings. In between, I sadly ate in my room the baguette with some cheese, or less and less frequently returned to the usual cheap bistros, where I cautiously read only the second column of the menu, the one with the prices. As for social life, worries about freshly laundered shirts or cab fare forced me to cut it to a minimum; contacts with my carefree friends from Switzerland and the jet set from my nightclubbing period with Faiza started to fade away.

In this alarming state of my personal finances I turned to our family friend Takvor Takvorian. As in Geneva, when thanks to him I could complete my studies, he helped me again. During the war, Takvor had lost fortunes in Bulgaria and Greece, but had recovered his position as a major French dealer of tobacco of all origins. "My boy," he told me with his typical mixture of boasting and kindness, "I'm the world's greatest tobacco man and I loved your father and mother. So I'll give you a fantastic opportunity. I'll take you in my company and make you a tobacco expert, a taster. Do you know what a taster is? Like with wines or perfumes, tobacco experts taste the leaves before we buy them and tell us about the quality. They're the best-paid people in the business. I'll give you a golden profession!"

Relieved and grateful, I started right away. The *"Societe Francaise des Tabacs en feuilles"* offices occupied a three-store town house on rue Vernet, not far from Champs-Elysees. There was a courtyard annex where packages of tobacco samples were stored, shredded in a small manual machine, and tasted. The blue-eyed, impeccably tailored Mr. Takvorian ran the company with the autocracy and panache of a benevolent sultan, assisted by less flamboyant but highly qualified men such as his partner, distinguished ex-League-of-Nations official Rene Charron, business veteran Robert Voisin, and director Mr. Blum. I was given a desk in a large office shared by three other employees, and entrusted to an old hand, a Monsieur Jeoffroy, to introduce me to the skills of my new profession.

Takvor was a big spender who loved bragging about his exploits at the casinos in Evian or Monte Carlo and about the prices he had paid for oriental kilims or jewelry. But he was anything but over-indulgent when it came to salaries to employees or allowances to daughters and nephews. As most successful self-made men do, he delighted in exhorting, for their benefit, the virtues of hard work and thriftiness, a welcome opportunity to proudly quote examples from his own youth. Thus, any candidate for pay-raise had to face not only a likely refusal, but also a long lecture on Takvor's early career in Plovdiv, Sofia and Paris.

My modest pay was barely sufficient to make ends meet, and the job was rather dull, but I labored conscientiously and patiently keeping in mind the prospect of a prosperous future as a high executive or tobacco expert. Or did I really? Looking back to these two tedious years at Rue Vernet, 8 to 12 and 2 to 6, with a sandwich in between, I should be honest to admit that the real reason to stay was simply that I didn't have another choice. It didn't take more than a few months for me (and which is worse, for my superiors) to realize that I wasn't very gifted for the commercial side of my work. Otherwise, how come that my colleagues *Monsieur* Tardy and *Monsieur* Hautefeuille (no calling by the first name in French offices, even if you work together for 20 years!), only by a few months my seniors in the company, advanced rapidly up the scale and were entrusted with correspondence with important clients? If, at least, my training as expert-taster were more encouraging! But...

Melancholy, rainy Parisian morning. At the alarm clock's odious ring, I wake up reluctantly and look through the window. The gray sky is down to the roofs of the houses. Except for the garbage truck and the milk delivery, the wet streets are still empty. I have a splitting headache and my mouth is dry and bitter: I had drunk too much the previous night and stayed up too late. The summary breakfast I take while dressing and shaving—Alka-Seltzer with a stale croissant—doesn't seem to help much. Umbrella in hand, I brave the rain. The office is not too far, four or five blocks away, but still far enough to get my feet wet. Another monotonous day is ahead, as dull as yesterday and as uninspiring as tomorrow, a day I'll count the hours and minutes until the slow-coming six o'clock.

The samples have arrived in the storage room, waiting to be tasted. "Exceptional Maryland, even the B and C grades are excellent this year!" exults one of my teachers, happily caressing a bunch of yellowish leaves. "Look at the color, look at size! Now taste the flavor, Monsieur Groueff! Try the "A" and you'll see what I mean." With my headache and my stomach in upheaval, smoking is the last thing in the world I would like to do. But obediently I choose a few leaves and shred them with the machine laying on the counter. Then I take cigarette paper, roll a cigarette with the shredded tobacco, as I have been shown, seal it with saliva, and light it. Slowly, I inhale a few puffs, trying not to choke or show my revulsion. "Isn't it great?" my instructor, a chain smoker, enthuses. "That's the quality we are ready to pay a lot for. Now, just to compare, try a "C." Acceptable, but we should bargain." We taste a few more letters, always for comparison.

"In no time, you'll be able to tell them blindfolded," reassures me my experienced colleague, as we switch from Maryland to Santo-Domingo, to Turkish tobacco and Brazilian Bahia. As we advance with the alphabet, my empty stomach is churning increasingly, but the lesson continues. "You should also know what tobacco to refuse," my torturer insists as he reaches for a sac marked "rejects." With the first puff, I get violently sick and rush to the toilets, to the dismay of my teacher.

The tasting sessions went on for several weeks, with no enthusiasm on my part. I used to smoke very little before, just to show off. I never smoked since. And I never became a tobacco taster.

*   *   *   *   *

Chapter 11

Neelia and Luttrellstown castle

I first met Neelia in Paris in the early spring of 1948. Sava's girlfriend Pamela Platt had invited me for a drink at the apartment she rented on avenue Montaigne, where she introduced me to a visiting friend from London. Aileen Plunket was a delicate looking blonde in her mid-forties, with ethereal white complexion and pale blue eyes, obviously a devoted customer of prestigious Parisian couturiers. A nervous twitch in her face betrayed an unusual shyness, and her frequent giggle and unfinished sentences ending in mumble didn't help much the conversation, especially that my English at that time was less than rudimentary. But she made an honest effort, used some French and a lot of her teasing type of humor, and I found her quite pleasant, if a bit weird, which I thought of most English people I had met. (She was actually not English but Irish, Pam informed me, but in my ignorance it didn't make any difference.)

A couple of days later Aileen called me and, in spite of my total panic when speaking English on the telephone, managed somehow to convey the message that her 18-year-old daughter was staying in Paris with family to study French, and would I come to a party "for the young." I was not particularly thrilled by the idea of escorting 18-year-old schoolgirls; my fantasies in that period floated around gorgeous fashion models and intriguing femmes-fatales. It's only with age that men seem to discover the aphrodisiac quality of early youth. The vanity and insecurities of the immature man of 26 that I was, probably needed the reassurance that experienced, sophisticated, and already recognized beauties can offer.

Anyhow, I went to the party at the Rue de Berry apartment of Vicomte et Vicomtesse de Lamotte, where the Plunket girl was staying. The first thing I noticed was how tall she was—she measured barely one inch less than my 6 feet,—and it was a somehow apologetic tallness, not the kind flaunted by haughty amazons. And yet she was rather pretty; I wouldn't say "tall <u>and</u> pretty," but "very tall yet pretty:" lovely blue eyes with long lashes, exquisite small nose, a friendly girlish smile. Her name was Neelia, "my mother's name spelled backwards," she explained in her upper crust English. The rest of the conversation with the painfully shy Irish teenager, the two Lamotte girls, who were her age, and the few extremely polite young men and girls *de bonnes familles* whom they had invited, hardly reached a more sophisticated level. Neelia told some cute stories about her longhaired dachshund "Schnapps," Jacqueline and Helene de Lamotte described a movie they had just seen, and everybody laughed when Lavinia, a redhead English girl, related some supposedly mischievous boarding-school pranks. What on earth was I doing in this juvenile company, I thought, feeling more and more out of place, especially when the conversation turned to fox hunting, a subject in which Neelia seemed to excel and which intimidated me immensely. Indeed, there is no more treacherous trap for outsiders than to speak about "*chasse a courre*" without using the right terms: you just call a red jacket "red" (instead of "pink"), or say "the deer" or "fox" (instead of "the animal"), and any true gentleman would know that you're nothing but an ignorant plebeian, an imposter who "doesn't belong." In foxhunting vocabulary, for instance, the fox's tail is called a "brush," its head—the "mask," and the foot is a "pad." I already knew better than to open my mouth. As I remember, my unique contribution to the conversation that evening consisted of a few bits of information on Bulgaria, including the name of the capital Sofia (not to be confused with Bucharest or Budapest!) and the curious Bulgarian way of saying "yes" with a left-right-left nod of the head, and "no"—with a up-and-down nod, a cute bit of trivia which always seems to amuse foreign audiences. And also the proud fact that yogurt is a Bulgarian invention (Latin name: *Bacillus Bulgaricus*.) I doubt that this briefing enriched significantly the company's general culture or established me as a fascinating raconteur, but I was asked again at Rue de Berry. This time we had lunch with the Vicomte and the Vicomtesse, charming people who showed sincere interest in Eastern Europe and asked many intelligent questions. Neelia was there too, shy but animated, and she told me later that the Lamotte parents had declared me "*un jeune homme bien.*" So I was accepted and more invitations followed.

Aileen also invited me with Neelia at the *Ritz*, where she was staying during the spring fashion collections, and she took us to three-stars restaurants. She teased me about my mispronunciation of English words and joked about Neelia having a crush on me. She was obviously amused by the whole situation and pleased that her daughter was seeing me. During the day, I was at my 8-to-12 and 2-to-6 job at Takvor's *"Societe Francaise des Tabacs en Feuilles,"* but a few evenings I took Neelia to the movies or to some of the cheap bistros I could afford. She always acted delighted to see me, was extremely appreciative and unspoiled, and very attentive to everything I was telling her. And. I admit, I was quite longwinded, a bad habit which seems to have stayed with me all my life. But I was rather lonely during that period, Sava was constantly with Pam or away, and finding patient and truly interested listeners wasn't that easy.

Especially that I was going through difficult times. My sister Radka in Bulgaria was in real danger: she was working as a nanny for the children of an American military attaché in a villa outside Sofia and didn't dare leave the house for fear of being arrested by the Militia, which tried to enlist as informers all Bulgarians working for foreigners. Separated from her, my mother and brother were forced to live in appalling poverty in a village, Robertovo, where Boubi worked in a factory. The news I was receiving sporadically through foreign diplomats was extremely depressing and the messages brought back by Monsieur Voisin, a director at Takvorian's company who had just visited Sofia and talked to Radka, caused me to have nightmares. Never had I felt so upset, helpless, and guilty, and the evenings with the lovely, innocent Irish girl were moments of relief and much-needed change of mood. Even her ignorance and naivety were refreshing and soothing, her unawareness of the world's evil and atrocities, of communism, and Bulgaria, and war, and misery.

Neelia's feminine gentleness appealed to me. She had an Irish sense of humor, a kind I was unfamiliar with, but amused me. When telling funny stories, she laughed uncontrollably, like a child, long before the punch line. She was emotional, overly sensitive, and often touchy. Tears came easily. She was totally, but charmingly, insecure. She was romantic to the point that I thought she was only now beginning to doubt about Santa Claus and was still dreaming of Cinderella.

And trusting, with all the naivety and purity of an old-fashioned virginal girl. Compared to most young ladies one saw in Paris, Neelia was a lovable, vulnerable anachronism.

We started calling each other every day. Although a little embarrassed about "dating children," I began to feel happy each time I was going to see her after work. Before long, my amused curiosity, my patronizing friendship, as well as my flattered male ego, turned to a genuine affection. She stayed in Paris for the rest of the spring, then in June joined her mother in London, to be presented to the Court and take part in the other glamorous events awaiting the "debutantes" during the famous social "Season." By that time I had realized that I had become very attached to her and missed her. But I was torn by conflicting feelings. Before leaving, Neelia had spoken shyly about engagement, about "our future," had dreamt aloud of small, idyllic country houses with many children, dogs, and horses. It had flattered and touched me enormously, and made me happy. At the same time, it had made me feel guilty: she was so inexperienced, so trusting and vulnerable, but was I really in love? Did I have the right, me, the penny-less refugee, to talk about marrying a rich girl who had been used to all the luxury of the world? She had cried many times when I avoided direct answer to her love questions. Before leaving, she had made her mother invite me to Ireland for the Dublin Horse Show in August, together with the Lamotte girls and a few other friends, and I had promised to try hard to get the visa and the money for such a visit. At the same time, the news from Bulgaria was getting worse and there were days when I couldn't think of anything else but worry about my family. And as Neelia began to write to me every day or two, the waiting for the mail—the one from London and the one from Bulgaria—transformed my life that summer into a schizophrenic agony.

*   *   *   *   *

I had a pretty good idea of mother's and Simeon's miserable life in Robertovo, where they were living in the last year and a half. In the rare letters smuggled out of Bulgaria, she was always trying to sound cheerful and not to worry me, but the true picture was transpiring. "Our room is good, in a new building, bright, with two windows," she wrote. "I'm very happy to be near Boubi and am doing everything I can to make it pleasant and comfortable for him. The village is 3 kilometers from the railroad station, where his factory is. Boubi works 24 hours and rests 12 hours. My main worry is for him to have proper food, as his work is heavy and the air he breathes is foul. Refinery of organic oils. I haven't been there, but they say that the air is horrible. His clothes and shoes smell of grease. They make now working clothes for them, because their own shirts and clothes are filthy; I'm constantly boiling his shirts, but the stains are greasy and cannot be cleaned completely..."

"I received your presents and am very touched, Here the peasants prefer to barter rather than to sell for money. If I had kerchiefs for the head, I could have butter, eggs, cheese, etc. Here they wear scarves of one color, without flowers—light blue, pink, green, gray,—generally soft colors. They like bracelets, necklaces, earrings and other junk jewelry, cheap but fancy. Also lace tablecloths, round or square...Boubi needs a flashlight very much, the village roads are very dark and muddy, and some canvas bag to carry the food I prepare for him, it's difficult to carry it in his hands. And a toothbrush. For me, if you insist to send me a present, could you send kerchief for head (I don't wear hats), I prefer gray, a necklace of white beads to freshen up my dress. Knitting needles Number 3, for stockings; also Number 3 for sweaters, they're difficult to find here, and I do a lot of knitting..."

"I'll go to see Radka in Sofia soon, but it's difficult to walk to the station here—an open field, very strong winds and terrible mud. Poor Boubi, he has to walk this road every second day. He comes from work exhausted and falls asleep at the dinner table. He doesn't complain, says that it not too hard, but as mother I suffer for him. I only pray that his health be good!..."

Hotel Claridges, London, June.

"...went to a ball for Nadina Bowes-Lyon, who is a first cousin of Princesses Elizabeth and Margaret-Rose. It was very royal and rather too pompous; all the men had to come with their decorations. The King and the Queen were there. She's is so heavenly and looked so lovely in a huge black crinoline. No one danced cheek-to-cheek, because if you do, you go automatically onto a black list

*and you're not asked anymore. Princess Elizabeth nearly did it with Philip—
very shocking!*

> *Your loving Neelia.*"

Claridges, London, June 13,
"*...As soon as Lavinia arrived, I whisked her off to a cocktail party given by
a girlfriend of mine...It was very gay and amusing. We then rushed home and
changed into our most glamorous dresses for the Kemsley dance...The dance was
terrific, very well dressed, and Princess Margaret-Rose was there. She looked very
sweet...The day after was the (Buckingham Palace) Garden party, and I made
my curtsy to the Kind and Queen without falling flat. We had a wonderful tea,
I'll always remember it...After the party I went to the Dorchester in a party to a
ball, great fun, but nothing out of the ordinary...Last night I went to the theatre
with a party of ten, a musical comedy...We all had dinner at the Savoy Hotel
afterwards and danced until midnight.*

> *Your Neelia.*"

Sofia, U.S. Legation.
   "Dear Stephane,

   I must write you by this courier to urge you to act immediately, I repeat—
immediately,—the situation is growing more serious every day, and the Colonel
and I fear that unless a Frenchman or Swiss arrives very soon, with whom your
sister can make a marriage, the law we all fear will be passed, prohibiting all marriages of Bulgarians to foreigners. Things are worse now than when Radka last
wrote to you.

   Your brother was let out of prison, it is true, but only after he had put himself
in the hands of the militia to be their tool. Yesterday he came here. He has lost his
job and has little hope of finding another. The militia refused your mother an
exit permit but I have urged her to try again.

   About Radka, there are only three hopes:

   1. Marriage with a Frenchman or Swiss.

   2. Adoption, and that is for you to arrange from France.

3. Smuggled out—if unsuccessful could be fatal.

Let me say again: you cannot act too fast. And I beg you to find a way somehow before it is too late. Also, please let me know by return courier.

Mrs. Gratian Yatsevitch."

She was the American assistant-military attaché, Col. Yatsevitch's, wife, and I received other letters from her.

"Dear Mr. Grouev,

I must write you again and yet again to beg you to make the necessary arrangements to get your sister out of Bulgaria, and also to repeat once more, so that you will make no mistake about it: nothing can be done from here.

Evidently M. Voisin didn't give you a true picture of the utterly desperate situation of Radka, because after that you had apparently seen him and even received some letters on this subject, you still cabled her to do what she could in Sofia. Both colonel Yatsevitch and I fail to understand you—is it possible that you are still ignorant of her present situation and the terrible treatment she will surely receive should she again fall into the power of the cruel Militia; or, is it possible that you actually do not care enough for your sister to make the necessary arrangements outside of Bulgaria to get her out of here? Need I repeat that her very life depends upon the speed with which you make arrangements to get her out—very soon there will be strict law simply prohibiting people from leaving Bulgaria, exactly like the Soviet Union. (Do you know how it is there, read the first hand account by Kravchenko.) And when that condition prevails here, you will not be able to help save Radka. Any day the law against marriage to foreigners will be in force. Even now the British, French, or Swiss minister must ask the President of Bulgaria several times to allow the marriage of a 2nd secretary to marry a Bulgarian girl; after that comes permission from the Militia for an exit visa, even more difficult to get, and before longer—impossible.

The people highest in three diplomatic legations are willing to help get Radka out, provided the initiative comes from outside, because there is no possible way here—no one to marry, if that is still in your mind.

America does not give a passport in that case...That is the reason I suggested to you to send in a Swiss man who will marry her, but with a very secret understanding of marriage blanc, otherwise she would not get a visa...or an Englishman...or a Frenchman...

The only other solution is adoption. Why can't you arrange that? The French Consul here assured (us) that if you find in France the person to adopt Radka, get the papers, and send them in soon, he can push the adoption through here...

From you we have no word at all that you really understand the importance of efficiency and speed on your part. No letters sending assurance from you that you do understand and indication of what you are trying to do, if anything. Why can't you write to her? Why can't you reply in a businesslike way, which is in keeping with the gravity of the situation? No one needs lipstick and nail polish, they need hope.

Poor Radka is absolutely desperate, and for some reasons of her own. Probably her lifelong devotion and loyalty to you and her faith that you will act to save her. Col. Yatsevitch and I have no such reasons to be optimistic about anything you can accomplish."

I remember that my hands started shaking as I read this letter. I had no way of finding someone to marry or adopt Radka, not a cent to my name, nothing to offer. And, as if I didn't feel guilty enough, the letter of Radka's employer and protector went on:

"...Just for your enlightenment: Did you know that the last time the Militia got your sister, in order to force her to do their filthy espionage work, they tortured her? She was in Militia headquarters for three long weeks—and horrible tortures they were. And if they caught her now, it would be far worse because we have had to keep her hidden from them for nearly a year. They are always making attempts to arrest her. Therefore she is a virtual prisoner with us—can never go off American property without the Colonel or myself, and in an American car at that and directly to another American villa. If they caught her and insisted she do espionage on us and she refused as she surely would, they would practically kill her by torture and if that failed either, really kill her (and they certainly have tortured people to death—we all know the case of the 23-year-old secretary of the escaped Dr. G.M. Dimitrov). Radka would probably be sent to work in a tunnel or coal mine until she died there. To get her out of this villa when the Colonel was 10 days in Turkey, was their aim in arresting your brother and holding him—luckily he was not tortured, just mentally, of course—and neither did they take your mother. But with the best advice of three Ministers, I refused to allow Radka to go out of the villa. One Militia man came here posing as a friend of your brother's, trying to urge her off this American property, telephoning her once or twice a day to meet him—plenty of psychological torture for her—when she didn't know what they were doing to her brother. For some weeks now things have been quiet, but I can assure you that their brains and schemes are not quiet, and something is going to happen very soon.

I protected her that time, but I cannot always do so. Suppose we leave suddenly—suppose they let her know that they have sent your mother and brother to a camp or to do heavy labor until she promises to meet them unprotected and outside of American or foreign property? Then what will they do to her?

Now have I hinted at enough to stir you to produce results. Plead, bribe, or use any means you possibly can think of to get her out of here! The safety of your mother and brother depend on her as well and if no help comes, well, draw your own conclusions.

I am praying all the time for your success, but soon, and wish you all God speed.

Mrs. Gratian M. Yatsevitch.

P.S. At once Radka says she will marry anyone to escape, and now appears (because there has been no immediate terror) to think otherwise. But you go right ahead with plans for her adoption or marriage.

*   *   *   *

Guilt. An immense, oppressive feeling of guilt was eating my heart out for weeks each time I received such news. The guilt and total helplessness of the poor, powerless refugee, a little nobody, struggling at his pitiful job, barely making ends meet. And yet, people back home had heard about my Egyptian royal friends, had received from Paris press-clippings with my picture at glamorous parties, and Sofia's gossip had created the image of "the successful Bulgarian abroad." The well-connected, well-to-do relative who could help his family. If only he wanted to help…Depression revisited me again, with the old phobias and panic-attacks that I had known at the time of my father's death. Among the rare joys in that gloomy period seemed to be the pale-blue envelopes addressed in an immature handwriting, which arrived every day in my small hotel.

"Claridges, London, June 23rd.

"Darling,…I told someone last night that I was engaged to some-one in Paris, because he was getting troublesome…So now I'm a little worried that soon it will be all over London…So if you hear I'm engaged, don't be worried! Your loving Neelia."

Claridges, July

"I went today to a wonderful wedding of a friend of mine, Raine McCorquadale. She was the most beautiful debutante to come out in London last year, and married someone called Gerald Legge. She had sixteen bridesmaids and two pages, so they hardly fitted into the church, especially as they all wore huge crinolines. She looked lovely but a bit too actressy, with a huge crinoline and tiara of diamonds, etc. They are going to Paris for their honeymoon.

"This evening I had dinner with a rather pompous bore in a small house—lovely, but far too full of beautiful things. It was the sort of house one hardly dares move in, in case you knock over a valuable bit of china or something. The other people there were all very nice and pompous and the dinner was very good (for London…). Love and kisses, Neelia."

At the same time, other letters, from Sofia:

"Stefo, my dearest,

I hope you received the letter I wrote you last week. Mrs. Yatsevitch is writing a long letter to you now and I believe you will understand how critical the situation is.

I saw Boubi yesterday. He told me that he is fired from the factory and now he is looking for some job. That's extremely difficult to find and in the same time he got to work because of the law against the idlers. Fortunately I make enough money for all of us. He was very sick last week, but he's all right now. They have to live in Sofia now and it will be very difficult to find a place to live.

Will you please write to Mrs. Yatsevitch or me as soon as possible? We feel like if anything will be done it has to be done fast. I'm looking forward for your answer with impatience and hope that something could be done. Love, JOY. "(The way Radka signed when writing in English.)

        *   *   *   *   *

Neelia wrote almost every day, and beside the frivolous chat about the London social season, her letters became more and more affectionate, beginning with something sweet, ("Darling, it was lovely to get your letter today. I read it about six times since I got it and am looking forward for the seventh time just before going to sleep…) and ending with something touchingly loving. I missed her too, but the possibility of me going to Dublin in August seemed more than remote. Indeed, I could barely spare enough francs to send medicine, clothes, or food parcels to my family, let alone to travel to Horse Shows…

The luck, the same incredible luck that continued, God knows why, to help me in most unlikely ways, struck again and decided things for me. I wouldn't blame anyone for thinking that I made up the story that follows, but it is so fairy tale-ish that I certainly would've invented some-thing less corny, if I had to. A few days before the famous Derby, Neelia, a horserace fanatic, wrote me: "…I'm backing the horse *My Love* five pounds each way for you in Derby, and also for myself." How sweetly romantic, thought I, never having heard of a horse with such a name. I would repay her when I see her, if I loose, she wrote.

Then, the next letter: "…I'm so excited about the Derby, as now you will have to come to Ireland to collect your wins! I did even better than you, as I had the horse that was third as well…I never put so much money on a race before. You made 62-and-a-half pounds and I made 112-and-a-half!…We are having a ter-rific time already ordering tents for the party Horse Show week. We have let get-ting seats for the show a bit late and only have six on the good side at the moment and 16 on the not quite so good. I think with a few strings however it will work out."

Sixty-two pounds! That was a real fortune! Soon after, I received a call from the Irish consulate. Neelia had talked to some family friend at the Foreign Ministry and I was granted Irish entry visa. Then a beautifully engraved envelope arrived at my hotel: Aileen Plunket's "official" invitation to the Dublin Horse Show week. She had also discreetly enclosed a Paris-London ferryboat ticket and an Air-Lingus ticket from London to Dublin. Should one fight Destiny?—Not that kind of destiny, I thought, as I started packing, very excited, for my first trip to the British Islands.

*   *   *   *

Seeing England for the first time was a notable and long-awaited event for me. I felt I was arriving, as I had always expected, in a very different world, the almost mythological world I had heard so much about since childhood, from history books and from newspapers, from Shakespeare, and movies, and Dickens, and Sherlock Homes. I was, of course, thrilled when first discovering Switzerland and France, but it was a different kind of experience. I was enchanted by their beauty, their culture, and the novelty, but not by their foreignness; I spoke French and these countries were somehow familiar and not intimidating to me—my father had studied in Grenoble and there were always French books and old magazines around our house. But England was another story.

My preconceived ideas of London were of a haughty, intimidating metropolis, a totally foreign-looking center of the world's most powerful empire. In the world I had grown up, Great Britain was the leading world Power, the center of the Universe with which I hadn't had any personal contact: I barely spoke the language and had only scant knowledge of its history and culture. Europeans in general had little understanding of the British and their behavior, mentality, ways of dressing and speaking, and customs. Odd chaps, a bunch of snobs and eccentrics, a nation of stuttering guys with folded umbrellas and bowler hats, and bony, toothy, badly dressed ladies. To me, this was a truly foreign, but nevertheless tremendously impressive land. And I was pleased with myself, proudly self-conscious,—the "Albion, here I come!" feeling,—ever since the moment, at dawn after a dreadful night of fighting sea-sickness, when I saw the contours of the Dover coast from the crowded deck of the rusty, smelly ferryboat.

The discovery of the Anglo-Saxon world however almost ended in disaster at the customs office, when the officer, holding my passport, asked me how many times I'd been in England before. "This is my first visit, Sir," I replied cheerfully. "But you've already been here, three months ago," the man contradicted me rather defiantly. "No, never," I insisted. The officer looked again in my passport and his face took all the official gravity of His Majesty's civil service, which he was representing. Suddenly it occurred to me what had happened and that I was in trouble.

A few months before in Paris, Sava had awakened me in the middle of the night, terribly upset. He and Pam, who had gone back to London, had had a bad fight on the telephone and she had declared that she would never see him again. Sava was desperate. "She refuses to talk to me," he said in tears. He didn't sleep the whole night, trying to reach her, but she had disconnected the phone. The next day he came to me with a crazy idea: "I must go to London! I can't live without her and I'm going!"

"You won't get British visa, it'll take several months, with our old Bulgarian passports."

A mischievous gleam lit his face. "Yes, I know. But you, you already have a visa." Indeed, in anticipation of my future job at *Intraco* in London, a job that never materialized, I had applied for British visa and, after several months, had received it.

"Sava, you must be mad!"

"Are you saying that you won't help me, you, supposedly my best friend?"

"Do you know that we can both go to jail?"

"You have no heart, I always knew it. O.K., I'll go without visa, I'll try to enter illegally, but I will go! And if they arrest me, you'll have it on your conscience."

"Sava, we don't even look alike."

"Thank God that I don't look like you! But everything in our passports is the same, isn't it?—Both born in Sofia, on the same day, same year; both tall, same University, same address in Paris…"

"You have brown eyes, mine are blue…"

"Big deal, nobody will notice the eyes. Oh, I beg your pardon, I see: ever since Ella Trayanova said that yours are '*le plus beau bleu du monde*,' you can't get over it. You don't think that the customs people too will rave about your big cow's eyes, do you?"

"Shut up, you idiot! I'm not going to commit crimes because of you and your silly girlfriends."

"Some friend you are!…" And Sava slammed the door angrily.

That day, I pretended that I had left inadvertently my passport on the table in my hotel room. We were not in speaking terms. I pretended I didn't notice him making his suitcase in the next-door room. When I returned late that night, I didn't even bother to check whether Sava, or my passport, or both, were missing. I went to bed with a smile, but also rather nervous, and kept my fingers crossed under the sheets for a long time.

*   *   *   *

"Your passport shows that you've already been in England," the customs officer said.

"Oh, you mean <u>that</u> visit? Yes, Sir, of course, I came once before. But now I'm in transit, going to Ireland. What I meant was that it's my first time going to Ireland…"

"I asked you about England, not Ireland." The man sounded suspicious.

"Sorry, Sir, me no speak English good."

"You can say that again!" Disgusted, he stamped my passport and let me go.

*   *   *   *

Just crossing London on my way to the Air-Lingus flight and spending a few hours sightseeing, confirmed my feelings about the Empire's grandeur. Today, now that I know London pretty well, I realize that the city I saw on that first visit was not the real-life London, but simply a vision, a reconstruction and pasting together of thousands bits of previous knowledge, postcards, and book pages, stories heard or imagined, stored for years in my memory and subconscious. True, the gray walls of the majestic buildings were real, and so were Piccadilly, and Buckingham palace, and Hyde Park, and the red two-deck buses, and the Guards' bearskin bonnets; they provided the perfect container into which I poured all I had wanted to be London. It was a case of idealized reality, which usually makes us happier, because in it we invest some of the best that we have in us. Some women have this quality, often without being aware of it: to serve as magnificent containers to our most romantic imagination. Akin to London in my case, they may remain admirable even after we begin to see them objectively, but then we're talking about a different feeling...

Neelia met me at the airport in Dublin, beaming with excitement, adorable in her awkward shyness, blushing and stuttering animatedly. There are few things in life more rewarding than spontaneous, enthusiastic welcoming, whether demonstrated by a small child, a pet dog, or a person not hiding a genuine liking of you. She drove me across the city in her small car, traversed the vast Phoenix Park, and then headed West through the emerald-green countryside toward Clonsilla, the exclusive residential area where her mother had her estate, Luttrellstown.

"Everybody is already here," Neelia announced happily, referring to the houseguests from Paris and London, invited by Aileen and her daughters for the Horse Show week. "But you have enough time to change for the party Mummy's giving tonight for the teams."

A few miles further on the country road, she pointed to a tall stonewall on our left. "That's Luttrellstown," she said. For several minutes we drove alongside the old wall and there was still no sign of a building or a driveway. Behind the stones, half-covered with luxuriant vegetation, one could guess sizeable woods and meadows, glens and crop fields, gardens and riding alleys. Finally she slowed down and we found ourselves in front of the estate's gates. A smiling old servant came out of the gatehouse, taking off his tweed cap to greet us. As we followed the well-groomed alley through the park, my enchantment was growing by the minute.

There, behind the huge lawn, I recognized the crenellated turrets and the ivy-covered Gothic facade of the early-19th-century castle. Luttrellstown. I had seen a few photos of Aileen Plunket's estate, but I had not imagined such an impressive mansion. I didn't know that it was one of the most famous and beautiful Irish castles, still fully staffed and impeccably kept as a family main residence. In fact, I knew very little about the prominence of Aileen's family. I knew, of course, that she was a Guinness heiress, one of the three daughters of Sir Ernest Guinness, but one had to visit Ireland or England to really appreciate the importance of the Guinness family and the immense popularity of its main product, stout. In Europe, I had never seen or tasted in Europe this dark, velvety beer. It didn't take me long to find out that being a Guinness in Ireland was like being Henry Ford in Detroit, Agnelli in Italy, or Oppenheimer in South Africa, only more so. The family fortune was colossal, which permitted Aileen's father to buy the rebuilt medieval castle as a wedding present to his daughter, when she married in 1927 the Honorable Brinsley Plunket, second son of the fifth Baron Plunket. (He was killed in action during World War II, leaving Aileen a widow with two small daughters.)

Since that memorable summer of 1948, I have stayed in a number of magnificent houses, visited many stately homes. But, probably because of the particular circumstances, no other home affected me as strongly as Luttrellstown did. Its spell nearly changed the course of my life and it pursued me for several years, wherever I went. Not only because of its luxury, the army of footmen, valets, maids, and stable boys, permanently at the disposal of the family and the guests. Not only because of the sumptuous decor—the stately bedrooms, the signed pieces of furniture in the ornate salons, the immense ballroom with damask-covered walls, 18th-century crystal chandeliers, Regence and Louis XV chairs, the oak-paneled library with leather-bound volumes. As if the decoration were not magnificent enough, Aileen had commissioned a well-known designer, Felix Harbord, to entirely redo the dining room. The work was going on in full during my first stay, but when it was finished the following year, the room was palatial, with a gorgeous fresco on the ceiling, tapestries with idyllic scenes on the paneled walls, a huge Bessarabian carpet, and the round dining table which could be expanded to seat thirty guests. Felix, a refined and sophisticated chap, was the first interior decorator I met in my life; before that, I didn't know that such profession existed at all. Such was the decor into which I, the "Displaced Person" (that was my legal status as a refugee), was temporarily displaced.

$$* \qquad * \qquad * \qquad *$$

The same ritual was meticulously repeated every morning. The pompous valet would knock discreetly on my door, enter the room without waiting for me to answer, and silently place a wake-up cup of tea on my night table. Then he would pull open the heavy curtains and announce in a most impersonal monotone: "Lovely morning, Sir!" no matter whether it was a bright morning or a hurricane. He would then go to the bathroom, run the water in the tub to the right temperature, carefully unscrew the cap of the toothpaste and apply the paste on my toothbrush, as if to save me the effort of doing it myself, and spread my robe on the nearest chair. With that, he would silently leave the room, letting me enjoy a few more moments in bed.

A few minutes later, a new knock on the door, and the valet would reappear with the breakfast tray, set with exquisite china, massive silver, and impeccably pressed linen. And a single flower in a small crystal vase. While I enjoy the soft-boiled eggs, the toasted bread, the bacon, butter, and jam, the Lapsang Souchong tea and fresh orange juice, the imperturbable valet would mumble the ritualistic question: "Which suit it'll be today, Sir?" The first few mornings I wondered whether the man was being sarcastic or merely stupid: apart from the dinner-jacket, there was only one suit in the closet, hanging next to my worn-out tweed jacket and old gray flannel pants. But soon I realized that the absurd question, like the invariable "Lovely morning, Sir!" were merely part of an obligatory formula for the little morning ceremony which every conscientious valet had been taught to observe. Nevertheless, this and the continuous snatching of any shirt, underpants, sock or handkerchief laying around after being worn for as little as one hour and their being sent immediately for laundry and pressing, were a source of some embarrassment, since my modest wardrobe consisted of a pitiful minimum of such items. Each time the blue shirt (the one and only) disappeared for pressing, I felt that asking "Shall we wear the white shirt today, Sir?" (the only one left in the drawer) was rather superfluous, if not tactless. But the valet didn't seem to think so. Nor did he see the absurdity of his question every evening, when I was changing into the obligatory dinner-jacket: "Which cufflinks did you choose for tonight, Sir?" as if I possessed more than a single pair...

But there was nothing I could do, without hurting his feelings. His duty was to serve me and he thought he knew how a gentleman should be served. To him, I was simply the guest of Miss Neelia, therefore a gentleman, a member of a different class, almost a different human species.

*   *   *   *

My life was now temporarily so different: the carefree hours on the lawn in front of the castle's library, sipping a cool drink and playing with the girls' dachshunds; the afternoons in the elegant box at the Horse Show or to some popular point-to-point race, wearing a hat, binoculars in hand; or, wearing britches borrowed from Neelia's friends, riding the horse assigned to me for the duration, even enjoying—a suicidal enterprise!—a foxhunt, desperately trying to keep up with Neelia, her sister, Doon, and the other galloping amazons. Those were the days of my initiation to Guinness stout and to gin-and-tonic at the Royal Hibernian bar; the lunches downtown at the Russell or Shelbourne hotels; the black-tie evenings at Luttrellstown or at Plunket's friends' homes; the shiny Irish silver and heavy crystal glasses on the impeccably polished mahogany table at Mont and Penny Kavanagh's, at Honor and Frankie Svejdar's, at Charly Judd's,—where everybody was curious to meet Neelia's "Bulgarian boyfriend;" and, at the end of the meal, the smell of Havana cigars and the taste of port ("You should never pass the bottle to the neighbor at your left, it's terrible luck and terrible manners; port is always served from left to right!" was one of the first important tips of savoir-faire that I was given.)

It was all so different. Was I impressed?—Of course I was. I loved Luttrellstown, I still think it was one of the most beautiful houses I've ever known. But, as I already said, it was not only the comfort, the luxury. I had suddenly found myself on a different planet, whose existence I had long ago ceased to suspect, a planet untouched by the war and the cataclysms of the previous decade. I had fallen through some Alice-in-Wonderland rabbit hole into an enchanted, unreal world, where I was discovering a new kind of happiness. In that world, called Luttrellstown, innocent jokes could make the Plunket girls laugh with the spontaneous, contagious laughter of happy 10-year-olds. Then they could also cry to break your heart because a horse was hurt or a puppy died. Human feelings—love, compassion, even ambition (to win ribbons at the dog show, for instance)—were the same like elsewhere, only the subject matters seemed to be so different.

They knew fright and horror too, but their own kind of horror: the time for it was before going to bed, when ghost stories were told in front of the fireplace. Luttrellstown had, of course, its own resident ghost—the "Grey Lady," supposedly seen quite often, roaming through the rooms by night. Five centuries or so ago, the castle belonged to the Luttrells, a much hated family collaborating with the English in torturing the poor local Irishmen. Terrible things had happened before the castle burned in a fire that left only one wing intact. Luttrellstown was rebuilt several times, but a few rooms of that wing still exist, especially "the haunted room."

I don't believe in ghosts and banshees, but everybody in Ireland did. When I say I don't believe, I mean by daytime and when I'm out of Ireland. When I am there, I'm less sure, especially in spooky nights in old castles, with the bedroom miles away down the squeaky corridors. After the fireside ghost stories, you say goodnight and you start turning the lights off behind you, one by one, as you walk alone to your room. You go to bed trying to ignore the weird sounds of the wind shaking the tree branches outside and the creak of windows and doors. And the worst: the distinct sensation that you're not alone in the dark room, the impending appearance of something frightful. It's pure imagination, a self-feeding autosuggestion. The ghost never appears. Everybody in Ireland has a friend, a mother, and an uncle, who has seen a ghost. ("She's the most honest, reliable person. Why would she lie?) But I'm still waiting to hear a reliable testimony given in the first person singular, "I saw the ghost. Not my cousin, not our maid, but I, myself, I saw the Grey Lady, or the Hoofed Gentleman, or whatever. I laughed when Neelia one wrote me from Ireland: "...*Last night, having tried for quite a long time to make tables turn unsuccessfully, we all decided to visit a castle nearby called Lepp, which is reputed to be very haunted. It was about two in the morning and we were all petrified. When we all got out of the car and walked towards it, both Doon and I and the other man were too frightened to get beyond a tree, about fifty yards from the castle. Some of the party were too frightened to come at all. So the two other boys, who had the courage of all nineteen-year-olds went in alone. They stayed for about ten minutes and then came out insisting we should all come in. When we got to the door, which was closed, it swung open of its own accord, so we were too frightened. Actually, the castle was burnt down about ten years ago and no one has been in since. So I am not sure the ghost still exists.*"

What a ridiculous superstition, I thought. But I wish I could say that the next time I spend the night in an Irish castle...In fact, I was tested once, and I didn't like at all. We were having late supper on trays in Aileen's bedrooms and she was telling us some Grey Lady stories, when she noticed how skeptical I was. "If you're so sure, why don't you go downstairs to the "haunted room" and bring us The Book? You know where it's kept," she challenged me. (They all believed that the very old volume inside the bureau's drawer had belonged to the cursed Sir Luttrell.) It was past midnight the castle was pitch-dark, all servants had retired to their quarters, and we had had several drinks.

Male pride being one of my faults, I had no choice, although the little nocturnal excursion in the grave-like silence of the empty castle didn't particularly appeal to me. As I walked down the large staircase and lit lamp after lamp in the corridors and rooms on my way to the "cursed room," my heart seemed to beat faster. Was it because of the many after-dinner whiskeys, or was it the restless soul of the abominable old Luttrell? Some difficulty in finding the light switch in the haunted room added to my cowardice, and I was frankly relieved, almost surprised, when no ghost slapped my hand as I opened the desk drawer to pull out the infamous volume.

Back to the ladies upstairs, I scoffed at the entire affair, as any rational person should. But I didn't sleep well that night and wasn't very proud of my thoughts. I felt as though somebody was watching me in the dark.

         *   *   *   *

Such were the bits and threads of which my imagination, so starved for gentleness and peace, wove the enchanted tableau of Luttrellstown—a sentimental tear here, a childlike giggle there, a harmless prank, the terror of a good ghost story, the suspense at the horse race, the gossip about Princess Margaret-Rose, the butler's pride in a ship-shape household. It was an unrealistic world, an anachronistic oasis, but it was so soothing! To me, reality has been the other world, the one ravaged by war, deprived of joy, a cruel, unjust, and cynical place inhabited by hard-working, anxiety-ridden survivors. The oppressive world of persecution and misery, in which my family lived; and its less dramatic, gray version, where I was living, the lonely, uprooted young man with his dull job and worries about money.

I didn't resent the luck of Luttrellstown's privileged people, neither was shocked by their insouciance. On the contrary, I was delighted to discover that Alice's Wonderland did still exist. More than that, this discovery touched me deeply. Not so much the opulence, but the kind of purity and innocence I found in Neelia and which I had begun to forget. Often, listening to her during our promenades in the castle's park, along the romantic stream that joins the Liffey near the walls of Luttrellstown, I could hardly believe that a modern girl can be so charmingly naive and inexperienced, and say the things she was saying. We would reach the "wishing seat" perched over the brook and she would talk about her childhood, about her father she missed so much, about the problems with her spoiled, fickle mother. She would speak of the small country house she wanted to have one day, the many children, the horses, of course, and the many, many dogs. Then we would follow the stream to the nearby glen and admire the reflection on the water of the decorative Doric temple, erected in the 18th century, and the obelisk commemorating Queen Victoria's two visits to Luttrellstown. "I don't know why I'm telling you all that," she said, blushing. "I never tell these things, to anybody!" Then she would ask countless questions about my life in Paris and before, about my family, about Bulgaria. She wanted to know whether she could write to my sister and how. She wanted to know how one says "I love you" in Bulgarian and learned to write it in Cyrillic letters. I had told her that I was not happy with my job and was determined to look for something better. Also that I had started writing Bulgarian radio-scripts for *BBC* in London and that they encouraged me to write more. Of course, she didn't doubt for a minute that I was going to have very soon a big-salary job and also be a *BBC* star, and she already calculated excitedly my future income. "Then Mummy will let me marry you!" (Until the age of 21, she needed Aileen's permission.)

Aileen treated me openly as her daughter's boyfriend, different from the other young guests at Luttrellstown, and gave me the impression that she liked me. To Neelia's great joy, her mother agreed to send her again to Paris, at the Lamottes, for the entire autumn. Before I left Dublin, Aileen invited me to come again and stay at Luttrellstown very soon, when Neelia was going to return home for a while.

On the way to the airport, Neelia couldn't hide her excitement. "I talked to Mummy last night, she likes you very much," she said. "I think we'll get married by Christmas!"

*   *   *   *   *   *   *   *

Chapter 12

My debuts at "Paris-Match"

Wing Commander F.F.E. Yeo-Thomas, G.C., M.C., was one of the most daring and effective British intelligence agents during World War II. Born in England but educated mostly in France, where he lived and worked as a director of the famous Parisian dressmaker Molyneux, he had volunteered at the age of 38 with the RAF. Parachuted in Nazi-occupied France, he operated as an important liaison with the Free French underground, under the code names of "White Rabbit," for the British, and "Schelley," for the French Resistance. Yeo-Thomas took enormous risks, until he was finally caught by the Germans in Paris, beaten savagely, tortured repeatedly during months of interrogation and sent to the Fresnes prison. He ended in Buchenwald and the death camps of Gleina and Rehmsdorf, and survived only because he was assigned, with other prisoners, to the sinister task of carrying corpses daily from the camp hospital to the morgue and the common graves. After the Allied force liberated the survivors, Yeo-Thomas became on of the principal witnesses at the trial of the Buchenwald torturers.

Fascinated as the "White Rabbit" story may be, one could ask what it had to do with the story of my own life? I happen to subscribe to the theory that every act, every movement of anyone in this world somehow affects the rest of us. In this particular case, the link was the fact that one of Yeo's important contacts in the French Resistance was a prosperous Parisian pearl-dealer, Jean Rosenthal, who was sent often from London to be parachuted in the Lyon area, and who operated in the underground near the French-Swiss border. He also survived his dangerous missions and after the war the two men remained in touch, the one in England, the other in Paris.

I had never heard of Monsieur Rosenthal, and yet this wartime comradeship indirectly affected the course of my life. That's how it worked: "Yeo" suffered from severe migraines, as a consequence of the tortures at the hands of the

Germans. His doctors insisted that he go and live in the country. He was recommended to Aileen Plunket, who badly needed a manager for her Dublin estate. Yeo, a military man and good organizer, was the perfect choice. But he was bored and isolated in the carefree world of the Irish gentry. He missed talking about the war, and there were not many listeners around Luttrellstown. I could listen for hours his stories, and in turn he was interested to hear about Eastern Europe and communism. He happened to be a convinced anti-communist who, at the end of the First World War, at the age of 18, had fought with the Polish forces against the Soviets, had been made prisoner and sentenced to death, but managed to escape the day before the execution. I think I won his sympathy when I told him about my involvement with anti-communist exiles in Paris.

Yeo was a discreet man and never asked personal questions about my relationship with Neelia, but he did know that I was looking desperately for a better job. "Why don't you call a friend of mine in Paris, who can give you some good advice," he suggested.

Jean Rosenthal received me in his office near the Opera. A charming, courteous gentleman, he put me at ease right away. He asked me about Bulgaria, about my background, education, and interests, and promised to talk to some of his friends. When I visited him again the following week, he mentioned a few possibilities: insurance company agent, salesman for an industrial firm, etc. I am totally lacking in business sense, so it didn't look promising, and Mr. Rosenthal realized it very quickly. "What would be your real interest, if you had a choice?" he asked. I knew it wasn't realistic, but I told him about my short newspaper apprenticeship in Sofia, my news bulletin in Geneva, and the emigre newspaper in Paris. "My dream would be to be a journalist," I said.

Rosenthal thought for a moment, then smiled and reached for the telephone. I never forgot his opening sentence, which I plagiarized later on many occasions when I had to recommend someone: "Herve," he said, "I'm not sure whether I'm *asking you* for a favor, or I'm *doing you* a favor." Then he suggested that his friend receive me.

"Herve Mille is one of the top journalists in France," he said when he put down the receiver. "He's Jean Prouvost's right-hand man. You've heard of Jean

Prouvost, haven't you?" I had not. But later, when I mentioned this name to a few people, everybody seemed to know him.

*   *   *   *   *   *

From what I had heard about the social status of French journalists, the aristocratic Rue de Varenne didn't sound like a typical home address. The elegant *hotel particulier* at number 73, not far from the Rodin Museum, seemed an even less likely building. It occurred to me that it was a wing of the house of Lord Granard, which I had seen briefly during my jet-set days around Princess Faiza. And yet, when I asked for Monsieur Mille, the young man in valet's vest who opened the gates invited me without any hesitation to follow him and offered me a drink while I waited.

The high-ceiling, gilded salon was truly impressive, decorated lavishly in excellent, if somehow theatrical, taste. No visitor could miss noticing the authentic Boulle-Louis XIV bureau, or the blue 18-th century Persian carpet, or the original Houdon sculpture. The duplex had all the opulence of a rich French apartment, but the precious antique furniture, expensive carpets and heavy curtains, ancient wall-paper and cushions, objets-d'art and bibelots, didn't have the tired, worn-out look, which in those post-war years characterized most homes of French impoverished aristocracy. On the contrary, everything looked shiny and prosperous, arranged with imagination and maintained with constant care.

My host appeared in a few minutes, a tall and svelte, impeccably dressed gentleman in his mid-forties, a rather reserved man with worldly manners and an occasional warm smile. Dark but with blue eyes, Herve Mille had the unhealthy complexion and even the facial expression of someone suffering from liver or bad stomach. His diction was often unclear and he lisped, but his conversation was remarkably brilliant, a fireworks of literary quotations, witty remarks and *bons-mots*. He was obviously a man of considerable culture and sophisticated, almost decadent, tastes, "*un dandy, un Proustien, un raffine,*" according to the description of his close collaborator Gaston Bonheur. A raconteur with a penchant for the colorful historical or literary anecdote and good political and society gossip. "As Gide says…" he would quote an aphorism with a mischievous smile, or "It reminds me of Talleyrand's mot to Napoleon when…" To me, this quick, elegant, and slightly bitchy repartee represented the essence of the famous *"esprit Parisien."*

Mr. Mille interrogated me thoroughly, charmingly polite but exuding authority, his penetrating eyes examining me carefully as we talked. At the end he told me that "an important press group" contemplated launching a new publication—"just a project, nothing decided yet"—and that if there are some openings, I might be considered… "Call me in a week or so!" he said.

This last sentence I had to hear again and again for a couple of months. "Nothing decided yet. But call me in a week or so!" It was discouraging and I had to surmount my shyness and my feeling that he was just being polite. But in the meantime he invited me one day for tea with other people, and then for lunch, occasions at which I met some interesting guests, as well as his younger brother, the interior decorator Gerard Mille. I learned that they were both born in Istanbul, the sons of a well-off French family which had for a few generation s lived and done business in the Turkey of the Sultans. When the family left Turkey during the Balkan wars, Herve and Gerard spent their adolescence in Lausanne, before moving to Nice and then to Paris. Herve, the more intellectual of the two, began a career in journalism. The more frivolous Gerard became a successful interior designer, which explained the spectacular Rue de Varenne apartment. Both bachelors, the brothers lived together and seemed to be extraordinarily attached to each other. But while Herve had this dignified air of wisdom about him, Gerard, equally elegant and witty, had all the flamboyance of the extrovert homosexual decorator that he was. Mercurial, impulsive, gregarious, quite a ham, he was continuously making jokes, usually quite naughty but always funny, and indulged in all sorts of follies. He filled the distinguished *hotel particulier* with unconventional artists and actors, eccentric ladies and colorful outcasts. Herve was the amused spectator, watching his brother's shenanigans with the affectionate and forgiving eye of a mildly shocked parent.

Between the two, they knew everybody in *"Le Tout Paris,"* from the Rothschilds to Prime Ministers, from Cocteau, Colette and Louise de Vilmorin, to Marcel Pagnol and Serge Lifar. Herve was a close friend of Coco Chanel, who was still living in a semi-exile in Lausanne. The moody Marlon Brando, unshaven and in worn-out jeans, became a frequent visitor in the Milles's sumptuous salon. Later, inspired by Brando, Herve imported and co-produced in Paris Tennessee Williams's *A Streetcar Named Desire*, then *A Cat on a Hot Tin Roof.*

Beside celebrities and titled guests, some less elegant characters could be seen at the Milles's apartment. There were, of course, the regular number of Bohemians and longhaired Left-Bank types brought in by Gerard. But there were also a few quite different young men, looking more like commandos than like socialites or artists, who seemed to feel at home *chez les Mille*, playing cards on some corner sofa or pouring themselves whisky from the hosts' bar. By age, physical aspect, culture, and manners, they had little in common with the Mille brothers; in fact, some of them were frankly uneducated and ill mannered. But they were all handsome, strongly built, full of vitality, amusing, and outrageously irreverent. They bantered continuously with Gerard and teased each other mercilessly, but in Herve's presence they behaved like admiring disciples around their guru, fascinated by his anecdotes and parables. I was mystified by the unlikely relationship. Litle did I suspect that soon some of them would become my friends too.

Guessing Gerard's "sexual orientation," as one says today, and Herve's indifference to ladies (except for intelligence, taste, wit, and elegance), one could've suspected some homosexual attraction. But no one could be further from being "gay" than these red-blooded, tough guys, all shameless womanizers.

Homosexuals, generally despised by the average French of the epoch, had nevertheless influence and a certain appeal among the intelligentsia. Talented writers such as Jean Cocteau, Andre Gide, or the convicted thief Jean Genet, intrigued the young intellectuals, and Cocteau's boyfriend, actor Jean Marais, was a matinee idol. Oscar Wilde was in vogue again, and Tennessee Williams's plays were the new rage. But all was still "in the closet." As for myself, coming from puritanical and "macho" Bulgaria where "pederasty" had the worst stigma, homosexuality belonged to the books about "sexual deviations" in which we read about perverts who do it to sheep, corpses, or other men. I had known personally only one Bulgarian "gay," a charming and highly cultured diplomat, for whom I felt the same compassion one has for a dear friend afflicted with incurable disease. (Rumors about the existence of lesbians were received in Bulgaria with the same hilarious incredulity we reserved for the tales that Chinese women had "it" slit horizontally, rather than vertically...)

Herve's connections in the post-war political and press milieu were impressive. But he had always avoided the limelight, never owned a newspaper, never tried to be in the government or the parliament. A superiorly intelligent, clever, somewhat manipulative man, a virtuoso of the Byzantine intrigue, he was more of a Machiavelli than a Churchill. He had opted for the behind-the-scene influence of an *eminence grise*, rather than the pride and vanity of power. Just before the war, he had found his prince and seigneur in the person of a genius of the press, and now he was the *eminence grise* of this aging, paternalistic tycoon, Jean Prouvost, who had the reputation of turning into gold every publishing venture he touched. Having worked for Prouvost's newspapers since the 1930s, Herve had earned not only his total confidence, but also his affection and friendship.

I was loosing hope, and the prospects of marrying Neelia soon were evaporating when, on day in March, Monsieur Mille surprised me with a different answer to my routine telephone calls. "It looks like Monsieur Prouvost will launch a magazine," he said. "Come to see me at 51, rue Pierre-Charron." I was elated. My dream was about to come true! At last, I'll be a journalist!

Alas, my joy was premature. Things turned out to be not so rosy. At the shabby office where Mr. Mille received me—a far cry from rue de Varenne,—he spoke very frankly not to say bluntly. Yes, a new illustrated magazine is starting; but not in the "Time" and "Newsweek" model, with regular departments, where he had thought I could be used in the "East Europe-Communism" section. They had decided in favor of the "Life Magazine" formula: lots of photos, no regular sections, few foreign news, except for an extensive weekly piece by the famous Raymond Cartier. Sorry, Mr. Groueff, but no room for you...

"But can't you use me for something else, not necessarily foreign news? Just try me, I'd do anything!" I must have looked so crushed that Mr. Mille took pity. "It's very risky to leave a secure job, even a small one," he sounded paternal. "It may not work. But it's your decision. If you insist, do try! But I'm warning you, it will be difficult financially." It was a tough decision for a penniless refugee. The reason was saying "no," while the heart was screaming "yes!" For several days I couldn't sleep, I was sick with indecision. I even felt guilty for wanting to leave "Uncle" Takvor, who'd been so kind to me. But at least these scruples proved unfounded: when I finally took all my courage and submitted, stuttering, my resignation, Takvor showed such understanding that I should have felt insulted if I weren't so relieved. He took me warmly by the shoulders and wished me much luck. I know he had affection for me and sincerely wanted to see me happy. But I also realized that my departure was hardly a cruel blow for his *"Societe des Tabacs en Feuilles."*

*   *   *   *   *

Jean Prouvost had already published a *Life Magazine*—type weekly just before the war. It was called *Match* and in its short year-and-a-half existence it had enjoyed an extraordinary success with the French public, reaching a weekly circulation of 1.8 million. But the German occupation put an end to this venture and *Match* was closed. The best-selling women's magazine *Marie-Claire* was also a Prouvost's creation, and so was the phenomenally successful tabloid *Paris-Soir* (2.5 million copies daily in 1939). Herve Mille had participated actively in all these success stories. Before the war, "Le Patron" or "J.P.," as Jean Prouvost was called, had become the most important press baron in Europe.

The unusual thing is that he has begun as an outsider, and only after he was 35-year-old. A very rich man, he belonged to a well-known family of industrialists in the North of France, one of the most important woolen textile businesses in Europe. "J.P." however, being the second son, was less interested in devoting his life to the family business. A rather adventurous bonvivant who preferred the cosmopolitan Parisian life to the austere and hard-working existence of his inbred relatives in Roubaix, he had been considered somewhat of a black sheep of the Prouvost family. What seemed to interest him particularly, was journalism, a profession for which the rigid, dignified *"bonnes familles"* in the North had not much respect.

Nine years after the demise of the first *Match*, Prouvost, already 64-year old and having lost all his newspapers during the war, decided to revive it. He surrounded himself with some of the best journalists from his former papers, men like Herve Mille, Philippe Boegner, Raymond Cartier, Gaston Bonheur, etc., hired a few trusted old-timers to run the business and administration sides, which interested him much less personally, and in March 1949 *Paris-Match*, successor of the old *Match*, was born.

The team represented something unheard of in European journalism. After filling the key desk jobs with first-rate professionals, Prouvost and his lieutenants boldly applied most unorthodox, often absurd, criteria for selecting the acting reporters and photographers, thus making *Paris-Match* the talk of the international publishing world. They didn't look for graduates of journalism schools (I don't know whether there were such schools in France in those days). They didn't ask for previous experience; on the contrary, the idea was to break with the old stereotype of the journalist, the aging, cranky, unshaven looser with the perennial cigarette butt in the mouth, drinking countless cups of black coffee while typing his copy in a gloomy office. Prouvost, determined to create a new type of journalism in France, preferred to form from scratch young men without professional "bad habits" acquired elsewhere. He had his clear idea of the kind of reporters he wanted for his new venture, like the head of movies' central casting knows what physique, personality, and lifestyle to look for in the actors. It would be nice, of course, if the future *Paris-Match* recruit had also talent for writing or taking pictures, but this was not absolutely indispensable. With this model of reporter in mind, Prouvost's directors succeeded in recruiting the most unlikely and unprofessional bunch of colorful young men that any publication had ever assembled.

"Le Patron" was, of course, clever enough to insure himself by hiring some experienced press photographers, such as Kitrosser, Izis, Maurice Jarnoux, and Pierre Vals, as well as a few new paparazzi-style stars, like Walter Carone, Jean Mangeot, and Willy Rizzo. But apart from them, there were very few in the original team who had worked in the press before. Former paratroopers, actors, playboys, soldiers, and poets were promoted "reporters" and "photo reporters," some of them never having had a camera in their hands before: Michou Simon, Jean-Pierre

Pedrazzini, Daniel Filipacchi, were just kids of 18 or 19. There were other young men with good records from the anti-German Resistance, some of them highly decorated: Andre Lacaze, Jean Roy, Rene Vital, joined soon by their wartime boss, Joel Le Tac. They had tried different professions after the war—Jean Roy went to Hollywood as a scriptwriter, Vital was trying as an actor, Le Tac enlisted as a professional paratroops officer. Roger Vadim was an aspiring moviemaker, while Andre Frederique was a pharmacist and poet. Beside myself, there was another East-European refugee, the Hungarian Mathias Polakovits, who was preparing himself for a career of opera baritone, when *Paris-Match* discovered his amazing talent (or chutzpah?) for approaching people and getting familiar with celebrities. Another genius for making friendships with famous people and beautiful ladies was Benno Graziani, a charming and well-read playboy who was just demobilized from the French troops in Austria and was now importing fabrics for the big Parisian fashion designers.

The best-known qualities of new photographer Pedrazzini, a strikingly handsome, tall and blond daredevil, were that he skied well and drove sports cars like a maniac. He fitted perfectly the image of the new-look reporter, including his trench coat, sense of humor, and funny slang. As writing was not his forte, he was promoted photo reporter, his total lack of experience with a camera notwithstanding. Another novice in that profession was Michou Simon, a bespectacled, likeable kid who practically lived in the caves of St. Germain-des-Pres and was a personal friend of many Left Bank celebrities. As for Daniel Filipacchi, a handsome youngster interested in modern art, he had access to his father's remarkable collection of jazz records, and was very knowledgeable about American blacks' jazz, which was maybe not the most logical qualification for becoming a photographer. But *Paris-Match* editors believed that any bright and enterprising young man can learn photography technique; it was more important to have guts, drive, and an eye for a good story. The new recruits were given a camera and put in the hands of established photo reporters like Rizzo or Carone, street-wise, imaginatively aggressive and nevertheless artistic professionals, who taught them *le metier* the tough way.

What did this disparate bunch had in common? I think that they corresponded to Jean Prouvost's vision of a modern magazine reporter: First, they were young. At 27, I was one of the oldest. Second, they loved adventure and traveling, and had a natural curiosity. Not only were they available at any hour of the day and the night, but they were eager to be sent on an assignment. (Marriage was thus a handicap.) And third, they were sociable and had an easy contact with people. Good sense of humor was a must, and a keen interest in girls was considered a very good point.

We all came from very different backgrounds, but we all shared the pride of belonging to the *Paris-Match* team, like one is proud to be a member of a glamorous, successful sporting club. We dreamt of "scoops" and "exclusive stories" with our by-line. The photographer's role model was Robert Capa, the dashing American whose extraordinary pictures of the D-Day Normandy invasion and later of the frontline combats in Indochina became classics of the action photojournalism. The fact that Capa was killed in Indochina only added to his cult.

"Le Patron" encouraged this spirit and gave us good working conditions. Compared to the rest of the press, *Paris-Match* reporters were better paid. Reporters were generally disdained in France. It was Prouvost's merit to inject glamour and romanticism into the profession. He made reporting not merely a job, but an adventure. His reporters had fun, assignments became a favorite sport, a hobby, a way of life—an exciting life full of surprises. When they had no assignment for several days, they grew restless and bored. The old man knew what he was doing and knew how to do it. He wasn't above enjoying competition, even rivalry, among his collaborators. He closed his eyes when reporters padded their expense accounts, pretending not to notice it. ("*La Sucrette,*" or sugaring the bills, counted among the favorite perks in an assignment.) "Reporters are thrilled much more by one-thousand francs *sucrette*, than if a gave them a ten thousand francs bonus for a good story," he told me one day, several years later, when I knew him better. "It's part of the trip's attraction…"

Rapidly, a "Paris-Match spirit" was created, an *esprit-de-corps* that even the French "Legion Etrangere" would envy. To our romantic search for adventure, a "commandos" technique was added, and to the pride of belonging to the team—the thrills of competition. Any obstacle became a new stimulus, any difficulty—an incentive.

The mere mention that "Nobody else succeeded in taking this photo" became an irresistible challenge. Boasting about ingenuity and courage in front of the colleagues became part of the *reportage*, and the reporters got caught in the game. The accounts of impossible missions, of seducing exotic princesses in order to obtain the interview, or disguising in priest's cassocks to get inside places off-limits for the press, were often greatly exaggerated and embellished, but always entertaining. Often, the "commando approach" was quite unnecessary; why, for instance, enter through the window when the door is wide open? Or why try to sneak without a permit when anyone can get it easily?

But it was so much more fun, we thought, and so thrilling. Reporters were frankly disappointed when an assignment was too easy, for instance when a press-officer simply handed the press release, or a celebrity gladly agreed to be photographed. And I'm certain that stories done under the delusion of living an adventure were always better than those done with the cooperation of press agents and official authorities

Within a year, *Paris-Match* affirmed itself as the most successful magazine in France. But you'd never guessed it by looking at its offices in the shabbiest apartment one could imagine. Located on the second floor of an old-fashioned five-story building at 51, Rue Pierre-Charron, in a distinguished section of expensive hotels near the Champs-Elysees, the flat was much too small and illequipped for editorial offices. So small, that none of the services had its own room. The directors and the managing editor were crowded in two rooms, where anybody entered at anytime without knocking. There was a total lack of formality and everybody was called by his first name. A slightly better furnished room was reserved for Le Patron and supposed to be kept locked. But in the absence of J.P., who usually came in late in the afternoon, his office served as conference-room, waiting room for distinguished visitors, or occasionally, being the only quiet place, as studio for taking photos for the cover. Sometimes, it was used for naughty purposes: a photographer would offer the "privacy" of Prouvost's office to a model to change her clothes, or even better, to try bathing suits, leaving her gentlemanly alone for a few moments. Meanwhile, several of his pals would pile up at the door's keyhole in the adjoining room and enjoy the peep show. But due to the unrestrained giggles and appreciative whistles of the unruly voyeurs, the scam was discovered quickly and the shocked Administrator, Andre Roux, put an end to it.

The largest, corner room was reserved for the layout. On the night of the weekly *bouclage* (the closing of the issue), most of the team jammed around the wide table, looking over the shoulders of Philippe Boegner, Gaston Bonheur, and the layout technicians, commenting loudly on the selected photos, giving advice, protesting or joking, talking and smoking, until the morning. Without exception, the *bouclage* was always late, causing hysteria to the technical services and countless threatening calls from the printing house. Somehow, the weekly miracle of closing the book was achieved, but the lesson was never learnt. The same crisis was repeated the following week, barely ending by sunrise. On closing days, the *Paris-Match* editors were simply incapable of starting to work before dinner.

While they were making the final selection, each reporter and photographer defended his story, arguing to get a maximum pages for it. The process couldn't have been more democratic, but also more disorderly and time wasting. Often Le Patron appeared at the *bouclage* after some black-tie dinner, accompanied by his handsome, elegant companion Elisabeth Danet, to oversee the work in progress. In such occasions, some silence and order were restored for an hour or so. J.P. was the supreme, final authority, the incontestable boss in editorial matters as well, and an extremely competent boss with that. Everyone was in awe of his uncanny gift to guess what subject and which photo would fascinate the readers that particular week.

The rest of the apartment, i.e. the other three rooms, was for the writers, reporters, photographers, and everybody else. The more important ones had a desk, which they could claim as more or less their own. Beginners like me only had a drawer. We had no personally assigned typewriters; a few matronly typists typed our handwritten copy. Each room had one or two telephones, not automatic, of course; we had to go through operators, located in a windowless former maid's room, next to the antiquated toilets. These patient ladies had to dial the numbers for us and page us in a motherly way when we had a call: *"C'est pour toi, mon p'tit!,"* or *"Mais il faut patienter, coco!"* But no one cared about the inconveniences of the offices: if we had to write seriously, we did it at home or at the cafe *La Belle Feronniere* across the street. The noise and disorder at the office made it practically impossible to concentrate.

For a visitor, the scene was hardly believable. From 10:30 or 11 A.M. on, when everybody started arriving leisurely as if coming to a club, the place was in a state of continuous uproar, with ebullient young men running noisily in the corridors, as they chased each other; girlfriends waiting at the reception desk; reporters' dogs lying on the floor; idle photographers playing cards in a corner. (One day, as General Weygand, the octogenarian former French Supreme commander, was being led to Prouvost's office, a bunch of galloping reporters ran into him in the corridor and pushed him unceremoniously aside, shouting *"Pousse-toi, Papa!".)* In an office, Willy Rizzo and Rene Vital, the best comedians of the team, would improvise some uproarious show: Willy would step on top of a desk and imitate a hysterical speech of Mussolini, while we would scream "Duce! Duce!"; or Vital would pretend speaking Vietnamese or Arabic, pronouncing in perfect accent words invented by him. With my arrival, he included Bulgarian dialogue in his act, imitating the diction so well that for a long time many colleagues were convinced that he spoke with me in my tongue. Some of the reporters' practical jokes were crude or pure slapstick, sophomoric as in the lycee years. The Administration's mild attempts to establish some order in the untidy offices had only short-lived effect, like when indignant pedestrians on Pierre-Charron and Francois-I side-walks complained of being hit by "waterbombs"—grocery paper bags filled with water,—dropped from the second-floor windows by mischievous journalists while writing articles on the French economy or the United Nations problems. Or when the dignified administrator Monsieur Roux, an older man who wore spats and was the only per-son at *Paris-Match* to be called "Monsieur," tried to stop the silly game of "toilet-paper raids"—boisterous, screaming gangs of reporters, armed with several rolls of toilet paper, bursting into the offices and unfurling the rolls over desks, books, and heads of working colleagues. As a drastic measure, Monsieur Roux discontinued the toilet-paper supply, until a delegation of innocent-faced reporters remitted a petition, describing in rather unappetizing detail the consequences of such a violation of the personnel's human rights. The paper was restored, but not before "*Le Pere Roux,*" who didn't lack of humor behind his severe appearance, issued a much-celebrated "Memo to the Personnel," rationing the commodity in question: 3 to 4 pieces per person, and exceptionally, up to 6 pieces in case of stomach problems. We laughed for weeks, but, somehow, the raids ended.

Taming the *Paris-Match* reporters was a hopeless task. I suspect that J.P. and his directors encouraged implicitly this spirit (except for Raymond Cartier, who liked discipline and was not amused by such a behavior). Because, when it came to cover a story, these colorful characters proved unbeatable, as far as nerve and ingenuity went. The magazine could then ask them anything and be sure that they'll accomplish it with gusto. If they needed direction, it was to restrain the excess of eagerness, rather than stimulate it. Having dreamt of a commando of adventurers, Le Patron had no use of conventional employees obsessed with security, 40-hour workweek, and health-care and pension benefits.

The handsome Pedrazzini was a typical *Paris-Match* guy. Between reportages, he could be seen driving wildly his Citroen (with, I don't know why, a Monaco license plate), his insolent smile showing how much he enjoyed using the Paris streets as automobile-racing course, blowing his loud police-car siren as he approached the *Paris-Match* headquarters. "Here comes Pedra!" the amused customers at *La Belle Ferroniere* terrace would say, curious to see whether he would get another traffic ticket. He was a guy on whom the *Match* gang could always rely in fistfights, pranks, or adventure. He could kill for the gang's boss, Jean Rigade, the soft-spoken Chief of the Photo department, the only authority the photographers obeyed, and more than the directors, more even than Le Patron himself. Rigade entrusted "Pedra" to his older pals Carone and Rizzo as their "assistant," a position between a trainee, camera-bearer, bodyguard, and slave. In a few months in this kind of Match version of a Marine Corps boot-camp, Jean-Pierre learned the essentials of news-photography (there was no need to become an artist *a la* Cartier-Bresson or Karsh), and was launched to fly on his own. As we'll see later, this bold, seductive, and competitive novice's professional exploits became news in themselves.

Jean Roy was one of the wildest, an indomitable, insanely bold adventurer and a master of the witty slang and four-letter-words. And also a talented writer with unexpected sensitivity. He had an extraordinary war record as a volunteer with the U.S. Army and the French Resistance, was captured by the Germans and sentenced to death. We were told that he was sent before an execution squad, but survived by miracle. The rumor was that as a result, he had a small platinum plate implanted on the skull, under his hair. After the war, he had tried his luck as a scriptwriter in Hollywood, and married the sister of the movie star Maria Montez (actor Jean-Pierre Aumont's wife). Back in France, he continued to write, and his talent, as well as his lifestyle and personal charm, brought him to the attention of the Paris-Match recruiters.

The greatest thrill for Roy was to defy Destiny, showing a total contempt for physical risks. With a provocative smile on his handsome face, he was constantly in search of danger, and as each time his lucky star seemed to protect him, he took greater and greater risks, sometimes bordering on the suicidal. Thus, in the company of ex-paratroopers and tough right-wingers, he went one year to confront the traditional Communist party's annual march from La Bastille to the Place de la Republique. As the front rows of the huge procession appeared on the boulevard, Roy and his friends slowly walked towards them. Finding themselves face-to-face with the Party leaders, Jean attacked the red-flag bearer and, in full sight of hundreds of startled spectators, slapped his face. It was a crazy action, and while Roy's friends rushed to save him from the fury of the demonstrators, scores of noses were bloodied and teeth broken in the indescribable melee that followed. Out of breath and bleeding, but happy and content, Jean had once more his skin saved.

Sent as war correspondent to French Indochina (today's Vietnam), Roy and photographer Jacques de Potier assured a spectacular coverage, but also caused great headaches for *Paris-Match*. Roy was in his element on the battlefront and always managed to mount to the advanced lines, often defying the military command's interdiction. The Army headquarters sent many complaints to Rue

Pierre-Charron, but to no avail. No threats of disciplinary measures and expulsion from Indochina succeeded in taming the recklessly bold reporter who, according to witnesses, had the annoying habit of standing up under the worst enemy fire and shouting insults, as in some sports contest.

Miraculously, bullets didn't seem to reach him, which made him ever so more daring.

*   *   *   *   *

I looked often for an explanation of the irrational boldness of men like Jean Roy. Maybe I was fascinated because physical courage has not been among my most noticeable qualities, although I always admired it and was intrigued by it. Knowing that even the bravest men can suffer from the natural, very human, feeling of fear, makes acts of courage ever so more admirable. But Roy was a rare case of a man entirely deprived of this normal instinct. Either by birth, or, as some friends suspected, as a result of his trepanation in the Resistance days, he was afflicted by what amounts to be almost a physical infirmity, like other people are deprived of normal sight or hearing. So we shouldn't expect cautiousness and prudence from a person who doesn't know the feeling of fear, no more than we can expect a colorblind driver to stop at a red light.

Such people are a rare exception. In fact, apart from Roy, I have met only one similar case: the young Marquis Alfonso ("Fon") de Portago, a dashing Spanish grandee who lived then at the Plaza Athenee hotel in Paris, and had become a close friend of Sava's. The courage and audacity of this spoiled brat of a nobleman were already proverbial. At the age of 15 or 16, he had already flown, for a bet, a small airplane under the London Bridge; he was a car-racer; he had fistfights in nightclubs at the slightest provocation, or without provocation; he rode as gentleman-jockey in the most murderous horse race in Europe—the Liverpool Grand National, where only a tiny percentage of riders and horses reach the finish without broken legs or necks; and he used to court most openly and impudently any woman whose looks he liked, whether she was accompanied or not, married or not, known to him or not.

In his tireless search for ways to break his neck, Fon was in those days racing as professional jockey at the Paris hippodromes. Sava and I used to see him at lunchtime at the Relais bar of the Plaza, opposite our small hotel, where he arrived in an old open-neck blouse, his dark beard unshaven for two days, to eat his regular row meat steak-tartare, with no bread or anything else. This was his diet, as he wasn't allowed to go beyond the regulation weight at the pre-race weighing of the jockeys, all midgets next to him. After telling a few naughty stories and winking at some unknown lady at the next table, Fon jumped into his sport scar and headed for the hippodrome.

Failing to break some limb on horseback, Fon moved to the ski slopes of St. Moritz for the winter sports season, in company of his American buddy Ed Nelson, another daredevil, to train for the bobsled events and to enjoy the thrills of the world-famous icy Cresta run, the kamikaze variety of the sled sports. In the spring, they switched to automobile racing.

Even after marrying the beautiful American model Carroll McDaniels and becoming a father, Fon continued his pursuit of danger, unaware that Nature had deprived him of what normal people call fear. *Only God knows why and how He postponed for a few more years to call the intrepid Marquis to His heavenly kingdom. But finally, when the press announced one day that Fon Portago and his co-driver Ed Nelson met their death in an auto-race accident, the news saddened me, because they were both great fun to be with, but I wasn't surprised a bit.*

$$*\qquad*\qquad*\qquad*\qquad*$$

In a totally different genre, another typically *Paris-Match* phenomenon was Andre Frederique, one of the funniest characters in the team. This poet-pharmacist, very appreciated for his wit and knowledge of literature, had already published absurd poetry and written a few comedies, some of which, *Dugudu* and *La Plume de ma Tante*, had been quite successful in the Paris theaters. Fred used to spend two nights a week at *Match*, doing "re-writing" and stories on the Parisian nightlife. The rest of the time he worked at his family's pharmacy. Even there, he couldn't resist his vocation of humorist, preparing, for instance, "patriotic" tricolor suppositories, especially for "War veterans."

Once in every few months, Le Patron used to summon the magazine's top brass and give them hell for spending too much and keeping too many people on the payroll. Then he demanded a list of less-essential staffers to be laid off without delay. We, the little guys, used to hear immediately about these tempests on

Mount Olympus and waited with heavy hearts the announcement of the next *"charrette."* The sinister term dated from the bloody day of the French Revolution, when horse carts ("charrettes") brought the condemned to the guillotine. Being just a contributor, Frederique's name was always on the list for the next personnel reduction, but due to his popularity, the execution was each time cancelled at the last moment.

There was a period when Fred disappeared from work for several days and we assumed that serious business problems had forced him to concentrate all his attention on the running of the pharmacy. Just at that time, J.P. had ordered one of his periodic cuts. As unpleasant as it was for his directors, they thought it fair to start with Frederique, who wasn't coming to work anyway.

The news shocked us enormously, and a wind of revolt and indignation was blowing over Rue Pierre-Charron the evening when Fred, genuinely upset, irrupted into the offices. "I can't believe my ears!" he exploded. "Have you heard? Not only they decided to fire me, but also they give me the most absurd reasons. Can you guess what they accuse me of? They punish me for working as a pharmacist! I would understand it if they said a thief, a criminal, if I had done something shameful. But to be punished for working most honestly in a pharmacy!..." We found his logic most convincing. Highly indignant of the injustice about to be committed, we all pledged unconditional solidarity and support. Under the pressure of the entire staff, the directors retreated and Frederique kept his job. (Incidentally, notwithstanding the regularly staged explosions of Le Patron and his threats, no journalist was ever fired at *Paris-Match*.)

*   *   *   *   *

My first weeks at Match were totally confusing and demoralizing. Herve Mille introduced me to his co-director, Philippe Boegner, a distinguished gentleman, a scion of a most prominent French protestant family, whose conservative looks and demeanor of a bank president contrasted strangely with the anarchy and the sloppiness which reigned at the place. Boegner sent me to the *Redacteur-en-Chef* (Managing editor) Gaston Bonheur, after which I didn't see them again. Except once, at the end of the first month, when the entire personnel was lining in front of the cashier's window and I discovered that there was no check for me, nor any trace of my name being on the payroll. Alarmed, I rushed to Mr. Mille, who acted a little embarrassed but instructed the cashier to give me a "provisional advance," just enough to pay my rent. Advance against what? I began to doubt whether leaving my small job at the tobacco company had not been a foolish move.

The worst was that I was being totally ignored, with nobody asking me to do any work, or even explaining what I was supposed to do. After Monsieur Bonheur, a rotund, charming poet with a strong meridional accent, handed me to another Southerner, Georges Pernoud, I found myself in a smoke-filled room with half-a-dozen other aspiring journalists, who were spending their time playing belote and reading newspapers. They didn't know more about what was going on than I did. Pernoud was a pleasant, remarkably well-read editor, but too busy to talk to us. Bonheur was unreachable. Mille and Boegner?—Does a private disturb the generals when the cannon is rolling? Indeed, for *Paris-Match* the grand offensive had begun and the frantic men in shirtsleeves, always several hours behind their deadlines, perpetually trying to solve one crisis after another, had no time to pay attention to apprentices.

So the hours passed, the days passed, in reading newspapers and anxiously waiting to be called. From time to time the door would open and a "real" reporter or re-writer would show his head, arousing our hopes for an assignment. "Get me yesterday's article about the new *mec de la mère Piaf!*" (the famous singer's new boy-friend), he would asked hurriedly, usually with no further explanation and certainly with no "please!" Or, "Find out at what time is the conference and where exactly!" Woe to you if you asked "what *mec?*" or "which conference?" "Are you stupid or what?" would be the most civil among the likely answers.

Among the busy "real" reporters, the true *insiders*, I recognized a few of the Rue-de-Varenne belote players—Jean Rigade was there, surrounded by impertinent paparazzi; and Walter Carone and Jean Mangeot, packing their Leicas and Rolleiflexs; and the reporters' reporter, "Dede" Lacaze, describing in tough-guy's argot how he outwitted his competitors on a story.

My first jobs were hardly Pulitzer-prize stuff: Once I had to identify on a photograph a group of diners at *Maxim's* in black ties and evening dresses; ("from left
to right, Count X., Signora Y, Madame Z...") another time I translated captions
of Russian and Bulgarian cartoons, for an article on anti-Western communist
slogans; and so on...

Is that the way my journalistic career is going to be?, I asked myself. Luckily,
even the humblest professions have their little joys and rewards. Willy Rizzo, covering a fashion collection, brought me one day to Balmain's, across the street
from Match, to take the names and some biographic data from the models he
was photographing. The gorgeous girls, in great hurry to change from one dress
to another, weren't paying any attention to the helpers in the dressing room, who
were anyhow completely *blasé* of seeing young ladies in panties, garter belts and
bras (or no bras). As for me, I was breathless with excitement and didn't stop
blushing while trying to concentrate and interview the half-naked mannequins.
Those were memorable hours! Alas, I never had the same luck again: all reporters
were fighting for these assignments and other guys always managed to get them
before me.

With time, Pernoud started asking me to look for amusing short items in
American magazines, for a section he edited. My selections seemed to please him
and he encouraged me to make suggestions for adapting interesting foreign subjects. It was mostly a clipping-and-pasting job, no original reporting, but I
enjoyed devouring a dozen or so English dailies and American magazines every
day. Some of my suggestions brought me to the attention of the managing editor.

Gaston Bonheur was a most delightful and humane boss, adored by the entire
staff. Easy-going, warm, and friendly, his Mediterranean slowness was proverbial.
His well-rounded figure betrayed his devotion to gastronomy and great wines, in
his case a cult or art form, practiced with remarkable erudition and inspiration. A
favorite place where he officiated almost daily was *Chez Joseph*, a select restaurant
located diagonally opposite Paris-Match. He would arrive by 1:30, accompanied
by three or four of his close associates, for a lunch of *aperitif*—three courses—
two wines—coffee—and *digestif,* during which many editorial ideas were born.
To watch Gaston select, order, taste, eat, and comment a meal, was a fascinating

and highly instructive experience. As some of his table-companions were no dilettantes either, I was lucky to find myself accepted into such an exclusive league, feeling as humble as a village science-teacher would be at a convention of Nobel laureates. They were all earnest and refined connoisseurs of good wines. They didn't "drink," in the Anglo-Saxon sense of the word, with its booze-and-alcoholism connotation. The non-negligible quantities consumed notwithstanding, I wouldn't think of saying that Gaston was a drinker, no more than I would call Michelangelo a wall-painter, or Coco Chanel—a seamstress. Gaston was a troubadour of the great vintages and a virtuoso taster.

The French speak of wines as if they were talking about human beings, using adjectives such as "honest," "tender," "gay," "nervous," "funny," "amusing," or "triste." A good wine is "eloquent," has a "conversation amiable;" a bad one "has nothing to say." If too young, it "has not yet passed the threshold of the dialogue." A wine can have "character," "charm," "love," or good "cuisse" (thigh) or "corsage," it can "sing," "flatter," "cajole," or "caress." I've heard colleagues of mine admire some "noble," "elegant," or "aristocratic" wine and speak with contempt of wines whichwines that are "vulgar," "treacherous," "plebeian," or simply "fatigued" and "boring." I was present at a luncheon when Herve challenged Gaston to identify the wine he was serving. Gaston accepted the bet and as he took the glass to examine visually the wine's color, sparkle, and consistency, the suspense in the room reached such a degree that even Raymond Castans stopped cracking jokes for a few minutes, which is saying a lot. Gaston then closed his eyes and passed the rim of the glass at an inch from his nose. After sniffing a few times, the first pronouncement came: "It's a *Bordeaux*, of course." So far, no one except myself was impressed: for the others, this was as elementary as describing a rose as "a flower," rather than a plant or vegetable. Next, Bonheur took a small sip and retained it for a few moments in his mouth, without swallowing, his eyes turned up to the ceiling so only the white of the eye could be seen. Only true connoisseurs can perform this ritualistic pose without looking phony. "A *Medoc*," he proclaimed. "Not quite ready, but an excellent cru." The moment of truth approached. Gaston's lips sucked slowly and sensually from the precious liquid, as in a kiss; he took a sip, rolled his tongue over the roof of the mouth, thought for a moment, then swallowed a second sip, and a third. Revelation illuminated his chubby-cheeked face, while all eyes were fixed in expectation on him. "A *Pauillac*. Tastes like 1942, not my favorite year, but this must be an exceptional bottle." Loud applause greeted the verdict. Once more, Gaston had guessed right.

Jean Prouvost, of course, had not hired Bonheur because of his oenological talents. The consensus among all *Paris-Match* writers was that he was the best among them. Considering that next to opera singers and famous surgeons, writers are the most egocentric and jealous profession, this unanimity was surprising. It was also a key factor in the smooth running of the magazine. Gaston was an amateurish executive, a hopeless organizer, and the antithesis to an authoritarian commander. If his authority had to depend on hierarchy and on his title of managing editor, the weekly miracle of producing a magazine under the indescribably messy conditions, disorder and temper tantrums at Rue Pierre-Charron would be unthinkable. Neither the wild mustang-reporters, nor the prima donnas writers would accept much coaching or censoring. But there was no discussion when Gaston said "Your opening paragraph is too slow. Rewrite it and start with the anecdote on page 6!" or "I want to see more of the little girl crying in the corner. That's where the story is, not in the disaster itself!" And, for finding an original, appealing "angle" in treating a story and coming up with an enticing title, Gaston was unbeatable.

From his South, Bonheur had brought with him a few of his pals, "*les copains*"—from Nice, the urbane Pierre Galante, who had worked with Maurice Chevalier in Hollywood; from Sete, the mustachioed Roger Therond, a 24-year-old movies-and-photography aficionado, as well as the jolly Raymod Castans, a humorist and debuting playwright, and the layout artist Victor Laville; Pernoud from Marseilles,—all from the sunny pastis-and-petanque world of Marcel Pagnol's stories. Incidentally, the author of *Marius*, *Topaze*, and *Cesar*, was their role model and admired older friend. For the "Meridional Mafia," as we called them, the highest among all human virtues was loyalty to the friends, (as it is with most other mafias…) Gaston would protect and defend his reporters and writers in any conflict with outsiders or with the magazine's management, whether they were right or wrong. He valued loyalty above any laws, rules, or the company's interests, and had little use for Socrates' dictum *"Amicus, Plato, sed magis amica veritas."* ("You're a friend, Plato, but for me Truth is a greater friend".) Bonheur entertained very good professional relations with Prouvost, but his first loyalty was to *"l'equipe,"* the team. "Le Patron is a crocodile with a heart of *midinette**," he used to say, a good description of the shrewd press-baron who nevertheless felt better than anyone which romance or celebrities-gossip made the readers dream and cry. In fact, the archetypal *midinette* was Gaston, the unabashed sentimentalist who could spot a touching human story in any news item, be it an earthquake or a royal wedding, a rugby game, a scientific discovery, or even a financial statistics.

Success had not erased the perennial smile from the face of the dreamer-child from the Midi, who grew up living in various village schools in the Carcassonne area, where his mother was a teacher. His father, also a teacher, was reported missing in action in the first month of the war of 1914, before Gaston was one-year old. The child and his elder brother were raised on the meager schoolteacher's salary of their mother, a hardworking lady who insisted firmly on their solid education and respect for the republican institutions. After studies at the *lycee* of Carcassonne, Gaston received a scholarship for *La Sorbonne* and, at the age of 18, and having already written some poetry, he discovered Paris. At first, the poor, unsophisticated poet with his heavy meridional accent and his rope-soles sandals felt lonely and intimidated by the glamour of the capital, but he was quickly adopted in the world of writers and artists. He was introduced to publisher Paulhan, actor Louis Jouvet, writer Cassou, art critic Christian Zervos, became close friend of future star-chansonnier Charles Trenet and playwright Audiberti. At 20, he published a book of poetry. Before he was 21, he got married and the

---

**Midinettes:* young women working in the garment and fashion industry in Paris, reputed to be sentimental and naively romantic.

great publisher Gaston Gallimard bought his first novel, but being still a minor, his mother had to sign the contract. But after he became a father, the following year, poetry and song lyrics could not feed a family, and he tried journalism. Pierre Lazareff hired him at *Paris-Soir*, where Herve Mille, Lazareff's co-editor, noticed his talents et became his mentor. Later, during WW2, Gaston joined the exiled Prouvost team in Lyons. When Paris-Match started in 1949, one of the first editors to be hired by Le Patron and Herve, was Gaston Bonheur.

I liked Gaston ever since I met him. He was friendly to me and showed interest in my work. I learned a lot about journalism from him. Often he asked me questions about Bulgaria. My country intrigued him, especially that he was interested in the history of the Cathares (or Albigeois), the medieval religious sect which had been very strong in his region, Southwest France, and whose origins were traced back to the Bulgarian "Bogomil" heresy.

I was lucky that Gaston Bonheur was among the men who later gave me my chance.

*   *   *   *   *

Chapter 13

End of my Irish romance

In addition to my first trip to Ireland, August 1948 was marked by another important event in my life: the arrival in Paris of the Panitza family. After living for four years through the humiliations and perils of dispossessed "class enemies" under the Communists, and after several unsuccessful applications for exit visas, Mika, Stati, and 17-year-old Dimi had finally managed to leave Bulgaria. Mrs. Yablanska had died in the meantime. To me, it meant that I was going to have a family again, and I was overwhelmed with joy.

The Panitzas' departure from Sofia was the result of a clever plot, masterminded by the close family friend Jordan Peyev, who had succeeded in leaving Bulgaria one year before them. "Dancho" Peyev, the brilliant young officer who had been Sava's and my platoon commander in our Artillery regiment, had a aunt married to an old French doctor, who happened to be an influential member of the then-ruling Christian-Democrat party. Using their connections, the good doctor Mathieu and the childless aunt adopted Peyev legally, and got him a French passport. Once in France, Dancho put all his efforts into implementing the plan the Panitzas had discussed with him in Sofia. It sounded farfetched, but it was relatively simple: Stati Panitza had been Norwegian honorary consul in Sofia, which involved not much more than entertaining a few Oslo visitors passing through Bulgaria, issuing a visa or two, and hosting the National-day reception, on which occasion the Norwegian flag flew proudly from the balcony of the family house. With time, some of the diplomats who had enjoyed his hospitality had become important men in Oslo. Upon hearing of the difficulties the Panitzas were having with the Communist authorities, they had expressed concern for the fate of their charming Bulgarian representative. From this, to the idea of rescuing a loyal friend in trouble, there was only one step. "Maybe having so many contacts with foreigners was a source of the Panitzas' trouble with the Bulgarian

Secret services? But it was the result of 'our man in Sofia' performing his duties well!" was the Scandinavians's reasoning, consistent with their well known philanthropic attitude. Friendly Norwegian officials discreetly established contacts with the Panitzas, who at that time lived in the attic of their own house, after their home was requisitioned. The first exchange of communications was followed by an energetic campaign waged from France by the devoted Dancho. At the end, Norwegian passports were issued to the "consul," his wife, and their teenage son; thus they were reunited with their other children, Sava and Harri, in the West.

And myself, I must add. Because, ever since I had left Bulgaria, the Panitzas had considered me as another son. Now, as I no longer had my own parents, "Aunt" Mika and "Uncle" Stati took their place. As soon as Neelia joined me in Paris for another stay at the Lamottes, I introduced her to the Panitzas, and, to my delight, they liked each other at first sight. The tenderness and unusual closeness between the parents and their son Dimi, a serious young man near her own age, touched her. The family's warmth and ways of externalizing affection contrasted sharply with the Anglo-Saxon reserve in Neelia's world, and won her heart. Mika, the perennial romantic, was thrilled to see me in love and, being a most rewarding listener, as well as an inquisitive questioner, became my confidante.

Finding themselves with very little money abroad, the Panitzas had to be extremely careful with expenses. At first, they moved in with Stati's sister, Bobbie, who lived at La Tremoille, a quiet little hotel, which in those days was not yet the de-luxe place it became later. "Tante Bobbie," who had managed to escape from Russian-invaded Vienna, was a highly peculiar lady, straight out of some Charles Addams' cartoon. Her face, or what one could see behind her black lace veil, was covered with a thick layer of white powder, weirdly contrasting with the dyed black curls of hair and the heavy eye makeup. A face from the shadows. Since her beloved husband's death, she slept during the day and lived by night, if "living" is the exact term for her persistent, solitary attempts to communicate with him and other relatives in the after-world. I'm not certain she succeeded, yet at times she had a strangely satisfied look about her...

I still feel guilty about "Tante Bobbie," a lack of loyalty guilt. She was a gentle and generous person with polite manners and always extremely kind to me. She dressed in extravagant clothes made to order by a favorite dressmaker of the best silk, satin, and lace, with matched accessories and jewels. Fancy outfits. But of *la mode 1900*, when her husband was alive, and in our eyes, instead of admiring this touching expression of marital fidelity, it was comically eccentric. It was an absolute embarrassment to walk with Tante Bobbie the short distance between La Tremoille and our usual modest bistros, the rare evenings when the nice old lady expressed a desire to leave her hotel and join us for dinner. Stati and Mika were very attentive and kind to her, and behaved perfectly normally on those occasions. Sava was the worst coward, and I wasn't much better, both giggling and walking far behind the trio, pretending not to be with them. Once inside *Cnez Andre* or *Doucet*, Bobbie's appearance caused a sensation, conversations stopped, and an ordeal began for Sava and me, especially when some acquaintances or pretty mannequins were in the restaurant. Red-faced, we could hear them whisper to each other: "What's that? A *bal masque*, or what?"

After a couple of months, the Panitzas moved into a rented apartment on Boulevard Suchet, and the life of refugees began for them. Mika, who'd never been near a kitchen in Sofia, started cooking and, to her own and everybody's surprise, turned out to be an excellent cook. Dimi found a job as a small clerk in a bank. The apartment was too small to have a room for me, so I continued renting rooms with private families, changing addresses every couple of months, but I started taking my meals at the Panitzas, at "The Round Table," as Stati liked to call it. Another daily guest at the Round Table was Dancho, often late for meals, or disappearing mysteriously for several days. It was some time before I realized that he had been deeply involved in secret anticommunist activities. Then, a few months later, he invited me to join him and asked me to write articles on current Bulgarian subjects. At that time my family was having serious problems with the Militia in Bulgaria and had begged me to be extremely discreet and careful, so I declined Dancho's offer. But I ended by writing the articles, signing with the pseudonym "Pavel S." and making Peyev promise me full anonymity. In the beginning of 1949, after recruiting a third editor, Dianko Sotirov, my former boss at "Intraco" and colleague at "Le Peuple Bulgare" clandestine newspaper, a former lawyer and diplomat who was now a refugee in Paris, Dancho launched the ideological monthly *Vazrazhdane* (Renaissance). The Panitza home, which soon moved to Rue Franklin, became a sort of clandestine headquarters of the new review. Its first issues were printed at a small Russian printing house in Paris and paid by Peyev, with money he obtained from his aunt and her husband, the French doctor from Savoy.

*   *   *   *   *

Meanwhile, my romance with Neelia was blooming. In Paris, where she spent a few months, I saw her every evening after work, taking her to small bistros or to the movies, driving around Paris in her little Austin she had brought from Dublin, or seeing friends—some of my compatriots and a few Parisian *jeunes filles de bonnes familles* we had befriended, such as Brigitte and Patricia Brian, Paola and Francesca Saint-Just, Cynthia Balfour, and Lavinia Lambton, all attractive girls of her generation, with many pleasant young friends. Then I was invited to Ireland again, and once more, enjoying the wonderful life at Luttrellstown, becoming closer to the family, to the adorable kid-sister Doon, to cousin Caroline Blackwood, cousin Honor Svejdar…On one my visits, I was accompanied by Dimi, Neelia's favorite among my friends, and for a whole week we enjoyed silly Bulgarian jokes in the privacy of our luxurious quarters and laughed heartily behind the back of the snooty personal valet, like boys in school.

When separated, Neelia and I wrote to each other almost daily. She wrote about her riding and going to the races, about Doon, and the friends, and the parties and the dogs, and how much she missed me; but no wedding date was mentioned. Her mother had always tremendously intimidated Neelia, and now that Aileen was postponing the date or simply avoiding the subject, she couldn't gather enough courage to face her and insist, although delaying it made her very unhappy. In a way, I could understand Aileen. Here is one of the richest heiresses in Ireland, who wants to marry an unknown refugee from some exotic country, without a penny or even a promising job…What mother wouldn't be worried?

She didn't say "no," but the plan for a Christmas wedding was postponed to spring, and we agreed that I should first try to find a better job.

Everything looked better when in March I started working for *Paris-Match*. Now everything was just a matter of a few more months! Or so we thought. By the end of the same month, Neelia wrote to me that her grandfather had died suddenly and all her plans for coming to Paris had to be postponed. Arthur Ernest Guinness was the younger brother of the Earl of Iveagh, the head of the Irish branch of the colossally wealthy Guinness family. When in Dublin, he and Neelia's grandmother lived in Glenmaroon castle, a stately estate two miles away from Luttrellstown. "A fascinating but hideous house," Neelia had written to me. "Fascinating, because each time we go there, there is some new electrical device or mechanical gadget that makes an organ play, panels in the wall open, or something unusual happen." Later, I stayed there, during Luttrellstown's renovation, when Aileen had temporarily moved to Glenmaroon, and I saw what Neelia had meant: the place was a veritable castle of Oz, outfitted with electronic gadgets and musical gimmicks. I remember also that after Luttrellstown's style of life, which I thought quite fabulous, seeing the lifestyle of Sir Ernest, the man with *the really big* fortune, reminded me once more of the relativity of everything in this world…

Sir Ernest had three daughters, Aileen, Maureen, and Oonagh, each one more spoiled, helpless, and charmingly irresponsible than the other, three heiresses cursed with terrible luck in their marriages and messy love affairs. Extravagant spenders, they lived way beyond the generous revenues from their trusts (Aileen was constantly trying to break hers), but it didn't matter too much, in view of the huge fortune they were going to inherit. Especially that their father, in order to avoid the extraordinarily high inheritance taxes, had divided his estate while he was alive and had earmarked it as a gift to them. (It was estimated at about 3.5 million pounds, an enormous sum in those days.) But alas, he died too soon, ten months before the minimum period required by the law for such gifts. The inheritance was going to be taxed at a devastating rate. To raise the cash, houses, land, factories, jewelry, Sir Ernest's two yachts, his private helicopter, and much more were probably going to be sold. Aileen panicked, crying about "being ruined," (which reminded me again of the relativity of things…) talking about selling her personal jewels, maybe even Luttrellstown.

The thought that the timing of Sir Ernest Guinness's death could have any effect on the life of a Bulgarian refugee he never met, should normally be discarded as preposterous. People's biographies, however, not always follow "normal" scenarios, and in my case the premature demise of beer tycoon did change the course of events. Neither Neelia nor I suspected it when she wrote to me on March 26: "…*The funeral service was very beautiful. The cathedral was packed and the choir very lovely. On the way, all the streets were lined with people. I have never seen such crowds. It was probably because the brewery was given a half-holiday. The flowers were very impressive too…Poor Mum breaks down all the time. Darling, don't be impatient with her any more, please! She really is ill and so thin and pathetic at the moment…*" But the truth is that as far as the wedding plans were concerned, the momentum was lost. Neelia's visits to Paris had to be shortened. The family lawyer working on the question of her own trust and allowances before she becomes 21, (she wasn't yet 20), shelved the case, pending the solution of the new problems. Aileen was too upset and preoccupied to even talk to her daughter or to me about the wedding.

Meanwhile, we were considered engaged. In June, during a Neelia's one-week stay in Paris, I offered her an engagement ring. It had been a problem causing me a lot of worrying: I couldn't afford even the cheapest trinket, let alone an engagement ring for a Guinness heiress! Yet I knew how important it was to a girl like Neelia! It was again my dear "Aunt" Mika who came to my rescue. The previous year when Harri had visited Sofia (she already had a Swiss passport), my mother had given her my father's old ring and a pair of gold cufflinks, the only pieces of his jewelry she had saved. How well I remembered this ring, since my earliest childhood! It brought tears to my eyes when Harri handed it to me. I don't wear rings, but I treasured it more than any of my possessions. Unfortunately, it was too masculine to offer to a fiancée—a large "tiger-eye" stone, set in a heavy gold frame. So Mika brought me to a jeweler she knew, who remodeled the ring, took out the "tiger-eye," and replaced it with a pretty blue aquamarine stone of her own. I was deeply touched by her generosity, especially that I knew how precarious her financial situation was. "But you're like my son, aren't you?" was all she said to my protestations, as I hugged her. The ring turned out quite attractively, Neelia was delighted and I was proud to see her showing it off to her friends. I was sure that my father didn't mind that I had sacrificed his gem.

Then, she had to go with her mother and sister to London. The "Season" had started, and Doon was a "debutante" that year. In July I took a ten-day vacation, (in those days *Paris-Match* didn't care what I did and I wasn't missed too much…) and joined them in London and Dublin for a whirl of balls, dinner-dances, and night-clubbing, being introduced everywhere as "Neelia's fiancé." But not a word was said about the wedding. I was back to Paris when Doon was presented at Court and had her debutante dance. "…*Doon's party last night was very good. I climbed into bed at 6:30 AM…*" Neelia wrote me from *Claridges* on July 22nd. "*Princess Margaret and the Duchess of Kent came to our dance, also the Irish Horse Show team…I'll tell you all about the party when you come to Dublin. Tomorrow we go to Ireland and I'll be able to be in the sun and think of you all day, also all night…*"

The next letters from Ireland sounded differently. Neelia was obviously worried, disturbed. She had found her mother reticent, reluctant to talk about the wedding. I foolishly reacted in the wrong way. Being overly touchy on the question of "marrying a rich heiress," I wrote back angrily, showing my impatience and irritation with Aileen, blaming Neelia for not acting more resolutely, pressing her with words like "if you really loved me…" instead of showing her more understanding and love. These were our first quarrels; by letters only, but nevertheless hurting and spoiling the happy tone of our relations. Things were repaired by mid-August, when I took another vacation to Ireland, two marvelous weeks spent in horseback riding, driving around the countryside, attending horse shows and races. We stayed at Glenmarroon, the grandparents's house, and in the enchanted Luggala, Neelia's aunt Oonagh's estate, located at the bottom of a picturesque geological fault, looking like an illustration from a nursery rhyme book of "The Queen of Hearts." We had a great time, but as soon as we talked about our future, worries and quarrels started again.

I didn't feel happy when I returned to Paris, on August 29. I also missed Sava, who was married that same day in Johannesburg, where he had joined Pamela, just before I left for Dublin. A few days later, he wrote me a long letter, describing in detail his first weeks in South Africa and his new life as a married man, and asking: "How are your love and matrimonial problems? Mommy told me on the telephone that you were not very happy and things were not quite alright…"

Then Neelia told me that the *Evening Standard* had written about our engagement and that Aileen was very displeased. As the information came from *Standard's* Paris correspondent, Sam White, she wondered whether I hadn't indiscreetly originated the article. That upset me enormously. I called White and made a big fuss about it, which was, of course, a useless over-reaction. Soon after, *France-Dimanche*, the sensationalist mass-circulation weekly, ran a ridiculous Princess-and-Poor-Shepherd type of love story, under the title "THE QUEEN OF ENGLISH BEERS DOESN'T RESIST THE SLAV CHARM" and with large snapshot photographs of both of us. I felt utterly humiliated. At 27, I was too inexperienced and overly sensitive to deal with that kind of situation, and I'm sure that my wounded pride showed too much in my letters to Neelia. Doubt was slipping into our relationship, slowly driving out the sunny, fairytale side of it.

Aileen seemed to have second thoughts about the wedding. She succeeded in convincing her daughter to take a trip to Spain with friends, and give herself a chance to think everything over, instead of returning to Paris and to the same old problems, the very thought of which was becoming painful. An unexpectedly frank letter of Neelia informed me that she was going to consult her older, wiser cousin Honor *"whether I was right in the decision I took. And, darling, I must admit here and now that it was me who took it. You can condemn when you hear it, but don't before, please! Maybe I grew up slightly…I love you and only you. Please love me!"*

Late in October, she went to Spain and it hurt me badly. I think I was also jealous, because I learned that among the traveling companions, her mother had also invited an eligible young man. November was a sad month for me. On her way back from Spain, Neelia passed through Paris, apologized, explained, swore that nothing had changed. Then in December she came for a longer stay, and everything seemed to be forgotten and just like before—the lunches at the Panitzas' or the Lamottes', the evenings out with Dimi and George Revay, with Lavinia, the Brians and the Saint-Justs. Neelia was as loving as ever. She told me that Aileen had finally said "yes" and had even found a Greek-Orthodox church for the wedding in Dublin. She was expecting me at Luttrellstown for Christmas, when the official announcement would be made.

I was relieved and happy again, but doubts continued to eat away at my heart. Were we really in love? Weren't the differences in our situation, personalities, and background too big to overcome? After one-and-a-half year, wasn't the romantic love turning into something less exciting, as it seemed to be the normal fate of all love affairs? If so, wouldn't marriage be a mistake? I know that Neelia was going through similar doubts, but neither of us knew then that almost everybody goes through some such agony before a wedding. The difference between us was that she had no one to share her fears and uncertainty, no confidant, no really close friend for intimate advice or consolation. While I had Mika to pour my heart out, and Sava to write to, without trying to protect my pride. His devotion and concern for me were touching, and he was quite a good psychologist, in his outspoken and realistic way. *"I worry a lot about you and your stupid Neelia, and I begin to be pessimistic about the whole thing,"* Sava was saying for a long time. Now, after Neelia's Spanish escapade, he was advising a more energetic attitude: *"You're too naive. You'd better listen to me: Out of sight, out of mind! When you are together, you're the king of the situation. But if you aren't constantly with her, you'll loose the girl! I know that it doesn't depend on you, but if you're having one of your idiotic Stefo's illusions that this may last this way, without marriage, until she comes of age, you'd better go and jump into the Seine! Those things don't work from a distance, especially when the mother is against it. You must give N. an ultimatum: if she's serious and really in love, she must say straight to Aileen, clearly and unequivocally, that she's definitely decided to marry you. I'm convinced that Neelia doesn't dare say one word to her mother. If she doesn't, then I'm not sure she's that much in love, and I would understand, to a point, Aileen's attitude as mother. If N. doesn't act after your ultimatum, the situation is clear. Then cross out the whole thing and forget her!"*

I gave no ultimatums, because everything seemed to work well again. We had a wonderful Christmas and New Year at Luttrellstown, exchanging presents around the tree, listening to carols, enjoying the company of festive (usually hard-drinking) Irish friends, in front of roaring chimney fires. Neelia and Doon were aglow with excitement, like two little girls waiting for Santa Claus. Aileen was friendly again. She was in a sentimental mood, listening to records of the new American musical South Pacific. She, Neelia, and I wrote drafts for the official wedding announcement. Only the exact date was needed before sending it to the London *Times*. It had to be decided any day now. In the meantime, I had to start looking for an apartment in Paris and Neelia had to make the final financial arrangements with the family lawyer. Hooray!, Neelia and I exclaimed, overwhelmed with joy.

After the New Year, we took a trip with friends to the West of Ireland, across the solitary, weird Connemara, to the apocalyptic coast at Galway and Clifden, where the Atlantic makes one feel a witness to the time of Creation, and to the romantic Ballyconneelly, where the Guinness sisters owned a small cottage on the cliffs. I couldn't have dreamt of better or more Irish background for celebrating our engagement.

I returned to Paris a happy fiancé, accepting congratulations and looking at apartments for rent. Sava was already anxious to know who was going to be my best man. "I insist on Dimi, who'll do in on my behalf," he wrote from Johannesburg. Neelia wrote that all her doubts were over and she had meetings with the lawyer. "I wish you would come over for Easter as then we could really announce our engagement officially." Then, an even better news: Aileen had more or less fixed a date in April for the wedding, either Easter Saturday or Monday! But just when I thought I had seen a convenient apartment, another letter arrived: *"I am so excited about the flat! I do wish I dared tell Mummy about it though I just don't know how to keep her on to the marriage at the moment. She is difficult. I ask her about the lawyer and she says she doesn't know yet, and one is inclined but doesn't dare to say "Are you really asking?"...As you see, depression has set in...Darling, if by any chance the wedding is in May instead of April, you can live in the flat, can't you?"*

This seesaw exercise, putting the wedding date off and on again, continued all through February and March. Loving letters alternated with letters of despair or by long, unexplained silences. Neelia was obviously deeply disturbed, loosing hope of ever obtaining her trust allowance or her mother's blessing. Maybe also fed up with my new moodiness, my continuous blaming her and her family? And disappointed by the immaturity of outbursts of the kind "If I'm not good enough for your mother, tell her to go and buy you some stupid lord!" Then, as Easter approached, I received the letter I expected the least: *"My own Stefo, we have got the money! I don't know how soon we will actually have it, but anyway it is possible to get it."* Deeply relieved, I smiled broadly and continued to read. *"Darling, I have an awful confession to make. I am worried now that everything is really nearly settled, do I love you enough for always or not. I'm not sure anymore. If you want me like that, you can have me, but otherwise it's up to you to break it off…I'm sorry to write you like this, but I have been thinking a lot now that it's certain we've won, and it's got me worried. I haven't talked to anyone and it's up to you to take a decision. And if you decide against me, don't blame me too much, as circumstances in the past haven't been fair. All my love, Neelia."*

This was her last letter. I went to Ireland on Good Friday, as planned, not knowing whether I really wanted her "like that," as she had said, but hoping nevertheless that when we would see each other, everything would miraculously be solved. It wasn't. We were both too proud to speak openly, both waiting for the other one to say the things we wanted to hear. On Easter Sunday, we all stood tense and silent in the family pew in St. Patrick Cathedral, Neelia humming her hymns through tears, Aileen avoiding to look at us, and myself thinking that tomorrow was the day we were supposed to get married. It was the saddest Easter and Luttrellstown had never looked gloomier to me. After three days, during which we either quarreled or wept, Neelia drove me silently to the airport and we said goodbye to each other. But I made sure that she knew that I was going to stay for two days in London, at my old friend "Shoo" Stancioff-Guepin's house. The day was April 12th, exactly four weeks before Neelia's 21st birthday.

I confess that for two days and two nights I secretly hoped that an airport taxi-cab would stop in front of 68, Drayton Gardens and Neelia would jump out of it, mumbling "Sorry…I love you!" Or that Shoo would say that a Miss Plunket had telephoned from Dublin.

But Miss Plunket never called.

*   *   *   *   *

Chapter 14

The unusual ways of "Paris-Match" and its Patron

I'd been working for *Paris-Match* for several weeks, before I saw "Le Patron" for the first time. From distance only, of course, because Jean Prouvost wasn't the kind of boss that a cub reporter like me would be in direct contact with. I saw him a few times as he was entering the building, or when leaving his office, if I happened to be in the corridor. But even so, I was thrilled, as when one bumps unexpectedly into a celebrity. And by then he was already a legend to me, and also the man who was paying us. Although I suspected that some of the stories we had heard about him were apocryphal or at least highly embellished, the Jean Prouvost saga was central to the *Paris-Match* mythology and I was eager to see what this fabulous press-tycoon looked like in person. I wasn't disappointed: the man certainly looked the part.

Lean and erect, over 6-foot tall, with a spring in his step rare for a man in his late 60-s, well-dressed in conservative three-piece suits and impeccably polished black shoes, he had the unmistakable demeanor of a grand-seigneur. A prominently long upper lip, as well as a high, bald cranium, conferred certain severity to his narrow, equine face. The word "Patron" came somehow naturally just by watching the self-assurance in his gestures and hearing the tone of authority in his nasal, slightly high-pitched voice while instructing or interrogating his interlocutors. Indeed, lacking totally of small talk and impatient when listening to stories which he didn't ask for, giving directions and interrogating were the only two modes in which he conversed. Plus a third one, silences. Long, uncomfortable, oppressive silences, during which nobody knew what was coming next, a compliment or a reprimand. Unsmiling, absorbed in his thoughts, he never made the slightest effort to put his listener at ease.

Everybody feared Le Patron. Yet, like a strict but respected and generous father, everybody admired him, and most *Match* people liked him sincerely. When I first came in his presence—it was during one of those nights when he came to oversee *le bouclage* of the issue—and he looked at me with his penetrating, clever small eyes and asked my name, I was simply petrified. *"Ah, c'est vous, Droueff, le Bulgare.* Herve told me about you." And that was all. Although Gaston respectfully corrected him, saying that the name was Groueff, Le Patron continued for several months to call me *Droueff.* He didn't like to be corrected. He was also touchy about his hearing, and although he didn't hear well (especially when he didn't want to), he used to scold people: "But don't shout! I'm not deaf!" *"Oui, Patron!,"* was the usual reply. The obligatory formula *"Oui, Patron!"* was a ritual in the paternalistic Prouvost empire, but was applied differently by his subjects. For the troops, it meant an obedient "yes," an order one didn't discuss. The version *"Oui, Patron,* but..." was the privilege of his top lieutenants, and could mean anything, including *"Non, Patron!"* Herve Mille, Boegner, and Bonheur were masters of this respectful form of disagreement, pushing it often to its supreme refinement, which consisted in doing the opposite of what Prouvost had said and presenting it as his own idea or wish. Surprisingly, it worked in many cases; maybe because Prouvost, in spite of his imperious ways, was a man who changed his mind often, and the polite resistance of his directors provided him with good ways to save face. But not always: when, at the end of the first year of *Paris-Match,* Herve disagreed openly with J.P., he had to leave the magazine for a couple of years; the same fate was shared later by Boegner. The only one among Prouvost's closest collaborators who sometimes was saying undiplomatically *"Non, Patron,* you're wrong!" was Raymond Cartier, which caused several conflicts, quarrels, and difficulties for the impetuous director. Describing the qualities and faults of his "egocentric" and "parsimonious to the extreme" boss, Boegner wrote: "This man, capable of being odious, rude, aggressive, unsupportable, ungrateful, knew nevertheless how to transform into servants totally devoted to his person—more than to his enterprises—people of very different conditions and levels who, while feeling an aversion toward him, admitted their inability to resist him."

Few men in my life had intimidated me to the degree Jean Prouvost did. My regret is that it took me years before I could talk and act normally in his presence. He used to make me exceedingly tense, his silences rendered me hopelessly inarticulate, the impatience I used to read in his critical eyes discouraged anything original or amusing that I could've said. Yet, his prodigiously successful career and his obvious genius to communicate with the general public fascinated me.

A product of a rigid, bourgeois family in the strait-laced milieu of rich industrialists of the North, he had always had the courage of trying the new, the risky and unorthodox. To begin with, his very involvement in the woolen manufacture was a rather unconventional thing to do for a younger brother: family businesses were traditionally reserved for the first-born sons. But at the end of World War I, in which he served first as motorcyclist-courier and then as apprentice-pilot, he returned to Roubaix and took over a part of the business, modernizing it by importing young cadres of specialists from Paris and applying new methods, and increasing it three-fold in five years. He opened a branch in Czechoslovakia, then went to the USA to learn about American and Canadian methods. Impressed, he started, associating his elder brother, a *peignage* business, (wool-combing), a departure from the family routine, and it soon became among the most successful in America. But J.P.'s greatest business success came in 1926, when he had the idea of promoting knitting among the women in France, starting in Roubaix a mass-production of wool-balls. The country was soon inundated with home-made sweaters, socks, and scarves, knitted with high-quality wool *Pengouin*, Prouvost's trade-mark. To his part of the old family wealth, the younger son added the considerable income of his own new fortune.

He needed it. Because in the meantime Jean Prouvost had discovered his true vocation: journalism. In 1924 he had been offered an insignificant Parisian newspaper, *Paris-Midi,* circulation 4,000, which he had bought for a song. Ever since, he acted as full-fledged editorial director, not a mere capitalist. He put the accent on stories of popular interest, and to the strong stock-market and racing pages, he added an exciting "Parisian Life" gossipy page, which he entrusted to a street-smart 18-year-old drop-out, Pierre Lazareff. (Lazareff later became a key figure in French popular journalism.) In no time, *Paris-Midi* was selling 120,000 copies daily. Surprisingly, the grand-bourgeois from the North and scion of a privileged industrial dynasty was showing a remarkable affinity with the popular masses.

There was nothing even remotely plebeian, however, in his personal lifestyle and tastes. In his thirties, the young man from Roubais had already become part of the elegant Parisian life, a rich bachelor who lived very well, had amusing and influential friends, and romantic successes with talked-about ladies. Pierrette Madd, for instance, a famous actress, was his girlfriend in a period he moved in theater circles. Everybody knew that Prouvost, like most members of old-fashioned, traditionalist families, had gone through arranged matrimonium with a heiress of a related clan, at the early age of 20, a marriage that had lasted for about one year, the time to produce his only son, but nobody talked about that. Although he hadn't seen her for 30 years, and didn't want to hear about her, he had never divorced. First, because Catholics in the North didn't divorce, and second, because they were married under the regime of "*communauté des biens,*" i.e. everything J.P. owned had to be split by half in case of a divorce, and that was the last thing he wanted to do.

His career of great press lord really began in 1930, at the age of 45, when he acquired *Paris-Soir*, a newspaper that was losing money and had a circulation of 60,000. It took Prouvost a few years before it could compete with its infinitely more powerful rival, *L'Intransigeant,* which was selling 350,000 copies a day. But by 1934, he had found the right formula for his *Paris-Soir:* a lot of dramatic, generously displayed photographs, which was a novelty for the French dailies; popular subjects, directed to the large public, not only for the elites, and written in vivid style, by first-class journalists; serialized fiction, feuilletons about historical personalities, preferably great mistresses of kings, actresses, or murderesses. With this formula, *Paris-Soir* began to climb spectacularly. By 1934, it reached one million copies. Prouvost had won the battle. Young Herve Mille, who assisted him next to the dynamic Lazareff, remembers how Prouvost used to see the role of the great daily papers: "There are two ways of covering the news. The more obvious way is to try to tell, as much as possible, everything that's going on in the entire world. That's the way of *Le Temps, Le Monde, New York Times* or *Times* of London. *"Paris-Soir"* has very different ambitions: There are, every day, two or three major events that interest the entire public, without distinction. They have to do with politics as well as with crime, love, and local topics. To these events, we must give maximum space and devote all material and human resources, beginning with talent."

The fantastic growth of his newspapers forced Prouvost to look for additional capital, especially for the supply of newsprint for the enormously increased daily circulation. He found it from another North-of-France family of industrialists, the Beghins, leading manufacturers of sugar and paper. Thus, the Beghins became fifty-fifty co-owners of all present and future Prouvost publications. But J.P. kept exclusively the total editorial control for himself, which explains the odd fact that I, no more than most of my colleagues, never met a Beghin, although they paid half of all *Paris-Match* expenses. Not only didn't the Beghins feel very welcome at the editorial offices, but also editorially, *Match* ignored them totally. Thus, in an article about American dietitian Gaylord Hauser, our Georges Pernoud deplored the disastrous effect of sugar on human health, under a bombastic headline in bold letters: "Don't Eat Sugar!" When the outraged Ferdinand Beghin demanded apology and the head of Pernoud, Le Patron pretended to share his indignation, but his malicious smile indicated that he wasn't displeased by his sugar-producing partner's vexation.

By the mid-thirties, Jean Prouvost had become a powerful press baron, the proprietor of the biggest daily, *Paris-Soir*, then of its former rival, *L'Intransigeant*, then, in 1937, of the first women's magazine, *Marie-Claire*, a huge success since its first issue. *Marie-Claire* became Le Patron's favorite toy. To the great annoyance of its editors Philippe Boegner and Marcelle Auclair, J.P. was interfering constantly, suggesting stories, bluntly discarding material that he judged boring, exulting at dubious "great ideas," such as adding in the magazine's celebrated test "Is Your Husband A Good Husband?" the question whether he squeezes the toothpaste in the middle or by its end. Once again, he was proven right: the readers loved the test. Each Wednesday, the day *Marie-Claire* came out, Prouvost took the rapid train Paris-Lille-Roubaix for his weekly visit to his factories and the editors waited in anguish for his late-afternoon call. For as soon as he boarded the train, the great press tycoon walked through all the cars, counting the passengers reading his magazine. If his telephone call started with "<u>Our</u> issue this week…" the editors knew it was a success. (He always shouted when speaking on the phone, repeating several times "Allo! Allo!") But if he said "<u>Your</u> issue this week…" there was consternation at *Marie-Claire:* the Patron was displeased and there was going to be some storm the next day. In addition to attracting some of France's best journalists, J.P. asked many celebrated literary lions to cover news stories for him— Georges Simenon, Jerome and Jean Tharaud, and Colette wrote on murder trials, Francis de Croisset covered King George V's Jubilee, and Louis Gillet—George VI's coronation. Joseph Kessel became a regular contributor. Maurice Decobra and Pierre Mac Orlan described Germany of the 1930's. Jean Cocteau wrote a series "Around the World in 80 Days" for *Paris-Soir,* following Phileas Fogg's itinerary, and Saint-Exupery interviewed Goebbels in Berlin and sent reportages from the Soviet Union. The idea was always the same: narrate the news story as a novel, by first-rate writers. Even Maurice Chevalier wrote a dozen of stories for *Paris-Soir,* the first one describing an execution in a prison, which the famous chansonnier happened to witness.

Soon after the success of *Marie-Claire,* Herve Mille and Lazareff, already Prouvost's closest collaborators, convinced him to start a new popular week-end paper, with emphasis on entertainment and leisure reading. Thus, *Paris-Soir Dimanche* was born, a hugely successful weekly resembling some of today's "yellow press" tabloids, but written with talent. Typical scoops: the American "Memoirs of the Sing-Sing executioner" and "The Memoirs of the Siamese Twins." When it was reported from Hungary that several young people committed suicide after listening to the song *Somber Sunday, Paris-Soir Dimanche* rushed its reporters to Budapest, had the lyrics translated, and made the song an enormous hit in France. A most valuable discovery made at this Sunday paper was Gaston Bonheur, the young, penniless poet newly arrived from Carcassonne, whose talent to romanticize any small local news caught the eye of Prouvost and Mille. Herve called him "*un poete du quotidien,*" a poet of the everyday and made him editor of *Paris-Soir Dimanche.*

The next success was the pre-war *Match, an* illustrated news weekly inspired by the American *Life Magazine.* A part from the old-fashioned *Illustration,* a lifeless album of static photos, no such publication existed in France. Prouvost was fascinated by the successful new formula of his American colleague Henry Luce, but, as usual, spent a long time to decide to import it to France, changing his mind every week, agonizing between the pros and cons of such venture. As Herve Mille said, "one of Jean Prouvost's principal qualities is hesitation, which is the opposite of stubbornness." But finally he made his decision and then nothing could stop him. He owned a small sports weekly, called *Match.* In September 1938, he transformed it completely into a news magazine, going from Tour-de-France bicycle race and boxing to spectacular photos of Hitler, Mussolini, and Chamberlain. It was the period of Munich, the Spanish war, and the growing anxiety about German mobilization, and the public received warmly the new magazine. The first issue sold 150,000 copies; three months later, its circulation doubled; by the spring of 1940, it reached 1.8 million. Prouvost had guessed right: the French definitely adored double-spreads with "photos-choc," indiscreet pictures of celebrities, and narratives of events "as if you were there." But the war put an end to the triumph of *Match,* and in June 1940 it ceased publication. At that time, *Paris*-Soir was selling 2.5 million copies and *Marie-Claire*—1.5 million.

Then things began to turn badly for Prouvost. During the crisis following the defeat of the French army, Prime Minister Paul Reynaud asked Prouvost to go secretly to London and find out from his fellow-press magnate Lord Beaverbrook, Churchill's closest associate, what Britain intended to do next. At his return to Paris, Reynaud reshuffled his cabinet and pressed J.P. to become Minister of Information. Although he had always kept out of politics, Prouvost saw the offer as his patriotic duty, and reluctantly accepted. On June 6, 1940 he became a member of the cabinet. Another new member was Colonel de Gaulle, appointed Under-Secretary of State for Defense. Four days later, as the Wehrmacht marched toward Paris, the government left the capital for the South. All Prouvost journalists followed the exodus, to Clermont-Ferrand in the non-occupied zone of France, then to Lyons. In occupied Paris, the Germans seized the *Paris-Soir* building, installed their own personnel and continued printing it, under the same title, until the Liberation.

At the advice of its High command, the French government asked for an armistice. Reynaud resigned; disagreeing vehemently, de Gaulle left for London. The Germans occupied Paris and the North, Marshal Petain, the WW I hero, formed a government in the non-occupied zone, and Prouvost kept shortly his post at the Information, until he joined his team in Lyons. (Later, he was going to pay dearly for the few weeks of association with the Petain regime...)

In Lyons, he regrouped his effectives and resumed publication of a reduced version of his *Paris-Soir*, which had to fight every day with the Vichy censors or invent ruses to outwit them. With the ex-*Match* journalists idle in Lyons, he also started a smaller and cheaper newsweekly. "*7 Jours*" resembled more a popular London tabloid than *Life Magazine*, but its success was immediate, due mostly to a newcomer, Raymond Cartier, a remarkably erudite editor with a phenomenal capacity for work. Offering a rich variety of news stories from abroad to the deprived of information Free Zone, *7 Jours* was avidly read by 800,000 Frenchmen. The trick was simple: Cartier was writing almost single-handedly the entire magazine, drawing on his encyclopedic mind and using American magazines left over in the passengers' cabin on the flights from New York to Geneva. *7 Jours's* man in Annemasse, on the Swiss border, picked them regularly at the Geneva airport and rushed them to Lyons, a true goldmine for Cartier and his assistants, Max Corre and Marcel Haedrich. (After the war, both young men became directors of successful magazines.) Prouvost, of course, took active part, as demanding as ever, changing stories and outlays at the last moment, making life hard for his editors, but also taking good care of them. He continued *Paris-Soir* until November 1942, when the Germans entered the Free Zone and he ceased publication in protest. When ordered under threat to resume publication, *Paris-Soir* had to obey, but printed only 100 copies a day. Then in May 1943 it stopped appearing.

Meanwhile, Prouvost had discovered a new interest: the cinema. He opened an office in Cannes, hired two renowned movie-makers, Marc Allegret and Marcel Achard, and started producing films, the best one being "L'Arlesienne," with Raimu, Gaby Morley, Louis Jourdan, and Gisele Pascal.

J.P. remained in the Free Zone until one month before the liberation of Paris, when he returned to the capital. While in Lyons he was in good terms with the Free French, contributing large sums of money, through Herve Mille and other close associates, active in the Resistance. (Once, for instance, an important contribution, 16 million francs, was obtained through the same Jean Rosenthal, the man who later recommended me for a job at *Paris-Match*. He was the Resistance boss in the Lyons region.) Some journalists of the Prouvost group had been arrested or deported by the Gestapo, or had died in German camps.

But it didn't help J.P. much during the turbulent days of revengefulness, mutual accusations of collaboration with the enemy, and ugly, arbitrary acts, which followed the Liberation. The Communists, who always hated Prouvost, occupied forcibly the old *Paris-Soir* building on Rue du Louvre on the day on which its German occupants left, and started using it for their own newspapers. In order to expropriate Prouvost's press holdings, they accused him of collaboration and demanded that he be prosecuted for having voted in favor of the armistice as Minister of Information, for serving in Marshal Petain's government, and for publishing newspapers during the occupation. They omitted, of course, to mention that not only had the Lyons' *Paris-Soir* nothing to do with the false *Paris-Soir* stolen from Prouvost by the Germans, but it had kept a distinct pro-Allies and anti-German line, in spite of the Vichy censorship. Neither did they mention that the collaborationist press viciously attacked Prouvost and his papers as tools of Anglo-American capitalism and Jewish international conspiracy. (Wasn't his top editor Lazareff a Jew?) Prouvost's name was put on the Communist black list, and as the Communists emerged very powerful at the Liberation, a warrant was issued for his arrest. Fearing for his life, Prouvost went into hiding on September 1st 1944 and didn't surface until July 1947, when the High Court not only cleared him completely, but also commended him for his help to the Resistance.

The malicious defamation marked Le Patron for the rest of his life. It forced him to spend three years in hiding, like a fugitive from justice, with the police searching for him and his name and photograph displayed on "Wanted" posters, changing clandestine domiciles, living in constant fear to be discovered. He survived, his name was cleared and most properties recovered thanks to three men who devoted all their time and efforts to his cause: his most trusted director of the textile empire,

Marc Midol, and his closest collaborators in the press, Herve Mille and Philippe Boegner, my future bosses at *Paris-Match*. They knew well that the political climate of the day precluded any protection from the mob or guarantee of a fair trial, and that the essential thing was to remain in hiding and survive, until the passions calmed. They hid their Patron, taking enormous personal risks. Midol was kidnapped and submitted to rough interrogation, then put in jail for many days, as were other associates of Prouvost. Plainclothes policemen constantly followed Boegner, Mille and M-me Danet, J.P.'s great love, with whom he could only communicate through secret messages. Living under the false identity of "Monsieur Martin-Picot," Prouvost changed at least nine hideouts, in Paris, in the suburbs, and in the province of Vendee. Some of his hosts, who took considerable risks, were personal friends, such as Missia Sert and Don, the cartoonist. Others were present and former associates—Midol, the baroness Anne de Mareuil, Andre Roux, Louis Dechizeaux, and Hubert Giron. But even people who not only didn't know him personally, but disapproved fully of his "sensationalist and vulgar" press, gave him asylum, just because they were outraged by the excesses of the postwar witch-hunt. Thus, the countess Helene de Suzannet and the marquis de Saint Pierre offered him hospitality for several months in their chateaux in Vendee, although they found it difficult to converse with him and rather disliked him. Meanwhile, Boegner, Mille, and Midol lobbied unremittingly every judge, prosecutor, politician, and journalist they could buttonhole and hired the best lawyers in France. After three years, their devotion and perseverance paid off. Acquitted by the High Court, the fugitive "Martin-Picot" became again the magnate Jean Prouvost, "Le Patron." He was 62 and the exciting venture of *Paris-Match* wasn't to start but two years later.

THE TEAM

It was amusing to see how this colorful bunch of unruly guys with no respect for authority, gladly and unconditionally obeyed their soft-spoken leader, Jean Rigade. It reminded me of movies about Prohibition-days Chicago in which hot-headed gang members, much fiercer and tougher than their mild-looking boss, behave like lambs in his presence. *Match* photographers not only strived to please Rigade professionally, but they also looked for his approval of their lifestyle, their love conquests, their new suits and new jokes. He was not yet 30, but his authority was indisputable. The photographers, who often resented orders by the *Match* hierarchy and sulked about unpleasant or unglamorous assignments, never disputed Rigade's commands. "You leave for Lyons tonight, *coco,*" he would say softly, "and *demerde-toi!*" (polite translation: "Try to manage!") Or, "Go and take pictures of that boring big shot! And if he plays the prima donna, just tell him to shove it!" "Yes, Jean," the usually insubordinate reporter would reply meekly. For the photographers, what counted most was that Rigade like their pictures, whether the editors were satisfied or not. And they were crushed if he would bluntly say "*c'est de la merde!*" His verdict, as the rest of his conversation, would be delivered in a mixture of vagabond argot and the cheeky street-urchin's wit of a "*titi parisien.*"

Tall and slim, conservatively dressed, Jean Rigade was a rather good-looking young man with intelligent eyes and a pleasant smile. Women found him attractive and rumors about his various girlfriends circulated at Rue Pierre-Charron, although, unlike the usual *Paris-Match* boasting Casanovas, he was discreet and limited himself to smiling mysteriously when teased about some starlet or fashion model. Jean was a Breton, the son of a late *super-prefet,* or chief regional administrator, and he had grown up as a half-orphan: his mother had died when he was a child and, not getting along with his stepmother, he had drifted around without much of a family life. Like the rest of the photo reporters, he had a rather scant formal education (almost none of them had been to college), but he certainly had accumulated a copious real-life experience during his eventful youth, including a bout with tuberculosis. He still was going through periods of depression, which probably explained his quiet, slightly melancholy disposition. From time to time, he went away for a treatment and these were the days when the gang demonstrated its total devotion to the chief. Reporters were taking tours to visit him daily and brief him on the goings on at rue Pierre-Charron, reporting each incident and gossip, asking for advice, cracking jokes to boost his morale. Once, returning from a reportage with Rene Vital, we nearly missed the story because Vital insisted on leaving one day earlier so he could pay a visit to Rigade at the clinic, and there was nothing I could do to make him change his mind. This amazing loyalty became quite a problem later, when Rigade had to be absent for a very long time. After several weeks, as the job of Chief of the Photography service was vital for the magazine, the management began, regretfully, to consider Jean's replacement. The gang's reaction was vehement and categorical: if Rigade is replaced, we stop working! A compromise was reached, with the photographers delegating a representative, Daniel Filipacchi, to temporarily assume Rigade's desk duties, acting in his behalf, until Jean returns. But it was made clear that the title remained Rigade's, and neither Daniel, nor anyone else, would replace him.

Apart from his *super-prefet's* genes, Jean Rigade's authority owed a great deal to the unmitigated support of his inseparable buddy Andre Lacaze, the magazine's most popular reporter. If somebody could personify the style and characteristics of the *Paris-Match* reporter of the first team, that would be "Dede" Lacaze, the daring, imaginative, and amazingly resourceful journalist whose professional exploits had won him the admiration of his colleagues. Dede lived with *Match* and for *Match*, with the same passion he had shown, as teenager, as a right-wing activist first, then as a hero of the Resistance. Now, Lacaze was Rigade's alter-ego. If the photo reporters's band was a corporation, Rigade would've been the chairman of the Board, and Dede, its chief executive officer. The editors loved him, because hardly a week passed without Lacaze bringing ideas for a scoop or for some "photo-shock." All reporters dreamt of emulating his ingenuity in surmounting obstacles. His trick at a Sugar-Ray Robinson fight, for instance, became a classic in *Paris-Match's* folklore. The *Vel d'Hiv* stadium was packed to capacity on the night of the Robinson-Villemain match. Dede had no ticket and the security service was impenetrable. He suddenly sees at the gates a good-looking young black woman, who is also struggling to get in. "Come with me!" he tells her. Then, pushing her in front of him, he forces his way across the crowds, the ushers and the police, shouting "Let Mrs. Robinson pass! Please let Mrs. Robinson pass!"

A tall, muscular guy quite proficient in boxing and "*la savate*" (kick-fighting), fearless, disrespectful, laconically foul-mouthed, this 30-year-old product of the Parisian streets and Nazi labor camps had the kindest smile and the charm of an innocent child. Team-spirit was his religion, and he was ready to die for a *copain* in trouble, which showed in the witty four-letter slang by which he demonstrated his affection for his buddies. Indeed, the first time I felt really "accepted," was when one day he noticed my presence in the room and, assuming a mock boxing stance, dared me, with a smile: "Defend yourself, Bulgar!" I could, of course, think of better ways of committing suicide, so I prudently dodged the coming blow. "Not bad, Bulgar!" Lacaze said approvingly, and in a friendly gesture, hit me affectionately on the shoulder, which was enough to keep it blue for a week. It was like little kids hitting each other when they don't know how else to be friendly, but from then on Dede and I remained on excellent terms.

Lacaze's father used to have a fencing school on rue de Grenelle where he taught swordsmanship to the sons of good Parisian families. In summer, the Lacazes went to Dinard where he gave gymnastics courses on the beach. Prefet Rigade's family was also spending summers in Dinard, and that's where the lifelong friendship of Jean and Dede began. Since the age of 15, Jean sometimes visited his friend in Paris and being penniless, often slept in the locker room of Maitre Lacaze's fencing gym, then the two boys explored the streets of Paris together. As the writer Guillaume Hanoteau, who joined *Paris-Match* a few years later and who knew Rigade from the cafes of Saint-Germain-des-Pres, remembered, Dede the Parisian "had nothing new to teach to the Breton Rigade, who already knew all the exits in the Metro through which one could enter without a ticket."

Lacaze was the youngest Frenchman ever decorated for Merits to the Resistance. He had become a member of the clandestine cell of a young man, Joel Le Tac, whom he had met at stormy political rallies, where they had fought, physically, on opposing sides. After exchanging some blows, they had become friends and later, Le Tac enrolled Dede in his unit in occupied Paris. Lacaze took part in operations of parachuting arms near Rennes, then installed and manned a radio-transmitter at rue de Seine, until the Gestapo discovered it and arrested him. He was twenty-two years-old. He spent fifteen months in the Fresnes prison, being brought to Paris almost every day for interrogation. He tried to escape one day by jumping from the Gestapo van at boulevard Raspail, a territory he knew perfectly well, but cracked his head on the pavement, was recaptured and finally deported to the S.S. camp of Mauthausen. The conditions there, working at the construction of a tunnel, were abominable, but Lacaze survived and was able to see the Liberation. It was from the prisoners, many of them common-law criminals, that Dede learned the argot of "*le milieu*," the slang of the underworld, which he transmitted to Rigade, and which became the *Match* photo reporters' dialect. Sometimes I found it difficult to under-stand Carone and Vital, Mangeot, Rizzo, Roy, or Pedrazzini in their non-stop banter, and that was probably a reason I never quite felt like a full member of their exclusive club. They were all fluent in these truants's lingo, but even in linguistic matters they all recognized the superiority of Dede and Rigade, *les grands maitres.*

In liberated Paris Lacaze found his wartime boss Joel Le Tac, who had also survived, after so many exploits, that General de Gaulle named him *Compagnon de la Liberation*, the highest honor of the Resistance. (Not long after *Paris-Match* started, Joel joined our team as a reporter.) Lacaze was also reunited with his old pal Rigade, who had been spared much of the war's ordeals because of a broken leg. Jean had joined in the Free Zone his father, who worked at the prefecture of Lyons. There he met the group of exiled Prouvost journalists and soon was discovered by Herve and Gerard Mille. They liked him immediately and took him under their wing. Thus, after the war, Rigade saw them again in Paris and became a *habitue* of the rue de Varenne.

Back in Paris, Rigade and Lacaze became inseparable again, naughtier than ever, living it up, making up for the lost war years. The early postwar adventures of the duo are not well chronicled, and even if they were, they would probably not all be printable. All we have heard is that they were very colorful, sometimes wild, and not always observing the rules. But we do know that when Rigade brought Lacaze to the Mille salon, rue de Varenne, Herve found that Dede was like "a son of Jeanne d'Arc and of d'Artagnan." And we were told that the freres Mille brought Rigade and Lacaze for a weekend at Saint-Jean, Jean Prouvost's country house in Sologne, and Le Patron was "taken by their vivacity and enthusiasm." The prototype of the future *Paris-Match* reporter was found.

*   *   *   *   *

With daredevil reporters, there was a price to be paid. One of the earlier dramas involved, predictably, Jean Roy, and, to a more tragic degree, his teammate in Indochina, photographer Jacques de Potier. In December 1952, French troops surrounded in Na-Sam, in the Thai-Noir sector, decided to break the Viet circle with paratroopers dropped behind the enemy line, in the jungle at a place called Co-Noi. Roy and Potier volunteered to join the dangerous operation. Roy jumped with the 800 "paras," 65 of whom were wounded at landing; he sprained his ankle and had to limp for a few days. Potier arrived the next day by jeep from Na-Sam and while Roy was nursing his ankle, he joined a Foreign Legion patrol on a clean-up mission. In the thickest of the jungle, the patrol fell into a Viet ambush. The lieutenant was killed and three legionnaires were wounded badly. While Potier and an Army photographer, Jean Peraud, attempted to assist them, two machine-gun bullets hit Jacques, shattering his thigh and leaving him lying down in the tall elephant-grass, bleeding profusely. Risking his life, Peraud managed to pull Potier out and drag and carry him across the jungle. After a terrible ordeal, when they reached the post in Co-Noi, Jacques's leg was already beyond repair. A helicopter flew him to Na-Sam, from where a plane evacuated him to Hanoi. The doctors wanted to amputate immediately, and it was only the categorical, and at times menacing, opposition of Jean Roy, who had joined his buddy and refused to leave his side, that the amputation didn't take place. Flown back to Paris, and surrounded by "the team," Potier underwent a number of operations and spent several years of treatment before he could use his leg again. The Army issued him and Peraud citations for heroism and they received the Croix-de-Guerre.

It was the first decoration to a *Paris-Match* reporter in action. Jacques de Potier became the first of our casualties, but, as we shall see, he was far from being the last.

      *   *   *   *   *

Chapter 15

The ordeals of my sister Radka

As she walked in the cold, wet city streets, Radka felt particularly hungry that day, hungrier than she had been used to feeling in the last several weeks. When hunger becomes a constant state, one gets somewhat accustomed to it, but only to a certain degree, like a chronic illness, never sufficiently to ignore its pangs when they strike the body and invade the mind.

The month of March can be quite unpleasant in Sofia, with winter still holding on, alternating rain and sleet, brief promises of spring and frigid, penetrating fog. For Radka, having painfully survived the year of 1945 in concentration camp and forced residence in unfamiliar places, and a winter of despair back in Sofia, where her homeless, wrecked family had returned, there was not much hope left to escape from the bleakness and hostility around her. Yet she couldn't afford to sink into despondency: not only did she have to make a living, however pitiful, for herself, but she had also to help Mama and Boubi, who had found temporary refuge, penniless, at the home of distant relatives in Bourgas, on the Black Sea.

Suffering had pursued the family ever since my father had been killed and Mama and Radka liberated from the camp in Dobrudja. The first couple of months they were ordered to reside in Vratza, a city totally unknown to them but luckily near enough to Sofia for friends, such as the Savovs and the Balabanovs, to help them periodically with money and food. These were risky gestures, as contacts with "people's enemies" were dangerous, and many relatives and old friends preferred to avoid them, fearing for their own safety. They had no other means of support; Boubi was still in military service in Sofia.

One day, Militiamen came to their humble room in Vratza and ordered them to pack and leave immediately for a new destination. No reason was given, no explanation. Thus, the two women spent the entire fall in the desolate hamlet of

Pomezhdin, without money, with no job for Radka. They had to live from the charity of the peasants, kind, compassionate people for whom mama, a knitting expert, made socks and sweaters. These very poor, uneducated villagers showed great sympathy for the Communists' victims and never left them hungry. But Mama fell quite ill and spent a long time in bed, in the miserable room with no sanitary facilities that she shared with Radka. The local doctor certified that her kidney illness required urgent hospitalization. His certificate was added to Radka's and Boubi's application to the authorities to authorize Mama's transfer to the capital, but no reply was received. In Sofia, Boubi was desperately knocking at the doors of family friends still untouched by the new regime, but in 1945 most of them were powerless or vulnerable themselves. The Queen, despite her affection for him, could not be of much assistance, as she was isolated and confined at the out-of-town palace of Vrana; anyhow, any royal intervention at that time would only have aggravated things. It was better to look for people uninvolved politically (operetta super-star Mimi Balkanska and soprano Nelly Karova, for instance, tried to help, and so did our old Uncle Mitcho, who happened to know one of the new big shots from his student days). Under the new regime, the only connections that counted were those with some party-member or fellow-traveler, and every family in trouble was searching for one among former schoolmates, neighbors, or in-laws.

It will never be known whether the friendly interventions helped or not. The fact is that as winter was already on its way, Mama and Radka were told one day that they could go to Sofia, with no more explanation than the day when they were sent to Pomezhdin. Another ordeal began for the homeless women in the unfriendly city, by then overcrowded with "proletarian," hostile crowds brought from villages. For several months, night after night, week after week, they had to look for a place to sleep. Bouby was still in the Army, and myself, still a student in Geneva, had almost no news from them, nor any possibility to help. In the beginning, thanks to the Queen's intervention, Mama entered a Catholic hospital, while Radka slept in kitchens, hallways, even staircases, of friends and relatives. By then, most apartments were taken away from proprietors, or unwanted tenants were placed in every unoccupied room. This homeless life continued after Mama left the hospital. During the long, cold winter, they shared the modest homes of countless cousins, aunts, friends and acquaintances, all very kind and understanding, but themselves living in overcrowded quarters, and constantly worried about the Militia and the Communist in charge of the building, as it was strictly forbidden to shelter unregistered people overnight. A few times, when kindhearted relatives let them use a room for a longer period, the hosts received warnings not to receive "fascists," and the search for a bed resumed. Meanwhile, Radka took all sorts of small secretarial jobs, grateful to be given temporary work at still non-nationalized businesses of brave enough friends. The pay was hardly enough to support herself and Mama, so very often she had to skip meals. There were times when she hadn't eaten for two or three days. Boubi finished his service and also started looking for a job and a place to live in. But it wasn't before long that friends warned them that remaining in Sofia without permit was becoming risky. Rather than being deported forcibly again, Mama and Boubi decided to leave the capital voluntarily and stay for some time with cousins of Mama in Bourgas, the Djapunovs, who received them warmly. At that time Radka had a job, so she stayed in Sofia, the only breadwinner in the family.

*   *   *   *

"I think you could find a better job, Radka!" Elie said. "It's a pity to see a girl like you struggling so hard!"

Elie Trayanova, a former flirt of mine, was an attractive young woman, a little older than me and far more sophisticated than most of our Sofia contemporaries. Daughters of a diplomat, she and her sister Neda had lived abroad and by Bulgarian standards were totally westernized and emancipated, which made them intriguing for the men and sometimes shocked the local matrons. During the first couple of years of communism, they still managed to move in the set of foreign diplomats in Sofia, with relative impunity. Elie, still joking about "her blue-eyed love Stephane," had shown much friendship toward Radka in that difficult period and had even given her some clothes. "The wife of an American assistant-military attaché is looking for Bulgarian lessons," she said that day. "Mrs. Yatsevitch, a very distinguished lady. You speak English, so you'll be perfect for the job. The

Americans pay very well. Go and see her, they live in the Peyev's villa in Boyana! A few lessons a week, and she'll serve you tea." With that, Elie handed her money for the tramway fare.

Tea! Tea with cake, and probably sandwiches, cookies! That did it for Radka, hungry as she was that day. She hesitated for a moment—she knew that contacts with foreigners were to be avoided, especially by "people's enemies" like herself. But the temptation was too big and she called the lady. The first encounter was very promising. Mrs. Yatsevitch was a charming, cultured American, obviously from a refined background, and the tea and cakes were delicious. Radka was hired and after a few lessons, her pupil made an offer: she needed a fulltime nanny for her two small boys. The salary, translated in local currency and after the misery of the last two years, sounded fabulous. "And during your off hours, the Colonel and I will, of course, treat you as a friend and a member of the family."

An offer one couldn't refuse, a solution to many of Radka's problems, a solution for Mama and Boubi too, she thought. And, who knows!, maybe a possibility of getting out of the country one day! She accepted and for the two years that followed, she was glad she did. Until…Until she lived to regret it.

Radka's new employers kept their promises fully. Colonel Gratian Yatsevitch turned out to be a highly intelligent and worldly young man who treated her as a lady and who quickly won her respect and total confidence. He and his wife also grew attached to Radka and sincerely tried to help her. Mama and Boubi, back to the suburbs of Sofia, visited her often in the comfortable villa in Boyana, formerly belonging to friends, prominent chocolate industrialists, and they were always received warmly and with great consideration. Boubi was working at various badly-paid manual jobs, and he and Mama were almost entirely supported by Radka. Her life improved immensely. Again she was among civilized people, able to eat well, dress nicely, and fall asleep without fear; most important, she felt like a human being again, like an attractive young woman of 22, respected and well-liked. Not only was she included in all parties at the Yatsevitches, but the Colonel and his wife introduced her to friends in the diplomatic corps and often took her to dinners and receptions at other Western missions. She met the British minister, the French and the Swiss ; young diplomats and cultural attaches began to invite her; everybody seemed to like her.

Her boss was particularly considerate and didn't hide his concern for her safety. To Radka's great shock, she soon became aware of the fact that every single Bulgarian working for foreign diplomats—secretaries, chauffeurs, valets, nannies and cooks,—had to submit regular reports to the Bulgarian State Security about the goings-on at the embassies. She was equally shocked to learn that every embassy was not only perfectly aware of that, but expected it when hiring its personnel, and in many cases helped the employees with preparing the reports. Col. Yatsevitch warned Radka that this might happen to her too,—at least the Militia would try to enlist her,—and therefore she should avoid leaving the premises unaccompanied by some American or other diplomat. But in case that happened, he gave her specific tips and detailed instructions how to behave and what to say. Radka was frightened, but her wise boss's advice gave her some reassurance, especially after a few of her close friends also working for foreign embassies confided in her that they were all compelled to serve as informers for the feared Militia. It was mostly about trivia—who were the dinner guests and what they talked about, does the boss drink too much, does he get along with his wife,— the only things that a chauffeur or a housemaid might notice in a household of diplomats too cautious to ever discuss politics or embassy business in front of the local staff. Nevertheless, the very idea of having to report was repulsive and frightening enough for Radka to make her decide not to ever leave the villa alone. It gave her a disturbing feeling of living in a cage, but at least it was a warm, friendly cage in which she had found some joy and understanding, and it was a screen against the brutal outside world which had wounded her so badly. Life was slowly becoming more normal, worth living, even pleasant at times. Then, in 1948, a telephone call brought her back to the dreaded reality.

The Colonel was away on business to Turkey. His trip coincided with the first official visit of Tito to Sofia, received with great fanfare by his then friend and ally Dimitrov. Radka was alone in the villa with Mrs. Yatsevitch and the children. The sinister voice on the phone, coarse and vulgar, belonged unmistakably to "one of them," Radka thought right away and it gave her shivers. The anonymous man informed her that Boubi had been arrested and if she really cared for him, she could help him, but she should meet a person who would come to see her with a note from Boubi. Soon after, Boubi himself called from jail, confirmed the message and asked her to send him food through that person—some cheese, he said, some salami and bread. Radka panicked, and sick with worries, went for advice to Mrs. Yatsevitch. The situation was really very serious, the American lady realized, and it was unfortunate that the colonel wasn't there to tell them what to do. It wasn't clear whether Boubi's arrest was part of a mass round-up of potential "security risks" during Tito's visit, or had some other reason. Needing the advice of some trustworthy friend, Mrs. Yatsevitch drove Radka and the children (to make the visit look less suspect) to the residence of the Swiss minister, an experienced diplomat who knew Radka's case well and had sympathy for her. He advised her to follow the instructions Col. Yatsevitch had given her strictly, namely not to leave the villa's grounds unescorted, no matter what the provocation. Radka remembered another of her boss's advices: if blackmailed by threats to the family, she should pretend that she didn't care for them, even if this sounded monstrous.

The man came to the villa, and indeed he was bringing a brief note from Boubi, saying that he was in a predicament and imploring Radka to help him. Please, he wrote, if you love me, do what this messenger would ask you. She was shaking while reading the letter, but the signature gave her a clue that the plea was a fake: Boubi had signed "Simeon," which was his given name, but which we never used in the family. The man wanted her to come with him, so she would visit her brother. Asking him to wait until she prepared the parcel, she went to inform Mrs. Yatsevitch. Then she handed him the food and said that she couldn't leave her job that day, but that she would think it over and would try another day.

Anonymous characters called her again and again, and each time she refused to go out to meet them. Tough as it was for her, she managed to convey the impression that she didn't care so much for her brother and that his difficulties were, after all, his problem, and not hers. When Boubi called again, saying that his fate depended on her, she found enough strength to turn him down coldly: "Sorry, Boubi, but I can't help you. I'm not going to lose my job because of you!" Meanwhile, the fear and guilt that he may be hurt by her fault didn't let her have a moment of peace. She was immensely relieved when he was freed, unharmed, and especially when he told her, when she saw him again, how he had hoped that she wouldn't fall into the trap. Weeks and months passed by, and the shock caused by the sinister plot began to heal slowly. Maybe it won't happen again, she hoped and prayed. But her boss was pessimistic. Col. Yatsevitch, a non-career officer whose duties at the US military mission in Sofia were rather unclear, but whose background and skills were uncommon (Polish-born, British educated, speaking foreign languages, including Russian and Serbo-Croatian), seemed to know much about the methods of State Security services and Militias in Communist countries. He warned Radka that these services would probably try again and may succeed the next time. Therefore, insisting that she be as prepared as possible for such an unpleasant ordeal, he intensified his coaching her in the art of surviving interrogations. Radka was immensely frightened; the horror stories of the tortures and beatings of a number of Bulgarian employees working with the British and the Americans, and refusing to cooperate with the Militia, were a public knowledge, and she knew a few of the victims personally. But the worst was that there was no exit, no way to resign and leave the job: the Militia wouldn't allow it. A few Bulgarians were lucky to marry foreign diplomats, even only pro forma, just to leave the country. The Yatsevitches and other foreign friends tried hard to arrange such a marriage (they pleaded with me too to find some "fiancé" in France), but it didn't work; in the meantime, there was a new law: changing nationality was no more allowed. Radka was now trapped. The only solution, a temporary one, was to take advantage of the extraterritorial status of the diplomats's homes, and not to leave the house without a foreign official.

It was a hard way to live, but there was no choice. By 1948, the last pretense of a "coalition government," of opposition parties or press, and of Anglo-American right to veto any Soviet or Bulgarian violation or excess, had disappeared. Despite all post-war agreements, the Western Allies ended by miserably abandoning Bulgaria to the Russians, whose representatives in Sofia no longer even bothered to keep informed their British and American colleagues in the Joint Commission or to answer their daily protests. Communist rule had become open and total. The police terror, bloody and savage since September 1944, was practiced now with no apology, and allowed no recourse for protest or appeal.

Radka's numerous foreign friends had no delusion that they could do much for her if she ever fell in the hands of the Militia, but they were willing to help prevent such an occurrence. Staying with the Yatsevitches became particularly dangerous—as an American military attaché, the colonel had become a prime target,—and it was high time to look for another job. Long before the Yatsevitches had to leave for another post, they made sure that some trusted colleagues, preferably not Americans, hired their *protégée*. The response of the British diplomats was admirably warm. Minister Mason and his wife offered the hospitality of their own residence, while looking for a job with some family from the embassy. Thus, during the following years, Radka worked as nanny at a number of British diplomats—the Greenhills, the Dunnetts, the Coxes,—all aware of her case and treating her, after the hours of household work and taking care of the babies, with respect and understanding. Before leaving their post, each family, as well as the always thoughtful Masons, made arrangements for Radka to be taken by another British family.

She seldom left home, except when visiting diplomats' houses, and always accompanied. With time, the vigilance was gradually relaxed, the fears began to appear exaggerated, paranoiac. Her bosses, noticing how hard she worked, always confined to their home, kindly suggested that a young woman like her should have a day off every week away from work, with friends and family. Her long confinement had become burdensome and Radka accepted the offer with gratitude. Again she could see old friends and spend a few hours with Mama and Boubi, when they came from the nearby village where they lived! Occasionally, to break her monotonous life-routine, she stayed to sleep in town, enjoying the luxury of a duty-free night.

*   *   *   *   *

One night, she was going to sleep at Elena Beneva's, a relative who had sheltered her many times before. She had crossed the small garden in front of the "Sveti-Sedmochislenitsi" church and was walking on "6th of September" street, when a black car pulled along Elena's entrance. Two men in civilian clothes jumped out and grabbed Radka. "Get in!" they barked and pushed her into the car. She was driven to the State Security headquarters at the "Lions' Bridge," the most dreaded building in town. Inside, as her taciturn escorts led her through the long corridors, they ordered her to turn her head toward the wall each time they crossed other persons, lest she see them or be seen. She was ushered into a nondescript room, where a man in uniform was waiting. The plainclothes men took seats next to him, remaining silent during the interrogation.

The Militia officer started by speaking slowly, trying even to sound polite. "Comrade," he said, "we're sure that you love your country and would be ready to do something for it..." He was addressing with the familiar "ti" ("thou"), rather than using the polite "you."

"Of course I do," answered Radka. While petrified with fear, she remembered Col. Yatsevitch's lessons: "Don't start by refusal to talk, by antagonizing them or talking back," he had said. "It will only aggravate your situation and they'll immediately proceed to violence. Try to gain time, try to learn what exactly they want and how much they know about you!"

"Good!" the officer said. "Because you care about our Fatherland, we need your help, as a good patriot. It's sad, but your employers are no friends of Bulgaria, they're working against Bulgaria. They're here to spy, to slander our country and help its enemies."

"I didn't know that," Radka said. "I've never heard them speaking against Bulgaria." The uniformed man gave her a severe look. "Listen, we know everything! And you'd better be truthful with us. Now tell us all!" The interrogation lasted several hours. He wanted her to tell them everything about the Dunnett family, their habits, their visitors, the things they talked about. Radka tried to be as vague as possible, without nevertheless to appear that she was hiding something or lying. She told them about the children and the household chores, but insisted that her bosses didn't talk much in front of her and that she stayed in the nursery when they had guests. But the officer, looking increasingly skeptical and displeased, repeated the same questions again and again, as if he was dismissing the answers she had already given. He asked about each one of the other

Bulgarians employed by the British, most of whom, she knew, were reporting regularly to the Militia; he was obviously checking on their reports. How come, he berated her, that she had recommended "fascists" like the cook Nasko or the chauffeurs Stefan and Kosta, all formerly employed at the Royal Palace? "Whom else would I know, when foreigners ask me to recommend a servant?" she tried to justify herself.

The hours passed by, the inquisitor's mood was switching from icy and menacing, to oily and seducing, and back to ominously official. She was getting tired and hungry—only a glass of water had been offered to her, and finally a cigarette, which she foolishly accepted, forgetting that smoking on empty stomach would make her sick. The session didn't seem to be ending, when she recalled another advice she had been given: "It's getting terribly late," she said looking at her watch, "and if I don't return now, my bosses will be mad and will fire me…Do you want me to lose my job?" The word "firing" had a magic effect. "No, comrade, absolutely not! It's imperative that you stay with the British!" She discerned a genuine concern on the Militia-men's faces.

It was late in the evening when they let her go. But not before she had to pick one of the code names they suggested for their future contacts. ("Tatiana, if I must have one," she said, thinking of "Evgueni Onegin".) And not before she had to sign a pledge to report each time her employers "speak or act against Bulgaria." She hated signing it, but the wording gave her some consolation: her definition of "Bulgaria" differed indeed totally from the Militia's.

As she walked in the empty, dark streets back to Elena's apartment, she saw a certain hope in the discovery that the dreaded Militia was, after all, not as omniscient as it boasted to be. Indeed, some questions that night indicated that there were many things it didn't know. But it was a meager comfort. The inquisitors' last words were still ringing in her ears: "We'll talk again. Soon. God help you if you tell anyone about this meeting!…"

      *   *   *   *

She didn't *tell* Mr. Dunnett. The following morning, she just put in front of him a note: "I was with them." The Englishman read it, look at her in silence, and tore it. Later, far from indiscreet ears and, hopefully, from hidden microphones, Radka's tale was heard by Mr. Robb, the embassy's First secretary, to whom Yatsevitch had entrusted her before leaving. She told him everything, and she kept reporting to him when the Militia contacted her again repeatedly, at irregular intervals. The Security agents persisted asking the same questions about the British, and Radka tried to answer by the same bland, anodyne generalities. Although the subjects sounded unimportant and harmless, she was extremely disturbed, hating herself for having to inform on people who had shown her so much understanding and trust; all the assurances of the British that it didn't matter because they expected it as part of the game, did little to allay her feeling of betrayal and ingratitude.

Things worsened when the Dunnetts left and Radka moved to the Cox family and the Militia ordered her to report once a week, on a fixed day. She would be told to go to a certain place, each time different, at a certain hour, and wait. "Be in front of the Russian monument! You'll see a tall man in a gray suit and a blue shirt, wearing sun glasses and carrying a brown suitcase. He'll turn around the monument three times, and then you'll follow him, pretending you haven't seen him." Radka would walk at a distance behind him and follow him into some house (usually a cooperative apartment building, but never the same one). While the man would knock on some door, she should stay way behind, in order not to see or be seen by the person who opens the door. Once inside the apartment, the agent would introduce himself by an obviously phony name, pull out a list with questions and order "Comrade Tatiana" to write. During the hour or two that took her to write her answers, the man wouldn't say much, nor would he read her report when she finished. He would simply put it in his briefcase and escort her to the door. Until the next time. Then, a new meeting place, a new face, a different apartment. But more and more often, the new Security man would start by admonishing her about last week's "home work." "What did you mean by writing this rubbish, comrade Tatiana? You'd better answer the questions properly this time, or else… Don't try to fool us, because you'll be sorry, I'm telling you! Now get to work!"

The situation was becoming serious. Indeed, Radka's long-winded "free compositions" were a cope-out, pages after pages of generalities about what the children ate, what color was the visitor's dress, how the dog got sick. With each weekly meeting, it became clear that the technique for outsmarting the Militia would no longer work. The agents' tone changed, it became rude and menacing, the questions became more precise. "What was the reaction at the diplomat's home to the news of Comrade Georgi Dimitrov's death?" "Describe exactly Mr. Cox's eating and drinking habits! Does he have a girlfriend? And Mrs. Cox, a boyfriend? How close are they to each other? How does he treat his children?…"

Disgusted, Radka went through agony each time she had to write her report, an abject violation of her human dignity. But the British insisted that she play the game, they even assisted her with the answers, as they did with the rest of their Bulgarian personnel. Then the Militia put new demands on her: she was enrolled in a course where some 15 or 20 young Africans and Arabs, men and women passing officially for "foreign students," were trained for subversive actions. Each week, the group would meet for "theoretical studies" at a place known as "The Fourth Kilometer," just outside Sofia, or be driven to some meadow on nearby Mount Vitosha for outdoor drills. Radka, not particularly gifted for sports, found herself being trained in the skills of stalking an "enemy" (an agent always played "the imperialist spy"), hiding weapons, dodging pursuers, shooting with pistol, even climbing up vertical ladders (she was helplessly clumsy at that one). The "students," who all spoke Bulgarian, would be placed in view of a passing train and taught, stop-watch in hand, how to count the number of railroad cars and evaluate the speed. Questions about other "students" ' origin or destination were strictly forbidden. At the end of the course, written exams and target-shooting tests were held, which Radka failed miserably, inviting insulting remarks from her contemptuous instructors.

She reported everything not to her boss, Cox, but to his superior, the First secretary Robb, a wise and discreet gentleman whom she trusted fully. She used to see him alone at his home, preferably outside or in a room with the radio or the phonograph blaring, usually on the third day after each Militia contact. Robb lived on the ground floor of the old Malinov house, on "Evlogui Georgiev" street, conveniently near the Cox apartment where she lived. The pretext for the visits was that Robb had asked Cox to "lend" him Radka to teach his new house-keeper how to organize dinners, set tables and arrange flowers, know-hows for which Radka had a good reputation among the British and American diplomats.

But her nerves couldn't take it much longer. She was scared and knew that the vise was closing in on her. Robb, also worried about her safety, agreed that some way should be found for her to leave the British, without arousing the suspicion of the Militia, which was categorically opposed. But how? It was decided to try some medical pretext. An English doctor suggested that faking a kidney ailment would be least likely to detect. Radka received detailed briefings on the symp-toms and began acting as a person suffering from serious kidney problems. For the benefit of servants and visitors, she pretended to have kidney attacks and pains, then went on a strict diet. She also made sure to mention it to her Militia contacts. The "crises" became frequent, until the Embassy's Bulgarian doctor was summoned. As Radka went through the act, he examined her thoroughly, then closed the door and whispered in a friendly voice: "Now tell me, Radka, what do you want me to put on the certificate?"

Finally, she told Mr. and Mrs. Cox that she was too sick to work and resigned officially. Unfortunately, something unforeseen happened, which disturbed the plans. Since the Coxes weren't in the know, they were genuinely alarmed and rushed to the Minister and his wife, pleading with them to find a shelter for poor, sick Radka. The Masons immediately invited her to stay in their own home until she recovers. This created a problem: Radka couldn't refuse the invitation, but it was putting in jeopardy the entire plot. Desperate, she turned to Mrs. Mason and begged her, implored her, to find a credible pretext to chase her out.

The agreed-upon "scandal" erupted two days later, as Radka was having tea with the nanny and the Mason children, while some servants were working around. Suddenly, Mrs. Mason busted in, mad as a fury, and turned on Radka, screaming: "I don't want spies in my house! Get out of here right now, you, traitorous Communist agent!" With Radka sobbing hysterically, Mrs. Mason escorted her down to the entrance. "I don't want to see you ever again!" she shouted, then turned to the stunned servants: "Never let her in! She is a Militia spy!"

Once in the street, Radka could hardly control her joy. Walking to Elena's apartment, she was thinking, highly relieved: "At last, I'm free! The Militia nightmare is over. I outwitted them!" The next day she didn't go to the weekly State Security appointment. Nothing happened. She missed the following date too, and there was still no sign from the Militia. She decided that she'll never see them again, and started looking for a job. Mama and Boubi, who then lived in Sofia, resumed visiting her at Elena's apartment, where they were showing my letters, photos and parcels from Paris to each other and happily discussed my Irish romance with Neelia.

*   *   *   *   *

It was an evening when Mama and Bouby were about to come, that the Jeep stopped in front of the house and two plain-clothes agents came to the apartment. "Come with us!" they ordered Radka rudely. They acted very angry. "What do you mean by not coming to the rendezvous?" they asked in the car. "Do you imagine that you can play tricks on us? You'll be sorry!"

"You know that I'm sick. You know that the English kicked me out..."

"We know nothing!. You'll have a lot of explaining to do now!..."

The officer in uniform at the State Security building received her with an outburst of fury and insults. Rude and abusive, he shouted a litany of accusations—why did she let herself to be fired by the British; how dare she try to cheat the Militia; why didn't she keep her appointments... his ugly face was distorted by hatred as he interspersed his tirade with ominous remarks, such as "We'll teach you how to obey!..." Hatred and fanaticism also filled the eyes of the plain-clothes agents flanking the officer, as well as the two sinister looking youngsters sitting silently on a long bench in the corner.

"Now get undressed!" the officer ordered and the young men jumped to their feet and seized their victim. Nothing had ever felt as degrading as being stripped stark naked in front of these man. They put her on the bench, face down, and tied up her wrists and ankles with leather belts. Then the beating began.

She couldn't see what she was being hit with, she only felt the atrocious pain. It was something very heavy, not a whip, not belts, nothing sharp; they didn't use their fists either. Later on, she learned from friends who had gone through the same torture, that the Militia "beaters" used long, narrow sacks filled with sand, which didn't leave scars. At the beginning, she was determined not to cry or scream, no matter how bad the pain. But as the blows rained over her back and buttocks, the pain became unbearable and she started screaming. At certain point, she fainted and the "beaters" poured a bucket of cold water over her to revive her. When she regained conscience, she expected that the beating would resume. But the torture ended and she was untied. "Get up and get dressed!" the boss shouted. Staggering across the room, she put her clothes on. Everything ached and she found it difficult not only to walk, but even to collect her thoughts. In a fog, she heard the officer hissing: "Is it clear now that you'll do what we tell you to do? Get out of here and remember well this lesson!..."

There is more than a mile from the Lyon's Bridge to the "6th of September" street, and with no buses in service after midnight, the long walk turned into another ordeal, the back hurting at each step and the swollen feet dragging pathetically. It was already dawn when Radka collapsed on her bed. "I worried about you. Where were you all night?" Elena greeted her the next morning. "A boy-friend?" She gave her a conspiratorial wink. Radka nodded affirmatively. "Good for you! But what shall we tell your mother and Boubi? They were here last night, waiting until late, and left very worried."

Indeed, Mama and Boubi were extremely upset when they came two days later. My brother fulminated: "How could you stay out so late? How can you do such a thing? Where have you been?" Mama was weeping. "I spent the night at my boyfriend's," Radka answered calmly. They were stricken. "Your father would turn in his grave!" Mama cried out. And Boubi, shocked beyond belief, could only say: "Shame on you! You're dishonoring the Groueff name!" before he slammed the door.

It was very painful for Radka to hurt those two beloved people, who already had their own share of suffering and sorrow. But she felt that she shouldn't tell them the truth. It would be too much of a burden; under this police regime, sharing a terrible secret could only mean endangering the loved ones and adding to their worries and troubles.

Before letting her go from the State Security building, her inquisitors ordered her to resume working for foreign diplomats. They rejected her excuses that nobody would hire her after the scandal with the British, which everybody had heard of. "Don't you worry, we'll take care of that! We know exactly what vacancies there are at each embassy, and we'll find you a job!" With that, they gave her a rendezvous for the following week. In a way, Radka was relieved. She knew that Mr. Robb had asked all British and Americans not to hire her, and had spread the rumor among the Western diplomats that Radka was probably an informer. But she also knew that the Militia officer was telling the truth: exclusively, the Bureau for Assistance to Foreigners, controlled by State Security, supplied all Bulgarian personnel at the foreign missions.

When she arrived at the rendezvous at the back door of the "Sveti-Sedmochislenitsi" church, an unknown man addressed her as "Comrade Tatiana," gave her the name of an employee of the Bureau at the Ministry of Foreign Affairs, and instructed her to go and see him right away. The Bureau sent her for an interview with a French family. During the few days she had to wait for the answer, Radka prayed with all her heart that the French would refuse. She was greatly relieved when the negative answer came, but the Militia didn't give up. Another interview was arranged, this time with a Swiss family. The same anguished wait, the same reply. Thus, a long, exhausting series of job interviews followed, bringing Radka to other Frenchmen, to Argentineans, to all sorts of Western diplomats. Luckily for her, no one showed interest. Meanwhile, Radka, acting disappointed, was telling the persistent Militia: "You see, it's not my fault if everybody refuses to hire me! Do you think it's easy for me to be jobless and starving? You know that I'm ready to take any job—nanny, chamber maid, kitchen help,—but nobody wants me. Your Bureau is also trying, and they're failing too. I think everybody suspects me to be working for you…"

Did the Militia finally realize that Radka had become useless as an informer? The fact is that one day, after several months of persistent but unsuccessful efforts by the Bureau to place her with some Western family, the regular weekly rendezvous on a street corner ended without the agent fixing the hour and place of the next meeting. Still afraid to hope too much, she waited for another week, then another. State Security had cut the line. No sinister voice called to ask for "Comrade Tatiana" anymore.

*   *   *   *

Chapter 16

"The Free Bulgarians". Radio "Free Europe"

As a platoon commander in the Fourth Battery, Second-lieutenant Jordan Peyev was an object of unanimous admiration. I knew him before I went to serve my military service, at the home of the Panitza-Yablansky family, where he was invited often and had impressed the hosts, as well as their guests, not only with his good looks of a dashing officer, but also with his worldly manners and, for his age, the unusual maturity and political savvy. Mrs. Yablansky, who could be quite an intimidating old lady, loved to discuss the international situation with him and often she and her bridge partners would interrupt their game to heard some opinion from the brilliant lieutenant. While Sava and I, 19 years of age, wouldn't have dared to intrude in conversations about politics between older persons such as Prime Minister Bogdan Filov, the opposition leader Nikola Moushanov, and a scattering of foreign diplomats, also frequent guests to that home, "Dantcho," only five or six years older than us, didn't hesitate to air his opinions and even express, respectfully and eloquently, some disagreement with them.

Like most officers of that period, Peyev was an ardent patriot and convinced anti-communist, deeply concerned about the Soviet threat to Bulgaria, without sharing however many of his colleagues' admiration for the impressive victories of the German army. His sympathies, albeit discreetly, were on the side of the Western democracies. Descendent from a family from North Dobrudja, Dantcho had lost his father at an early age and had grown up worshipping his uncle, the former Chief-of-Staff general Peyev, assassinated recently under un-clarified circumstances. Another decisive influence in his youth was that of his aunt and her French husband, who lived in France and thanks to whom he had learned French and was reading French books and publications. He had befriended Sava and me, but it was a friendship based more on respect than on complicity in amusements or chasing girls, for which he appeared more serious than us.

Once we donned our soldiers' uniforms, our relationship took a different dimension. Since the very first day, we realized that in the regiment the friend "Dantcho" ceased to exist; he became the commander, to be addressed by "Yes, Sir!" and "Permission to speak freely, Sir!" Only in the rare moments when we found ourselves alone with him, could we address him by his first name. Then he would give us the avidly expected news from our families and friends. But as far as the service was concerned, he was much more demanding toward us than toward the other soldiers. In the matter of a few days, Dantcho won my total respect and became the role model for the entire battery. Indeed, he possessed all the qualities with which a commander wins the admiration of his subordinates. To begin with his impressive appearance, a tall (6 ft.2), svelte officer in a well-tailored uniform and dapper, custom-made high boots. Soon, one noticed his good education and solid knowledge of history and the Bulgarian classics. Peyev spoke to his soldiers with all the authority of a real leader, combined with the ardor of a preacher and the spell exercised by a favorite school teacher. His skill in shooting with rifle and pistol was unmatched in the regiment, and his virtuosity and audacity when driving a car or a motorcycle astounded the soldiers. Although we were a motorized unit, Peyev kept his own horse in the regiment and rode him around during the lunch recess, a welcome show in the monotonous day of the barracks. But most contagious of all were his 'boy scout-ish' enthusiasm for civic and military virtues and his cult for the notion of duty and service to "our just national cause." One must note that such a combination of rectitude, solid education, patriotism, and sense of duty, characterized the majority of the alumni of the Royal Military School before the war. It used to be a remarkable educational institution, whose contribution to the formation of Bulgarian elite is yet to be fully appreciated. In this respect, Peyev was no exception. But in addition to these qualities, he was blessed with the intangible, indefinable gift, which makes a star only a few chosen ones among equally talented actors, politicians, or sportsmen. No doubt, Dantcho possessed this "star quality." And it was so shattering for me to see him, some four years later, at the railroad station in Paris. The fat, half-paralyzed and gray human ruin that came out of, or, rather, was carried down from the train car, bore no resemblance to the dashing officer I knew before; this wreck had nothing left of the star of the Sofia artillery regiment. I learned later that Peyev had been involved in some risky conspiracies and been caught when trying to smuggle people across the border (among them was the Russian refugee in Bulgaria, Prince Lobanov). During the interrogations, and then in prison, he underwent severe torture, which broke him physically and which he refused to discuss with us. Luckily, he was punished only for the smaller infraction (attempt at illegally crossing the border), while, thanks to his exceptional willpower, he didn't succumb to the pressure to confess the more serious crime (conspiracy against the government). Finally released, with the help of his French uncle, Peyev came to France for medical treatment. After long months under the care of his aunt, and still walking with canes, he moved to Paris, where we were reunited again around the recently arrived Panitza family.

If the slender figure of a lieutenant from the glory days was gone forever, none of the patriotic flame and leadership qualities seemed to be affected during his transfiguration into a political refugee. On the contrary, his personal experience in communist Bulgaria had given him a new stimulus and had proven invaluable in his determination to launch himself into the resistance cause.

My very long exile taught me that while our emigration abounded with excellent privates and the anti-communist "train" was composed of first-class "wagons," extremely rare were the people who could serve as "locomotives." The latter requires special talents of organizer, initiator, and leader, and they are not necessarily to be found in every ardent patriot or wise statesman. I would put myself, as well as most of my ideological friends into the category of sincerely dedicated activists, ready to join and contribute to the struggle, even at some personal risks. In other words, the category of the "railroad cars." But in all those long, somber years in exile, I hadn't met more than a handful of "locomotives," those who say "Let's go!" who know how to organize, who decide where the others will assemble and at what time, and who will push them and send them a reminder the night before. I'll list a few names, without trying to judge their ideas or activities. The Agrarian party leader Dr. G.M. Dimitrov was such a "locomotive." Ivan Dochev, of the national Legions, was another one. I know that the Macedonian organization's Ivan ("Vanche") Mihailov was a powerful "locomotive," although I never succeeded in meeting him personally, as I didn't meet Prof. Alexander Tzankov, who was followed by many patriots abroad. Among the people with whom I shared the same political credo, the man who emerged as the most successful "locomotive" was Jordan Peyev, who revealed himself such an energetic and effective organizer, that in a short period of time he succeeded in rallying an impressive part of the exiles' elite.

His first initiative was the monthly review *Vazrazhdane* ("Renaissance," "Revival"), which Peyev started with Dianko Sotirov and myself in the beginning of 1949 in Paris. Dianko had already won himself a good reputation of a bright and respected believer in democracy, always ready to help anti-communist initiatives. As for myself, Peyev chose me because he trusted me since Sofia, knew about my previous participation in the Paris group around the newspaper *Le Peuple Bulgare*, and was aware of my active contacts with prominent Bulgarian exiles. Our first issue was published in January. "Our brethren in Bulgaria are deprived of free press," we proclaimed, "and unfortunately the Bulgarians abroad are not informed in an objective way either, and have no efficient means to express themselves. Fully aware of the imperative need for free publications, we are offering our modest contribution to the missing periodical literature of enslaved Bulgaria."

The small format review had a gray cover and each issue contained about 40 pages in small print. It was produced in a Russian printing house and we used the old Bulgarian orthography, keeping the few letters of the alphabet that were abolished by the new regime. Our pages, however, were open to free discussion of the orthography controversy, provided that the conflicting opinions were well argued. As editors, the three of us insisted particularly on literary language, dignity in the tone, and respect for differing opinions. Some articles were also printed in French translation. Such was, for instance, the case with our political platform. "The struggle for liberation from Bolshevik captivity, as well as the defense of the national interests, are the duty and the right of every true patriot...We want full restoration of the (pre-Communist) Tirnovo Constitution...All litigious questions concerning the form of government shall be settled after the Liberation and according to the democratic procedures prescribed by the Constitution itself...The leadership of the liberation struggle and the representation abroad of the Bulgarian nation should be assured by a supreme national body, comprising the most prominent, respected, and active personalities among the Bulgarians in exile...Therefore, we insist on an acceptable agreement between the different political groups, and on the inclusion of refugees not belonging to any organized group or party."

So far, so good; few people would quarrel with such principles. But the paragraphs that followed brought to the open some of the controversial issues that divided the emigration. A number of refugee activists belonged to the former Agrarian Union and to groups that had worked with the "Fatherland Front," the Communist creation which overthrew the last legitimate government. Soon disappointed, they had turned against the Communists and had been brutally persecuted by them. Some managed to flee the country and were organized in Dr. G.M. Dimitrov's "National Committee." Now they claimed to have received from the Bulgarian people an "exclusive mandate" to represent the nation. The rest of the emigration, consisting of people never involved with the "Fatherland Front," could not, of course, accept such exaggerated claim of monopoly, especially that Dr. Dimitrov and his entourage belonged mostly to the group *Pladne*, a leftist, minority faction of the Agrarian Union. Most emigrants were skeptical as to how much "Pladne" represented the mainstream of the Agrarians, whose last legitimate government (Premier K.Mouraviev's) it helped to overthrow...Without denying the courageous contribution to the anti-communist cause of Dr. G.M. Dimitrov and many of his collaborators, *Vazrazhdane* didn't hide its disagreement with their methods and left-wing ideas, and rejected categorically their claim for having a "mandate" to represent us abroad.

The three of us—Dantcho Peyev, Dianko Sotirov, and myself—prepared the platform, as well as most of the material for the first two or three issues of "Vazrazhdane," with the enthusiastic assistance of Stati, Mika Panitza, Bontcho Dimitrov, and the new, 18-year-old refugee, Dimi Panitza. Immediately after the publication of the first issue, numerous friends and other compatriots expressed their approval and readiness to help. Bulgarians in Paris, so far uninvolved in any organization, established regular contact with us, among them the businessman

Kyril Bougartchev, the philology professor Christoforov, and the former secretary at the embassy, George Damyanov. Students, such as Matei Hroussanov and Dimitry Panev, joined us, as did a cheerful, adventurous youth from the port city of Bourgas, Steftcho Apostolov, recently escaped with his accordion, disguised as a sailor on a foreign ship. Christo Shishmanov, a former royal diplomat well respected for his integrity and moderation, became a regular and very wise adviser, and, of course, we could always count on the friendship and assistance of Evgueni Silianoff. From England, the entire Stancioff clan, plus my childhood friend Liliana Daneva-Brisby, offered their collaboration, and so did Christo Boyadjiev and his group in Rio-de-Janeiro, and also my old friends in Geneva. There was no doubt that "Vazrazhdane" had touched a sensitive chord in many Bulgarians not belonging to any party.

For the first issue, I wrote an article entitled "September 9th -a bright, or a black date?" and signed "Pavel S." (the pseudonym I used, out of concern for my family in Bulgaria), In it I maintained that the Soviet-backed coup of September 9th, 1944, glorified as a "Liberation" by the new regime, was in fact the starting point for the destruction of the traditional Bulgarian values, the suppression of freedom and human rights, and the beginning of the monstrous terror. A shameful, baleful date. Many well-intended Bulgarians admitted later that the Fatherland Front had fooled them, and many paid dearly for their naiveté or mistake. No one should, of course, deny them the right to join the struggle; but we cannot accept the insistence of former Communist collaborators that only they had been right, while the Fatherland Front's critics were nothing but "fascists" or "reactionaries."

The readers' favorable reaction to the ideas expressed in *Vazrazhdane* stimulated us to double our efforts. Our meetings in different Paris cafes or in Panitzas' home became more frequent and the time Dianko and I devoted to the review began to fill a considerable portion of our day. At that time, Dianko was without a job, but with his characteristic sense of dignity and always neat appearance, nobody would've guessed that he and his wife Mimi were under financial strain and had to make ends meet only with her modest salary. As for myself, I was in the midst of my Irish romance, and since the spring, was working at *Paris-Match*, therefore I had, outside of *Vazrazhdane*, a busy private life and career. Neither had I neglected some hobbies: I continued attending jazz concerts of visiting American musicians, such as Louis Armstrong and Rex Stewart, and spent late nights at *Le Vieux Colombier*, mesmerized by the soprano-sax of my jazz idol, Sidney Bechet. Sometimes I tried my clarinet with George Damyanov, an eager guitarist, or with Steftcho Apostolov, whose talent on the accordion and the piano matched his carefree, bohemian charm. Nevertheless, my interest in Bulgarian affairs remained intact. Thus, for instance, each time I went to Ireland, I made a stop in London, where I discovered a great sympathy for *Vazrazhdane* among the local Bulgarian colony, including, surprisingly, prominent critics of King Boris' policy during WW2, such as the famous *BBC* commentator Mrs. Vlada Karastoyanova, and Michael Padev, a Bulgarian who had established himself as an influential British journalist.

As far as private life or recreations were concerned, Peyev was different. *Vazrazhdane* had absorbed him totally, had become his 24-hours-a-day obsession. Having put everything else aside, progressively neglecting his physical appearance, sleep and regular eating, Dantcho lived exclusively with and for *Vazrazhdane*. His only relaxation were the meals around "the Round table" at the Panitzas, where he would arrive lugging his heavy leather briefcase, bursting with papers. But even there his conversation turned inevitably to the review. During the first year of publication, *Vazrazhdane* was financed entirely with his private money, the allowance received from his aunt. Not only did Peyev write articles and edited the review, he also took care of the printing (he had a passion for printing presses and was quite knowledgeable about them), the galley proofs, the mail, and the constant search for collaborators, subscribers, and sponsors.

Vazrazhdane continued in the spirit of tolerance and objectivity, always ready to quote from publications of other anti-communist groups, even when we had reservations about some of their leaders and opinions. The approval this moderate approach received from the readers surpassed all our expectations. It was as if the emigration was waiting for the creation of such an unbiased forum, to give it immediately its trust and to flood us with enthusiastic letters. Praises were coming from everywhere, Former Premier Kiosseivanov congratulated us from Switzerland. New York's bishop Andrey sent his blessing. Former ministers N.P.

Nikolaev and Sava Kirov accepted readily to join our circle. From the Royal palace in exile, colonel Maltchev, aide-de-camp of the Queen and the child-king, wrote me that we were "on the right track." And what encouragement were to us the compliments we received from almost all exiled former diplomats and public figures we held in high respect! But more than anything, the touching letters we began to receive from unknown refugees in camps in Greece and Italy, warmed our hearts.

The number of people sharing *Vazrazhdane* ideas was growing rapidly, like a snowball rolling down a steep hill. Heartened by the success, Dantcho extended his activity in other, parallel directions. Thanks to his uncle's connections among the European Christian-democrats movements (it was the period when they governed most of Western Europe: Schumann in France, Adenauer in Germany, De Gasperi in Italy, Van Zeeland in Belgium), Dantcho founded a Bulgarian section at the *Nouvelles Equipes Internationales* and through it we were included into the nascent initiative for United Europe. A summer issue of *Vazrazhdane* was thus dedicated to the European idea. Particularly enthusiastic about United Europe were our friends Silianoff and Zdravko Tsankoff. Peyev and Sotirov gave public conferences in Paris, well attended by the emigration. At the same time, Dantcho tried to organize a small communal farm for newly arrived Bulgarian refugees, at Herouville, just outside of Paris.

Until September, we represented just an ideological circle around our review. But the idea of creating an organization that would activate politically all Bulgarians living in freedom and coordinate the activities of the existing different patriotic groups, was ripening perceptibly and many of our adherents urged us to realize it. As a result, Dantcho, Dianko and I drafted a project for an organization and sent printed invitations to all Bulgarians in Paris to come and discuss it with us. The reunion was to be held at the Geographic Society on boulevard St.-Germain, on the 10th of September, at 8:30 in the evening. When we arrived, the auditorium was filling rapidly. But in addition to the public we had expected, we noticed a number of unfamiliar faces, casting rather hostile looks in our direction. To our surprise, the rostrum on the podium to which we headed, was already occupied by Milka Ghenadieva-Boeuf, Tsenko Barev, and a few of their followers, none of them friends of *Vazrazhdane*. Before we could understand what was going on, a bunch of burly toughs guys grabbed us and barred us from taking our places at the dais. Some of their confederates, obviously men freshly arrived from the refugee camps, blocked the exits. As Peyev was trying desperately to read his introductory remarks, Milka's and Tsenko's cohorts rudely prevented him from speaking, while the usurpers of the dais announced that this meeting had in reality been called by the Bulgarian legation with the purpose of sabotaging the liberation movement. But Dr. G.M. Dimitrov's National Committee, sole leader of the struggle, was not going to permit this provocation, they said. "We have information that the communist legation wants to use as front an association which calls itself "The Free Bulgarians," That's why we decided to come here to this meeting and declare that the real Free Bulgarians, that's us!" announced Milka, without batting an eye.

We couldn't believe our ears, hearing such monstrous accusations from the mouths of people who knew us sufficiently well and with whom we used to collaborate! But Tsenko and Milka's words were met with loud applause by the long mistreated refugees, aroused by the G.M.'s committee, which had met the same afternoon and had given orders to its troops to "seize the gathering." The menacing expression on their faces indicated that they didn't have the slightest idea who we were and that they believed sincerely that we were helping the communists. As we insisted on being heard, someone hit Dantcho and a rain of blows fell over Dianko and myself. Our friends rushed to our rescue and in a moment the auditorium of the venerable Geographic Society was transformed into a rowdy arena, resounding with angry screams and foul Bulgarian curses. Frightened ladies and gentlemen tried frantically to leave the premises, only to find the doors barred. Others opened windows and started yelling "Help! Police!"

Menacing hombres encircled me and my chances of escaping without serious corporeal damages appeared extremely slim when, diving over the melee, Christos Sarbov, who had come with the Agrarians contingent, took position at my side. "Don't touch Groueff!" he roared to my assailants, as he took a boxing posture. "Don't you touch him, or you'll have to deal with me!" The bullyboys stopped dead in their tracks, wondering on which side this prominent member

of their committee was fighting. But his powerful shoulders proved to be a sufficient argument for them not to insist further. Protecting me with his iron fists,
Christos escorted me out to the boulevard, just as the police were invading the
building and putting an end to the free-for-all. He was visibly ashamed of the
behavior of his fellow-partisans. "Don't judge them too harshly!" he whispered as
we parted. "They aren't bad guys, but they've been misled."

Disheveled and out of breath, some with bleeding noses, the friends of
Vazrazhdane were leaving the building and converging on the sidewalk. I was
shaking with indignation and shame, and tears were rolling down my cheeks.
Everybody was deeply shocked and it took us some time to recover. But then
something unexpected happened. Instead of disbanding and going home, we all
headed for a nearby cafe, where, still agitated, we spontaneously voted to form a
new organization. That was how the Society of the *Free Bulgarians* was born on
that September evening in Paris. The next morning, the by-laws were filed with
the French authorities. The first elected officers were Jordan Peyev, president;
Dianko Sotirov, vice-president; Stephane Groueff, secretary; and Bontcho
Dimitrov, treasurer. It was the first time I came out officially with my name.

In October, we rented a club in the center of Paris, not far from the Bulgarian
legation. The apartment at 174, rue de l'Universite had a spacious room for
reunions, but as it was too big and expensive for us, we sublet a room to a Polish
emigrant, Volsky, while I moved into the other bedroom, for which I paid one
third of the rent. The organization grew incredibly fast and in one month after its
creation we counted over 100 members with paid dues. In addition to the officers,
a Council, including former ministers Kirov and Nikolaev, Evstati Panitza, Christo
Shishmanov, Prof. Christoforov, Kiril Bougartchev, governed the Free Bulgarians
and a few other respected Bulgarians. Bishop Andrey, who came from New York
for the occasion, solemnly inaugurated the club on October 28th. Over 120 people
attended the ceremony at which Bishop Andrey blessed us and said: "I'm happy to
see you so inspired and united in your love for our people and our Holy Church,
and I came to bless you and encourage you. You founded your organization of The
Free Bulgarians to serve the common cause of the entire nation, without succumb-
ing to any partisan bias. Keep your purity and your idealism, and you'll always have

God's blessing and the support of the Church. Keep the same purity and Christian values you have in your review; it's because of this spirit and style that *Vazrazhdane* is received with joy by all those who read it in America." A week later, Bishop Andrey blessed also our commune for refugees in Herouville. With these two ceremonies, the only Bulgarian high church dignitary in the free world put all his prestige and influence behind the Free Bulgarians.

Having a club facilitated greatly our organizational work and allowed us to meet regularly every week. *Vazrazhdane*, enriched by many new contributors, continued publication through 1950 and 1951. Our "elder statesmen"— Nikolaev, Kirov and Shishmanov—became increasingly involved. With the help of Bishop Andrey, we founded a church community in Paris," Saint-Ivan-Rylski," with Evstati Panitza as president. At the same time, a Youth section was added to the organization. With the rapid growth in membership and prestige among refugees and foreigners, The Free Bulgarians imposed themselves as one of the three important exiles organizations, gathering the moderate and the non-party émigrés of the center of the political spectrum, and filling the space between Dr. G.M. Dimitrov's "National Committee" on the left, and the National Front, on the right.

The United States, the only great Power at that time to show some interest in exiles organizations, had given its exclusive support to Dr. Dimitrov's committee, which didn't recognize any other group or organization. Disappointed, but not discouraged, The Free Bulgarians opened negotiations for cooperation with some National Front leaders, such as the older statesman Christo Statev and the brilliant intellectual Stefan Popov, as well as with a former Agrarian Union member of Parliament, engineer Toncho Tenev. Tenev, who had severed all ties with G.M. Dimitrov's left-wing faction *Pladne* and was trying to organize the Agrarians of the centrist core of the Union, had escaped to Paris, where we established good relationship with him and launched together a few common initiatives.

In October 1950, Stefan Popov came to visit us in Paris and we agreed to commission representatives of *The Free Bulgarians*, the *National Front*, and Tenev's agrarians, to explore together the possibilities of unifying our activities. In discussions about eventually forming a united National representation abroad, a few names seemed to get a general consensus: Kiosseivanov, Bishop Andrey, former ministers N.P. Nikolaev, Sava Kirov and Christo Statev, industrialist Ivan T. Balabanov, former head of military intelligence, Colonel Kostov. All of them were well-known personalities who refused to work with G.M. Dimitrov's *National Committee*. We also agreed to seek the approval of the Royal palace in exile. Our wishes to see the Americans revise their policy of according a monopoly to Dr. Dimitrov were somewhat encouraged when Kiosseivanov and Ivan Balabanov were discreetly invited for conversations in Washington. But with, or without American support, we were determined to try to unify the emigration. To that goal, The Free Bulgarians gave a mandate to Kirov and Shishmanov to sound out ex-Premier Kiosseivanov. We were all cautiously optimistic as to the feasibility of creating a sort of government in exile accepted by all, and the first part of 1951 was devoted to conversations and negotiations concerning this initiative.

The fact that the most respected public figures in exile were writing to me personally, trusted me, and sometimes even asked for my opinion, filled me with pride, but at the same time placed a heavy burden on my young (I was just 27) shoulders. I couldn't help feeling flattered when receiving letters from ex-Premier Kiosseivanov, Bishop Andrey and ministers and diplomats from my father's generation. "Your initiative to unify the emigration outside of GMD's *National Committee* is reasonable and useful, although it comes rather late," Dr. Nikolaev wrote me from Sweden. "You must hurry and not waste valuable time in trying to convince some particular individuals. As the proverb says, 'While the wise are making up their minds, the crazy are frolicking to their heart's content'. Anyhow, they (meaning Dr. Dimitrov's group) managed to register themselves before the Western world as the sole 'mandataries' of the Bulgarian people and to collect the gate money. Thank you for the honor of asking me for my opinion… Gather all valuable forces, and since this isn't possible without some compromises, be careful in the process not to betray our basic beliefs and not to lose complete hold of the general leadership. The participation of 'neutral' people, such as Kiosseivanov, Ivan Balabanov, etc. is very welcome. Your position concerning GMD's committee (after this projected unification, to look for an all-Bulgarian unification), is very correct…"

As teenagers, we were always intimidated by the prominent industrialist Ivan T. Balabanov, the very strict father of daughters with whom we used to play, and later to flirt. Now the same formidable parent was writing me from Italy: "I'm invited to participate in a European Movement conference. Please talk to Shishmanov and Kirov and tell me whether I should accept." Another time he commented on my letter about our unification initiative: "The way you project it, I'm not only ready to take part, but I'll put into it all my energy and abilities—but as a private only! I don't know anything about politics. But my impulsive character and blunt candor are incompatible with a leading position in a political action. How do you imagine putting in a responsible position a man like me, who wrote to Prime Minister Filov that his economic policy was driving Bulgaria to a disaster? Who asked dictator Georgi Dimitrov, in the presence of nine people and two stenographers, whether he was lying, or it was his government that followed a policy differing from their announced program? A man who wrote to the Communist leaders that nationalizing the economy would lead to a catastrophe?..." And the important international businessman concluded: "You took the right road, which no serious and good Bulgarian could criticize, and I congratulate you!"

The Free Bulgarians started with high hopes. Hopes for unification of all Bulgarians in exile; hopes that the Western democracies were beginning to understand us and would, sooner or later, come to our rescue. Early in the 1950s, all this seemed feasible and realistic. Myself, and my friends, we had no doubts that our country's 'nightmarish' regime was only a temporary aberration. In those years, we still believed in "the Liberation," expected it, and deluded ourselves that we were working for it…

*   *   *   *   *

RADIO "FREE EUROPE," MUNICH

When Bill Rafael of *Radio Free Europe* looked me up in Paris in the summer of 1951, I thought it was in connection with the few scripts I had written for that station. I went to our appointment very willingly, because I liked working for them and also because earning any fees was a welcomed supplement to my modest *Paris-Match* salary.

As soon as he greeted me with a few warm words and shook heartily my hand, Rafael won me with his charm. He was a friendly, outgoing American in his mid-thirties, with a warm smile and lively eyes, exuding energy and humor. His voice was the marvelous baritone that only American radio announcers seem to possess, and he spoke convincingly and with great authority. At the same time, when animated, his round face turned rosy with the shine of a shy adolescent which added to his charm and betrayed a highly emotional nature.

After a few compliments for my radio scripts, Rafael went straight to the true purpose of his visit. The New York based *Radio Free Europe*, he said, had recently moved its news services in Polish, Czech and Hungarian languages to Munich. The bulk of the programs—political commentaries, ideological articles and polemics,—remained in New York, where the headquarters of the radio were located. Only the information bulletin, broadcast to the three countries, was prepared in Munich, with no editorializing or comments. Rafael was the program director for these news services. "Now we decided to also transfer there the Bulgarian and Rumanian information bulletins," he told me, as he went on with a detailed presentation of the mission and the goals of *Radio Free Europe*.

It was one of the most brilliant and inspiring pleadings of the enslaved nations' cause that I had ever heard from the mouth of a foreigner. Not only did his analysis of the problems show a remarkable knowledge of communism in general and the internal situation in these countries, in particular, but the concrete radio program he was proposing, revealed a dash and imagination that filled me with enthusiasm. Rafael was in his element, inspired, convinced and convincing, bursting with original ideas and practical suggestions. While he spoke, his eyes were burning with the spark of a missionary in full action. At the end, he looked me straight in the eye and said: "We're proposing to you to come with us to Munich and take charge of this new service."

The unexpected proposition surprised me and disturbed me profoundly. Although I was flattered, and our ideas seemed to be in full accordance, it would've been absurd for me to accept. If the offer had come a year or two earlier,

I probably wouldn't have turned it down. But now? Just when things were beginning to look bright at *Paris-Match,* when my journalistic dreams were coming true and my private life seemed finally to be better organized! Indeed, 1952 was a good year for me. My work was becoming more interesting and promising. *Paris-Match* was sending me frequently to London, where I made many friends. In the spring, I went to represent the magazine on a wonderful junket for journalists in Spain, Morocco, and Tangiers. Then I also covered stories in Marseille and elsewhere in France. In the meantime, the organization of The Free Bulgarians, whose secretary I was, was growing very successfully. We had left the club premises at Rue de l'Universite, but were meeting regularly at "Cafe des Sports" at Porte-Maillot; our review *Vazrazhdane* was doing well, and we were also helping the new Bulgarian Students society. And, with the radio scripts I wrote for the *BBC* and, recently, for *Free Europe,* my budget had become less strained.

My personal life was full of variety and excitement, and I had found a real new home and family warmth at the Panitza's apartment on 27, Rue Franklin, where I lunched and dined every day. That February, and for the first time in the five years since I lived in France, I could afford a ten-day skiing vacation at the still-unknown little resort Meribel-les-Allues. And, as I gradually recovered from the pain caused by the break-up of my engagement to Neelia, the reaction had thrown me into the other extreme. It was a period, when my rekindled interest in the so-called "tender sex" had taken uncontrollable proportions; a period of a few rather lasting romantic involvements, but also of countless ephemeral adventures. It was as though the hormones had gone wild and were pushing me to unholy thoughts and actions at the sight of every second skirt. While in such a state, humans are liable to do stupid things and then no efforts at self-discipline are of great help. To be honest, I didn't overdo it with such efforts, but then the life of a young bachelor reporter in Paris was not very conducive to that.

"What would you say?" Rafael asked.

"Thank you very much for the invitation, but I'm afraid I can't accept it." The American heard my arguments patiently—my obligations to *Paris-Match,* my career, my family and friends in Paris, and so on,—but a cloud passed across his face and extinguished his enthusiasm. "I see," he murmured as he got up, ready to leave.

"It's a pity!..We thought that…But never mind, it's your business, after all, of you, the Bulgarians. We only wanted to help…" He was visibly disappointed. "But think it over! Some colleagues of mine will come through Paris soon and will contact you again."

Indeed, two other young Americans from *Radio Free Europe* called me in August—John Wiggin, Rafael's assistant, and Creighton Scott, the head of the News department. Meanwhile, my conversation with Rafael hadn't left my mind. Somehow, I felt guilty, although all my friends with whom I had talked about it, unanimously advised me not to risk my promising career for an adventure with uncertain future. Especially when we knew well that the Bulgarian section of *Free Europe*, headed by D. Matzankiev, was entirely under the influence of Dr. G.M. Dimitrov's *National Committee*. "Why would you join them too?" my friends asked me. "Weren't you saying that you don't approve either their ideas, or their methods?"

Wiggin, a well-dressed, reserved gentleman with a carefully trimmed mustache, and the good-natured, witty "Scotty," a casual professional journalist, reiterated *Radio Free Europe*'s proposition. Their style was different from the inspired talk of Bill Raphael, a born leader. Completely different was also the style of the political adviser of the radio, Bill Griffith, who I met a little later—an academic-looking young professor with a bow tie, rimless glasses and caustic humor concealed behind his serious, official facial expression. But all four men belonged to this human species of the American Idealist, which I had not met before and which is often misunderstood in the rest of the world. There were, of cause, plenty of idealists in Europe and elsewhere, but they seemed to be found mostly among the poets, the thinkers and the dreamers, generally among people who live in the clouds. A beautiful, pure race, but somehow unrealistic. The type of the "practical idealist" was unknown to me, and it was a revelation to meet as representatives of super-materialistic America some of the sincerest and most unselfish idealists that were still left on our wicked Earth. Coming from the land of the ruthless business and greed for profit, were altruists who not only were compassionate, but also had the will, the organization, and the means for concrete action.

People like Rafael, Wiggin, and Scott made me feel that my cause was really their cause too. With the difference that they were acting, while I was only talking. To my objection that the Bulgarian section of the radio had become a partisan monopoly, they confided into me that *RFE* was determined to change that situation and it was one of the reasons to turn to me, with a guarantee for total independence vis-à-vis the New York desk. In Munich you'll act with absolute autonomy and you won't have any contacts with Matzankiev's desk," they assured me.

I repeated to them that it was impossible for me to leave my job, but the enthusiasm of these "practical idealists" had obviously had a strong effect on me. The new meeting only exacerbated my guilt feeling. "We complain," I was telling myself during the following nights, "that America doesn't give a damn about us, or only supports leftists exiles. O.K., now they do invite us, offer us a powerful radio-station and independence in broadcasting, and what is my reply?—I only think of my personal career at *Paris-Match* and of the hot Latino lady with whom I was involved at that time in Paris."

At the end of August, I received an insistent telegram from Munich saying that *RFE* expected me "urgently, for a vital mission." In September, I informed Gaston Bonheur that I was leaving *Match*. It was one of the most painful decisions that I have ever made in my life. When I mentioned my understanding that my salary was to cease, Gaston interrupted me with his familiar charming smile: "First you go now to liberate your country, and don't worry about these trivia!"

On October 3, I said goodbye to the people who had become my family— Mika, Stati, and Dimi,—and to my "comrades-in-arms" Dantcho, Dianko and Bontcho, and boarded the evening train to Munich. "Why, oh why, did we have to part again," Mika said in tears. I spent most of the night at the car's window, with my eyes fixed on the impenetrable darkness outside, and my heart was heavy at the thought that once more I was going to be all alone.

*   *   *   *

And alone I was indeed in Munich. Alone in my assigned room at hotel *Regina*. Alone, and with only scant knowledge of German, in the not fully reconstructed after the war city, where I didn't know a soul. Alone in the rooms allocated to the Bulgarian service, in the new building of *Radio Free Europe* in *Englischer Garten*, a functional construction of utilitarian offices and aseptic studios. I was the first Bulgarian at the radio and there was an urgent need of a secretary, Bulgarian typewriters and dictionaries. Rafael, Wiggin, and Scott welcomed me warmly and introduced me to my new colleagues, most of them cordial young Americans, open to new friendships. I also met the heads of the other national desks—the aristocratic Hungarian count Dessewffy, the prominent Czech resistance activist Pavel Tigrid and the Polish underground hero Ian Novak. A pioneering spirit of inspired volunteers, enthusiastically encouraged by Bill Rafael, permeated the whole place. There was a feeling of an eve before a crusade, and that was exactly what I hoped to find in Munich. As at *Paris-Match*, the absence of routine and bureaucracy appealed to me.

I was consulted about the appointment of a second newsman in the Bulgarian desk, according to the *RFE* plan, and ten days after my arrival the Americans introduced me to their candidate, who impressed me very favorably. The following day, Evdokim Evdokimov a 30-year-old exile from the Danube city of Vidin who had studied in Germany, was appointed as my colleague. Collaborating with Evdokim proved to be easy, effective, and with no frictions. A hard, conscientious worker, he was a calm and quiet man, sharing none of the typical for many émigrés excitability and tendency to rash, intolerant generalizations. Soon after, we found a secretary, a young girl with no professional experience, but eager to work and bursting with enthusiasm. In no time, Gilda Koevesh, a half-Hungarian raised in Sofia, learned to type and to organize the avalanche of information pouring out from Scotty's service, which Evdokim and I selected and edited for our daily news bulletin. Emotional and loquacious, Gilda's exuberance brought some animation to the otherwise businesslike quietude in our offices.

After a few draft tests and rehearsals at the microphone, the news broadcasts to Bulgaria started on October 17th. We read the bulletin every evening, three times a day, for 10, 15 and again 15 minutes, after which an office car drove us to the hotel, quite tired, by 10 P.M. The routine was monotonous and our life—rather ascetic. Every day a car picked me up from the hotel before noon and brought me to the radio, where I spent the whole day and the evening. The day started with a briefing for the desks' chiefs, with Bill Griffith commenting the main news and giving the official *Free Europe* line on the important political developments. For lunch and dinner, usually cold hamburgers and Coca-Cola, I ate at my desk, while selecting the news items and preparing the bulletin. Evdokim and I took turns to read at the microphone, and we also took turns for duty on Saturday and Sunday. The only variety during the day was brought in the few moments of recess, spent in the company of our new friends—the Rumanians from the next door office, Coca Romanos and Gregorian, and the American secretaries in our section, Margie Jacob and Janet Quin, very likable and friendly girls, fresh from their native small towns and still thrilled by the discovery of Europe and the exotic world of Czechs, Poles, and Hungarians, and now—Rumanians and Bulgarians. Sometimes we all met after dinner with other Americans at the bar of *Regina*, talking about our countries until late in the evening. I still knew very few Americans, so I was genuinely amazed by the quantities of gin and whisky some of them were capable of consuming. But generally, because of lack of free time, I lived inside an enclave of Americans and émigrés, seeing practically no Germans, except for two or three cosmopolitan Mincheners, recommended by friends in Paris. Evdokim introduced me to a few local Bulgarians of the National Front organization, the most impressive among them being Dr. Dimitar Valtchev. They had welcomed my nomination at *RFE*, but their hopes that I would influence the Americans to modify their cool attitude toward the Front, were soon frustrated. Unfortunately for them, in the States, as well as in France and England, nationalistic émigrés were still suspected as being "Germanophiles," and the authorities were denying them political contacts.

My main diversion in the monotony and solitude of this life overloaded with work were the ski-weekends. When free, I liked to go to nearby Garmisch-Partenkirchen, or to the highest mountain in the area, Zugspitze, alone or with some colleagues. Twice I went skiing with friends in Kitzbuhl, the Austrian ski resort across the border. When in the mountain I felt happy, but weekends ended too fast and the return under the rain to the gray, foggy city used to revive the familiar Sunday-nights melancholy of my old school days. Decidedly, Munich in winter wasn't meant for souls prone to depression.

*   *   *   *

To create and sustain audience interest with a public totally deprived of objective information wasn't a particularly difficult task for us, and Scotty provided us with sufficient material from the world's news agencies. Our concern was to build a solid reputation for reliability. I hoped to achieve this by two means. First, by purging the information items from all propaganda, slogans and clichés, from adulatory or insulting adjectives, grossly overused in totalitarian propagandas, to the point of rendering them counter-effective. "The facts, the pure facts, with no comments!" became my motto. And second, I was ready to sometimes broadcast in good faith also news unfavorable to the United States. We were in the middle of the Korean war and occasionally the American troops suffered minor setbacks. Why, some critics wondered, should I report them too? "It's simple," I answered, "this is a good way to convince our listeners of our objectivity and reliability. And it doesn't cost much: we all know that our side is winning the war and those are only temporary difficulties. If we don't hide the reverses now, the listeners will believe us hundred-percent when we'll be announcing the victories; and those are certain." Rafael and Griffith gave me full support, and reports from Bulgaria indicated that our bulletin enjoyed the listeners' trust. I was also encouraged by the support I received from people whose opinion meant very much to me. "I would've preferred to see you here in America, rather than in Munich," wrote Bishop Andrey from New York. "But I'm happy that you're taking in your hands the radio service in Europe. We live in a time when, with the suffering of our people and the possibility, whatever it be, to help it, we will sacrifice a lot; sometimes our personal interests and hopes, very dear to us." Stefan Popov, the inspired patriot and philosopher of European class, whose unyielding rectitude I had admired since my student years in Switzerland where I met him, wrote to me: "I congratulate you from all my heart for your decision to take up radio *Free Europe*. Let's hope that under your leadership it will become a symbol of sound Bulgarian political thought." Encouragement, although with a few caveats, came from the wise, always cautious minister Kiosseivanov: "I'm happy that you agreed to undertake this task of public utility, although I consider it a thankless job. I don't want to discourage you, but I don't believe the promises of full independence. Don't count too much on them, if you don't want to be disappointed." And the former Premier, whose invitation to visit the United States continued to be delayed, explained his skepticism: "The Americans are peculiar people. No doubt, good intentions inspire them (but isn't is said that the Hell is paved with good intentions?); but the trouble is that when it comes to implement them, they begin to ramble hither and thither. Whether because of lack of experience, or political myopia, or simply by a 'kind-hearted naiveté' they commit big or small mistakes, and sometimes, unfortunately, can cause damage. The words if quotes aren't mine; I'm quoting a foreigner with long experience with them. According to him, the Americans love to say that they don't want to interfere in the internal affairs of other countries, but in fact that's exactly what they do, intentionally or not, and without any embarrassment stick their nose wherever they should or should not…But that's how they are. And still, we should forgive them everything. Because it's exclusively on them that are pinned now all the hopes of those who are hurt, humiliated, repressed, and enslaved, and also those fearing a similar faith. Nobody can deny that America, and only America, disposes of the necessary means and potential to set right—alas, by fire and sword!—the tragically entangled (to a great degree by her fault) world situation. Amen!"

At least during the first few months, Kiosseivanov's fears didn't materialize. The Americans kept their word and indeed, the Bulgarian desk in New York didn't interfere at all in our work. Besides, it became known that Matzankiev split with Dr. G.M. Dimitrov and left him. Disappointed, the royal ex-diplomats Nikola Balabanov and Milio Milev also quit Dimitrov's *National Committee*, and looked again for contacts with us, *The Free Bulgarians*.

*   *   *   *

But our Paris organization was causing me serious worries. Its mover, Dantcho Peyev, our "locomotive," as I used to call him, was lately behaving peculiarly, which became a matter of concern for the rest of us even before I left Paris. Quite uncustomary for him, he began to miss meetings and appointments and to neglect his duties concerning the printing of our review. A period followed, when he used to disappear mysteriously and no one could find him for several days. His physical appearance and state of health made us worry about him: he looked terribly tired and complained of continuous headache. Even his visits to the Panitzas became less frequent, and when he came for dinner, he was despondent and often fell asleep on his chair. It was obvious that some serious worry was bothering him, but he obstinately refused to talk about it. At the same time, he began to borrow money, supposedly "just until tomorrow," debts which he continuously delayed paying back. In other words, Peyev was no longer the same man we all knew.

As secretary of *The Free Bulgarians*, I was spending many nights in my hotel room in Munich writing reports, statements, articles and letters to our important members, but Dantcho's letters became more and more rare and irregular. The organization's work fell progressively on the shoulders of Dianko Sotirov, our vice—president, but he too began to complain about Peyev's absences. "I received money from Angel Boyadjiev (a wealthy Bulgarian industrialist in exile), who also entrusted me with a sizeable sum to be distributed to needy and sick Bulgarians. He's been very helpful and promised to continue helping us," Dianko wrote me. "Dimanov" (a rich Bulgarian living in Madrid) sent us 200 dollars, so our cash register is in good shape for the moment. We must publish *Vazrazhdane* new issue, but Dantcho continues to be remote and invisible, and I really don't know what to do with him…" The mystery surrounding Peyev was getting thicker. Had he contracted some strange disease? Or had he become involved with some plots with foreign intelligence agents? Or, God forbid!, was he being blackmailed by Bulgarian secret agents? Two days before Christmas, Dimi Panitza and Anni Tchaprachikoff called me from Paris, very alarmed, saying that Dantcho was on the verge of total breakdown and I should go there without delay. I asked Evdokim to replace me for a few days and rushed to Paris, where I learned the sad truth about my friend Peyev's downfall.

I was startled to hear that Dantcho had taken to gambling and as a result had found himself into an incredible financial mess. After losing all his money and contracting enormous debts, and being afraid to confess it to anyone, he had spent countless nights at gambling houses, determined to "make up" for the losses and return his debts the next morning, without anyone noticing. And, as it always happens with addicted gamblers, the more he tried, the deeper he sank until he reached total impasse and even the thought of suicide.

I was profoundly shocked, and so were Mika, Stati and Dimi Panitza, for whom Dantcho represented the model of the near-perfect man of whom we all were very proud. It was extremely painful for us, and a true tragedy to him, to hear the pathetic confession of this once proud and valiant officer. Unable to conceal it any longer, he told us through tears how, in his obsessive search of funds for the organization and the review, he succumbed one days to the temptation to try his luck at the casino. (It must be said that Peyev wasn't in the least interested in getting rich personally, material things weren't very important to him.) The unexpectedly easy winning that night enticed him to try a second time, and a third and a fourth time, until he suffered his first considerable loss. The rest of the story, a pitiful stereotype in every tale about gamblers, was easy to guess.

As Dantcho's friends, our first priority was to help him cure himself, to rescue him, and to avoid the scandal that menaced our organization. Two days after my arrival in Paris, the leadership of *The Free Bulgarians* met at *Café des Sports* and decided that Peyev had to find a pretext and resign, as discreetly as possible, from the presidency. We all agreed that Dianko Sotirov should replace him.

*   *   *   *   *

My work in Munich went on with no essential changes, although the radio increased its broadcasts, using new and more powerful antennas. There were discussions about hiring a third person for the Bulgarian service and the Americans asked me for names of potential candidates. But the decision was dragging on, although Evdokim and I barely managed to cope with the ever-increasing programs. There were also rumors about moving the entire radio to Istanbul or to Portugal. I was getting accustomed to life in Munich, to my skiing weekends, and the pleasant evenings spent with colleagues from the radio. Occasionally I managed to find time to take out my local flirt Jean Daly, the pretty secretary to

Bill Griffith, a bright and beautifully mannered Florida girl who was telling me about the delights of life in Palm Beach.

I was then pleasantly surprised to discover that, in spite of my formal quitting, *Paris-Match* continued to consider me as a collaborator. Thus, Gaston Bonheur called me one day and asked me to go to London for a story on the young Scottish Duke of Buccleugh, a close friend of the royal family. Rafael, always kindly disposed to me, allowed me a five-day furlough, and I did the reportage, with *Match* photographer Daniel Filipacchi. Another time, when Raymond Cartier, one of *Paris-Match* directors, came to Munich, I accompanied him during his visit to a nearby German refugees' camp and assisted him in the research.

These renewed contacts intensified the nostalgia for my reporter's job and for my friends in Paris, and I began to ask myself whether the time had not come for me to leave Munich. After spending six months at the radio, I considered that I had done my duty. The Bulgarian news service has been built, the format of the programs established, and the bulletin broadcast smoothly and regularly. Evdokim and Gilda, who in the meantime had also learned to read on the microphone, were perfectly capable to do the job alone, without me, provided that we found another journalist to fill the vacancy. There was also something else: as it's normal with any developing institution, radio *Free Europe* was becoming better organized and more regulated, with less improvisation and less spontaneity. The pioneering spirit, which had attracted me in the first place, seemed to yield to the routine and the professionalism. We were already talking about our rights to yearly vacations, about salary increases (the foreigners' pay was incomparably lower than the Americans'), about medical insurance, and even about future pensions. All this was, of course, very understandable and indispensable. But... Didn't we run the risk to be transformed, with time, from selfless volunteers in a patriotic cause, into employees in a bureaucratic establishment?

In March, in a frank, friendly talk, I informed Bill Rafael about my decision to return to Paris, and we started looking for a new colleague of Evdokim's. In the beginning of April, one of the candidates, Mandikov, was approved and hired. Margie and Janet gave a farewell party for me, where I said goodbye, not without regret, to the colleagues, who had already become true friends. On the 7th of April

1952, I left for Paris, carrying with me the best memories of radio *Free Europe* and the people, who had sincerely dedicated themselves to its noble mission.

Chapter 17

The Egyptian revolution: my first scoop

Professionally, my big chance came in the summer of 1952.

Since my return from Munich, I was doing quite nicely as a reporter, but *Match* hadn't sent me yet on any really important story. That summer, Egypt became hot news. King Farouk's arbitrary rule and outrageous behavior had reached shocking proportions and had become an inexhaustible source of scandalous stories for the international yellow press, while the growing outcry for radical reforms had led to an open political crisis. As I was interested in Egypt ever since I had met Faiza, I found myself reading and clipping stories about it and briefing my editors about the situation there. My knowledge about the country was minimal, but at *Match*-reporters' level, anybody who knew anything beyond Farouk's most recent wife's name and the year of Napoleon's campaign to the Pyramides, could be labeled an Egyptologist.

So on July 23rd, when a flash announced to the world that a military coup had taken place in Cairo, I became much in demand at the editors' conferences. I was digging out the sparse information on the mysterious "Free Officers," their unheard of leader general Naguib, and the old politician Aly Maher, the new Prime Minister, for an article my colleague Jean Farran started preparing for the next issue, when, on July 26th, we heard the sensational news: Farouk had abdicated and left the country!

The news had all the ingredients for an ideal *Paris-Match* story: drama, conspiracy, royalty, corrupted regime, repudiated King's wives and mistresses, casino gambling at fabulous stakes, fanatic young officers…All this with a photogenic background of lavish palaces, the sphinx, and Bedouins on camels! No wonder that our editors were excited. The story was too late for the current issue, already going to print, but it was imperative for *Match* to send its own team to Cairo immediately.

The editorial conference, to decide whom to send, began as an exercise in humiliation for me. Being just a junior reporter, I had no place around the long table, but I was standing up in a corner, with the Egyptian files under my arm, listening silently as the editors discussed. It was a very hot summer day and they all looked worried. They had just assigned Willy Rizzo, one of the ace-photographers, to fly without delay to Cairo, but were unable to reach any of the "grand-reporters" to go with him. The stars were either busy elsewhere, or vacationing in places out of reach. Dede Lacaze was covering the Helsinki Olympic games, with Carone and Filipacchi; Jean Roy had left to chase Farouk and his family in their exile in Capri, with Jacques de Potier. The telephones of the others simply didn't answer. Editor-in-Chief Gaston Bonheur was really annoyed. "I don't know why we pay so many people, when there is no one when we need them!" he grumbled. "Nobody! Not a single reporter available!" "Yes, it's scandalous!" others echoed his words, "Not a single reporter! They're all on vacation!"

My feelings were really hurt. Here I am, willing and ready, and they ignore me totally, as if I didn't exist! Finally, I took all my courage and shyly mumbled something to the effect that I would gladly accompany Rizzo, at least, you know, to organize things before a "grand-reporter" arrives, I mean, why not try…The thought hadn't even occurred to the editors, but they looked at each other and, after some hesitation, said: "That's an idea. While we look for a reporter, why not send Stephane to assist Willy?" I didn't detect any particular enthusiasm in their voices, but I was overjoyed. Although in Paris-Match lingo to "assist" a photographer meant to carry his bags, arrange his appointments, and put his exposed films on the first available plane to Paris. The next day Willy and I were on the *TWA* flight to Rome and, after taking two of the airhostesses to dinner at Trastevere, we boarded the 2 AM plane to Athens and Cairo.

Cairo was incredibly hot, but totally calm. There was no sign of the dramatic events that had taken place only a few days before. The scene however changed completely when we went to the headquarters of the victorious junta. The hectic place resembled a command post on the eve of a great battle. Jeeps loaded with young officers in combat gear were arriving and departing at full speed. At the gates, tough-looking soldiers with automatic weapons checked the visitors' passes. In the overcrowded large hall on the ground floor dozens of journalists waited to be received by the "Savior of the Fatherland," as the Egyptian radio was calling General Naguib. He was much too busy to give interviews, but contrary to Farouk, who hated reporters, Naguib showed them consideration. To the heavily perspiring journalists packing the waiting room, he offered bottles of Coca-Cola, bought, we were told, with his own money.

In addition to the excitement and the heat, I was overwhelmed by inferiority complex. Indeed, all the top guns of the international press were there: the fabulous *Life* magazine reporters, role-models to us; *Associated Press* and *UPI* veteran correspondents; the guys from *Magnum, Life, Time,* and *Newsweek,* plus representatives of every major publication in the world. I recognized a few of the famous names of international journalism, whom I had admired for longtime. Now I was going to compete with them for the same prize: a personal interview with Naguib.

We had all deposited our requests with aides-de-camps acting as the general's press officers, and everybody was watching his rivals with ill-concealed suspicion and apprehension, lest they pulled some trick and gain unfair advantage. Pushiness and bluff are great trumps in that game, and I'm afraid I'm not good at it, so I relied entirely on Willy's experience and nerve. As things turned out unexpectedly, there was no need for it.

A press-officer reappeared, holding the long list with the journalists' names. In the silence that followed, he read out loud and clear: "*Paris-Match*. Will you please come in!" To the angry shouts "It's unfair!" and "Why them?" and at the risk of being lynched by the mob of rivals, Willy and I were led to the office of the man who had overthrown Farouk.

I never understood why general Naguib gave us such preferential treatment. I suppose he didn't want to identify himself with Anglo-Saxon publications: Egyptians were sensitive about their recent status of British protectorate. On the other hand, favoring German or Italian magazines could send a wrong political message: the memories of totalitarianism were still fresh. A French connection sounded neutral and most convenient. Hence, *Paris-Match*.

Naguib was sitting behind a large desk covered with files and no less than five telephones which rang continuously. He wore his khaki uniform with open collar and his dark, unshaven face betrayed great fatigue. In spite of his rugged looks—thick, black hair cut short, bushy eyebrows, weathered dark skin,—he gave the impression of a warm, accessible, and sincere man, probably because of his friendly smile. He was rather short, well fit, and looking younger than his 53 years of age. Through the half-open door to the adjoining room we saw an iron field-bed; that's where the general took his naps when he could. We learned that during the previous week he didn't sleep more than three hours a night.

We didn't need an interpreter: Naguib spoke French pretty well. He had also taught himself English, German, and Italian. While we spoke, the door opened every minute and busy-looking young officers in battle-dress, rolled-up sleeves and gun on the hip interrupted us, giving the military salute to the general and delivering messages in guttural Arabic. Naguib conversed with them in a friendly manner, warmly shaking hands with them before dismissing them. They were all very young—lieutenants or captains; we didn't see any superior officer. As a matter of fact, all generals had been dismissed after the coup of the "Free Officers," who only trusted the veteran desert warrior Naguib.

I had done my homework and started respectfully with a few concrete questions, to reassure him that we were no paparazzi looking for sensations. He relaxed and answered readily. I felt no longer intimidated, not to speak of Willy who didn't know what the word "intimidated" meant. The interview was off to an excellent start. I must say that the friendly atmosphere was due to a great degree to Willy Rizzo. This short, mischievous French-fried Italian, with his locks of reddish-blond hair and impertinent twinkle in his eyes, was a born comedian and rarely failed to amuse the people he worked with. His special talent for putting the personalities he photographed at ease and becoming immediately cozy, almost intimate with them, had always amazed me. Whether a movie star, a statesman or royalty, Rizzo took liberties which would be inconceivable in the case of other reporters; any other photographer would appear overly pushy, indiscreet and too familiar. But directing his subjects where to sit, how to pose or smile, and what not to do, came so naturally to Willy, with such a matter-of-fact authority and humor, that people had no time to object or resist. Before Naguib had a chance to realize what hit him, he was literally in the hands of Willy, who was moving his chair, fussing with wrinkles in his uniform, rearranging tripods and lamps, all the while grinning in the general's face and almost patting him approvingly. I was slightly embarrassed and immensely amused by Rizzo's nerve. The extraordinary thing was that Naguib obeyed with docility and didn't seem to mind.

Our time was up and we felt that we had a good story in our hands. But I already saw the possibilities for a better one, a real scoop that our limited time had not permitted us to achieved: I wished that Naguib told us, in the first person if possible, the day-by-day, the hour-by-hour tale of what exactly had happened during the dramatic week of the coup, how the coup was executed, with colorful anecdotes and human details, with quotations of what Farouk said and what Naguib said, and where exactly, and at what time. In other words, the *Paris-Match*: to reveal the human side of the great headline event. This, no one had told so far. I didn't think it impossible, because somehow I had felt that Naguib had liked me and trusted me. I felt it particularly when my questions had turned to his personal biography and background. He told me that he had served for a longtime in the desert, in remote oases, with just a few Bedouin soldiers and their camels. Talking about those years, his face lit up and he made no effort to conceal how much it meant to him. Noticing my fascination, he let himself go, and for a moment the formidable junta leader sounded like an inspired poet. "Have you ever spent a night in the solitude of the desert, under the starry sky?" he asked me. I confessed that I hadn't, but when he went on describing the unique "communion of Man with Infinity and Eternity," I ventured that it might be similar to the "cosmic" feelings one discovers in the solitude of the open sea or the high mountain, which I had experienced a few times in the Alps. "How interesting!" he said, as if talking to a friend and not a reporter. "Too bad we cannot talk more. But, you see, I'm under terrible pressure and must leave you now."

I liked the man. It surprised me, because I had come prepared to dislike the conspirator who was Faiza's enemy and had put, I feared, her security and even her life, in serious danger. I didn't care at all for Farouk, who had gotten what he deserved, but reading the excessive attacks in the revolutionary press, I worried about my favorite Egyptian lady. I had, of course, called her home as soon as I landed in Cairo, but was told that she and Ali were in Alexandria.

Back to the *Metropolitan* hotel, I worked on my article and spent the next three days in Cairo, talking to French diplomats and some officers at Naguib's headquarters, visiting the pyramids, the Sphinx, and the fabulous Cairo Museum for the first time. I was relieved to hear some officers say that Princess Faiza was highly regarded by them and that nobody blamed her for the misbehavior of her royal brother. An attractive cavalry major, Hussein Khairy, turned out to be married to her cousin, Princess Hadidja. We quickly became friends and he introduced me to a few of his colleagues of the "Free Officers," who gave me extremely useful information about the junta. In addition, he put me in touch with Faiza and Ali and we were all delighted to hear each other's voices on the telephone. "Come to Alexandria!" they asked me. So, when my work was finished, Willy took the plane to Paris with his films and my paper, while I left for Alexandria excited and happy, as I hadn't been for a longtime.

$$* \qquad * \qquad * \qquad * \qquad *$$

No stage could've been more appropriate for the romantic mood was in than Alexandria during those hot August days of revolution. Many novels and films had told me about the city's colorful, multinational population, beautiful beaches, and its air of international intrigue, but I found this metropolis on the Nile's estuary even more exciting than anything I had expected. No wonder: while pursuing my appointments with a few officers of the new regime, I spent all my evenings at Faiza and Ali's, with their friends of the old regime. They were all bitter and worried, and extremely critical of the "Free Officers." All, except Faiza.

I was thrilled to see her again, several years after my Paris infatuation. She had changed considerably. Not physically: if anything, I found her even more beautiful now than she was in Paris. The vivacious, frivolous girl had matured into a more reserved, reflective young woman, calmly, even detachedly, observing the cataclysmic events that were sweeping away her class and the world she was accustomed to. Alone among the friends and relatives I met in her house, she had accepted the inevitability of the change, with no anger. She even expressed, to the disapproving amazement of her guests, a certain sympathy for the cause of the Naguib's junta, especially for their love for Egypt and their revolt against shocking social injustices.

Freshly arrived from the "enemy camp" and full of news from Cairo and Paris, I became a center of attention in Faiza's circles, in Alexandria first, then in Cairo, where we returned together for the last three days of my stay. I was with them every moment when I wasn't pursuing my inquiries in meetings with officers of the new regime or old politicians. I felt that I was beginning to loose my head again, or rather my heart. The sad look in Faiza's eyes, her pensiveness and melancholy smile intrigued me and disturbed me deeply. Was I falling in love? The events were developing too fast and the surroundings were much too glamorous to permit a sober assessment. Those dinners at her house during the hot, balmy nights, when she always made me sit next to her; those car rides in the desert around Cairo, where she wanted to show me the eroded Sakkara pyramid; or visiting the Sphinx by moonlight; or lying on the sand of Agami, the marvelous beach in Alexandria...One doesn't have to be overly romantic to imagine oneself enamored in such 'quasi-Hollywoodian' setting. By night, thinking of her, I dreamt of myself in the role of some latter-day Douglas Fairbanks, rescuing the Princess-in-distress from captivity, by heroically snatching her in a plane provided by accomplices among my new Egyptian friends...But when I mentioned to Faiza that she may be in danger and should probably consider leaving Egypt, she just said: "Don't be silly! Nobody wants to harm me," and made me feel stupid.

I left Egypt saying "*A bientot!*" rather than "Goodbye," sure to return very soon: Naguib's office had assured me that the general may grant me, before the end of the month, the exclusive interview he had promised *Paris-Match*. Elated, I flew back to Paris, where Gaston Bonheur complimented me warmly on my work. A Paris radio-program invited me on a round-table discussion on Egypt with prominent experts, such as Edouard Sablier and other distinguished arabists. When the anchor-man introduced me as "Monsieur Groueff, the well-known specialist of Egyptian politics," not only did I have to blush, but my illusions about the depth of knowledge of most media "experts" went out of the window, for ever...

While waiting for the word from Cairo, *Match* sent me to London, with photographer Jean-Pierre Pedrazzini, to cover the wedding of elegant bachelor Anthony Eden, Churchill's Foreign Secretary and heir presumptive, with the old warrior's niece, Clarissa Churchill. Traveling with Jean-Pierre was always great fun, and on this occasion the juxtaposition of the formal outfits, titles, and Eton accents at the wedding, and the insolent irreverence and outrageous argot of "Pedra's" private remarks, was hilarious. On my way back to Paris, I stopped for two days in Geneva, to see my old friends and tell them about Egypt. The Belinoffs had me for dinner with Harri, Dimi Panitza, Tania and Jean-Pierre Cellerier, and Johnny Stancioff, and as usual we never stopped laughing at the same old Bulgarian jokes, as if we were hearing them for the first time.

Naguib's much expected consent finally arrived and on August 29, Willy Rizzo and I boarded the *TWA* flight to Cairo. At noon the next day we were at the General's headquarters, panting and sweating in the atrocious Egyptian heat. Naguib, in greenish safari shirt with general's epaulets and ribbons of many military decorations sewn over the left chest pocket, greeted us as old friends, smiling and offering us the unavoidable Turkish coffee. To me delight, he was ready and willing to tell his story and answer all my "how exactly?" and "what happened then?" questions. From time to time he had to slow down to give me time to take notes and spell some name correctly. He told me how, by 1947, a group of young army officers, exasperated by the way King Farouk treated them, formed the secret organizations of the "Free Officers." Naguib, already a senior officer, was not invited to join. But then came the disastrous war in Palestine, the greatest humiliation for the Egyptian military. They blamed the King and his corrupted regime bitterly for the catastrophic defeat which, they were convinced, could have been avoided with a better strategy and supply, and, above all, with more dedication to Egypt.

Mohammed Naguib was a hero of that war, a frontline commander wounded three times and venerated by the army. By 1949, the "Free Officers" invited him to become their older brother, their leader. He knew about conspiracies: in the very early days of his career, he had participated in a secret anti-British plot.

The many petitions and formal protests sent to the government and the Royal palace had no effect, and in the beginning of 1952, when Farouk decreed the closing of the Officers' Club, whose president was Naguib, the junta decided to pass to action. It was a period of great political instability, with Aly Maher, Hilaly, and Sirry succeeding each other as Prime Ministers. When Farouk imposed his brother-in-law as Minister of Defense, the Free Officers struck. In the night of July 22nd, 300 officers, leading 3000 soldiers, occupied the Army headquarters and Cairo's radio, railroad station and telephone central offices, while tanks were placed at street intersections and at the airport. "We proceeded to arrest all superior officers, without exception," Naguib said. "I didn't hesitate to arrest my own brother, general Aly Naguib, the commander of the Cairo region. He's one of the most brilliant cavalry officers we had. He's not against us, but I hadn't informed him about the coup: in case of failure, I thought one victim would be enough from our family. So that night I found myself the only general at freedom." Because of the element of surprise, the coup was bloodless, or almost: only two soldiers were killed in front of the Army headquarters, and six of the Royal palace guards were wounded."

Smoking his pipe, Naguib continued his tale, consulting his pocket notebook from time to time. He told me that at dawn the government, which was in the summer capital, called from Alexandria to inquire as to what was going on in Cairo, and Naguib reassured them that everything was calm. At 7 AM, the radio broadcast Naguib's proclamation, announcing the success of the coup. In Alexandria, Prime Minister Hilaly offered his resignation to the king, who refused to accept it, insisting that he remain in power. Meanwhile, the Free Officers sent Farouk a list of demands, including the nomination of the old statesman Aly Maher, a man they respected, as Prime Minister. Naguib went to Maher's home and asked him to form the new government. Farouk, realizing that the junta is already in full control, accepted Hilaly's resignation and summoned Maher to Alexandria. The following day, the Maher government was sworn in and Farouk reluctantly appointed Naguib Commander-in-chief of the armed forces.

"But did you personally talk to the King before he abdicated? Where and when? What did you say and what did he say?" I asked, worried that the interview would end without me learning much about the dramatic tête-à-tête. But Naguib seemed to enjoy our conversation. "It's getting late now. But why don't you come tomorrow night to my house? We'll be able to talk better there, and I'll tell you the rest of the story." That was more than I could've hoped for and I tanked him profusely as we took leave. But Willy, fresh as usual and always looking for new story angles, asked without any hesitation: "*Mon general*, will your children be home? I'd love to photograph them too."

The evening at Naguib's modest suburban house was even more successful than the interview at his headquarters. When we arrived, he was playing chess with a civilian friend who wore a fez, but he interrupted the game to greet us and offer us coffee. Then, very relaxed, he told me the story of Farouk's abdication. "We, the twelve members of the junta's Central committee, had decided the night before that the King must go," he said. "As we didn't know in which of his two Alexandria palaces, Montezah or Ras-el-Tin, he was, our troops surrounded both places. We also watched his yacht, *Mahroussa*. In the morning of July 25th, I arrived by plane in the Mustapha-Pasha barracks in Alexandria, where the Navy officers came to assure me of their support. After spending the evening with the new Prime Minister Maher, the committee met late at night and drafted an ultimatum to Farouk, demanding his abdication the next day, July 26th, and his departure for exile before 6 PM that day. At dawn, assault units with tanks and artillery advanced to the gates of the two palaces, but at Ras-el-Tin a young officer mistakenly placed his foot soldiers in front, instead of behind, the tanks. As they reached the harem area of the palace, the royal guards opened fire and six soldiers were wounded. Fire ceased, but the king was awakened and when he received the ultimatum at 9 AM he had already realized that any resistance would be useless. Aly Maher went to the palace and it took him twenty minutes to convince the king to accept the ultimatum. But Farouk demanded that the American ambassador, Jefferson Cafery, come and guarantee his and his family's personal safety. At noon, Farouk was no more king."

Naguib stopped for a cup of coffee and to answer a phone call, while I was burning to hear the rest of the story. By then, Willy had taken over and the living room looked already like a photographer's studio, strewn with cameras, strobe lights, tripods, and unwrapped film rolls. He was in his element, especially after the general, at Rizzo's insistence, called in his three sons and introduced them to us. For the next half hour all conversation stopped and the startled host and his sons became obedient, if slightly clumsy, performers in a *Paris-Match* photographic production. Willy started by bossing the boys around, acting as he were their closest uncle, and soon they felt comfortable with him. But although he took as many photos as he wanted, he didn't looked satisfied. Suddenly, to my horror, he turned to the host and asked: "General, you say you're deeply religious, a true believer in Allah. Do you do your daily prayers regularly?" Surprised, Naguib replied: "Yes, I do." And Rizzo: "Right here, in this room?" "Yes, sometimes in this room too..." I couldn't believe my ears when I heard my partner say: "Show us! Let's do it now!" And as the general hesitated, Willy prodded him: "It would be great for people to see what a pious Muslim you are! Everybody will feel happy and reassured!" He was already leading him to the other corner of the room, and helping him to go on his knees. "But you take your shoes off, don't you, general?" Totally confused, Naguib took his shoes off and followed Willy's directions. I could've died of embarrassment when Willy, never satisfied, ordered the boys to kneel behind their father and start bending in prayer, their foreheads almost touching the carpet. It was an incredible scene, which was later reproduced in every magazine in the world: Egypt's new strongman and his sons, praying on the floor of their living room, while *Paris-Match's* photographer shouts his orders, as if he were directing models in his studio: "No, general, turn the head a little more to me!...That's fine! But you, boys, bend more, and don't move now!"

When Willy was finally satisfied, the interview resumed. Naguib described how by 5:30 that afternoon queen Narriman, crown prince Fouad and the three king's daughters boarded the *Mahroussa*, while Farouk was saying goodbye, at Ras-el-Tin palace, to his sisters Fawzia and Faiza (that name I wrote correctly without waiting for the general to spell it for me...) and their husbands, Prime Minister Maher, and American diplomats Caffery and Simpson. "I wasn't there,"

Naguib said. The ex-king left the palace and walked slowly to his private dock where a motorboat was waiting to take him to the *Mahroussa*. A band was playing the national anthem, while the royal standard was lowered, folded, and presented by an officer to Maher, who in his turn handed it to Farouk. The palace servants were crying aloud. Cannons fired a 21-gun salute. At 6 PM precisely, as the officers stood at attention and saluted, Farouk boarded his yacht.

"So now you know the whole story," Naguib said to me, signaling that the interview must end. It was already 8 PM and we had been there since 6 o'clock.

"But, Sir, the story would be incomplete without your personal last encounter with King Farouk," I insisted. "Did you say goodbye to him?"

By then it was obvious that the general like us. He looked at his watch and said: "It's too late now. But come tomorrow early in the morning, and I'll tell you the rest." Luckily, we had one more day before Willy had to fly to Paris with our reportage (I had other plans: I had asked *Match* for two weeks vacation in Egypt if we deliver a scoop). I spent part of the night editing my notes, and Willy—arranging his cameras and films.

Our new "friend" Naguib didn't disappoint us the next morning. In fact, I had felt that ever since our conversation about solitude in the desert and "communion with the Universe," he welcomed occasional remarks about private thoughts and feelings. His last meeting with his former sovereign, whom he deposed, was certainly an emotional experience for him. "Farouk had demanded to see me before he left for exile," Naguib told me. "I would've done it anyhow, I considered it my duty as an officer." He wanted to attend the farewell ceremony at Ras-el-Tin and left in a car on time to arrive before 6 o'clock. But his chauffeur not only got lost, but also didn't foresee the extraordinary crowds jamming the streets around the palace. The euphoric crowds recognized the general and hundreds of hands were reaching through the car's windows to greet the hero of the coup. "When I arrived at Ras-el-Tin, it was exactly 6:04 PM. The king had just left." Naguib was determined to say goodbye to Farouk; otherwise, it would look as if he came late on purpose. So he immediately commandeered a Navy motorboat anchored near the palace and headed for the bay where *Mahroussa* was getting ready to leave.

Naguib and the four officers who accompanied him boarded the royal yacht and gave the military salute to Farouk, who waited on the bridge, dressed in white admiral's uniform. The ex-king returned the salute and shook his hand. "At that moment, something strange happened to me," Naguib told me. "Suddenly, I didn't know what I wanted to say to him, and I think Farouk, obviously moved, couldn't say anything either. A painful silence followed, which lasted for one minute. Everybody remained standing at attention and one could only hear the sound of the waves breaking against the ship. There was something solemn, touching, and terrible in this silence that none of us wanted to break. Then I spoke. "*Effendi*..." I started. (*Effendi* means *Sir*, and this word pronounced by me and heard by him for the first time, had for both of us a strange resonance.) *Efendi*, do you remember that when, in 1942, the British surrounded your palace and forced you to sign the nomination of Nahas Pasha, I gave my resignation? I felt wounded by the humiliation inflicted to my king."

"Yes, I remember."

"We were all loyal to you then, and we wanted nothing else but to remain loyal. But since 1942, many things have changed..."

"Alas! Yes, many things have changed."

"But it's mainly you that changed. It's you who forced us to do what we just have done."

"I wish you to succeed where I did not succeed," the ex-monarch answered. Then, another silence. I saluted again and shook his hand for goodbye. He shook the hands of my officers. "Your new task is very hard," said Farouk. "It's not at all easy, you know. Anyhow, if you hadn't done what you did, I was going to do it myself, and right away." These were his last words. I never understood what exactly he meant."

*   *   *   *   *   *

Our story had an enormous success. *Paris-Match* with a portrait of Naguib by Willy Rizzo on the cover, and huge headlines: "*NAGUIB'S COUP DESCRIBED BY HIMSELF. Our special envoys in Cairo cable the fascinating tale of General Naguib.*" The several pages with my text and Willy's photographs opened with a picture of myself taking Naguib's dictation, and closed with a picture of Willy shaking hands with the general. A few days later, the Egyptian press published my interview in-extenso, as "the official version of the events, as told in exclusivity by General Naguib to Stephane Groueff." The photos and the story were sold and resold by Match all over the world, and for the first time I saw my signature and my photo in dozens of foreign publications. But, in addition to the joys of the vanity, the syndication of the scoop brought me an unexpected award, which, as we'll see later, had to play a very important, and lucky, role in my private life. The practice was that Match and the reporters shared the proceeds from the resale. As a result, by the end of the fall, I found myself in possession of a few thousand dollars, a real fortune for me, the first money other than my modest salary that I ever had in my life. How I spent this money and how it brought me luck, is another story. For the time being, let me stay with my Egyptian venture.

*   *   *   *   *

I spent the first two weeks of September between Alexandria and Cairo, mostly in the company of Faiza and Ali, and I had as happy a time as I had had the previous month on my first visit. Happy and disturbing. The closer our friendship grew, the more clearly I saw the absurdity of my romantic yearning. But there was little I could do about it: the appeal of an impossible dream is notorious. So, rather than resist, I let myself drift down the bittersweet stream of entertainment offered daily by my generous friends. Pleasant lunches and dinners with their friends, sightseeing by car along the Mediterranean coast as far as Aboukir, after-dinner movies at Faiza's Cairo home at Gezirah, on the Nile, visits to Ali's ranch for "Gamuz" cattle, or picnics on Agami beach. One evening we all had dinner there and when it became late and the group was about to leave, I looked at the immensity of the desert behind the dunes and remembered my conversations with general Naguib. I suddenly felt a strong desire to be alone. My friend Major Hussein Khairy agreed to return and pick me up in a couple of hours, and everybody drove back to Alexandria.

Left alone, I proceeded to walk slowly into the desert, enjoying thoroughly the silence and the new serenity I felt. The stars above me seemed brighter and bigger than any stars I had seen before, and much, much more plentiful, as if I were looking at the sky of some different, miraculous planet. I sat on the ground and, my eyes fixed on the firmament, tried to imagine that I was the only existing person now, a soul suspended somewhere between infinity and eternity. It was a weird experience, I thought, wondering whether this was what Naguib meant when he talked about the long solitary months he spent on customs duty in the desert. I felt like lying down and spending the rest of the night contemplating the starry skies, but it was getting chilly and after a while I walked back to the place where Hussein's car was waiting for me.

A few days later, near Cairo, the desert treated me to another, completely different, aspect of its fascination. This time it had to do with Faiza. The princess used to ride horses from a stable located in the vicinity of the Sakkara pyramids, and once or twice she took me along, together with a couple of friends, all incomparably better horsemen than I. Horses and riders could hardly wait to get out of the enclosure, as eager as thoroughbreds at the start of a race when the automatic gates are about to be pulled open. Then, once they sensed the desert, they let themselves go, intoxicated with speed, bewitched by the open, unobstructed infinity of sand before them. Faster, faster! I just clung to my mount's neck, not even trying to control the runaway horse, saying my prayers and abandoning my fate in God's hands.

Running in the lead, as if daring her companions to catch up with her, Faiza rode at full gallop, out of breath, the eyes sparkling and the cheeks flushed with excitement, her black hair flying freely in the air. It was a thrilling sight, the sight of total liberation of someone who, exhilarated, was escaping from everything and from her own self too. I can't explain why or how, but I knew that it definitely had to do with the desert, and that the enigmatic desert was part of her, a part which I will never be able to reach.

When I returned to Paris, my position in *Match* had improved greatly. I was promoted "grand reporter", which meant that I was given interesting assignments regularly, traveling mostly to England, sometimes to Munich, Bonn, Geneva. I had overcome most of my shyness, gained better assurance with the girls and was enjoying myself enormously. Life of a 30-year-old bachelor-reporter of the glamorous

Paris-Match who is interested in girls, going out, and traveling, seemed to be made in heaven. Maybe not particularly serious or praiseworthy, but it surely was great fun. And yet, during these months of excitment and quick successes, my thoughts would be drifting back to Egypt. Was I in love? I certainly didn't behave like someone in love, but on the other hand, I was constantly plotting to be sent again on some story to Egypt. Winter came and friends started asking me to join them to some ski resorts, a great temptation for me, especially that now, for the first time in so long, I was able to pay for myself a couple of weeks in the mountains. My pals from the old Swiss days, Daria Mercati and Teresa Thyssen, both St.Moritz *habituees*, had even arranged with their friend Andrea Badrutt, the owner of the super-chic *Palace-Hotel*, to give me a very special price for a small room at his luxurious place. To the frustrated ski enthusiast that I was, it sounded like a dream, but I didn't hesitate a minute to cancel my reservation for the end of January, when the opportunity came again to go to Egypt.

Cairo again. As soon as I unpacked at the *Semiramis* hotel, I rushed to *Zohria*, Faiza and Ali's house in Gezireh where I received a most warm welcome. I had arrived just in time: the same evening they were leaving for the Upper Egypt…I was crushed. We spent the whole day together and as I was bidding them goodbye, they suggested that I should join them in Assouan or Luxor. I was eager to do it, but it seemed impossible: I had come to Cairo to find out about the mysterious "Committee" of officers,rumored to be the real rulers of Egypt, as Naguib was reduced to a figurehead role.

The next day, when my attempts to contact my "friend" Naguib were politely discouraged, I sensed that the rumors might be true. A few conversations with people I knew from my previous visits confirmed this impression. But who ran the Committee?, I inquired. That's when I heard the name of Lt.Colonel Gamal Abdel Nasser. I asked to see him, and thanks to my friend Major Hussein Khairy, Faiza's cousin's husband, and some of his colleagues, a meeting with the Committee was arranged for the following week. I was overjoyed: not only could this be another scoop, but the date was giving me seven free days. I spend three days in Cairo, seeing some French and American diplomats and Egyptian acquaintances, and attending polo games at the Gezireh Sporting Club with Hussein and his wife, Princess Hadidja. Then I boarded the night train to Luxor.

Night trains have always brought out the dreamer in me. There is something intrinsically romantic in their racing through the darkness of invisible land-scapes; the glimpse of distant village lights or some solitary lit window making me imagine all sorts of scenarios of human activities and dramas; the train whis-tle piercing now and then the silence of the world asleep. As an incantation, the hypnotic beat of the railtrack seams beneath the wheels puts me under its spell, almost carrying me to some altered state of consciousness. It had often happened to me, even in familiar lands. But now, in the exotic world of palms, camels, and noisy crowds in djellabas, being aboard the Cairo-Luxor sleeper, puffing along-side the Nile across moonlit deserts, was an especially inspiring experience for romantic imaginations such as mine. I don't think I slept much; but the dreams were not less colorful than if they were made in sleep.

This state of romanticized reality lasted for the three days I spent in Luxor, a place of such mystique it could hardly be overstated. I didn't make any effort to sober up. On the contrary, ever since I arrived at the *Winter Palace* hotel, where Faiza, Ali, and about ten of their friends were staying, I did everything I could to feed this euphoria, -digging out in my mind and glamorizing faded remem-brances of school courses, museums, and novels on Ancient Egypt, while fanta-cizing about my hopeless, impossible infatuation. The grandiose Colossi of Karnak, the superb temples, the ruins and the frescoes in the mysterious tombs in the Valley of the Kings and the Valley of the Queens, became a stage set for my personal (alas, only imaginary) romance, as did the snake-charmers in the *Winter Palace's* gardens and the primitive sailboats on the Nile, on board from which we admired the sunsets.

But the day of my appointment with the officers' junta approached, and to gain one more day in Luxor, I returned to Cairo on the very last evening, by plane. Faiza and her group remained in Upper Egypt and I already wondered whether I'd ever see her again.

*   *   *   *

The first thing that impressed me when I was led into the conference room in the army barracks in Abassia, a suburb of Cairo, was the age of the men around the table. They were all in their 30s, all majors or lieutenant-colonels. Some of them I had seen before, at Naguib's headquarters: I recognized the thin, elongated face of Major Abdel Hakim Amer, the General's chief of cabinet, and also Lt.Col. Abdel Moneim Amin and Major Khaled Mohieddine, two officers with whom I had talked last summer. Then I saw the best known member of the junta, Salah Salem, 32, a.k.a. "The Dancing Major", in his perennial dark glasses. Newspaper photographs showing him performing soudanese danses at some public celebration had made him a celebrity. I had seen him a few times at Faiza's, whom he obviously admired, and he always seemed uncomfortable in my presence, not sure how discreet a journalist I was. This time, caught in a totally different scene, we both chose not to recognize each other. With him was his brother, Gamal Salem, a pilot war-hero, now in charge of the agrarian reform. All men wore British-style mustaches and uniforms, and for a moment could be mistaken for British officers, weren't it for a few dark skins among them, especially the black face of Anwar El Sadat, a perfectly groomed gentleman. Little did I suspect then that this attractive, brilliant lieutenant-colonel would one day become a major player on the world scene…

There was no need for me to be told which one was Gamal Abdel Nasser: the 35-year-old, tall lieutenant colonel with thick short hair and a black mustache, presided the conference with undeniable authority, althouth the atmosphere was one of relaxed camaraderie. The young officers had reached the stage when their anonymity was no longer needed, and they readily answered most of my questions. Yes, their committee did hold the absolute power, and they were about to announce it publicly, and call it "Supreme Revolutionary Committee". Yes, they were thirteen members, (they listed the names for me), plus General Naguib, whom they venerated as their spiritual "father". But he was absent at that meeting. It was clear that the real boss was going to be Nasser.

It was fascinating to listen to them talk about their plans and goals. The men were highly motivated, inspired by their beliefs, youthfully optimistic. They had no illusions about the enormity of the task they had accepted—rebuilding their hopelessly poor and backward country and curing its congenital corruption and diseases. They had few allies among the political and Islamic forces, and none in the Estabishment and knew that in case of failure they were risking their heads. Did they have any competence, did they have any chance of success? Obviously, I couldn't judge. But I had no doubt about the sincerity of their idealism and about their determination, and that's what I reported in my article. I wrote that their conviction that it was high time "to do something", as well as their desire to "change the world", had gained the Egyptian youth. And knowing how Faiza and her cousin Hadidja felt, I added: *"One notices that even Princesses of the Royal family don't conceal their sympathy for the regime that dispossessed them"*, which I probably shouldn't have written…

Why did the secretive Nasser accept to talk to me? Why did the 13 Officers decide to reveal the existence of their Committee to a French magazine, before they announce it officially? I suppose they needed a forum like *Paris-Match*, they were eager to tell the world of their motives and intentions. And, after our previous articles, they trusted us not to deform their words. Be what it may, we were capable of printing: *"Paris-Match has been authorized to reveal, in a world exclusivity, the secret of the Free Officers…If Egypt is today a dictatorship, the real dictator is not Naguib."*

Exactly one week after my interview with Nasser, I packed my skis and left for St.Moritz.

*   *   *   *

Chapter 18

Glamorous St.Moritz. Meeting Lil.

I was slightly annoyed when Daria Mercati invited me for a quiet dinner at the *Palace Hotel* just on the night when most of my friends were going to the Press Ball at the nearby *Suvretta Haus*. "You'd do me a favor, I need you tonight", she had said, "I've asked an American couple who just arrived today and who'd been awfully nice to me when I was in New York. Please, don't let me down!" She must have read the "How boring!" expression in my eyes, because she added quickly: "Anyhow, they'll be tired after the trip and we'll finish very early, I promise. Then you can go to your ball and join the pretty girls, if you want."

I owed Daria so much, that it was impossible for me to deny her such a small favor. Indeed, ever since my student years in Geneva, she had been touching in her generosity and friendship to me. Besides, I really liked her company, her sophistication, her ladylike manners and discipline; even her extreme self-consciousness and nervous powdering of her nose every two minutes, didn't irritate me and rather amused me. If I was now vacationing at this millionaires' winter-sports Mecca, it was to a great degree due to her: the cosmopolitan Countess Mercati, a Greek-born divorcee of a wealthy Swiss industrialist, had been for years an established feature of St.Moritz's social life, a good, if a bit fussy, hostess, always chic and perfectly coiffed, but also an outstanding skier who used to ski with people like Swiss champion Rominger. I was very lucky to have her as my cicerone in this exclusive resort. It had taken just two words by her for the *Palace's* owner Andrea Badrutt to give me a "secretary's room" at an exceptional price. (It was just an euphemism for the rooms for the personal maids and valets of exotic potentates and foreign super-tycoons who used to spend three months each year in the Engadine's winter paradise; modest cells along long corridors lined with Vuitton wardrobe-trunks and superb leather luggage, but more than adequate for an unspoiled skier like me.)

The bar, where we had to meet before dinner, was almost empty when I arrived, but I noticed a good-looking, very well dressed young woman sitting at a table across the room. I had never seen her before, although, after being a whole week in St.Moritz, I thought I knew most of the attractive faces around the *Palace*. This was a strikingly beautiful face, the kind one sees on fashion magazines covers. "That's my tough luck, wouldn't you know!", I sighed wistfully. "Instead of having to make polite conversation to some boring Americans tonight, why couldn't I be with an attractive thing like that!..."

The young lady was with a tall, handsome man in dinner-jacket. Two minutes later, my hostess Daria appeared from the other side of the bar. Before I could salute her, she rushed to the couple and greeted them ebuliently: "Oh, you're here! How wonderful to see you! Did you already meet Stephane? No? Stephane Groueff, a dear old friend of mine. He's having dinner with us." Their name was Phil and Lil Isles.

So, these were the Americans! My mood changed immediately. Delighted, blushing, I awkwardly mumbled something as we shook hands and followed Daria to the dinner table.

*   *   *   *

I should've been very tired that evening, after skiing for hours with Teresa Thyssen and Tony Page, an expert skier, who was showing us how to handle the deep newly fallen powder snow. The previous night, Tony, a wealthy American-born businessman from Zurich, and his wife Eliane, whom I knew from my student days in Geneva, had taken us for dinner at the fashionable *Chesa-Veglia* and we had stayed terribly late, as everybody did in St. Moritz. The day before was another day of hard skiing at Celerina and a very late night at the *Palace* grill with Daria, the Stagni brothers, a Parisian friend of mine, Cle-Cle de Maille and some friends of hers. And so on and on, with no rest in between. I don't know when we, the skiers in this Dolce Vita, slept at all: we were out every night until the wee hours, dancing, drinking, or just hanging around the *Palace* bar. It seemed that the February weeks didn't have enough evenings for the St. Moritz hostesses to give their parties, each one more lavish that the other. With many husbands away and a great number of single women, extra men were the rarest commodity, so my only social problem was how to avoid uninteresting invitations without being rude. The "*apres-ski*" afternoons were equally busy, with teas in the main hall, cocktail-parties at the bowling alley, or drinks at the *Suvretta. Kulm, Steffani,* and the other hotels. At the end of the day, I had barely time for an one-hour nap and a shower, before changing into dinner jacket and rushing out for dinner.

And yet, the next morning on the slopes, I always felt fresh and eager to ski. Being young helps, of course, but there was also something else: the invigorating power of St. Moritz's air is famous. Situated at an altitude of 1,800 m., (6,000 ft.) this Engadine valley village has a crystal-clear air containing, I was told, 18percent less oxygen than sea-level air, forcing visitors to breathe faster and deeper. Skiing much higher, on the runs of Corvatsch, Corviglia, or Piz Nair, causes such exhilaration, that fatigue is totally forgotten. Because of its climate and its mineral springs, St. Moritz had been for a century a well-known health resort. When a few luxury hotels were built, it became the winter home of the very rich; after World War 1, with the new popularity of winter sports, it became one of Europe's most fashionable resorts, described as "the gleaming and bejeweled playground of the *haut monde.*"

I had heard a lot about the celebrities going regularly to St. Moritz—people like King Albert I of the Belgians; the Nizam of Hyderabad, supposedly the world's richest man; the not-much-poorer Aga Khan, whom, it was said, his adoring Ismaili faithful used to reward in gold and jewels equaling his weight; Barbara Hutton, the richest heiress; or the Duke of Alba, Spain's noblest grandee. It also attracted Hollywood's aristocracy: Norma Shearer, Paulette Goddard, Merle Oberon, and Rita Hayworth. Magazines wrote about the extravagant sums of money spent by partying Greek ship owners like Onassis and Niarchos and South American millionaires. They reported how the Aga Khan, upon his arrival, would leave $ 10,000 with the concierge, to be handed to him each time the Aga needed pocket money. They described the lavish seated dinner for 211 at a specially repainted and redecorated salon in Suvretta Haus, given by Princess Fawzia, the Shah of Iran's first wife and King Farouk's sister, with a gift watch for each guest and thousands of white roses flown from Rome for the occasion. In a different vein, my friend Sava, who'd been in St. Moritz before me, had given me briefings on the female population of the place, that left me drooling: apart from the millionaires' wives and mistresses in Balenciagas, Diors and necklaces from Cartier, the scene abounded with fantastic young girls and models, he said...

The public I found that season was up to St. Moritz's reputation. True, it was more "cafe-society" than *Almanach Gotha*, more of what one calls today "the international jet set;" but glamorous it surely was, and rich, and devotedly hedonistic. There was Niarchos, and banker Loel Guinness, and gregarious Chilean magnate Arturo Lopez with his best-dressed wife and his permanent companions, Baron Alexis de Rede, and Princess Ghislaine de Polignac, and scores of other pleasure-seeking tycoons, international playboys and playgirls. Beside them, the flower of Europe's "golden youth" was also having a great time on and off the slopes—Fiat's heir Gianni Agnelli, Baron Heini Thyssen, Gunther Sachs, Lord Porchester, Marquis Fon Portago, Prince Tino Liechtenstein,—each young man more attractive, richer, and fun-loving than the other. In the afternoon, an elegant, multilingual crowd filled the hall of the Palace, the ladies showing off fashionable apres-ski outfits, the men playing gin—rummy, canasta, or backgammon. Even the plaster casts on broken legs of skiers walking on crutches, (the *Palace* hall was nicknamed "Boulevard des Invalides") had an aura of elegance about them. Bored of the hotel's regular dining room, where meals were included in the price of the rooms, chic guests preferred to dine, at a steep extra charge, in the Grill Room, or in the old country-pub atmosphere of the paneled *Stubbli*, or in the candlelit ambiance of the *Kegelstube*, the bowling alley. The available menu, no matter how exquisite, never seemed to offer a sufficient choice, and competitive hostesses would make a point to order something special and original. As the best Iranian caviar, served in copious portions inside a hot boiled potato, was a standard first course in such dinners, some *blasé* guests would ostensibly scrape out the caviar and only eat the potato...No need to say that I never reached this level of sophistication.

*   *   *

All during dinner that evening, I couldn't take my eyes off my American table companion. The name of the petite, blue-eyed New Yorker with the most delightful small, turned-up nose was Lil, and she was really as bright and full of charm as she was beautiful. Beautiful, but rather reserved; warmly polite, but somehow elusive, unlike her husband, a convivial banker, who was openly friendly. In fact, I shouldn't say "but," because, as the evening progressed, I found that her reserve only added to her charm, giving her an intriguing air of feminine mystery.

I was so taken by her, that I regretted that I had to go to the *Suvretta* ball. Before leaving the table, I heard Daria arranging with the Isles to move after dinner to the bar, where some friends were expecting us. "I'll join you there in an hour!" I volunteered enthusiastically and rushed to *Suvretta*. After a dance or two, I couldn't wait to go back to the *Palace*. But my heart sunk when, entering the bar, I saw that Lil was not with the group and heard Phil say: "Come and join us! Lil is sorry, but she was very tired and went to sleep."

The next morning, as I was riding up to Corviglia, I saw her from the train window, skiing downhill behind her instructor, looking terribly cute in her skiing outfit. As soon as I reached the top, I put on my skis and rushed full speed down the run, hoping to catch up with her. I did, but just as she and the guide were boarding the train up for another run. To my joyous, animated greeting, she replied with nothing more than a nice, polite smile, then turned back to her instructor to resume their conversation, giving me no encouragement to join them. Obviously, I had made no impression on her the previous night, I thought sadly. That day, South-African friends of Sava's, the Hawthornes, took me for lunch to the *Corviglia Club*, the sanctum sanctorum of the smart set atop the mountain. The club's rigorous exclusivity was jealously protected by a snooty but highly competent staff, supervised by Vicomte Charles Benoist- d'Asy, a distinguished-looking French aristocrat with a well-groomed mustache, whose icy politeness would give an inferiority complex to any plebeian or non-member attempting to enter the premises. People were still talking about last year's incident, when Eleanor Roosevelt had been turned away at the door. The former First Lady, never known for her elegance, and an equally un-chic-looking friend, were visiting St. Moritz as tourists and simply wanted to have a snack on the mountaintop. "This is a private club," a disdainful receptionist stopped them, after taking one look at their shabby costumes. Mrs. Roosevelt insisted: "But we came all the way from the States! Let us at least take a look inside!" After a repeated refusal, the friend said: "But do you know who this lady is?" and she told them. Unimpressed, the staff finally called Monsieur le Vicomte. "I'm sorry, Mesdames, but the club's rules are very strict, and you're not members," Benoist-d'Azy said.

Luckily for me, John and Flaffie Hawthorne were members, and so were many of my friends, so I never had to experience poor Mrs. Roosevelt's problems. In the club, packed with sun-tanned men, ladies in fur coats and sunglasses, pet dogs, and private ski-instructors, I found the usual carefree, happy crowd, having drinks, laughing loudly and agitatedly describing their last ski-run or last night's party. Then I suddenly heard someone calling me from the other side of the room. It was an exuberant American lady I had met a few days before, Momo Pershing, having cocktails with friends at the bar. "Come and join us!" she summoned me cheerfully. As I was crossing the crowded room with my full glass in hand, I saw Lil sitting at a nearby table and my heart beat faster. She greeted me warmly and her friendly smile disturbed me so much that just as I was over-eagerly reaching her table, I tripped miserably, spilling my drink and knocking glasses and trays all around me. Everybody burst into laughter, as I, blushing and mumbling apologies, was trying to recover from my humiliation. It was a pitiful sight and I beat a retreat without daring to look at my dream-lady.

Luckily, we knew some of the same people and I saw her at a few parties to which I was invited. The evening of my clumsy performance, we met at a glamorous dinner the Duchesse d'Aremberg gave at the *Cresta*, and Lil didn't mention the incident; on the contrary, I was delighted to see her acting as if she liked me. A few nights later, at a huge dinner for 80, given by an older couple, the Stanley Mortimers, we had a chance to talk at length, and she seemed to be genuinely interested in my job and in my native country. I saw her many times on the mountain, always in tow of her ski guide. That week I took several practice runs for the guests' ski-races for which I had bravely subscribed, although I was not half as good as some of the other participants, and going up and down the mountain,

I always kept one eye looking for her. On the day of the downhill race at Piz Nair, I was relieved to find out that Lil hadn't been watching, as I took a terrible spill in the first half and never reached the finish. Four days later, I was luckier in the giant slalom and unexpectedly finished in fourth place. I was bursting with pride, but when I saw Lil at the Arturo Lopez's party that night, I realized that she didn't even know that there had been a race…By then, anyhow, I should've known that this kind of exploits wouldn't impress or interest her at all.

But what did interest her?, I was asking myself. What was her life, what was she thinking and dreaming of? Why didn't she seem to be really happy? This young, beautiful woman who had, I learned, three small children, a very wealthy, attentive, and attractive husband, a lot of friends everywhere…She and her husband became very friendly with me, inviting me often for dinner and lunch with Daria, with Ernesto and Carlo Stagni, the Hawthorns and other friends of mine. They introduced me to the Kennedy girls, Pat and Jean, with whom they were often together, a lively, amusing sisters act with their inside jokes and teasing humor. I had already heard a lot about their glamorous brother, the young Senator John F. Kennedy. We shared many pleasant hours with Phil and Lil Isles, and during the long conversations I had with her alone I was immensely attracted by her intelligence and sensitivity. But the more I saw of her, the more intrigued I grew about the real personality hidden behind her lovely smile.

When the time came for me to leave St. Moritz, I felt very close to her and I had the wonderful feeling that she also liked me and was interested in me. A new, marvelous friend-ship, which had enriched my life, I thought. Only ephemeral, alas, like many beautiful things in life. For it wasn't likely that we would meet again. Unless I happened to be in Paris when they passed through on their way to the States. Otherwise…She had her family in New York, and it wasn't in the cards that I should ever go to America, a country that I had never been to.

*   *   *   *

I was in Paris in March, when the Isles came for a few days after St. Moritz, and they did call me. It was lucky they found me, because it was a period when I was constantly sent on *Paris-Match* assignments and didn't stay much in Paris, where I was sharing then a small apartment with Dimi Panitza. Thus, three days after returning from St. Moritz, I went for a week to London on a story about Tito, interviewing, among others, Churchill's wartime envoy to Yugoslavia, Fitzroy McLean, now a member of the Parliament. (He impressed me very favorably, but I was shocked by Churchill's cynical pragmatism and total lack of concern for the fate of the Yugoslav people in case of Tito's victory. "Why, do you intend to live there?" he had cut short McLean's warnings about the dangers of Communism.) Back to Paris for just one day, we learned, on March 4th, that Stalin was gravely ill. It changed the plans for the current issue and I went, two days later, to Munich, where *Radio Free Europe/Liberation* had the best documentation on the Soviet Union. I had hardly returned to Paris, when I received a message that the Isles were in town and were having dinner at the *Perigord*. Excited, I rushed to the restaurant, where I found them in the company of the Kennedy sisters and another friend, Arkadi Gerney. Lil looked beautifully suntanned, and we were happy to see each other and glad to go night-clubbing at the *Elephant Blanc*. I knew that in two days I had to leave for Malta to do a story on Lord Mountbatten, the new Allied Supreme commander in the Mediterranean, and it was a pity to be away during the week Lil was about to spend in Paris. That left me with only one more day to be with her and show her around town, but I was grateful even for that.

They sing romantic songs about "April in Paris," but I can certify that the town is not less romantic in a spring-like, mid-March afternoon around the banks of La Seine. I drove her around the narrow Left Bank streets in my tiny, second-hand Renault-4Chevaux, we had tea in a cozy tea-room on St. Julien-des-Pauvres with a view on Notre Dame, we walked along the bouquinists's stands on the river, talking, and talking, and talking. For the first time she told me about herself and her life in New York and I gathered that her marriage was no longer a happy one. He was a considerate, exemplary husband, and she adored him as a person, but with the years, they had grown in different directions. Now they shared a deep affection and friendship, but it made her restless and not happy. I told her, without mentioning Faiza's name, that I thought I was in love with a woman who lived far away and whom I could never have, and that I was very mixed-up about my feelings.

There is, under the bridge Henri-IV, a pocket-size islet, a peaceful wooded park with benches facing the two sleeves of the Seine. That's where we kissed for the first time. It came quite naturally, as an inevitability that was destined to happen. We both stood without saying a word, looking at the water, deeply moved, confused, somehow surprised of what we had done. I didn't even try to understand my own feelings, and I don't think she did either. I was still profoundly perturbed but thrilled later in the evening when we joined the rest of the group—Phil, Dimi Panitza, Pat Kennedy, Carlo Stagni,—for dinner at *Dinarzade*. The Russian nightclub, with its balalaikas and gypsy music, could not have been a worse—or better?—place for my mood that night. We continued at *Jimmy's* until very late, and when elated, half-drunk, and totally confused I went to bed, I was still musing on the mysteries of the human heart in general, and my own, in particular…

On the next morning, I took the plane for Malta with Pierre Vals, a quiet, good-natured *Paris-Match* photographer.

*   *   *   *

The week we spent in Malta was quite successful, in spite of my big, and premature, disappointment at our first visit to the Fort Lascaris headquarters, where Sir Louis Mountbatten received us with all the charm and politeness of the great gentle-man he was, but warned us in his commanding voice: "There will be no photographs of me!" I was crushed. The main point of our reportage was to take pictures of this superbly handsome uncle of Her Majesty, the famous ex-viceroy of India with the looks of a movie star, now dressed in his immaculate admiral's uniform. "But Sir…" I started, but he interrupted me with an imperious gesture of the hand: "You can photograph my headquarters, but I repeat, no photos of me! Now, I'll be glad to answer your questions." Reluctantly, I pulled out my notebook and started my interview.

To my surprise, Pierre Vals didn't look overly upset by the refusal. He sat quietly on a couch in the corner, his Leicas and Rolleiflex on his knees, patiently listening to our conversation. My interview lasted for quite a long time and Mountbatten succeeded in putting me completely under his spell. But watching this most photogenic man talking and gesticulating against the backdrop of the magnificent port of La Valette, only made my frustration worse. Then I looked at Pierre. Quietly, unobtrusively, he had pointed his cameras at the admiral and was steadily taking pictures. Sir Louis pretended not noticing him, yet he was already adjusting his collar, turning his better profile to Pierre, striking more and more dramatic poses. Increasingly nervous, I continued with my questions. At a certain moment, Mountbatten whispered something to an aide-de-camp, and a gorgeous, gold-emblazoned admiral's peaked cap was produced. Fixing it carefully on his head, he led me to the balcony behind his desk. "Come, I'll show you some of the ships here!" With that, he leaned over the old-fashioned field glass mounted on a tripod on the balcony and scanned the waters in a most theatrical manner. Vals nearly had an orgasm: that was The Picture, a photographer's dream come true! Still pretending to not seeing him, Sir Louis repeated the scene, to make sure that Pierre got him well in focus. As we were leaving, he shook our hands, smiled, and apologized: "I'm really sorry, gentlemen, but that's my rule: no pictures of me!"

Back in our hotel *Phoenicia*, Pierre, a veteran photo-reporter, gave me a valuable professional tip. "Never forget that men are much more vain than women! They all love to be photographed, but the trick is not to mention it and let them pretend that they didn't know…"

I was eager to return to Paris before Lil left for the States, and we flew back as soon as the story was completed. She was still there, alone at the *Ritz*, for only one more day. But it was amply worth it. It seemed that I had never before seen the Bois-de-Boulogne with the eyes I saw it that afternoon with her, and had never felt the magic of Place-du-Tertre, as on that night, when we dined alone at the foot of Sacre-Coeur. And when she took the Le Havre train at the St. Lazare station before boarding her trans-Atlantic liner, I was already missing her. I didn't know whether I would see her again, when, or how. We just promised to keep in touch and write to each other.

*   *   *   *

I did write, or rather sent postcards as I continued traveling all through April and May. I wrote from London, where I did a story on Churchill's relationship with the Kremlin, then from Munich, from where I reported on the rivalry between Beria and Malenkov. While in Munich, I took a weekend in Garmisch with friends from *Radio Free Europe* and did some late-April skiing on Zugspitze. Lil sent me a few humorous post-cards from *El Morocco* and other New York nightclubs, co-signed by Phil and other friends I knew from St. Moritz. It was anything but love correspondence, just kind reminders of the sort one writes to faraway friends whom one may not see again for years. At the end of April I went to Cairo again, ahead of photographer Jean Mangeot with whom I was going to do a story on the Suez Canal, threatened to be nationalized by Egypt. Again I spent most evenings at Faiza and Ali's, always with a lot of their friends; again we visited the Pyramids; again I joined her for horseback riding in the desert. But this time I felt that my infatuation had gone, replaced more and more by an affectionate friendship. Had I grown up? Grown out of my juvenile romanticism? With all that had happened to my sentimental life in the last several months, I had given up analyzing my complicated feelings. All I knew was that we both felt more at ease this way, and continued to enjoy each other's company like before.

Mangeot arrived and the same morning we left for Ismailia. There we took a dilapidated taxicab to Port Said, on the northern end of the Canal, where, shortly before midnight, we boarded the French ship *Pasteur*.

*   *   *   *

It took *Pasteur* thirteen hours to cross the 100-mile-long canal from Port Said to Suez, a narrow route through which interminable caravans of slow-moving tankers of all flags seemed to be floating on the sand. It was a fascinating sight and even the blasé, cynical Mangeot found it difficult to suppress a few admiring exclamations, such as "*Merde!...*" or "*Ca alors!...*" In spite of his tough guy's argot and his indignant disbelief that I, or any civilized person, could even consider having a meal without at least a half-bottle of wine, he was a very good companion and we worked well together aboard the ship, at the *Compagnie du*

Canal de Suez headquarters, and at the camp of the British military controlling the canal zone, where we shared a tent over-night. Mangeot was a mixture of a feisty street urchin and a Left-Bank Parisian sensitive to the arts, who had friendships with people like gregarious Gerard Mille and sophisticated intellectual Louise de Vilmorin.

Mangeot was also a *bete noire* of Monsieur Roux, the *Match* administrator, with whom he waged continuous wars over expense accounts. That's why I was surprised to see the diligence with which he collected receipts for the smallest expenses and kept records, down to the cent, of every tip and purchase of a newspaper. I found it exaggerated when he demanded receipts from illiterate taxidrivers and porters, and especially when he asked for copies in Arabic of our hotel and restaurant bills. Had he repented, after Monsier Roux's repeated accusations of padding his expense accounts?, I wondered. Or had he decided to shed off his reputation of virtuoso of "*la sucrette*"?

"*La sucrette*" was considered an art in the reporters's quarters at *Match*. Its techniques were often the subject of long and heated debates, opposing partisans of the two preponderant schools of thought, both claiming to be based on psychology. The first recommended writing of short and vaguely formulated expense accounts. "Just write 'Travel'—so much; 'hotel'—so much; 'food'—so much; but no details, not much explanations. And don't forget 'Miscellaneous'! And claim a maximum for each category! *Le Pere Roux* may contest the figure and he would have the satisfaction of having cut it down, but even the reduced figure will be quite bigger than the actual expenses." The second school disagreed. It aimed at wearing down M. Roux by flooding him with receipts and overly detailed bills, with pages and pages of minute descriptions and uncontrollable items, such as tips, bribes, mid-road car repairs, flowers sent to secretaries, tickets at scalpers' prices for sold-out shows, replacement of stolen films…

A few days after we returned to Paris with our Suez Canal story, M. Roux called me in his office. He was holding our expense account, prepared by Mangeot. "It's a pity that an honest *garcon* like you lends his signature to Mangeot's machinations," he said in a fatherly tone. "He thinks he's so clever, but this time I've had him! He thinks that because he gives me all these receipts in

Arabic, I'm not going to check them. But a-ha!" he added triumphantly, "I'm sending the whole thing to a certified translator at the *Ecole des Langues Orientales*, just to teach him a lesson!"

He did. And when the expert's report arrived, it said that every single figure was rigorously exact, to the last penny. Mangeot had worked for days to prepare his naughty trap and, to his delight, Monsieur Roux had fallen in it.

*   *   *   *

When I returned from Egypt, *Paris-Match* was already all excited about the forthcoming Coronation in London, and Gaston Bonheur and Editor-in-Chief Roger Therond assigned me to prepare articles on the life of Queen Elizabeth. I was lucky that my St. Moritz friend "Porchy," the grandson of the famous Earl of Carnarvon, the discoverer of Tut-Ankh-Amon's tomb, was visiting Paris. From Young Lord Porchester, a personal friend of the Queen and Princess Margaret, I learned many amusing details and anecdotes of their life, nothing indiscreet, of course, as in those days friends of the Royal family were extremely loyal. I was getting ready to leave for London as a member of the large *Paris-Match* team for the great June 2nd event, when a message came from Lil and Phil from New York. They had received my Suez postcard, and were informing me that Lil was going to…guess where, of all places?—to the Coronation! This was a wonderful surprise. I hadn't had any advance knowledge of my going to London, and even less about hers, and I had already reconciled myself with the idea that I wouldn't see her for a long time, if ever. So I was very excited when, ten days before the Coronation, I arrived in London with the *Paris-Match* gang.

Phil and Lil had given me her address, in case I happened to be around London, (she was going to stay with friends, actress Glynnis John and her husband, corporate executive David Foster) but it was too late in the evening when I arrived to call. But early in the morning I took a taxi and went straight to the Fosters' residence. I didn't know them, but I was too impatient and didn't want to rely on delayed telephone messages. The uniformed maid who answered the door acted surprised when I asked to see Mrs. Isles, making me feel that the hour was too early for visits, but nevertheless offered me a seat. After a wait during which I began to wonder whether I hadn't blundered, Lil appeared, with a most surprised, but I guess delighted, expression on her face. The household sounded still asleep and she wasn't at all ready for visitors, so we agreed to meet later for a drink at *Claridge's*. From that moment on, I was engulfed in a breath-taking 10-day whirlwind of Coronation pomp, feverish work, and flourishing romance. We saw each other every free moment we had, which demanded almost acrobatic efforts, with her unremitting social engagements and my rushing between appointments, writing, and meeting the other *Match* guys at the office of our London correspondent Jacques Sallebert.

The very first evening Lil introduced me to the Fosters, who were giving a big party in her honor. She seemed to know the half of London and was obviously very popular. She took me to several cocktail parties, dinners and dances, we went to the theater and to nightclubs, always in a crowd, but we managed to have a couple of brief tête-à-tête rendezvous for lunch or tea. When the Marlboroughs invited her for a weekend at *Blenheim,* I went with Porchy to his family castle, *Highclere*, and maneuvered it so that he and his father took me for a visit to *Blenheim*, one of the greatest estates in England, where I surprised her at teatime. *Highclere*, where I spent the weekend, was no slum either. The elder Porchy Carnarvon, a jovial, stocky man who, like many English lords, was usually a rather nonchalant host, treated me quite attentively: he used to court Daria Mercati and she had spoken about me. "So you're the Bulgarian boyfriend of Daria?" he asked indiscreetly with a grin.

On Coronation day, my assigned place was outdoors, on the packed Mall, from where I had an excellent view of the procession. It was an incredibly cold morning for a 2nd of June, but the magnificence of the pageantry was hundred times worth all the shivering I had to endure since the break of dawn. My long piece on the personality of the new Queen was already being printed for the *Paris-Match* special issue, and I was now enjoying the splendid spectacle and taking notes of things seen and heard in the festive crowd. And trying to imagine which gilded carriage was passing at that moment in front of Lil's eyes, which resplendent Horse Guards regiment or exotic head of State in spectacular full dress. I knew she was watching the cortege from the perfectly located offices of

MCA, the huge U.S. talent agency, in company of its owner Jules Stein, his wife Doris, and a bevy of Hollywood stars, and I couldn't wait to see her to exchange impressions. But this had to wait until tomorrow, as the whole afternoon and evening I spent, like the rest of the dozen of our reporters and photographers, shuttling frantically between photo-labs, picture agencies, and the telexes and telephones at Sallebert's office. It was not before 10 PM when Pedrazzini, carrying the super-precious cargo, took the plane to Paris, where the editors spent another sleepless night, putting the finishing touches to an issue which reached one of the largest circulations in *Paris-Match's* history.

Two days after the Coronation, with frenzied London still incapable of calming down, I said goodbye to Lil and went back to France. But this time I left with elated heart: she had arranged to come and stay for ten days in Paris.

*   *   *   *

That's where things changed for both of us. After the four months of near innocence, the charming flirtation became a serious romance, and the simple thrill of seeing each other grew into an aching, insatiable need to be together all the time. Imperceptibly, we were overcome by that feverish state of alternating bliss and anguish, the affliction known as being in love. Ten days of heaven, and ten days of dreading the imminent separation. Being in Paris, in the most gorgeous season of the year, only exacerbated both.

People in love are superstitious, eager to see omens of some divine blessing. Were we superstitious, we too? I don't know, but something curious happened to us just after we bid goodbye to each other. Lil had left Paris on a Monday, to spend four days in London before taking her plane to New York. Unable to bear it, I flew on Wednesday to London, just for the day. It was only when I returned home, that I realized that she had gone, left for good, and was struck by the new emptiness I found in Paris. Luckily, I didn't have much time to mourn: on the Friday, the day Lil was leaving London for the States, I had to go to Coventry with Jean Mangeot, to do a story on the Jaguar automobile factory.

We left Paris by an evening plane. Mangeot saw that I was very sad, and we remained silent during the flight. He recognized the *"chagrin d'amour,"* and it was one of the few things *Paris-Match* reporters had respect and compassion for. By 8 PM we landed at London airport, where a Jaguar chauffeur had to meet us to drive us to Coventry. As we waited, I couldn't help not thinking of Lil and sadly reminiscing of happier times connected with that airport. But now, she was flying somewhere over the Atlantic, further and further from me...

Then suddenly, she appeared in front of me. She was as surprised to see me, as I was to see her. "What are you doing here?" she said. "What are you doing here?" I said, hardly able to believe. The way we threw ourselves in each other's arms was enough for Mangeot to understand everything. "I'll wait for you in the restaurant," he said, as he withdrew discreetly.

A miracle?—She had just missed her plane and was on her way back to London, after making arrangements to take the next day's flight. She had had no idea that I was changing transportations at that same airport, on that same day, at the very same hour. We were too happy spending the providential gift of an extra hour together, to muse about "coincidences" and "predestination." But later that night, in the car rolling to Coventry and in the plane taking her to New York, we both felt the sweet tingle of some unhoped-for, mysterious promise...

****

Chapter 19

Discovering New York and my mentor Cartier

O.K., I know you'll say that I am making it up! And I can't blame you. It seems that each time when things begin to look hopeless for me and I reach an impasse, I pull a *Deus-ex-machina* and my life story's plot is set again in the desired direction. But honestly, that is exactly what happened in that summer of 1953.

I had, as I said, fallen in love. But Lil had gone home to New York, for good, and I had stayed in Paris, for good too. So, as far as that romance was concerned, it did look like a hopeless situation, an impasse. By the end of June, I resumed my old activities—traveling for *Paris-Match*, attending meetings of *The Free Bulgarians* and keeping a voluminous correspondence with Bulgarian exiles, seeing my friends, having a busy social life. I cannot say that it was a sad life, or a dull one. In July, Match sent me with Rene Vital, one of our most amusing photographers, to Portugal to do a story on Don Juan, the pretender to the Spanish throne, who lived in exile in Estoril. A very attractive gentleman and an accomplished sailor, he received us most graciously in his villa *Giralda*, and also on his yacht, and we did a good story on him, his wife and children. What a tragic curse had pursued the family of King Alfonso XIII, don Juan's father!, I thought as I read his bizarre story. Alfonso dethroned; two sons born hemophiliac and another, don Jaime, deaf and dumb; his eldest son killed in an automobile accident; then don Juan's daughter born blind…no wonder that some people fear the number 13! Luckily, our handsome and intelligent host, as well as his son Juan-Carlos, seemed to be splendidly fit and healthy. (Soon afterwards, however, the younger son, "Alfonsito," killed himself at age 11, while playing with a loaded gun…)

Later in July, I returned to London, again on a story about the Royal family and Balmoral castle. Royalties have always been a main *Paris-Match's* staple. Our shrewd "Patron," Prouvost, no monarchist at all, knew well that no one was more fascinated by kings and princesses than the staunchly republican French readers, and he kept them happy week after week with stories about British, Belgian, or Monaco princesses. It wasn't a particularly intellectual journalism, but I enjoyed every opportunity to go to England. Meanwhile, I also worked on news stories, such as "Malenkov and the H-Bomb" or "Mossadegh's Referendum in Iran." That summer Dimi Panitza and I lived in his parents's apartment on Rue Franklin, while they were visiting Sava in South Africa. Upon their return in August, we rented a small furnished flat on rue Marbeau. Dimi was working as a junior member of the *Readers' Digest* Paris office and was also active with *The Free Bulgarians*. I had just bought my first new car, a *Citroen-11*, and our bachelor life was very busy and not at all unpleasant.

However...

There is a Bulgarian saying: "A man in love is like a torn sack," pathetic and of no use. That's how I must have looked to Sava, who was trying to get used to the discipline of married life and the routine of a boring job in Johannesburg (he worked for a musical records company, and hated it). Although happy with Pamela and crazy about his baby-girl Marina, he had moments of great nostalgia for his glamorous bachelor's days in Europe, for his social successes as a popular single man, for his frequently refreshed collection of girlfriends. Pouring out his heart in lengthy letters, he didn't stop envying me for the life I was having now. How can you be so stupid, he wrote, not to take full advantage of the great luck you have, instead of poisoning your life and wasting your time with hopeless, un-shareable, and probably imaginary loves, first for Faiza, and now for this married woman in America! Maybe he was right. But I just couldn't get Lil out of my mind, and that was spoiling my otherwise wonderful summer.

Then one day Gaston Bonheur called me in his office. "Cartier wants you to do a few stories in America, and it's O.K. with Le Patron. What about going for a couple of months to New York?" he said. I couldn't believe my ears. Of all possible assignments, I was being sent to the city where *She* lived, without even asking for such miraculous favor! I remember leaving his office with the biggest grin on my face, feeling like singing as I ran up rue Pierre-Charron to share my joy with the

Panitzas. Life appeared beautiful again, so exciting and full with promises. This exhilaration didn't leave me for the rest of the summer. It felt great to be happy, and know it. My veins were pulsating again with the sensuous influx of youth, optimism and health. There is nothing as invigorating as this physical feeling of well being and I savored it with every breath, fully aware of it. It was a time when I walked, as a song said, "with the kind of walk one walks when one is loved."

My departure for the United States was fixed for the end of September. In the meantime, I was really spoiled that summer, both professionally and as far as having a great time. After Portugal and England, I was sent to Rome to interview empress Soraya during the August crisis with the Iranian monarchy, while my friend Benno Graziani followed the Shah. A master in using connections and charm, Benno managed to board the Shah's personal plane, with photographer Descamp, and talked with the temporarily exiled monarch all during the flight to Teheran, thus adding another scoop to his impressive score. Graziani had to jump on the plane without any luggage and as his shirt was torn during a scuffle at the airport, His Majesty graciously lent him one of his own.

One week later, I flew to Dublin to write a story on Irish President De Valera. I stayed with Mont and Penny Kavanagh, who were seeing Neelia quite often. She had been married for already two years and wasn't in Dublin that week, but the Kavanaghs called her at Balliconeelly and we spoke on the telephone. Then, at the beginning of September, Queen Giovanna invited me to Cap d'Antibes, where she had taken the *Villa Cypress* for a vacation with her children, King Simeon, 16, and Princess Maria Luisa, 20. I loved every hour of the week I spent with them at the Cote-d'Azur. Since the Queen started, three years ago, inviting me to join the family when they came to France or Switzerland, I had become deeply attached to her, and with my growing devotion and affection for her, she took a very special place in my life in exile. For one thing, she knew my parents so well,—for fourteen years, until his death, my father had been extremely close to her,—she loved him, she loved Bulgaria, and we could talk for hours about the country and the people we knew there. With her, I could relax completely when talking about my unhealed wounds, about my homesickness, about my worries and fears for my family, and she would understand me perfectly. She also showed

me a real affection, which warmed my heart. To have a person of her moral forti-
tude, self-discipline, and deep religious convictions, genuinely caring for me, was
a most reassuring and rewarding feeling, and I loved her for that. In addition, we
seemed to enjoy the same kind of humor: she loved to tease me and was the best
audience for my stories. In between her European visits, while the exiled Queen
resided in Egypt, and then in Spain, our friendship was sustained by a regular
correspondence. In those pre-long-distance-telephone days, some people still
favored this most rewarding way of communicating, the personal, handwritten
letter, and both the Queen and I were among them.

The royal children were growing up and my relationship with them was evolving. "Mr. Groueff," their mother's guest, became "Stephane," the storyteller and
companion at excursions and games. Between Simeon, Maria Luisa, and myself,
we developed a long repertoire of inside jokes, newly coined funny words, and
imitations of people and accents, and we could laugh for hours. I must admit that
I didn't always behave my age, but we had great fun. The exiled king was still too
young, but for Maria Luisa that summer I became a true older friend and the person she was allowed to go out with. She was a remarkably bright girl with a strong
but charming personality, amusing and bursting with vitality. Having been
brought up very strictly, she was only beginning to enjoy her emancipation as a
young woman and to have romantic interests, and I often played the role of a
trusted confidant. As I had come with my *Citroen*, Maria Luisa and I loved touring the Coast, going to swim at Eden Roc with Simeon, dining with friends and
dancing in Cannes or Monte Carlo, listening to my jazz idol, Sidney Bechet, at
Juan-les-Pins, always having a marvelous time together. Thus began one of the
great friendships of my life, only to become closer and deeper with every year that
passed. (One among its countless rewards came several years later in Toronto,
when I had the joy and honor to represent her family and walk her down the aisle
at her wedding to Broneslaw Chrobok, her second husband.)

By September 10, the Royal family and the aide-de-camp Colonel Maltcheff
left for Spain. After four more days gallivanting between Cannes and Monte
Carlo, I drove back to Paris, giving a lift to the Queen's lady-in-waiting, Helene
Petroff-Tchomakoff, a dignified, Western-mannered spinster who had served at

the royal palace since before I was born. Ten mornings after returning to Paris, Stati, Mika (in tears) and Dimi Panitza as well as my *Free Bulgarians* friends Dianko Sotirov and Boncho Dimitrov, were hugging and kissing me goodbye at the Gare St. Lazare, as I took the train to Le Havre. A few hours later, as excited as a child on Christmas Eve, I was unpacking in the comfort of cabin 214 on s/s *Liberte*, for which *Paris-Match* had paid the sum of 470 dollars.

*   *   *   *

I envy anyone who is about to make his or her first discovery of America, a unique and, in the modern world, an absolutely indispensable experience. The thrills of the maiden trip will never be fully equaled, like a second cup of the best coffee never tastes the same. And if the person is lucky enough, it should be done the old way, by ship. It doesn't have to be a Christopher Columbus galleon, just any luxury liner, the kind that used to take six days to cross the Atlantic and was dethroned by the airplane in the 60s and the 70s. In fact, besides comfort and speed, the modern discoverer of America has a specific gratification: in contrast to the men of *Nina, Pinta, and Santa-Maria*, who had reached the New World by mistake, so to speak, and were disappointed to find a *terra incognita* instead of India, we, the new travelers, are arriving finally at a destination we were always striving to reach. To us it was a *terra* very much *cognita*, from what we had heard and read and seen in movies, a land perhaps idealized and mythologized that we couldn't wait to see. Impatient, we were coming with great expectations. Wittingly or not, USA had made enticing, generous promises to the rest of us. Reality, of course, was not always the same as the myths, but I have never been disappointed. Not since the first glimpse of the Statue of Liberty, after a week of a most pleasant crossing on the beautiful French boat, with its excellent food and amusing dinner-dances in attractive company.

I couldn't have staged a better entry to the New World. A gorgeous Indian-summer morning welcomed me with clear, blue skies that only New York can have on a 1st of October. As the cab took me cross-town from the Hudson River pier, my eyes were popping out with excitement when we passed Broadway, the Rockefeller Center skyscrapers, Fifth Avenue, and St. Patrick cathedral. At the

New Weston hotel, on the corner of Madison Avenue and the 50th Street, a message was already waiting for me: the Isles expected me for dinner that night. Before even unpacking, I called Lil and the unmistakable joy that transpired through the shyness of her voice was one of those things that make being in love such a bliss. We had lunch alone at a small French restaurant on the Third Avenue, *Le Bistro*, and I felt like pinching myself to make sure that I was really in New York and we were together again.

In the afternoon I paid my first visit to the *Paris-Match* office, a modest room in the *Daily News Building* on East 42nd Street. My new boss, Raymond Cartier, wasn't there—he was traveling in Africa,—but his assistant, Countess Mara Sherbatoff, a Junoesque Russian lady, greeted me warmly and briefed me about the bureau's work. She inspired respect and I liked her immediately.

With the Isles as guides, my exploration of "New York by night" started under most glamorous conditions. The first night they took me and two attractive young friends, K.K. Hannon and Patrick Guinness, to dinner at "21" and dancing at "*El Morocco*," where every second table with the zebra-striped banquettes could boast each night with at least one celebrity. The second night, we went to "*Le Pavillon*," known as the best restaurant in town, and to "*El Morocco*" again, this time with a budding British tycoon, Bill Hanson, and the adorable Audrey Hepburn, whom he was dating at that time. Lil, for some reason, wasn't crazy about this most fashionable of all nightclubs. But maybe because it was all new to me, (or was I more frivolous?) I found it quite amusing to watch the Duke and Duchess of Windsor having supper with Elsa Maxwell, or Clark Gable talking with Douglas Fairbanks, Jr., Aly Khan with a new girlfriend, Onassis and Niarchos entertaining some bankers, Errol Flynn flirting, Zsa-Zsa Gabor dancing flamboyantly, the naughty Cassini brothers giving the business to the ladies on the dancing floor…Many celebrities from the tabloids, the "cafe-society" from the social columns, the best looking women, and the most expensive jewels and fur coats could be seen nightly at Mr. Perrona's "*El Morocco*."

The weekend came, and Phil took me on his motor yacht from the East River pier to their country house in Sands Point, a beautiful place on the Long Island Sound, where I met their daughters Jill, 9 and Tina, 8. Seeing Lil in her own surroundings, in the background of the lovely home she had created, revealed a new dimension of her personality—the nest-maker, the hostess, the decorator,—and this discovery enchanted me. On Saturday, Lil and Phil brought me for dinner to country neighbors, the Paleys. I had read, of course, a lot about Bill Paley, the founder and owner of CBS, and his stylish wife Babe, reputed the *chic*-est and best-dressed New York socialite. Other dinner guests had no less familiar names: Mrs. Astor, Averell Harriman, the wartime envoy to England and Moscou, the Alfred Vanderbilts. The next day, young Truman Capote, a witty brat already spoiled by his literary successes, came for a swim at the pool, and in the evening we enjoyed a movie screening at the estate of Phil's uncle, banker Robert Lehman, the owner of one of the world's best private art collections. And so I went on and on, meeting more and more of Lil's rich and famous friends and social acquaintances. It was all very interesting and enjoyable. But at the same time I was realizing how different her world was from mine, how difficult it was for a struggling journalist to be part of the life of a woman who seemed to have everything. It was a disturbing and painful thought.

*   *   *   *   *

While trying to keep my evenings and weekends free in case Lil could see me, my days were fully occupied with *Paris-Match* work. Or rather work for Raymond Cartier, as his requests had absolute priority over all other assignments, and were always urgent. He returned from Africa nine days after my arrival, and after receiving me very courteously in his Manhattan House apartment, he put me to work immediately.

Long before I left for America, colleagues warned me that working with Raymond Cartier, *Paris-Match*'s autocratic viceroy in New York, wouldn't be easy. He's a most difficult boss, they said, a tyrant, a slave driver. A lot of stories circulated about his exacting demands, his bad temper, and his tempestuous outbursts of rage. Nobody questioned his awesome intellect and erudition, or his immense talent ; he was the undisputed star of the so-called "serious" part of the magazine, the incomparable master of turning most abstruse political or scientific subjects into highly readable thrillers. But he intimidated the reporters and the directors, even Le Patron himself, avoided contradicting him openly.

Cartier, a rotund, bespectacled, bald man of 49, had indeed very little in common with the typical Paris-Match journalist. For one thing, he lacked totally of frivolity or any kind of hedonistic interests. Completely absorbed by reading and work, he shunned rest and pleasure, despised vacations, and couldn't understand how intelligent people could waste time lying idle on a beach, or playing golf. Indifferent to fashion and gastronomy, clothes (usually baggy pants and checkered shirt) were to him a mere protection against weather's inclemency, and food—a boring, if necessary, supply of nutriment and calories. As a bachelor in New York, he fed himself at his desk with messenger-delivered hamburgers, while typing or reading a book. He needed only a few hours of sleep, and had the ability to wake up at any hour of the night and resume instantly reading the paragraph where he had left the page before falling asleep. He read endlessly, and read everything he could put his hand on—books, newspapers and magazines, statistics, maps, business annual reports, even comics. Less fiction, but everything concerning history, politics, geography, the sciences, biographies, economy. In between, for a brief rest, he amused himself learning to draw Chinese characters, or to solve problems from books on mathematics. An exceptionally fast reader, he read at least one book a day, and as he did that since childhood, the material absorbed in 40 years of continuous reading was staggering. Moreover, he was gifted with an almost super-human memory. Every fact and figure that entered his phenomenal brain, seemed to remain there forever, clearly catalogued and ready to be retrieved at any moment. He still remembered entire pages of the logarithmic tables he had learned by heart in high school. As a child, he used to amaze teachers when they asked the class to concentrate and memorize some long poem in one hour; only a few minutes after the assignment, little Raymond would get restless and raise his hand, which disturbed the rest of the class. As the annoyed teacher was about to scold him, Cartier would simply announce that he had already memorized the verses. Called in front of the class, the boy would indeed recite the poem word by word, after having read it only twice.

Coupling his extraordinary gifts with a workaholic's passion for writing, Cartier had become one of Europe's most read journalists, and also one of the most controversial. Politically, he was a man of the Right, a bold, unabashed adversary of left-wing ideas, a formidable challenger of what he considered "liberal hypocrisy" and conventional wisdom accepted by the so-called "public opinion," which he held in contempt. Had he lived today, he would've been a most outspoken denouncer of "political correctness." As he didn't mince his words, and these words were brilliantly articulate, original, and solidly documented, his articles often provoked waves of indignation, but of admiration too. Le Patron didn't always agree with Cartier's views, (J.P. thought, for instance, that Raymond went sometimes too far in lashing out at the United Nations, or was too harsh when exposing some French flaws) but he admired the brilliance of his writing, and also was shrewd enough to realize that the provocative, often outrageous ideas and splendidly argued petulance of his opinionated top writer were what made the public buy the magazine.

Yet Cartier couldn't care less about his popularity and was making no concessions to his compatriots. On the contrary, he deplored their chauvinism, their lagging in joining the technological and industrial leaders of the postwar world, choosing instead to sleep on the old laurels of an alleged French superiority in taste and culture. Above all, he accused them of myopia, of not realizing that the true destiny of France was, he was convinced, to be the central pillar of an United Europe. To such point he disagreed with the old-fashioned, nationalistic mentality of many Frenchmen, that at the end of the war he chose to reside in the country he admired, the United States. America the Mighty; America looking forward; America proud of its successful institutions, its industrial and scientific achievements, its victories; the dynamic, unapologetic America, the triumph of White Man and his civilization.

He wrote for *Samedi-Soir* in New York, when in 1949 Jean Prouvost, his former boss from the wartime *Sept-Jours*, offered him to become the American correspondent for his new *Paris-Match*, and also a director of the magazine. Cartier rented a one-room office, hired Mara Sherbatoff, who had worked as a journalist in France during the war, and started sending his dispatches. It wasn't just a regular weekly piece. It was a downpour of articles, columns, features, book reviews, captions, adaptations, suggestions for stories. Mara could hardly catch up with feeding him documentation, interviewing sources, and typing his torrent of illegibly handwritten prose. The indefatigable Cartier provided single-handedly an impressive part of each issue's texts.

When I arrived in New York, the *Paris-Match* bureau in the Daily News Building consisted, apart from Mara, of the photographer Nick de Morgoli, his apprentice-assistant Paul Slade, a trainee-reporter, Michel Duplaix, and Morgoli's wife Monique, who helped with the office work. Cartier worked in his apartment and appeared only rarely at the crowded office. He traveled extensively across America and around the world and was so busy with his own articles, that Match decided to send a reporter from Paris, (me) to do reportages that Cartier had no time to do himself. The bureau welcomed my arrival in a most friendly way, and a pleasant camaraderie began right away between me and the wise, ladylike Mara.

The relationship with my new boss was more complicated. Apart from being so impressive intellectually, Raymond Cartier was not easily approachable as a person. There was a kind of pride in him, a sense of dignity, or maybe shyness, which prohibited any display of intimate feelings or human weaknesses, forming a protective fence around his privacy. At the first contacts, our rapport was purely professional, one between a senior and a junior; polite, mutually respectful, but reserved. There was no question of the usual *Paris-Match* familiarity and convivial comradeship, and it wasn't only because of the age difference. It was, to a large degree, due to the fact that I was frankly intimidated by him and couldn't relax in his presence without feeling frivolous and superficial. Therefore we only talked about events and about ideas. Or, rather, he did the talking, and I listened dutifully, like a disciple listening to his teacher. And as he was the most profuse and fascinating talker when a subject interested him, I had the benefit of learning a lot from him.

In Paris, I had seen Cartier only a few times at *Match*, without ever exchanging more than a few words with him. My first real contact with him took place in February 1952, when he came for three days to Munich while I was working at

Radio Free Europe there. I accompanied him on a visit to the Waldkreiburg camp for Sudeten German refugees, and was impressed by his knowledge of their history and their problems. The camp officials were equally impressed. Cartier had taught himself German and read it fluently, but refused to speak it, because he was embarrassed by his strong accent. (He had the same complex with the English language, although his vocabulary and grammar were better than those of many Americans.) We had drinks with him and veteran photographer Kitrosser at the *Park Hotel;* bar, pleasant meals at *Hofbrauhaus* and *Rumplemeyer,* and a cocktail party Prince Constantin of Bavaria gave for him, and I discovered with pleasure that he could be a fascinating companion, not half as cranky as he had been described. His impatience however showed a little when he was dragged to hear *Tosca.* Opera was not among his favorite ways of spending an evening. "The only operas I like are *Aida,* because of the procession with the trumpets, and *Prince Igor,* when they bring a live horse on the stage," he confessed candidly. And when asked which kind of music he preferred, he loved to shock the questioner: "The shortest," he would answer with a chuckle.

In New York, I understood why he had the reputation of a difficult boss. Never sparing himself, he expected his assistants to do the same, which wasn't easy, given his unusual working capacity and endurance. Knowing how demanding he was and admiring the quality of his writing, I made a special effort to satisfy him and worked hard in order to provide him with a maximum of research. He was tough, his criticism was blunt, but he was also appreciative. One late evening, soon after my arrival, I had deposited at his building an enormous package with dozens of press clippings, notes from interviews I had made for him, and a few books on the subject he was writing about. I had spent several days at libraries and archives and talking to people, and long nights reading and taking notes. I went to bed rather pleased with my work. Now, this will keep him busy for a longtime, I thought. With that material, Cartier could write not an article, but a whole book! It was so different from Paris, where our average Match writer would be satisfied with two-three press clippings and a couple of pages of notes. Early in the morning, Raymond woke me up, ready for work. He had already read everything during the night, books and articles and all. "Very interesting, the things you sent me," he said cheerfully. "It's excellent! Now we can start. When do you think you can do THE research?"

After a few weeks, he showed that he trusted me and appreciated my collaboration. I began to think that, in his undemonstrative way, he even liked me, or that was what Mara told me. I was lucky, because working with him, I had an unique opportunity to profit from his encyclopedic erudition. Whether he was by nature a teacher, or he found in me a good sounding board for testing the ideas of his next article, he liked to keep me for hours each time I brought him my folders and notes, sorting out aloud his thoughts, vehemently challenging imaginary contradictors, trying to prove some provocatively unconventional point. These un-edited rehearsals were far more violent than the final printed version, itself hardly a model of complacency and conformity. I heard him fulminate against despicable United Nations practices, such as having the sinister Andrei Vishinsky, the Soviet prosecutor responsible for thousands deaths, preside over the U.N. Commission on Human Rights; or against Third World "crooks and ignoramuses" who pose as statesmen and are plundering miserable African and Asian countries, after getting rid of the European colonial powers. Intellectuals such as Jean-Paul Sartre and similar "decadent and arrogant crypto-Communists" irritated him immensely, and he despised "demagogues" like Pandit Nehru, a "phony who had the nerve to criticize the Western democracies, while in his India they still had 'untouchables,' people were dying like flies from starvation and epidemics, and 'sacred' cows lying in the middle of the streets stopped traffic. I was sometimes shocked by the vehemence of Raymond's views, but I never left his company without having learned a lot. He was so well documented, that contradicting him convincingly was extremely difficult. The debate would inevitably reach a point when the opponent, confronted with an avalanche of statistics, quotations, and historical examples, would have to admit ignorance of a certain figure, name, or date, and thus look rather silly, arguing without knowing his facts. I heard him once discussing the Civil War with an American from Atlanta. The man seemed very knowledgeable and was explaining some famous battle, when Raymond animatedly interrupted him to contest his facts. "No, no!" he said. "General Sherman was not there that day, it was

General so-and-so! You're talking about the wrong battle!" And he proceeded naming the exact units and their commanders having fought on that particular front. Startled, the Southern gentleman discovered that Cartier was a Civil War buff and had read dozens of books about it. Other hobbies were the French Revolution, ("I'm ashamed, as a Frenchman, to have for National Day the infamous Bastille Day and celebrate that bunch of despicable criminals and whores...) and Napoleon, whose every battle he knew in greatest detail.

It seems ironic that this exceptional man, who taught me more than anybody else in my life, was in effect so different from me. He was highly opinionated, while I am a compromiser, a man who sees the other point of view ; he had a strong, domineering personality, which I don't have at all; he was decisive, while I have difficulties to make up my mind; I am sentimental, while he would've rather died than show his feelings; he was a fighter, a man who spoke bluntly and didn't try to please people, and I'm the conciliator, the appeaser, the diplomat; I love music, the theatre and the movies, nightclubs, parties, leisurely vacations,—things that he absolutely didn't care for; he was brave, I'm cautious...I can go so on and on, the list of our differences is very long.

We had, of course, many interests in common: world affairs and a passion for the news was probably the main link between us at the beginning, and we shared the same aversion for communism. But the so-called precise sciences—physics, math, chemistry, geology, astronomy, etc.,—didn't figure among my interests. They seemed to fascinate Raymond, an avid reader of *Scientific American* and popular science books, but they used to leave me indifferent, if not frankly bored. Even at school, although I was quite a good student in most other subjects, I had a blind spot for science and math. Maybe I had never had teachers capable of arousing my interest.

Raymond was the first to show me the close link between these seemingly dry, technical disciplines and the great philosophical questions of the existence, of the mysteries of life and Man's destiny, which had always fascinated me. At first, I was surprised to find out that the un-romantic realist Cartier, this paradigm of rational thinking, was deeply intrigued by the "whys" of the Universe, a domain I thought reserved to philosophy, metaphysics, or poetry. He was genuinely preoccupied by questions such as the genesis of matter, the birth of new stars, the secrets of the oceans' depth or the origin of Man. To him, the enigmas of salmon's migration or the blind navigation of bats were infinitely more exciting than any spy thriller. Listening to his illuminating discourses on these subjects, I began to perceive the connection between them and the prosaic definitions of the physical sciences, between the secrets of the Universe and the tedious Table of Mendeleyev, between the splendor of a starry firmament and the boring math classes that I could hardly stand. From Cartier, a man who had no use for religion, metaphysics, abstract philosophy or poetic dreams, I learned that there were other, unsuspected by me, roads to exploring the big "Whys" and "Hows" of existence, and that these roads were not less stimulating and beautiful. This discovery aroused my curiosity vividly. But it also made me feel ashamed of my ignorance.

The shame turned to real embarrassment when Raymond asked me to prepare the documentation for an important article on the *Nautilus*, the first nuclear submarine. Everybody was talking about this historic breakthrough and everybody seemed to know a lot about atomic energy. It just happened that I was totally ignorant in that field; it had been among the blindest of my blind spots. I had about a month to do the research, and I panicked: I didn't have the slightest idea about atoms, neutrons, or chain reactions; I didn't even understand the terminology, let alone write an article about it. So I started from scratch. I spent long days at the library, I bought books and magazines about atomic energy. And as I couldn't understand them, I turned to school textbooks and even read comics for children, with cartoons of atoms, electrons and protons. The Atomic Energy Commission sent me elementary brochures for the layman. Surprisingly for someone who prided himself for being only interested in "the humanities," I found myself spellbound when learning how physicists had broken the secret code of matter and had even released artificially energies Nature had kept locked up since Creation. My reading was decidedly becoming more interesting. Phil Isles knew an important member of AEC, Gordon Dean, who had written a book on the basics of nuclear energy, which I read. After a couple of weeks, when I knew more or less what questions to ask, Phil arranged a lunch with Mr. Dean, who kindly gave me all the information I needed. Finally, I remitted the huge file to Raymond, for his article.

When the detailed story of the atomic submarine and its colorful "father," admiral Rickover, was printed under the title "The Revolution of the Nautilus," people at Match could not believe their eyes: the by-line, in fat letters, read: "By Raymond Cartier AND Stephane Groueff"! Gaston Bonheur and Therond congratulated me on the telephone: "You must know that Raymond personally insisted that you be signed with him. It had never happened before!"

Apart from working for Cartier, I did a couple of stories on my own, including an interview with Louis Bromfield at *Malabar*, his model farm in Ohio. I had admired his best-selling novel *The Rains Came* since my days in Bulgaria, and was thrilled to spend two days with the great writer. But my main assignment in the States was to do a story on a great American university. We selected the University of California and in the beginning of December I left with Nick de Morgoli for San Francisco and Berkeley. In a way, this was a good time for me to leave New York, because Lil was about to go with her children to Switzerland, and we couldn't be together anyhow.

Morgoli, a Russian émigré like Mara, was a good photographer and a charming companion, with a pronounced penchant for comfort and civilized living. A well-groomed man in his late 30-s, with worldly manners and discriminating taste, he refused to settle for second-rate hotels, fast food, or cheap wines when on assignment, which would've been fine, except for one annoying problem: Nick was permanently broke. This didn't seem to bother him particularly, but it created problems for Mara, the bureau's paymaster, who liked him but had to constantly cover up for his debts and non-reimbursed cash advances. Cartier used to make a scene each time Morgoli presented his expense account, and he would've fired him long ago, weren't it for Mara's intervention. "This is the last time I'm helping you!" she would scold him like an older sister, and Nick would promise to reform. When we traveled together, I tried to convince him to be reasonable with our expenses and avoid unnecessary luxuries. But he was too much of a grand-seigneur to even discuss such plebeian matters as accounting. "We'll talk about that later," he would say, ordering a second glass of some rare brand of whiskey. "I cannot be distracted when I work. To be creative, I need my comfort." And creative he was indeed, always coming up with some imaginative idea for a photo. He was a good professional, and pleasant to work and travel with.

I was very impressed with Berkeley. The University was exactly what we were looking for: a model of a great American school for higher education, and very unlike our European universities. It wasn't only the scale that was different, although figures such as 1,000 colleges in the USA, and 33,382 students at the U. of California alone, sounded astronomical by Old World's standards. The existence of campuses (this university had eight of them!) was something new to us, and so were the fraternities and sororities, the Berkeley's gigantic stadium for 80,000 people, the futuristic "Bevatron"—one of the world's most powerful cyclotrons, even the beauty-queens and the football team with its cheer-leaders and pom-pom girls,—all this being part of the university! What a far cry from the Sorbonne or my Swiss Alma Mater! But what impressed me mostly was the type of the Berkeley professors and their relationship with the students.

There were no less than six Nobel laureates in the faculty that semester. Most of the professors were young and very informal in their appearance, manner and rapports with the students. None of the pedestals and striped-pants solemnity of European professors. I met the first one at the basketball game the Berkeley "Bruins" were playing in their gymnasium against the team of San Jose. Glenn Seabord, 41, a tall, skinny chemistry professor and sports official at the University, acted as excitedly as his students, encouraging loudly his team and screaming with them "Gr-r-r-rah, rah, rah!" at each point won by the "Bruins." I interviewed him the next morning, not so much about basketball, but because he happened to be the man who had discovered Plutonium, the second man-made element in Nature, for which he was awarded the Nobel Prize. Then we went to meet and photograph his colleague Edwin McMillan, another Nobel laureate, who had produced Neptunium, the first artificially made chemical element. He was 32 when he made this discovery. I couldn't help thinking of the chemistry lessons in school and the little I remembered about the "Periodic Table of the Elements" we were forced to study. Imagine: here is the good old planet on which, for billions of years, there existed 92 chemical elements, not one more, not one less. And then comes this guy McMillan, who is now sitting opposite me, talking to a group of kids in blue jeans and sneakers, and he adds a 93-rd element to God's list! And after him comes the other guy, Seaborg, the one from the basketball game, and he adds another man-made element, Number 94, Plutonium! Two ordinary-looking, easy-going men, who have changed, so to speak, Nature's established order and with whom we now eat hamburgers and drink Coca-Cola in Berkeley's cafeteria...For a day or so, the very thought of it left me in awe. Then one gets used to it: because there was also Professor Wendel Stanley, (Nobel Prize) who had just isolated the polio virus; and famous physicist Ernest Lawrence (Nobel Prize), the inventor of the cyclotron and one of the fathers of the atom bomb; and pioneers of the computer, working with the *Zwac*, an electronic brain; and the astronomers at Lick Observatory with their 120-inch telescope; and many other scientific luminaries and fabulous equipment unheard of in other countries. All this was part of the University of California, and was shared daily and in the most informal atmosphere with the students, who were actively involved in the professors' research and took full credit for their discoveries and publications.

The two weeks I spent at Berkeley and UCLA in Los Angeles opened my mind to new vistas and gave me a first insight into the world of scientists. Little did I know then that a dozen of years later these early contacts would prove invaluable in my future work.

*   *   *   *

Chapter 20

Assignments in the USA, 1954-1955

It was already ten years since I had been living as a "stateless" person, a man without a country or nationality, a "Displaced Person," or *D.P.*, according to the official terminology. Now, that I started shuttling between my last port of call, Paris, and New York, I found myself even more displaced than before. I had little reason to complain: sharing my time between France and the United States was hardly an unpleasant fate. Nevertheless, a *D.P. I* was. A U.N. agency, the International Refugee Organization (I.R.O.) had issued me an identity document and I resided in France as a "*Refugie d'Origine Bulgare;*" instead of regular passport, I traveled with a "*Titre de Voyage.*" It required entry visas for every country and each trip, a considerable handicap for a working reporter like me. Yet, in comparison with millions of less fortunate refugees, I was extremely lucky, especially that my recent displacements were not because new persecution or fear, but for new opportunities and love.

Cartier had been pleased with my work in the States and I could have stayed much longer in New York. That would have been the reasonable thing to do at that stage of my career. But people in love don't always act reasonably and on the day after New Year's Day 1954 I flew for Paris, because Lil was spending the winter with her children in Switzerland.

I've never "done drugs" in my life, so I'm no authority on drug-induced "*altered states of consciousness,*" a fashionable subject since the 1960s. But there are obviously other situations in which the mind passes into a different level of perception of reality, into states where "normal" reasoning ceases to apply, states with their own reality. To different degrees, alcohol, fever, religious exaltation, or extreme physical exhaustion, cause such changes of consciousness. Sometimes, even high altitude, incantations, or simply the spell of music, can temporarily divorce the consciousness from the logic of our so-called "sanity." Being in love must be one such state. How else explain the reckless behavior of a normally reasonable, decent young man like me, respectful of the established morals and conventions, suddenly losing his head in a forbidden, insoluble love affair? It made me feel guilty, and at moments the guilt made both Lil and me unhappy, although Phil had by then resigned himself to the failing of their marriage. But no matter how distressing, the remorse was powerless to extricate me from my "altered state" and bring me back to the reality of "normal" reason and morality. Of course, I must add, it was also a marvelous state, a paradise discovered at last, after having suspected its existence, a nirvana hard to renounce voluntarily. Lil had become part of me, the better part, and like many people in love, I was struck by the revelation, so well formulated by Plato, that full human beings are actually composite creatures, of which only one half is born at a time—a half as Man, a half—as Woman. Scattered around the wide world, they're both compelled to spend their lives searching for each other, in order to realize themselves. A desperate search against the odds, with only a very few lucky ones succeeding. The rest, the enormous majority, will never find their missing component and will never become full human units.

I felt that I had found my soul's missing half. Maybe that explained why our thoughts, perceptions and feelings were operating on such an amazingly similar wavelength. And why the very idea of a permanent separation seemed simply inconceivable. From now on, I felt, I would not function normally and be at peace unless I was with her. As much as we disliked hiding and being deceitful, we schemed and maneuvered to find ways to meet that winter; first in Paris, "officially," then secretly on a short but heavenly skiing escapade. We headed for Davos, but when we caught sight of someone who knew us, we retreated in panic to another Swiss resort, before he saw us. That's how we discovered charming Wengen, where we knew no one. Its snow-covered streets closed to car traffic, the bourgeois peacefulness of the hotel's dining room, the ski runs from the top of Kleine Scheidegg and to Grindenwald,—they all became thrilling pages of a fairy tale romance. When we had to say goodbye, the beautiful oneness that had just been achieved according to Plato's formula was painfully torn apart, and the unit's halves resumed their separate roads, one—she to Gstaad, to her children, and I—to my job in Paris. Luckily, the separation wasn't long, as later in February I took my "official" two-week vacation and went—you guessed it—to Gstaad. Again bliss and agony took turns, the joy of being together and the pain of hiding. Especially after Wengen, where open cohabitation had spoilt us...Now I had to content myself with seeing her *en famille,* after a day of skiing, at their gingerbread-like chalet *Bambi.* Watching the snow falling outside the windows, we would sip our tea and make pleasant conversation with the children or a visitor, dying to touch hands and looking furtively into each other's eyes, while the same soulful record would play again and again, Bobby Hackett's *For Lovers Only* or romantic French singers. The mountain would be already asleep when, my heart aching, I'd walk alone on the snow-covered path back to my hotel, feeling both happy and sad, sad and happy.

Then back to Paris again, and Lil coming there briefly for the spring fashion collections. The happiness was increasing each day, and so were the pain and the feeling of hopelessness. By end of March, Lil and family left Europe and returned to the States. Two weeks later, taking advantage of Cartier's offer to spend the rest of the year at his office, I was on the *Air-France* flight to New York.

My work for Cartier was exacting but very interesting. He had just married Rosie, a bright, poised and artistic Belgian lady he was seeing for a longtime in New York, and I found him a happy man in an excellent mood. True to his professed disdain for sentimentality or conventions, he had made a point to have his wedding in a tongue-in-cheek way, during a trip with Rosie to Las Vegas. They walked into a marriage office, where customers were gambling at slot-machines while waiting for their tour to be married, and when the official pronounced them husband and wife, Raymond pulled the lever of the distributing machine to get the bridal roses. But in spite of the casino decor, this marriage turned out to be unusually successful.

It had taken several years for Raymond to overcome his skepticism about marriage and conjugal bliss. He had been marked previously by a disastrous experience: married briefly at an early age, he had gone through a bitter divorce, refusing to ever see his wife again. A son was born, who grew up with his mother, barely knowing his father. Now the son, Jean-Pierre, a gifted young writer, was working at *Paris-Match* in Paris, but he and Raymond rarely saw each other.

The marriage with Rosie was a success from the start. The metamorphosis in Raymond's looks and habits became noticeable right away. Imperceptibly, the gruff, antisocial bachelor who couldn't care less where he lived and what he wore or ate, as long as he had his books and enough writing paper, started wearing well-tailored suits and enjoying good restaurants. Rosie had fixed the apartment in Manhattan-House attractively and gave Raymond a taste for collecting Atlans, Poliakoffs, and other abstract artists. She followed the old tradition of clever European women who unostentatiously run their husband's life by remaining, or pretending to remain, always in his shadow. In Rosie's case, it wasn't difficult: not only did she have a limitless admiration for Raymond's intellect and respect for his work, but she was the kind of woman who found fulfillment in devoting herself to "her man." On the subject of Raymond, she was what the French call "*entiere*"—unconditionally loyal, intolerant to any criticism of her husband, ready to fight for him like a tigress. If anyone said something unpleasant about Cartier, he was likely to explode, get angry, counter-attack furiously; but he would quickly forget and forgive. Not Rosie. She would put the offender on her black list and would remember forever and never forgive, long after Raymond had completely forgotten the incident. Cartier was not easy to tame, but Rosie knew how to handle him; she learned to never, but never!, disturb him when he was working, and with a lot of patience, she taught him to enjoy a personal life, until he became totally dependent on her for everything outside his work.

Paris-Match had then no office in Washington, and Cartier used to send me there often, with the photographer Morgoli or alone. We usually stayed at the old Willard Hotel, near the White House and that spring we covered many of the infamous Senator McCarthy hearings, as well as press conferences of President Eisenhower, including a visit of Churchill and Eden. I went several times to State Department, the Pentagon, and elsewhere for briefings. But the main attraction of the Washington assignments for me were the weekends in Urbana, a village near Frederick, Maryland, one hour away from the capital, where the Stancioffs lived in their small farm.

After leaving Switzerland, Ivan and Marion Stancioff packed their seven children and went to America, Marion's native country, where, with the help of her mother, the wealthy but rather strict Mrs. Mitchell, they bought their Urbana home. It was a huge, old house with a long porch and a lot of Southern charm, to which a few Stancioff's pieces of furniture added some European flavor. The family didn't have much money and lived modestly, doing their own cleaning, gardening, repairs and repainting, cultivating their own vegetables and milking their cow. But the unpretentious country house had become a favorite gathering places for diplomats and Europeans living in Washington.

In spirit and the way it was run, the farm was not much unlike a family commune. The host and hostess seldom knew, or cared about, the exact number of its inhabitants, which changed daily. On weekdays, it included at least a dozen of Stancioffs and friends, plus a few resident outsiders, mostly European refugees, impoverished Russian and Polish aristocrats, or temporarily homeless friends of friends. Each time a foreigner with a recommendation letter to the Stancioffs was stranded on the shores of Washington, he was given temporary asylum in Urbana, the word "temporary" being used very loosely. Some of them had fascinating backgrounds, for instance a brilliant Jewish (!) Jesuit scholar from Egypt, whom I met there on one of my visits. Another longtime resident was an Estonian, or Latvian, supposedly a very bright intellectual, which none of us could unfortunately ascertain, as he only spoke his Baltic language. At each visit that spring I was mystified by the presence of another polite man who came to table very promptly, ate in silence, helped clearing the table, and disappeared into his room. Finally I asked the Stancioffs who he was. They didn't know. "I don't have a clue!" Marion told me. "He was sent by a good friend of ours, saying that he had just arrived and had no place to sleep. We invited him to spend the first night here. It was several weeks ago..."

During the weekends, the farm's population doubled and tripled. As the guests arrived, each one was given a pair of sheets and towels, assigned a bed, (which, of course, the guest had to make himself) then lent an apron and sent to the kitchen or the garden to help prepare the meals. The ladies assisted the Stancioff girls with the cooking, the men helped the boys to peal potatoes, shuck corn, or split wood logs. I've seen elegant French ambassadors do the barbecue and dignified British diplomats cheerfully wash the dishes with the rest of us. The intellectual conversation around Marion was so stimulating, Ivan's charm as raconteur so entertaining, and the lively atmosphere around the seven sons and daughters and their numerous friends so joyous, that everybody wanted to be part of the Urbana weekends. There was always some amateur entertainment after dinner: an improvised show acted by guests and the family, a makeshift costume party, a comical sketch written by Marion and the older children, limericks and songs in every language, performed and enjoyed by all ages, from grandmothers to the youngest Stancioff, Andrew, age 16. And often, nostalgia supplanting this international atmosphere, Dimitri or Johnny would strike up some Bulgarian patriotic song; Ivan, Peter, and myself would join enthusiastically and the Urbana living-room would resound with "*Edin Zavet*" and "*Velik e Nashiat Voynik*," the military marches way back from the country we thought we'd never see again.

*   *   *

Don Diegue: "Rodrigue, as tu du coeur?"
Don Rodrigue: "Tout autre que mon pere
                    L'eprouverait sur l'heure."
Don Diegue: "Agreable colere!
Digne ressentiment a ma douleur bien doux!
Je reconnais mon sang a ce noble courroux"...

It's been almost half-an-hour since Raymond, who's driving the car, started reciting, line after line, scene after scene. He seems to know by heart all of Corneille's "*Le Cid*" and never stops to search for a forgotten verse. Last night it was the same with Victor Hugo's epics. "It keeps me from falling asleep when I drive," he explains.

There is magic in the balmy stillness of the hot, humid summer night, with the starry skies and the nonstop chorus of the cicadas—or is it frogs?—on both side of the pitch-black road. As we roll along in the dark, Don Rodrigue avenges

his father by killing the Count, and now he's in deep trouble with the Count's daughter, his beloved Chimene. Raymond's voice goes on, monotonously:
  "...Don Rodrigue: "O miracle d'amour!"
  Chimene: "O comble de miseres!
  "Don Rodrigue: "Que de maux et de pleurs nous couterons nos peres!"...
  Decidedly, Cartier should never try to be an actor, but at least the recitation keeps him awake. In a moment, it will be my turn to replace him at the wheel. On the back seat, Rosie is asleep, tired after the long drive across the Carolinas in the terrible June heat. "To really know a country, one should always visit it during its typical season: Russia in winter, the South in summer," Cartier had said as we began our two-week exploration of the Southern states. As for Rosie and myself, we were grateful that the brand new Lincoln was air-conditioned. We had left New York two days ago and after spending the first night in Richmond and crossing Virginia and North Carolina, we headed for Atlanta, Georgia, on our way to New Orleans and the Bayou country. Raymond was in excellent mood, very talkative, excited about every town and road we were passing, full of information, dates and statistics. Passing by the sites of famous battlefields, from Delaware down to Atlanta, Rosie and I received most detailed history lessons on every battle of the Independence and Civil Wars. Advancing into the South, I was thrilled to see this celebrated region we Europeans had loved to read about, since *Uncle Tom's Cabin* and Huck Finn and Tom Sawyer, and recently, *Gone with the Wind*, a bestseller just before the war, everywhere, including Bulgaria. Europe indeed had a special feeling for the American South and its ante-bellum houses with neo-classic white columns, its cypress trees draped in Spanish moss, its cotton plantations with black croppers singing Negro spirituals. Europeans felt an affinity for the lifestyle, taste and cuisine of the Old South, such as they rarely had for the Yankees, whose achievements they admired and envied, but whom they judged overly materialistic and less civilized. Even the indignation for the way Blacks were treated in the South, (segregated schools, buses, hotels, restaurants, and waiting rooms still existed in the South, and we saw an embarrassing number of signs "No Colored!" and "Whites Only!") did little to shake this preference for the South.

Europeans were sincerely outraged, but it was like criticizing and condemning relatives. The Yankees, they were simply strangers.

As an admirer of Dixieland jazz, and influenced by books and movies, I shared some of these romanticized ideas of the Old South, and we saw enough of it to make me happy. We talked to old plantation owners, trappers and jazz musicians and watched Southern belles with parasols dispense their charm; we visited exquisite old houses in Natchez, well-appointed with precious French furniture and English silverware; we spent an afternoon with relatives of Margaret Mitchell, the creator of Scarlet O'Hara and Rhett Butler, and visited her grave; we met defiant men proudly flying the Confederate flag, still refusing to recognize the Civil War defeat. But we also saw the reverse of the coin: miserable slums in Savannah, "Tobacco Roads" in Carolina, decadent "white trash" in Alabama, brutal white supremacists in Mississippi.

There was nothing very original or unexpected in my first impressions. But again, the clichés and conventional "truths" could not satisfy Cartier's inquisitive mind. He appreciated, of course, the picturesque-ness of the South, but looked for things beyond the obvious charm. In the Gulf of Mexico he was more interested in the novelty of offshore oil drilling than in beautiful seascapes with pelicans that Rosie and I were avidly photographing. On the Mississippi, he was less intrigued by tales about steamboat gamblers, than by the navigation on the new canals; while we were thrilled by New Orleans' jazz-bands and its streetcar named "*Desire*," still there, oddly enough, he inquired about new industries and atomic plants ; and as we admired the beauty of myriads of blue jacinth flowers literally covering the surface of several Mississippi tributaries, Raymond was seriously alarmed that their monstrous proliferation was endangering the navigation in the delta.

We often discussed the South of Faulkner, Erskine Caldwell, Tennessee Williams and the new literary rising star, Truman Capote. Raymond had read them all, although not always impressed by them. By the end of our trip, he said one day: "You see, they prove once more that novelists are incapable of being anything else but historians. Because the South they continue to describe, exists no more." And he elaborated: "We're witnessing a second Civil War, an industrial war, and the South is winning it. In the last few years, this rural, colonial South, this nonchalant South of the Spanish moss, is emerging as the new site of more than 15 percent of all US factories".

This transformation was far from upsetting him. Quite the contrary: although a staunch conservative, Raymond was enamored with modernity and technological progress. Few things irritated him more than lamentations over "the good old days." "What was so good about it?" he would explode. "Ridiculous! Even taking into account all the imperfections of today's advanced societies, human condition in the past was incomparably worse. Except for the privileged elites, the people lived miserably, with no rights or hope of improving their lot. And even for the privileged few: let's talk about longevity, hygiene, and medicine—how can you compare? Remember Washington's wooden teeth, and Louis XIV's syphilis ravaged body; and surgery without anesthesia, and the stains from the emptied nightspots on the walls of Versailles! Think of the shocking infantile mortality in the past, of the average population dying in their fifties, of the women accepting old age once they had one child or two!..Yes, tourists and artists rave about the charm of dilapidated Left Bank tenements, but would they live with the filth, rats, bedbugs and non-existent plumbing?"

"But Raymond..." I would try to defend the past, "material progress is not everything. Weren't old civilizations morally superior, their spiritual values, their ethics?.." Raymond would interrupt me impatiently. *"Mais voyons, Stephane! Un garcon intelligent* like you, how can you believe such nonsense?" And he would go into tirades on how more cruel, socially unjust, and morally callused the old societies were, compared to modern age. "We have horrible wars, I grant you, we have Hitler and Stalin and Buchenwald. But at least our society condemns them categorically, rejects them as abominable, criminal aberrations. But in the past, atrocities and massacres were condoned as normal part of warfare, even glorified, and nobody would even think of regrets or apologies. Remember our history lessons: King so-and-so ate the heart of his enemy, bravo! And another one beheaded his rival and drank wine out of his scull, and everybody applauded. Don't tell me that they were morally superior to us! Even most admirable statesmen like Thomas Jefferson owned slaves and it didn't bother them in the least..."

In spite of his reputation for irritability, Cartier was very courteous to me and listened politely, if sometimes slightly impatiently, when I occasionally formulated some objections. Only twice during our trip he lost control and showed his bad mood. The first time was an evening at *Le Vieux Carré* district in New Orleans, when we stopped for a drink in a Bourbon Street jazz-bar. As the black musicians were letting themselves go with "*Muscrat Ramble*," "*Royal Garden Blues*" and similar Dixieland classics, Rosie and I beamed and our feet found it difficult to resist tapping the beat. But Raymond's face grew more and more somber. He clenched his powerful jaws and his silence became ominous. After a few more wild numbers and drums solos, he exploded: "How can you stand this savage noise?" he scolded us angrily. With that, he stood up and we all left the bar. Not a word was spoken on the way to the hotel and Raymond didn't make any effort to conceal his displeasure. It happened again during our visit to a offshore drilling platform in the Gulf of Mexico. We had spent the night in Grand-Isle, on Bayou Lafourche, and at 5 o'clock in the morning we boarded the motorboat for the eight-mile crossing. Raymond was in an ebullient mood: nothing could have made him happier than exploring the primitive bayous of Cajuns speaking archaic French, and then being transported to the ultramodern world of the latest technology! But after ten minutes of very rough sea, his face turned pale, then green, and he locked himself into an impenetrable silence. I committed the imprudence of asking him whether he was alright. "Of course I'm alright!" he barked at me angrily. Rosie knew better and never asked questions nor offered sympathy, although her man was getting sicker and sicker. "Just ignore him and don't look at him!" she whispered to me. When we arrived at the platform, Raymond recovered a little and bombarded engineers and oil-drillers with questions about their work and technique. But not once did he talk to us or even look in our direction. He hated us for having seen him sick and not up to the occasion, as he obviously hated himself. His moroseness remained unchanged for the rest of that day and he went to bed hardly saying goodnight to me.

I remembered then several remarks he had made about the human body. Cartier, always in awe before the miracle of human brain and its admirable achievements, didn't think that the Creator had done a very good job with the rest of the body. In fact, he resented the imperfections of the body. "Some masterpiece!" he would say sarcastically, almost angrily. "Think of its pathetic vulnerability, of the indignities of disease and infirmity, of the decay in aging! It's disgusting!" In his pride, Cartier couldn't resign himself to the idea of the inevitable deterioration of the body. In his contempt for weakness, any kind of weakness, he despised the process of aging, but at the same time was fascinated by its mystery. "Aging is not a normal process, as most people had reconciled themselves to believe," he used to say, half puzzled and half irritated. "It just doesn't make sense. Look, the body's cells are rejuvenating themselves continuously; therefore, the tissues they form should in principle be immortal! There must be something else, not age, which happens in the course of life and interrupts the normal rejuvenation. But what?" And Raymond sounded annoyed that science, in all probability, would find out the answer when it'll be too late for us...

Being an agnostic, his protestations took sometimes blasphemous overtones. In those cases Rosie, a good Catholic, would be upset and ask him to stop. On the subject of religion, Raymond didn't contradict me when I expressed my admiration for Christ's philosophy and moral teachings: he readily accepted Jesus as one of the greatest thinkers in History; but a *mortal* thinker, a historical figure, not a divinity. One day, probably irritated by my conventional Christian ideas, Cartier interrupted me impatiently: "Look, Stephane, I'll guarantee that if you lived in the time of Christ, you would've been entirely on the side of the Romans! You're such a law-abiding man and supporter of the Establishment, that you'd have sympathized with Law-and-Order; and if you had heard of Jesus at all, (which is not sure) you would've consider him just a troublemaker..."I protested vehemently, I even felt a little offended. But when I went to bed that night, I thought for a longtime about what Raymond had said, and wondered whether his opinion of me was correct...

I stayed the entire summer in New York and in spite of the atrocious heat, I was happy there. Working with Raymond and listening to him was extremely stimulating and instructive; he adored explaining and I was learning from him more than if I had gone to another university. The office in the *Daily News*

Building building, with Mara Scherbatoff and her small team, offered a very pleasant atmosphere for work. Except that there were too many days of heat waves, when the small room with no air-conditioning became unbearable, making it impossible to concentrate or even to think properly. But the rest of New York was no better in those early years of air-conditioning and there was little relief to be found anywhere, certainly not during the stifling, sweaty nights in my small sublet apartment when the 90-plus-degree heat, absorbed during the day by buildings and pavement, transformed the city into a humid oven.

As for Lil, she was spending the summer at Sands Point, but drove often to Manhattan to see me. Some weekends the Isles would invite me to the country and for two days I would swim, play tennis and enjoy the company of their guests—Anita "The Face" Colby, Audrey Hepburn and Mel Ferrer, the Robert Lehmans, NBC's young genius-president, Silvester "Pat" Weaver, Lil's best friend Flo Smith…Then back to sizzling Manhattan. In the evenings, I saw Bulgarian friends. I was still very active at *The Free Bulgarians*, (in fact, when Dancho Peyev resigned as president in Paris because of his personal problems, I was elected in his place) and we were starting a US chapter of the organization. This took much of my time.

Some evenings I went to listen to jazz: one could hear Roy Eldridge at "*Jimmy Ryan's*", Dizzy Gillespie at "*Birdland*," Gerry Mulligan at "*Basin Street*," Red Allen at "*Café Metropole*." Such evenings had a double-edged-sword effect on me: they exalted my jazz passion, and at the same time made me feel utterly inadequate and hopeless. I used to bring my clarinet to George Damianov's, the former diplomat who played the guitar and we occasionally held small jam sessions. One problem was the repertoire: while I wanted to try blues and Dixieland, he was partial to sweet sentimental songs, popular radio-programs' hits with lyrics consisting of any combination of the words "my heart" and "in the night." He actually composed such songs himself, sang them with pathos, and insisted that I play along. Far more serious however was the second problem: George and I were equally poor instrumentalists. With one difference: I knew it, and I left each session discouraged with my playing, wondering whether to touch ever the clarinet again; George, on the contrary, thought we were great and couldn't wait for our next session.

In July, Anni Tchaprachikoff received her American emigration papers and came from Switzerland as permanent resident. Thus, in addition to my friends from Sofia now living in New York—Mattey Hroussanov, James Agura, Peter Orahovats, Liubo Dellin,—I was happy to have a person as close as Anni near me. In August, the Cartiers left for Europe and didn't return to New York until October. Before leaving, they did something that few of Raymond's critics would expect from him: handing me the keys of their apartment, he mumbled something like "Why don't you move in here, you'll be more comfortable..." Before I could thank him, (he hated to be thanked and was awkward in such occasions) he also handed me the keys of the brand-new Lincoln, his proud possession. "You won't smash it, would you?" was all he said, then gave me a few blank personal checks already signed. "In case of emergency..." he muttered. From that moment on, I knew that he had given me his total confidence and his friendship. This, coming from the man who had impressed me intellectually more than almost anybody I had met in my life, made me feel very proud.

*   *   *   *   *

Like a sonata's different movements, human feelings go through various keys, tempos and modes too, and being in love is no exception. In our case, after our passion had played in all possible minor and major keys, alternating between adagios and allegros, it had reached an intensity that cried for a finale. The need of a solution, any solution, seemed less urgent when we were in the same town and could meet, or at least talk every day. Routine, even in chronic diseases, makes somehow pain bearable; one postpones decisions, one accommodates. It takes an interruption of the routine to realize the gravity of an impasse. To us, it came when, in mid-September, Lil went for two weeks to Europe.

The separation hurt me immediately. *"Today is my first day without you in New York,"* I wrote in the first of my long letters I sent her every day to the Ritz in Paris. *"The weather is sad, rainy and cool and I didn't know what to do with myself. I was so used to you, to your phone calls. After you left, I even didn't know whether I missed you or not—I was unable to feel anything, like a dead person…Last night, it was a lonely and depressing evening. I hated the apartment. All the time I am looking at my watch, adding the six hours difference, and thinking where you are and what you are doing.*

I feel that you are as confused as I am. All my feelings are crying for marrying you, and all my reason and logic scream against it. Sometimes I feel that marriage would be a mistake, having all the odds against us. But at the same time, I cannot imagine my life without you…I must confess that sometimes I'm so worried about the obstacles and the doubts about marriage, that I begin to doubt in my love…I know that you have such moments too, and this is wrong, because I know that our love is true. But we are still not quite sure about the marriage."

Then, listing once more our problems: *"1)your breaking with your family and kind of life. 2)making Phil and the children unhappy. 3) our age. 4)the financial difficulties and insecurity… But we don't think that those are the only reasons of our doubts and confusion. There is in us another terrible doubt, which comes from our previous experience and from our intelligence. We are afraid of the future of our passionate and romantic love, of its end… Science, statistics, common sense, experience, all show that such "love" does not last. Do you think that ours will last after 5 or 10 years? What will happen afterwards? Normally, "being in love" is replaced by "loving," a wonderful friendship, habit, common interests and fun, etc., take the place of sex and romance.*

But will you be happy with that? You proved to be a most romantic and sentimental girl, and I am afraid that what you need is not so much me, but is <u>to be in love.</u> <u>Now</u> things are wonderful and the idea of an end of our romantic love seems impossible. But when (or if) that happens? Will you be happy with the same, too well known husband Stephane, or your heart will beat faster and you'll dream of other romances each time there is sentimental music or a full moon?…If you had doubts about the future, don't feel remorse, because sometimes I have the same doubts. And I know that I love you. We are too romantic, both of us, and we don't want to surrender to this logic which wants romance to finish after a year of marriage.

It's not very cheerful, my letter, is it? But darling, if you feel a sort of wakening-up from a dream, like getting sober after a night of drinking, then don't hesitate and let me know! Because, if it is happening, now is the right moment to tell me... There is no deadline and no ultimatum. If you don't reach another solution, we'll try to go on like before."

I continued writing every evening and, thank God, not always the same kind of moaning and gloomy analyses. I wrote also about my work, my weekends in Connecticut at our friends Bettina and Bill Ballard's, my interviewing Alfred Hitchcock, on location for a movie in Vermont, about asking to meet writer John O'Hara...But each letter said how much I missed her and how eagerly I was expecting her letters. I knew that something very serious had happened to me, because, beside declaring my love, I felt a need to share other most intimate thoughts with he, an irrepressible urge to confide feelings, which I was hiding even from myself. Thus, musing one lonely night upon the many books in Cartier's apartment, I wrote to her:

"...These books are giving me an inferiority complex, a feeling of guilt and jealousy. I begin to think how ignorant, superficial and useless I am at times, I worry whether I am using well the few hours God gave me to spend in this world. Am I on the right track? Where am I going? Isn't it a terrible waste of time, of energy and feeling, this life I am having now? The days fly one after the other, the weeks and months too. Everyday I am preparing myself for something. But what is it and when will it come? In the meantime, the years go by. Before I was 20, there was an easy answer— I knew that "life" was ahead, I was preparing myself for this famous "life." But yesterday I was 25, today I am 32, tomorrow...But what is it, to "live really"? I'm saying simply that I'm sad and angry if I'm losing precious time by not doing the right things. But what the hell are they? And why all those thoughts are always connected with you? Why do I feel that you are one element of the solution?"

I had to tell her everything, as though she held the key of all the mysteries of existence...Isn't that a sure symptom of being in love? "'I'll say something even more surprising," I confided in her, "last week I woke up twice in one of these most terrifying and perfectly clear states of mind, when one realizes precisely what one is, and that sooner or later we will die and disappear, and nothing, absolutely nothing can spare us from that. I can talk to you about it, because I know that you too, you felt often this icy fear of non-existence. And both times I thought of you and somehow it *reassured me. I don't know why, no more than I knew why, as a child, I thought that my father could protect me from that. But thinking of you definitely calms me down…Each time I find my real self and am faced with the true things in life, when I am alone with myself and with my God, there is always the image of you that I see…"*

In the meantime, Lil received my first letter, with all my doubts about our love and future, and, naturally, it disturbed her. I already regretted having sent it, but it was too late. Her reply, in which she called me weak, insecure and immature, was like throwing an ice-cold water on me. Very upset, I wrote immediately that I had felt it my duty to give her a chance, "probably the last opportunity of saying 'no'," but that I was now sure of my feelings, etcetera. Then the agony began of waiting for her next word. (I didn't want to call from Cartier's phone, because the bills were going to the office, with the name of the called person, and everybody could gossip about my calls to Hotel *Ritz*…) When no further news arrived the next day, I panicked. Nothing came the following day either. Then, sick with worry and spending the entire weekend next to the telephone, (I didn't dare go out for fear of missing her call) I wrote the longest, most desperate and pathetic love confession. *"This morning there was no letter. Hundreds of thoughts came to my sad mind,"* I said. *"Did you change? Did you realize that it was all illusion and dreams and in reality you are not in love? Did you decide to give me up? What a torture, without any escape! I carry it everywhere one goes, when I sleep, when I eat, when I talk."* I had sent a cable at 2 PM, urging her to call me, and now it was past six. Eleven in Paris. She's probably dining some-where in town, God knows with whom, I continued torturing myself. And if she doesn't call? What an unbearable night it would be! I was writing all these thoughts, line after line. The radio was playing the Cesar Frank's symphony we had listened together that summer at the Tanglewood open-air concerts. *"I think they do it on purpose, to torture me,"* I wrote. *"Everybody wants to torture me. I opened a book on color photography, just to have something to do, and immediately found a picture of you (by somebody called Rawlings?)—in front of a porcelain cabbage, in long dress, a full-page photo. I have it in front of me now."*

Then I went on about the symphony: *"I was listening and thinking: "You, idiot Bulgarian fool, why didn't you enjoy it more? While lying on the grass next to her and listening to the music, did you realize how happy you were? Did you realize that these moments will never come back and hundreds of times in the future you'll cry over them? Why weren't you happier, more in love, more grateful for what you had? Yes, I was very happy then, but at the same time I was thinking about the wonderful moments we spent together in the past. Switzerland, Paris—always the past! How could I waste even one minute in regrets for the past, when I was having the most beautiful present? Now that I am alone, I am sorry for every second we spent in regrets for the past and in worries for the future, instead of enjoying the present."*

I went on and on, how much better I would love her now if she were with me, how slowly time went when waiting for her call l *("…it is seven o'clock now, it is quarter to eight,…one of the worst 8-o'clocks I've ever known"..then 11:30—it's 4:30 in Paris …"I feel miserable and tired, and disappointed, and sick with jealousy. I shouldn't have asked you to call me, it hurts too much to be disappointed.")* While waiting, all sorts of memories came to my mind, and it relieved me to put on paper and share with her a few of them that night; small, insignificant episodes which I treasured because they were connected with her. I don't remember at what time I fell asleep. But there is a P.S. at the end of the letter, written the following day, shortly after noon: *"At last you called! I don't know how I would've been able to stand the day if you didn't l…I'm so thrilled about the news of your coming back on Wednesday, isn't that the best news!.."*

*　　*　　*　　*

When the Cartiers returned in October, I moved to the *Beekman-Tower* hotel, then to a studio in the *Beaux-Arts* hotel, near the United Nations. It was there that I took my courage and invited a dozen of friends for a drink—Mara and her cousin Georgie Vassilchikoff, UN's star simultaneous interpreter; Anni; *Harper's Bazaar* and *Vogue* editors Bettina Ballard and Cathy McManus; writer Romain Gary, now with the French UN delegation, after serving in Sofia, from where he brought me news from Radka; and a few others. But my real purpose was to find an occasion to introduce Lil to the Cartiers. She and Phil came and were both very interested in meeting the famous journalist I had talked so much about. Raymond, who hated cocktail- parties, made an exception for me, and I was nervous trying to guess whether and how much he knew about my romance. Although I was already very close to the Cartiers, they were not the type to ask personal questions. But I was pleased when he told me the next day that he had found Lil "*tres jolie et intelligente.*"

I still lived with the naive illusion that nobody knew about our "affair" when my mission in New York expired and, two weeks before Christmas, I left for Paris. I had told everybody that I was taking the plane. But in reality I sneaked into a cabin I had secretly reserved on the s/s "America," hours before boarding time, and remained locked inside until the transatlantic liner raised anchor. Then I knocked on the door of a cabin whose number I had memorized very well. Excited by our own audacity, jittery because of the risks we were taking, but radiant, Lil opened the door.

From then on, and for a whole week, we floated in paradise, in a secluded heaven between two continents.

*   *   *   *

Back to Europe, we enjoyed many more happy days that winter, in spite of the frequent separations and the constant worries about our insoluble problems. We were separated during the Christmas holidays. (Lil was with her family in Gstaad.) Unfortunately, she broke her ankle just on her birthday, the 27th of December, but still managed to come, with the ankle in a cast, on a brief visit to Paris later in January. I was still sharing the Rue Camoens apartment with Dimi, the perfect company and a good shield against feeling lonely.

In February, I took my yearly vacation and went again to Wengen for two weeks, then for another two weeks to Kleine Scheidegg, the adorable isolated hotel on top of the mountain where the ski runs begin. It was a lovers dream hideaway—no village, not many guests, no telephone,—just an old Swiss inn with cozy rooms with fireplaces and puffy eiderdowns, and cretonne-covered walls, which shook when a snowstorm raged outside. Lil's ankle had healed and she joined me there. We had some magnificent skiing, went many times down to

Wengen and Grindenwald, returning home at the end of the day on the mountain train, and took trips on the Jungfrau funicular up to the vertiginous altitudes of the eternal snows. With a guide, I skied on the Eiger glacier and one beautiful sunny day we took Lil with us, maybe too prematurely, to the glittering Eismeer glacier, where she lost control of her skis, fell, and rolled down the steep slope for about a hundred yards. To me, watching in horror but helpless, the fall seemed to take an eternity. Luckily, the virginal powder snow was several feet deep and she emerged intact when the guide and I rushed down the hill to rescue her. But she was badly shaken for the rest of the day and she never recovered her skiing courage again. But one of the most memorable features of Kleine Scheidegg were the delightfully early nights, when, after a very active day outdoors, the one's eyes burn and it was then difficult to keep them open after 8 PM.

Then a new separation through most of March. And again, the old doubts and moments of depression. True, my trips to America and the Swiss skiing escapades were exciting, but they were exceptions. My regular work at *Match*, interesting at times, but with periods of frustration, was not giving me complete satisfaction. I felt restless, feeling that I was not "doing things," and not even knowing what "doing things" really was. *"As you already know, that is an old trouble with me,"* I wrote in a letter to Lil. *"Am I too ambitious and not modest at all, am I too full of myself, or simply am I a man who doesn't know what he wants? But anyhow, I don't have the feeling that I'm doing much for the moment. A few articles, and some research, even when serious and on interesting subjects, are not, and cannot be, all I should do. It is not enough. I'm absolutely sure that it is not my life, it is only a pleasant occupation that I love and enjoy. But what is "The Real Thing"? And when will it come?"*

Luckily, Lil didn't have to go to New York that winter, as the children were in school in Gstaad, so we could steal a couple of brief clandestine rendezvous in Paris and in Zurich. In the meantime, I covered a few stories for Paris-Match in London (traitor Pontecorvo and the H-bomb; the conflict between Labour Party leaders Attlee and Bevan; Churchill definitely leaving 10 Downing-Street) and in Bruxelles, where Peter Townsend, Princess Margaret's love, had been exiled. I went with a photographer to Stratford-on-Avon to take pictures of Vivien Leigh and her husband, Sir Laurence Olivier, the famous actor on whom Lil had a secret crush (maybe that's why I wrote to her: "...*Sir Laurence behaved like an ass, and I hope for him that he is not this way all the time. Excuse me if I'm spoiling another of your dreams! But she was charming and very nice...*")

In Gstaad, Lil and Phil were pursuing their sad but frank discussion about the state of their marriage and he had begun to accept the inevitability of a breakup. I felt badly about him, but at the same time a new hope, still indistinct and even scary, was filling me with unreasonable optimism. Elated, I wrote her to stop worrying any more, because this was her *last* holiday without me. They'll separate now and in April she'll come to me in Paris, I suggested. In May she'll go back to the States, *not for very long*, I insisted, just to arrange the legal separation, and then she'll come back for good...And after?—I didn't know too well, it was all still too vague and exciting, but somehow, I thought, somehow it will end well, with her in the role of Mrs. Groueff.

*   *   *   *   *

Vacations in Koprivshtitza: Boubi, Radka, mama, grandma and I (circa 1929)

Christmas tree in Sofia, with my father, mother, brother, sister

My father Pavel Groueff with the U.S. envoy George Earle III

Pavel Groueff (in the middle, behind Queen Joanna and Princess Evdokia) at the opening of the Parliament

King Boris's "Throne speech" at the opening of the Parliament. At his right, Prime Minister G.Kiosseivanov; at his left-Pavel Groueff

With mama in the winter resort Borovets

Princess Faiza of Egypt; Neelia Plunket

Nightclubbing with Princess Faiza, her husband Bulent Rauf and friends, Paris 1946

Coming of age of exiled King Simeon of Bulgaria, press conference in Madrid, 1955

With the Bulgarian Royal family in exile, in their Madrid residence: Queen Joanna, Princess Maria Luisa, King Simeon

Lil, then Mrs.Philip Isles, when I first met her in 1953

The Eastern-Orthodox wedding in New York, by Bugarian Bishop Andrey

At our wedding, with Lil's daughters Jill and Tina

The club-atmosphere at the "Paris-Match" New York offices: with Anni Tchaprachikoff,
Philippe de Bausset, Myles Herbert, Paul Slade

My best childhood friend Sava Panitza, Johannesburg, 1961

with Dimi Panitza, as exiles in Paris

The golden wedding anniversary of Stati and Mika Panitza, who became my family in exile

Members of the "Paris-Match" team. Clockwise from bottom: Lacaze, Rizzo, Groueff, Therond, Rigade, Mezerette

At the 1960 Democratic convention in Los Angeles, with Henry Fonda

With Marilyn Monroe and Paula Strasberg in Hollywood

With Jackie Kennedy

With President J.F.Kennedy at the White House

With Fidel Castro, soon after Castro took power

My mentor, the great French journalist Raymond Cartier

My sister Radka in Sofia in 1961, after 17 years of ordeal

In Southampton with little Paul and my brother Simeon (Boubi) at his first visit to USA in 1962

In Antarctica

"Paris-Match" owner Jean Prouvost (the third from right) during a visit to New York. The other "Match" men, from l. to r.: F. Farkas, Dominique Farran, Paul Slade, Jean Farran, Stephane Groueff, Alain Danet, Jean-Paul Olivier

With George Soros, the founder of "Open Society"

With King Simeon II and fellow-director of the "Free Bulgarian Center" Dr.Peter Orahovats in Washington DC

With my son Paul in Koprivshtitsa, during my first return to Bulgaria after a 46-year-long exile in 1990.

Chapter 21

Bandung. Saigon. First taste of the world of Science.

In real life, things rarely happen according to pre-designed plans, and it wasn't surprising that in our case events didn't follow the timetable I had set for resolving our imbroglio. Before Lil had a chance to answer my suggestions about coming to Paris in April, *Match* unexpectedly sent me on an important assignment to Indonesia. The leaders of the principal "Third World" countries had proclaimed their desire to stay out of the cold war between the West and the Soviet bloc, and had called a neutralist summit conference in Bandung, in the island of Java. Apart from the host, Indonesian President Sukarno, the conference was to be attended by such stars of international politics as India's Jawaharlal Nehru and Krishna Menon, China's Chou En Lai, Egypt's Colonel Nasser, Yugoslavia's Marshal Tito, Philippines' Carlos Romulo, Burma's U-Nu and other top leaders from 29 nations. It was going to be an international event of capital magnitude and had galvanized the world's media. I was disappointed to have to postpone my reunion with Lil, but was, of course, very excited to be given this assignment, my first opportunity to visit Asia and the Far East. Wouldn't it be fantastic, I wrote to Lil impulsively, if she could somehow arrange to meet me at the end of the conference somewhere in the Orient? In Bombay, for example (round trip from Paris $ 620 in tourist class, 841 in first class, I informed her after calls to travel agencies). Or Bangkok ($ 856 and 1083 respectively). I knew it was almost impossible,—how was she going to keep such a trip secret and explain her absence?—but still, it was nice to fantasize…

I was delighted that photographer Rene Vital, a favorite of mine, would be my companion. Working with him was always very rewarding. Rene was among the best comedians in the *Paris-Match* team and his sense of humor came particularly alive in moments of difficulties or danger. His taste for adventure provided him with ample opportunity to demonstrate it. A tall, handsome daredevil with a mischievous smile, Vital had covered the Korean war for *Paris-Match* and recently had served as war correspondent in Indochina, where his exceptional courage earned him a military decoration. Four months before our trip, general Salan, the French commander-in-chief in Indochina, had issued an order to the Army citing for gallantry Vital who *"in the course of several reportages in Indochina took part in numerous operations with infantry and armoured units. At the end of 1950, he distinguished himself during ambushes against convoys on Route RC4, between Cao-Bang and Lang-Son. Won again the admiration of all combatants on July 3, 1954 at Phu-Ly, showing exceptional calm and courage during the worst moments of a Viet-Mihn attack and a counter-attack by our forces.. This citation includes the bestowment of the War Cross with the Vermeil Star."*

We flew through Amsterdam and Geneva, and after a short midnight stop in Cairo, continued via Karachi, Rangoon and Bangkok. Just before leaving, I had a bad inflammation of a wisdom tooth, but there was no question of postponing the trip, which soon turned into a nightmare. The toothache and the swelling worsened so much, that during our 3-hour stay in Karachi I had to be rushed to an airport dentist, who unceremoniously pulled out the tooth. The interminable flight finally ended at 2 o'clock in the night in Jakarta, which struck me as being the hottest and most humid city I had ever seen. Exhausted and full of painkillers, I tried to sleep on the sweat-soaked sheets, but even Vital's jokes did-n't' t help much that night.

We were happy to leave that steam bath of a city the next morning and fly to the resort town of Bandung and its pleasant mountain climate. The conference hadn't started yet, but the town was ready to welcome the expected 3,000 delegates. The streets were washed and scrubbed, the houses repainted, the walls decorated with flags; even the beggars and the prostitutes were sent out of town and the schoolchildren dressed in brand-new uniforms. We registered at a charming family pension with verandas in front of each bungalow and a garden full of flowers, the *Van-Hengel*, and joined the other 350 foreign correspondents arriving from every corner of the globe.

We spent two hectic weeks in Java, the first three or four days shuttling between Bandung and Jakarta's airport and trying to photograph the arrival of the major delegates. Everybody was, of course, competing ferociously to get near the same personalities—Nehru, Tito, Chou En Lai, Nasser,—and they were, of course, the most severely, not to say brutally, protected by the security services. It was in such situations that *Paris-Match* photographers showed their skills and incredible nerve. Vital was in his element and I was in awe of his ingenuity, dexterity, and hustle in coping with crowds, bodyguards and competitors. He was past master in the art of seducing female assistants, of dropping names to intimidate officers, posing as a member of a delegation, (even one of Blacks or Orientals) enacting phony tantrums or simply jumping athletically over barricades. A couple of times, after taking some forbidden photo, he was wrestled by policemen and forced to surrender his film, and at such occasions he would assume tearfully his innocent face of repentant cherub. But no sooner than we were out of sight, he would hand me, with a naughty smile, the genuine film: he always kept unexposed films handy, to be substituted with prestidigitator's adroitness in case of trouble. Eventually, Vital photographed every single one of the conference's stars.

The conference was solemnly opened with great pomp at the *Merdeka* (Independence) Hall on April 18th and lasted for an entire week during which speaker after speaker denounced colonialism. The greatest success, the most popular star of the conference, was incontestably Chou, as enigmatic as his country, a courteous man projecting intelligence, and authority and, unexpected to me, a certain charm. Although the experts claimed that in reality he had little personal power inside the Communist structure, the suave foreign Minister in his elegant buttoned-up, pale-blue Mao jacket,—an ex-actor in his early bourgeois youth, I was told,—served as a respectable, pacific and polite facade for his redoubtable regime.

I was taking copious notes and cabling them every night to Cartier at the *Raffles* Hotel in Singapore, where he wrote his articles and was also receiving the wire services and the reports of our Tokyo correspondent, Smoular. Raymond had no interest in chasing delegates and interviewing them personally, and no taste for the hosts, Sukarno and his regime, who, he believed, only substituted one form of colonialism to another, much worse. For Cartier, Indonesia, a huge archipelago of disparate islands hostile to each other, was a false nation which never existed before the Dutch "fabricated" it. In the name of "Independence," he said, Sukarno and his clique managed to reduce this fabulously rich and happy "paradise on Earth" into an area of misery and oppression...

To make sure that my material would reach Raymond, and Rene's undeveloped films would arrive in Paris on time, took a lot of effort, time, and worrying. Every evening Vital and I had to rush to the telegraph office and then to the airport to find reliable flights, passengers or airhostess to entrust with our precious packages. A couple of times, with no connecting flights from Bandung, we went all the way to Jakarta, sent the packages, and returned, dead-tired, the same night to Bandung.

There were relaxed, pleasurable moments too, parties by different delegations in folkloric costumes, receptions with Indonesian music and Balinese dancers, dinners with colleagues from other papers. Under the tropical sun and daily showers of exotic Java, the conference, with its extraordinary variety of racial types, colors and indigenous attires, was a most colorful sight, a real feast to the eye. But to Cartier, it was the symptom of something far less cheerful, the self-righteous signal of the end of an era, a harbinger of grave events to come. He was indignant against the hypocrisy of a conference which ferociously assaulted the European remaining colonial powers, France in the first place (many Algerian, Moroccan and Tunisian activists found full support in Bandung), while any mention of the worst colonialism of modern times, the Soviet Union's, was quickly dismissed. For that, Cartier mostly blamed Nehru, "a haughty, irritable, intractable man, nasty with the journalists, rude to the ushers, condescending with the other delegates, believing that he was the salt of the Earth, a false democrat if there was ever one..."

Summing up the results of Bandung, Cartier titled his articles "An Indictment of the White Man."

*　　　*　　　*　　　*　　　*

While we were in Bandung, alarming events were taking place in Indochina, today's Vietnam, then a French protectorate. The powerful Binh Xuyen sect had rebelled against the government of President Ngo Dihn Diem and a shooting war had erupted in Saigon between Diem's troops and the sect's forces, led by general Le Van Vien, its supreme leader. Raymond Cartier, who knew the situation in Indochina well, left urgently Singapore and went to Saigon. Vital and I received our marching orders to join him immediately. We already had a correspondent stationed in Saigon, Jacques Chancel, but the events were of such importance to France and our readers, that Paris Match dispatched also the veteran combat reporter Joel Le Tac, as well as our Tokyo correspondent, Smoular.

Finding airline connections wasn't simple, and it took us three days to fly from Bandung, via Singapore, to Bangkok, where I spent two nights, and from there, by a Thai plane via Pnom-Pehn, to reach Saigon. As the taxicab was taking us from the airport to Hotel *Continental*, we realized that the fighting had spread all over the big city: one could hear the crackle of small arms and see smoke over Cholon, the Chinese quarter. Thousands of people from the poor quarters where their straw houses were burning were rushing towards the central boulevards, frightened people carrying babies and loads of pitiful belongings. They were joining other thousands of refugees from the Communist North Vietnam and the city was overcrowded with a miserable crowds living on the sidewalks, sleeping, eating and washing in the streets. The sidewalks in front of the *Continental* were covered with sleeping bodies, mainly women and children, and we had to jump over them to enter the hotel.

Rene knew the place pretty well and he led me from our hotel to the *Majestic,* where Raymond and Rosie were staying. I found the center of the city very pretty, with its large, tree-lined boulevards and nice French-style buildings, giving it a feeling of an elegant South of France town. The Cartiers were lunching on the roof terrace with Chancel and his wife, Le Tac and Smoular. After welcoming us warmly and congratulating us for our work in Bandung, they briefed us on the situation in Saigon. As we were talking, several detonations shook the air; from the roof terrace as we watched in the distance parts of Cholon were burning, a hallucinating sight for me, the newcomer.

As fighting continued during the following days, the sound of machine guns and howitzers became part of the usual street noises and didn't disturb me as much as in the first day, especially that there were no combats downtown. But things were different when we had to go and take photos of the action in other neighborhoods. Once we found ourselves caught in cross fire, with bullets whistling around and we throwing ourselves on the ground. To see bullets tracing luminous tracks in the air in front and behind me was quite a new experience for me, fascinating but hardly reassuring. "Run in zigzag, don't walk in straight line like an idiot!" Vital was shouting as I followed him in the deserted streets, imitating his movements, not knowing where I was. I was definitely scared, and rightly so: that day many people were killed, among them two correspondents—an American fellow and a French woman.

What made things worse was that I couldn't figure out who was fighting whom. The French troops kept neutrality and although present everywhere, this time they didn't involve themselves in the shooting. As to the belligerents, not only did they look alike, wore the same uniforms, and had similar names (general Van Vy, general Van Ty, etc.) but it appeared to us, foreigners, that they weren't quite certain why, for what and against whom they were fighting. Internal Vietnamese politics and rivalries were so complicated and constantly changing, that it took me many days and several briefings at both headquarters to begin to understand anything. Luckily, Cartier knew the scene well and had personally met many of the principal actors, including President Diem and general Le Van Vien, but even he found some events confusing and incomprehensible.

At secret briefings of the rebellious sect's command, which I attended with great precautions a couple of times, I became acquainted with a friendly senior officer, who was as bitter and convincing in his anti-government grievances, as he was willing to cooperate with me and see them aired in *Paris-Match*. One can imagine my stupefaction a few days later when I attended a governmental press conference and saw the same officer sitting at the table of the officials! Assuming that he was spying there, I pretended not to know him, but he recognized me and greeted me most cordially. At the end of the briefing, I took him aside.

"Didn't you tell me the other day that so-and-so...?" I confronted him. "Yes, I did," he replied.

"But you seem to be friends with these people here, and they're telling a very different story..."

"So?" he asked, sounding very sincere.

"I don't understand. You shoot at each other, they're your adversaries, and you're still friends?"

Now he became impatient. "Yes, and we'll continue to fight. By the way, my unit is waiting for me, I'm late. But you, Westerners, you're funny. For you everything has to be black or white. Nothing is black-or-white in life, remember that!" And he left for the battlefront, leaving me quite perplexed.

A couple of days later, another experience put my Western logic to a similar test, this time shared with Raymond. The fighting had subsided in Saigon, but another sect, the Cao-Dai, had taken arms against the government and heavy battles were raging in the area, with many casualties on both sides. Raymond had arranged an audience with the Cao-Daist "Pope," His Holiness Pham Cong-Tac, at his capital of Tay-Ninh, in the mountains, and Rosie and I joined him. The first surprise was that our "secret" pick-up place in Saigon was...at the Defense Ministry building! This was a week when the government troops, commanded by a Caodaist renegade, general Trinh Minh-The, were engaged in bloody battles against the "Pope's" forces. An officer from the Ministry, who introduced himself as a member of the sect, drove us to the airport, where a small government airplane (!) was waiting to take us to the enemy's headquarters! It was rather confusing, but our official guide was charming and informative. Upon arrival, he took us around Tay-Ninh and showed us its strange cathedral, where, next to large, rather naive frescoes of Jesus Christ, Buddha, and other "Great Initiated," we saw the familiar bearded figure of Victor Hugo in uniform of the Academie Francaise.

But we waited and waited, and there was no sign of the "Pope." Finally, an apologetic assistant appeared to express Pham Cong-Tac's deep regrets that the audience he had promised Monsieur Cartier had to be cancelled, for reason of the sudden, tragic death of a extremely close, beloved person. His Holiness was profoundly affected by this loss, the assistant said. Raymond was annoyed, but there was nothing we could do but return to Saigon. It was only in the plane, when our guide told us the identity of the much-lamented deceased, that we could measure the difference between our logic and theirs: the "beloved person" was the "Pope's" archenemy, general Trinh Minh-The, killed that day in Saigon. I was still puzzled, when our Cao-Dai escort drove us to our hotels, wished us goodnight and returned to his office. Incidentally, we had learned the government was paying his salary, like the salaries of the other rebellious offers.

After a week or so, the fighting stopped and some sort of truce was signed between President Diem and the leaders of the sects. The shooting ceased, the tremendous tension relaxed, the all-night curfew was lifted. The night before I left Saigon, we decided to celebrate and Raymond took us for a Chinese dinner at the "Arc-en-Ciel" restaurant. We were all in a great mood and after dinner the Chancels led us to a nightclub, *La Cabane*, packed with journalists, French officers and civilians, out for the first time after the cease-fire. As the band was playing and couples were dancing happily, Jacques Chancel jumped on stage, grabbed the bass fiddle and joined the orchestra, quite aptly. Delighted, our table applauded noisily and Lucien Baudard, a well-known French correspondent, complimented Raymond: "Not bad, your man!" Equally surprised, Raymond answered proudly: "Yes, our *Match* boys can do anything! Tell him, Stephane!"

"Of course, we do!" I answered and at that moment one of my Walter-Mitty-dreams came true. To the infinite surprise of Raymond, Rosie and the rest of the table, I stood up, walked to the bandstand and borrowed the clarinet from one of the musicians.

By chance, the band was playing *"I Can't Give You Anything but Love,"* one of the few pieces I knew and liked to play. I'll never forget the expression on the faces of Rosie and Raymond, who had never suspected that hobby of mine, when I started blowing. They remained speechless until the number was over, then, flabbergasted, joined the applause.

*　　　*　　　*　　　*

The letter Cartier sent me to Paris in the beginning of June arrived at a most crucial moment. Lil had been in Paris since mid-May, arriving just two days after

I returned from the Far East. On my way back from Saigon, I had stopped for three days in Calcutta, profiting of the opportunity to see a little of India, a country which had always intrigued me. I cannot say that I liked Calcutta. It fascinated me, moved me, impressed and shocked me maybe more than any other city I had seen, but I wouldn't use the word "liked." Mostly, I was shocked. Calcutta's indescribable misery, filth and human degradation affected me to a point of making me feel sick and deeply depressed.

God knows I had seen poverty and appalling living conditions, but it took me several days to recover from the things I saw in Calcutta.

So, after being separated for more than a month, Lil and I were reunited in Paris. In the meantime things had gone very far: she had had very frank talks with Phil and they had decided to try a separation. Not a divorce, for the time being, but an amiable and legally arranged separation. He had been very understanding and gentlemanly, and they had agreed that she would move into an apartment of her own; in order to avoid interrupting the children's school routine and lifestyle, which Phil alone could afford, they would continue to live in the present home during the weekdays, with their governess Miss Fischer and the servants they were accustomed to, but would spend their weekends and vacations with their mother. Lil felt in a way relieved to put an end to her double life and have her freedom, but couldn't help being apprehensive of the radical change of life that this arrangement was going to mean for her. Mostly, she was deeply perturbed by the idea of being separated from the children. But both she and Phil agreed that there was no other solution, unless she gave me up completely and tried to patch up their failing marriage.

We were both disturbed, unsure of what to do and worried about the future. But one thing seemed inconceivable: to say goodbye forever. For the moment, Lil was going to try and spend as much time as she could in Paris and, as staying at the *Ritz* was going to be financially excluded from now on, she looked for a small apartment to rent. She found a furnished one on the top of an old building on Avenue d'Iena, near L'Etoile and the *Paris-Match* offices, and made her debut as a Parisian housewife—shopping at the neighborhood stores, preparing meals, trying her French on the cleaning woman. To me, this was something overwhelming and un-hoped for—an exceptionally attractive woman, blessed with everything money can offer, was ready to give up so much and risk everything, to change her life totally,—all this for me, the penniless, insecure, unimportant me!...I was overcome by happiness, by gratitude, but also by an enormous sense of responsibility and fear of failing her.

And now this letter. "Let's do the series on the World—its origin, its essence, its destiny,—let's do it together, cher Stephane!" Raymond wrote from New York. "I'm very excited by the subject, and now I think I know how to approach it. Try to come before Rosie and I leave in July, so we can discuss it in detail!" The idea wasn't new to me, Cartier had mentioned it before and I remembered how surprised and delighted I was to hear this man, whose mind I admired but thought impervious to metaphysical or purely philosophical problems, concerning himself with things such as infinity, eternity, and the whys and hows of life. He soon corrected my misconception, by pointing out that he didn't mean metaphysics, religion, or abstract philosophy, but was talking about the precise sciences, about experimental research and concrete scientific observations. What a fascinating subject it would be, he said, to describe this research and sum up the results, as of today!

The idea appealed to me very much, but the subject was totally beyond my competence. To penetrate the world of scientists who explore the mysteries of Creation and Existence!..Wait a minute, I thought, what do WE know about Science? Myself, I knew almost nothing. Even the great Cartier, with all due respect for his phenomenal erudition,—he was no scientist; wouldn't be too immodest, if not absurd, for outsiders like us, journalists, to try to answer the great eternal questions? "Can you imagine more important questions than 'Where the World comes from, where is it headed to, what is Life?'" Raymond elaborated on the telephone, when I called him eagerly the next day. "Every person has asked them and always will. So there is no more fascinating subject to explore. We won't claim, of course, to give answers. We can't, and nobody can. But every generation, every civilization, have tried to solve the enigma. The present generation is no exception; on the contrary, today's scientists have the benefit of incomparably better tools, of unprecedented experience and accumulated observations. Let's see what they have found out so far, for what it's worth! Don't you see that as journalists, we are best equipped to investigate, to interview and describe the scientists, their methods and results, in comprehensible language that the average educated layman would understand and enjoy reading? Not in esoteric jargon, Latin and mathematical formulas, as experts usually do."

Cartier was so convincing that at the end of June, when I joined him in New York, I found myself more stimulated than I had been by almost any other subject before. We drew a general plan for the series, which had to consist of ten long articles, richly illustrated in black-and-white and color, to start by the beginning of 1956. This allowed me six months for organizing the investigation and preparing the documentation for the first three or four articles by Cartier. Most importantly, it allowed me a couple of months for my own elementary education, which, in view of my quasi-total ignorance of the Sciences, turned out to be painfully inadequate. Meanwhile, I was excused from any other *Paris-Match* work and didn't go to the office, except for a couple of hours in the afternoon, when I could. My presence wasn't needed, as by then Mara Scherbatoff was given two new collaborators: the quick, flamboyant reporter Mathias had been sent temporarily from Paris, and Anni Tchaprachikoff, who had impressed the Cartiers and Mara very favorably when I introduced her to them, was hired to help with the office work.

Cartier did me another favor. *Radio Free Europe*, whose headquarters were still in New York, had some problems with the Bulgarian desk and was in the process of reorganizing it drastically. Since the winter of 1951/52 when I worked at the Munich *RFE* News desk, I was on excellent terms with them, and now they asked me to take over the direction of the Bulgarian services. The offer was very tempting, especially that it involved much creative work with the projected reform of the entire program. But this time I was too committed with *Paris-Match* and didn't succumb to the enticement of my charming ex-boss Bill Rafael and his colleagues, as I did in 1951. I kept Raymond informed about my conversations with *RFE* and he, the ardent anti-communist, sympathized fully with my frustration at missing such a stimulating opportunity. "You should accept," he told me, to my surprise, a few days later. "Not full-time, of course, not as director—we have much work to do now, you and I,—but why don't you do it on half-time basis?" A prodigy of work himself, he thought it perfectly normal that other people do several job at the same time.

He turned out to be the right advice. *Radio Free Europe* and I found a compromise solution and I was named "consultant" to the Bulgarian desk, with vast powers to hire, fire, and create a new program. It was agreed that I would work at the RFE offices on West 57th Street in the morning only, leaving me the rest of my time to *Paris-Match*. On July 20, Rafael assembled the members of the Bulgarian desk and introduced me officially. Most of them welcomed my appointment and gave me a warm Reception. But the desk's old leaders, predominantly supporters of Dr. G.M. Dimitrov's "National Committee," were less happy. In those days, they considered me and my *Free Bulgarians* friends as being too conservative and "right-wing," while we viewed them as "leftists" and former fellow travelers.

As soon as I arranged my time-schedule and settled in the cozy East-side bachelor's studio of Mara's cousin, Georgie Vassiltchikoff, which I sublet for the summer, I plunged into Cartier's project. To start, I perused the entire collection of *Scientific American* for several years, as well as the science-pages of *The New York Times, Time, Newsweek* and other publications I could understand, taking ample notes, copying book titles and names of top experts. Then I bought several books and read dozens of others at the 42nd street's Public Library, where I spent most afternoons. The reading room wasn't air-conditioned in those days, and the Xerox facilities were still primitive or non-existent, so I used to copy by hand, page after page, until I couldn't hold the pen any more. Many texts were just Chinese to me and I had many moments of discouragement. But other pages were true revelations, and a delight to read. Thanks to highly stimulating popularizations written imaginatively and in accessible language, I quickly fell under the spell of Cosmology. George Gamow, a great Russian physicist, who had emigrated and worked in the States because of the heavy-handed intrusiveness of Soviet pseudo-scientists of the type of the infamous Lysenko, was one of the authors whose exciting, often witty, writings changed many ideas I had about some great topics in science. The idea about the Universe, for instance. I had always assumed, like an axiom, that the Universe was eternal and infinite, something that had always existed and that had no limits. Not so, I read, to my surprise. It <u>did</u> have its limited, measurable dimensions. It <u>did</u> have a beginning, and scientists were even trying to determine the precise date and hour when it was born. They thought they knew exactly how it happened. In Gamow's books, I read for the first time, in total disbelief of course, some rather detailed descriptions of that event, which he was calling the "Big Bang." I think it was Gamow who coined the term, soon to become used universally.

After weeks of intense reading, I contacted Columbia University, Hayden Planetarium, Lamont Observatory and similar research centers in and around New York, making appointments with scientists. One of the secrets of successful interviews is to do one's homework before meeting the person, so I always considered it an elementary politeness to know the brief biography of the interviewee and at least the titles of his publications, in addition to the correct spelling of his name. In the States, the reporter's job is immensely facilitated by the presence in each university and laboratory of a public-relations office, paid to help journalists like me with the necessary background material. We weren't used to such treatment in Europe, where men of science considered any kind of "publicity" as being beneath their dignity. As soon as I noticed that the scientist was pleased that I had heard of him and his work, the real interview began. Dealing with unfamiliar subjects, I learned quickly that nothing paid off better that the candid admission of ignorance. "I should be embarrassed by my ignorance, Sir," I would start, "but I confess that I have no idea whether the center of the Globe consists of super-hard material (because of the incredible pressure), or is liquid (melted under those temperatures), or is gaseous (evaporated by the heat)? Yet such an elementary question…I'm sure we learned it in high school, but who remembers those things!… Would you please tell me?"—It never failed. We all enjoy teaching people who know less than us, and scientists love it when laymen show interest in what they do. Then you can't stop them talking. Thus I learned extraordinary things about the Earth, and the stars, and Life, and Nature. But beyond the facts and the theories, I learned even more unexpected things about scientists themselves and about Science. I was surprised to hear that, for instance, they too were unsure about the consistency of the center of the Earth, a question that had seemed too childish to me to even ask. They didn't agree either on whether our planet was created extremely hot, cooling progressively ever since Creation, or, on the contrary, started as a cool body, which is gaining heat. Professor Harold Urey, a world authority in chemistry, the discoverer of Deuterium and a Nobel laureate, had recently stunned the scientific community by formulating the latter hypothesis. I read everything I could find about him in the non-specialized press, and just when I was about to be convinced by his brilliantly constructed hypothesis, he declared that he didn't, of course, believe much in his own theory, but it had the great merit of not being absurd. Proving it totally wrong would be extremely difficult, he was proud to state. The mid-1950s were also a time when scientists were beginning to make less fun of the fantastic theories of Wegener, who believed that the continents were not fixed on their permanent locations, but were drifting like colossal rafts over the world's oceans. Most scientists I interviewed in 1955, referred to his ideas as being science fiction, "not serious," even "ridiculous." (In the 1970s, when I worked on my book on the Earth, no scientist talked about "fixed" continents any more...)

I was amazed to find similar changes of axioms and doctrines, often total reversals, in most sciences, whether we talked about Life, Evolution, the Cosmos, the atom, or origin of Man. The more scientists I interrogated, the more I was tempted to assume that they didn't know much more about the fundamental questions than we, the laymen, did, that they were almost as ignorant as we were. And yet, their incertitudes only increased my respect for them. Because there was an enormous difference: their ignorance was still articulate, beautifully formulated, informative, even brilliant; one always felt a challenge and a stimulating restlessness in it; while our lack of knowledge, the common man's ignorance, is unimaginative and tongue-tied, simply a deficiency of mind and education, pitiful and depressingly dumb. There is a difference when an uneducated or uninterested person says that he doesn't know how the universe began, and when an eloquent astronomer admits the same thing.

California, that's where I continued my research in the fall, visiting Mount-Palomar and Mt. Wilson observatories, which then had the largest telescopes in the world, interviewing their astronomers at the Carnegie Foundation offices in Pasadena, where they worked, and talking to scientists at the California Institute of Technology (known as "Cal Tech"), a Mecca of advanced science, also in Pasadena. It was during that trip that I had my first taste of the true nature of modern cosmology, which left me both enthralled and astonished. Enthralled, because its poetic and philosophical aspects had always attracted me immensely, and now I was discovering that their empirical exploration was not only quite possible, but had already begun, not long ago, circa 1924, to be precise. Amazed, and a bit disappointed perhaps, to see the prosaic, matter-of-fact techniques used for this most grandiose of all human quests. Indeed, I realized, the present knowledge of the Universe and its origin, of the galaxies and the vertiginous distances between them, of the composition of the heavenly bodies and their destiny, owed less to inspired stargazing than to a pedestrian, specialized instrument called spectrograph. I was disillusioned to find out that even with the 200-inch giant atop of Mount-Palomar, the astronomer on duty does not "watch" the galaxies; he simply photographs them and analyses their "red-shift," recorded by the spectrograph attached to the telescope. "Red-shift." That's the key to the entire modern cosmology, the word I heard everywhere where cosmology was discussed. I wanted to hear about the Creation of the Universe, about fantastic worlds astronomers were discovering thanks to the new, incredibly powerful telescopes, about beautiful theories and visions of the infinite skies, and all I was getting was some technical talk about spectrum analyses and red-shift. Rather dense and boring talk. What could the most sublime subject have to do with? Wasn't I wasting my time?

Luckily, I didn't give up. Like any Shakespeare admirer should forever bless his parents for forcing him, as a child, through the tedium of the alphabet, I owe a debt of gratitude to those who had the patience to explain to me the basic principles of light spectrum and red-shift, and their significance in cosmology. It's quite simple, they said. When you make light go through a prism, it is decomposed into a spectrum of all colors, going from the violet to the red. Like the rainbow. But scientists noticed several fine, vertical lines in each spectrum (called "Fraunhofer lines") and, curiously, they were different for different sources of light: sunlight spectrum's lines are not the same as, say, the lines in candle light, or starlight, or light coming from burning oxygen or carbon. Next discovery: each chemical element has its specific lines, as unmistakably different as are individual fingerprints. Hence, the spectrum of any star tells you a lot about its chemical composition.

I was fascinated. So, I thought, that's how any astronomy freshman can tell you how much helium or iron or carbon a star contains, just by analyzing its spectrum! But that wasn't all. When better telescopes allowed taking spectrograms of heavenly bodies at great distance, astronomers discovered that the Fraunhofer's lines were slightly displaced toward the violet end of the spectrum when a star was approaching us, and, on the contrary, were moved to the red end of the spectrum, when a star was receding, moving away from us. It's similar to the change of pitch of a train whistle: it gets higher as the train approaches the station, and lower when it goes away, although in reality the whistle's sound is the same. The Fraunhfer lines' "red-shift," I learned, indicated that an object was flying away from us.

So what's so important about it, the layman might think. So far, it's purely technical talk of specialists. This tedious information however became crucial when, in 1924, another Californian astronomer, Edwin Hubble, made a totally unrelated discovery: using the Mt. Wilson 100-inch telescope, he established that the Andromeda "nebula" was not part of our galaxy, the Milky-Way, as generally thought, but was another, independent galaxy, a world apart, consisting itself of billions of stars and located at a distance of 900,000 light-years! Astronomy accepted as a new truth that the Cosmos was much larger than our Milky Way and contained countless other galaxies, "archipelagos-Universes," separated from each other by unimaginable distances.

The story was getting more and more interesting, I thought as I continued reading it as a thriller. Then came a real *coup-de-theatre*: Mt. Wilson telescope succeeds in taking spectrograms from Andromeda, with painstakingly long exposures, lasting entire nights, because of the galaxy's faint light. When the spectrum's lines are analyzed, what does one find?—A red shift! Andromeda is receding, flying away from us at a vertiginous speed! Hubble and his team, mostly with his collaborator Milton Humason, measure the distances and analyze the spectra of many other galaxies. There is no doubt: they all show red shift, they are all receding. A most disturbing, sensational conclusion comes to mind: all galaxies, every piece of matter in the universe, are scattering away at enormous speed, like the fragments of an exploded bomb. If one calculates the distances and the speed of dispersion—which the scientists did,—one concludes that all those fragments come from the same original explosion, a cataclysmic event occurred several billion years ago, when all existing matter was concentrated in one piece. The primordial "Big Bang." As fantastic as this hypothesis sounded to me, I realized soon that almost every scientist I talked to, subscribed to it or was beginning to accept it.

Modern cosmology's revelations had a great impact on my thinking, and I developed a strong desire to learn more. For years after our *Paris-Match* series was published, I kept reading articles on the subject, dreaming of doing one day a more extensive study of the state of the present knowledge. This chance came much later, but in the book on cosmology I published in 1975 in France, I included the following paragraph, which summed up my feelings during my first visit to the Californian astronomers:

"It is strange to think that the solutions sought by what is the most beautiful, noblest, and most elevated in human spirit and heart, should come from reading of recordings as coldly technical and fastidious as are the spectrograms! One would love, in moments of "communion with the Cosmos" which one feels sometimes in the solitude of certain starry nights, that the answers to these disturbing "since when?" "to where?" and "why?" were revealed to us in the style of Homer, or with Wagnerian accords. One is therefore a little disappointed to realize that the major part of the Book of present-day knowledge of the Universe is written in a very different alphabet, an alphabet in which Fraunhofer's lines, those vertical black lines on a rainbow background, serve as letters..."

Visiting personally the scenes of this great scientific epic—Mt. Wilson, Mount Palomar, Hubble's Pasadena office at Santa-Barbara Street,—and meeting some of the protagonists I was reading about—Milton Humason, V.M. Slipher, Ira Bowen, Rudolf Minkowski—was a memorable experience. Sometimes rich of surprises. I read, for instance, so much about Hubble's principal co-worker, Humason, one of the architects of the Flight-to-the-Galaxies theory, the man who supplied most of the red-shift data. Now this famous astronomer is in front of me, ready to answer my questions. A mild, unassuming, almost humble man. "Tell me, Dr. Humason..." I begin. He interrupts me: *"Mister* Humason, I'm not *Doctor."* "But what university degree do you have?', I ask. He smiles politely: "None. I haven't been to college." Then the story unravels. Humason hasn't even finished high school. He dropped out of the Pasadena school when he was sixteen. I begin to sense a *Paris-Match*-type story..."Then, Sir, how did you become an astronomer?"—Dropping high school, he went to work as a mule-driver on the construction of the Mt. Wilson observatory, carrying provisions up the hill, he told me; sort of first, albeit indirect, contacts with the world of astronomy...Then he fell in love with the daughter of one of the engineers, married her when he was 20, and as they both loved the mountain and had no money, he accepted the job of janitor of the observatory. Working with the big telescope required long vigils (sometimes films were exposed for 60 or 70 hours!) and when a tired, hungry astronomer had to leave his watch for a brief rest, he would call the nice janitor to replace him. Often, Humason gave the astronomers a hand with re-positioning of the telescope, loading a camera, developing a film. Meanwhile, fascinated by their work, he was asking questions, reading articles, and learning more and more. As he proved to be exceptionally reliable, precise, and meticulous when helping with the films and spectrograms, he became in a few years very much in demand. He became an appreciated expert not only in taking photographs and spectrograms, but also in analyzing them. His unusually sharp eye and imaginative interpretations in examining spectra was noticed by the observatory's director, George Hale, who appointed him "assistant observer" in 1920. Then Hubble was so impressed by the ex-janitor's thoroughness, that he entrusted him with most of his special projects. The rest is...yes, I read the rest in every history of modern astronomy.

*   *   *   *   *

In between visits to universities, observatories, and labs, Lil joined me in Los Angeles and took me to a lavish Hollywood party given by her friends Doris and Jules Stein, the founder and owner of MCA, the world's largest talent agency. Jules was a shrewd self-made tycoon with great common sense and wisdom. He had started as a poor Jewish student in Vienna putting himself through medical school by playing the violin in the cafes. He was so good in negotiating the working conditions for his band, that other musicians sought his help, until he became Hollywood's super-agent. But having obtained his doctor's diploma, his heart remained with ophthalmology. He built the best eye clinics in California (and also in Israel), and that was the occasion we were invited to celebrate. Nothing pleased this successful multi-millionaire more than to be addressed as "Doctor" Stein and to speak at ophthalmologists' conferences. Although Jules and Doris were considerably older than we were, they were very fond of Lil and he was always ready, in his quiet way, to give her some wise advice. Apart from our friendship in New York with their daughters Jean and Susan, the elder Steins became good friends of ours.

In Los Angeles Lil and I also attended a glamorous dinner party at Rocky and Gary Cooper's. I was, of course, quite excited to meet the movie star whom I had admired since Bulgaria, and found him even more charming, modest and genuine than I had imagined him from his films. Right away I liked his gentlemanly, rather shy, manner and we had a very pleasant conversation. The Coopers, their lifestyle and their friends—a sort of Hollywood elite—were visibly far more distinguished than the rest of the movies' capital and had little in common with its flashy, publicity-crazy celebrities.

The next morning Lil and I drove to Prescott, Arizona, and spent a day and a chilly night at the Lowell Observatory in Flagstaff, the most famous center for Mars studies ever since Giovanni Schiaparelli had announced that he had observed "man-made canals" on the red planet, thus triggering a world-wide furor about Martians, and Percival Lowell built the observatory in order to verify the alleged discovery. The Flagstaff astronomers gave me very useful material about the Solar system, their specialty, but I left with my belief in the myth of "canals" and intelligent Martians irreparably shaken…

After a day in Las Vegas, where we were both appalled and amused by the incredible display of garishness and bad taste, we flew to San Francisco. While I was inquiring in Berkeley about photo-synthesis, viruses, and the borderline between living and inorganic matter, Lil was enjoying re-visiting beautiful San Francisco, where she had and Phil had lived for a year during the war and where her daughter Jill was born. During our stay, we went to Sacramento to have lunch with Lil's sister, Shirley, and her husband, Harvey Johnson, who lived there with their three children. I had already met Lil's father and mother in Long Island; now I was introduced to the rest of the family. It was really getting serious…

Indeed, Lil had already found an apartment in New York. It was a small and pretty flat on Fifth Avenue, facing Central Park, with rooms for the children. On December 3rd, she moved into her new abode, and her daughters spent the first night with her. I was living then in a sublet apartment at 21 East 65th street and that weekend I played host to Dimi, who had come for a few weeks to the States for the *Readers' Digest*.

For the better or the worse, a new life was about to begin for Lil and myself.

By that time, I had completed my research for the first two articles of the series, "The Cosmos" and "The Solar System," and handed the voluminous files to Cartier. While he started writing, my investigation continued: "The Earth," then "Life," "Evolution," and "Man." The first article appeared in *Paris-Match* in February 1956, and the series ran for a year, under the general title of "The World: Where does it come from? Where does is goes to?" Raymond Cartier signed it, with the mention "Research under the direction of Stephane Groueff." As the articles were well received by the public, we continued with the same formula with "The Dawn of the Civilizations," "The Animal Mystery," "The Vanished Civilizations," and then, through 1957, "Man and the Earth," "Aging and Death," and the last, the twelfth, article, "The End of the World."

*   *   *   *

Chapter 22

The extraordinary saga of "Paris-Match"

Conceived by its father, Jean Prouvost, to be a French imitation of Henry Luce's *Life Magazine, Paris-Match* quickly acquired a very distinct and indeed a most colorful personality, making it, by the early 1950s, the talk of the publishing world and a model for many other publications. It inaugurated a new style of journalism and, even more spectacularly, a new breed of reporters, who injected excitement and glamour into the magazine and won it a unique popularity. In France, *Paris-Match* became not only a great success, but also a sort of a fad, a fashionable conversation piece, and the "in" thing. To be objective, this wasn't entirely due to the quality of its articles, although they were mostly quite good, and some were excellent. But there were other magazines in the world with equally good, if not better, articles, and yet none of them had caught the public's attention in the way Match did it. The impact of its remarkable photos counted, of course, for much of the success. But the lifestyle of its reporters, the excitement and gossip their behavior kept stirring up, became the real trademark of *Paris-Match*. Indeed, among the most fascinating, moving, fanciful, *Match* stories was its own story, the never-ending saga of its reporters. While reporting the news, *Match* was news in itself.

Roger Vadim, for example, was a re-writer in the original *Paris-Match* team when he discovered Brigitte Bardot and launched her career. He was the sexy teenager's boyfriend, then her fiancé, long before anyone had heard of her. Brigitte used to come regularly to our offices, rue Pierre-Charron, or at the Belle-Ferronniere cafe opposite, and all *Match* reporters knew her. Another movies celebrity, Leslie Caron, the future "Gigi," was totally unknown when her lovely face appeared on the Match cover, where Gene Kelly saw it for the first time. Bettina, the Paris top model, just divorced from Benno Graziani when he joined the magazine, but she continued to use his name. At a Cannes Film Festival,

Match's Pierre Galante met Olivia de Havilland, the memorable Melanie of "Gone with the Wind," who had already won two Oscars. In April 1955, the great movie star became Madame Galante. "Le Patron," Jean Prouvost, presided at the wedding ceremony, in his capacity of mayor of the village of Ivoy-le-Marron, and Gaston Bonheur was the best man. Two years later, again at the Cannes Festival, Paris-Match reporters played Cupid in the most celebrated romance of the decade.

The star at Cannes that year was Grace Kelly, at the top of her career and beauty. Match had dispatched Pierre Galante to cover the festival with our Cote-d'Azur correspondent Jean-Paul Olivier and photographers Michel Simon and Edward Quinn. With the enormous competition in Cannes and having covered the festival year after year, the problem was to find some original idea, some fresh "angle." The Match team had an inspiration: why not photograph "the princess of Hollywood" at the palace of a real prince, Rainier of Monaco? Galante knew both of them and succeeded in arranging a visit of the star for 3 o'clock the next day, May 6th. The four Paris-Match men picked up Grace Kelly at the hotel *Carlton* and drove her to Monte Carlo, only to receive a message from the prince, apologizing for being delayed and asking the to start the tour of the palace without him. Without wasting time, the reporters did just that, photographing the actress in some of the sumptuous salons, including the salon of the Throne. As the tour proceeded, a door opened and Rainier appeared and greeted his guests. Smiling charmingly, Grace Kelly did a discreet curtsy when she shook the Prince's hand. Rainier was obviously taken at first sight by her beauty and gallantly offered to personally show her the rest of the palace. He took her to his gardens, showed her the old carriages, and led her to his private zoo. She was impressed, he was delighted, Pierre Galante and his colleagues were ecstatic, and it was a real scoop! Little did they know then that the following year, when Miss Kelly and Prince Rainier would marry and the entire world would be thrilled to tears by this fairy-tale, *Paris-Match* will already have, taken in advance, the exclusive photographs of Princess Grace posing in front of the throne of Monaco.

The magazine's notoriety didn't arrive from association with romance and glamour only. Its daredevil reporters took care of constantly connecting the name of *Paris-Match* with stories of battles, adventure and risk. After the daring, often reckless, coverage of the Indochina war, they became fully involved in the dramatic, bloody events in French North Africa, giving the same impression of looking for and enjoying risks. The spirit of *Magnum* agency's war photographer Robert Capa, a Humphrey-Bogart-esque role model in the eyes of many of them, was still very much alive in their mind. Capa was killed in the spring of 1954, 40 miles from Hanoi, while taking action photos for *Magnum*. These spectacular images, published in *Paris-Match*, had a great impact and inspired considerably our Jean Roy, Joel Le Tac, Rene Vital, Michel Descamps, Charles Bonnay, Daniel Camus, Pedrazzini and others who were looking for trouble anyhow on different war fronts.

Dramatic events place in 1954 in French Indochina (today's Vietnam, Cambodia and Laos). The war against nationalist Vietminh, led by Ho Chi Minh, was already in its 9th year, when the French command decided to go for the definitive battle. The plan was to solidly fortify the camp of Dien-Bien-Phu by gradually parachuting a force of 10,000 men with artillery and tanks, then lure the redoubtable General Giap's main forces there and destroy them. Alas, the strategy didn't work. In the spring, the Viets massed 81,000 troops around the camp and the fortress was transformed into an infernal trap for the French. The agony of the garrison, relentlessly bombarded from the surrounding hills by the artillery Giap had brought in detached pieces through the jungle, lasted 56 days rich in remarkable feats of heroism. In the devastated camp, looking like a scene of Verdun, the French suffered very heavy casualties. Holding its breath, the world followed the drama of the siege. For France, Dien-Bien-Phu became a national symbol, a tragedy affecting every Frenchman. For a few months, the nation was suspended by the news from the beleaguered camp, and *Paris-Match* was the best source. The public couldn't wait to see the spectacular photos of the aristocratic general de Castries, the commander of the garrison, calmly reassuring his exhausted, hungry men, or the tough, impetuous commandants Bigeard and Touret, or the "Angel of Dien-Bien-Phu, the nurse Genevieve Galard, the new national heroine. Besides the Army's communiqués and agency news about the military developments, *Paris-Match* was reporting moving human-interest stories, glimpses of heroic actions, bravado and personal misery, sent by reporters Joel Le Tac, Michel Descamp and Rene Vital. But the great journalistic feat was that after Dien-Bien-Phu became totally, hopelessly encircled, *Match* continued to publish photos taken _inside_ the besieged inferno. Two daring Army cameramen, Daniel Camus and Peraud, achieved these scoops. Daniel, a *Paris-Match* photographer, was doing his military service with an Army's cinema unit. Gentle and timid, unusually taciturn, this tall, strongly built young man of 23 didn't seem to belong in the Match photo reporters team of flamboyant, bragging jokers. But when it came to courage, and particularly to parachuting, few could compete with Camus. A few days before the great battle for Dien-Bien-Phu started, Camus parachuted into the completely sealed camp. Thus he was able to cover not only the activities at General de Castrie's headquarters, but also the desperate fighting at French outposts resisting the repeated onslaughts of Viet-Minh's suicidal units. Dien-Bien-Phu fell on May 7, 1954 and all survivors were take prisoners, including Camus and his colleague Peraud. Under indescribably inhuman conditions, the pathetic column of starved, exhausted prisoners in rags began the long march, barefoot on the muddy roads to the prisoners' camps in Tonkin, a 300 kilometers (200 miles) walk. Daniel spent three months in the camp and when he left, he was a living skeleton. It was only then that he saw his Dien-Bien-Phu photos published in *Paris-Match* and in all magazines in the world. Peraud was killed when trying to escape from the camp. After regaining his health, Camus resumed his work for *Match*. One year later, his name was again in the news. In August 1955, he broke the world parachuting record of landing on high altitude by jumping over Mont Blanc and landing on the snow at 4,400 meters (about 13,200 ft).

As for Joel Le Tac, after the Dien-Bien-Phu disaster and after the Saigon rebellion the following year, when he joined Cartier, Vital and myself, he found himself covering the events in French North Africa. He followed the Foreign Legion in full operation and no wonder *Match* had the best first-hand reports from the battlefronts: with his extraordinary record of founder in 1941 of one of the first Resistance cells in occupied France, of being the second licensed parachutist of France-Libre, a holder of the highest honor granted by General de Gaulle— "Compagnon de la Liberation," then serving as a company commander in the

French battalion in the Korean War, and also being among the last Frenchmen to leave Haiphong when the Viet-Minh occupied the city, Joel had seen action as much as the most experienced fighters. With him in Indochina and then in Algeria and Morocco, *Match* had no problem covering the French commandos in action: Le Tac was one of them. Apart from wars and adventures, the *Paris-Match* style of covering news,—not always according to the rules,—began to attract the public's attention. More and more stories about *Match* reporters' mischief circulated in Paris and in international press circles. People were amused to hear how, at a solemn Vatican occasion strictly off limits to photographers, Walter Carone doned a priest's cassock and piously joined the procession; at the crucial moment, he only had to lift the skirt to reach for his camera and start shooting. Or how, at the Melbourne Olympic Games, Jackie Garofalo dressed as member of the Italian fencing team—mask and all—to gain access to the main event and take pictures of the French champion Christian d'Oriola's victory. At the same Games, Garofalo was the only photographer to follow the marathon victory of another Frenchman, Mimoun: his car flew the flag of a race official, picked from only Jackie knew where...

Sometimes the tricks and ruses to outsmart the services of order didn't work and the reporter was in trouble. But even those defeats added to *Paris-Match's* reputation for dealing with obstacles. The picture of a disheveled Jean-Pierre Pedrazzini in torn clothes being roughed-up by Bahamian policemen during a 1955 visit of Princess Margaret to Nassau appeared in all tabloids in the world. Pedrazzini had been arrested when he tried to disembark from a rowboat just at the moment when Margaret's yacht was docking ceremonially. Shocked by the police brutality, the Princess demanded that he be released immediately. In addition to the publicity, Pedrazzini had all the photos he wanted (*Match* published six pages of them).

Timidity was not among the faults of the fresh, handsome Jean-Pierre, as ven the Soviet leader Bulgarian could ascertain. In February 1956 Pedrazzini was with the group of French journalists accompanying President Vincent Auriol on his state visit to the Soviet Union. During a reception at the Kremlin, he went straight to Marshal Bulganin and, in the presence of Voroshilov, Molotov and

Mikoyan, asked through an interpreter: "My friend and I would like to tour USSR in automobile next summer, and bring our wives with us." The friend in question was Dominique Lapierre, one of the most enterprising *Match* reporters and a master of the persuasive hyperbole. In those years, the request sounded absurd, no Westerners were allowed to travel freely across the country. But six months later, a white *Simca-Marly* station-wagon marked *Paris-Match* in big red letters and carrying the two reporters, their wives and tons of photographic equipment, was causing sensation on the routes of Russia, Ukraine, Crimea and Georgia. They spent two months driving over 12,000 kms. taking pictures and talking, through a guide assigned to them, to hundreds of Soviet citizens of all ages and professions, a record for Western journalists and a real scoop for *Paris-Match*, made possible only because of their extraordinary seductive talents. Friendly and gregarious, cracking jokes, paying compliments and entertaining everybody with fascinating tales, Jean-Pierre and Dominique made a hit everywhere their car stopped. Even the security agents who arrested them once for inadvertently taking pictures in a "restricted zone" couldn't resist to their humor and palaver and freed them after several hours of interrogation.

The world's press became more and more interested in *Paris-Match's* success, not always without certain jealousy. *Newsweek Magazine* wrote on Feb.7, 1955:

"*The biggest journalistic news in Europe lately has been the rise to prominence of a colorful French periodical named Paris-Match. A splashily covered weekly that calls itself a news magazine, but looks to veteran barbershop habitués like a foreign-language combination of Life and Look, Match has flared up to a roaring 1.3 million circulation inside of a fast five years...*

"*In charge is Jean Prouvost, an untiring moneymaker of 69...Its staff of 84...A quarter of them are former paratroopers, and most of them own very fast sports cars. (They are the best-paid journalists in France; Match's reporters average close to $ 150 a week, vastly more than the Paris average), They all have to be very fast men with a story, and the staff turnover is notably high. The characteristics of Match which have greatly helped make it a success, after all, are an appearance of timeliness and an air of authentic knowledge concerning absolutely all the inside dirt...*"

In April 1956, with the wedding Rainier-Grace Kelly, *Paris-Match* established a new all-time record for the French press: its issue Number 368 was printed in 1.9 million copies.

      *   *   *   *

I was in Paris that day of June 29 and feeling very sad, although 1956 had been so far a very good year for me. My work was doing well—the first installments of Cartier's series on the eternal questions about the Universe, Life, Existence, etcetera, had been published with enormous success, I had been duly credited and praised for the research, and now I was continuing with the research for the remaining articles. Meanwhile, a few news stories were published with my by-line. Sava and Pamela Panitza came on a visit to Europe for the first time since he had emigrated to South Africa and I was very happy to be reunited with my best friend after such a long separation. In February we spent ten days together in Gstaad, where Lil was with her children. In April, Dimi and Yvonne Fourcade became engaged, and I fully shared the joy of the Panitza family. At the end of May, Lil and I spent a quiet week in the French Riviera, discreetly we thought, until we bumped into people who knew us, including Rocky and Gary Cooper. After that, and for years, she never stopped teasing us about our escapade. We returned to Paris for Dimi's wedding in June, at Fourcade's country house in Monsoult. In the meantime Lil had found a superb apartment on the Left Bank, in the Rue du Bac *hotel-particulier* where Madame de Stael had lived. As location, decoration and architecture, the place, sublet from the Prince of Monaco's father, represented everything that Lil had dreamed about Paris, and she was delighted to move in by mid-June.

Why then was I unhappy?

We were both sad because we knew that we were in an impasse. In July, Lil had to return to her children in the States and there was no possibility for me to go to New York, at least in the foreseeable future. Now that Lil had an apartment in Paris, she would come more often, great!, but it was unrealistic to think that she could come and live on Rue du Bac for good. As her departure date approached, the anguish increased, with no solution in view. Should we accept reality, be brave, and say goodbye?, we were tearfully asking each other many times. And as things were becoming hopeless, a most unrelated event changed the course of our lives: on June 29th, in Connecticut, Marilyn Monroe married Arthur Miller.

I remember clearly every detail of that fateful evening. We were going to dinner at Andy and Bea Embiricos's lovely house at Porte Dauphine and I was dressing in my small hotel room, when the telephone rang and an excited *Paris-Match* operator told me to come to the office immediately, because "something terrible had happened to Mara Sherbatoff in America," that she was in hospital and I was needed to communicate in English with the emergency room. I called Lil at Rue du Bac and told her to go ahead and I would join them as soon as I could.

At the Rue Pierre-Charron offices I was told that Mara had been in an automobile accident as she, Paul Slade and Paul's brother were following the bride and groom's car before the Monroe-Miller wedding. From his home, Le Patron was frantically trying to reach Cartier, who was in charge of our American offices, but as Raymond was traveling somewhere in Africa and could not be located, Prouvost asked me to find out more about Mara's condition. I called New York and finally had Anni and Michel Duplaix on the phone. Mara was in critical condition, they said the first time. When I called a little later, she was dead. I liked Mara very much and I was deeply shocked. I informed Le Patron and he asked to come and see him the next morning. Then I went to my dinner. Philippe de Croisset, director of our women's magazine *Marie-Claire* and close collaborator of Jean Prouvost, was also at the Embiricoses', and for the rest of the evening we talked about Mara.

The next day we learned the details. The famous movie star, age 30, and the playwright, age 40, were married in the evening by a judge in White Plains in a ceremony which lasted less than five minutes. Only a few persons attended the wedding. But before the wedding, the couple had given a press conference in Roxbury, Connecticut, where Paul Slade's brother drove Mara. The car lost control around a sharp turn and smashed into a tree, hurling Mara through the windshield. She and the driver, who suffered minor injuries, were taken to New Milford Hospital, where Mara died at 3:30 PM. *New York Times* wrote the next day: "*...The playwright and his bride-to-be halted when the crash occurred and helped to carry Miss Sherbatoff from the wreckage. Mr. Miller then called an ambulance.*" (Four years later, when writing a story on Marilyn Monroe, we talked with her and Arthur Miller about the tragic accident. "Yes, I remember it too well..." Marilyn said. "When we returned to our car, I saw a blood stain on my skirt and I thought 'It's a bad omen'...")

With Mara's death and Cartier traveling around the world, the New York bureau found itself suddenly without chief. Journalistically speaking, it couldn't have happened at a worst moment: grave events in Hungary and East Germany were putting the United States to a test; in Manhattan, the Suez crisis was looming over the United Nations ; and the "*Andrea Doria* was sinking off the American shores. It was all too important to the magazine, yet the American office was without a Bureau-Chief. "Stephane, you must go to New York right away!" *Paris-Match* told me.

Once more, as unexpectedly as many times before, somebody else was pulling me out of an impasse.

*   *   *   *   *

When Lil left, as planned, for New York in July, we were no more agonizing over the long-dreaded "final separation;" she was now happy to return to the States. Because of Mara's sudden death, Lil's repatriation meant the opening of a new chapter in our viciitudinous romance. As of the end of July, when I joined her, I was no more a hopeless long-distance suitor, separated from her by my work and an ocean; I was now a resident of <u>her</u> city, I was the new *Paris-Match* Bureau Chief in New York.

1956 turned out to be a dramatic year for *Match*. Unfortunately, Mara Sherbatoff's accident was not the last tragedy to hit our team that year. The next victim was one of our most popular photo reporters, the happy-go-lucky Jean-Pierre Pedrazzini. It happened in October, during the insurrection in Budapest, the most sensational event behind the Iron Curtain in more than a decade. In the New York office, everybody was very excited, especially Anni and myself, and we were spending our time glued to the radio and the UPI ticker machine, hardly daring to believe the news we were hearing. Talking on the telephone with the Paris office several times a day, I knew that *Match* had sent to Hungary the reporters Paul Mathias (who was originally from Budapest) and Vick Vance, with the photographers Pedrazzini and Franz Goess, and we couldn't wait to hear their reports.

Late on October 30th, somebody said that Pedrazzini seemed to be hurt, but the information was very confused and I couldn't learn any detail. Then we were stunned the next morning to read in the *New York Times* that "*During the storming of the Political Police headquarters, Jean-Pierre Pedrazzini, photographer for the magazine "Paris-Match," received a burst of machine-gun fire in the stomach and leg, while Tim Foote, photographer for "Life," was slightly wounded in the hand. They were fired on by A.V.H. tanks. Not long afterward a numbed of political police, who had been captured by the revolutionaries, paid for their resistance with their lives.*" But how serious was Jean-Pierre's condition? It was quite bad, the Paris office told me. "Pedra" was hit by Russian bullets in the stomach, the back, and in one leg. Hungarian freedom-fighters had helped Mathias transport him to the Petofy hospital where the local doctors were doing their best to help him, but they urgently needed medicine.

It was 2 p.m. when Jean-Pierre was hit, and 6 p.m. when *Paris-Match* received the bad news with Mathias' and Vance's SOS through the French embassy. From that hour on, and for three days and nights, an unprecedented rescue operation was spontaneously organized to bring the wounded Pedrazzini to Paris. In a splendid show of camaraderie, the entire *Match* staff—reporters, editors and writers, secretaries, telephone operators and messenger boys—was moblilized to help Jean-Pierre. The first task was to find a way to send immediately to Budapest Pedrazzini's brother-in-law, Doctor Dieckman, a prominent Paris physician. Mathias called again and again, insisting that Dieckman bring medicaments and instruments. The same evening, the radio station *Europe-1* offered its plane to ransport the doctor to Vienna, but in the meantime the Prime Minister put a sanitary aircraft at his disposal. The American Hospital in Paris provided the necessary medicine, and at Orly airport a departing *Air-France* plane delayed its take-off to let the sanitary aircraft use the runway. Our photographer Michel Descamp waited for Dieckman at the Vienna airport and, with the help of the French ambassador and the president of the French Red-Cross, a convoy was formed with destination the Hungarian border. Dr.Dieckman arrived on time to revive his brother-in-law, but the operation couldn't be performed in the Budapest hospital.

It was crucial that Jean-Pierre be transported to Paris. But the Russian troops were already occupying the airport. Again *Match* put all its resources and connections in a state of alert, an Austrian airplane was requisitioned, and Dr.Dieckman and Mathias managed, with the help of the French ambassador's wife, to obtain the Russian authorities' permission for the aircraft to leave. Once in the air, at 10 o'clock in the evening, Dieckman proceeded to give instructions by radio to Vienna, where a blood transfusion was performed at 11 p.m., to Le Bourget airport, for a second transfusion at 3:30 a.m., and to the hospital in Neuilly, where the anesthetist waited for Pedrazzini at 4 o'clock in the morning.

Never had a press organization shown more solidarity and esprit-de-corps, and more love for a friend in distress. Like a close family around a beloved brother, the Match team mounted an around-the-clock vigil at the Neuilly hospital, and for an entire week all other preoccupations were pushed to the second plan. Gradually fading but always brave and trying to smile at his visitors' jokes, Jean-Pierre continued to live with the magazine. He was asking about his pals and the stories they were covering. He wanted to see the photos he had taken in Budapest. When he died, in the morning of November 7, there was not a dry eye at the Rue Pierre-Charron offices. Two days later, looking at the sad faces of the tough reporters and war-correspondents assembled for his funeral at the Saint-Philippe-du-Roule church, one could guess what the loss of the 29-year-old star-photographer had meant to them all.

Many of Jean-Pierre's colleagues couldn't attend the funeral—that week they were covering another war story, risking their lives in their turn, this time in Egypt. Indeed, the bloody Suez war had started only three days before. In spite of the strong opposition of the United States, the Soviet Union and most other countries, France, Great Britain and Israel attacked the forces of Gamal Abdel Nasser, who had nationalized the Suez canal. Paris-Match, of course, sent some of its best war-reporters with the invading armies: Jean Roy and Daniel Camus, both ex-paratroopers, and Charles Favrel, (a reporter who had worked many times for Match in Korea and Indochina), joined the French commandos about to attack Port Said and Port Fouad; Benno Graziani and Tony Saulnier joined the Israeli army advancing in the Sinai.

Early in the morning of November 5th, Camus and Favrel jumped near Port Fouad with the 1,000 paratroopers of Colonel Conan taking off at Cyprus. Their mission was to take over the bridge leading to Port Said, over which the Allied seaborne force, disembar-king the next day, would advance in the direction of the canal. It was a difficult landing, with the Egyptians receiving the commandos with violent artillery and machine-gun fire, and both sides suffering heavy casualties, but the bridge was taken and Port Fouad surrencered. At 7 o'clock the next morning, a formidable Franco British armada of 200 ships reached the beaches and started disgorging the Allied main force. Among them, aboard a landing craft, was Jean Roy. He was, like Daniel Camus, in his element, wearing a commando's camouflaged jump suit, full paratroopers' gear, red beret and all. Most of the "paras" knew both *Paris-Match* men from Indochina and Algeria, and widely admired the proverbial courage of Daniel, the taciturn hero from Dien-Bien-Phu, and Roy, his insolently bold colleague. This time, the reporters really outdid themselves. Camus never boasted about his bravery, but his behavior that day was well described later in the Citation issued by the Minister of Defense, who decorated him and Favrel with the Croix-de-Guerre. The citation read: *"Camus, Daniel, reporter photographer, whose name is famous in the paratroopers' and shock units. Volunteer to jump at Port Fouad (Egypt) during the airborne operation on November 5, 1956, he proceeded immediately to the most dangerous points in order to accomplish his mission, under violent mortar fire hitting the landing zone. Took the automatic rifle of a dead paratrooper and used it until he was able to hand it to an officer and resume his work as a photographer."*

The Franco-British invasion lasted only a couple of days. As the Egyptian resistance was collapsing and Nasser appealed to the United Nations, public opinion in Great Britain turned vehemently against Prime Minister Eden, the Soviet Union threatened to act, and President Eisenhower refused to give his support to the Allies. A cease-fire was declared and the invasion was brought to a halt. Waiting for further developments, Jean Roy, the incorrigible adventurer and prankster, had a field day. He quickly "captured" a few abandoned Egyptian army cars and, after painting on them the *Paris-Match* telephone number, *BALzac-00.24*, drove around the combat zone, taking notes, talking to frightened townspeople or helping children, joking with commando friends and other reporters. He had unearthed somewhere an Egyptian officer's gala uniform and for a few hours delighted his buddies by pompously parading in it.

Jean Roy didn't care much for rules and regulations, and it's possible that, on November 10th at noon, he just ignored the warnings of the British sentries frantically waving at him to signal that his jeep, passing by their advanced post, was entering a "no-man's zone." Or he might have not noticed them, involved in conversation with his companion, the American photographer David "Shim" Seymour. With Roy at the wheel, they were headed south, hoping to cover an Egyptian hospital train, supposed to evacuate wounded soldiers. The car roared by, in the direction of the front line, along a road flanked on one side by the Suez Canal, on the other by an irrigation canal, then speeded passed an Egyptian outpost, some 1,000 yards down the road. The British soldiers, following them by binocular, heard a burst of gunfire, then saw the jeep zigzagging out of control and falling into the irrigation canal. It was only the next day that an Egyptian liaison officer announced that the two reporters had been killed. And only four days later that their bullet-ridden bodies were brought to the French camp in Port Fouad, where paratroopers, Marine commandos and Senegalese riflemen rendered military honors.

This is what *Time* magazine wrote the following week:

"By the time most correspondents got to Port Said, the fighting was virtually over and Paris-Match reporter Jean Roy, 34, had the situation well in hand. The big (6 ft.,190 lbs) handsome Frenchman (real name: Yves Leleu) was living up to his legend as the fire-eating knight-errant of war journalism. In the 24 hours since he had landed with the first French ground troops, Roy had take over two jeeps and a Chevrolet truck, daubed each with a new license plate, "Bal-zac 00-24" (the phone number of Paris-Match) and whirled through a typical swashbuckling round of good deeds and derring-do.

"When Roy heard that hundreds of wounded Egyptians were suffering for lack of water and medical facilities in a hospital, he browbeat the French command into sending a water truck. When a French-speaking Egyptian woman pleaded for milk for her five small children, Roy rammed his jeep through the iron blind of a locked milk store. British MRs warned him that pillaging was a crime for which he could be shot. "O.K., go ahead and shoot!" said Roy. He gave one case of powdered milk to the woman, delivered a jeep to a hospital.

"For his fellow correspondents, Roy commandeered Port Said's second biggest hotel, the Eastern Exchange. They found nothing to eat, so he drove to French headquarters and traded his Chevrolet truck for three cases of French rations and three bottles of Chianti."

Every correspondent seemed to have some colorful story about Roy. *Newsweek's* man reported that when Jean ran out of gas in Port Said, he approached British Army headquarters with an official-looking document signed, he announced haughtily, by the "highest French authority." As he drove away, tank filled, the British officer got around to glancing at the signature. It read:" Philippe Petain, Marechal de France." He had a "lust for trouble, a lust for danger," was the diagnosis of his colleagues from *Time* magazine, telling how Roy, as a WW II soldier parachuted in occupied France, landed in the Normandy invasion and was badly wounded at Bastogne, for which he won the Silver Star. "As a civilian, he kept going to war," *Time* wrote, listing a few of Roy's exploits: In Guatemala during the anti-Communist revolution, he climbed over street barricades carrying not only a camera but a .45 Colt. During Tunisian riots, he calmly snapped pictures in the middle of a pillaging mob looking for Frenchmen to kill. In Indochina, snipers bullets ripped his uniform without touching him. In Algeria, he was often as much as five hours ahead of advancing French troops. In Moscow, he stepped up to a high-ranking Soviet officer in the street, plucked off his shoulder boards and said "Thanks, I'll keep these as souvenirs."

We were terribly upset by Jean's death, especially that it came only three days after Jean-Pierre's and four months after Mara Sherbatoff's fatal accident. But we were hardly surprised. He died the way he had lived. This could hardly be said about the gentle, civil and peaceful David Seymour, who had the bad luck to be

Roy's companion that day. At 45, "Shim," a Polish-born, Sorbonne educated American, was one the most famous world photographers, a founder, with Robert Capa, Henri Cartier-Bresson and Werner Bischof, of the celebrated *Magnum* agency, *Paris-Match*'s great competitors. There had always been a mutual admiration between the two teams. Now the professional rivalry about who gets the best news photo, seemed to be tragically moving into another area: which team suffered more casualties. Indeed, by a strange coincidence, Bischof was killed in an accident in South America on the very day his colleague Bob Capa was blown by a landmine in Indochina. And now "Shim..."

At *Match*, the effect of the casualties was, if anything, to boost the esprit-de-corps of the reporters. Many photographers felt that they had to live up to the daring of Pedrazzini and Roy, an attitude that could lead to recklessness that began to worry the editors. No wonder that Lloyds of London decided to raise insurance rates for *Match* reporters: henceforth, they announced, a parachute jump by a *Paris-Match* man will cost $ 2,500 in premiums; a Cyprus flight, $ 1,400. For others, they remain $ 1,000 or less. *

The spirit of belonging was among the most striking characteristics of the *Match* team, a really touching belief in and reliance on *"le journal."* Wherever we went, we felt reassured when we could call the office and hear the familiar voice of one of the lady-operators: *"Allo, allo, iciParis-Match, Balzac 00.24!"* This telephone number was the symbol of everything that united us. That's why Jean Roy used it as a license plate for the jeeps he "borrowed" in Suez. That's why the last words of Jean-Pierre Pedrazzini, dying in the Neuilly hospital, were: "Doctor, please call *Balzac 00.24*; they'll get me out of here!"

*　　　　*　　　　*　　　　*

---

* *As reported in Newsweek Magazine of Dec.3, 1956.*

Chapter 23

Bureau Chief in New York. Wedding.

Although Lil was legally separated and living in her own apartment, she wasn't considering divorce, unless Phil asked for it. He had always been kind to her, she said, a good husband and father, and she didn't have the heart to cause him more pain than she had already done. We were happy to be together in the same city, seeing each other openly every moment we could, with no more hiding. I met Lil's parents, who accepted me politely, although they were upset by the breakup of their daughter's marriage, especially since they liked Phil very much. Lil's father, Lester Fox, a World War I veteran, started slowly warming up to me when I showed interest in, and some knowledge of, the great Battle of Verdun, in which he had fought as a US artillery captain. Like all participants in this bloodiest war slaughter, he had never gotten over the ten-month-long inferno, but after 40 years of reminiscing, his tales were finding less and less attentive listeners, including (and especially so) his own family. So he welcomed the visit of someone like me who had seen the historical Verdun battlefield and who asked questions about the German offensive, Petain's heroic defense, or the caliber of the Krupp artillery pieces. Lil's mother, "Honey," a matronly, friendly lady of Irish descent, received me graciously, but it was obvious that both parents were disturbed about their daughter's decision and torn by the loyalty they felt for Phil.

When I say that Lil and I were seeing each other openly, I should make a reservation. Whether the accepted mores were then stricter than today's, or we felt it improper for non-married people to live together, especially when children are involved, the fact was that I continued to live in my bachelor's apartment on East 80th Street, and to worry about Lil's doormen, and even more about her maid Maggie. A native of North Carolina, Maggie, an imposing black lady of nondescript age, was also a Baptist deaconess and her silences could be intimidating. She was totally devoted to Lil, in a protective and rather proprietary way, and I didn't know whether she approved or disapproved of me; she just tolerated me, I felt.

I respected Lil's decision not to be the first to ask for a divorce if her husband didn't want it, but this was putting us in an awkward, often painful, situation. The incertitude about the future of our relationship was a cloud over our happiness. Then, unexpectedly, the solution, once more, came from outside. Phil asked Lil to have lunch with him and told her that he was seeing someone who worked at the United Nations; the relationship had become quite serious and he considered marrying her. Wouldn't it be better for everyone if he and Lil started a divorce procedure soon? He had already consulted his lawyers, he said, and they advised a divorce in Sun Valley.

In those days, a divorce by mutual consent was permitted only in the states of Nevada (in Reno) and Idaho (in Sun Valley). The catch was that it was valid only for residents of these states. To become a resident, one had to prove an uninterrupted residence of a minimum of six weeks. There were, of course, worse things in life than to spend a month-and-a-half in Sun Valley in the middle of the winter-sports season! What followed was the friendliest divorce that one could wish for. Generous as usual, and eager to get married himself, Phil made arrangements for Lil at the comfortable Sun Valley Lodge, where she arrived on the 21st of February. Jill and Tina took turns for two weeks of skiing with their mother in perfect snow and weather conditions, and Phil called them frequently to make sure that the rooms were good enough and that they liked their ski-teacher. As soon as the daughters left, it was my turn to keep company to the future divorcee. It was time for my yearly vacations and I couldn't have been more delighted to spend three weeks in the ski-resort of which I had dreamt since I had seen, when still in Bulgaria, the Sonja Hennie movie *"Sun Valley Serenade."* My arrival however turned into a near-disaster: just when I was leaving New York, I suffered a terrible wisdom-tooth infection, which made my flight an ordeal. At the stopover in Salt Lake City I had to rush to the first available dentist who extracted the tooth, transforming my face into a huge, ugly balloon. But when Lil greeted me in Sun Valley, she managed somehow to conceal her shock at the sight of her pitiful-looking Romeo, and after 24 hours of fever and compresses, the romance resumed in full. I loved Sun Valley. Maybe the romantic mood I was in had a lot to do with it, but I found the place as beautiful and idyllic as the corny Hollywood film had depicted it. In those days, the remote winter paradise, created from scratch near the village of Ketchum by Averell Harriman and his Union Pacific Company with the help of Austrian experts (some of them were still running the prestigious local ski-school), was still pristine and unspoiled. Weather that month of March was gorgeous, the ski conditions extraordinary, and our skiing companions most attractive. Lil's friends Liz and "Pat" Weaver, the brilliant innovator-president of NBC, were there, and it was also on the "College" and "Canyon" ski-runs that began our friendship with Elise and Basil Goulandris, the most charming and refined of the great Greek ship owners. Lil had her own ski-teacher and I took a few lessons with a Swiss, Otto von Almen, of the well-known family of racers, but most of the time we skied together and had a most marvelous time on the slopes of Baldy Mountain. During my last week there, the place filled with top international racers, arriving from everywhere to compete for the "Harriman Cup," and it was exciting to watch the training runs of world champions such as Molterer, Christian Pravda, Beaulieu, and the phenomenal Tony Seiler.

I left Sun Valley with great regrets, but thrilled that the next time I was going to see Lil, she would be a free woman.

*   *   *   *   *   *

Lil received her divorce in April, and in May we married. First, in the most prosaic banality of the New York City's Marriage License Office, and then in the colorful and rather exotic (to Lil) Eastern Orthodox church ritual. The way I'd been brought up, a wedding without a church blessing wouldn't be a real wedding. Lil, although an Episcopalian, knew how much it meant to me, and had no objection to getting married in the Bulgarian church. Bishop Andrey, the Bulgarian Metropolitan for North America, had known my parents well, and my very religious mother had admired his sermons, which had won him considerable popularity in pre-war Sofia. I had met him during his visits to Paris and he had given great support to our *Free Bulgarians* organization and I maintained friendly contact with him in New York. I introduced him to Lil and a few days before the wedding, he came for dinner at her apartment and gave her the necessary instructions.

Wise and eloquent, the soft-spoken Bishop Andrey was a highly cultured and cosmopolitan man. He also had a politician's mind, which served him well both in gaining influential and wealthy friends for his diocese, and in navigating around the Byzantine intrigues of the Church's high hierarchy. This latter quality proved to be of crucial importance during the Communist rule in Bulgaria, when the Church's supreme authority,—the Holy Synod, headed by the Patriarch,—had been reduced to a powerless, frightened body controlled by the regime. Bishop Andrey was abroad when the Communists took over, and the persecutions, humiliations and in many cases physical torture suffered by his colleagues were spared him. Maneuvering aptly, he managed to preserve his diocese's independence.

The wedding took place on May 11, 1957 at the Bulgarian church in New York. We wanted to get married in the strictest privacy and didn't invite anybody, outside of Jill and Tina, accompanied by their governess, Miss Fischer (Philip was away at boarding school), and our Eastern Orthodox witnesses, Anni Tchaprachikoff and Boubi Petroff, an exile friend recently arrived from South America. A most unexpected protocol incident surprised us just one day before the wedding, when Jean Stralem, Phil Isles sister, called. "Lil, how could you do that to me?" the ex-sister-in-law complained, deeply hurt. "We learn that you're getting married tomorrow, and you didn't invite us! You can't go to the church by yourself, with no one from the family! Donald will come and be your witness. And after the service, I'm expecting you all here, for the wedding lunch." (Donald, a Wall Street banker, was Jean's husband, and both Stralems had been particularly warm to me ever since I met them.) I was as deeply moved as I was surprised: coming from a part of the world where families of divorced husbands carry a lifelong vendetta against men who took away the wife, I couldn't believe that former in-laws would behave in such a civilized manner. (From that day on, and until her death, some 37 years later, Jean Stralem always introduced me as "my brother-in-law" and "my favorite relative".)

Indeed, as Bishop Andrey, in gilded vestment and miter, began the Eastern Orthodox service, Donald Stralem, the banker from a prominent "Our Crowd" family, was the one who gave the bride away. Anni and Boubi Petroff held the crowns over our heads, while the two little girls, Jill and Tina, followed wide-eyed the unfamiliar ritual. (Our "crowns" were in fact two hastily made wreaths of flowers, which Anni had to improvise with the help of a next-door florist at the last minute, when Bishop Andrey discovered that the church's regular wedding crowns were somehow missing that day...)

The intimate lunch at the Stralem's Park Avenue duplex was a happy affair. Lil looked radiant and I still remember how my heart was beating wildly from emotion. Bishop Andrey, a worldly man who appreciated the arts, was highly impressed by the Matisses, Picassos, and Rouaults in the apartment and had a great success with the host and the hostess.

After lunch, we rushed home to change and pick up our suitcases, and then took the plane to Palm Beach. Flo, Lil's close friend, and her financier husband Earl Smith, had a charming house, which they kindly offered to us for our honeymoon. They had just returned to New York at the end of the Palm Beach "season," and we had the house all to ourselves, except for their baby-boy Earl and his nurse. One could hardly dream of a better honeymoon hideaway than the comfortable villa in the fashionable resort of the rich and leisurely.

We had hardly unpacked, when Dolly O'Brian called to remind us of the dinner she was giving us at her home. Dolly, a famous beauty of the so-called "international jet-set" and mother of Lil and Phil's friend Jack Heminway, was a most colorful character. A merry, seductive septuagenarian with several much talked-about romances to her credit, (she had had the distinction of having turned down Clark Gable, among others), she continued, ignoring age and public opinion, to still naughtily consort with attractive young men. We had already dined with her in Paris with the Duke and Duchess of Windsor and Rocky and Gary Cooper, and had seen her at many parties in New York, always vivacious and having a good time.

Dolly O'Brian's party was our first as Mr. and Mrs. Groueff and I was tickled to hear myself referring to Lil as "my wife," quite a new feeling. We greatly enjoyed the evening—a huge wedding cake, amusing toasts, photographer and all,—and were introduced to quite a few local characters. An excellent hostess, Dolly looked very attractive that night, a champaign-blond coiffure and a glamorous dress complimenting her youthful figure, the naughty expression never leaving her eyes. Her current boyfriend, a young automobile racer at least half her age, looked rather jealous as she was playfully flirting with the guests.

The key word in Palm Beach was "parties," and new faces were in limited supply, so we, the young newlywed couple, had ample opportunities to mingle with local well-known residents. Most of them were attractive, civil gentlemen and ladies of taste and manners, spoiled but inoffensive, well brought up but with few interests outside golf, card games and gossip; mostly inactive people who neither worked, read, or cared about the rest of the world, but nevertheless amusing at parties and fun on the golf course. For a short vacation, I found Palm Beach quite a pleasant playground, and as Lil and I could afford being alone whenever we wanted and exploring it together, we enjoyed our 8-day honeymoon thoroughly. But we were also impatient to return to New York and start our new life of a married couple.

* * * *

Whether it was something to deplore or boast about, the fact is that the *Paris-Match* office in New York reflected fully the ambiance of the Paris headquarters. This wasn't helped much by my questionable managerial talents. I was a casual, permissive Bureau chief, and it was a lucky thing that in spite of the laxness and the frequently erratic behavior, the office functioned quite efficiently. Moreover, the camaraderie one felt around it made work stimulating and rewarding. Compared to most American offices, the bureau looked sloppy and badly organized. To begin with, during the long years I directed it, I could never convince or force my collaborators to arrive on time in the morning. I was equally unsuccessful in establishing clearly that business during the working hours had priority over personal chores and conversations, coffee breaks and lunch, visits by friends, or dentist appointments. As a result, the unassuming townhouse apartment on the second floor of 22 East 67th Street had all the coziness of a lively private home and none of the businesslike air of a functional correspondent's office.

There are people born to be bosses and give orders, good administrators who establish discipline in their outfits, who can say "no" and fire inadequate personnel. I definitely didn't belong to that species. I behaved more as though I were "one of the guys," or ran it like a benevolent, permissive father runs a disorderly but likeable family. I knew that a good executive would act differently, but I would never have the heart to replace our secretary Gaby just because she was a poor, two-fingers-only typist; or dismiss Flora, the other secretary and an excellent typist, just because she spent hours on long-distance telephone when infatuated romantically, which happened quite often, being a very romantic girl. Talking about romances, I considered being in love a legitimate enough reason for photographer Paul Slade's occasional absences from work, the way a teacher would accept a medical certificate to excuse a student missing a class. When Paul disappeared for a few days, he never lied to me, he wouldn't say he had been sick or there was an accident ; he would just come to my room, close the door, and mumble, with teary eyes, "You know, Genevieve's in town and she's been so mean to me..." Then I would try to console and advise him, as an older brother, "Now, now, Paul, pull yourself together! You know how women are..." I loved Paul, with all his show-off postures and his aggressive vulnerability. And, of course, I loved too much my old-time friend Anni, who was the manager of the office, to insist that she try to come to work before 11 A.M. Worst, I was too weak to ask Paris to recall Mathias, an excellent reporter but exasperating colleague, and thus be relieved of a heavy cross which myself and the office had to carry for years.

When Raymond Cartier was in town—about twice a year for a couple of months—or when he worked on American subjects, the atmosphere in the bureau was different. There were less absences and less erratic behavior. During such periods, his article had absolute priority and the office worked almost entirely for him. This didn't always please the other editors in Paris, but none of them dared challenging Cartier openly. Periodically, someone would complain behind his back to Le Patron that other American stories were being neglected because "Cartier monopolized the bureau," but Jean Prouvost, who didn't dislike some little intrigue and jealousy among his collaborators, would mischievously pretend to be helpless: "I know, I know! But that's how Raymond is!..' Anyway, they all agreed that his weekly article was the *piece de resistance* of each issue and didn't protest too much. By then, in addition to his formidable journalistic reputation, Raymond had gained a new celebrity with his provocative ideas about disbanding the French colonial empire. In the midst of a passionate national debate, he took the position of granting independence to all colonies. But not for any of the traditional liberal reasons. On the contrary, the shocking but undisputable statistics and crushing examples provided by Raymond's ivestigations tended to prove that France, rather than exploiting its colonies, was in reality being taken advantage of by them and would be much better off to "get rid" of them and spend the immense subsidies at home, where they were badly needed. Even General de Gaulle became fascinated by some aspects of the "Cartierism" and borrowed them in his reforms. But the mutual admiration was short-lived. Raymond, feeling himself more a European than a French nationalist, never forgave de Gaulle for missing the golden opportunity for France to become the leader of the nascent European community and preferring instead the narrower goals of oldtime French chauvinism.

Cartier worked at home and only paid occasional visits to the office, usually to relax and chat with us, in good spirits, when his piece was finished. He had let me in full charge of the bureau and our relationship, both professionally and as friends, was most cordial. We talked with each other daily, and Lil and I saw Raymond and Rosie quite often.

Beside the work for Cartier, the bureau functioned very well and Paris, including Le Patron, seemed to be pleased with our work. With all our shortcomings, we shared a tremendous dedication to the magazine, a cocky assurance that we were the best and no competitor could cover stories better than we did. And, somehow, it worked. I never had a case of a reporter objecting or even sounding grouchy when I woke him up in the middle of the night—no matter whether it was a Sunday, Christmas, or at the height of some family celebration,—and asked him to rush to the scene of a developing story. I was myself, of course, constantly awakened by Therond's or Lacaze's telephone calls: with the 5 or 6 hours time difference, morning in Paris meant 4 AM in New York, and nobody wasted time to apologize for the disturbance. Once on a story, the reporters behaved like excited hunting dogs on a game's trail; for a few days, nothing else counted—personal safety, fatigue, police restrictions; nothing but the deadline and the fear of being outsmarted by a rival. As different as they were from each other, all reporters who took turns for a year or more at my office— first Benno Graziani, Dominique Lapierre, Philippe de Bausset, and Mathias, then Bernard Giquel and a few others who stayed for shorter periods,—they all donned the same personality the moment the telex or telephone sounded the tallyho. They became the archetypal *Paris-Match* reporters: irreverent but dogged, ingeniously resourceful, charming and funny when possible, aggressive when needed. They carried the old Rue-Pierre-Charron embellished lore, its fierce esprit-de-corps and taste for adventure and independence. Even our American-born photographer, Paul Slade, was totally converted to this spirit and to the tricks, jokes and mannerisms of the Paris gang.

With the eagerness of my collaborators, no prodding from me was ever necessary. When launched on an important story, the reporters' zeal contaminated the rest of the office, transforming it into an anxious, united team. For a few days, the bureau would live with and for the story. Anni and I would spend weekends at the office or on the telephone, Gaby and Flora would stay working way beyond the office hours, somebody would always volunteer to go to the airport to entrust the package with the reportage personally to the Air-France personnel. Sometimes, in case of a scoop, Paris would call to congratulate the bureau and we would rejoice, like a proud family.

Then the next day the bureau routine would resume. Everybody would be late again at the crammed office with the shabby, second-hand desks. As I arrived, I would greet Gaby and ask whether we had telexes from Paris. She would put down the telephone receiver for an instant, briefly interrupting the lively chat with her best friend, just the time to smile at me and hand me the message, before resuming her talk: "...Yes, Esther, isn't it great about Sarah's daughter?..." Gaby, a friendly Jewish young woman from French Tunisia, had become such an integral part of the office, which we grew accustomed to her amateurish typing and incapacity to take dictation. Her religion presented another problem: her husband, a pious Orthodox Jew from Rumania, served at the synagogue and wouldn't even consider a member of his family working on Sabbath, even handling money or telephones on a Saturday. We observed, anyhow, all official and religious holidays, both American and French, *Quatorze-Juillet* as well as Fourth-of-July, Labor Day and Thanksgiving as well as Pentecote and La Fete de Jeanne-d'Arc. But come September, Gaby's appearances at the office were reduced to a strict minimum, her empty desk signaling Passover and Yom Kipur, Rosh Hashana, Hanukah and Purim. There was a time when I made a few half-convinced attempts to correct that situation, but Gaby would just smile and shrug her shoulders helplessly: "Would you want me to divorce my husband?" she would say. No, I didn't want her to divorce, the rabbi was a nice guy and a good husband and father. I stopped trying. The hell with efficiency!, I rationalized. Who wants robots that type with the speed of light but wouldn't understand the *Paris-Match* ways? Wasn't it more important to preserve the family atmosphere at the office? We felt cozy with Gaby, we liked her, we trusted her, and she was, after all, one of us.

So was Flora, a luscious brunette with a most pleasant disposition, always cheerful and ready to help her colleagues. The extraordinary thing about this young girl of Assyrian descent ("Not Syrian! A-ssy-rian! Didn't you learn at school about Assyria and Babylon?" she proudly corrected anyone who would confuse the races), was that her rather chaste personality of a sentimental, credulous good girl didn't correspond at all to her Playboy-Centerfold physique. Indeed, the Mesopotamian, or whatever, gods had lavishly endowed her with a bust of such striking dimensions, that one couldn't help be in awe, like as before the Tower of Pisa, of this prodigious defiance of the laws of gravity. There was seldom an incomer—be it a delivery man, messenger boy, or visitor,—who wouldn't be stopped in his tracks at the sight of Flora's overfull sweater when first entering the office, and who wouldn't take a second peek and a deep breath. Flora would blush, lower her eyes and continue typing. We anticipated the visitors' legitimate surprise and were each time greatly amused by their reaction. Meanwhile, only half-aware of the lustful thoughts her shapes were provoking,

Flora was absorbed in romantic Gothic novels, Hollywood fan magazines and social columns, having crushes on movie stars, and waiting for Prince-Charming. But apart from some periods of dreaminess, Flora was an excellent worker and the bureau was lucky to have her.

Past the secretaries desks, I would take off my jacket and join my colleagues. Here was Miles Herbert, busy reading recipes in some cookbook and, to judge by the epicurean anticipation in his eyes, already savoring the delicious dish his French wife would serve him that night. Occasionally, stricken by some sudden gourmet fantasy, he would dial his home and whisper sensually in the phone: "Cherie, shall we try it with champagne sauce…and then sear it quickly?…No, not that long, just a soupcon! And don't forget the truffles!" Before hanging up, he would invariably make with his lips the noise of "kiss-kiss" and tenderly say "je t'aime!"

Among us, Miles was the best in French spelling and grammar, always ready to explain a word's etymology, a master in the use of the *subjonctif passé*. Yet he was a pure American who had taught himself to speak both literary and colloquial French faultlessly and with no accent. Beside gastronomy, French was his principal hobby and he delighted in discovering some new slang word or unusual idiomatic expression. He wrote very well, and having never worked at *Paris-Match* in Paris, he had a more serious attitude toward his job, or shall we say, he was a more orderly and compliant collaborator.

The sight of Janie Bonheur's dog leisurely stretched on the floor behind her desk added to the homey atmosphere of the place. Janie, editor-in-chief Gaston Bonheur's daughter, had been sent to the New York office as an intern and to learn English.

A few times a month we had a visit of Ira Slade, Paul's kid brother. A law-school student, he helped us with the accounting, insurance policies, and filing taxes. A thankless job, because such duties seemed somehow to go against the grain at "Match" and were received with unconcealed skepticism, if not hostility. Ira's insistence on having some order in the bookkeeping, and especially his annoying habit of retaining a portion of the paychecks for income tax, did not meet with much cooperation from the staff. But we found him to be a nice guy and, despite his odd profession, we considered him a member of the family.

For all its unprofessional ambiance, our office must have had some attraction for a number of young men, especially aspiring photographers. Not unlike "groupies" following a rock band, they seemed to be happy to hang around, no matter how small the chance of getting an assignment. A good example of this was the tenacity of Chuck Rapoport, a bright, witty New York kid, who practically lived at the office, savoring every bit of "Paris-Match" lore, drama, and gossip, with no remuneration except a rare job whenever Paul Slade was busy elsewhere. His perseverance paid off: his big chance finally came and Chuck ended as a good photo reporter in his own right.

As if the fraternity-house atmosphere at 22 East 67th Street were not enough to dispel any suggestion of serious business being accomplished on the premises, our landlady, whose busy real estate agency occupied the ground floor, happened to indulge in a hobby hardly typical for her guild. Indeed, the Valkyriesque Pat Palmer dreamed of a career as an opera singer and worked quite assiduously at it. So, a few times a week, a retired voice coach used to come after office hours and sit in front of the upright piano in an office facing the elevator. Then for an hour or so the whole town house with the marble-floored hall and staircase resonated with Pat's overpowering *bel canto,* sporadically interrupted by a critical *"No! No! Start again!"* from the old maestro.

Miles's habit to whisper when speaking on the telephone was a blessing in a bureau where Mathias's overbearing presence was hard to be ignored. When our Hungarian colleague was in the office, his powerful baritone could be heard from the elevator's hall, sometimes exultant, even singing, other times in a fury, always excited and loud. Privacy was a notion totally unknown to Mathias; he neither respected it in other people (which made him a formidable reporter), nor ever practiced it himself (which made him an embarrassing colleague to share an office with). "Marella," he would say loudly on the phone, talking to the wife of the famous Italian tycoon, puffing on his strong cigar, his feet comfortably on the desk, "wasn't it great fun last night at Lee's? But I don't think Jackie looked at her best in that dress. And did you notice how Slim turned livid when we mentioned

Truman? Oh, boy! The story is that Babe Paley had said to Diana…" And on and on the social talk went, with Mathias immodestly reporting the latest gossip about Pamela Churchill, or Charlotte Ford-Niarchos, or some Rothschilds, while the rest of us, feeling highly uncomfortable, pretended to be writing and not to listen. It was partly lack of prudence, partly a childish need of boasting, unnecessary in his case, since the whole office knew from the social columns that Mathias was a favorite "walker" of internationally famous society ladies.

He knew most of the rich and famous, and if he didn't, he made a point to know them and was very good at that. A bright, good-looking and very socially minded bachelor, he was an amusing dinner guest, always arriving from, or about to leave for, some fascinating reportage, keeping the table entertained with first-hand tales about astronauts, revolutions, or great international scandals. And, of course, a few indiscretions about what some Rothschild told him, or Kennedy, or La Garbo…He was a snob, all right, but not the distant, blasé, haughty type; on the contrary, he was noisily gregarious, openly nosy, easily sentimental and familiar. Everybody at *Paris-Match* and among his friends and social acquaintances had colorful stories about the mercurial, temperamental, and incredibly brazen Mathias. As he expressed his opinions with passion and was capable of throwing tantrums in the midst of formal dinners, explosions around him were not infrequent, including at the office.

The value of Mathias was that he put all his talents, social connections, and even his personal faults, to the service of the magazine. He would use anything and anybody in order to open a door or get a favor for *Paris-Match*. When General de Gaulle came on official visit to Washington and no reporter was admitted to his private breakfast with President Kennedy, *Match* asked us for all the details of the meeting. As we agonized over how to get the information, Mathias picked up the phone and called the French Embassy. "I would like to speak to Monsieur l'Ambassadeur Herve Alphand," he said. "I'm a friend of his, Mathias Polakovits" (he had never met him). A long pause. "Yes, Mathias, M-a-t-h-i-a-s…Of course, he knows me. No, you can't, its personal. Yes, it's important." Another pause. Then, to my amazement, I hear: "Allo, Herve? Comment vas-tu?" (Alphand was a very formal diplomat, rather snooty, and few people would call him *Tu.*) "Oui, mon ami, c'est moi, Mathias! Oh, we had such fun together at Berthe David-Weil's! (Mathias knew about that party.) Nicole (Alphand's wife) looked lovely, I think it's her best color, tell her that I said that! And I'm still laughing at your imitation of the senator!" (Alphand's talent as an after-dinner impersonator was famous.) After establishing the authenticity of their social "friendship," Mathias continued: "Le Patron (Jean Prouvost) just called from Paris and ask me to call you…He's very curious to know what the Presidents had for breakfast at your place. Tea? Fried eggs, bacon? Oh, come on, Herve, *tu* can tell him, the old man will be terribly amused, you know how he is!…" Five minutes later, Mathias had a full description of the breakfast and a good idea of what was said.

Sometimes the requests from Paris were much easier to take care of. Send us the photo of the new Algerian UN delegate as he attacks France, for instance, or something similarly simple. Gaby would make a call and the picture would be delivered a few hours later. But Mathias would first send a telex, announcing great difficulties, "but I'll do my best." A second telegram would build up the imaginary obstacles but add that, as an exceptional favor to him, an important friendly diplomat might help him. Finally, Paris would receive a long, self-glorifying message, pointing out that, uniquely because of Mathias's personal connections, the "exclusive" document had been obtained.

At the beginning we only laughed, but this outrageous self-promotion ended by irritating the rest of the office. Although most telegrams were signed collectively "*Le Bureau de New York,*" his, with his role greatly embellished, were always in the first person singular and signed "Mathias." A few times, when I caught him sending behind my back collective office work under his own name, I had to reprimand him and we had some painful talks in private. But no sooner that we closed the door of my office, and he would burst in tears and deliver a self-flagellation performance worthy of the best Dostoyevsky. "I don't know how you can stand me! I really behaved like a *merde!* Can you forgive me?" he implored me, tears rolling down his cheeks. Startled, I would be so embarrassed for him that I wouldn't know what to say. Freudian confessions followed, making me regret hundred times my unfortunate decision to act for once as a "real Bureau chief."

"I know I have a terrible character, I know I'm difficult to live with…No, no, don't try to contradict me, you're so good!…But I was always so insecure, since childhood, my parents always preferred my sister, Vera had all the attention, all the affection…" It made me so uncomfortable to listen, that I would end by stupidly putting my arm around him and consoling him. Once calmed, he would gratefully give me his word of honor: "It'll never happen again! I swear to you!" And for a week or so, he would keep his promise and be the most charming and considerate colleague. Until the next time. Oh, how I hated to be Chief of Bureau, chief of anything and anybody! So I would tear up my request for Mathias's recall, and continue in my old ways, the poor executive's ways…

Now I know that I was wrong, that inability to say "no" or implement unpleasant measures is often nothing but weakness, the easiest way out. But I must say that our Paris editors were not of a great help either. They were perfectly aware of Mathias's foibles and shenanigans, but they also knew that he delivered, that he seldom came empty-handed. And also, they were impressed by his connections; lines such as "Jackie told me…" or "I'll ask Jackie," dropped abundantly by Mathias, were not only impressive, they were usually true.

My failure to tame Mathias however was detrimental to the work of the bureau. One after the other, Slade, and Giquel, and Anni, and Miles, started refusing to work with, or around, their explosive, egocentric colleague. The malaise came to a peak when he moved to live in one of the office rooms that had a bathroom. At first, I gave him permission for a few nights, just the time to take possession of a new studio he was about to rent, after he was asked to move out of a friend's Park Avenue apartment where he had lived, free, for a whole year. (Mathias's stinginess was proverbial, and he himself was telling funny jokes about it.) So he moved his dinner jacket and a few suitcases into the office, "very temporarily," while waiting for the contract to be signed "tomorrow or the next day." Tomorrow was slow to come and in the meantime Mathias ensconced himself comfortably in the pleasant office, fully enjoying his hot showers, the free telephone, and above all, the delight of paying no rent. Weeks passed by, then months, and we found ourselves in a pretty embarrassing situation, with the secretaries bumping into Mathias in pajamas and slippers in the morning, or visitors being surprised by the appearance of a man in a bathrobe and the face covered with shaving cream. "Just a few more days!" he swore each time I demanded that he leave. "The painters promised to finish by Monday." It took a lot of insistence, threats, and finally complaints to Paris, to force Mathias out of the premises.

Paul Slade was the one who suffered the most. Emotional and explosive himself, he was often engaged in violent shouting matches with Mathias. A few times they ended by exchanging blows, which sent Gaby running for cover to the bathroom in tears and with severe palpitations, while I tried to separate them. Each time they both solemnly threatened to resign if the other guy was not fired at once, but only a couple of days later they were together again on some assignment. And they were a terrific team. It was difficult to say which one had more nerve or could be more pushy when in action. Paul, considerably younger than Mathias, was unbeatable in crowds or in "no-press-admitted" situations. He combined the street-smart toughness of a Lower-Eastside Jewish boy with the naive sentimentality and warmth of the kindest heart. Ever since his debuts as a humble camera-bearer of the seigniorial Nick de Morgoli, Slade had found his path and destination. Although he had never been in France, he fell in love with everything French. He taught himself the language, spoke it with a very nice accent, and in spite of the many errors and the difficulties he had during the first few years, he insisted on speaking French to us, even when we addressed him in English. He had one religion—"Paris-Match;" one dream, nay, determination-to equal *Paris-Match* star-photographers Walter Carone and Willy Rizzo, to amount to *Magnum's*" Henri Cartier-Bresson, and *Life Magazine's* Eugene Smith, his idols. He was so passionately motivated in his work, that at certain occasions I had to put some brakes; no goading was ever needed with Slade.

Paul in action was quite a sight. His corpulent frame laden like a Christmas tree with an arsenal of cameras, lenses, light meters, strobes and bags with films, sweating profusely, huffing and puffing, he cleared his way through the crowds with the delicateness of an assault tank. When positioning himself at the best vantage spot, he had no qualms pushing backs that obstructed his view, stepping on feet that had the imprudence of being on his path. And usually he succeeded in securing a first-row place for *Paris-Match*, in "being there" as the event was unrolling. On less competitive assignments, he was all smile and charm, palsy with the guys, flirtatious with the ladies, showing off his French and telling tall stories about *Paris-Match* incredible exploits. I did myself several stories with Slade as photographer and each time we had great fun traveling together. He was a really nice young man, pure and decent, unsophisticated but learning quickly. There was something touching in his eagerness to use Parisian slang, in his determination to sound and behave as French as possible, in his childish desire to sound important each time he was trying to impress fellow-photographers or airline stewardesses (incidentally, though I've been occasionally embarrassed to listen to him boasting in my presence, I can witness that Paul scored with air-hostesses and pretty starlets much more frequently than people would suspect...) But apart from the fun, he was one of the most conscientious and thorough professionals that I have worked for. No matter how tired, he would spend hours during the night meticulously arranging and labeling his films, charging the cameras for the next day, cleaning the lenses, and worrying. He suffered from the classic photographer's nightmare: dreaming that there was no film in the camera during the crucial shooting, and waking up in cold sweat. Although there was not much sleep for me when we had to share a motel's room, I enjoyed Paul's company. For him I was not only the "boss" (as he called me when it wasn't "Steve"), I was an older-brother figure, the adviser and the father-confessor. This last role was sometimes amusing and made time fly faster on a long trip, but it could also be a tremendous burden and responsibility. Especially in two cases: when Slade was in love, which happened quite often, and when he complained about insufficient recognition and unfair treatment by Paris, which periodically brought up to surface all his fears, suspicions, and insecurities. In both cases he would come to me and ask pathetically: "Why?" and "What should I do?" It was difficult, of course, to tell him what to do; but I hope that I helped him in a few cases by advising him what not to do, namely not to act impulsively or do something foolish, as he was often tempted to. I think Paul trusted me fully and had a sincere affection for me, and I became very attached to him.

*   *   *   *

Back from our Florida honeymoon, Lil and I were faced with a problem. It was end of May, Lil had the children for the summer, and with New York's hardly bearable heat and humidity, there was no question of keeping them in the city. On the other hand, there was no question for me taking two or three months vacation in order to be with her, nor being separated for the summer, just after getting married. Looking for a solution, we thought of renting some place in the Hamptons, so the children could enjoy the ocean while I work in Manhattan, less than three hours away from them. Our first choice was Easthampton and one weekend we drove there, looking for houses. The ones we liked were too expensive for us, so Lil's friend Brunie McKnight took us around Southampton, where she and her husband Bill had a house and were members of the local clubs. We loved the place immediately and were lucky to find a small, modest house that we were able to afford (the rent was $ 1,000 for the season). We spent three marvelous months there and made numerous new friends. Philip, Jill, and Tina were with us, and Maggie, our cook, came too. I came every Friday afternoon by the train, spent Friday, Saturday, and Sunday night in Southampton, and left Monday morning on the early train. Very often Lil would join me in New York for a night or two during the week, so we weren't really separated during the entire summer. It was a most convenient, lucky arrangement. With the magnificent ocean beaches, the attractive new friends and very active social life, and with the children happy around us, Southampton was a wonderful beginning for our married life. As the years passed, and after changing a few houses, it became our real home, one of the many good things that have happened to us.

****

Chapter 24

Mama finally comes out of Bulgaria

It's a dark, cold December night and as I drive to Le Bourget airport, I find it difficult to calm down. For thirteen years I dreamt of this impossible reunion, and now that the moment approaches, I still cannot believe that it will happen. Is it possible that, after all that has happened during those years, I'll see my mother again, and see her here, in Paris, free? But the telegram is in my pocket: "Arriving tomorrow night, Mama." It came yesterday, addressed to the Panitzas, so the whole thing is true. And yet…There have been so many disappointments, unrealized hopes and false alerts! Such as the cable I received eight days ago in New York: "Arriving Paris evening fifteenth, Mama." I nearly had a heart attack, I was so excited. The same evening I boarded the *Pan-American* flight to Paris, where I received a second telegram that the trip had been postponed…The following days, the suspense was unbearable. The Panitzas waited with me until the last minute, but yesterday they left for Geneva to spend Christmas with Harri and the grandchildren.

I'm going to the airport alone. Maybe it's better this way. There are moments one has to experience things in total privacy. The worries, which preoccupied me during the last eight days, reach their paroxysm. How does she look now? So many things have changed, we have changed so much, she and I…Is she really very sick, or was this urgent need of operation just a pretext to apply for her passport? Why are they letting her out now, after so many categorical refusals? And what is she going to tell me about how they live, she and Boubi and Radka, the real story and not what they've been telling me in their censure-controlled letters? Indeed, I know so little about their life in Bulgaria. I know, of course, the "official" stories: mama lives in deep poverty with Boubi in the outskirts of Sofia (their address is "Dobar-Yunak" street, 10). Boubi changes constantly miserably paid menial jobs, anything he can pick up. Radka married two years ago to a quiet man, Sasso Rizov, another victim of the regime: his father was in jail, where he died not long after. It was a sad marriage of two lonely, persecuted young people with nothing to hope for in life. He works hard, making keys, until late in the evening; she gives English lessons during the day and does the cooking, cleaning and laundry in the evening, in their poor room at the "Chaussee Volokolam," 65, just outside of Sofia. Last year they had the baby, George, and Radka is absolutely crazy about him. I'm receiving photographs all the time and detailed descriptions of every move and sound the baby makes. I send him clothes Lil buys at "Lord and Taylor" in New York and the parcels bring Radka, the proud mother of "the best dressed baby in Sofia," as she puts it, into a state of ecstasy.

They know pretty much about my life in New York, about my travels and some of my *Paris-Match* work, but I have to be careful what I write. Last September (1956), Tania Cellerier, who has a Swiss passport, visited Bulgaria and was able to give them detailed news about me. It was a great event for them, and when she returned, I went to Geneva to see her and at last hear firsthand news about them from this trusted old friend. But there were still enormous blanks in my information of what they had gone through and what was happening to them now. With great impatience, and no little apprehension, I waited to hear what mama was going to reveal.

Last October, I wrote to them about Lil for the first time and sent photos of her. Radka was delighted and wrote me a long, loving letter. She and Boubi wished me much happiness, but decided to postpone telling Mama, since she was quite sick then with a kidney stone attack, and also very upset by the latest refusal by the Militia to give her a passport. Her doctors had recommended an operation, but she refused to have it before seeing me again. Meanwhile, I repeatedly sent her dully-legalized invitations to come and be operated in Paris (not New York, since the US was labeled "progressive" Bulgaria's worst enemy) and affidavits of support in France. But they were ignored. When her latest application to travel was turned down, she had a premonition that she would die "without seeing my Stefcho again." By December she still wasn't told about Lil. Radka wrote me again, confessing her and Boubi's concern that Mama, belonging to another generation, might be disappointed and shocked by my romance with a married woman, a mother of three children. They were wrong. When Mama was finally told—only three months later,—she wrote me a most touching letter, giving me her full blessing and telling me how happy the news had made her. "I was only saddened," she wrote, "to realize how little my children (Boubi and Radka) know their mother..."

In the meantime, her health has worsened. The doctors warned that if not operated, she may suffer serious complications; but she continued to refuse. All through 1957, worries about her condition cast a constant cloud over the many happy events which seemed to follow me that year—my promotion to Bureau chief, my marriage, our exciting life in New York, Paris, Sun Valley and Southampton, our belated honeymoon in Spain, the first contract to write a book with my colleague Dominique Lapierre. All I could do was to mail medicines unavailable in Sofia and gifts Bulgarian citizens were permitted to receive, and carefully send small sums of money through compatriots with relatives in Bulgaria, who needed foreign currency—a risky, punishable practice. (Parcels could not be registered nor insured, and were frequently "lost;" customs restrictions changed constantly: in some periods weight was limited to one pound, precluding mailing of a pair of shoes, unless sending each shoe separately. Once I offered to give my brother a typewriter; he regretfully declined, because of the prohibitive customs duties...) I had to be very careful about sending books. Luckily, the lavishly illustrated *"Le Monde: d'ou Vient-il, ou Va-t-il?"* for which I collaborated with Raymond Cartier, arrived with no problem and was a source of great joy and pride for the family.

Suddenly, hopes for obtaining passports were revived by rumors that Bulgaria was going to relax its policy a little. The government was, we heard, interested again in reopening diplomatic relations with the United States, cut recently after violent mob demonstrations against the US embassy in Sofia and vicious anti-American campaign by the authorities. Now the communists needed to reestablish relations with the US, but Washington wanted first to see proofs of change of attitude. Denying that its citizens were prohibited to travel, the government granted passports to a few people. Paradoxically, they were mostly relatives of prominent anti-communist exiles, an obvious move to discredit their allegations of civil rights violations. Thus, the families of anti-communist activists, such as the Agrarian leader Dr. G.M. Dimitrov, chairman of the Bulgarian National Committee in Washington, and the head of *Radio Free Europe*'s Bulgarian section, Dimitar Matzankiev, were unexpectedly allowed to leave. As a member of the *Free Bulgarians'* leadership, known by then as a French journalist, could I be put in the same category?—I doubted very much. My real concern had always been the opposite: that my anti-communist activism was endangering my family. I knew that this was the principal reason for denying my mother her passport, and often I felt guilty.

I had absolutely no contacts with representatives of the Bulgarian regime, and was determined to keep it this way. But a mysterious character, some Bulgarian called Mr. N…approached me one day, saying that my mother had asked him to call me and had given him my address. He had arrived in Paris and wrote to me in New York, then sent me a telegram, asking for francs, that he would repay in levas to my mother. He seemed to know much about her, had obviously met her, and as the sum was reasonable, I transferred it to him. Some time later, my mother confirmed by coded words that she had received the money. N…did it again, and told me on the phone that he had a "friend" who could arrange for my mother to get a passport. Again I sent him money, which he gave to my mother. But this time he also asked for a small sum for "the friend." I obliged readily. Mr. N…came a couple of times to France, assuring me each time that the passport would be granted. Once he asked me to buy a raincoat for "the friend." The requests were modest, less than a couple of hundreds of dollars in all. (According to rumors, passports could be bought for a few thousands of dollars, but I had never found such a channel.)

In the meantime, I insisted that Mama keep applying for a passport, no matter how many times the authorities refuse. It sounded useless, especially when an official at the Militia told he rudely: "Didn't you understand, comrade, that you'll never get it? Never! You're wasting your time and ours!" I never knew whether N…'s friend helped at all, whether the authorities intended to exploit my case and cast doubt on my credibility, or whether the doctors' concern prevailed. The fact is that in mid-October I was surprised by a telegram announcing that Mama had received a passport for France. I was beside myself with excitement and the same day arranged, through *Paris-Match*, the immediate issuance of a French visa. In spite of the special French treatment, it took four weeks for the visa to be stamped on Mama's passport, four weeks of daily disappointments, absurd formalities and petty chicanery on the part of the Bulgarians, which turned into an unbearable ordeal for Mama's nerves and a painful suspense for me. Not to mention Radka, who had to do it all, with Mama sick and no one to leave the baby with. Radka's weekly reports on this bureaucratic torment read like a most depressing Kafkaesque nightmare.

Now all hurdles were cleared, or so we hoped. In a few hours, Mama was going to be with me. In a way, my life was about to change. Missing her during these painful thirteen years of separation, had become a way of life. Expecting her letters, getting upset, emotional, worried or relieved when reading them, was already part of a chronic sorrow, almost a routine, and so was my feeling sorry for her and for them, my preparing parcels, my looking for opportunities to send uncensored letters; and my vain, obsessive attempts to lift the mystery that still veiled their life in Bulgaria, the forbidden country from which I was cut and banned forever. Maybe some of this will change tonight? Maybe Mama's arrival from the world of shadows and nightmares, reappearing in flesh and blood into the real life, will liberate me of some of my burden?

*   *   *

It was 11:30 in the evening when the *KLM* flight from Sofia landed and the first passengers began to walk out of the plane, mostly a homely bunch whose ill-fitting clothes of cheap fabric identified their Eastern-bloc provenance. My reporter's pass allowed me to meet the plane at the gate, beyond the customs check-point, and I started scrutinizing the arriving passengers one by one, trying to recognize the silhouette of my mother among them. At first sight, no one resembled the figure and face I had kept in my memory. I looked closer, beginning to fear that she might have missed the plane or been forbidden to leave at the last minute. Then suddenly I saw coming down the ladder a short, plump old woman in a faded overcoat and worn out flat-heel shoes, and my heart sank. Still unsure, I rushed toward her to take a good look. The lady wore a hand-knitted woolen hat and her face without makeup was so swollen that her eyes had almost disappeared. Could this be Mama? This woman was much too small, blown-up and old to be her…Only when she burst into tears and eagerly opened her arms to hug me, did I recognize her. "Stefcho, my dear Stefcho, God has been good to us, to see you again!" she sobbed as she kissed me repeatedly. I cried too. I cried for joy, and also for pity and compassion. Her poor physical condition touched me tremendously. The once handsome, svelte and vivacious lady, the distinguished looking wife of the King's Chief of cabinet, was now a broken old woman with an extinguished look in her eyes and the pale smile of a sick person. My heart cried when I saw her hands, the rough hands of a charwoman, and all fingernails black from some fungus, which, she told me later, she contracted long ago when working in the fields.

It's curious how sometimes the sight of commonplace objects can trigger the strongest emotions. Mama's frayed dress and threadbare scarf, her worn homemade sweater, the mended nylon stockings, obviously the best she owned, and even the pitiful old suitcase,—put together they overcame me and filled me with infinite tenderness and love for her.

I brought her to the *Franklin Roosevelt*, a small hotel on Rue Clement-Marot, one block away from *Paris-Match*. She still acted dazed, hardly believing that she was in Paris, reunited with me. A private bathroom, with hot water day and night? And a telephone on the night table? The modest hotel, with me in the next room, seemed like a dream to her. We didn't sleep much that night. There were too many questions to ask, too much news to update. How are Boubi and Radka? How is Radka's baby, "Boozy"? And Lil, tell me about her, is she as beautiful as in the photographs? I wanted to find out about how serious mama's kidney ailment was, while she was anxious to transmit the greetings of relatives and friends, aunt Mara and Verka, and aunt Minka—you know, she's not well with her phlebitis,—and cousin Gosho (he gave me a letter for you), and uncle Mitcho, and, oh, I nearly forgot uncle George and Louchko, who always ask for your news…

Mama was too excited to stay in bed after 6 AM and too tempted by the luxury of having her own bathroom, so she spent a whole hour in the very hot tub, a pleasure she had enjoyed all her life but had not indulged in for thirteen years. After we had our room service breakfast together—another long-for-gotten luxury,—I took her shopping in town. I remember it as a great day in my life. Playing Pygmalion, by transforming at least the physical appearance of a beloved person, is one of the most rewarding experiences one can enjoy in this world. No wonder this privileged role had been celebrated in mythology and in fairy tales, and from George Bernard Shaw to *My Fair Lady*'s Professor Higgins!

What a pleasure it was to take Mama to *Madelios* on Place de la Madeleine and watch her excitement as we were choosing a new coat and a couple of dresses, blouses, cardigans and whatever, down to stockings and underwear! Still incredulous but obviously delighted in front of the mirror, she was repeating: "But isn't this too much? Are you sure it isn't too expensive?..." And how impressed she was by the variety of selections at the shoe shop, a very average one, which looked to her like a cornucopia of superabundance! The best part, and the most delicate, was the beauty parlor, where, faced with the curious stares of both hairdressers and customers, she panicked a little. "That's not for me!" she mumbled, feeling insecure, and pulling me to get out. But I took a friendlier-looking hairdresser aside, explained the case, handed her a tip, and commissioned her to give my mother "the works"—wash, haircut, setting, facial, manicure and all. "I'll pick you up in two hours," I told Mama, who gave me the alarmed look of a child left with the teacher on the first day of school.

The woman I found when returning, after deposing the packages at the hotel, looked so different that I gasped at her sight and we both started laughing. It wasn't exactly the metamorphosis of poor Eliza Doolittle into the elegant Audrey Hepburn having tea with the gentry, but the change was striking, almost comical: the look was certainly no longer that of a refugee from behind the Ion Curtain. The coiffure was a little overdone and too much make-up was applied to her face, unused to cosmetics. For the next few hours she acted self-consciously, having difficulties to get accustomed to her new clothes and new face, but after a few corrections with her own comb and a towel, she managed to relax.

Not completely. When we sat for a snack on a terrace on the Champs-Elysees, her behavior became very peculiar. She often interrupted herself with sudden silences in the middle of a sentence. Each time I mentioned words such as "communists," "militia," or even "America," she would ask me not to talk so loud and, after looking furtively at the tables around, would lean toward me and answer in a whisper. As I couldn't understand her edginess, she said in a conspiratorial voice: "Don't look now, but I think the man behind you is eaves-dropping!" Of course, he wasn't; it was simply a Frenchman reading his *Le Figaro*. When that man left, Mama transferred her suspicions over another one. "Doesn't he look Bulgarian?" she asked. "He can hear us." Finally it bothered me. "Mama, we're in Paris and nobody cares about our conversation. They don't understand Bulgarian. And even if they did, it's too bad for them, France is luckily still a free country!" But she remained unconvinced. "You don't know *them!*" she said with a sigh, as if she were talking to a very naive person. "And don't forget that Boubi and Radka are still there!" This last reminder brought me back to the realities in my country and upset me. It was also upsetting to see my mother afflicted by the same paranoia I noticed in all those who had lived in communist Bulgaria. Indeed, for months after her arrival in the free world, she continued to act as though microphones were planted in every room and Big Brother was constantly watching.

It was the holiday season, the day before Christmas Eve. I was sad to be away from Lil on the first Christmas after our marriage, but the occasion was too extraordinary to leave us a choice. I spent Noel alone with Mama, taking her to the small restaurants in the neighborhood, *Chez Andre, Doucet, Café des Theatres, Rome*, all familiar bistros where I used to eat during my ten bachelor's years in Paris, never expecting that one day she would see them. Most of the people she knew in Paris were away for the holidays, so we spent the entire week all by ourselves, just mother and son being together after a painful separation, barely having enough time to tell each other what had happened to us during those 13 years. Then friends began to return and she was happy to spend the New Year's Day with Dimi and Yvonne at Yvonne's family country house in Monsoult, to lunch at her old friend Takvor's, to go to the movies with Rosie Cartier, and then, to celebrate Bulgarian Christmas with the Panitzas, an emotional reunion at their

Rue Franklin home. To my delight, the transformation—or shall I say transfiguration?—I could observe in her, was striking, beyond any Pygmalion's dream. The shapeless figure of a pitiful, poor old woman was fading away, a smile reappeared on the tired face, and a spark in the deadened eyes. She still cried often, when thinking of Boubi, Radka and other relatives in Bulgaria, but there were many moments when she looked really happy, albeit hesitantly at first, as if relearning a long-forgotten skill. One day I was surprised to see her enjoying genuinely a small custom-jewelry necklace I gave her. Surprised, because I had assumed that long suffering, deprivation and inhumanity, and witnessing the precarious nature of all worldly things, kill any residue of frivolity forever. Wrong! That day I knew that mama was going to recover. I stayed with her in Paris until January 10, then returned to New York, while she waited for her American visa. Lil and I rented a studio apartment for her on East 84-th street, and Lil furnished it in ten days, just in time for Mama's arrival in New York. She fell in love with America immediately and already felt and looked better. Nevertheless, our doctors confirmed their Bulgarian colleagues' diagnosis and soon she underwent a kidney operation, followed, a year later, by removal of her gall bladder. But her health improved in an amazing manner. In no time, she recovered her energy, figure, and high spirits. To watch the well-dressed, smiling lady of 65 on her daily walks of 20 or 30 city blocks, or eagerly attending her English-language classes, one would hardly recognize the defeated, heartbroken pariah from the Communist world.

*　　　　*　　　　*　　　　*

In those days, our social life was extremely active. As a recently married couple, we were invited out several times a week and often we had friends for cocktails or small dinners at home, which delighted Lil, a born hostess. In addition, my job as Bureau chief demanded that I see people from the media, the theatre, or the United Nations, and also entertain visiting *Paris-Match* colleagues and directors, including Le Patron himself. Mama's arrival didn't change the hectic tempo of this amusing, sometimes very enjoyable life. She had her own studio apartment and was renewing old friendships and acquaintances with people she once knew in Bulgaria. But the long talks we had every day made me more aware of the enormous, even shocking, contrast between my life and the life of my family in Bulgaria, and this revived the old feelings of guilt, although there was nothing I could do to change the situation. Mama wanted to assure me that the fact that I was living better gave them more hope. "How lucky we were to have you abroad and doing well!" she used to say. "All these years we breathed through you, you were the only bright ray in the darkness. Otherwise, we who had remained in Bulgaria would have been left in total gloom and despair." Her reasoning made me feel better, yet, hearing her tale I couldn't help asking myself: "Why was I spared, and not the others? Weren't we the same family, the same blood and background? Why had I been the lucky one to escape this hell?"

Mama's tale was a sad one. I remember a Sunday afternoon, soon after she arrived. The director of *Marie-Claire*, the urbane Philippe de Croisset and the jovial Raymond Castans, assistant-editor of *Paris-Match*, were visiting New York and we asked them for a drink. A few other people dropped in, among them glamorous Jackie Kennedy (JFK was still senator). We had a pleasant time and the usual cocktail-party chat about exhibits, fashion, Broadway shows and gossip was still ringing in my ears when, after they left, Mama came home for dinner. We stayed late and talked long after Lil went to bed; talked, as usual, about their life in Bulgaria. That night she told me about Koumaritza, a small railroad station outside Sofia, a filthy village where they were once interned during their repeated expulsions from Sofia. She described their quarters in a dilapidated shack, where they had two rooms—one for Mama and Radka, the other for Boubi. There was no running water and they did the cooking on a portable heater. To wash themselves, they used to fill a tin barrel, suspended outdoors, with an empty bucket beneath it. The smelly outhouse was at a distance from the rooms.

Now we were talking about this, sitting comfortably in our cozy, English-style decorated living room; a Renoir and a Matisse, belonging to Lil's children who lived with us, hung on the walls; outside, one could see Central Park blanked with snow; from time to time, a limousine or taxicab would stop in front of the quiet building and our uniformed doormen would greet the last tenants returning home.

I remember also the time she told me about their next internment. Lil and I had returned from a weekend in New Jersey, where we were the guests at the Far Hills country estate of Charlie Engelhard, the industrial tycoon for whom Sava worked in South Africa. Jane Engelhard, the elder sister of my Paris friends Brigitte and Patricia Brian, was an accomplished hostess who entertained lavishly and thought of every detail, to begin with sending a chauffeured limousine to pick her guests up and then driving them back to New York, having a crack staff to unpack our suitcases, press our clothes, and pack them beautifully just before the weekend was over, and organizing a busy program of promenades, lunches, cocktails and dinners for her guests with clockwork precision. On Sunday, the Engelhards took us for lunch at the mansion of Governor Robert Meiner, in the company of Adlai Stevenson, Marietta Tree, Aileen Guinness Plunket and her new husband, Valerian Rybar. I was impressed by Stevenson's intelligence and culture, and fully understood the fascination this presidential candidate held among Democrat intellectuals (but it was also obvious, that the civilized, non-partisan thinker possessed none of the drive and ruthlessness, needed to win political campaigns.)

When Mama asked "How was your weekend?" how much could I, should I, tell her? The Bulgarian tale she resumed that evening was like from another planet. For example, how two Militiamen arrived unexpectedly one day in the shack in Koumaritza, two rude, un-talkative brutes, who only ordered them to pack everything and leave in a few hours. Why? Where?—Shut up and don't ask questions, just be ready! It was useless to pro-test, to complain. Complain to whom? The three of them-Mama, Boubi and Radka—were already used to this kind of abuse. Worried, but resigned, they boarded the freight car and the train raced toward the unknown destination. It was very far away, somewhere in Dobrudja, where they were ordered to disembark. They had never before heard the name of the village, Gueshanovo. Another dusty, God-forsaken village of very poor but friendly land laborers. Then another year of poverty and isolation, struggling not to surrender to the despair.

"Let's not talk about it, it's much too sad!" Mama said. "I'd rather hear about your friends. Elena Beneva read in the paper that you went to a party at Henry

Fonda's? Tell me, what kind of a person is he?" She was pleased to hear that Gary Cooper, whose looks she liked the best among the Hollywood stars, was a really kind man. ("Did you tell him that we used to watch his movies in Bulgaria?…") Indeed, some of Mama's friends read the social columns and called her each time when our names were mentioned. She would ask then who were these people whom we were seeing and whom the newspapers made sound so glamorous. In a way, she was proud, but at the same time certain comparisons were difficult to evade when talking about "our people back home," a constant subject of conversation.

Mama used to pick me up sometimes from my *Paris-Match* office on East 67th street for a quick lunch in some coffee-shop in the neighborhood, and often I would ask her to tell me more about those 13 years, when we were separated. "What happened after Gueshanovo? How long did they keep you there?" Then she would tell me how Boubi and Radka had to work in the fields and how hard it was to find anything to eat. I learned how, one year later, they were told to leave, with no more explanation than when the Militia sent them there. They went back to Koumaritza, then back to the insecurity of unauthorized sojourns in Sofia, sleeping here and there, at homes of charitable relatives. The previous year in Koumaritza, Radka had met Sasso Rizov, a quiet, decent young man whose family, also interned, lived across the untidy, dusty backyard. Now, returning to the same village, she saw him again. Two lonely, uprooted casualties from the same upheaval, badly in need of friendship and home. It wasn't a passionate romance. Just finding someone to trust and be with. The two families knew and liked each other. At the end of 1954, they married. A no-frills, no-thrills wedding, with no great illusions, like many marriages in Bulgaria in those days of police terror and housing shortage. Radka sent me a snapshot of herself taken in front of the first house she lived in as a young bride. All the shabbiness and desolation of a Third-World hamlet showed in this photo. Their next home, where the baby was born, a tiny proletarian "studio" on a highway in the outskirts of Sofia, was hardly less depressing, but at least it was in Sofia, where Sasso had a job as a locksmith, and Radka could give French lessons, if she could entrust the baby to someone for a couple of hours.

It was a discomforting contrast that the same evening after such conversations with Mama, I would don my dinner-jacket and go to some lavish party, hosted, say, by young heiress Peggy Bancroft, a new star on the New York social scene, where one would mix with Aly Khan, Elsa Maxwell and similar jet-set celebrities. And later we'd go on to dance at *El Morocco* with old friends of Lil's, some of whom had become also my friends. Or to cozy, informal Sunday evenings at Jean Howard's, where we'd have great time with her Broadway friends—Leonard Bernstein, Arlene Frances with Martin Gable, Adolphe Green with Betty Comden, Lauren Bacall with Jason Robards. Mama's arrival in New York coincided with a period when the week didn't seem to have enough nights for us to go out and meet entertaining people.

The weekends were not less active, especially in summer, when Southampton transformed itself into a seaside jet-set playground. Although we used to rent rather modest houses and couldn't compete with the summering multimillion-aires, our low-budget, improvised parties usually enjoyed a great success. *"In the good offbeat vein, the Stephane Groueffs gave a Left-Bank 'caveau' party in their cellar, that owed its fantastic success to the host's ingenuity and the hostess' skyrocketing enthusiasm,"* wrote "Town and Country" magazine in an article on the art of entertaining. *"In a season of rather lavish and extravagant Southampton parties, the cellar idea gave everyone a free-wheeling feeling from the start. There were French posters—'Defense d'afficher' and other familiar French 'defenses'—crayoned around the walls, red-checkered cloths on the tables, candlelight, nothing but a phonograph with particularly hot records to dance to. There were spaghetti, salad, and cheese to eat, red wine, and the usual hard liquors to drink—and guests who came dressed comfortably as Left bank characters (which everyone has dreamed of being at one time or another) already conditioned for fun. They weren't disappointed. It was a spontaneous hair-letting-down evening that strong men like Henry Ford and Gary Cooper and, in fact, all husbands found exactly to their taste. The next time Lil and Stephane Groueff give a party, no wife will have to ask her husband if he wants to go—it's a foregone conclusion."*

We, of course, had a great time too and danced wildly in the hot, cement-walled cellar until the wee hours. Yet, when back to the city…With Mama's tales and the letters arriving from Bulgaria, what normally sensitive person wouldn't feel it a little indecent to enjoy too much such frivolities?

       *   *   *   *

Chapter 25

Book on the Mafia. Some celebrities in my new life.

It was late in the radiant morning of October 25th, 1957, when the notorious gangster Albert Anastasia entered the barbershop of Hotel Park Sheraton, on 55th Street and Seventh avenue, took off his brown over-coat and his perennial gray fedora, and sat on his usual chair, ready for the customary ritual of haircut, shave, facial massage, manicure, and shoeshine. A thick-set man of 55, with a somewhat sinister face and strong Italiano-Brooklynese accent, he enjoyed a certain popularity among the personnel and the habitués of the salon, due perhaps less to his crude pleasantry than to his lavish tips and the fact that he was, after all, a celebrity.

As Joseph the barber started officiating, two masked gunmen burst in, brandishing their pistols and shouting: "Nobody moves, or you're all dead!" They rushed to Anastasia's chair and, with him watching them in the mirror, opened fire, point-blank in the back of his neck. As the victim collapsed in a puddle of blood, the assassins coolly put their guns in the pocket, left the barbershop and disappeared into the crowd in the street. Nobody has seen their faces, and they were never caught.

Anastasia's midday assassination in the center of Manhattan caused a furor and my *Paris-Match* editors asked me to send an article in the lines of the one I had written five months earlier on the assassination attempt on another top gangster, Frank Costello. Indeed, when the so-called "Prime-Minister of Crime" was shot in May, also in New York, I had quite a good time digging out several colorful details and describing some rather amusing aspects of the sordid world of organized crime. I wrote of Costello's flashy diamond rings and custom-made silk shirts with embroidered monograms, of his mirror-shiny pointed shoes, his deep attachment to Mom, family, and the Catholic church, his generosity in charities, and, after a long career in rackets and crime, his touching striving for respectability, which made him limit his social involvement with old confederates of the type of Jack "Dirty-Fingers" Gusick, "Big-Jaw" Levin and "Dandy Phil," and look instead for somewhat more distinguished society. He invested in "legit" businesses, moved to residences in elegant neighborhoods, and left the Brooklyn greasy-spoon eateries for "L'Aiglon" and similar classy joints. He even started going to a fashionable Park Avenue psychoanalyst...And above all, I was impressed by his fanatical aversion to answering questions, any question, by journalists or police. Even when it was for his own protection, like when asked to describe his aggressor who shot him facing him squarely, from a distance of two feet, staring at his face (the bullets pierced a hole in the front of Costello's hat, missing the forehead). "I didn't see him, I have no idea what he looked like," insisted Costello. "Anyhow, it must be a mistake. Who would like to kill me? I only have friends, I have no enemies, I swear!" "The guy who shot you has strange ways to show you his friendship!..." retorted the exasperated police inspector.

As in Costello's case, reporting the facts in Anastasia's murder wasn't particularly difficult. Edition after edition, New York's tabloids inundated the readers with the most minute and gruesome details. But again, I found it more interesting to focus on the bizarre mores and rituals of the Mafia and the idiosyncrasies of its principal characters. Albert Anastasia was a perfect subject for this kind of anthropological study: the 17-year-old son of poor Calabrian family who enters the US illegally by jumping boat in New York harbor and who brings in, the next year, six of his brothers by the same channel; the hired gun, who climbs up the Mafia hierarchy by participating in some 100 murders, thirty of them executed by him personally. The ex-prisoner of Sing Sing, arrested repeatedly, five times for murder, and once sentenced to death. But the Mafia lawyers managed to obtain a retrial; when it started, all witnesses had miraculously disappeared, having suddenly left either this country, or this world, prematurely. Acquitted for lack of corroborated proofs, Anastasia continued his career, this time on a higher level, as manager of murders, rather than a simple killer. At the same time, he never ceased to be the perfect son who spoiled his Mama in Italy with lavish presents and a luxurious house and, when she died, built her the best mausoleum in the village cemetery. The faithful husband and concerned father who sent his children to the best schools and hired private tutors to teach them philosophy.

In Anastasia's biography, it was the gangster's professionalism that fascinated me particularly. It wasn't for nothing that he reached the highest position of "Lord Executioner" and boss of the infamous "Murder, Inc.," the punitive branch of the Mafia, which provided "torpedoes" (out-of-town contract killers) to member-gangs in need of assassins difficult to identify locally. Albert's professional conscience in preparing each job was impressive. He proudly considered himself an artist in his field, never allowing the slightest emotion—hatred, anger, or vengeance—to interfere with his work. Cool and dispassionate as a surgeon, this technician of assassinations planned and studied in advance every detail and contingency, and had a contempt for killers acting out of passion, or amateurish torpedoes doing a sloppy job. This, and other typical, almost comical, oddities in the underworld's lore, amused me a lot and made my research quite pleasant. They also amused some of my friends with whom I shared the best anecdotes. Nobody enjoyed it more than my new friend Dominique Lapierre, a bright 26-year-old reporter full of life and humor, which *Paris-Match* had sent to work temporarily with me at the New York office.

Not only was he fascinated by the American underworld's saga and melodramatics, but they gave him some professionally practical ideas. No sooner had he returned to Paris at the end of his tour at my office, than he surprised me with a concrete proposal. "Steve," he called me in late October (in our banter about Mafiosi, he liked to call me "Steve," a more tough-guy-sounding name), "what a great subject for a book! I already see it: Murder Inc., Costello, Anastasia and all the gorillas and torpedoes...And his kid-brother, "Tough-Tony" Anastasia, with his longshoremen...just think of Marlon Brando and "On the Waterfront" movie! We'll tell the history of the Mafia, and "Scarface" Capone, and Abe Reles, the stool-pigeon who betrayed the Mafia's secrets and was thrown out of the window of the *Half-Moon* hotel..." And we both chuckled on the phone, recalling the sinister underworld joke: "Abe Reles could sing, but couldn't fly..." Dominique was in his element. "We'll have such fun writing it, you and I, and I guarantee you that all Paris publishers will be fighting over our book. What do you say, Steve?"

I hadn't thought of a book. I had never written one. Dominique had—a few short books on his travel adventures. The idea appealed to me, and also, I didn't know many people who could resist Lapierre's enthusiasm. He was a born salesman, a natural promoter, bursting with exciting ideas and self-assurance. I'm sure that phrases such as "He could sell you the Brooklyn bridge" or "He could charm a snake" were coined for people like Dominique. But his was an attractive talent, not at all the pushy hustler; he had the conviction and warmth of an eminently likeable personality, a happy man who genuinely liked people and made it easy to be liked in return. Also a sincere friend who could be trusted. After he wrote me that he would take care of finding a French publisher and negotiating the contract—for which I had no experience or talent,—I gladly said yes and a most enjoyable and productive collaboration began across the Atlantic.

I read all I could find on the Mafia and sent books to Dominique to read. I interviewed a few New York law enforcement officers and federal agents specialized in organized crime, but I still found it difficult to believe that such a powerful, well-structured and well-functioning confederation of gangs, did really exist in America. That it operated with quasi-impunity, had its own government, its rules and by-laws, its strictly demarcated "turfs," its councils and kangaroo courts. The whole story sounded too much like a Hollywood script, like an embellished tale of imaginative journalists. Then suddenly, as Dominique and I were drafting the book's table of contents and deciding who would write which chapter, and as he was offering it to French publishers, another sensational news brought us the proof that the clandestine organization did exist indeed. Occurring just twenty days after Anastasia's assassination, the unexpected event came as a bonanza, as a custom-ordered new episode for our scenario. On November 14th, the police surprised 65 top gangsters assembled for a summit conference at an unlikely pla-ce: the country house of a Joseph Barbara, in the upstate New York hamlet of Apalachin (277 inhabitants). Most stars of the underworld's Who's Who were there, their sumptuous Cadillacs and Lincolns sneaking in by the dirt roads across the bleak rural landscape: Vito Genovese and

Joseph Profaci, reputed big bosses of the Mafia, Joe "Bananas" Bonanno, Vincent Rao, Miranda, De Marco, even Lewis Santos from Havana, who had arrived especially for the conference. The state troopers blocked the exits and apprehended them all, many of them while running in the woods in their delicate Italian shoes, and submitted them to interrogation. As expected, they all told the same story: they'd heard that good old pal Joe Barbara was sick, so they came to visit him and eat barbecue with him. All in the same day, independently from each other? Yes, what a coincidence, isn't it amusing? But is there a law forbidding visits to a sick friend? They were all released.

I had a field day writing my *Paris-Match* article about the Apalachin summit, obviously called to assess the Mafia strategy after the Anastasia and Costello shootings and to redistribute the turfs. With Dominique, we were already savoring the new chapter. To the juicy gangland "classics", we could now add the Apalachin sequence with the stampede through the woods of the bosses in expensive suits and wallets packed with crisp thousand-dollar bills, hiding in the thorny bushes and climbing trees!

Finding a good publisher is always difficult for new authors, but not when one has Dominique Lapierre as a partner. By the end of November, in the midst of my excitement about my mother finally receiving her passport to leave Bulgaria, a letter from Dominique announced that he had met with Rene Julliard, the upcoming Parisian publisher. "Although extremely busy, he kept me for a whole hour," Dominique wrote, which didn't surprise me at all, knowing well his irresistible talent of raconteur. "*Accord total et enthousiaste pour l'idee.*" A few days later, the contract arrived, my first contract for a book, a particularly thrilling "first" in my life. It coincided with my departure for Paris, where I met my mother just before Christmas. It was also an excellent opportunity for Dominique and me to discuss the final details of the project and to begin the real work.

During the following few months, we worked very hard. His good spirits, a penchant for adventure, and airs of glamorous *Paris-Match* reporter notwithstanding, Dominique was an extraordinarily hard, methodical worker. He wrote half of the chapters, and I—the other half, then each of us read, commented, and corrected the pages of the other. An easy, pleasant collaborator as he was, we never had the slightest disagreement about the text and readily accepted each other's remarks and suggestions. We knew, of course, that it wasn't great literature, and wrote our small book (226 pages) with tongue in cheek, sharing many good laughs in the process.

The book was published in June 1958, with a photo of Al Capone on the yellow soft cover, and with the title *"Les Caids de New York."* (A "Caid" is a chief in Arabic, and the term is used in French slang for "boss" or "tough guy".) Not a great title, and I never knew who chose it, but I was so happy to see my first book published, that I didn't object. (*Eleven years later, Julliard and Paris-Match jointly published a new, updated version in hard cover, under the title "Les Ministres du Crime."*)

Our mentor and boss Raymond Cartier did us the favor of writing the preface, which, in view of his enormous prestige in France, was not a bad idea commercially and considerably helped the sales. Commending "my friends Stephane Groueff and Dominique Lapierre" for the strict respect of the truth and for the exactitude of our narrative, Raymond wrote: *"They should hardly be congratulated for that. First, because for good journalists, this should go without saying. And then, because they've made the most astute choice. Indeed, where would you find, in our limited capacities for invention, the equivalent of what reality offers?"*

****

A VISIT TO CASTRO

Paul Slade and I had all the reasons to be excited as we arrived at Havana's hotel *Nacional* on that hot August day: we had an appointment with Castro on the following morning, a rare opportunity those days for journalists coming from the United States. Indeed, eleven months after the victory of his revolution, Fidel, still little known abroad, disliked most newsmen and refused interviews. And yet, the world was greatly intrigued by the enigmatic personality of the 38-year-old leader and puzzled by his new regime and its intentions. Since the US had severed diplomatic relations with Cuba, I applied, as a French correspondent, for an interview with Castro through the Cuban mission to the United Nations, which seemed to be well aware of the impact *Paris-Match* had in

Europe. After several attempts and much insistence, the word finally came from Havana: yes, the Leader of the Revolution will receive you and your photographer next week.

As soon as we arrived, we asked the hotel operator to connect us with Castro's office in order to work out the details of the interview. "Which office are you looking for?" she said. "I don't know," I said, "Just give me the Presidency." "What presidency?" I was getting annoyed. "Look, I want to talk to Fidel Castro's office, to his secretary, or aide-de-camps, or whatever." Total blank. "Sir, I don't know where he works," the operator answered, to my dismay. "What a stupid girl!" Paul and I thought as we took a taxi and rushed to the Foreign ministry. "Where are President Castro's offices, what is the telephone number?" we asked half-a-dozen people there. Amazing as it was, no one seemed to have the slightest idea. We spent the rest of the day running around the capital and asking the simplest question: what is the Head-of-the-State's address. We began to worry, realizing the ridiculousness of our situation: Fidel Castro was supposed to be waiting for us and we, the smart *Paris-Match* reporters, were unable to find his office!

Our concern increased when we contacted a few local journalists whose names were given to us in New York. "Fidel's address?" they said, indicating they felt sorry for us, "Are you kidding? If you manage to find him, will you please tell us ? He has no official office, no desk, and no fixed schedule. He's constantly on the move, he decides things on the spur of the moment, wherever he happens to be."

"But we have a confirmed appointment with him, tomorrow!"

"Ha-ha! Good luck to you, guys!"

Deeply disturbed, we spent the evening and the night trying to locate the head of government. We approached a few bearded, uniformed officials of the regime and some of them showed sympathy for our unusual plight. "Try Celia Sanchez's house!" said one. (Celia Sanchez was Castro's close friend and adviser.) But there was no trace of him when our taxi driver located that address. "Your best chance is at Hotel *Havana Hilton*, was the advice of an insider. "Not the apartment they keep for him on the 23rd floor, he seldom sleeps there, but go to the kitchens downstairs. Fidel loves to pass by there between two rides in town and get a few spoonfuls directly out of the pots, while he chats with the cooks."

Slade and I spent hours in the kitchen, but no Fidel that night. Another Castro man told us that the Chief works often at the new building of the Agrarian Reform, his pet project. "He doesn't have an office there, but just arrives unannounced, pulls a chair at the desk next to the director and reads the reports." We tried that too, we also followed a tip that he went regularly to the military airport to visit the Air Force chief, we even looked for his brother Raul, with whom he supposedly stayed frequently, but we had no luck. More and more concerned, we spent the next day on the telephone and in taxicabs, but with no success. It was a most embarrassing situation. How were we going to explain to our editors that we missed the appointment with the Prime minister because we were unable to find him in his own capital?

We were already anticipating the cruel teasing by our *Paris-Match* colleagues when, on the third day, a tremendous excitement interrupted the lazy, resort-like atmosphere of the *Nacional* hotel. Announced by loud shouts, car sirens and screeching brakes, a couple of military jeeps raced into the hotel's yard and spewed out carloads of noisy, heavily armed kids in guerilla fatigues. They were teenagers, with all the cheerfulness and menacing look of juvenile delinquents headed for a street gang battle. They were followed by another jeep from which a huge bearded man in olive uniform jumped out and rushed energetically through the lobby. Castro himself! When the general excitement subsided a little, we understood that the leader of the Revolution had come to pay his respect to the widow and the daughter of a recently assassinated prominent Chilean leftist.

Brandishing our French press passes, we managed to follow Fidel's entourage up to the hotels corridor and planted ourselves in front of the room he had entered. With the rudeness of the suspicious and ferocious-looking bodyguards, this wasn't an easy achievement, but somehow we succeeded in convincing them that the boss had agreed to see us. We were still arguing with them when the door opened and Castro came out. An aide informed him that the two French reporters pretended having an appointment with him and he walked toward me. He didn't stop until he was only a few inches away from me, practically breathing in my face.

My first impression was of a powerful, massive presence in front of me. Not only was Castro much bigger and stronger than what I had expected, but he emanated a palpable, almost animal, strength and authority. His manner was self-assured and bossy, and his way of standing so close when he talked to people, gave one the feeling of a towering, intimidating wall of rock. His face also seemed different from the photographs: I noticed that his nose followed down the straight line of his forehead, with no curve at the bridge, like the profiles in ancient Greek sculptures. He spoke to us politely but authoritatively, showing no desire to please and making it clear that he didn't have the slightest interest to listen to our questions, opinions or criticism.

Nevertheless, I tried a few questions, to which he impatiently gave short, predictable answers. I wanted him to comment on the latest press reports describing him, in spite of his denials, as a covert Communist. Irritated, he scoffed: "You see how the papers print such American lies! How could one believe the press?" Then he cut our conversation short and stated, with a "take it or leave it" finality: "Look, I have no time for interviews! But if you want, follow me and you'll see for yourself what I do and what I say. You're welcome to come and photograph as much as you wish; but don't talk and don't ask questions!" With that, he turned his back and left.

As his rambunctious motorcade was getting ready to depart, Slade and I jumped into the first taxicab we saw and shouted to the old driver: "Follow them!" Easier said than done. Castro's escorts had obviously watched too many action movies with car chases. A mad race started through Havana's streets, with the careening jeeps cutting corners at full speed, ignoring red lights and slaloming between city traffic. Performing their special choreography around Castro's car, they passed it from the left side, then from the right, then riding ahead of it and blocking the other cars at the intersections. Grinning happily and showing off their machine guns to the passers-by, the longhaired "barbudos" were enjoying it thoroughly, while our scared cabby cursed the moment he had accepted the job.

At the suburb of Cojimar, the cars climb a narrow street to the top of a hill and we stop at the gate of a modern, single-floor villa surrounded by beautiful gardens and dominating the view of the entire area. It is one of the houses put at the disposal of the "Maximum Chief of the Revolution." The noon sun is hot and several "barbudos" are having their siesta under the large tree in the middle of the patio. They don't live in the villa, they are camping there, as they were used in the "sierra" during the guerrilla days. Machine guns hang on tree branches. The comfortable lounging chairs are empty, the men prefer lying on the lawn. Inside, others doze on the carpet, without removing their caps, boots or belts with handguns. Nobody makes a move when Castro arrives at the villa. To talk about total lack of formality and even elementary hierarchy in presence of the Supreme commander of the armed forces, would be an understatement. Castro climbs the garden stairs briskly, three steps at a time, and stops before a soldier sleeping on a mattress spread across the alley. The soldier wakes up, but doesn't move; he just looks up and winks familiarly to the Prime minister. "Hi, Fidel!" he greets him and goes back to sleep. Castro straddles over the mattress and walks into the villa, where some citizens were waiting for hours to present a petition. Their land had been expropriated unfairly, they claim. Fidel listens, as he puffs from his cigar, and examines briefly the documents. "O.K., a mistake has been made," he settles the problem. "Go to the Reforma Agraria and tell them that I want them to cancel the order!" The men leave, beaming. "Thanks, Fidel!" Everybody addresses him by the familiar "*tu*" and is on first-name basis with him. Not, of course, the dapper naval officer in his impeccable white uniform, who stands at attention while presenting an urgent report. Paul Slade's camera doesn't miss the contrast with the untidy informality of the dictator. While listening carefully to the lieutenant's report, Castro is changing his sweaty shirt in front of us, toweling his wet, hairy chest with one hand and holding his huge cigar with the other. A minute later, as he answers the phone, a young cook appears suddenly, without knocking on the door, a bearded adolescent wearing a filthy apron over his guerrilla outfit. "Fidel, do you want ice cream?" he asks. Castro, still half-dressed, grabs a spoon. The telephone is shaking under his commanding voice, some ice cream is running down the hairy chest, cigar ashes pile up on the floor next to him. But meanwhile some state business is expediently taken care of.

Now and then, Fidel signals us to leave the room for a while; some confidential matters are discussed, we guess. Next door, the guards are bored. There is not much to do, except to smoke cigars, doze, spit on the floor, and play with the weapons. To kill time, the barbudos are constantly loading and unloading their automatic arms, mechanically. They love their guns, one recognizes in their eyes the admiring look of a child handling his dream toy. Each time a newcomer enters carrying some unknown or newer model weapon, there is excitement in the room, and everybody wants to touch the gun and examine it and ask questions. Paul and I don't feel at home in this group, especially when the young barbudos point in jest a gun in our direction and, big joke!, imitate the sound of shooting: Tah-tah-tah-tah! They found the silly game even more amusing after they realize that we not only don't appreciate the humor, but are getting pretty nervous facing the machineguns' barrel; nothing could then stop the belly laughs at the expense of the two French sissies. These kids had followed their idol in the guerrilla war at a very early age and now they are the masters of the country, with one simple mission in life: protect Fidel; they wouldn't hesitate to shoot to kill at the slightest provocation or appearance of threat.

We took a few more photos of Castro and then, with no warning, he vanished in a hubbub of sirens, exuberant cheers and roaring motors. "I'll see you later!" he waved to us in a rather friendly manner, as we rushed out to catch up with him. But to see him where, and when?—We were again in the same predicament as in the previous days. The same wild-goose chase again: stalking Celia Sanchez's home; the *Habana Hilton* kitchens, late past midnight; the Reforma Agraria building in the afternoon. The chief of government without an office or a permanent residence was to be found nowhere.

Meanwhile, frustrated, we proceeded with the rest of our reportage on the New Cuba. It wasn't a very cheerful story. Less than a year after the revolution, the world-famous luxurious hotels and casinos were half-empty; the gorgeous beaches were deserted; revolutionary Puritanism had chased away most customers of restaurants and nightclubs; foreign tourists were not coming. We photographed the zealous confiscation of hundreds of slot machines, symbols of sin and decadence. We were bored at regimented ideological classes and interminable speeches on "liberation," and upset to observe the extreme caution with which Cubans who didn't like the new regime revolution spoke with us. When we had enough of revolutionary zeal and austerity, we escaped one night to the Tropicana, the district of casinos, Afro-Cuban dances, shows with half-naked girls, and other forms of debauched pleasure for which pre-Castro Cuba had been famous. "What a relief!" we thought, after a few numbers of bongo drums and pretty girls. But then came the "grand finale." The entire troupe, aligned on the front of the stage, deployed simultaneously the panels that each one was carrying. The huge letters formed a banderole, which read "Viva la Reforma Agraria!"

*　　　　　*　　　　　*

It was at that Agrarian reform's headquarters that the following day Slade and I almost lost control of ourselves and behaved in an utterly immature way. The cause of the ridiculous near incident had nothing to do with politics, it had to do with *spitting*. Yes, the common, if unattractive, human practice, defined in the dictionary as "ejecting saliva from the mouth, making a hissing or sputtering noise." Whether due to incessant cigar smoking or to some national custom, I had never observed more frequent and unabashed spitting in public than what I saw among the Castro followers. Campesinos, simple guerrillas and other uneducated "barbudos" did it constantly and everywhere, in the street, on floors or carpets; some, with better social conscience and respect for the fellow citizen, used the ubiquitous spittoons, the cuspidors conveniently placed in every room, office and public building in Cuba. (They were such indispensable furnishings, that a sincerely surprised man asked me one day: "But if you don't have spittoons in the U.S. and Europe, where do people spit?" I was at a loss for an answer…)

Men of distinguished manners, however, would always find ways to handle little personal problems with grace and discretion. Such a man was the official at the Reforma Agraria who received us, a neatly dressed gentleman who briefed me on Castro's ambitious land-utilization program, while Paul Slade was photographing him. He had barely spoken for a minute, when the familiar throat-clearing noise indicated that he felt an urge to relieve himself. At that moment, we realized that, for once, there was no spittoon in the room. Not in the least disturbed, our host smiled politely, pointing at his throat and said "excuse me!";

then, sliding open a drawer of his desk, spat inside, closed it, and continued the interview. "As I was saying, statistics show that the crop in 1958…" Two minutes later, the same gurgle and polite "Excuse me!" followed by the opening of the drawer to spit inside and the careful closing of the drawer again. "The sugar cane yield per acre…" he went on, only to interrupt himself a few moments later and repeat the same ritual. By that time, I found it increasingly difficult to restrain my desire to laugh. Pretending to concentrate on my note taking, I didn't dare to look at Paul, knowing that he too was about to burst with laughter. Revolting as the official's performance was, I couldn't help being impressed by a certain neatness and refinement in his act: he wasn't just vulgarly spitting at random, no matter where; indeed, the man was using always *the same drawer*, the second one on the left side. How sanitary!, I thought. And, a sign of good upbringing, he never failed to apologize with a charming, polite "excuse-me!"

The interview continued, but I was loosing track of the figures in the great land-reform plan. Mesmerized by the spitting manners of the agricultural expert, I only counted the number of times he opened and closed his left-hand-side drawer and waited for his next "excuse-me!" When finally I looked at Paul, I realized that we were on the verge of a public-relations disaster. Slade, absolutely red in the face, was suffocating with repressed giggle, tears pouring out of his eyes. It took just one exchange of looks between us and we were both out of control. In order to mask our laughter, Paul went into a loud, convulsive cough, while I rushed toward him and ushered him out of the room, mumbling some apologies to our startled host: "An asthma attack! Sorry, emergency! My colleague suffers from asthma!" Doubled up from uncontrollable giggles, we barely made it to the next corridor, where we literally collapsed and cried with laughter for a long time, before being able to take our breath and calm down.

*   *   *

Luck smiled at us again just a day before leaving, not entirely satisfied. It was midnight, while we were paying a visit to the newspaper *Revolucion* and talking to its young editor, Carlos Franqui, a close collaborator and speechwriter of Castro. Suddenly the doors of the offices banged open, with the delicacy of a police raid, and we recognized the juvenile faces of Fidel's devoted guards. Brandishing menacingly their automatic guns, they cast a searching glance at the room, before *El Jeffe* made his entrance. As he was giving Franqui a warm bear hug, he saw us and ebulliently greeted us with a *"Salud, amigos!* How's your story going? Did you find everything you wanted?" I admitted that we still wanted to talk more to him and were disappointed that we lost him the other day, which seemed to amuse him. "I told you that I don't like interviews," his voice roared exuberantly as he was puffing from his cigar, a few inches from my face. "You hear me speak in public, I say it all. If you want to know how successful the revolution is, just talk to the people!" Then, in Spanish: "Tell them, amigos, now isn't everyone much better off?" *"Si, s-i-i! Viva Fidel!"* was the enthusiastic, if not totally unexpected, consensus in the room. But Castro was in an excellent mood that night and did, after all, accept a few questions. With a self-confidence that wouldn't tolerate any contradiction, he listed a few points from his program, things which he had, indeed, repeated many times before in his marathon public addresses. The future was his, there was no doubt about it, because right was on his side, he stated arrogantly. As we talked, the noise of a short scuffle behind our backs distracted our attention. Slade had made a jerky move to reach for his strobe-light bag on the floor, which produced an unexpected flash. Before he could realize what was happening, the guards jumped him, brutally threw him, spread-eagle position, on the table, and started searching his pockets. I was horrified. There was no doubt that without Fidel's intervention, the eager Cerberuses would've killed my friend. Identifying the unfamiliar looking strobe and realizing their mistake, they let Paul go, patting him amicably on the back and smiling broadly, as if to reassure him: "No hurt feelings, *Frenchie!* Just a good joke!" Quite shaken up, his clothes badly ruffled, Slade resumed taking photos.

I left Cuba quite depressed. The police-state atmosphere made me think of my own country, of Communist Bulgaria, which I had never seen but about which I knew enough sinister stories. Although Castro was still denying being a Communist, the facts pointed increasingly to the contrary. In addition, I had ample private information from our close friend Flo's husband, Earl Smith, who was the last U.S. ambassador in Cuba before the fall of the Batista regime. A staunch anti-communist, Earl had been outraged by the naiveté of responsible "liberal" officials and politicians, who obstinately refused to pay attention to his warnings from Havana that Castro was a convinced Communist and a dangerous enemy of the United States. Having this knowledge, I must admit that during my visit, the thought that the Revolution's "Maximum Chief" might ask me where I was from, made me pretty nervous. Luckily, Fidel couldn't care less about the reporters who bothered him for interviews.

*   *   *   *

MARILYN M.

From the moment Marilyn Monroe entered the bungalow where I was talking with her husband Arthur Miller and offered me a drink, I found her extremely likeable. It wasn't only because of her celebrated physical attraction, which was, of course, obvious. There was nothing unusual that a normally constituted man like me wouldn't remain unaffected by the sight of such voluptuousness of the forms, and such seductiveness in the movements. We are human, aren't we? No wonder that she had become the "sex symbol" of the decade! Although she had already (this was early in 1960) reached full ripeness and, at looking closer, the legendary shape were getting a bit over-abundant. Indeed, today's fashion editors would've recommended that Marilyn should lose a few pounds. What really surprised me in meeting the star in her private life was her vulnerability. It didn't take five minute of conversation to find that my hostess was a charmingly gentle and insecure young woman, shy and sensitive, somewhat mixed-up, touchingly simple and not at all worldly. The kind of creature that men feel willing to protect.

Had this feeling led to the conquest of the serious intellectual Miller, the great American playwright? The unlikely combination of these two opposite personalities was fascinating. While we talked about world affairs (he asked questions about France and, upon learning about my Bulgarian origin, wanted to hear more about Communist Eastern Europe), Marilyn showed immense pride in her husband's knowledge and brilliance. Listening with the intensity of an admiring pupil, she was disarming in her humble admission of her own ignorance and lack of education, but she was doing it with all the cajolery and flirtatiousness of a playful kitten fully aware of its power over her master. They kept me for dinner and I told them how, quite unsuspectingly, their wedding had played an important role in my own life, with Mara Scherbatoff perishing in the road accident while chasing their car after the ceremony, causing my being sent to New York to replace her as *Paris-Match* bureau chief. Marilyn was quite moved by my story and said that she remembered the tragedy vividly. They had tried to help and when returning to their car, she had noticed a blood stain on her wedding dress; being superstitious, this had upset her tremendously. I told them that because of this tragic accident, I came to live in America and was able to marry Lil, who, now, was expecting our first baby. As the hours passed, the atmosphere *chez les Miller* became so relaxed and warm, that the intended formal interview turned to a pleasant evening of friendly conversation.

The interview had been arranged by our stringer in Los Angeles, John Bryson, a first-rate photographer with many intellectual and cultural interests, who enjoyed the trust of many Hollywood celebrities. *Paris-Match* had been for a long time eager to do an extensive cover story on Marilyn Monroe, and now that she was turning a movie with Yves Montand, another favorite of the French public, my editors urged me to go and "do the maximum," as we used to say in our magazine's jargon. John was making a lot of money in commercial photography, but preferred working for us, even at our incomparably lower rates, because he loved journalism and the way *Match* used his pictures. After several assignments I had given him in California, we became good friends and it was at his personal recommendation that Marilyn, by then increasingly reluctant to grant interviews, accepted to receive me at home and talk freely to me.

The morning after my first dinner with her, when John Bryson and I picked her up at sunrise from her *Beverly Hills Hotel* bungalow, she behaved as a friend already. A friend forgetting any vanity or protocol, allowing us to see her in a most unflattering state, half-asleep, with no trace of lipstick or make-up whatsoever, just a scarf covering her uncombed hair, dressed hurriedly in an old sweater and shapeless slacks. Being driven to the Fox studios ahead of time, she curled up on the back seat of the chauffeured limousine and fell asleep right away, while we kept silent, trying not to wake her up. There was nothing of the glamorous movie star in the young woman with the unmade, pale face, peacefully sleeping behind us. The scene certainly evoked no sexy lace nightgowns or *Chanel Numero 5* perfume she was supposed to wear by night, according to her publicists; it simply cried for a little girl's teddy bear to hug.

Once on the studio set however, the transformation was miraculous. It took, of course, hours, during which impatient actors and extras, frustrated technicians, and exasperated directors waited and waited for the star to leave her dressing room. Now I understood why she was notorious for always being outrageously late. As the time passed, with cameras all ready to shoot, people on the set were getting angry, resentment mounted. But when Bryson and I were admitted to take pictures in her sanctuary, I realized how little her lateness had to do with prima donnas' caprices, arrogance, or lack of consideration for her colleagues. Looking gorgeous in her transparent, sexy tights, surrounded by make-up specialists, hairdressers, and costume assistants, Marilyn was almost in tears, unhappy with the way she looked, shaking with insecurity, begging for reassurance from Arthur Miller, who was spending his entire mornings with her on the set, and from Paola Strassberg, the wife of "Actors' Studio" founder, who accompanied her as a trusted friend and adviser. "I hate this hairdo," she moaned, "And look at my lipstick, terrible!...I can't go out like this, can I, darling?" as everybody in the dressing room tried to convince her that she looked great. I felt somehow disappointed to see Miller, the great Miller whom I admired for his *Death of a Salesman* masterpiece, reduced to the role of his wife's assistant, patiently helping her overcome her stage fright.

And yet, once she appeared on the set, everybody's irritation was forgotten, everybody seemed to enjoy her presence, the friendliness she radiated, her constant flirting, her almost embarrassingly cute cooing and music-hall seductive poses, which characterized her acting. To be true, *"Let's Make Love,"* the light comedy she was making with Montand, didn't require Shakespearean actors, and as an entertainer Marilyn acquitted herself charmingly in her part. Personally, I found her adorable to watch, whether this was great acting or not. I knew that she was dying to be taken seriously as an actress, to be given a chance in some truly dramatic role, but the studio wouldn't permit it. For them, indeed, she was such a gold mine as a "sex symbol," that to lose it just to satisfy her artistic aspirations made no sense. And yet, she was very gifted, I was told. I'd heard it personally from Lee Strassberg, whom we saw at a few parties with our friends Henry and Afdera Fonda. Frustrated, feeling unjustly deprived of the opportunity to prove herself as an actress, Marilyn had joined the Actors' Studio in New York. Strasssberg told me that he was very impressed by her talent. "She's so gifted naturally," he said, "that she gave me the same feeling I had when Marlon Brando first came to study with us. It's a very rare quality. If Marilyn is allowed to devote herself to serious work, rather than be used for show business, she could become an exceptional actress." Could this happen?- Very unlikely, the wise drama teacher admitted sadly.

At the end of the shooting day, Marilyn and Miller took Yves Montand and me to a small projection room to see the "rushes" of the filmed scenes. It was a pleasure to watch her reactions of an excited child, unabashedly delighted by the scenes she found successful, loudly voicing her disappointment at the ones she didn't like. Everyone in the room wanted her to be happy. This was all that Miller seemed to care about, and so did Montand, and director George Cukor, and Paola Strassberg, and every present technician and stagehand. As if "M.M." weren't a most smashing world success, but some insecure debutante in need of encouragement and help.

Later, she sent me a large photograph of herself with me, taken backstage by John Bryson during a make-up session and signed: "I'm so glad we met." I must say that I was glad too. I returned to New York with a warm feeling. Later, when all her troubles—marital, professional, and emotional—began, I felt sincerely sorry for her. But not very surprised that she had been unable to cope with fame.

#   #   #

BIRTH OF PAUL

This had been a very special period for me. Lil was pregnant, which made me enormously happy, but also quite nervous. I had always hoped for a child, an essential part of my dreams for marital bliss. I had been deeply upset the year before, when Lil lost the first baby we expected and when, for a moment, it looked like we would never have a child, a thought that saddened me. Now I was happy again, thrilled and praying that this time everything goes well.

But something seemed wrong with my own health. Mysterious spells of dizziness, palpitations and stomach discomfort occurred more and more frequently, until I was forced to consult a doctor. Tests and thorough examinations didn't reveal anything wrong, and, perplexed himself, Dr. Lax could only prescribe a good vacation. "It's impossible at this time," I said. "My wife is seven months pregnant and we cannot travel now." "Pregnant? Why didn't you say so?" the old Hungarian physician exclaimed. "Now everything is clear!" And he told me that some primitive tribes, having observed that expecting fathers often go crazy, lock them up or even tie them to trees until the childbirth, for their own safety and the peace of the community. We laughed, but as my malaise worsened, the doctors strongly advised me to get out of town and away from Lil for a few days. It was March, the snow was still good, so I packed my skis and went, alone, to Mittersill, New Hampshire, to visit our friends Terry and Hubert von Pantz. The formula proved miraculous. In a few days my anxieties disappeared and I returned to Lil almost cured.

I felt well enough to accept an invitation to be the guest speaker at the conference of the American Society of Magazine Photographers on April 28, in Miami. With a selection of slides sent from Paris, I gave an hour-long talk on the history of *Paris-Match* and the unorthodox ways it operated. It was my first experience in public speaking and I was extremely nervous, but as the audience was warming up and seemed to be genuinely amused by the stories of the *Match* wild reporters' exploits and antics, the stage fright disappeared soon. By the end, the listeners' demand for "encores" stirred up the ham in me, and what had begun as an ordeal, turned into enjoyment.

Back in New York, I was able to manage "our" pregnancy in a pretty sane way, but insisted nevertheless on keeping a packed bag handy, ready for any emergency. As is the case with most emergencies, it happened without warning. Lil and I were enjoying a Sophia Loren movie at the East 86-th street theater around the corner, when she suddenly nudged me in the dark. "I something is happening," she said, calmly." We should leave right away." I froze. We walked slowly back to the apartment, grabbed some towels and the small bag, hailed a taxi and urged the driver to rush us uptown to the Harkness Pavilion of the Presbyterian hospital. I was sure that the baby would arrive any moment, right there in the cab. Never had a distance seemed so insufferably long as our journey up to 168th street that night. Never had I counted so many red lights, never was traffic so slow. Although Lil, remarkably composed, tried to calm me down by holding my hand and assuring me that the baby wasn't going to be born in the taxi, I was a nervous wreck when we finally arrived at Harkness. The admission formalities seemed unforgivably long to me, as if the unhurried, matter-of-fact people at the desk were dealing with some routine and not a momentous emergency. I suppose I acted as frantic as the crazed aborigine fathers who, according to Dr. Lax, had to be subdued by force.

The solitary hours I spent pacing the floor of Lil's hospital Room # 854, after she was taken to the labor room at 1 A.M., turned to an ordeal of unending wait-ing and anxiety. As the hours passed, the worst fears crossed my mind and soon I was near panic, praying pathetically: "Please, God! I beg you!…" With no partic-ular reasons, most tragic scenarios had invaded my mind, thoughts of losing the baby, and worse, of losing Lil. It was 6 o'clock in the morning, already daylight, when Dr. Equinn Munnell, Lil's obstetrician, entered the room. "You have a fine boy, congratulations!" he said with a broad smile and shook my hand. I waited for him to leave the room, and then, exhausted as I was, I cried with abandon, the happiest crying in my life.

*   *   *   *

I spent the next seven afternoons and dinners with Lil in the hospital, often bringing Mama and Honey to see her and the baby. I was immensely happy and proud, and didn't hide it, at times probably to the slight embarrassment of friends and colleagues. "Nobody, of course, had ever had a baby before Stephane!" I was teased for my over-enthusiasm. But it didn't slow down my very active professional, social, and private life. In addition to the frantic tempo at the *Paris-Match* office, my notebook for the weeks following the birth overflows with entries such as: "…*Jules and Doris Stein's party at their MCA offices on Madison*

Avenue...Leonard Bernstein concert at Carnegie Hall...Mike and Jan Cowles cocktails for Pierre Galante and Olivia de Havilland... Lunch with Raymond and Rosie Cartier: Jackie Prouvost (Le Patron's only son)*died in Paris...Karl von Leiningen* (Princess Marie-Louise's husband) *came to New York and we went to the piers to meet Queen Giovanna, arriving on the "Saturnia"...Cocktails at Jean Howard, with her Broadway friends...Dinner at Hank and Afdera Fonda's...Elsie Woodward's The-dansant on St.-Regis roof...Cocktails Tina Onassis...Jazz concert at Madison Square Garden..."*

I managed also, only a week after the birth, to fly for two days to Los Angeles, to receive the University of California's Foreign Press Award. Lil was still in the hospital and I felt badly to leave her, but the honor was too great to miss the occasion. I won the prize ($ 500 and an imposing brass plate) in a competition among foreign correspondents in the U.S., to which I had presented two recent *Paris-Match* articles: one on the shock the success of Japanese and European "compact cars" had caused to a complacent, arrogant Detroit, forcing American industry to switch also to production of more economic automobiles; the second, on the famous striptease star Gypsy-Rose Lee, an intelligent lady with an interesting life story, whom I had interviewed in New York after her new Broadway musical.

It was a very enjoyable trip. The award ceremony was in Hollywood style, with Loretta Young as guest of honor at the gala dinner and California's governor Pat Brown in attendance. *Paris-Match* was proud of my prize and published a "Letter from the Editor" about it, which gave me great satisfaction. But I couldn't wait to return to Lil and the baby and on the second day, after paying a friendly visit to Gary and Rocky Cooper, took the midnight flight to New York.

*   *   *   *

Only two months after this happy occasion, I re-visited Los Angeles, this time with Lil, for a most exciting event: the Democratic party's Convention of July 1960, which I covered for *Paris-Match*. With candidates such as the young senator with the *jeune premier* looks, J.F. Kennedy, the idolized guru of liberals and intellectuals, Adlai Stevenson, and Lyndon Johnson, the most powerful politician

in the Senate, the contest turned into the most glamorous presidential convention ever, a public media dream. For a week, Los Angeles became the meeting
place of top politicians and pundits, tycoons, movie stars, journalists and
socialites. On the personal level too, the ten days we spent there weren't less
glamorous, as Lil and I were the houseguests of Afdera and Henry Fonda, and
thus found ourselves in the middle of *Le-Tout-Hollywood*'s social life. Witty, vivacious Flo Smith, Lil's best friend, was the other guest at the Fonda's Belair cottage
at 242, Copa-de-Oro where, between attending the convention and partying, we
spent hours around the swimming pool, in company of movie people and visitors
from the East Coast.

The very first evening, at a big dinner party at Gary and Rocky Cooper's, we
met some of Hollywood's "high-society"- the Jimmy Stewarts, John Wayne,
David Selznick, and similar local "aristocrats." Gary had just recovered from an
operation, but looked well and as warm and charming as ever. Many of them
were Republicans, but the Democrats in attendance were divided in different
camps. Our host, Hank Fonda, and most intellectuals, supported Stevenson.
Like many industrialists and businessmen, Jane and Charlie Engelhard, Sava's
friend and boss in South Africa, rooted for Johnson. But most actors and visiting
socialites seemed to favor the rising star, Jack Kennedy. His entourage was, of
course, the most visible in and outside the Convention Hall, and the most colorful too, due to the activism of his Hollywood celebrities fans, especially his
brother-in-law, Peter Lawford, his "Rat pack" pals Sinatra, Sammy Davis, Jr.,
Dean Martin, and similar vocal sympathizers.

We were lucky to be included in some of the Kennedy camp celebrations. (Lil
and Flo used to know JFK since his college days, and Flo remained very close to
him; I had met his sisters, Pat Lawford and Jean Smith, in St. Moritz; and our
hostess, Afdera, was on excellent terms with all of them.) Thus, on our second
night, we attended a spectacular dinner party for the entire Kennedy clan at the
Lawfords. Only Jackie Kennedy, expecting a baby, was absent. I was seated next to
JFK's mother, Rose. At the end of the Lawford party we enjoyed one of the best
entertainments in our lives. It all happened spontaneously, as spirits were high
under the large tent and everybody felt happy, after many glasses of champaign

and the contagious beat of the band. Suddenly, unexpectedly, Frank Sinatra rose from his seat and started singing from his table. The effect was tremendous—all chatting and clatter of dishes stopped abruptly, as by command, and the romantic crooning filled the silence in the hot Californian night. Enthralled, we were still hearing the last words of his lyrics, when another magnificent voice resounded from a table at the opposite corner. It was Judy Garland at her best—touching, dramatic, pathetic as she stood up and sang extemporaneously, her voice trembling with emotion. The room went wild. We had no time to applaud, because at that moment Nat King Cole rose at his table and his sexy, velvety baritone challenged Sinatra and Garland into marvelous improvised duets. Other voices joined, other talents and famous names. To everyone's delight, the party lasted late after midnight, long after JFK and the politicians had left. It was 4:30 in the morning when we finally went to bed.

We saw many of that night's guests and other celebrities the following day, at the dinner the Fondas gave for 70 people on the eve of the convention's opening. Then, parallel to the sessions which photographer John Bryson and I attended as reporters, the social activities never stopped: private movie showing at Bill and Eddie Goetz's; Stash and Lee Radziwill's dinner at *Romanoffs'* for Jack and Bobby Kennedy, with Randolph Churchill, the Fondas, Fifi Fell, Flo Smith and us; lunch around Jean Howard's pool, with Joe Alsop, Louella Parsons, the Fondas, Anita Colby, Flo, Arlene Francis, and David Selznick with Jennifer Jones; a dinner at Milton Berle's; another one at Tony Curtis and Janet Lee's…I hadn't seen so many movie stars even on the screen.

Late in the evening on July 13, JFK was nominated, in a triumph. I spent the next day writing my article for *Paris-Match*, while outside of my window Lil, already badly missing her two-and-a-half-month-old baby left in Southampton, was sunning herself around the pool. Flo was, as usual, teasing and joking with Arlene Francis and the Radziwills, Jean Howard was taking more of her remarkable photographs, and Hank Fonda, suntanned and still looking superbly built and young in his swimsuit, was trying, with little success, to lecture his impulsive, unpredictable young wife, his "crazy Venetian," as he used to call her.

Back in New York, a busy schedule was waiting for me, barely leaving me time to recuperate the sleep I missed during this exciting week at the Los Angeles convention. Mathias had just arrived, to replace Philippe de Bausset in my office, and the Cartiers arrived for a month from Paris. Photographer Charles Bonnay was leaving for Bulgaria and I gave him messages and gifts for Boubi and Radka.

Twenty days after we returned from California, the baby was baptized at our home in Southampton. I was grateful that Lil, an Episcopalian, had no objection to the Eastern-Orthodox ritual, my religion, which meant a lot to me. She also made me happy by agreeing to the name I had chosen and which, according to the Bulgarian tradition, was my father's name—Pavel, or Paul, in English. We added a middle name, Simeon, which happened to be the name of both my grandfather and my brother Boubi, and also of my young king in exile. Princess Maria Luisa, the king's sister and one of my closest friends, was the godmother, and Bishop Andrey performed the service.

Maria Luisa came to Southampton with her husband Karl Leiningen and on the next day, August 5th, the Bishop baptized little Paul in the living room of "The Gables," our house on South Main Street. It wasn't without last-minute contretemps: Bishop Andrey hadn't brought with him the baptismal font in which the baby is immersed, and I had to rush to the village and buy an ugly laundry washtub. It was in this vulgar basin made of galvanized tin that my son was blessed into Christianity, but I was too happy and moved to mind. Such wasn't, however, the attitude of the baby's nanny, the stern and dignified Mrs. Spafford, who took a dim view of the Eastern Orthodox practices. She observed the repeated dipping with ill-concealed disapproval, and when, at the end of the ceremony, the aging bishop's trembling hand approached the baby's forehead with a pair of scissors in order to perform the ceremonial clipping of a hair-lock, she muttered in horror: "How barbaric!"

*   *   *   *

Chapter 26

My brother Boubi and sister Radka leave Bulgaria.

To be reunited with our families was, naturally, the most cherished dream for most of us, refugees, but in Anni Tchaprachikoff's case this desire had taken the proportions of a true obsession. Having studied in Switzerland during the last years of the war, she hadn't seen her widowed mother and her only brother Ivan since before the Communist takeover in 1944, and, like most of us, she worried enormously about their life as "class enemies" in Bulgaria. She had a good reason to worry: Ivan had been arrested a few times and had spent four years in the infamous concentration camp of Belene, a small island in the Danube river.

Anni and I saw each other all the time—we were extremely close in Geneva, then in Paris, and now in New York—and we had rarely a conversation in which she wouldn't talk about her mother and Ivan. She did the same thing to other people, to friends and acquaintances, to anyone who she thought could somehow help in bringing her family out of Bulgaria. Her flirts and romantic involvements were no exception. Being a beautiful young woman, she had many suitors, but no flirt would have a chance for more than one single date if the gentleman showed no particular interest in the fate of her mother and Ivan and in her plans for their rescue. And should a candidate have more serious intentions, he had better realize clearly that a future with Anni meant a future with what she considered her duty toward her Bulgarian family.

To get them out of Bulgaria had become the principal goal of her existence and she was constantly inventing new plans and devising most extraordinary schemes to achieve this goal. And what schemes! The gamut ranged from fake passports or smuggling across the border, to James-Bond scenarios, to interventions by world leaders. Many of her ideas were quite ingenuous and imaginative; but most didn't seem feasible, or sounded like pure fantasy. Once, for example, she played with the idea of hiring a small plane, which would take off somewhere in Italy, fly by night, and land for a few minutes on a prearranged meeting place in Bulgaria—some remote meadow, where the family would wait and signal its presence with lights. Anni found an adventurous pilot, a former British officer who had served in Bulgaria and knew the terrain well. They agreed on the price, to be paid by a rich Bulgarian exile with relatives inside the country, also willing to join the plot. She established a code and organized the synchronization with clockwork precision, sending messages and flashlights through Western diplomats, and receiving detailed maps, concealed inside salamis, sent from Sofia. The daring plan failed only because no insurance company accepted to insure the rented aircraft. When Nikita Khrushchev visited the United States, Anni prepared a detailed memorandum to his wife and, using her journalistic pass to follow Mrs. K.'s visit of Mt. Vernon, confronted the startled Soviet First lady and boldly presented the case of her mother and Ivan. I grew so used to Anni's constant schemes that I finished by listening with a great dose of skepticism; to me, they all sounded too fantastic and unfeasible. That's why, in the spring of 1962, when she told me that she had "a great idea" about getting her family and mine out of Bulgaria, my first reaction was an unenthusiastic "oh, not again!" But I listened carefully. And for once, I thought that this time Anni's plan sounded more realistic.

It was a period when hard economic realities had finally convinced Bulgaria of its critical need for Western currency. At the same time, the country had embarked in a major effort to improve and develop the facilities of its magnificent Black Sea resorts, potential important source of foreign touristic income. Thousands of new rooms were readied for visitors, but while multitudes of working-class East-Europeans and Russians with worthless rubles and zlotys were flocking to the incomparable Bulgarian beaches, hardly any Westerner knew about, cared for, or trusted them. It was partly due to the hostile, rude attitude of the Communist regime toward the "capitalist enemies" during the past 18 years. Now that it was ready and eager to spread the red carpet to guests with dollars, pounds and francs, the hour seemed to be too late. In the tough competitive world of international tourism, to attract prosperous Westerners to new, unknown resorts, required important advertising budgets and solid connections abroad. The impoverished and arrogant Bulgarian government had neither.

Like every spring, the *Paris-Match* editors were looking for summer vacations story ideas, for subjects a little more original than the perennial Riviera, Corsica, or Tahiti. One day we learned in our New York office, that Paris was thinking of a series in color on the theme "Unusual, little known vacation places," and was considering, among others, a story on Rumania's Black Sea. "Why Rumania? Aren't the Bulgarian beaches more beautiful?" was Anni's and my first, and maybe patriotically biased reaction. "Stephane," said Anni, "you're friends with Roger and the other Paris editors. The next time you talk to them, why don't you suggest doing Bulgaria rather than Rumania?" Which I did, and realized that in the mind of the editors, it didn't make much difference. But it did make a huge difference to us. The scheming wheels in Anni's head were already spinning. Shortly after that, her eyes gleaming, she told me about her new plan.

I knew that if there was a possibility to help us, Editor-in-Chief Roger Therond and the rest of the *Paris-Match* friends would readily do it. But how? It was here that Anni's bold thinking and dogged perseverance played their role. It happened that in May she was going to France on vacation, and once there, she wasted no time to implement her plot. Its first move consisted in convincing Therond and the editors, and then contacting the Bulgarian embassy in Paris. Nobody could've done it better than the discreet, courteous Jean Maquet, the magazine's assistant managing editor, who was entrusted with the confidential mission. A mild-mannered, prematurely white-haired man, Maquet was our top rewriter and authority on grammar and linguistic matters, a sort of a high priest of literary language who, in controversies about the correct use or spelling of a word, acted as *Paris-Match's*" one-man Academie Francaise.

One can well imagine the jubilation of the Bulgarian press attaché in Paris when the assistant editor of the most important European magazine called him to say that *Match* was interested in doing an extensive story about the beauty of the Bulgarian Black Sea resorts! To a country with a poor image in the West and starved for favorable publicity which it could never afford, the unexpected opportunity sounded like an impossible dream. "We would like to send our reporters and publish at least 8 pages, maybe 16, in color…Varna, Nessebur, Sozopol and other Black Sea beaches…We're also interested in the Valley of Roses, and Rila monastery…" Thoroughly briefed by Anni, Maquet sounded like an authority on Bulgaria to the impressed and flattered diplomats. An appointment with the Ambassador and the press attaché was immediately arranged for Maquet and Anni. What a brilliant coup it was for the Bulgarians! A prestigious magazine with circulation of 1.8 million and charging 25,000 francs for a black-and-white advertising page (39,500 fr. the color page!), doing public-ity for free, in its editorial pages, which has incomparably better weight and value! At the meeting at the embassy, Maquet presented the terms: we'll do a big reportage on your country's touristic attractions, you'll grant Anni's and Stephane's families passports to come and visit them in Paris. The Bulgarians got the message, and after reporting to Sofia, indicated verbally their consent.

With Anni in Paris guiding the operations while I was helping by telephone from New York, with Therond, Maquet, and a few others initiated into the "con-spiracy," and with the consent of Le Patron, the plot advanced and the moment came when the right person had to be found to execute it. From that moment on, its success or failure had to depend on the dedication, intelligence, courage, energy and ingenuity of the individual who was going to accept the unusual task. He also had to be someone who cared for us and was sincerely moved by the plight of our families behind the Iron Curtain. The choice of our emissary to Bulgaria turned out to be quite obvious. Just by enumerating the aforementioned requirements, one was describing almost perfectly our friend Dominique Lapierre.

Not only was Dominique one of the most enterprising and resourceful among the adventure-loving *Paris-Match* men, but he knew Anni's and my family stories very well. During the months he spent working with us in the New York bureau, we had become close friends and he had shown a genuine interest and compas-sion for our relatives. My friendship grew even deeper when we co-authored our book *"Les Caids de New York."* As soon as Lapierre heard about our plot, he vol-unteered for the mission with alacrity.

It took him no effort to charm the Bulgarian embassy's personnel, who thought that Monsieur Lapierre was the friendliest and most attractive

Frenchman they had ever met. Holding out to them the bright prospects of a *Paris-Match* extensive coverage, he fed the Bulgarians with juicy insides on the workings of the French press and entertained them with amusing anecdotes. At the same time, he missed no opportunity to mention how "popular and influential your compatriots Groueff and Miss Tchaprachikoff" were at Paris-Match. "And isn't it a pity," he would drop *en-passant*, "that, from what I hear, their relatives are denied permission to visit them after such a long separation!..." And while he insisted that it was none of his business,—he was "simply a reporter doing his job,"—he knew perfectly well that his words were dutifully reported to Sofia. Without talking explicitly about any deal, the Bulgarians had understood well that a favor shown to our families would considerably facilitate the publication of a major story on their country. For *Paris-Match*, of course, it had to be a first-class story, standing on its own merits. With Lapierre's talent and the assignment of our veteran photographer Maurice Jarnoux, nobody doubted that the quality was going to be superb. No politics, we all agreed, no concessions to the regime whatsoever. Just a good travelogue and spectacular photos.

On July 2, after Therond obtained the Patron's final O.K. and Monsieur Roux, by then also in on the plot, gave the money to Lapierre and Jarnoux, Dominique telephoned me in New York to say that he was leaving the next day for Bulgaria. I was quite excited, and also very glad to talk to him, for I had just mailed him a letter that he wouldn't receive in time before his departure. In it, thanking him from all my heart for what he was doing for us, I was informing him that my brother's latest application for a passport had just been turned down again. Indeed, both Simeon and Radka had applied numerous times to the authorities, but permission to leave the country had invariably been refused. Both Anni and I had also sent official invitations to our families to visit us, with affidavits for support. But now Dominique remained our last and only hope. Meanwhile, our families had no clue that Dominique was arriving. "*You'll probably see my sister, Radka Rizova, who lives in Sofia- 36, "Graf Ignatiev" street—and gives English lessons. She also speaks French. You can explain everything to her. My desire is for her to come with her 6-year-old son.*"

I also briefed Dominique about a new problem: *"As for my brother Simeon, the situation is more complicated. He works out of Sofia* (still denied residence in the capital, he lived in a small, impoverished monastery, Tcherepish, where he was making coffins), *and visits my sister only on weekends. He's a very bright guy, the intellectual type, but has no right to work except at manual jobs. He's extremely proud, with an unbelievable integrity, and is often not easy to deal with. Al-though suffering a lot in Bulgaria, he believes that if he came to see me, he should return, because all his friends and his people share the same fate. If, to come out, he has to promise to return, you can bet that he would keep his word…In other words, if my brother thought that his permission to leave was the object of some 'bargaining' between the government and 'Match', he's capable of refusing…A funny guy, indeed, but that's the way he is…So, I beg you to only discuss our plan with Anni's family and with my sister, but one shouldn't mention any "bargaining" to my brother. Don't carry this letter with you to Bulgaria, one never knows…God bless you, mon vieux, and may He assist you!"*

Knowing Boubi's intransigence, both Mama and I sensed some potential problem that could spoil our plans. Without suspecting any *Paris-Match* plot, he wrote us on July 1st, just two days before Dominique's departure: *"I'm touched that Stefo made demarches for me. It would really be a very good thing if we could see you both. But whether this is feasible is another question. As for me, I believe you know precisely, from my last letter, my position and my intentions, so I won't repeat myself. Stefo asks whether I shouldn't take some additional steps. I've already taken the steps required by the law, and received a refusal. I don't see what else I could do, and also I have no particular desire to do it, because I think that one shouldn't beg for trust, and trust cannot be forced on anyone. Let time give everyone the possibility to know me better!"* We did, alas, know his position. Six weeks earlier, while still waiting for an answer to his three-months-old application for passport, he had explained it quite clearly. He had asked no one for favors, he assured me proudly, and wasn't going to do it, even if an opportunity occurred. His reasons: *"1)I believe that every person should have the right to travel freely, and one doesn't beg for one's rights. 2) In order to receive a passport, I should be trusted, and one doesn't beg for trust either. If I changed my previous decision not to apply, I did it because I thought of a solution which would demonstrate certain things in a better and more eloquent way. Applying is not difficult. What is more difficult is to come to you, to have an opportunity for a better and secure life, and renounce all this by returning to Bulgaria. Thus, I would give an example and would silence all those, who now dare insult me with their mistrust. But whatever be the reply to my application, I'll accept it calmly. Seeing you, and then returning, would be wonderful, but to me this is not vital. Because a truth can be proven in many different ways. Don't worry if I receive a refusal. It won't be a disaster for me, because I have no intention of being anything else but Bulgarian; my life would have no meaning outside of Bulgaria."* Then, as if guessing my opinion that going back to the hell he was living in would be a folly, Boubi asked me tell him frankly if I disagreed with his idea to come on a short visit only and then return. *"Let's be entirely sincere with each other! If our opinions differ, we'll postpone our reunion,"* he wrote.

Was this letter written just for the censors' eyes, with the purpose of facilitating the issuing of his passport? Knowing Boubi's total incapacity and refusal to deceive, I had all reasons to doubt it. Nevertheless, I kept hoping that once outside of the Iron Curtain, once breathing freely, he would see "the truth" (I thought, of course, of _my_ truth, as we all do…). Anyhow, let's first get him and Radka out, and then we'll worry about the other problems!

*   *   *   *

From the day of his departure for Bulgaria, Dominique managed to keep us informed, Anni and me, with the touching thoughtfulness of a brother, who had taken our cause as his own personal one. "July 6th, Rome airport: waiting for my plane to Belgrade, where I'll change planes and will arrive in Sofia tomorrow night." It was a short, but very warm note, just to say that before leaving Paris, he had made the Quai-d'Orsay people ask, by the official channels, for an interview for him with Bulgarian dictator Zhivkov. Then, "Belgrade, Saturday morning, July 7: in a few minutes we're leaving for Sofia by Austrian Airlines." He had dined with the French ambassador in the Yugoslav capital and learned a lot about the current political situation in Bulgaria and about Todor Zhivkov. And Dominique ended his last letter before entering Bulgaria by writing: "My dear

Anni, I'm praying to God that the mountains of obstacles which you have been moving for so many years, will finally collapse. Have confidence and patience!"

Then we waited, and prayed, and waited more. Meanwhile in Bulgaria, Lapierre and Jarnoux spent ten frantic days of incessant work, traveling from town to town, photographing lovely landscapes and picturesque old houses, golden beaches around Varna and Nessebur and frescoes in ancient monasteries and churches. Near the Black Sea, they admired the water lilies of Ropotamo and Kamtchia rivers estuaries and took pictures of high peaks and thick forests on the Stara-planina and Rila mountains. One thing however they carefully avoided doing: contacting our families. They took more than 700 photos and when they returned to Sofia, they couldn't help exclaim: "What a beautiful country!"

It was a sincere admiration. It wasn't part of the masterful operation of publicizing *Paris-Match*'s presence in the country and ingratiating himself with the hosts, in which Dominique had been calculatedly engaged ever since he set foot on Bulgarian soil. Self-promotion was part of the plan, but salesmanship also came quite naturally to Dominique and he had a remarkable talent for it. But even when sincere, he couldn't help sometimes getting a little carried away. Later, when he showed me clippings with interviews and press conferences he gave to Bulgarian journalists, I was amused to read about the "eight million French readers" of *Match* and our "50 million readers" around the world. "Come on, Dominique, didn't you exaggerate a bit?" I asked. "Not at all," he chuckled. "Look, each issue is read by at least four members of the family; four times 1.8 million, it makes about 8 million, doesn't it? And many foreign publications have contracts with us to buy our articles. So, when you add their readers…" In an interview, he delighted the hosts by quoting a "well-known Bulgarian tale." I was delighted to hear it too. When God created the world, the story went, He summoned to Him all nationalities and distributed the lands among them. Only one person wasn't there, the Bulgarian. He'd been too busy working, and nothing was left for him. God took pity of him, cut a piece of His own paradise and handed it to this virtuous man. "Take this," God said, and you'll call it Bulgaria!" "Marvelous story!" I commented, patriotically. "Strange that I didn't know it. Where did you get this Bulgarian folklore, Dominique?" Lapierre smiled devilishly. "Maybe it's not exactly Bulgarian. To tell you the truth, I once used it about Mexico...and about Spain too...and else-where...You know, each time it works beautifully!"

During his two weeks in Bulgaria, Dominique made sure that everybody in the Foreign and Information ministries, in the Bulgarian Press association as well as in circles close to the Party, heard how influential *Paris-Match* was, how great were Jarnoux' 700 photographs, and how favorable Lapierre's impressions were. A born raconteur, he kept forty Sofia journalists spellbound for two hours at a conference "between colleagues," with tales about "how we do things in Paris." Officials were particularly impressed to see his reportages from an extensive tour of the Soviet Union, copies of which he was showing left and right. Everybody ended by loving him. At the same time, he was letting the right people hear about the problem with the families of his *Paris-Match* colleagues Stephane and Anni, and left a memorandum on the subject with the Foreign ministry. Soon, he had the clear impression that the message was understood and there were some encouraging signs that a favorable solution was possible. But this was not enough. Dominique knew that all depended on one single man, the dictator Zhivkov, and he had to obtain his personal consent.

To be received by Zhivkov proved to be much harder than Lapierre had hoped. In spite of his insistence and countless applications, the requested audi-ence was continuously declined. "The comrade First Secretary isn't available at this time," was the repeated reply. "The First Secretary is on a trip...Comrade Zhivkov is unable to receive you now." Time was flying, the reportage was fin-ished, and Lapierre was biting his nails, waiting in Sofia, determined to see Zhivkov. From a detailed letter Dominique sent us through a diplomat, Anni and I learned that he had finally seen Radka, Mrs. Tchaprachikoff, and Ivan, and had told them about his intention to take them out to Paris. To say that they were absolutely taken aback, thrilled, and shaken, would be a pallid understate-ment; they were totally overwhelmed. But after the first excitement, Radka fell back into deep pessimism. "They'll never let me and my child out. I have no illu-sions," she said. However, Dominique instructed them to stay ready, promising to call them back as soon as he talked to the dictator. Anyhow, your mother and brother, Anni, and your sister and nephew, Stephane, look very well and are in good shape, so don't worry too much about them, Dominique's letter assured us. And not to worry about their French visa, he was already arranging all this, just in case...The big problem was still the access to Zhivkov. "Now I'm thinking of nothing else but that," Dominique wrote. For Anni and me, the agony of the wait resumed.

Losing patience, Lapierre decided to try tactics of last resort. On July 17th, he gathered several important Bulgarian journalists and declared that, unfortunately, his good-will visit had to end with a big disappointment, because the First Secretary had declined to see him. The same morning, he deposited a letter directly at Zhivkov's office, informing him with regret that when back to Paris, he would have no choice but to report that the Bulgarian top leaders refuse all contacts with the Western press. The reaction was miraculous. Only two hours later, the Protocol office called Dominique to inform him that Secretary Zhivkov would receive him the next morning, at 9.30.

"The Big Tovaritch was alone when I was ushered into his huge office with Jarnoux and an interpreter," Lapierre told us later. The dictator was rather cool at the beginning, but Dominique wasted no time to do his spiel. First, trying not to be too unsubtle, he stressed the point of what a golden opportunity a *Paris-Match* substantive coverage would represent for Bulgaria and its tourism. Then, affecting a vivid interest in Zhivkov's stand on international and domestic affairs, he asked his host to kindly clarify for him some concrete points "which are causing many comments in the West..." That did it. Flattered, and eager to explain and boast, Zhivkov's face beamed and he never stopped talking. Although eminently bored by all statistics and examples of glorious Communist achievements, Dominique was all ears, his eyes lit with pretended curiosity, interrupting from time to time with a pertinent question, just to prove that he was devouring every word, dutifully taking notes and asking the speaker to repeat more slowly some "fascinating" sentence he missed to write down. The voluble Communist boss was in seventh heaven. Lapierre was a master in this kind of games, a true actor. But he also had prepared his homework. Before the interview, he had spent hours reading interminable Zhivkov speeches and articles. Later, when I was thanking him for everything he did for our families, he said: "Don't be silly, that was fun and I loved it. The only thing you owe me a drink for, is the excruciating tedium of the crap I had to go through. Have you ever read Communist reports on steel production or disarmament? That really requires courage, and it proves how much I love you and Anni."

They had talked for more than a half-hour, when Lapierre decided it was time to act. Politely, he asked permission to bring up a problem than only Zhivkov could resolve. "Go ahead!" the First Secretary said, and Dominique presented his plea for our relatives, which he had rehearsed several times before. Somber clouds covered the host's face. He stood up and picked a file lying on his desk. "You've already sent the Foreign ministry a note about this case," he said, visibly displeased. Dominique explained that it had been destined to his personal attention, and handed him a new note, written in Bulgarian. Zhivkov read it very carefully, then said that, not knowing the persons in question, he had ordered an inquiry and now had the results. Some of these people are enemies of the people, he said severely. Dominique respectfully expressed his astonishment that a frail, half-blind lady of 70 (Anni's mother), and a young woman (Radka), who was barely 19 at the time of the "revolution," could be a threat for the country. But isn't she married, Zhivkov asked. Yes, and that's precisely why she's applying just for a temporary visit, and only for herself and her child, not for her husband. The Boss began to listen with more interest. He didn't say anything about Boubi, obviously well aware of his harmless and pacific nature. But he had strong objections against Ivan, quoting from his file: prison sentences, illegal attempts to cross the border, "anti-people" convictions.." "But after so many years, Sir, isn't it now time to forgive past errors?" Dominique replied with an angelic smile. And wouldn't the public benefit from our reportage now far outweigh whatever harm these persons might have caused long ago?"

Zhivkov didn't give Lapierre the satisfaction of accepting his arguments. He only asked him whether he was leaving Bulgaria that night, as planned, and promised to let him know his decision later. But Dominique announced that he was in no hurry; he loved the country and would enjoy waiting for the reply here, so he be able to accompany his colleagues' Bulgarian relatives to Paris. The host didn't seemed very pleased, but made no comment. "You'll have my answer tonight," he said enigmatically as his visitors were taking leave.

That evening Jarnoux left for Paris with his photographs. Dominique returned to his hotel room to wait for the promised answer. The suspense was extreme, but he also felt relieved that Zhivkov had not asked the two things Dominique feared the most. First, if Groueff and Tchaprachikova want to see their families so badly, why don't they come here? They'll be welcome and free to leave whenever they want. Second, you, *Paris-Match*, will first publish the stories, and if we like them, we'll see about the passports… But he hadn't said that and Dominique felt more optimistic than he was before the audience.

At 6 p.m., the Deputy Foreign minister called and asked Lapierre to come and see him. The passports were granted. For all, except for Ivan, but his would be issued too at a later date, the Deputy minister promised. Dominique wasted no time to recontact our families that same evening. "We'll be leaving as soon as I book tickets on the next *KLM* flight, maybe tomorrow, maybe a day or two later!" he announced to the startled Mrs. Tchaprachikoff. For a moment, she remained speechless. The dream with which she had lived in the past 18 years was coming true! But then the expression of her face suddenly changed. "Tomorrow? No, it won't be possible!" she declared firmly. And as Dominique insisted that they shouldn't risk any delay, the distinguished old lady pointed to her hair: "Look at me! I can't go to Anni like this! I must find a hairdresser first!"

Dominique hurried to Radka's small apartment. Since noon, when he had told her that Zhivkov was going to decide by the evening, she had spent the day praying to God to grant her wish. "I opened the door and when Dominique, smiling, hugged me warmly, I knew, before he said a word, that the miracle had happened," Radka told me later. She burst into tears and it took her hours to calm down, still wondering whether she wasn't dreaming. Two hectic days followed, filled with packing, rushing for passports, visas, and airplane tickets (with money provided by Dominique), and saying tearful good-byes to just two or three close friends, adjured to keep it secret until she's safely in Paris. Meanwhile, Radka's husband, Sasso, rushed to the monastery, where Boubi worked, to announce the news and urgently bring him back to Sofia. Sasso's cooperation, vital to the plot, demanded an agonizing decision on his part and a real sacrifice, and he acquitted himself with nobility. Few people knew it, but the marriage had been disintegrating, and they had already agreed to separate. But they kept it secret: without keeping one spouse as "hostage," the militia would not permit the other to leave the country. Sasso knew that Radka and their 6-year-old son George would not return, but he also knew that the child would be infinitely better off in a free country. He gave his consent and thus facilitated their departure.

In the workshop of Tcherepish monastery, Boubi was in the midst of making a coffin, when his brother-in-law arrived unexpectedly and told him that he was leaving for Paris. Taken aback, he hastily collected his few belongings and both men hurried to Sofia, Boubi still perplexed and not understanding what exactly had happened and how. There he met for the first time Dominique, the new hero of the family, who was nervously waiting to take, practically by hand, his four charges to the plane. For Mrs. Tchaprachikoff, Boubi, Radka and George, it was the first flight in their life.

*   *   *

Early in the morning on Thursday, July 19th, I was awaken by a telegram from Sofia: "*Had interview with Zhivkov stop. Visas granted everybody except Ivan, but very optimistic ulterior visa for him stop Will all leave together for Paris soonest. Amities, Lapierre, Hotel Balkan.*" When I called Mama and Anni, they were almost unable to speak from emotion, and I, too, had to make an effort to control my voice. That evening I took them to an Italian restaurant to comment and discuss the next move. Mama, with her terrible experience with Communists, feared that the trip would be cancelled at the last minute, while Anni worried whether Ivan would ever get his exit visa. We exchanged cables with the Panitzas, who reserved hotel rooms in their neighborhood, and we waited for the next message from Dominique. It came two days later, while I was in Southampton: "*We'll be in Paris tomorrow Sunday 22nd of July.*" That Sunday I could hardly wait to call the Panitzas and learn all the details: Yes, they had arrived and they look very well; yes, they enjoyed the *KLM* flight via Vienna and Amsterdam very much; yes, uncle Stati Panitza met them at the Bourget airport; now they were happily resting in their hotel "Belles Feuilles," near the Trocadero. I called them right away and had a long conversation with Boubi. On Tuesday evening, Anni and I flew to Paris, where Dominique and Rosie Cartier met us at the airport and drove us to the Belles-Feuilles hotel.

*   *   *   *

Being the lucky brother, torn away from a stricken, close-knit family, had been a heavy responsibility to bear, involving much worry and pain. Eighteen years of fear and anguish, of homesickness and, sometimes, feelings of guilt; and frustrating waiting for news and constant preoccupation about sending parcels and money. For me, it had become a way of life, a permanent pinch of sadness, to be borne as one lives with a chronic illness. And yet, the reward on that Wednesday in July in Paris was so magnificent, that the years of trial seemed well worth it. When Radka, Boubi and I embraced for the first time after our long separation, I felt immensely grateful to have a brother and a sister. We all had lunch on a cafe-terrace on Place du Trocadero, eagerly questioning each other, examining with curiosity each other's looks and commenting on how we had changed during all these years. Radka, of course, was no more the high school girl I had left, and it was the first time I was seeing her 6-year-old son George; Boubi, the University student I remembered, was now a mature man of 41, with some silver in his hair. Their youth had gone, unseen by me, and the thought that they had never had a chance to be young, made me sad. Yet, despite the 18 years of separation, it took me only moments to find again the Boubi and Radka of yester-year, the brother and sister of my childhood. Was it a matter of genes, some animal sense of family "blood"? What makes this unique link between siblings? Some atavistic awareness, or subconscious residue from nursery days? Or just shared memories of happenings, faces and sceneries, of common experiences, inside jokes, and family folklore? Strange, I thought: I had made such great new friendships, closer and much more intimate than anything that these 18 years of separation had left of my family bonds, and yet, would anyone but us ever know how exactly it felt to be kissed good-night by my father—the tickle of the bearded cheek, the scent of pipe tobacco, the beloved voice? Would remembering the sound of the old phonograph ("*His Master's Voice*") playing the 1930's hit "*O, Dona Clara*" and driving our canary Figaro to a frenzy, mean anything to anyone, but us? Could we describe to outsiders the different taste of grandma's stuffed peppers, or her baklava ? And there were only three of us in the whole world, to giggle at the mention of Sozopol's street beggar Otto-Moto-Koleloto, or uncle Mitcho's umbrella, or the way an Americanized uncle pronounced the word "apartment," without having to explain who they were and what was so funny about it. A unique and very warming feeling, that made me very happy.

Serving as their host and guide around Paris was a very rewarding experience. They both spoke French, as also did Anni's mother, so meeting people presented no problem. The Panitzas received them with open arm, and one night Raymond and Rosie Cartier took them, plus Dominique Lapierre and Evgueni Silianoff, on the *Bateau-Mouche* for a spectacular dinner-tour on the Seine river, which thrilled them beyond words, especially young George. During the 12 days I stayed with them in Paris, I showed them Le Louvre, the Left Bank, and as many museums, churches and monuments I could. I brought them to many Bulgarian friends they knew in Paris—Sveto Radeff, Evgueni and Nina Silianoff, the Naslednikoffs, Lina Georgieva, Dobcho Palaveev, and others. Dimi and Yvonne Panitza invited us to her family's country house in Monsoult, where George was overjoyed to spend most of the day in the swimming pool. I even brought Boubi to a disco, "*Chez Regine;*" another evening, in male company, I was amused to watch his reaction to the nude showgirls at the "*Crazy Horse Saloon.*" (His eyes nearly went out of their orbits. It was clear that the austere years during which he was supposed to build socialism in Bulgaria, had not in the least dampened his decadent fascination with ladies' superb curves.)

Boubi didn't talk much about his hardships during the past years, he didn't like to complain. But there were little things he said which touched me profoundly. Enchanted with his hotel room, for instance, he revealed to me that it was for the first time in many years that he was sleeping in a room all for himself (he had always to share living quarters or dormitories), and had a private bathroom. Then, delighted by the car I had rented, he admitted that he hadn't been for years in an automobile other than a bus or truck! So every day I discovered more and more elementary things that in the West we took for granted, while people like Boubi had been totally deprived of.

Before returning to New York, I installed Radka, Boubi and George into a small apartment on rue de Varenne, which I sublet for one month from some Russian immigrants, descendants of the Tolstoy family. Then I introduced Radka to our aging administrator, Monsieur Roux, who gave her a flowery, sentimental welcome "to the fold of our *Paris-Match* family" and arranged for her to have a temporary job at the archives service. Meanwhile, Therond laid out Lapierre and Jarnoux's story. It was a magnificent, extensive reportage in the best *Paris-Match* tradition and giving an excellent idea of Bulgaria's beauty. Before sending it to print, and as we had agreed, I carefully read every line of the text and every caption, to make sure that they were totally untainted by any politics. The Bulgarian embassy was ecstatic. But before long, it began to inquire about the publication of the second story, the one with Zhivkov's interview. This worried Anni extremely, because we knew that Match would never publish such boring propaganda, and her brother Ivan was still waiting for his exit visa in Sofia.

My plans were to bring Boubi on a visit to America, while leaving, for the time being, Radka and George in Paris. Her Bulgarian passport was good for a three-months stay in France, but in her marital situation, an application for American immigration visa would've aroused suspicions in Sofia and could cause problems for the child's custody. Therefore, she decided to keep secret her decision not to return, and to try to prolong her passport each time it expired, for as long as would be possible. With this in mind, and after I brought Boubi to the American consulate to apply for a visitor's visa for the States, I left Paris on August 6, to return to my home and my job.

After seeing Radka, I had less worries for her. A hard and conscientious worker, plus speaking French and English, she quickly adapted herself to her new life and her job at Match. Before long, my Paris colleagues began to send me most flattering echoes about her work. Moreover, she was elated to be in France, in a free country, and tremendously relieved to leave the Communist hell, forever.

Boubi was a different story. He also loved Paris, its buildings, avenues and parks, the beauty of the Seine and the mood of Montmartre. He admired its monuments and museums, and walked for miles every day, taking notes and raving about the architecture. He was really happy to be reunited with me and, in a few days, with Mama, pleased to see old friends again and meet new people. But from the first day of our reunion, he was repeating phrases such as "When I go back to Bulgaria" and "When I return." At the beginning, I tried to ignore them. "He already loves it here," I thought, "and once he gets more used to freedom, he'll never think of returning to his horrible life in Bulgaria." A few times I brought up the subject, but Boubi became extremely agitated, touchy, and outright angry. "Of course, I'll go back! I'm a Bulgarian and my place is there," he almost shouted at me. "I've asked for a temporary visa and gave my word to return. Do you expect me to be a liar?" Reminding him that the Communists killed our father, destroyed our family, turned our country into a Soviet colony, reduced him, a bright, promising man, to a pariah humiliated daily and forced to work at the lowest jobs in order to make a miserable living, was to no avail, and I decided to be patient, still hoping. But Radka wasn't optimistic. "You don't know Boubi," she told me. "He means every word he says and nothing will make him change his mind."

Half-believing that he was talking seriously, all our friends who loved him tried to dissuade him, but he stubbornly refused to even listen to their arguments. In fact, they all—the Panitzas, Silianoff, Dimi, Anni, Dobcho, Sava (who passed through Paris shortly after I had left),—were sure that he'd never commit such folly, but were irritated by the fanaticism with which he defended such an absurd thesis. But most people simply assumed that he had good reasons to pretend that he was going to voluntarily return to his tormentors, and they discreetly asked no questions. And my Patron, Jean Prouvost, when informed that my brother, after being helped to escape from behind the Iron Curtain, was talking about returning there, had only one question: "But is this man crazy ?"

*   *   *   *

On September 20, after spending almost two months in Paris, Boubi came to visit us in the States. Mama had counted the days and the hours to this reunion and, religious as she was, had lit candles to thank the Almighty for answering her prayers. As we met him at the Idlewild (today "JFK") airport, she was in tears, overjoyed and repeating happily: "Thank you, God! At last, we're reunited, for good! All my children are free! The nightmare is over!"

Early fall is a marvelous season both in Manhattan and in Southampton, and Boubi seemed to be enchanted. Paul, a delightful, loving little boy of two, always smiling and ready to play, won him at the first sight. Lil, Jill and Tina, after hearing so much about my brother, welcomed him with a mixture of friendliness, curiosity, and certain shyness. Uneasy in English, and introverted by nature, he never relaxed completely with them, remaining warmly polite, but rather formal. He was very impressed by Manhattan's architecture and as soon as he learned more or less his way, he started taking long walks around town, returning to Mama's flat, where he slept, loaded with postcard, prospectuses and maps, and avid to share his impressions with me. Another favorite occupation was buying the *New York Times* in the morning, and spending hours deciphering it, with the help of a dictionary and diligently underlining passages and words he didn't understand, so he could ask me to explain them when he came to see me at the office or at home.

I introduced him to many of our friends, to Lil's mother and relatives, to my *Paris-Match* colleagues, everybody receiving him with great sympathy and listening to him with most genuine interest; in those days, they were, after all, not many people coming from Bulgaria, especially victims of the Communists. Although, looking at Boubi's appearance, there was nothing to suggest a victim. Meeting this well-dressed and rested man in our home, or at the Beach Club in Southampton, or at some party where Lil and I would bring him, our friends would have difficulty imagining that only two months earlier he was living and laboring in miserable conditions, separated from family and friends, deprived of the right to reside in a big city, constantly fearing arrest or deportation to another village, as it had happened several times to him. Now he could live as a free man, comfortably, taken care of by a loving mother, free from threats and persecution, and, because I was able to afford it, free from material hardships and worries.

We went to movies that he wouldn't be allowed to see in Bulgaria, to the theater, to restaurants. I introduced him to people with whom he could talk about world affairs, one of his main interests, such as our friend, Ambassador Angier Biddle-Duke, President Kennedy's Chief of Protocol, and Bill vanden Heuvel, of the International Rescue Committee. My mentor, Raymond Cartier, talked many times with him, and my colleague Mathias brought him to a few sessions of the United Nations. At a cocktail-party at philanthropist Mary Lasker's house, I introduced him to Adlai Stevenson.

In Southampton, he saw another aspect of my life: the cozy informality of the weekends with the family at our country house, *The Gables*, the mornings with Paul at the ocean, still warm enough for swimming, the tennis on the grass courts of the *Meadow Club*. Most of our friends met him with great sympathy. Some, such as Tommy Phipps, were fascinated enough to invite him to their homes to hear more details of his unusual life. It was a period when we used to play volleyball at Basil and Elise Goulandris' beautiful estate, *Andros*. We weren't particularly good, but our lively, hotly contested games seemed to give the shipping tycoon no less pleasure than did his super-luxurious yacht or the acquisition of his famous Cezanne, the first Impressionist painting to fetch more than a million dollars. To Basil, a charming man with delightfully simple tastes, winning a point (or a bet, or a card or backgammon game) was of utmost importance, and he and his fellow-Greeks playing with us, a highly competitive bunch, argued with passion and contested every shot. "*Exo!*" (Out!) would automatically shout the Greeks on the one team, even before the ball touches the ground, while the opposite team already screamed "*Mesa!*" (In!), just as a matter of principle, even with the ball falling way out of the court. Thus, we, the non-Greek players, quickly learned at least two Greek words. Apart from the Southampton regulars and countless Goulandris relatives, Basil and his twin brother, Nico, used to bring to the game employees of their firms, and we teased them that in order to have a winning team, each twin probably hired his accountants and bookkeepers mostly for their volleyball skills...Boubi came a few afternoons to watch our game and enjoyed the tea and delicious cakes the hostess graciously served to the exhausted, sweaty volleyballists.

I was happy to share some of the joys of my pleasant life with a brother who had had such bad fortune, and to see that he was enjoying it. It looked like I had all the reasons to believe that he would quickly forget his crazy idea about returning to Bulgaria. After a few weeks in New York, I wanted him to see more of the United States. Knowing that he would appreciate the beauty of Washington, I took him there, showed him the White House, the Capitol and several monuments, and left him for a week in the hospitable hands of Tina and Christos Sarbov and the Stancioff family. From there, still raving about the urban marvels of the capital, he embarked on a long *Grey Hound* bus trip to New Orleans and then all the way to California. It so happened that the grave Cuban missile crisis erupted at this time and I was not only seriously worried about the possibility of a nuclear disaster at any moment, but also extremely busy professionally, trying to obtain a maximum of information for *Paris-Match*. Luckily, I didn't have to worry about Boubi: he was on his sightseeing tour, calling me every couple of days, from Louisiana, Texas, Los Angeles and San Francisco. To everybody who knew about his life in Bulgaria, Boubi's visit to America sounded like a marvelous story with a happy ending.

I had, however, begun to see disturbing signs of strange behavior. At first, I tried to dismiss the thought that he suffered from the inevitable paranoia, characteristic for anyone coming from behind the Iron Curtain. In his case, it occurred on and off, in sudden, unexpected outbursts, erupting for no reason at all. He would then be convinced that he was been followed, spied on, or framed, and complained that people didn't trust him or suspected him. It resulted partly from his inability to understand the habits and workings of a free society, from having lived in a world of informers and betrayal. But was it paranoia or simply a matter of semantics, that he became so disturbed when I wanted him to meet Senator Javits, a friend of ours? At first, the perspective of talking to the bright Republican statesman thrilled Boubi. Until the day before the appointment, when he read in a newspaper that Javits was a "leader of the opposition." The word "opposition" upset him tremendously. "Stefo," he complained indignantly, "how could you put me into such situation? You know my delicate position, and yet you arrange meetings with opposition leaders!" The equation "opposition= conspiracy" was so strongly imbedded in his mind, that he never went to see the urbane Senator.

After a few weeks in America, Boubi learned better, but certain notions remained for him difficult to digest. Any American who criticized the US government was suspect in his eyes, and before guessing whether the person was simply un-patriotic, or was "sent to provoke" him, he would clam up and not say a word until the end of the conversation. He was very suspicious of people who criticized the authorities openly. Once, at dinner, my friend Philippe de Bausset, our Washington correspondent, told some jokes about President Kennedy and said that he didn't like his latest speech. Boubi became very tense and stopped talking. When Philippe left, he asked me: "Why is he against America?" I assured him that Bausset was, on the contrary, a very pro-American Frenchman. But Boubi kept worrying: "He meets me for the first time and tries to involve me in anti-Government talk."

He learned quickly that in USA citizens can criticize, even attack freely the President and the authorities, and that disagreeing publicly is not a subversive act. But he never learned to relax when military or security subjects were discussed. I recognized trouble when he got off the *Greyhound* bus in Texas and called me very excitedly from a telephone booth. "It's clear now that I've been framed," he said. 'Who ever arranged my itinerary wanted me to go through El Paso, can you believe it! Luckily, I realized it on time and got off!" "What's wrong with El Paso?" I asked. Although we spoke in Bulgarian, he answered in a whisper, as if suspecting that our conversation were tapped: "El Paso is on the border, didn't you know it? To send me into a fro-on-tii-er zone! Imagine!" It had never occurred to me that to a Bulgarian the word "frontier" had a sinister connotation of subversion and danger. He fought his phobias as long as he could. But on his way back from California, there was some mix-up with his suitcase: it had been mistakenly left over at one Greyhound stop, but recovered immediately at the next one. That did it. When he called me from a booth and said that he was returning right away, no persuasion on my part succeeded to convince him that there was no conspiracy involved and he should continue his trip. He returned, sure that "Big Brother" was still watching him.

Luckily, such cases were the exception. Meanwhile, he enjoyed more and more life in New York and his admiration for the American democratic system was growing every month. We spent a wonderful Thanksgiving together and Boubi was delighted to meet Rocky and Maria, Gary Cooper's widow and daughter, who came home after the turkey dinner, as did British actress Glynis Johns. The pre-Christmas weeks, always spectacular in Manhattan, were another happy time, with Mama and me showing Boubi and little Paul the fabulously decorated Fifth Avenue windows. On Christmas Eve the entire family was around our tree—Lil's mother, Mama, Jill and Tina with friends (only Philip was missing, he was in Gstaad), and Henry Fonda, whom Boubi had seen in many movies in Bulgaria, dropped in. "What a wonderful Christmas!" Mama was repeating, beaming with happiness as Paul was opening his presents. "And let's hope that Radka and George will join us very soon!" The next day we all had the traditional Christmas lunch at Lil's ex-sister-in-law's, Jean Stralem and her husband Donald, where Boubi, received as a true member of the family, was the center of attention. Then Lil and I flew to Palm Beach and celebrated New Year's Eve at a sumptuous private party oilman Charlie Wrightsman and his wife Jane gave for the President. Dancing all night amidst the boisterous Kennedy clan and the likes of Douglas Fairbanks Jr., Gianni Agnelli, Loel Guinness, Douglas Dillon and the French and British ambassadors—and knowing Mama and Boubi safely in New York, and Radka and George in Paris,—I had never felt so relieved from the Bulgarian nightmare.

But, alas, Boubi had surprises in store for us...

      *   *   *   *

Chapter 27

Boubi returns to Bulgaria

The place is rather peculiar for this kind of conversation, when I come to think of it. But here we are, the two brothers, in *Le Club*, the fashionable New York night spot, sipping our Scotch in the semi-dark room, with loud disco music for a background, and discussing his departure the next day. Boubi is nervous, but speaks calmly, matter-of-factly, while I'm trying to keep cool and not show too much emotion. He seems to enjoy this evening, as he thoroughly enjoyed the day we spent together. I notice that he's not quite indifferent to the good-looking girls on the dancing floor, and from time to time, between two grim sentences, his blue eyes sparkle with appreciation behind the eyeglasses, as he spots some pretty dancer.

My brother is neatly dressed, a conservative-looking, mild-mannered man with well groomed graying hair. The day after tomorrow he'll be turning 42 (his birthday is January 30th). The expression on his face is most of the time serious, but his slightly myopic eyes are warm and unusually gentle when he smiles. I almost wish he showed some anger or bitterness when, always moderate and detached, he depicts the monstrous universe that had victimize him. But, once more, I realize that some people are simply deprived, totally and maybe genetically, of any capability for hatred.

I can't stand it any longer.

"Boubi, for heaven's sake, can't you see what an enormous mistake you're about to make? It's a suicide!"

"I thought we agreed that we won't talk about it again."

"I know, I know. I promised. But…this is ridiculous!"

"You said you understood me."

I recognize the old, familiar stubbornness. He's letting down the steel armor that, since we were children, no one ever managed to break. That's the way, <u>my</u>

462

way, take it or leave it! One more word, and the communication will be cut. I capitulate on his terms. As I always did. I recover my calm and the conversation resumes, loving, brotherly, frighteningly lucid. Before coming to *Le Club*, I went with Lil to a dinner Jean and Donald Stralem gave for movie director Otto Preminger, so Boubi had dined alone with Mama, to whom he had also forbidden, after several painful arguments, to talk "about that," although for several weeks the poor woman wasn't thinking of anything else.

In a few hours, he'll be flying to Paris. Then, unnecessarily, voluntarily, stupidly—yes, stupidly!—back to Bulgaria, to the misery and the humiliations he's been enduring for the last 18 years. By his own choice, he'll trade the Brooks Brothers suit (and yet, when we went to buy it, he was so touchingly pleased!), for the pitiful rags of the outcast. After the comfortable months he spent as a free, civilized man in Paris and New York, how is he going to return to the depressing workers' dormitories, to the hard kitchen floors of charitable relatives, to the dilapidated monastery cell where he made coffins for a living? Those are unimportant things, he would answer. But what about the big, important issues, such as freedom, human rights, dignity? It's easy to discuss them here, to talk big, with a snooty maitre-d' bringing you the second glass of whisky and calling you "Sir"…Yes, it sounds so noble, so interesting—the fatherland, you know, the sacrifice, and not caring about comfort and material things. I'm getting progressively furious. God, I hope he'll suddenly sober up and change his mind! There are moments when I can hate all his nonsense, honestly! The worries he's causing to all of us, the ordeal for Mama. He really does not know what he is doing. The man just spent the weekend with us in Southampton, then a few days in Washington again, then this chic cocktail-party with all the art people, everybody very kind to him and everybody interested: "Tell us, Mr.Groueff, what is your opinion on this or that…oh, how interesting…what a remarkable gentleman…we should learn more about your poor country…"And imagine, talking en tête-à-tête to Adlai Stevenson, and the great statesman telling me the next day "What a gallant man, your brother!"

And then Boubi packs his suitcase, good-bye you nice people, good-bye Free World, I'm going home! Home! What home? No wife, no parents, no brother and sister, not even a girlfriend. No job, not an address either, no bed anywhere. To become again the zero, the non-citizen, the defenseless outcast that the lowest militiaman can insult and abuse, bully around, arrest or torture if he feels like it. No more "Monsieur Groueff" and "Sir." Illiterate brutes shouting at you "enemy of the people" and "fascist bastard."

It's pas midnight, but we are not sleepy and we both know that this could well be our last conversation.

"I'm sure that they'll arrest you the moment you cross the frontier. And, frankly, could you blame them if they don't believe you that you're returning just because you love the country? How do you intend to explain that after all the misery and squalor, you're leaving the comfort and security of Paris and America by your free choice? They'd be idiots not to suspect you. After liking it so much here? After meeting my capitalist and reactionary friends? Of course, they'll say that you're a CIA agent or something like that. Who wouldn't? With your family background? With an anti-communist brother like me? Let me laugh!..."

Flushed, suddenly all excited and upset, I look hardly like a laughing man. Boubi remains very calm, as he listens attentively.

"I agree. They'll probably not believe me. It's quite possible that they arrest me," he says simply.

"Don't tell me that you have no fear! You know too well what happens during some of those interrogations."

"Of course I do. It may be an unpleasant ordeal. But don't worry, it won't last long: they'll release me when they find that I'm not lying." And he explains that Bulgarian intelligence services are so well organized, that they'll find out quickly what he was doing abroad, whom he saw, and whether he's working for some foreign service. "They'll probably ask me about the Royal family; I'll tell them that I did not see them abroad; at first, they won't believe, but they'll check and find of course that I'm telling the truth."

Indeed, he has refused to see the Queen-mother Giovanna, a person whom he revered and who enthusiastically invited him to visit her in Portugal as soon as she learned that he had left Bulgaria. He also declined to see the young King Simeon, in exile in Spain, or his sister, Princess Maria Luisa, in spite of my insistence and

our family's close relations with them Mama and I were quite upset and embarrassed about his refusal and told him that he was being rude. "You see now why I
couldn't accept their invitation?" he says. "It would've been despicable to visit them
and then answer Militia's questions about how they live and whom they see."

I can't believe my ears. Why does he have to tell them that he saw the Royal
family? He doesn't intend to tell the hateful torturers, the kind of people who
killed our father and hundreds of our friends, he doesn't intend to tell them
whom he met and what he said when he was abroad, does he? Boubi's face
becomes grave, he stiffens in an almost defiant attitude. "You don't suggest that I
should lie, do you? I hate lies. Lies are wrong, no matter what the excuse. It
would be below my dignity. I've nothing to hide, nothing I should be ashamed
of. After all, isn't this the difference between "them" and "us"? Lying, that's their
kind of things. I won't have any part of it, I won't do it. If we want to prevail, we
should never use their ways, never go as low as they do. We should preserve the
difference and be proud of it."

He is a doomed man, now I see it. I know that he means every word he says.
He's indeed the only person I know who never told a lie. When children, Mama
was sometimes embarrassed when, not wanting to talk to some caller, she would
tell us "Say that I'm not home!" and little Boubi, blushing with indignation,
would refuse to obey: "Mama, that's a lie!" Even in our innocent children's plots
and pranks, we would never involve Boubi.

Le Club is getting emptier and only a few amorous couples are still dancing on
the darkened floor. I know I don't have much chance of convincing Boubi. He
looks so determined, so serene, entirely at peace with himself. It gives him an
unusual aura of strength. Or is it stubbornness? And, at that very moment, I also
realize how vulnerable and defenseless my brother is. How hopelessly un-savable
this fragile and sensitive man is. All my irritation and reproaches evaporate and
I'm overwhelmed by an infinite compassion. I feel as though a tremendous
drama is about to begin, as this pure and loving sole readies himself, with open

eyes, for his encounter with impending suffering. I love him now more than ever. And yet, there is nothing I, or anyone, could do to divert him from his destiny.

*   *   *   *

That same night, the quietude of Mama's tiny, cozy apartment on East 95th Street has the color of despair, the taste of swallowed tears, the sound of suppressed sighs. With the volume of the TV set turned down to the minimum, Mama's favorite entertainer, Johnny Carson, and the guest of his *Late Show* seem to be engaged in some hilarious dialogue, but she doesn't notice them. The flickering light of the television screen throws flashes to the corners of the darkened room, intermittently illuminating the dozen school-notebooks and dictionaries, piled on the table, the icons on top of the commode, the framed portraits, crowding each shelf, the pots with geranium and Bulgarian "zdravetz" on the window sills. It is a warm, comfortable New York studio apartment, but unmistakably an immigrant's home.

The notebooks' lined pages are filled with the homework of the 69-year-old student of English, penciled in the painstaking, studious handwriting of a stubborn foreigner determined to learn the language of which she didn't know a word five years ago. Words, copied 20 times, 50 times: *"Delicious...delicious...delicious..."* then, in the margin, in Cyrillic letters, her own interpretation of the correct pronunciation, something sounding like *day-lee-shoss.* Or sentences copied patiently ad infinitum, until mastered properly, some of them of questionable utility: "What is the score of the first half time, please?" or "The aurora borealis is a luminous phenomenon."

And the collection of portraits and photographs! There is, of course, the entire Royal family: an old picture of the late King Boris with his Bourbon nose, handsome mustache and intelligent blue eyes, taken during a parade in Sofia; a portrait of Queen Giovanna, gentle and aristocratic, with inscription "To dear Dafinka, Merry Christmas, Estoril, 1960;" recent family photos of young King Simeon with wife and babies in Madrid, of his sister, Princess Maria-Luisa, with husband and babies in Toronto, all signed for "the dear Mrs. Groueva."

The royal souvenirs are only part of mama's cherished display, a real private iconostas. There is no formal portrait of my father (most of our personal belongings have disappeared in the whirlpool of events in Sofia), but the many photographs and newspaper clippings, some of them framed, some simply resting on the shelf, keep him ever-present in the Manhattan room: here, the King's Chief of Cabinet in his resplendent gilded uniform the chest covered with medals, the white-plumed bicorn on his distinguished head, the ceremonial thin sword with mother-of-pearl handle on his side, as he accompanies in pomp some new foreign ambassador on his first visit to the Royal palace; there, the kind-faced, old white-bearded man walking slowly with his cane on a sunny Sofia street; next to it, the same blue-eyed face, but when the beard was still blond and the features younger, in a group of smiling friends in old-fashioned costumes.

The gallery includes, of course, Mama's three children: Radka with her little George; Boubi, in an old portrait, looking very serious; and many pictures of me, my two-year-old Paul, and Lil. How proud Mama is of her American daughter-in-law, of Lil's photos in *Vogue* and *Harper's Bazaar*, of our Southampton house, of the parties we give, of the mentions in the social columns! I was often embarrassed to see her collecting these columns, after some of her friends informed her that *Journal American* or *Daily News* had mentioned our name, usually in connection with some party we had attended. At first, I was surprised that someone who had been through persecution and forced internments would keep the slightest curiosity for such frivolities. But with time I realized how reassuring this must have been for her shattered feeling of security, and how well it fitted into the fairy tale she had built around her perfect, ten-foot-tall son, his glamorous American wife, and their golden wunderkind son. This naive adulation and unconcealed pride made us uneasy and annoyed Lil, but Mama would never understand it.

It's late in the night when I drop Boubi at the door of Mama's brownstone house off Central Park, and I know that she's still awake, waiting and worrying. In fact, she hasn't slept much since his arrival in New York, four months ago. It's ironic that just now, when her ardent prayers have been answered and all her children are finally safe and out of Bulgaria, she has to go through the pangs of new, unexpected agony. All these weeks I have watched her recently won happiness giving gradually way to the new fear. Growing anxiety swept the fragile peace away from her mind. The ghosts of the past returned and invaded the little paradise she thought she had found in the security of her American family. In the usually smiling eyes of the alert, handsome lady, I recognize the defeated old woman with the swollen face I met at Le Bourget airport five years ago, when she arrived from Sofia.

Most of the drama in the small 95th Street apartment evolved in silence, because Boubi is a taciturn man, reluctant to talk about his feelings and plans, and Mama is intimidated by his moodiness. Long, tense, restless nights. Mother and son pretend to be asleep, staring at the ceiling, tossing and turning in their beds, only a few feet from each other. Theirs thoughts are filled with images and voices from the same country, yet the chasm is unbridgeable between them, between her black nightmare about Bulgaria and his bright dreams about the same Bulgaria.

I'm familiar with her nightmare. Or, more exactly, I know it like one knows a story one has read or heard. But the terror in a nightmare, which petrifies you and makes you wake up in cold sweat, cannot be really transmitted second-hand. Mama had described—often emotionally, always disjointedly,—the grim scenes of the collapse of our world, Dad's arrest and prison, Radka's and hers concentration camp, the monstrous "People's tribunals," the execution of Dad and hundreds of our friends, the years of destitution and internment in remote villages. I knew the events, but could I feel the sensations, the sounds and smells of terror? How could I? It wasn't *my* face that turned ashen, it wasn't *my* heart that stopped beating when the Militia broke into the apartment. I didn't see the look in my father's eyes behind the bar during the short prison visit, nor did I hear the sound of his whisper. I didn't smell the stench and breathe the foul air in the overcrowded prisoners' trains. The sub-zero cold in the Dobrudja camps did not freeze *my* body, and it wasn't *my* hands that bled from tearing thorny hedges to feed the pitiful fire during the blizzards. Yes, that very month of January 1945 I was cold a few times, but only because I was skiing in Davos…And how could I comprehend the intangibles—the hatred in the eyes of the mob, the smell of imminent danger in the air, the chill of rumors about torture or persons who had disappeared, the despair of being helpless, the relentless fear? I've been spared these horrors, but I imagine how these memories must haunt Mama's nights since Boubi began talking again about returning to Bulgaria.

Returning to Hell, that's what it meant to her. She had almost succeeded in exorcising her demons, and had tried hard not to think about Bulgaria, she told me, to erase it from her mind. She didn't want to hear about that country again; she wanted to forget it forever. "It's too painful to remember," she told me several times. "Everything I loved there is gone, dead. They took away my husband, they destroyed us; for thirteen years I was hurt, persecuted, humiliated, destitute, and my children—for eighteen years. Isn't that enough? Are we going to be punished more? Are you going to let Boubi return to Hell? He won't survive. They'll destroy him."

I haven't lived Mama's nightmare, but Boubi has. And yet, he's determined to go back. Mama is stunned, desperate, she can't believe it. Why, why, why? The moment he turns his back, she starts crying and praying." Please, God, bring him back to his senses! Make him see the light!" There is no more use imploring Boubi: after he scolded her angrily a few times and became extremely upset and uncommunicative, she doesn't dare bring up the subject again. Nobody does, and I have to be very careful when trying to dissuade him, lest I lose his trust that I'm the only one who can, and should, understand him.

*   *   *   *

Friends who hear about Boubi's bizarre intention, cannot believe their ears, or listen with unconcealed skepticism. Oh yes, he'll go back to Bulgaria, sure, sure!…Then, the knowing wink of the accomplice who is aware that these things shouldn't be discussed in public; that, if one has to protect someone left there, behind the Iron Curtain, it's always safer to pretend that one will return. Being in love is the most plausible supposition, and the most romantic: he can't live without "Her," they swore never to part, so he will not abandon her before she too can leave the country…Other possible explanations come to mind, some political, even conspiratorial ("Simeon Grouev is probably involved in some opposition group or plot against the regime"), some purely personal ("Many refugees cannot adapt themselves to the Western life, some even dislike it. Maybe Simeon is disappointed in America and disapproves of it?") Or, is he too proud to put him-self in full financial dependence of me, to accept the life of being just "Stephane's brother"? Other suppositions, or rather suspicions, reported to me, are clearly unattractive: "First of all, how did the Communists let him get out, and why? Why would they let the son of Groueff go visit his brother in America? Don't be naive! In 18 years, they can brainwash anyone. Simeon will return because he was sent here with some mission..." I was very hurt to hear the other day that one of the extreme-rightwing refugees in New York, Kalin K., had said that he expected Boubi to be used by the Sofia propaganda, when he returns, and to make anti-Western public statements and revelations.

But I must admit that most of these hypotheses could make sense. One of them must be the correct one, otherwise this whole talk about returning *voluntarily*, when he has it so good here, sounds absurd. I spent countless hours trying myself to guess which was the real, the truly compelling reason. I knew that he had no fiancée or great love left behind; he was not involved in any political action, let alone a conspiracy committed to forceful overthrow of the regime—he abhorred violence and terrorism; he certainly wasn't disappointed by what he saw in the West,—quite on the contrary, he became a true admirer of democratic societies, especially the American one." In the past I occasionally had moments when I wondered whether a free society was not just a utopia; now I *know* that it's possible, and I hope that we'll have it one day in our country too..." he told me. So, there was no question of disenchantment with the West. Nor did the financial considerations seem to be a decisive factor in his decision: my boss, Raymond Cartier, had offered Boubi to use him in some research work, at least in the beginning; on the other hand, the Bulgarian desks at *Radio Free Europe* or *BBC* would gladly hire a reliable non-Communist intellectual, just fresh out of Bulgaria. No, in Boubi's situation, it was difficult to figure out a logical reason for wanting to return.

Maybe I should say a "conventional" reason, or a credible one, the kind that motivates "normal" human actions. And one day, I saw the truth, I finally discovered that Boubi's reason was much simpler than any hypothesis that I had struggled with, and that's why, perhaps, it had been so hard to understand. Boubi, simply, was in love with Bulgaria! Emotionally, intellectually, almost mystically, in love. What psychiatrists call an "obsessive love." And can anyone reason with a person in love? I thought of Pirandello characters, who had left such an imprint on my early youth, I thought of the play I tried myself clumsily to write at age 19—who's "normal," what, after all, is "logical" and what is not?,—and Boubi's universe appeared less bizarre to me. When he was saying that he couldn't possibly live outside of Bulgaria, that he couldn't imagine life without Bulgaria, and all joys, rewards, and values he cares for— spiritually, esthetically, morally, even hedonistically,—made sense to him only in the framework of Bulgaria, it might sound corny and overly patriotic, but in his case it was absolutely true. Not without awe, I realized that I was in presence of a quasi-religious devotion, total and inflexible. There was no use fighting against it, it would be like trying to make a fish live outside water, though it may be contaminated water.

The next day, January 29, 1963, I drove Boubi to the airport, where he took the *PANAM* flight to Paris. Two days later, he wrote me from France: "*You and I, we met for a few months, and once again our destinies separate us. But I hope that now we know each other better. From now on, we'll resume writing letters, longer or shorter letters, according to the mood and the opportunities. But I don't want you to think that I don't understand how much you did for me.*" And to Mama he wrote: "*I was very happy that you understood me entirely and could accept our new separation. Naturally, it will be painful for you, as it is for me too, but it's better when there is a full understanding between us. Also, let's hope for a happier future! Now, that I'm far from New York, I begin to realize that I got used to that city and begin to appreciate it more deeply. It's always like that: we have to go away from something, in a way to lose it, in order to understand better its value.*"

He spent four weeks in Paris with Radka and little George, while waiting for an Italian visa. I wanted him to see Rome and Venice on his way back to Sofia, hoping, as the last resort, that the beauty of these cities would seduce him…It did, but not to the point of changing his plans. Rome, where our family's friends

Ivan Balabanov, Ivan, Marion, and Feo Stancioff received him warmly and showed him around, left him ecstatic. (*"My legs are exhausted from walking, but my soul is filled with the beauty and poetry of this city. It is indeed "the home of all Arts," Byron's words which I read on his monument at the Pincio..."*) He dropped the traditional coin in the Trevi fountain, in the hope of returning one day to the Eternal City, but all this admiration didn't make him cancel his ticket to Bulgaria. On February 27, leaving for Venice, a city which enchanted him no less, he wrote me his last letter before re-entering the world of darkness and censorship: *"It was a great joy for me to see you, to meet Lil, the children, and especially marvelous Paul. You and I had a few arguments and perhaps we still see some things differently, but this is entirely understandable. For 20 years we lived in completely different ways and under different circumstances. You had experiences, which I didn't share, and vice-versa. But I want to emphasize that for me you remain my brother, a good brother.*

"The thing I desire is the well-being of Bulgaria. I agree that there are many ways for attaining a goal. I believe that, under the present circumstances, the way I've chosen could turn out to be the most fruitful. But I repeat, this goes for me only, not for anyone else. It's always hard to open new ways. But there are times that call for new ways. I think we're living in such a time. The problems are not only Bulgarian, they are worldwide problems." Had he overestimated the significance of Khrushchev's sensational reforms, I asked myself while reading Boubi's letter, and was he gambling on the idea that Communism was about to collapse? Or did he hope that Bulgarian authorities would be moved by the nobility of his selfless act and would appreciate his patriotism? In both cases, that would be a huge, tragic misjudgment. *"If people always understood me correctly, I would have been very happy,"* he went on. *"But I have a big flaw: I cannot stand it when people don't trust me. If anyone really wants to know me, he should be aware of that; otherwise there will always be great misunderstandings."* And, quite in character, he replied to my suggestion to use some code words in our future correspondence: *"I don't think it would be correct to establish any cipher between us. I reject any conspiratorial ways of action and don't want to give cause for any suspicion."*

So, to the utter disbelief of everybody in Bulgaria, my brother returned. Voluntarily. Someone else had filled his place at the coffin-making shop in Cherepish monastery, and he had to look for work. After a couple of months of unemployment and short-lived miserable jobs in Sofia, Militiamen knocked one morning at the door of Radka's husband Sasso, where Boubi slept, and took him away. Thus, a long journey through stone-quarries, labor camps, forced residences, and hospitals began for him. A curtain of silence fell over him and hid him from us, the family abroad.

*   *   *   *   *

Chapter 28

Writing "Manhattan Project"

My desire to write books on my own came both from frustration with my job and fascination with a particular subject that I grew eager to explore. The frustration, which was gaining on me gradually, was due to the realization that, while my position as bureau-chief was quite enviable, I had reached a ceiling and things were going to stay the way they were. I was becoming more and more an administrator and less and less a reporter or writer, which was the thing I really liked. Directing and assigning most stories to others, rather than doing them myself, taking care of expense accounts, insurances and vacations, listening to complaints and small office rivalries, didn't interest me much, and I certainly had no taste for bossing anyone. I loved journalism, but apart from a few stars like Cartier, allowed to choose their subjects and write them as they liked it, a magazine is mostly an editor's medium; the reporter or correspondent simply provides the ingredients. In our case, it was Gaston or Therond who had the really creative role—deciding what went into the magazine and how it was edited and cut and balanced with the rest of the material. I suppose the same goes for newspapers too, and journalists have to resign themselves to see some stories unpublished, or mutilated, with the wrong emphasis or with the by-line omitted. But such is the newsman's mentality, which it takes one prominently published and signed article, and all unhappiness is forgotten. Until the next time...

So in such a period of professional frustration, I found myself intrigued by a subject which I felt would do a great book. During the ten years since I had first worked on articles related to nuclear energy and atom bombs—subjects then totally new to me, but which had aroused my curiosity enormously,—I could not understand why so little had been written and known about the fantastic obstacles surmounted during the construction of the first atomic bomb and about the Herculean endeavor it had required. There were books on the scientific side of the project, on the first splitting of the atom, the discoveries leading to the nuclear chain reaction and the design of the bomb, and one knew the names of the principal scientists involved. But twenty years after Hiroshima, very little, if anything, was known about the production of the bomb-ingredients and the actual building of the weapon, feats declared unfeasible by most experts of the time. The more I read, the more surprised I was that no book existed describing how exactly this had been done and who were the individuals who solved the supposedly unsolvable problems of this titanic enterprise. Secrecy was one explanation. But a few documents began to be de-classified, and some isolated descriptions were gradually appearing in carefully censored articles with reminiscences by former participants including the memoirs of General Leslie Groves, the wartime head of the super-secret project. This excited my curiosity, and smelling a good story, I started calling people and writing to the Atomic Energy Commission in Washington.

The replies were very cautious, but not negative. The AEC wanted to know more about me and my intentions. A long pause followed—I guessed they were investigating my background,—and then they answered some of my inquiries, but not all: my first request was for about 25 documents, and I only received four or five, the rest being still "Classified." But having learned names of companies that had participated in the project, such as Union Carbide, for instance, or Dupont, or Chrysler, I contacted their public relations offices and asked for the names and present addresses of their wartime executives, if they were still alive. When I started calling them on the telephone, their reaction was identical: at the mention of the Manhattan Project, they all—former company executives, engineers, Army officers,—would suddenly become silent and extremely cautious, if not outright suspicious. "Could you call again in a couple of days?" they would say. I knew exactly what happened each time: as soon as I hung up, they would call AEC and report that a man with a foreign accent and a name ending by—eff just called and was quite nosy about the wartime work on the Manhattan Project. The AEC office, which by then knew me, would reassure them. "He's OK," they'd answer, "You can talk to him. But, of course, you keep in mind that such-and-such part of your work (the material used for the diffusion "barrier," for example, or the pumps' design, or the shape of the filter, or whatever) is still strictly classified!" When I called back, the voice was usually friendlier, and in most cases they accepted to be interviewed.

After several interviews, my assessment of the magnitude of Manhattan Project was largely confirmed. In the opinion of most engineers, scientists and industrialists, the grandiose wartime undertaking represented the greatest single achievement of organized human effort in history, comparable to the building of the Pyramids and the China Great Wall. Though such superlatives are usually exaggerated, a further study of the Manhattan Project convinced me that the scope of the performance was indeed without precedent. As a journalist, I saw that the subject deserved much more than a series of articles. It was surprising to me that the Americans themselves were still unaware of the prodigious adventure into which their country's industrial power was launched, secretly and boldly, at a colossal cost and with an unprecedented effort, in order to produce the bomb. So I decided to write this book. Not so much about the scientific discoveries, relatively well known by then; and not about Hiroshima, nor the moral and strategic aspects of he atomic weapon. But about how the first bomb was built, by whom, and under what circumstances. It was going to be the story of the men who, in the summer of 1942, received the order to go ahead and build, with extreme urgency, the first nuclear weapon (they were convinced then that Nazi Germany was already ahead of them). The story of determined men who did not suspect the incredible difficulties of the task and who did not know how immensely different the problems of the laboratory would be from those related to the actual manufacturing of the bomb. Besides, I saw it as a superb illustration of the way the American system operated in the early 1940s, the manner in which America reacted to a concrete danger, to a precise task. The enormous majority of the people involved did not know what the final product of their effort would be. For them, there was a gigantic challenge to be met, an apparently impossible job to be done, and they carried it to an end splendidly.

This is the gist of what I wrote in an outline for potential book publishers, and in a letter to General Groves, by then retired in Washington DC. It was not without apprehension that I called him the following week: the formidable commanding officer of the Manhattan Project had the reputation of being a gruff man who distrusted civilians, suspected foreigners and disliked what he called "intellectuals," which included journalists. To say that he was charming the first time on the telephone would be an exaggeration, but he was cautiously polite and listened. He didn't say yes, but didn't say no either; he wanted to see me first and hear more about my project. So, on a hot August day of 1964 I took the train to Washington and at 11 AM I rang his doorbell in the big apartment building at 2101 Connecticut Avenue.

The soft-spoken, stout man with full graying hair and mustache who received me wore civilian clothes, but there was an unmistakably military air about him. The authority in his demeanor, the clarity and purposefulness of his statements, and his good, articulate English seemed to be typical of the West Point pre-war graduates. He was definitely a sober, patriotic, right-wing officer with a solid education.(I knew that he was the son of a regimental chaplain and had studied engineering at MIT.) As we talked for an hour, his bear-like attitude began to mellow, his original suspicion of the French journalist with the Bulgarian name gradually dissipated, and I felt that he liked the way I intended to present the Bomb-construction epic. When he agreed to be interviewed the following week, and gave me addresses of former assistants to contact, I knew that he would cooperate.

The cooperation turned out better than anything I had hoped for. Week after week I used to arrive at the Connecticut Avenue apartment and, my tape-recorder on the table, to listen to the most fascinating details of the grandiose undertaking. Our conversations spanned over a period of one year, and by the end of 1965 I had accumulated an impressive collection of taped interviews and notes. With time, the General became very friendly, and besides the invaluable information he entrusted to me,—some of it heretofore classified and most of it never published before,—he relaxed enough to discuss all sorts of general, political and philosophical subjects, even to give me personal opinion on colleagues or events.

Meanwhile, I proceeded with uncovering many surviving participants in the Project and asking them to describe the unclassified part of their wartime work. Each time I learned about an important meeting or a crucial decision, I asked for the date and applied to the AEC for the corresponding document. Much of the records were still secret and many requests were turned down, but quite a number of documents were declassified as a result of my application. A major problem with records was not only their secrecy, but the difficulty in locating them among millions of pages of papers, memos, letters and drawings. You couldn't simply apply for documents related to the atomic reactor built at the University of Chicago; you had to ask for precise letters from, say, Fermi to Compton, or for the minutes of a conference on that subject; but to do that, you had to know, of course, whether such letters and meetings existed, and what was their exact date. It was almost a detective's work, but it fascinated me, and each interview provided new leads.

Thus, I met some extraordinary characters and uncovered some unbelievable facts. To my delight as a writer, I realized how rich in anecdotes, in cases of ingenious improvisation, intuition, serendipity and shear luck the story of the bomb creation had been! I saw that my narrative was going to involve as many colorful episodes and human stories, as it did physics and engineering, if not more, and that encouraged me greatly. Who would've imagined, for instance, that the makers of the "Chicklets" chewing gum had contributed to the solution of a seemingly unsolvable technological problem that had eluded the world's top scientists? That a staffer from "House Beautiful" magazine had been used in solving another insurmountable obstacle of advanced physics? That at a crucial moment when an entire process of producing Uranium-235 was reaching an impasse, a miraculous solution was suggested by the fabrication of Bakelite, a most mundane plastic? These people didn't have a clue that they had, unwittingly and indirectly, helped in the building of the first atomic bomb. Some of them learned it for the first time *from me*, 20 years after WW2. One could imagine the faces of the "American Chickle" officials when I visited the chewing-gum factory in Long Island City and told them the story! Some of them remembered vaguely the irruption one day in 1943 of a group of Army men who, showing requisition orders signed by the highest authorities, took over one of their label-printing machines and brought in two civilians who, under the protection of armed MPs, proceeded mysteriously with some bizarre activities. After five months, a detachment of MP's swarmed over the place, cleaned and carefully removed every bit of evidence of the work, and the group left as abruptly as they had come, without any explanation. I also enjoyed meeting Leonard Shazkin, the former *House Beautiful* employee, now a successful publisher, and hearing the unlikely story of his accidental involvement, he, merely a printing expert, with physicists and chemists on a top-secret mission at the Columbia University. I was enormously thrilled when a Connecticut ex-decorator and house painter, Edward Norris, told me about his unexpected, but major, contribution to the Bomb. By the end of 1942, a crucial aspect of the Project, the so-called "Gaseous diffusion" process for obtaining fissionable Uranium, was in deep trouble: in spite of long, all-out, top-priority efforts, no satisfactory filter, or "barrier," could be developed for the diffusion of the extremely corrosive gas, and this failure was holding back the entire Project. Having tried all possible techniques, desperate scientists noticed a spray gun that Norris had built long ago for himself because he didn't think the sprayers on the market gave fine enough and even enough painting on the walls. A British scientist asked him whether he could produce a similar, but even finer mesh, and Norris came with a small sample, a half-inch- square with a half-million holes in it. Before he knew what was happening to him, he was dragged to Columbia University's lab of Dr. Dunning and Dr. Adler and commissioned to make a larger sample to their specifications. When he produced two better samples in his home workshop, Norris, who had no training in chemistry, was moved to Dr. Adler's laboratory, given several assistants and all the equipment he needed, and hired as Dr. Adler's collaborator. The "Norris-Adler barrier" which resulted from the collaboration of the house painter and the Columbia chemist was a major breakthrough in the Uranium-235 production.

My research lasted through 1964 and 1965 and involved several trips to Oak Ridge and Los Alamos, towns built from scratch and in total secrecy especially for Manhattan Project. I interviewed scores of people at the Universities of Chicago, Columbia, Princeton, MIT, Cornell and CalTech. I visited Dupont in Wilmington, Chrysler in Detroit, General Electric, Eastman Kodak, Westinghouse, Union Carbide and other companies; also the Argonne National Laboratory near Chicago and the Radiation Lab at Berkeley. I tracked retired executives and scientists to Florida, to Indiana, to Minneapolis, Santa Fe,

Charlotte, N.C. and Pennsylvania, and listened for hours to their reminiscences. Most of them were delighted to find an avid listener and eager to receive some overdue recognition. And in Washington I met several of Groves' Army officers. Before my research was over, I had had the rare opportunity of spending hours in tête-à-tête conversations with two former advisers of President Roosevelt (Alexander Sachs and Vannevar Bush), and several of the world's top nuclear scientists, luminaries of the stature of Hans Bethe, Harold Urey, Glenn Seaborg, Eugene Wigner, John Wheeler and Richard Feiman (all Nobel laureate at the time, or soon after), J. Robert Oppenheimer, Lew Kowarski, James Conant, George Kistiakowsky, John Dunning and many others.

Such an extensive research required, of course, much time and considerable expense. For the time, I had to thank *Paris-Match*: whether out of friendship, or because of the usual disorder reigning in the magazine, the editors tolerated my frequent absences. My direct boss, Cartier, was so fascinated with my subject, that he encouraged me strongly. Once he said: "You know, Stephane, I'm a little envious of you. I should've thought of writing it myself!" The money was another question, and as soon as my book idea had taken shape, I started looking for a sponsor and a publisher.

*　　　*　　　*　　　*

It is one thing to write a book, and it is quite another thing to find someone to publish it. In those days, because of my position at *Paris-Match* and active social life, I knew many people in the publishing world. But although I tried hard, this didn't seem to help me. "Too many books about the war, the public is getting tired," Bennett Cerf, the genial head of *Random House* whom I knew socially, told me. "You're a French journalist, why don't you write about General de Gaulle? That's a subject that interests everybody!" I failed to convince him that my book *was not* a war book. Then Mrs. Knopf, *grande dame* of publishing who had been my table companion at social dinners, received me graciously in her distinguished office. "I don't think now is the right time to write about atom bombs," she told me frankly. "The subject scares people." Other publishers were either hard to contact personally ("Do send an outline and resume to our office...") or had no interest in unsolicited proposals ("We found your idea very good, BUT unfortunately...") My file with "But..." answers was growing thicker. For a while, like all turned-down authors, my ego took refuge in the mythology of tales about bestsellers and masterpieces missed by stupid publishers, (wasn't Proust rejected with contempt by every French publisher, before a clever one recognized his talents?...) I was getting discouraged when luck presented itself under the familiar features of my close friend Dimi Panitza. In the fall of 1964, Dimi, on one of his regular visits to *Readers' Digest* home office, became enthusiastic about my idea, discussed it with the magazine's book section and arranged a meeting with its editors.

The *Digest's* offices in the impeccably manicured park in Chappaqua exuded so much wholesomeness, that they could had come out of a Norman Rockwell illustration: tidy and cheerful, populated by earnest editors in blazers and Brooks Brothers button-down shirts, smiling receptionists and efficient, neatly groomed secretaries. The fine furniture in the silent, carpeted offices, the vases with freshly cut flowers on the desks and, mainly, the French Impressionists's originals hanging on the walls, gave the place an air of dignity and unmistakable prosperity. What a difference, I thought, from the mess and racket in the shabby *Paris-Match* offices! One wouldn't imagine a more fitting nursery for the kind of uplifting stories *Readers' Digest* specialized in, where the laudable American virtues of diligence, resolve, ingenuity and devotion to duty always prevail, no matter what the obstacles...?

During lunch at the homelike guesthouse, I was asked to elaborate on my project, as the half-dozen polite gentlemen listened and asked questions. After the coffee, they withdrew in a corner for a brief huddle, and then the question I feared most, came bluntly: "And what are your qualifications to write this story, Mr.Groueff? You were not in this country, and obviously were too young at the time of the Project. What is your scientific background?" My heart sank, I felt that I had lost. "No formal studies in the sciences. No personal connection with Manhattan Project," I admitted sheepishly. New huddle. Then the Editor-in-Chief smiled at me: "You're the right person to do it," he said. "Scientists tend to be too technical; former participants may be biased. We want the story reconstructed by a layman, for laymen. A human tale, told in their language. Can you do it?"

The contract we signed was very generous and the *Digest* editors behaved as true gentlemen. They gave me an advance and for two years paid for my trips and expenses, without ever questioning a single bill. They assigned me a research assistant (Nina Georges-Picot first, then Shirley Tawse), and when I was ready, an editor, Bob Rigby. During all this period I profited from the advice of the *Digest Books*'s head, Maurice Ragsdale, a charming, shy man, who stammered with inarticulate speech, as he was brilliant as editor. *Readers' Digest* bought the rights to serialize my story, but not to publish it in book form. A new search began, which came to fruition in a most unlikely venue, the opposite of the industrious and sober setting of the virtuous Digest: a Manhattan nightclub. Lil, I and our friend Flo Smith were in a particularly happy mood after a dinner party, when we decided to stop at *Shepherd's* for a last drink. On the sidewalk if front of the club, we were greeted by a group of revelers who were just leaving the place and were boasting noisily about the good time they have had inside. "If it's so great, why are you leaving?" Flo teased them. One of them, a nice-looking blond guy in a slight and happy state of insobriety, took the challenge. "You're right! May I offer you a drink?" He joined us and we had great fun together. That was how I met Stanley Hart, a young Bostonian who turned out to be not only an amusing companion but also an editor at *Little, Brown* publishing house. Before the night was over, and with Flo praising my talents in her publicity-agent hype, Stanley heard all about my work and showed interest in my current writing. Flo and her husband, Ambassador Earl Smith, were among the few friends who knew about my A-bomb project: at a recent dinner at their apartment I had told them about it and Earl, a tough and difficult man, had shown unusual enthusiasm. The next day, Stanley came home to discuss the book. After several more meetings, he grew increasingly excited about the subject, calling me frequently and inquiring about the progress of my writing. The exuberance of his involvement was just what I needed to stimulate me in moments of doubt, and his enthusiasm must have gained his bosses in Boston. It took some time, but one-and-a-half year after meeting Stanley Hart at the disco, with my first draft almost done, *Little, Brown* signed the contract for the American edition and Stanley started his editing.

Parallel to the U.S. version, I was negotiating with several foreign publishers. By the time the manuscript was ready, I had signed contracts with *Collins* in England, *Hayakawa* in Japan, *Presses de la Cite in Fra*nce, *Mondadori* in Italy, and *Bertesman* in Germany.

*   *   *   *

As my research advanced, it became clear to me that the book's main character should be General Groves. Not only was he the leader whose dogged determination and bold, risky decisions led the uncertain enterprise to a successful completion, but he also was the single participant through whose personal experience I could describe all aspects of the Project—the scientific, the engineering and the administrative. Therefore, beside my extensive interviews with him, I looked for facts and opinions about him from every source I could reach. The some 100 participants I talked to, provided ample material about the General. Many admired him, some criticized him, and a few even ridiculed him. But they all agreed that he was indisputably the overall leader running the show, without whose drive and single-minded determination the bomb would not have been produced. My inquiry established clearly that since 1942, the men who had the supreme authority about the A-bomb—President Roosevelt, Vice-President Wallace, Secretary of War Stimson and Chief-of-Staff Gen. George Marshall,—had given Groves free hand with all decisions concerning its construction. Together with Dr. Vannevar Bush, FDR's chief liaison with scientists, and his deputy James Conant, they formed the so-called "Top Policy Group," responsible for all major decisions. In fact, this group never met, I was surprised to learn. The White House relied on a special four-member "Military Policy Committee" (Bush, Conant, Adm. Purnell and Gen. Styer), who only acted as Groves's supervisors. But what shocked me, was to discover FDR's rather casual interest and involvement in the progress of the work, and the absence of any sense of utmost urgency and absolute priority at the White House, which such a momentous undertaking would warrant.

"I don't know whether Roosevelt ever inquired about the progress, but Bush saw him from time to time and kept him posted," Groves told me when I asked whether he felt urgent pressure coming from the White House. "Bush also talked to Harry Hopkins at times, but he didn't know any of the details. No pressure came from the War Department either. They all knew it was a big job that would take time to do. Marshall had a natural disposition not to interfere with subordinates. The President, Stimson and Marshall didn't keep direct contact with me, they depended entirely on the Military Policy Committee."

"How often did you report to General Marshall?"

"The first time was when I took the report to the President from the Military Policy Committee, early in December 1942. The next report was in August of '43, and I didn't take that over."

"So no report for nine months, and Marshall didn't ask..."

"No. I may have taken an occasional memorandum over to him, where I wanted him to do something. All he knew was that I'd been assigned to it, and he assumed that I was doing my best. It was very convenient from my standpoint, and it worked very well, but if I hadn't succeeded, it would have been a terrible affair, and I don't think anyone in his position should have allowed me to go free-wheeling as it were. Now, I did see from time to time on different matters Harvey Bundy, Stimpson's assistant, and he no doubt told his boss. But after my August report, there were only two more written reports, that's all...At that time, the atomic bomb wasn't an element of the war strategy. Marshall's idea was that we would fight the war without it, and if it came, why, then we would be prepared to use it. The bomb may not work, one shouldn't count on it as a sure thing. I started seeing Stimson only in the fall of '44. Then by April '45 I saw him all the time."

"But for two years you wouldn't see either Stimson, or Marshall, or the President?"

"No, I only saw President Roosevelt once."

I found this hard to believe. "The public imagines that while America was preparing this new secret weapon with which to finish the war, the men in charge—Roosevelt, Stimson, Marshall—lived in an almost unbearable suspense, waiting impatiently, constantly asking "is it ready or not?" eager, pressing...and you're telling me that for two years they didn't inquire and you didn't report, day by day!"

"Remember that Bush was talking to the President from time to time and undoubtedly each time he told him about this. But he didn't go to see him for this particularly."

I talked to Bush. He told me that regular White House conferences on the progress of the bomb never existed. In fact, there had never been *any* conference at Roosevelt's or Stimson's level, devoted specifically to the bomb's construction! Bush briefed the President from time to time, in a very general way, personally in private meetings at the White House, which lasted about 15 minutes and covered several topics, of which the A-bomb was not necessarily the first nor the most urgent. Important people were constantly competing for FDR's time and attention, and while Bush eagerly counted on each one of his precious 15 minutes, the President sometimes wasted time in passionate dissertation on some completely different problem. Once Bush had to listen in deep frustration to a long tirade against General de Gaulle. Another time Mrs. Roosevelt entered unexpectedly, greeted the visitor with a friendly "Hi, Van!" gave a kiss to the President and asked to join them. The scientific briefing continued, with Eleanor interrupting from time to time to ask a question, with FDR patiently and lovingly trying to explain. Usually, Bush would bring a summary of the major problems requiring immediate action, with proposals of the course to be taken. Very often, but not always, Manhattan Project's current problems would figure on this memo. The President would glance at it, sometimes asking a few questions, sometimes not, then would scribble his "O.K.—F.D.R." on the paper. Were there occasions when Roosevelt would disagree or question the suggestions?, I asked Bush. "No, never."

How far this was from our stereotype ideas about History-making!, I couldn't help thinking. The successful building of the bomb was less due to the official decision-makers, than to the real "doers," Groves and his men. I realized also that the General was never *given* the extraordinary powers he used; he simply *took* them. Each time precise instructions were missing, he didn't ask, he acted.

*   *   *   *

I was intrigued by Groves's personality, the private man behind the leader. His wife was, of course, the obvious best source. After several visits to their apartment, I felt that Grace Groves, a pleasant, well-educated lady from a distinguished Southern family (her father used to command the regiment whose chaplain was Leslie Groves' father), was favorably disposed to me. With the General's approval, I interviewed her once when he wasn't home. Mrs. Groves, who played the piano, spoke Spanish and German and enjoyed literature, joked about her husband's lack of interest in the arts. Did he read novels, poetry?—No, only history, biographies, she said. I had noticed that he knew the Civil War and WW1 well, and had read a lot about Napoleon. "Napoleon is his hobby, if he has one. You'll see his pictures all over this apartment. He loves Napoleon. We go to Paris and we spend our time in the Invalides, we walk up and down this gloomy place by the hour—he loves it. But the arts…no! He doesn't like theater, he can't bear movies. It just doesn't mean anything to him. Television?—He'd look at sports, that's all. He was a good tennis player. He adores football, he goes to every Army football game." And what Americans he admired most?—"Gen. MacArthur, for sure. Not Eisenhower. And certainly not Roosevelt. He has a kind of affinity for Truman—he has his faults, as we all know, but he's a real American, he's more understandable to us than a person like Kennedy or Roosevelt, for whom we have no respect whatsoever." Groves, of course, had no use for left-wingers, Socialists, or wishy-washy people. "He's what you might call patriotic to the very bottom," his wife said. "He really feels very strongly about what he considers to be the American way, which some people are out to destroy today, and very proud of being an American." I said that he gave me the impression of a man who never doubted anything, and she readily agreed. "Never! To him, there is just black and white, and nothing in between. He has this solidity, he never worries. He does what he thinks is right, and that's it. I've never seen him doubting, or hesitant, or missing sleep because of worries. I've never seen anyone like him!"

I felt that she trusted me and didn't mind discussing her husband. She was amused when I told her how disappointed I was as a writer when I asked the General to describe what I had imagined was "unbearable tension" the night of the bomb's first test in Alamogordo; he just slept, he said! Men like Fermi and Oppenheimer were on the verge of nervous breakdown that night, not knowing whether the bomb would destroy the entire state of New Mexico, or be a miserable dud, or cause an unstoppable worldwide chain reaction, and Groves just slept! He didn't even understand my astonishment. "What's so strange about it?" he said. "We were all exhausted after several sleepless nights, the test had to be delayed with a few hours because of a storm, and there was a cot in the tent; what's more natural than to go to sleep for a while?" Mrs. Groves laughed, that was her Leslie all right! (Or *Deeno*, as she called him.) "He can lie down, close his eyes and he's asleep, anywhere," she said. "It's very comforting to live with someone so steady, so decisive, the Rock of Gibraltar. I've always envied him tremendously. Oh, don't think I don't get awfully mad at him sometimes! But I still admire him very much." She was aware of his reputation of being gruff, and ruthless, and tactless. But he had mellowed, she said, now he was gentle and polite. "That's age!..I was used to have him much tougher. When he was young, he was very tactless, you might say, not endearing to most people. Whatever his mission was, he went after it and didn't care whom he had to step on to get there, and he was unquestionably not always considerate of people's feelings. He didn't care whether he was liked or not. And, of course, the scientists detested him because he didn't consider their feelings or opinions. He was just driving toward his objective and they had to put up with him. They thought he was a blustering soldier with no appreciation of their intellectual superiority."

I had already noticed that even in esoteric discussions with specialists, General Groves, a man with a solid engineering and mathematical background but certainly not a Ph.D., had never felt the least intimidated by scientists. The story his assistant, Col. Marshall, told me about their first visit to Rochester, where they used all their gifts of persuasion to enlist *Eastman Kodak* without however revealing the real purpose of the secret project, was typical. After the lengthy presentation, the two officers withdraw to an adjoining room to wait for the Board's decision. "How do you think I did?" Groves asked.

Marshall hesitated, then said: "It wasn't bad, General. But how did you manage to mispronounce, time after time, the same word—the key word! For heaven's sake it's "*isotope*," not "*isotrope*"! Dr. Mees, the director of research, squirmed each time you said "*isotrope*." I don't think your scientific explanations convinced him..." The Board however finished by accepting the ungrateful assignment. As they left the building, Groves was beaming. "How did you say it again," he asked Marshall mischievously. "It's not isotrope, but isotope, eh?"

I thought of another case, this time at the Chicago lab, at a briefing by a most impressive group of scientists, including Wigner, Szilard, and three Nobel Laureates—Fermi, Compton, and Franck. Noticing a mathematical error in one equation, Groves didn't hesitate to signal it and the scientist at the blackboard agreed and corrected it. Before leaving, immune of any inferiority complex, he bluntly told the illustrious company: "There is one thing I want to emphasize. You may know that I don't have a Ph.D. But let me tell you that I had ten years of formal education after I entered college. Ten years in which I just studied. I didn't have to make a living or give time to teaching, like most of you. I just studied. That would be the equivalent of two Ph.D.'s, wouldn't it?" There was an embarrassed silence. Groves had hardly left the room, when Leo Szilard, the Hungarian genius, erupted: "You see what I meant about that General!" he told his colleagues. "How can one work with people like that?" Szilard, whom most people recognize as *the* father of the A-bomb original idea, was the *bete noire* of Groves, who couldn't bear his erratic behavior of totally undisciplined and physically sloppy civilian. "A pushy, self-promoting troublemaker," he told me. "I wanted to get rid of him since the beginning."

"And yet I found that most of the great scientists worked very well with him," I said that day to Mrs. Groves. "Yesterday we talked about Oppenheimer for one hour, and although the General admitted that 'There are no two men so different and opposite as Oppenheimer and myself', he said that they got along beautifully."

"I knew Oppenheimer. After the bomb. A wonderful, a truly great man. You can't help being impressed. He has all this love of the beautiful, and this sensitiveness of an artist as well as a genius. He's very likable humanly, has a great deal of charm, I would say..."

"So how do you explain that the two men liked each other—the tough soldier who sees everything in black-and-white and doesn't care for poetry or music, and the artistic, hypersensitive intellectual?"

"It's simple: each one appreciated the integrity and the talent of the other. Remember the investigation, a few years ago? "

"Yes, the General took his defense. When they asked him: 'Do you think that Oppenheimer would be a risk, could be disloyal?', the General said: 'Definitely not! He's a loyal man.' Yesterday he was telling me that Oppenheimer made bad mistakes, like trying to protect his brother, but said that was understandable...I was somewhat surprised: I thought the General would be uncompromising...but actually he was the one who cleared Oppenheimer with the FBI, in the beginning."

"Yes, he did. He thought Oppenheimer was so valuable to them that it was worth taking a calculated risk. And it turned to be the right judgment. The General always knew what he was after and he kept his eye on the ball. He doesn't understand people who don't hold to the target. He doesn't understand weaknesses, insecurities and doubts. I know what Dr. Oppenheimer's like, I can guess his personal troubles, and his weaknesses. But the General wouldn't understand him in a thousand years. He doesn't understand nerves either, he thinks that's foolishness. He looks upon psychoanalysis, for instance, as a big piece of foolishness, he can't see why anybody would need that. He thinks it's just ridiculous. I don't mean that he's unsympathetic or anything like that, but he doesn't really understand. You have to experience things to understand them, and he hasn't..."

I must say that after spending so much time with Groves, I too ended by envying his incredible, almost shocking, lack of doubts and understanding of moral conflicts. Sometimes it was so disconcerting to me, that I was leaving his home furious with myself for not having found some better arguments and examples to shake his imperturbable certitude about Right and Wrong. I had never met another person to whom life seemed to be so uncomplicated, and ethical problems so simple to resolve. Usually, that's a blessing granted only to intellectually limited people, but the General was a highly intelligent man. The over-simplicity of his credo was striking, and it explained all his actions, his remarkable achievements as well as his most controversial and bitterly criticized decisions. Why did he often demand the impossible and pushed his men to the extreme, with no consideration for their feelings?—The answer was obvious: his orders were to build the bomb in the shortest possible time, and this had absolute priority. Why would he dismiss loyal, friendly collaborators and replace them with people he sometimes despised humanly?—Very simple: the job required the most efficient person available. Haven't some decisions been agonizingly hard to make ?—Not really, he said, when you keep in mind what your responsibilities are ; you just ask yourself which course of action advances the Project and which could delay it, and you discard the latter. "There is nothing that complicated about making decisions when you know exactly what your mission is," Groves assured me. With personal conflicts, or even rare moments of doubt, being unknown, I saw very soon that my interviews weren't leading to the kind of Shakespearean scenes of soul-searching that I, the writer, had anticipated. On the contrary: "Duties are perfectly clear, they are even spelled out in writing," the General insisted. "The U.S. Army regulations; the Constitution; the allegiance to the President, my Commander-in-Chief, to the country and the flag; the specific orders from my superiors. You stick to them, and you'll never be in trouble." "But, Sir," I protested, "Life is so complicated that anybody can be in trouble." Groves disagreed. "What's so complicated, if you follow the rules? Yes, there are accidents, and illness, and loss of a beloved person. But except for such tragedies, which are beyond our power, we deserve most of what happens to us. People don't respect the rules, and then they complain about the consequences."

"But, General, one can have bad luck, even the best get hurt. Look how much Oppenheimer suffered !"

"It all has some reason. Read the Ten Commandments, it's all spelt out there. You violate them, and you're in trouble. 'Thou shall not lie', it's said. But Oppenheimer did lie."

"His private life seems to be too complex, not very happy, so maybe…" I tried to find some justification. But Groves didn't buy that. "To begin with, what business did he have, a married man, meeting secretly that lady? (He was referring to the clandestine trip from Los Alamos to San Francisco where Oppenheimer spent the night with Jean Tatlock, a Communist and former girlfriend; security agents had followed him and reported his grave violation of the strict orders.) He broke a God's commandment, and also the Lab's regulations for which he was responsible as Director: the interdiction of leaving the super-secret Los Alamos site during those critical months."

What could I answer? How could I argue with a man who was almost apologetic when admitting that, while anxiously waiting for the Hiroshima news in his stifling Washington office on an unbearably torrid August day, he allowed himself to unbutton his uniform's collar, a violation of the Army's dressing code? A man, who resented my quoting him as saying on an occasion "I didn't give a *damn*." "I never use profanity," he corrected me. "I might have said '*darn*,' but I certainly didn't swear…" A man speaking in the same breath and in the same no-nonsense tone about Uranium isotopes and the Ten Commandments!…I hadn't met many people like him, but I understood better why he had succeeded in his impossible mission.

*　　　　*　　　　*　　　　*

It was ironic that Oppenheimer agreed to receive me only because General Groves had recommended me to him. Nothing else had worked. For two years I had tried in vain to have an inter-view with the famous physicist. Countless times I had called and written to his office at Princeton's Institute for Advanced Studies where he had succeeded Einstein as director. Many of his colleagues interviewed by me tried to arrange a meeting for me. "You cannot, of course, write about Manhattan Project without talking to Oppie," they all said. But the months passed by, I had already met most of the surviving leaders of the Project, and I still had no word from the Los Alamos former director. I had used the prestige of *Readers' Digest* and, playing on Oppenheimer's alleged Francophilia, my affiliation with *Paris-Match*; all to no avail. I was against a wall of protective secretaries who answered invariably; "Dr. Oppenheimer is not available. We cannot take any appointments at this time." "He won't see any journalist," people close to the reclusive scientist told me. "He's been hurt deeply and is a bitter man now. After what had been done to him, he hates the press. Moreover, he's not well, and he doesn't want to talk to anyone." By June 1965, I had almost resigned myself to not seeing him, when Oppenheimer's name came up again during one of my interviews with Groves. Although they were such opposites, the General held in high respect the scientist, to whom he had personally given a security clearance, in spite of the opposition of the FBI and Manhattan Projects security services, headed by Col. Lansdale. "With his background, and if we had observed all of the formalities of clearance, he'd now be still waiting…So, I merely wrote an order to our security people saying that Dr. Oppenheimer was cleared. He could not have been cleared in any possible way except by some such drastic action; you couldn't justify the clearance."

"In his case, it must have been a very difficult decision for you?"

"No. No decision is difficult, if you only make it."

"Why did you trust him?"

"In the first place, at that time he knew so much already that if he had felt that he had been unfairly treated, he could easily have become a menace. Then I would have become afraid. He knew so much I didn't want him out there, he could have easily, in casual conversation with fellow scientists given away so much information, particularly if he had animosity toward us. If he didn't have animosity, then no, he wouldn't. There was no reason to suspect him. The thing that is not realized today is that during the Depression years and during the Spanish war, all the liberals in this country and almost everybody excepting a hard core—5 or 10 percent, were in favor of the Spanish Communists. They saw nothing wrong with Communism, they approved of the recognition of Russia by Roosevelt, and they had no fears of Communism. One of the things people held against Oppenheimer was he had contributed a considerable sum, I think $500, toward ambulances for the Spanish Communist side. At that time, everybody was applauding that thing, excepting a small hard core like myself. Eleanor Roosevelt was out preaching that doctrine, and New York Times, and everybody of that kind. I said later at the loyalty investigation: "You should take the editorials of the Times of that era and say 'Why should Oppenheimer have been on this side when the *N.Y. Times* was so heavily down on that side? And Mrs. Roosevelt…How could you expect a young man to know more than all these very wise people?' Oppenheimer was politically very naive. He didn't know anything about such things His wife has had this terrible experience and

Communists had befriended her afterwards. His sister-in-law was an ardent Communist; his brother was a Party-member, which was not known at the time. And himself attended a number of meetings; he had associated with people that were wrapped up in it, but so had everybody else in the academic world. But I don't think he was a card-carrying member himself."

"Col. Landsdale was horrified at my clearing him. Well, he wasn't against that so much, it was later, when Oppenheimer reported to me about this Chevalier incident, and then Lansdale was horrified. But he eventually came to the opinion that I was right on Oppenheimer, that Oppenheimer was not a security risk. A calculated risk, maybe, but you risked it on everybody. You can't be 100 percent sure. And of course you have to watch out for blackmail; blackmail was one thing I was afraid about Oppenheimer.. Another thing is, and Ernest Lawrence made quite a point of it, he said that the average Jew had no moral principles on a lot of scores, particularly with respect to sex life. He said, 'You can't trust them. You take somebody that you think has been happily married for thirty years and you find him in bed with his stenographer.' That was a shock to me, but I learned to agree that that was so. You're not Jewish, are you?—I didn't think so, but I've told them the same thing: the trouble essentially is, in my opinion, that the Jew who gives up his father's religion doesn't have anything to cling to. He gave it up because he's a little bit ashamed of it, and that isn't a good thing...Now at Los Alamos, when we were getting sort of an affidavit that the man would observe the security rules, Oppenheimer suggested that in addition to having "so help me God!" and so on in there, that we have something like "on my honor as a scientist..."

"In Oppenheimer's case, were his moral values in doubt?"

"No, what was in doubt about him essentially was that his record was such that you couldn't say that he hadn't had Communist contacts, and he'd been so close to them and had reasons to be grateful to them through his life, that you couldn't tell whether maybe there's a setup there. You know that Communists used to make a practice of taking Communist girls and getting them to select certain young men and go out deliberately to entrap them..."

When telling me why he defended Oppenheimer at the hearings after the war, Groves expressed some understanding of his "foolishness" not to tell the entire truth in the famous "Chevalier case." "Oppie' had confided to him that Soviet agents had tried, unsuccessfully, to approach him through his friend Chevalier. "What he didn't tell me was that Chevalier had gone to his brother, Frank, and Frank had talked to him. That he left out, and in that sense he lied; he wanted to protect his brother…But outside of that, Oppenheimer's conduct was above reproach. He went beyond the call of duty when he told me that, considering it was his own brother. I always felt that the AEC made a horrible mistake when they carried on this (canceling his security clearance). That was really a vendetta against him."

"Was he friendly to you?"

"Oh, yes, always! Some people told me, 'Oh, you oughtn't to trust Oppenheimer. He says the most horrible things about you behind your back', and I said to them, 'Well, I was brought up in the Army and all my life I've heard criticism of the commanding officer. I've never known any who was any good. I'm not surprised that they say things about me which I'd rather not hear.' 'But you don't realize how bad it is!' And I said, "Well, it's nothing compared to what I used to say about commanding officers'. It didn't bother me at all."

Continuing our conversation, Groves asked me what Oppenheimer had told me about such and such case. He was very surprised to hear that I had not met him. "But you *must* talk to him! He's too important for your book." "I agree, General, and I've made a special effort to see him, but…"

"Hmm…" was all Groves said and we switched to another subject. The same night I took the train back to New York, and the next morning I was surprised by a most pleasant telephone call. "This is Dr. Oppenheimer's office," the voice said. "We understand that you would like an appointment with the Director. Would tomorrow, the 24th, be convenient for you? Yes? Then we'll expect you at 2:30 here, at the Institute."

I was well prepared for the interview—by now I knew in detail Oppenheimer's biography, had read the full transcript of the public hearings on his security clearance, had discussed his personality and work with dozens of his collaborators,—and yet I was quite nervous when I found myself face to face with him. After all, "Oppie" was the most controversial figure in the whole

Project, and also the most fascinating and enigmatic. People either venerated him (to his adoring assistants and students, especially the ladies, he was a cult), or condemned him vehemently. I'd never talked to anyone neutral about him: he was either "a genius" or "an arrogant, disloyal egocentric." The frail, gray-haired man who greeted me that afternoon in his office was very tense, as if he was making efforts to control some permanent fire burning inside him. He was unusually emaciated and this reminded me of the rumors that he was critically ill with cancer. But on the other hand, I knew that he had been extremely thin even when he was a young man. I remembered the first impression of the wife of Col. K. Nichols, Groves' second-in-command, when she first saw Oppenheimer, some 23 years earlier (she was, of cause, totally enchanted by him, as all women): "The first time my husband brought him home for dinner," she told me, "he called to warn me, which he had never done before. 'I'm bringing a scientist home and I just want to warn you: if he looks sick to you, please say nothing, pretend you don't notice anything.' And indeed, the man looked unusually frail, he gave me the impression of someone being loosely put together, who may fall to pieces any moment. But one immediately noticed an extraordinary mind and an unusual sensitivity. You know that you're in presence of a great man..."

I too was impressed. His voice was soft and his manners polite, but his penetrating, astonishingly blue eyes and his face, vibrating with sensitivity, were intimidating. He spoke slowly, choosing his words carefully. Between sentences, his hands played with his pipe or he paused to walk to the window of his ground-floor office and look outside at the park. He told me right away that he was receiving me at the request of Groves, because he had great respect for the General and his judgment; but it should be clear that no personal questions would be asked and that certain aspects of the building of the A-bomb were still classified. This he said with the severity and finality of someone who wouldn't stand for any journalistic nonsense. I felt the same authority when I took out my tape-recorder and he demanded to turn it off until I first answer his questions: what exactly I wanted to ask him, how much I knew about Manhattan Project, whom I have already talked to, what were the basic ideas I wanted to develop in my book. I talked for a long time, feeling a little like a student at an exam, while he listened without interrupting me, with no indication of approval or disapproval. Each time there was a silence, he would prod me softly: "Go on, go on!" and I would continue. When I finished, he walked again to the window, and after a long moment of reflection, pointed to my recorder, with a pale smile: "Now you can turn it on!" Obviously, I had passed the exam.

"Tell me, Dr. Oppenheimer, when exactly, and how, did you first learn about the secret project to build an A-Bomb?" I started my interview. Many other questions followed, questions about concrete details, descriptions of scenes and conversations, personal impressions of colleagues and events. He was answering readily and, of course, very intelligently, and I was learning many things I needed to find out. But from time to time, some unwelcome question would make the polite, cooperative physicist brusquely interrupt his fascinating tale, and the steel would appear behind the false fragility of his delicate frame. Thus, when he was telling an episode involving "a British scientist" and I asked whether he meant somebody called Oliphant, Oppenheimer gave me an icy look and snapped at me: "I will not provide the name. I said 'British scientist' and that should be enough!" After that, I became more careful with my questions. Minutes later, after relating some details about his early involvement with the Project, he became somber and cut himself short: "That's well recorded. I don't need to repeat myself!" And that's was that. But generally he was very cooperative, although he never relaxed, keeping the strictly official tone of the interview, as if afraid that I might get too personal. I left feeling great respect and not much warmth. He agreed to see me again before I complete my work, but his health deteriorated in the following months, and he died in February 1967.

*   *   *   *

By then the book was being printed. Meanwhile, I had to deal with another problem whose seriousness I had never suspected: the security clearance of the book. The people I had interviewed had all observed the strict interdiction to discuss any classified matters. But 25 years after the war, few of the retired executives, engineers and scientists knew exactly what was still kept secret, and what had been gradually declassified in the meantime. Moreover, considering the unusual length of my interviews, there was always the possibility of inadvertent slips of the tongue, or of saying more than one should.

I had sent pages of the draft to AEC, purely for checking the factual and technical accuracy; with the same purpose, I had submitted other pages to General Groves, mostly paragraphs with quotes from him. It was clearly understood that I didn't ask, neither would accept, any suggestions for editorial changes. But I had a real shock when, not long before going to print, an official looking envelope arrived from the AEC in Washington, containing a thin brochure entitled *U.S. Atomic Energy Act*. The accompanying short letter was simply but sternly advising me to read the Act's provisions very carefully. Reading a few paragraph almost made my hair stand on end. "Is punishable by prison for life…or for 20 years, or 10 years, and so on…" article after article warned, whoever divulges, transmits, propagates, even keeps in his possession, documents containing classified material concerning nuclear weapons…"Is punishable by death whoever…" *Death?!* Realizing that it was no joking matter, I rushed to the telephone and called my AEC contact, Chief Historian Richard Hewlett. Assuring him that I was perfectly willing to cooperate, we agreed that I would mail him the full text of manuscript and AEC would invite me a few weeks later to Washington to discuss it.

The security clearance meeting took place in June 1966 at the AEC building on H Street and lasted for nearly six hours. When I took place at the conference table, I saw that each of the three men facing me had in front of him a copy of my typewritten manuscript, with copious notes scribbled in ink on the margins of its several hundred pages. One of the men was from FBI and this worried me: frankly, many descriptions of the bomb and of industrial processes read like spy reports and I had been nervous even when I wrote them. I had described, for instance, the components of the first tested bomb, its detonation mechanism and its assembly, in such detail, that these paragraphs. I had described secret installations that no outsider had been allowed to see before. So, when the FBI man began his review, I expected most serious problems.

I had a surprise. Or, rather, two surprises. Almost all parts that I had considered extremely sensitive passed without any objection. On the contrary, paragraphs and sentences which sounded totally innocent, brought a most categorical opposition: the mention, for example, in the biography of a certain scientist, of the subject of his Ph.D. thesis; the *color* of a gadget, whose shape, chemical composition and exact measurement I was free to describe; the fact that shortly before a certain breakthrough, Dr. X had lunched with Y and Z, and even that he knew them. I never understood to this day why such innocuous bits of information would be a top secret, and when I asked, the answer was that the reason itself was part of the secret. But the AEC people were firm about it: I can keep these passages at my own risk only! They were extremely polite, they didn't threaten me, they didn't *forbid* anything; they only asked for my cooperation. I readily complied wherever the suggested corrections or changes didn't affect my narrative. But a few pages required serious changes. Those I re-wrote and re-submitted for their clearance; some paragraphs shuttled a few times between AEC and me, until we found acceptable compromises. On the whole, they were satisfactory and I had no complaint. I only was sad to forsake three or four very colorful episodes, which I felt would be excellent for my book. But when I realized that they touched on some of the last top secrets kept jealously not only from the Soviet Union, but also from the Allies, I didn't insist and voluntarily, if regretfully, dropped them. In order to protect myself from the draconian Atomic Energy Act, I went through my voluminous archives, collected all tapes and notes containing references to what I was told was still classified, and deposited them to AEC.

*   *   *   *

By February 1967, the book was printed and rough copies were sent to the critics. The first reviews began to appear in March and April, and they were extremely gratifying. "This is *must* reading for anyone who wants to know how the bomb was developed. Scientific background is not necessary to understand this engrossing story," General Groves was quoted in print, and then he joined me in a few interviews on radio programs. The officially launching took place at a cocktail party Lil and I gave in our apartment, to which we invited several of the people described in the book. As many of them had not seen each other since the days of the Manhattan Project, the event turned into quite a warm interesting reunion.

"General Groves was one of the most ebullient guests," the N.Y. Times reported the next day, April 2, 1967. *"His gray-blue eyes lit up as he was warmly greeted by Percival Dobie Keith, a Texas engineer who headed Kellex, the firm developed the key gaseous diffusion method to separate the light Uranium... Lanky industrial executives, bespectacled engineers and stocky technicians formed small clusters in the French period living room, while elegant society figures and famous authors and publishers milled around them, praising Mr.Groueff... 'I'm very glad somebody has come along with a broader account of the vast joint effort that developed the bomb', Groves said. "It was not only the academic scientists that should receive the praise, but also the inventiveness of the engineers, the technicians, and American management and Government that built the gigantic plants which produced the fissionable materials."*

A few days later, our friend Anne Ford kindly gave a party in my honor, which was marked by a rather comical near-accident, described the next day by social columnist Suzy Knickerbocker: *"General Leslie Groves, the man who for three years directed the titanic efforts to produce the atom bomb, almost went up in smoke in Anne Ford's exquisite French drawing room. The general, in the middle of a big cocktail party, leaned against a lighted candle and before he realized what was burning was himself, there was a big hole in his jacket down to the lining. He was a good sport about it. When you've lived with mushroom clouds, it takes more than a little old candle to make you blow your cool. Anne's party was in honor of Stephane Groueff and his new book, "Manhattan Project: The Untold Story of the making of the Atomic Bomb," a remarkable writing achievement which will become a part of history, enthralling, intensely readable history."*

Groves enjoyed the recognition he was receiving in the torrent of press reviews following the book's publication, and his brief involvement in New York's social life seemed to amuse him. "I never expected that building the bomb would bring me to mix with so many celebrities," he chuckled when shown the social columns. Indeed, Suzy, Eugenia Sheppard, and other columnists had reported the attendance of such social and media personalities as the Mike Cowles (*Look Magazine* owner), the Andrew Heiskells (*Time-Life* chairman), Margaret Truman and husband, Jean Kennedy and husband, Raymond and Rosie Cartier, the Jack Howards (*Scripps-Howard* Publishing), Mrs. Henry Fonda, Lady Sara Churchill,

Charlotte Ford Niarchos, Dolly Goulandris, Iva Patcevitch (*Conde-Nast* chairman), Jack Heinz II, and many other well known society figures.

The reviews made me happy. There were a few critical notes, but most of the reviews praised the book highly. My greatest satisfaction came from the reaction of the specialists and the veterans of the Manhattan Project, many of whom wrote me congratulatory letters. In a long review, *The Bulletin of Atomic Scientists* wrote: *"No one has until now turned the spotlight so fully on the vast, complex engineering and industrial side of the Manhattan Project..."* Dr. Vannevar Bush, President Roosevelt's chief adviser on the Atom bomb, said: *"Mr. Groueff has produced a volume that fascinated me. A swell book,"* and sent me kind personal letter. And years later, when *The New Yorker"* published an extensive profile of Nobel Prize laureate Hans Bethe, it quoted the great physicist as saying: *"One of the most vivid accounts of the making of the American atomic bomb appears in "Manhattan Project," a book by the journalist Stephane Groueff. Toward the middle of it, there is a remarkable passage,"* and Bethe recites three entire paragraphs in which I describe his tempestuous but mutually admiring relationship with impertinent young genius Richard Feinman. And to an interviewer for the *American Institute of Physics*, Bethe repeated his flattering words: *"For the Los Alamos atmosphere, I want to recommend to you the book by Groueff...It's extremely accurate. He captured it. He talked to 200 people, I think, and absolutely everybody who had been in the Manhattan Project and whom I have talked to, agrees that his part of the Project was pictured just incredibly accurately. The whole thing comes off very beautifully. It is very well written, and the characterization of General Groves is just marvelous."*

Not bad for the total layman I was! Not only did my vanity have a field day, but the success gave me the self-assurance that, with sufficient stimulation, time and means, I was able to handle the popularization of most complex subjects, far beyond anything that my education or experience had prepared me for. This didn't remain unnoticed by Raymond Cartier and the managements of *Paris-Match* and *Larousse*, the great French publishers, opening almost unlimited professional perspectives before me. But I'll come to this new exciting career later in these memoirs.

*   *   *   *   *

Chapter 29

My first Larousse book, "La Mer". Visit to the South Pole

Water, nothing but water, as far as the eye can reach. We have left Fiji five days ago, and the scenery has not changed: from starboard and from port, before the bow and behind the stern, we see nothing but the choppy surface of the ocean and the gray sky above it. Tomorrow, it will be the same, and the day-after-tomorrow too. We are sailing aboard the *Argo*, the research vessel presently on the scientific expedition *Nova*, which I joined in the South Pacific. During my insomnia hours, I'm glad to spend long moments in the oceanographers' cabin and muse upon the mysteries of the sea with Robert Fisher and Victor Vacquier, two American Ph.D.'s among the legion of scientists around the world who try to understand the ocean. The winds are strong, the sea is rough, and most of the time I find myself in this state of drowsiness, which usually precedes seasickness. But I haven't so far embarrassed myself by throwing up or spending the day lying in my berth. The latter, in fact, would not be much better than being sea-sick: the cabin (if I can call so the stifling, windowless cubicle I share with two sailors) would be a refuge of questionable merits, with its steel walls amplifying the constant clatter and banging, the hum of the engines next door, and its narrow bunks offering little relief from the nonstop seesaw of the raging waves. There is no question of going out to breathe some fresh air: huge columns of water batter the deck, making walking on it extremely hazardous. Reading doesn't come easily either. I just finished young Jacques Piccard's account of his historic descent in the bathyscaphe *Trieste* to the bottom of the Mariannas' Trench, 11,000 meters below the surface, the deepest point on the planet. Fascinating, especially since we are headed for the second-deepest submarine canyon, the Tonga Trench. The ship's library contains plenty of books and articles on oceanography, my new field of interest, but I have difficulties concentrating. Fisher and Vacquier reassure me: it's a problem for all oceanographers, they say; drowsiness is not conducive to intellectual effort, and it's a pity, because one has so much free time during the interminable days of bad weather.

Sleep doesn't come easily. In addition to the noise and the ship's rolling, a naked bulb in front of the door is glaring straight in my eyes. It's lit permanently, since the corridor leads to the lavatory, or "head," as they call it, a facility which the crew visit all night long with extraordinary frequency, as I had the bad fortune to discover. We can't close the door without suffocating, so I ended by improvising a sort of a curtain with the straw mat I had just bought in Suva at the foot of my bunk, in order to block the light. And just as I fall asleep, someone would come to wake up one of my roommates for watch duties. Then again I'd twist and turn and sweat in my bed. This is my second cruise in the last three months, quite a lot of sailing for someone not particularly used to the sea. But what a difference between the two voyages! Trying to make the best out of the rudimentary conditions aboard the *Argo*, I can't help remembering the comfortable cabins of the *Vagrant"* when we sailed leisurely between the Aegean islands, the yacht's exquisite luxury, the cozy, civilized mood around our hosts, the French chef's food, the way we were pampered by the large Greek crew.

*   *   *

At age 7, it was Paul's first cruise, and recalling now his boyish fascination with the sea, the boats and sailors, warmed my heart and made me miss him even more. For Lil and me, those were two carefree weeks of unmitigated delight. Our Greek friends and New York neighbors Dolly and Nico Goulandris had invited us for a second time to cruise on their yacht, this time with Paul, whom Dolly, an amicable, warm woman and a good amateur photographer, used to photograph since he was a baby. I was on a trip to Paris in June and flew to Athens to meet Lil, Paul and his French nanny as they arrived from New York. We spent the night at the Goulandris apartment, where Dolly kept her remarkable collection of Cycladic art, treasures that were later moved into a museum. The following day, we visited some of Athens' classic splendors and had lunch aboard Basil Goulandris's, Nico's twin brother, *Paloma*, one of the world's great yachts, which looked to me almost like an ocean liner. In the evening we moved aboard the *Vagrant* and while we slept, we lifted anchor and sailed away.

If I had to dream up an ideal way of seeing the Greek islands, I couldn't had done better. All the elements of the perfect formula were present: a charming hostess with great knowledge of the area's history and arts; a host with a passion for the sea and as competent as a professional captain; and a beautifully staffed and run private yacht. Dolly Goulandris was not only an important collector, she was also a willing and entertaining tour-guide, from whom we learned more about Delos, Myconos, Amorgos, Santorini, Ios, Patmos and all the islands we visited, than from any brochure and travel book. Nico, looking amazingly like Anthony Quinn in *Zorba the Greek* in his black turtleneck and captain's cap, was in his element at the helm, and even more so when going fishing with the crews of three fishing boats which he had instructed to follow us. As for the superb *Vagrant*, a white 117 feet, two-mast yacht, using sails and diesel engine, its streamlined and elegant silhouette attracted the general admiration in every port. Besides Yanni the captain and the chef, it employed three sailors and three stewards, all Greeks and vigorous *buzuki* dancers, to the delight of Lil who tried to pick up a few steps from Dolly and from them. Most of them were family men, obviously missing their children, so they adored playing with Paul and letting him hold the dinghy's rudder. (For longtime after, when asked which country he liked the best among the ones he had already visited, Paul used to answer without hesitation "Greece!'—a highly unexpected opinion on the part of a Bulgarian's son...But the little fellow was, of course, unaware of the traditional enmity which had for centuries opposed the two neighboring nations...)

In the abstract, I, myself, wasn't probably entirely untouched by the silly mutual prejudices existing between Bulgarians and Greeks. But when meeting Greeks in person, I almost invariably liked them. It was, of course, easy in the case of attractive people like Basil and Nico and their families. But in addition to their personalities, there seemed to be some Balkan bond between us, making us feel comfortable with each other; an affinity based I suppose on Orthodox liturgies, on baklavas and shish-kebabs, and heavy-accented *R-r*'s and *O-o*'s, things not shared with my Anglo-Saxon or West-European friends. Without knowing Nico that well,—a taciturn man who cared little for small talk and social amenities,—I felt the empathy for a pal from the old country, when he would take me on some of his fishing expeditions. We would board the small boats at dawn, while Lil and Dolly still slept, and for a couple of hours I would watch him work hard with the tough fishermen, drenched with salt water but fully enjoying himself pulling the heavy nets while out-shouting each other, sorting out the abundant catch, happier than I ever saw him at New York parties. It all looked, and sounded, and smelt and tasted so much like something from Sozopol of my childhood, with old Lefteraki and Ahmed and other local fishermen, with their mended nets and primitive "mauna" rowboats! The scene became even more familiar when we reached Andros island, the cradle of the Goulandris clan. Basil and Elise arrived at the same time on their *Paloma* and as we were engulfed in the warm, patriarchal world of innumerable cousins, nieces and relatives, and enjoying familiar Balkan food, customs and songs, pangs of nostalgia for my forbidden country came back to me on many unexpected occasions.

*   *   *

What a marvelous year 1967 has been so far for me!, I think, as I lie in my bunk on the *Argo*, counting once more my blessings. It started with my book "Manhattan Project" completed, printed, and already sold in six countries. In January, Tina had a baby, Timothy, Lil's first grandchild, and I was his godfather. Then Lil and I went to Sun Valley, staying at the Lodge and skiing for 15 days in gorgeous weather. In February Sava came from South Africa on business and we were happily reunited for several days in New York. My position at *Paris-Match* couldn't have been better, with Raymond Cartier as friendly as ever, and "Le Patron" showing me his appreciation. At home, everybody seemed to be very happy: Paul was the most delightful and rewarding child, Jill and her handsome Cuban husband Guillo were enjoying their *Dolce-Vita* routine, with swarms of carefree, fun-loving friends. Philip was engaged to be married to beautiful Alexandra von Moltke, a girl we liked very much. Mama, already ten years in the Free World, was more and more appreciating her life in America, although worrying about Boubi in Bulgaria, ("He's alright, and still working at the agricultural cooperative in the village of Gueshanovo," was the only news we received in April, from my aunt Minka in Plovdiv.) Radka had left Madrid, where she had spent one year in the service of King Simeon and Queen Margarita, and was back in Paris, working in a travel agency. It was a pity that she had to leave our Royal family, but the renewal of diplomatic relations between Spain and communist Bulgaria made it very unlikely for her and her son to ever obtain regular Spanish documents.

On March 27, "Manhattan Project" was launched officially, with the big cocktail party in our Fifth Avenue apartment, followed by a series of interviews, parties, and radio appearances. I felt I was on top of the world and I loved every minute of it. Each week brought some new excitement, each month offered another joy. How spoiled we have been this year! In June, we had our Greek islands cruise with the Goulandrises. From there, we went to the French Riviera, and spent all month of July in Sainte-Maxime, where we rented the house of *Vogue* director Alex Liberman (*Paris-Match* was really generous about vacations, I must say!…) In August, after Lil and Paul returned to New York, I went for ten days to Paris to report to Jean Prouvost and discuss new *Paris-Match* projects. Back to the States, the happy days continued—glamorous parties in New York, beach and tennis in Southampton, visits to Tina and Johnny in Watch Hill. A new joy in September: Jill had a baby-girl, Pauline, Lil's second grandchild.

So what am I doing here in this stormy October, at the other end of the world, half seasick on a rusty old ship? There are moments when I wonder whether I hadn't made a stupid mistake by volunteering for this rough expedition and whether it has been necessary at all. Sailing in the South Seas sounds romantic, but after my experience so far, you can have the South Pacific, thank you! But then I think of "our project" and I feel stimulated again.

It all started in early spring, as my "Manhattan Project" was about to go to print. *Paris-Match* company, immensely successful with its magazines, had tried to expand into book publishing, but had not succeeded: books were indeed a different business. This led to the partnership approach—Match would select the subjects and do the research and the writing, but production and distribution would be entrusted to experienced book-publishers. The chosen partner was *Larousse*, the prestigious publisher of encyclopedias and lavishly illustrated editions, a rich and powerful company. Looking for promising titles for the new co-venture, Raymond Cartier came with an old pet idea of his: an ambitious project of summing up, for the educated, interested layman, the present state of research and knowledge about the physical world we live in. Not textbooks, but journalistic narratives of scientific probes, their updated results, and the adventure of the men and women involved. (Twelve years earlier, Raymond and I had already published an embryo of the same idea: the long *Match* series "*Le Monde: d'ou vient-il, ou va-t-il?*".) "Now we can do it in a big way, Stephane, an entire volume per subject," he told me enthusiastically in March. "We have the publisher, we have the money, and you seem to have mastered the formula, with your Atom-bomb history. Let's do it!"

I was no less enthusiastic than he was. Together, we drew the plan: we would start with the exploration of the oceans, two volumes; we'd continue with the exploration of the Earth; and end with the Universe. By April, Raymond obtained not only the consent of Le Patron and of Larousse's chairman, Etienne Gillon, a friend of Cartier's, but also the necessary funds. To give me the necessary time, I was promoted a "Director" of *Paris-Match, Inc*, in charge of keeping Le Patron, Herve Mille and their services informed about developments and new projects in the US press, and maintaining contacts with the major American publications. Thus I was relieved of most day-to-day editorial responsibilities as Bureau chief. During my absences, they had to be shared between Mathias and Anni, which unfortunately didn't work well and caused frictions at the office. When Mathias managed to get the title "Bureau Chief," an open rebellion exploded at 22 East 67th Street, with Anni, Paul Slade, and Bernard Giquel refusing to work under him and threatening to resign. Our Washington correspondent Philippe de Bausset joined them and they all started bombarding me with long, indignant letters, which were reaching me in Greece and France, partially spoiling my vacations. The complaints implied, of course, that all was also of my fault, because as a boss I had been too indecisive and not strong enough to control Mathias's excesses and put him in his place. As this wasn't totally untrue,

I felt even worse about the whole situation. Now, nobody could reach me between Fiji and Tonga, at least one advantage of my isolation...

As Cartier was too busy with his other work, I was put in total charge of the five-year project's execution, with free hand to select the subjects, travel wherever I need, interview whomever I decide, hire assistants, buy books, and spend the budget at my discretion, as if Cartier and Gillon had given me a blank check. In other words, the dream assignment. I didn't I didn't waste time. By summer, I was involved in heavy reading and preliminary background talks with scientists and Navy people. Keeping modern scientific history for myself, I selected a *Paris-Match* colleague, Jean-Pierre Cartier, to write the historical part about old navigators, explorers and astronomers. Raymond gave his consent very reluctantly: the bearded, liberal Jean-Pierre, his total opposite both as character and as ideas, was his son, with whom he only kept rare and rather cool contacts. But my choice proved to be an excellent one and Jean-Pierre did a first-rate job, to the grumbling delight of his father.

It didn't take much reading before I realized, almost in panic, that I would never understand even most elementary oceanographic research techniques and instruments unless I go to sea and see with my own eyes. But how? I learned that the oceanography centers of *Woods Hole*, Mass., *Lamont*, in New York, and *Scripps*, in La Jolla, California, were among the most advanced and active, so I visited the three places, and applied to join some of their expeditions, just any expedition. I didn't have much chance to be accepted, and a few months passed without any word from them. Then, end of September, I received a call from La Jolla. "Somebody has to leave our *Nova* expedition at Suva, Fiji Islands, and we may have a berth for you on the *Argo*. But can you fly there right away?" asked the *Scripps*' director. Thrilled, I didn't hesitate: "Tell them I'm coming!" I said, only vaguely realizing that Fiji lay on the opposite side of the globe.

Shots and vaccinations by my friend, doctor Jay Meltzer. Reservations *TWA* to San Francisco and *PANAM to* Hawaii and Nandi, Fiji Island. Visit to baby Timothy (Tina and Johnny were touring Ireland). The last day, picking Paul from his *Madame-Corea* French school and bringing him to the *Paris-Match* office, which he loves. Going to say goodbye to Jill; strange, she looks disturbed and sad when I talk about Guillo; marital problems?- I dismiss the thought. Mama comes to play with Paul and stays for dinner. She tries to conceal her worry about my going away. Then, September 30th, I fly to San Francisco and take Lil's nieces Linda and Laurie for dinner to *Trader Vic's*. The next day I am in Honolulu, taking a nice evening swim on the beach in front of the *Moana* hotel. That night I fly to Fiji and when I arrive in the morning of October 3, my diary's page for "October 2nd" remains blank. Forever. The whims of the International Date Line have deprived me of that date, a day that was meant to never exist for me.

*   *   *   *   *

Life aboard the *Argo* is not very comfortable and the work is on the whole physically demanding, but gradually I'm learning some of the basics of oceanographic research. Now I know what "Nansen bottles" for taking water samples are, and can even use them. The expedition's scientists explain to me the principles on which the electronic depth-recorders work, and I listen to the "ping" of the impulses sent continuously to the bottom, and the "pong" of the echo coming back, while the stylus duly records on the slowly unrolling graph the profile of the sea floor. They show me how they activate the underwater air gun, as the seismograph records its discharges and the response from the ocean bottom. I try to understand the functioning of the magnetometers and the instruments measuring the earth gravity below us and I watch the readings of the deep-water thermometers.

A few days later, the *Argo* begins criss-crossing the waters above the abysmal Tonga Trench and the excitement increases. "19-th Parallel South," the captain informs me. "20th...23d...We are between the 171st and 173rd meridian West..." Then, at chosen moments, we proceed to what they call "a station:" the engines are turned off, the ship immobilizes itself. as much as the waves permit, and the real exploration work begins. It could be at midnight, or 4 AM, or any hour of the day or the night. Dredges and cameras are readied, instruments are set to action, and everybody rushes to his post. "3,200 fathoms!" announces the depth recorder. Screeching, the gigantic winch (it has a capacity of 30,000 feet!) begins to unroll the cable.

There is plenty of work to be done on the deck and every hand is badly needed, so I too pitch in—somewhat awkwardly, but trying hard to be useful. The crew, mostly grumpy old salts, accepts my help, but with no comments or encouragements. By now, I'm as filthy and unshaven as they are, my shirt and jeans stained with rust and machine grease, but they still don't count me as one of them; to them, I'm still the outsider, the writer, some sort of a big-city sissy. "Pull!" the man next to me at the winch would goad me, "One, two, thre-e-e! Again, one, two, thre-e-e!"

That night, the night of our successful "station," I realized, I felt physically, in a palpable way, how deep the ocean was. The time passed—five minutes, ten minutes, twenty, half-an-hour—and the cable continued disappearing rapidly into the bottomless blackness of the water. One thousand fathoms, two thousand—the winch wasn't slowing down. 2,500, 3,000, 5,000 fathoms…My God, I thought, but that's 9 kilometers, that's deeper than Mount Everest is high! The submarine trench under our ship kept on swallowing the miles of cable, with no sign yet of reaching the bottom. We were all exhausted when finally the dredger and the camera touched the floor, and exhilarated when, after the interminable hoisting up, the precious load of rocks and sediment was spilled out on the ship's deck.

During all this time, while miles of cable were rolling down in front of me, I tried to imagine the immensity of the ocean's depth and our puny speck of *Argo* dancing precariously on its surface. It made me think of *"L'Homme et la Mer,"* Man and the Sea, the title Raymond Cartier had chosen for our book. The ocean's depth was but one among many enigmas that kept me fascinated during the two years I spent for my research. They intrigued the oceanographers too, and continue to puzzle them. What is the origin of the oceans? Why the ocean's bottom, instead of being flat, is covered with the most gigantic mountain chains on the planet? Why does the sea floor consist of basalt, while the continents are made of granite? What actually are the currents and what's the mechanism of their movement? How could marine life exist in the abyss, under unimaginable pressures and in zones where there is no light, no possible photosynthesis, and consequently, no food? And why should those creatures have eyes and display bright colors? Can Man live underwater and will he be able one day to colonize the ocean floor? Could the sea provide enough resources to feed the entire world population? These, and countless other questions challenged the oceanographers, with each answer giving birth to new, unsuspected questions, and so on and on, without ever reaching the total knowledge. Before I knew it, I found myself deeply involved in their quest, not only professionally, but for my own curiosity's sake too.

*   *   *   *

I had found the challenge of writing a book on oceanography, a subject I didn't know anything about, most stimulating. Immodest?—Not necessarily, if one considers the mission Raymond and I had set for ourselves: not, of course, to come with some opinions and theories of _our own_, but to describe, journalistically, the people in the avant-garde of the scientific quest, to narrate their ventures, and sum-up their conclusions, for what they're worth. I felt I had the needed curiosity, and also the ability to portray the heroes of this new science. If one is ready to spend countless hours in libraries and archives, it's not too difficult to dig out fascinating facts and anecdotes about the pioneers of modern oceanography. My story started with the first systematic measurements of currents, temperatures, and winds, organized in 1845 by Lieutenant Mathew Fontaine Maury of the US Navy, followed the depth soundings by James Clark Ross, and described the first real oceanographic expedition, the voyage of H.M.S. _Challenger_ in the 1870s. The more I read, the more I became involved with the colorful characters and their discoveries. The saga of the other precursors was not less exciting- Prince Albert of Monaco's study of marine life; the "crazy" hypothesis of the "floating continents" of the German Alfred Wegener in 1912; the first "bathysphere" in which Beebe and Barton descended in the 1930s to 908 meters under the surface…What a novel of adventures!, I thought as I enthusiastically attacked the reporter's portion of the job—witnessing the developments underway, live interviews with the principal researchers and, in one word, "being there."

For the next two-and-a-half years, following oceanographers became my main professional occupation. I never became a diver myself. While vacationing with Lil and Paul in Ste-Maxime, I tried lessons with a local expert, a guy called Bruno, who provided oxygen bottles and rubber suits, only to realize that I was prone to claustrophobia, the worst peril in underwater activities. But I learned about deep diving, about the "bends" and nitrogen narcosis, from the mouth of the originator of underwater fishing and free diving, the French ex-Navy officer Philippe Tailliez, whom I visited in Toulon. He was part of the legendary trio Tailliez—Jacques Cousteau—Frederic Dumas, who popularized the new sport on the French Riviera during the years immediately before, and during, World War 2. I was mesmerized by his daylong tale of the *"époque heroique"* of diving and while Madame Tailliez kept me for lunch, I learned how a simple innovation—the underwater goggles he devised in the 1930s—transformed the relationship of Man and Sea forever. The naked human eye is almost blind under water, so the fantastic submarine vistas that the watertight goggles offered for the first time were a revelation for the three divers. Later, Cousteau wrote of his first experience: *"Sometimes we are lucky enough to know that our lives have been changed, to discard the old, embrace the new, and run headlong down an immutable course. It happened to me on that summer's day (in 1936), when my eyes were opened on the sea."* Listening about Cousteau, Tailliez, and Dumas' early exploits it surprised me to hear that Man began to swim underwater un-attached only since 1943, the year the trio started using the first "aqualung"! Capt. Cousteau's subsequent fantastic career figures prominently in my book, but I couldn't obtain personal interviews with him: preparing his own books and films, he was not about to share his stories gratis, before first publishing them himself.

As for marine geology, I was lucky to be initiated personally by *Lamont* Laboratory's Prof. Maurice Ewing, the geophysicist who introduced the seismographic method in exploring the ocean floor. Also at Lamont, on the Hudson river outside New York, his younger colleagues Marie Tharp and Bruce Heezen told me in detail how they discovered the existence of a continuous rift all along the crest of the under-oceanic mountain chain, a discovery which shook modern oceanography. Ewing, Heezen, and Tharp published the first map of the gigantic underwater ridge only in 1959, not even ten years before I met them. By chance, indeed, Raymond Cartier and myself had embarked in our book project at the precise moment when marine geology was undergoing a real revolution. Most scientists I had interviewed 12 years earlier, used to dismiss Wegener's hypothesis of continents "floating" like gigantic rafts as science-fiction, amusing and imaginative, but certainly not to be taken too seriously. Now the same scientists were subscribing to the new theory of a mosaic of "tectonic plates" in permanent motion and of spreading of the oceans' floor, where new terrestrial crust springs out at the rift of underwater mountains and old crust is engulfed into submarine trenches. "Don't even bother reading textbooks written before 1960!" prominent geologists advised me, referring to the ongoing revolution. Back in my school days, I used to consider geology a most boring subject, and now, here I was, absolutely fascinated by its unexpected findings! Acquiring firsthand knowledge from avant-garde researchers in full process of changing radically our basic ideas about the Earth, was for me a thrilling personal experience, and since my budget could afford it, I made a point to contact as many leaders of the new school in geology as I could. At Harry Hess's lab at Princeton, I was able to reconstruct the main episodes of his pioneering work in the Pacific by the end of WW2. Also at Princeton, I learned about J. Morgan's important contribution from his own mouth. Revisiting Ewing and Heezen at *Lamont*, I realized that in the meantime they had dropped their previous skepticism and also had embraced the new ideas. I went to England to talk to the young geophysicist Fred Vine, whose recent research on sea-floor magnetism had led to striking conclusions, then had most stimulating conversations at Cambridge with Sir Edward Bullard, with whom I'd already been in correspondence. He turned out to be a captivating raconteur. "I'd rather be wrong than boring," he confessed while playing with some of his unorthodox ideas, although few of his admiring peers thought him often wrong. As for Prof. J. Tuzo Wilson, one of the new school's apostles, he received me in Canada. Hearing him expose his theories was another intellectual highlight in my work on the oceanography story.

I loved the research. In addition to the intellectual rewards, it gave me opportunities for unusual travel and meeting interesting people Some of them became friends, like Jacques Piccard, the lanky Swiss who had descended to the deepest point on the planet. The son of the famous pioneer of stratospheric flight in balloon Professor Auguste Piccard, Jacques was a serious, disciplined man totally dedicated to the construction and piloting of his bathyscaphs and mesoscaphs. It turned out that we had been students in Geneva during the same years, but we didn't know each other then. After many interviews, in which I obtained full details of his exploits, I visited his mesoscaphe *Ben Franklin* during its construction in Long Island's Grumman plants and then, on its departure for the Gulf-Stream, I went to Palm Beach to see him off. It was a really bold adventure: with a crew of six, Piccard's mesoscaphe went under the surface, incorporated itself into the current, and drifted for an entire month with it, all engines turned off. The observations on Gulf Stream's nature and behavior were unique and invaluable. I followed the take-off on a small motorboat, until *Ben Franklin* submerged and disappeared in the Atlantic, a few miles off Palm Beach. What impressed me about Jacques at his departure was his lack of slightest stage fright, doubts, or even emotions. His basketball player size didn't seem to bother him inside the confined quarters of the submarine, where he was going to spend 30 days without surfacing, and which I had found extremely claustrophobic, when I visited him; I don't think he knew the meaning of the word. Cool as a cucumber, he was the efficient professional, too busy checking the last technical details. A Swiss engineer on a romantic venture, I thought. The mesoscaphe surfaced four weeks later, after having been part of the Gulf Stream for 2,700 kilometers. When I saw him, Piccard was very happy, but not at all surprised that *Ben Franklin* had performed precisely as he had expected it. He told me, however, that he had been deeply moved when learning about the historic event which shook the world above during his absence: on July 20, 1969, the submarine telephone informed the crew that the first astronauts had landed on the Moon. The fact that the two missions—those of the "deepest" man ever, and of the "highest" men in history,—were happening in the same time, gave me some food for thought. But then, don't we all like to see symbols even in mere coincidences?

Jacques Piccard's purity and dedication to his dream impressed me much and I also enjoyed his friendship. He visited us in Southampton and we visited his family in their home near Lausanne. We also saw each other in Gstaad, and apart from learning so much from him, I consider the time spent in his company a great bonus of my oceanography project. There were many other bonuses. The coverage of operation *Tektite* in the Virgin Islands, for instance. It was an under-sea habitat, where four researchers lived for 60 days, breathing a nitrogen-oxygen mixture. They needed no divers' suits inside the pressurized "house," but wore rubber costumes and oxygen tanks when swimming for their research outside of the habitat. The experiment was such a success, that five young women scientists, the first female aquanauts, succeeded the four aquanauts. They lived inside the *Tektite* for two weeks, and I went to the gorgeous beaches of St. John, Virgin Islands, to interview them before the start of the experiment. It was there that I was taken for the first time inside a diving bell, a steel sphere with windows, in which I was hermetically locked, all by myself, and slowly lowered to the sea floor. I must confess that the very idea of being sealed made me very nervous, but there was no way to decline what the aquanauts considered a very generous offer to a visiting journalist, especially one who boasted of being eager to taste the thrills of aquatic experience. Luckily, once I survived the terror of the bolts being screwed over my head, the indescribable beauty of the subtropical underwater world around me evaporated all traces of anxiety and fear. I was so enraptured by the splendor of lights, colors, and shapes of myriads of fantastic creatures passing by the sphere's windows, that I wished the descent to last for hours and sincerely regretted its brevity.

My trips offered several similarly enjoyable moments. When possible, I tried to mix work with pleasure. Thus, when my participation in the *Nova* expedition ended in Tonga, I took advantage of being in the South Pacific and took several days "vacation" by myself, visiting islands I always wanted to see: Pago-Pago, Samoa, and of course, Tahiti—Papeete and Morea. I would've gladly stayed longer in that enchanted part of the world, but I had to rush back to New York in time for my stepson Philip's wedding with Alexandra: he had asked me to be his best man, which had pleased me so much that I wouldn't have missed it for anything.

I witnessed some drama too. The breakthrough experiment in sea floor living, *Sealab-3*, which I attended on San Clemente island, off California, turned to tragedy, when young aquanaut Berry Cannon died in a diving accident. Before that unfortunate night, the Sealab program was running beautifully. Following the 1962 successful experiments with underwater habitats in the South of France (Edwin Link's *Man-in-Sea* and Cousteau's *Precontinent 1*), then *Precontinent 2* in 1963 in the Red Sea and *SPID*, with Robert Stenuit and Lindbergh's son Jon in 1964 at Key West,—the US Navy had launched the ambitious *Sealab* program. The first two American habitats had broken many records. In 1964, sitting at a depth of 58 meters off Bermuda, *Sealab-I* had housed for 11 days four aqua-nauts, able to swim for the first time under such enormous pressure. The follow-ing summer, near La Jolla, *Sealab-II* became the submarine home of another team, led by the famous astronaut Scott Carpenter, who lived an entire month at 62 meters under sea level. In order to prevent the "bends" before the final re-emerging to the atmospheric pressure, they had to spend 35 hours in a decom-pressing chamber. At the same time, in the *Precontinent 3* in the South of France, six men of Cousteau's team spent twenty-one days at 100 meters, breathing helium. Their decompression lasted for three-and-a-half days.

Something went wrong with the compressing of the American aquanauts, that day of February 1969, at the start of operation *Sealab-III*. While the empty habitat, a huge, 50-ft.-long cylindrical tank, was lowered to a record depth of 185 m., the nine aquanauts of the first shift were being prepared for the pressure, in the sarcophagus-like compression chambers, installed aboard the auxiliary ship *Elk River*. The previous evening, we had met these young Navy men with crew cut hair, all superb, experienced divers bursting with vigor. Now we were watching them on the closed TV circuit inside the compression chamber as they were making funny faces, yawning and swallowing exaggeratedly to relieve their ears and noses from the gradually increasing pressure. They were cheerfully dis-cussing the last details of the forthcoming dive, but their voices, affected by the gas mixture they were breathing, sounded ridiculously high-pitched and distorted—the so-called "Donald-Duck-effect" of helium. Several hours later, the instruments aboard the *Elk River* revealed an unexpected small leak in the shell of the empty *Sealab-III*, already waiting on the sea floor. Somebody had to be sent to close the leak, and as four of the nine divers were pronounced sufficiently "saturated," they were dispatched down in the small capsule, which had to serve as an elevator between the ship and the underwater house. Berry Cannon was one of them, but when he reached the habitat, his breathing gear became entangled and the team, half frozen, had to be hoisted up to surface without repairing the leak. Later the same night, after some rest in the compression chamber, the same men were sent down again. As soon as they left the capsule and started swimming toward *Sealab-III*, the underwater TV camera showed that Cannon was in difficulty. Then a most horrible ordeal unraveled on the screen: the heroic efforts of the divers, restricted in their frogmen suits, to help their comrade; the entanglement of their clumsy equipment; the feat of loading Cannon's inanimate body into the exiguous "elevator;" the interminable, 40-minute-long, ascent of the capsule—during which the aquanauts desperately massaged Berry's heart with their frozen fingers and gave him mouth-to-mouth breathing. Piled around the command post where the project directors watched the screen and kept us informed, we followed the drama all along through the divers' ascension to the compression chamber and to the final announcement: "heart failure." At 6 in the morning, Cannon was pronounced dead. *Sealab-III*, the most ambitious program of underwater habitat, was cancelled. I was quite shaken when I left San Clemente island. For the remaining eight aquanauts of the first shift, a new ordeal had begun: distressed, their dream shattered, they found themselves condemned to spend the following seven days and seven nights stretched on the narrow bunks inside the decompression chamber, lest they die of the bends.

*   *   *   *   *

It took me almost three years to complete my research. Did I learn everything about the sea? Of course not. Did I understand most of its mysteries? I'm afraid, new causes for puzzlement were added to the already considerable awe in which I had always held Nature. The more I learned, the more my awareness increased of the immensity of my ignorance, like a flashlight in a pitch-black tunnel: the further its beam reaches, the greater the sense of the darkness around.

But those were marvelously rewarding years, rich with exciting trips, contacts with stimulating men, and novel experiences. Pursuing any concrete goal—in this case, the writing of a book—is already half of the recipe for what is generally called "happiness." So, one can say that during the period I worked on "*L'Homme et la Mer,*" I was a very happy man.

****

To the South Pole

The signboard under the American flag, planted into the ice at the precise geographical point of the South Pole read: "Medium yearly temperature: 49 degrees below zero Centigrade; altitude: 2,790 meters above sea level; ice thickness: 2,700 meters." Our *Hercules C-130* had just landed on its skis and we hadn't walked more than a hundred steps on the frozen snow, but we were already out of breath because of the altitude and the cold air cutting our lungs. In spite of the special equipment required for Antarctica—fur-lined parkas with huge hoods, isolating rubber boots worn over our ski-boots, elbow-length leather mittens, above two other pairs of gloves, and protective goggles covering the cheeks,—our faces and fingers had started freezing in a matter of a couple of minutes.

The day was January 27th, 1970, the height of Antarctica's summer, and the glare of the sun in the cloudless sky was reflected so blindingly by the snow that it would be impossible to keep your eyes open without the thick, black welders' goggles we all wore. But at the same time a piercing wind savagely swept the flat plateau of the Pole, spread out to the horizon, a boundless, desolate plain with none of the striking beauty of the rest of the continent. "We're lucky with the weather today," said the American lieutenant who escorted us. "It's only 25 below, which is rare for the Pole. In winter, of course, it gets unbearable. The record here is minus 80. The human skin cannot take such temperatures, not even for one minute, so for six months the personnel doesn't even show their noses outside the station."

Next to me, my boss Raymond Cartier couldn't hide his excitement. "Just think that no matter in what direction we look—left, right, forward, back—it's North everywhere! Indeed, we were standing at the exact point where all meridians converge at the bottom of the globe. At the entrance of the station, arrows nailed on a pole pointed with a kind of Polar inside humor to all possible directions: "Miami, 8,000 miles; Athens, 15,030 kilometers; Washington DC, 8,411 miles…"

I was no less moved. I was particularly thrilled at the thought that ever since the world existed, only ten men—just ten!—had reached the South Pole by land (if we can call so the incredibly thick layer of ice), and this happened only once, in December/ January 1911-1912. No one, before or since, had repeated the feat of the five Norwegians of Amundsen and the five Englishmen of Captain Scott. Only recently, just 13 years before my visit, other humans set foot on the Pole again, but those were visitors brought by airplane. Since then, only about 3,000 people, including my group, had seen the true Pole. (As different from visitors to the other stations on this enormous continent, twice as large as Europe. By then, the total of visitors to Antarctica from all countries was still under 23,000.) I felt also a particular pride to be the first and only Bulgarian setting foot on the South Pole.)

Half-frozen, we couldn't wait to find refuge inside the station, built under the ice. Named "Amundsen-Scott" and belonging to the USA, it was well equipped and heated. Before entering, a last glance at our *Hercules* reassured us: the engines were running and the propellers still turning. Without admitting it aloud, the memory of Admiral Duffek's first flight was still vivid with all of us. When the *DC-3* of George Duffek and his team of five landed for the first time on the Pole on October 31,1956 and they hurriedly deposed a few scientific measuring devices and planted the American flag, the motors refused to restart. The sort of this historic flight (the plane's name was "Que Sera Sera," after a hit-song title) was in mortal "danger." The pilot activated four emergency fuses *Jatos*, but to no avail. Another four, and the motors still remained silent. There were only 7 *Jatos* left.

Four more were attempted. No result. The crew was already almost frozen in the minus 50-degree cold as desperately the last three devices were lit and, miracle!, the engines started coughing noisily and the "Que Sera Sera" took off over the Beardmore glacier. Thus began the modern conquest of the South Pole. But after Duffek's near-disaster, the pilots never turn off the engines during the many hours of their visits to the Pole.

The only possible way to reach the South Pole was by US Navy plane taking off from McMurdo, the American Antarctic base situated on the Ross Sea. There is no other way out and the few non-American visitors—Russians, British, Argentineans, and other nationalities—had entered and left uniquely as guests of the Americans. The three-hour flight form McMurdo over snow-covered gigantic mountains, glaciers, and canyons, offered the most fantastic sight I gad ever seen in my life. I don't believe there is a more dramatic land relief anywhere on Earth, with vestiges of titanic geological cataclysms and an amazing spectrum of silver, white, blue, and aquamarine gleams of snow and ice. From a bird's eye view, one realizes the immensity of the Antarctica continent, boundless and pristine. I shivered at the thought that since Creation no one had ever disturbed the peace of this eternal snow desert—no man, animal, bird, not even a bacteria or a plant,—and that it will probably remain this untouched forever and ever.

Flying over the Antarctic mountains, the grandiose ranges of Queen Maud's land and the Beardmore glacier, I couldn't help not admire the exploits and superhuman ordeals of Capt. Robert Falcon Scott and his companions. We flew at a low enough altitude to be able to clearly see the crevasses, canyons, precipices, and steep walls, crossing the glacier, as terrifying as some illustration for Dante's Inferno. To think that five exhausted men, frostbitten, starved, and thirsty were capable of traversing these obstacles on skis and by foot through storms and blizzards, pulling overloaded sleds, was mind-boggling. The Siberian ponies that Scott unfortunately had preferred over the polar dogs, had not survived the nightmarish conditions and had quickly died during the two-month-long trek to the Pole, before the five martyrs started the return trip on this polar Golgotha. And I imagined their despondency when, reaching the geographic Pole on 18th of January, they saw there the Norwegian flag already floating: their rival Roald Amundsen, favored by excellent weather and 56 robust polar dogs, had outpaced them and already arrived, by a different way, on the 14th of December!

Now we were flying over the scene of this epic drama, relatively comfortable and at considerably less risk (although it was mandatory each time we left MacMurdo to carry a knapsack with first-aid and survival equipment, in case of vehicle break-down or sudden change of the weather, which happened all the time). Admiral Duffek's flight had traced the first itinerary and only two months later two *DC-3*'s had reached the Pole unloading the first team of well-prepared military specialists from the US Navy *SeaBees* construction battalions, with eleven dogs. The construction of the South Pole station, a remarkable engineering feat by the *SeaBees* and a team of scientists with machinery and prefabricated components brought aboard *Globemasters* huge cargo planes and dropped on the ice by parachutes, began in November 1956. At the end of the polar summer, the first station named "Amundsen-Scott" was built and on March 21st eighteen volunteers, all men, were the first to see the sun setting behind the Pole's horizon, never to rise again for the next six months.

During my visit, most of the 20-member winter crew had already arrived. Some of them were scientists, intending to study the atmosphere, the ice, and the climatic conditions, as observed from this unique and still totally unspoiled post, as well as the geological history of our planet. The maintenance of the station was assured by a unit of the US Navy, responsible for the living quarters, supply, heating, electric station and transportation. NASA was also represented: indeed, the only places on the globe where the future colonizers of space could already test their equipment and experience life under extremely hostile conditions were only near the South Pole and inside the bathyscaphs operating on the oceans' floor. Equally logical was the presence of NASA psychiatrists, and not only because of risks of claustrophobia or depression. When a group of people are locked together for several long months in very narrow quarters, such as spacecraft, cohabitation becomes almost unbearable; the small habits of each neighbor begins to irritate you, his cough, the way he laughs or brushes his teeth, his snoring—everything takes abnormal proportions and threatens the teamwork. The psychiatrist was dutifully taking notes of the most seemingly insignificant human reactions.

The physical conditions of life "underground" were better than satisfactory. Refrigerators were packed to capacity with steaks and varieties of food. The sleeping quarters were warm, cozy, and pleasantly decorated. The library offered hundreds of books and magazines, while the selection of records, various games, and films shown in the spacious living room (with new movies every night), could satisfy all tastes.

Nevertheless, the volunteers had to accept the total isolation and be resigned to the thought that no matter what happened during the long winter—a crisis, an illness, a heart attack—nobody would be able to come to the rescue. I interviewed several men as to why they had chosen this risky mission. For the scientists, it was easily understandable: as researchers, they had reached a ceiling in their specialties from where they could advance only if they came to the Pole. The especially high pay tempted other men. "When I finish with my military service, I'll have enough money to buy myself a small house," a young sailor confessed to me. Perhaps still others came in the hope of healing some great personal disappointment or unhappy love. But in all of them I detected considerable desire for adventure.

This I could understand. True, I came in a primarily professional mission: I was working on my book on Earth sciences and for me visiting the fantastic natural laboratory that was the Antarctica continent was certainly a wonderful opportunity. But I was also stimulated by my thirst for a new adventure. However, being included in the American *Deep-Freeze* program wasn't easy. And it was, as I already mentioned, the only way to go to Antarctica. (Some touristic tours were beginning to be organized, but only to the shores of the continent and passengers remained aboard ships, without disembarking.) The exception were the 33 polar stations belonging to ten different countries. Among them, only three American stations (*South Pole, Byrd, and Plato)* and the Russian *Vostok* were located in the interior, far from the shores. And since everything—personnel, supplies, and material—was imported, each pound of cargo counted. Each airplane seat was carefully assigned several months in advance and no amount of money could buy it. Therefore I was elated when *Deep-Freeze* invited me as a guest.

The trip, on a military propeller plane from California to New Zealand, was interminable. First from San Francisco to Hawaii; the next day from Honolulu to Fiji; finally, flying over half of the Pacific, until *Deep-Freeze* base in Christchurch in New Zealand. There we underwent a thorough medical examination, although we already had all the required health certificates and vaccinations. I asked why they took so many X-ray pictures of the teeth. The answer was hardly reassuring: "For identification in an autopsy, in case of accident. Moreover, we cannot afford the luxury of dealing with unexpected infections." It appeared that dental inflammations and rupture of appendix, both unpredictable crises, were the two risks most feared by our Antarctica hosts. We also had to fill in forms with many indiscreet questions, such as "Do you sometimes wet your bed during your night sleep?" and "Do you have homosexual tendencies?" (This in view of the extremely narrow bedrooms.) The next step was the fitting of clothes and equipment by a strict sergeant, a ritual that evoked memories of my military service in Bulgaria. The American sergeant made us undress completely and leave all our clothes in consignment, in exchange for polar uniforms, made of special thermal materials. He visibly had little respect for our civilian equipment, which some of us brought from ski resorts and sports shops. The new outfits certainly didn't look like made-to-order garb, but were warm and perfectly weatherproof.

The flight over the Polar Ocean from Christchurch to McMurdo was extremely long, ten hours, and quite tiring. Because of the atmospheric conditions, an average of two-thirds of the old, propeller-driven *Hercules* planes equipped with skis were usually forced to return in mid-flight. Once over the ocean, there was no possibility for emergency landing or refueling. The hours passed slowly and nothing interrupted the monotonous sight of the infinite ocean except for chunks of floating ice and a few gigantic icebergs, majestically moving under us. In the plane's cabin, our admiral was explaining *Deep-Freeze's* mission and answered questions. "If we had some break-down during the flight, what would be our chances for survival?" asked one passenger, pretending to be half-joking. The admiral's answer came calm but definitive. "None. In these waters, the human body can only last three minutes." A silence followed. I realized that we were given no instructions for use of lifebelts and rafts. They were obviously considered superfluous. We all then pretended to be sleeping, but I supposed that like me, everybody was keeping their fingers crossed.

Luckily, all went well and in the evening the plane landed at Williams Field, McMurdo's improvised airport on the ice. The evening?—A glaring sun was shining from the blue sky and it kept shining, without setting, during all the days and nights of my stay. In the beginning, it was rather disturbing and in spite of the thick black curtains on the windows of the hut, where I was billeted, sleep didn't come easily. Of course, this was also due to the euphoric effect of the crystal-pure dry air (Antarctica's climate is among the driest on Earth), and to the excitement of the new experience. But the cold wasn't worse than any winter at home. McMurdo, the largest base on the continent, was truly a tiny village, with it's muddy, snow-covered alleys between the sleeping huts and dining halls, its laboratories, nuclear reactor for heating and electricity, and water desalinizing station. There was even a *Playboy Club*" hut and quite near it, probably for moral counterbalance, a small wooden chapel. During the super-busy summer season, the population reached two thousand, then almost all inhabitants were to leave in March, before the fall of the Polar night.

I wouldn't describe the base itself as attractive. But the beauty of the surrounding nature surpassed everything I had expected to see. Contrary to the North Pole, which is nothing more than a geographic point in the middle of an eternally frozen ocean, Antarctica is a true continent made of rock under a blanket of ice, at places almost one mile deep, with mountains higher than the Alps. Two of them, the volcanoes Erebus and Terror, dominated the landscape behind McMurdo. During the summer thaw, the abundance of life on the shores is prodigious. Thousands of seals rested lazily on fragments of ice floating in waters teeming with fish, shrimp and algae. At a visit to Cape Royds, we saw cliffs literally black with tens of thousands of penguins, roaming busily through their noisy colony, excited and angry at our visit. Such penguin "rookeries" abound at many points on the seashore.

But less than one mile away from the coast, all traces of life disappear in the interior to the continent and one enters a colossal white desert, majestic in its impenetrability, like some different, sterile planet, totally indifferent to time or to the existence of the human race. I had the opportunity to make a few short excursions into this strange, but hypnotically attractive kingdom of eternal silence. But on a plane, of course, or with helicopter, or aboard the icebreaker *Burton Island*. We visited the *Byrd* station with its impressive tunnel dug into the snow, as well as other laboratories displaying remarkable technologies. But the romantic atmosphere of the epoch of explorers-adventurers I think I found only in the modest New Zealandese base, not far from McMurdo. Inside the hut, red-cheeked mustachioed men with British accents, in old, home-knitted sweaters, calmly smoked their pipes and drank tea around a blazing tin stove, into which from time to time they threw a lump of coal. Outside, a few dozen huskies, attached to long chains, lounged on the snow and howled, looking forward to their portions of seal meat. In the American stations, snowmobiles and helicopters had long replaced dogs, sleds, and skis.

The heroic past I found, almost intact, in Captain Scott's hut, still preserved at Cape Evans, some half-hour by helicopter from McMurdo. It was there that Scott and his companions had spent the winter before leaving for the Pole, and it was there that the rest of the expedition awaited, alas in vain, their return. Totally exhausted, with gangrene on their frostbitten feet and hands, half-blind from the blizzards and faint with hunger and thirst, they all died on their return trek. Scott kept his diary until the end. Before dying, he carefully stowed it under his jacket, together with a dozen farewell letters, slipped inside his sleeping bag, and fell asleep. He was only nine miles from his pre-deposited cache of provisions...

Knowing the history of this hero from my young years, I was deeply moved when I entered the hut and saw his bed and sleeping bunks, the shelf with medicine, the clothes, harnesses, and cupboards with supplies. Everything was well preserved, as if in an icebox—canned food, biscuits, flour, onions, grains spilled on the table. I looked at the dates of the few English magazines: 1910. At the exit, the corpse of a dog lay on the veranda, its fur fully conserved. Only the rictus on its muzzle indicated that it was dead. Dead long ago, in 1913, when the unlucky expedition left Antarctica.

Outdoors, the un-abating polar wind continued to drift snow over the abandoned hut.

****

Chapter 30

Boubi's strange and tragic life in Bulgaria

News from Boubi became extremely scarce and, unfortunately, always upsetting. He had stopped writing, and also our friends and relatives had turned silent, either because of the strict censorship, or because they too knew little about his whereabouts. Mama suspected the worse and became progressively silent, but it was obvious that she was suffering a lot.

Our aunt "Lemi," Boubi's closest person in Bulgaria, who had learned to fear the communists and was extremely careful in her letters, now wrote even less frequently, although we wrote to her regularly, with questions about Boubi between the lines. "I know that something had happened to Boubi," Mama often voiced her somber thoughts. "I feel it. Something bad..."

In July 1964, a relative of ours, Christo Roussev, had managed to go on a business trip to Helsinki and he sent me a letter from there, without passing through the censorship. *"Your brother was expelled again, three months ago, to the village of Krupen, in the region of Tolbukhin,"* Christo wrote. *"We had a family council in our house and decided to send grandpa Mitcho Mintchev to plead Boubi's case- to bring him back to Sofia and to restore his Sofia residence. I wrote to your brother in detail and asked him for his consent. I don't know whether it was because of pride or of some scruples, but he didn't agree. Yet, grandpa Mitcho is 84-year-old, speaks persuasively, and, most important- nobody can do him harm, at his age. And Boubi has a very strong argument: he returned from abroad voluntarily! If only the municipal service big bosses knew this fact, it will be sufficient to grant him a permanent Sofia residence. He however replied that they, the big shots, have the obligation to know that and to solve his problem on their own initiative. In principle he's right, but let's not forget that there are many petty people, who wouldn't think of that, or would do something out of spite. Boubi's work is very hard—crushing rocks and loading trucks at the quarry in*

526

Krupen. I have an idea: can't <u>you</u> ask the people of your magazine to drop a word in favor of Boubi to the proper instances?"

New worries for me, new feelings of remorse..."Can't you?..." How could I explain that in emigration I had become involved to the neck in anti-communist activities, that the Bulgarian services are perfectly aware of, that the authorities hadn't forgotten that "Paris-Match" never published the second, the political, part of the reportage on Bulgaria, for which they had let my family and the Tchaprachikoffs leave the country? I thanked Christo and our relatives (by then we already knew about Boubi's expulsion, through a letter from some friends of Mama), and I wrote to him that *"my brother is a curious and stubborn guy, and when he puts something in his head, it's impossible to make him change his mind: the best example is his return to Bulgaria. He has his own ideas about duty and patriotism, and in the present case, it's very difficult to help him...This winter we have heard that contacts with the West, and especially with the USA, had suddenly and again, become very dangerous and suspect in Bulgaria, and I wonder whether Boubi didn't suffer because of that. He definitely cut all contacts with us. That's why I didn't want to write to you sooner. I didn't know whether, on account of the sudden deterioration, I wouldn't, instead of helping, do more damage."*

And when we learned that the heavy physical labor at the stone quarry had caused problems with Boubi's heart, I turned to an old friend from Sozopol, Boris Naslednikov, then a Paris lawyer. I asked him whether his brother Liuben, an attorney for the Holy Synod in Sofia, could intervene officially in order to restitute the Sofia residence to Boubi, for purely humanitarian reasons. Boris took the case to heart and not only did insist with his brother, but personally appealed to the newly appointed Bulgarian ambassador to Paris, Topencharov, whom he had known from before. The ambassador replied that there was a new amnesty law in Bulgaria, concerning expelled people, but that Boubi had to file an application. He was surprised, he said, that Boubi wasn't taking steps officially and concluded that "it seems that this man is some kind of an eccentric..." After a few vain attempts to put Boubi in touch with his brother, Boris also lost hope. "If Boubi himself refuses to cooperate, we can't do anything for him," he told me.

Indeed, according to information we were receiving from various relatives and friends, Boubi was refusing to "beg for something which represented his natural right." But the years were passing and we were hearing less and lees from him. On Palm Sunday in 1967, for instance, Lemi wrote us a long letter, full of nostalgia for the past. She was already 82, in poor health, resigned to the solitude and poverty of her modest room, where she had squeezed herself after our family house had been expropriated because of the death sentence against her brother, my father. Her only entertainment was to watch the sparrows through the window, the unknown passers-by, and the change of the seasons. And to read, of course, preferably French novels and poetry, as much as her eyes permitted. But the two pages, filled with her illegible, old-lady's handwriting, didn't answer any of our questions about Boubi, except in a two-line post-script: "*Boubi is still in the village of Gueshanovo; a few days ago I had a letter from him. He's alright and continues to work in the TKZC* (cooperative farm)." But why in Gueshanovo again? And since when?, we were puzzled.

In her next letter, Lemi wished us a Happy New 1968 Year, but with not a word about Boubi. Then she wrote for Easter, sadly reminiscing Palm Sundays of long, long ago. "*Today my mother celebrated her name's day. How wonderful it was, when we all were around her! When the house was full of life; in the garden, the trees and the bushes were heavy with blossom; lilac, tulips, hyacinths…Now is also spring, but it only inspires sadness, it only resurrects Nature, but where are my beloved ones, where are they?…*" Only a mention, at the end: "*I had a letter from Boubi recently; he writes that he's in good health and continues to work in the fields.*"

But why didn't he write to us, why did he keep silent for several years? These questions tortured us, Mama and me, and we were in vain asking ourselves whether we hadn't somehow hurt his feelings and he couldn't forgive us some word or some action. I suppose Lemi had talked to him about that, because finally he wrote to us, from her room in Plovdiv. It was a short letter, somehow formal: "*Plovdiv, 26 September 1968. Dear Stefo, after my arrest in April 1964, I deemed it the right thing for me to do was to interrupt my correspondence with you. I believe that you'll understand that I had very serious reasons to do it. I hope that you are alright and you advance continuously in your job. As far as I'm concerned, I have again a new profession—I'm studying agriculture, as a worker in the TKZS in Gueshanovo, where I live since the summer of 1966, as I was not allowed to stay in Sofia."*

More concrete news arrived in the beginning of December 1968, in a registered letter from Lemi. It was bad news. *"I know that this letter will upset you, but I beg you to read it with calm. For quite a long time Boubi is with me, because he doesn't feel well. According to the neurologists, there is an over-fatigue of the nervous system and they recommend rest and medical treatment. How are we going to persuade him, and what kind of treatment it will be, we have no idea. Here, in our country, I'm his only close person. To every question I ask him, he only answers with a slight shaking of the head, as if he wanted to say "What's the use? There's no sense." He feels and knows the state he's in, a state which doesn't permit him to work, and this torments him much. He feels no other desire. My love and respect, my devotion to him, are of no help. And the miserable conditions in which I live don't offer anything to cheer him up, they only inspire dark thoughts.*

"I know, Stefcho, that all this will alarm you, but I consider it my moral responsibility and my duty to inform you. Boubi cares very much for me, but despite all his love and esteem for me, he doesn't tell me what's oppressing him. In fact, he doesn't have to tell me anything, I know the causes of this state very well. Boubi will stay with me for a longer time, therefore please write to him to my address. He doesn't know about this letter, and I think he shouldn't know that I wrote to you."

I asked myself whether I should tell Mama. But seeing her so worried, I decided to keep it the bad news myself, especially that she had gone to visit Radka in Florida. Ten days later, Lemi informed me that Boubi had entered the neurological clinic at the Plovdiv University hospital. Following all the alarming news, I was highly relieved to receive a longer, warm and calm New Year's letter from Boubi himself, thanking me for my Christmas presents and for my invitation to meet somewhere out of Bulgaria, or at least to talk on the telephone. *"It was unfortunately impossible to speak on the phone, as now I'm under treatment in a Plovdiv clinic—nervous exhaustion. You're writing that we should meet. I think there's no need for me to tell you what a great joy it would be for me to see you, to see also Mama, Radka, Lil, and the children! But whether this is possible or not—it does-n't depend on me."*

Meanwhile, the news worsened. A relative of ours from Plovdiv, Vera Butchkova, a former hospital nurse who had for a longtime helped Lemi in a most touching manner, was now helping Boubi too, and started writing me detailed letters about his medical condition. She thought that the only solution was for him to come and join us in America. This was also the advice of my cousin and former classmate, Gosho Panov, whom I had implored to try to do something to help Boubi. The situation became critical when Lemi fell gravely ill and had to be send to a hospital, and then to an old people's home. Then Boubi finally consented to apply again for a passport to go abroad. In view of his med-ical condition, Vera, as well as Gosho, volunteered to escort him on the flight to Paris, if the authorities allowed them. Naturally, all expenses had to be paid by me, for which I provided a duly notarized affidavit. By that time, I was already sending money to both Boubi and Lemi. However, after repeated attempts, Boubi's application was turned down again, which was a new blow to him. Feeling deeply and unjustly hurt, he declared that he would no more humiliate himself and beg for a passport. It became more and more clear that he would never be allowed to leave the country again.

*   *   *   *   *

But why had he cut all communications with us during four-and-a-half years, although he was aware from our letters that we worried so much and Mama was sick with sorrow? What were those "very serious reasons," mentioned in his brief letter? I wonder which had been harder on me: having been kept that long in total ignorance and fearing that we had somehow mortally hurt his feelings, or now, the horrible news about his health and mental state, which I had to hide from Mama? Indeed, the alarming letters I had begun to receive regularly from Lemi and from Vera Butchkova, distressed me enormously and cast a heavy cloud over the happiness of my otherwise happy life. I was also oppressed by the thought that my political activity in emigration had aggravated Boubi's fate and that he was probably persecuted to some degree because of me. At the same time, there was the remorse that I, who lived so well, was not capable of helping my own brother…

While we were beating our brains against the wall trying to find a raison for Boubi's behavior and made guesses about how and where he was living, his life during those years had been nothing but continual ordeal. Years later, fragmentary episodes and details from his strange and sad life (or should I rather say a *"passional"?)* started reaching me, enabling me to reconstruct the chronology of his trials. But it didn't reveal his intimate thoughts and feelings during his unending Golgotha. Even today I'm not sure that I fully understood the motives of all his actions and reactions, to begin with his obstinacy in voluntarily returning from America to Bulgaria in order to resume carrying the heavy cross, which he knew only too well.

After returning to Sofia in 1963, the Militia, as it was to be expected, didn't let him in peace too long. After having traded the comforts of Manhattan and Southampton for a bed in the modest lodging of Radka's husband, Sasso Rizov, Boubi found a temporary job in a workshop for steam radiators in a remote outskirt of the capital. It was an exhausting job physically, especially when two men had to carry on their backs 200-pound oxygen bottles up the floors. Then he started working on a construction project, until an early April morning when Militiamen arrived at Sasso's home and arrested him, with no explanations. Boubi suspected that the reason was a letter he had written a few days earlier to the Minister of Internal Affairs, interceding in favor of a young girl with whom he was then in love. One day, quite unexpectedly this girl had asked him some very strange (according to him) question. It was so uncharacteristic, that Boubi, being overly suspicious, jumped to the conclusion that the Militia was trying to forcibly enroll the young woman to spy on him. It reminded him of the odious tactics, a few years earlier, of the secret services when they attempted to coerce Radka into spying on her American and British employers. Without waiting for more proof, he wrote impulsively to the Interior Minister, asking him to order his services to let the young lady alone. ("What a curious, unwarranted reaction!" I thought when I first heard of it. But didn't those who were living in Bulgaria have enough reasons to be on the paranoid side?)

Only a couple of days later, Boubi was sent under militia escort to forced labor at a stone quarry in North-East Dobrudzha. After a three-day trip, the train deposed him at Krupen, a poor village near Kavarna, where a road was being built. There, he was enlisted in a group of 50 or 60 men, mostly alcoholics and common-law delinquents, with no more than two or three political "undesirables." They slept on bunk beds in an old hencoop, heated by a wood stove, for which they had to provide their own wood from the nearby fields. The quarry was located at 300 yards from the primitive dormitory. The work consisted in loading the empty trucks, which transported the rocks to the road project. From dawn to dusk, Boubi loaded trucks, and no matter how much he tried to select lighter stones, he ended each workday with his back aching from fatigue. Every night a militiaman proceeded to the evening verification, after which the light was turned off and the exhausted men collapsed to their bunks. There was no question of reading, not even of having a conversation with some more or less literate "colleague."

That's how Boubi has lived during one year and a quarter, through terribly cold winters and scorching summers. And despite the harsh living conditions and strict discipline, he always made a point to specify, "in the interest of the objective truth," that in Krupen he was not in a "camp," but only "on forced labor." Unlike the concentration camps, "in Krupen they paid us wages," he used to correct me, many years later, if I would say that my brother was sent to a camp... But could he leave Krupen?—Of course, not! It was forbidden even to go and buy something in the village. They were fed in the mess-room, with the price of the meals withheld from their wages.

But it wasn't the heavy labor nor the physical hardships, which oppressed my brother. He suffered above all from being deprived of freedom, from not being told why nor for how long he would be detained in Krupen. The uncertainty, the solitude, and the exhaustion took their toll on his mental state, with no outlet for him to share his worries, with no one to even talk to. After many unsuccessful protests and attempts to learn the reason for his punishment, Boubi declared a hunger strike and at the same time sent a detailed complaint addressed to the Parliament. For twenty days he refused to eat, spending his time in bed and accepting only water. He was not punished for stopping to go to work, but, of course, never received any answer to his petition. Meanwhile, the state of his health deteriorated so alarmingly, that he was sent for medical examination to Kavarna, where the doctor diagnosed a "defect in the heart." As a result, at the end of 1965 Boubi was released from Krupen and went at Lemi's, for a medical treatment in Plovdiv. After some rest, the "heart defect" turned out to be luckily nothing very serious.

After a few months however, following another refusal by the authorities to grant him Sofia residence, and in view of the miserable living conditions in Lemi's one-room dwelling (with no hot water and the outhouse in the court-yard), Boubi was forced to move out and look for a job. One of the few places he knew outside Sofia and Plovdiv was the cooperative farm in Gueshanovo, where he had already lived in forced residence with Mama and Radka, some 14 years earlier. Thus, in the summer of 1966, he left for this remote Dobrudzha village. He stayed in Gueshanovo for two whole years, going to visit Lemi in Plovdiv only for Christmas. The village, more and more abandoned by most young peo-ple, looked even poorer and more desolate than he had remembered it. A certain "Uncle" Vassil, who recognized him, showed him an empty room in an aban-doned, dilapidated house in the town's outskirts and Boubi moved in, to live there in total solitude. He would get up at dawn to join the TKZC's "brigade," where work was assigned at 6:30 in the morning. After a brief breakfast, all work-ers left for the fields. If the object was far away, they were transported on horse carts. They worked until noon and after two hours rest for lunch (Boubi used to bring his own bread, cheese and some butter), work resumed and lasted until 5 PM, when they returned to the village. There he had to face again the solitude, the darkness, and in winter—the cold, in his tumbledown dwelling. When in the right mood, he spent part of the nights working on a theater play, "The Mausoleum," which he had started before. (It wasn't his first literary venture: already in the 1950s, he had written a historical play, *Boyan*, in free verse, which he had re-written at least five times, while working at the coffin workshop in the Tcherepish monastery.) Now, in Gueshanovo, a village with no library, movie theater, or even a tavern, writing had remained his only divertissement. Beyond a handful of nice, but illiterate villagers, there was no one with whom he could speak. That's how two entire years of Boubi's life had passed!

When I think about it, I wonder whether it hadn't been for the best that he didn't write during those years. Maybe it was better for us that we didn't know how he was passing the interminable lonely hours of his days and nights that we were unaware of what he was thinking and feeling. This would've killed Mama, who was eaten away by black suspicions, but still could allow herself to rationalize that her dear Boubi kept silent only because he was a little bit on the eccentric side, and not because he was sick or suffering. I began to learn details only after he broke his nearly five-year silence, way after Gueshanovo. But up to this day I'm still horrified when I realize that my cultured, spiritually refined, brother, this mild, hypersensitive dreamer, had lived during some 40 months (if we add the time spent in Krupen and Gueshanovo) in a debilitating solitude and hopeless monotony, deprived of freedom, of understanding and any human contact, badly toil worn, frequently hungry, humiliated, forgotten in the depressing misery of unfamiliar villages and dormitories. While I, during that same time?...I can't help thinking of *my* life during those years, 1964, 1965, 66, 67, and the following years, each one happier than the other. And it pains me to think that we came from the same family and the same home, carried the same genes, and had a similar childhood. It pains me when I remember what a delicate and good child he used to be, how vulnerable in his idealism! And I ask myself, how does a human being with normal sensibilities outlive such ordeals, such a forced isolation? Myself, for instance, would I have survived, if I were in his place? How does the spirit survive, and the heart, and the soul?

In my brother's case, the sad answer to this question is nothing but too obvious. Physically, he did survive. But mentally...Here is what I learned, years later: It was during the fall. He was returning to Gueshanovo, after a leave spent at Lemi's in Plovdiv. It had been a very long, exhausting trip, eleven hours by train and bus to the city of Tolbukhin, where he stopped for dinner in a restaurant, before continuing to Gueshanovo. That's where he had the strange experience for the first time. An auditory hallucination. An unknown, but perfectly clear voice, was repeating distinct, unpleasant words in his ear. They were short sentences, some of them threatening, some sarcastic, expressed in rude, vulgar language. Shocked and frightened, Boubi returned in a terrible state to his village, where the hallucinations continued the following days. Extremely concerned and incapable to get rid of the importunate voice, he asked for sick leave and immediately returned to Plovdiv. But as he was passing again through the town of Tolbukhin, his attention was drawn by a tall antenna-tower on the top of the municipal park and exactly at that moment he heard the same voice in his ears. It was incredibly clear, as if someone were sending messages through the antenna's airways, directly to Boubi's brain. Fantastic as it was, a suspicion was born in his mind that some enormously important, but still secret, discovery had been made somewhere in the world: the possibility of sending words into other people brains!

It was with that idea, and not at all a fear of suffering some kind of nervous disorder that Boubi arrived in Plovdiv and it took the alarmed Lemi an enormous effort to convince him to look for medical help. Finally he consented to be examined at the Psychiatry department of the University clinic, where the consideration and understanding shown him by the doctors gained his trust and he agreed to enter the hospital. He was lucky that the treating psychiatrist, Dr. Boncho Kukladjiev, turned out to be a highly cultured man, who became sincerely interested in Boubi's case and, before long, a real friendship was born between them. After a three-months treatment with pills, the hallucinations disappeared and Boubi felt almost cured. The important thing was that, thanks to his complete trust in Dr. Kukladjiev, he realized that he was ill and needed treatment. His first letter to me, after his long silence, dated from this period. He stayed in the clinic for five months, but more as a boarder, free to go out whenever he wanted to see his aunt or look for a job. At the hospital he helped with the office work, continued his intellectual discussions with Dr. Kukladjiev and resumed work on his often-interrupted novels. In the spring, when he was discharged from the clinic, he found a job in a canning factory in Kritchim, a railroad station near Plovidiv, where he unloaded tomatoes by wheelbarrow. He lived in a workmen's dormitory and his health had improved considerably, but he suffered from total insomnia. After several weeks, at the insistence of Lemi and a cousin of ours, Magda Gerdjikova, he went for convalescence to Koprivshtitza, the old town of our ancestors, where he joined Magda. It was his first real rest since he had returned from the New York, and he spent the entire summer of 1969 in that picturesque small town, one of Boubi's favorite places. The pure mountain air, the surrounding peace and serenity, and the daily long hikes in company of Magda, had a highly beneficial effect on him, and soon he was able to sleep again, to eat regularly, and to think in relative calm.

The Gerdjikovs were among our most interesting relatives, and of them, Michel Gerdjikov, my father's first cousin and Magda's father, was the most colorful. A man with a remarkable culture and courage, he had gained fame as a legendary participant in the Macedonian uprisings in 1903, before ardently embracing the cause of anarchism and becoming one of the founders and inspirers of the Bulgarian Anarchist movement. Curiously enough, a special affection attached the two cousins during all their lives—the peaceable King's counselor, and the fiery revolutionary. By spirit and culture, Magda was a true daughter of her father. Although Boubi's senior by a few years, this bright, well-educated woman who read foreign authors and entertained many interests, was exactly the right company he needed now, hungry as he was for warmth and understanding after his years of seclusion.

But Koprivshtitza was not more than a brief interlude, just a moment to catch his breath. With the summer's end, the harsh reality was waiting for him in Plovdiv. Again unemployed. With no money and no permit to return to Sofia. He spent the winter sharing the dismal room of Lemi, whose health was worsening. His last hope remained to be granted residence in Sofia and find some job there, in the city where he was born and raised, and where most of his friends and acquaintances lived. But all his demarches and petitions remained unanswered, which, given his touchiness, turned into an obsession. After the Uncle Mitcho's failed attempt to intervene in his favor, other friends tried to help, but Boubi's stubborn intransigence was tying their hands. His stand was clear: he absolutely refused to *beg* for something (in this case, his Sofia residence), which he considered his right by birth and of which he was deprived illegally an without cause. Not only didn't he ask for a favor or merci on the part of the rulers, but he was voicing his indignation aloud and demanded full explanation for the denial of his requests. With the police regime reigning in the country, such language precluded, of course, any chance for receiving satisfaction. But to well-intended advice to be more flexible and diplomatic, or to use friends' connections with influential communists, Boubi replied indignantly with categorical refusal.

To this day, many are the people who could understand his refusal to accept the realities of life and who wonder whether he really had to go through the ordeals of Krupen and Gueshanovo, if he hadn't thrown himself in lost-in-advance battles against windmills. If he hadn't so naively insisted on receiving excuses for the injustices. But would these same people, including myself, return from New York and Paris, as he did, when he had the possibility of remaining there? If I ask the question whether all my brother's ordeals had been really unavoidable, and whether he himself hadn't contributed in some measure to part of them, then shouldn't I also ask myself to what extent the sufferings of the first Christian martyrs, headed *consciously* for their own slaughter, were inescapable? I confess that, although my brother and I share the same genes and upbringing, many of his actions and reactions will always remain incomprehensible to me. As, I'm certain, he wouldn't understand all in the behavior of his more superficial and hedonistically inclined brother.

Inexplicable for me is, for example, a decision he made after the long winter of unemployment and deprivations in Plovdiv. When a new refusal arrived from the Sofia authorities, Boubi was so deeply disappointed, that he decided to leave town right away and take any job, anywhere else. But where? At that point, a romantic image emerged in his mind. Longtime before, when he was traveling once to Gueshanovo, he met in the train car an adorable unknown girl. She radiated such an unusual purity, charm and warmth that, for a moment, Boubi forgot all the ugliness and cruelty of the world. They started a conversation and he became so enthralled, that he didn't feel how the hours passed and he had to get out at his station. "And you, how far are you going?" he asked. "I continue to General-Toshevo. That's where I live," she said with a lovely smile, before they he said goodbye. Long after that Boubi continued thinking and dreaming of her and each time the memory of their brief encounter warmed his heart.

Now, finding himself again with no home and no destination, he remembered the girl from the train, and the name of her town rang out as a bright symbol of some new hopes. Thus, with no other reason whatsoever, he took the train for the remote railroad station of General-Toshevo, almost the last town in Dobrudzha before reaching the Rumanian border. There he found a job with a minimal pay, as an unskilled worker at the construction of new stables for the local calves-fattening center. He rented a small room, where he spent all his evenings by himself, in reading and writing, seeing no one outside the construction people.

So far, many romantic natures may understand, more or less, this unusual behavior. Who, among us, following his or her heart, hasn't made unwise, and often absurd, decisions? But what makes Boubi quite different from myself and from the "ordinary" romantic natures, is his strange attitude afterwards. During the entire six months that he spent in General-Toshevo, he never looked for the young lady from the train, not once! Once or twice he saw her from a distance, in the street, but didn't go to talk to her. This example of extreme, pure Platonism, totally without any ulterior motives and not expecting anything in exchange of one's own beautiful feelings, was typical for my brother, but I admit, will remain a mystery to me.

After six months spent in quasi-total solitude in the unfamiliar town, Boubi felt the first warning signs of an approaching new period of depression. His landlord also noticed that something was not in order with his tenant and alerted the authorities. An ambulance was sent to pick him up and drive him to the hospital in Varna, where he described his recent medical history and the doctors contacted his psychiatrists in Plovdiv. But in the Varna hospital Boubi found none of the warm atmosphere of the Plovdiv clinic, nor the same human contact he used to enjoy with his former doctors. After three weeks of treatment, he asked to be transferred. The hospital showed understanding and even sent a nurse to accompany him on the train to Plovdiv, where Lemi waited for him. Boubi was admitted again to the University clinic. His old friend Dr. Kukladjiev gave the diagnosis of "Bleuler disease." There was some recurrence of hallucinations, but Boubi attributed them no more to "waves directed by someone from outside," he was aware of his illness. He spent two months in the hospital, at first confined in bed, in a room for four patients, and later under a more relaxed regime of "work therapy"—gluing envelopes and helping with office chores in the big lobby, where he was permitted to receive visits by Lemi and other relatives. In general, due to his incredible politeness and kindness, everybody in the clinic,—from the director, Prof. Todor Tashev, to the doctors, the personnel and the other patients,—were specially attentive to my brother, which contributed considerably to his recovery. The clinic turned out to be one of the rare places in many years, where Boubi didn't feel as a persecuted social pariah. In the beginning of 1972, recovering satisfactorily from his latest ailment, but already a man with permanently weakened health and nerves, Boubi left the hospital, returned temporarily to Lemi's and started procedures for early retirement. With the help of a certificate issued by the clinic, he obtained papers for provisional residence in Plovdiv, as well as a pension of 50 leva, the lowest possible for unskilled workers, and moved into an attic room at the devoted Vera's. In order to survive, I was sending him a little money, at the official exchange rate, i.e. one lev for one dollar, which was a real robbery, as the real rate of the dollar was at least four times higher. In addition, the authorities withheld a considerable part for the bank transfer and for various taxes, therefore he received only a portion of the money. But in his position, we couldn't take the risk for him to be accused of illegal exchange of currency. Thus, during the 1970s, Boubi lived in utter poverty in Plovdiv, renting dismal rooms found for him usually by the good cousin Vera, and still in daily touch with his beloved Lemi, the aging, ailing aunt, who was even poorer than him. His health was precarious and at times he chose, as a preventive measure, to return for a few days voluntarily to his well-known clinic. There his nerves calmed down and he didn't feel depressed or unhappy, especially when taken by the urge to write. Some evenings by 10, after all patients in the large common dormitory were asleep, he moved to the hall and wrote during long hours. Thus, at one of his stays, he had the idea of a new literary work, *Don Juan*, a long poem in free verse, on which he worked frantically during twelve consecutive nights. The satisfaction he felt when he finished it, made him forget for a longtime his illness and the misery in which he lived.

The sad, alarming letters of Lemi and Vera Butchkova during this period kept me more or less informed about Boubi's state, and they used to upset me deeply. But despite the formal invitations I continued sending for Boubi to visit me in the States or in France, and despite the official applications for a passport, which Boubi finally agreed to file again, the Bulgarian authorities invariably answered with categorical refusal without any explanations, or with total silence.

*   *   *   *

Chapter 31

Two more Larousse books: "La Terre", "Le Cosmos"

The elevator's cabin leaves the ground and, like a space rocket but headed in the opposite direction, is launched down into the subterranean depths. Finding myself for the first time so deep in the bowels of the Earth gives me a curious, uncomfortable, sensation. *Welkom* goldmine in Free State Geduld is one of the deepest in South Africa and shaft # 4 into which I'm plunging goes 1600 meters down—a full mile underground! The main galleries are quite wide, well lit and ventilated, and one should feel no more uneasy than in the Paris metro, if one can ignore the oppressive thought of being one-and-a-half kilometer below ground. But as soon as one leaves them to gain the lateral tunnels, which are passages of a claustrophobic narrowness, the only way to advance is by crawling on all fours. The darkness becomes total, pierced only by the light beams of the flashlights on our helmets, illuminating only a few yards in front of us.

The temperature rises, becomes unbearable; the coveralls are soaked, sweat pours from the foreheads. My heart beats wildly and I'm trying with all my strength to control my mounting panic. That would indeed be a disaster, because there is no possible way to stand up in this grave-like burrow, or to give up and go back: the shoulders touch the walls, my is back brushing the ceiling, and the person crawling behind me obstructs the passage entirely. Yes, I'm stuck. I feel buried inside this labyrinth that never ends, turning left, then right, then in another direction in the total darkness. And I ask myself why, oh why, did I volunteer to put myself in this spot.

When I think about it, these painful but short moments of anguish were just a very small price I had to pay for my otherwise marvelous visit to South Africa. Ever since Sava married and went to live there, that country presented a special fascination for me and visiting it had been a most cherished dream. In spite of

Sava's repeated and insistent invitations, I had never had the opportunity to fulfill it. Finally, the occasion came, or rather was instigated by me, in October 1971, when I included that trip in my research plans for the second volume of my *Larousse* books, *L'Homme et la Terre*, a book on the world of modern Earth sciences. Of course, going to South Africa was hardly a must, but as I had carte-blanche to choose my subjects and the people to interview, it didn't take much rationalization to convince myself that the South-African mines, being among the best and deepest in the world, were an excellent place to peek into the interior of Mother Earth. In other word, once more to combine professional duty and pleasure. Especially that Sava, working then for his friend Charlie Engelhard's industries, had befriended the most powerful man on the continent, *Anglo-American* and *De Beers* companies boss Harry Oppenheimer, owner, among countless other companies, of most of South Africa's gold and diamond mines.

I spent two delightful weeks at Panitza's lovely house in a residential outskirt of Johannesburg, where prosperous members of the Anglo minority live in great comfort among perfect lawns, swimming pools and, of course, black servants galore. Sava, Pamela, her daughter, Denela, and their daughter Marina showed me around (Nicky was away at boarding school) and I was introduced to many of their friends, all pleasant, sporty types with a taste for good parties and more than a couple of *gin-and-tonics*. Although obvious beneficiaries of the South-African segregation and accepting it as a reality which "they did not create," they all acted embarrassed by its excesses, deplored the so-called "petty Apartheid" and were strongly critical of the ruling Dutch descendants, the "Afrikaners," with whom they entertained very little contact. Pam and Denela took me on a two-day tour of the huge Kruger Park, where I could enjoy the sight of freely roaming herds of elephants and antelopes, of giraffes and all sorts of wild animals, and hear by night the majestic roar of lions near our cabins. I went by myself to Cape Town, one of the world's most gorgeously situated cities, and, perched on the rocks of nearby Cape of Good Hope, at the southern-most tip of Africa, and surrounded by annoying, noisy crowds of ugly baboons, spent long moments meditating on olden day navigators.

That night I dined with the celebrated Dr. Chris Barnard, and his beautiful young wife Barbara, to whom I had been recommended by Pamela. The glamorous surgeon had recently performed the first heart transplant, a historic milestone and had been repeatedly on "Paris-Match's" pages. We had quite an interesting conversation. Back in Johannesburg, Sava and Pam took me to a party every night, while during the day I was collecting information about the country, its regime, and its mines.

Among the most pleasant discoveries I made during my visit was Sava's 19-year-old daughter Marina. I had already met her briefly as a young girl in Paris, when some uncanny physical and behavioral resemblances triggered and revived in me, in a veritable shock, memories of Sava as a young boy. Recognizing in her the same traits which had attracted me to Sava when I first met him, recognizing my own feelings and sensations the way I had felt them *then*, I was suddenly transported back into these bygone days, and for a few moments *I was* that boy, with *his* self-awareness, and not my present one. It was a strange, very private thrill, and I was grateful to the unsuspecting child for that. Now in Johannesburg, her presence in the house gave me much joy and, having the opportunity to know her better, I developed a deep affection for this attractive girl and real interest for her bright, independent mind. If I had had a daughter, I thought, that was the kind I wished I had! She responded by making me her trusted confidant, which turned out to be a rewarding but highly delicate role: Marina was a rebellious modern girl, while Sava, like most former girl-chasers, was an overly strict and jealous father, refusing to accept that his daughter had grown into a young woman. Often I had to serve as buffer between their hot personalities, sometimes successfully, sometimes not, but always with love and caring enormously for both of them.

As far as my research work in South Africa went, the most important acquaintance I made, thanks to Sava, was that of the Oppenheimers. Harry and Bridget were obviously very fond of Sava, and he brought me to their magnificent estate, once with the families and a few guests, and the second time for tea, just three of us—Harry Oppenheimer, Sava and I. What surprised me in this fabulously rich and powerful man was his unusually modest demeanor. Oppenheimer, Africa's greatest tycoon, struck me as being not only extremely polite, but self-effacing and humble. I felt almost embarrassed each time when this shy, middle-aged gentleman opened a door for me and insisted that I pass first, or when he pulled a better chair for his guests and jumped to his feet to offer more tea and cookies. I was amazed to hear the political ideas of the mild, intelligent man who practically owned the country. He spoke as a convinced liberal, an ashamed and sincere enemy of Apartheid, an advocate of "colored" people's human rights, and an active adversary of the Boer government. Deploring the political inefficiency of his fellow "Anglos" of the opposition, he had formed his own third party, with representatives in Parliament, devoted to abolition of Apartheid. But not precipitately, and certainly not violently. His solution: begin by emancipating the Blacks through education and ownership! Give them first a real stake in the country, before giving them the right to vote, he preached. Long after we left him, I was still thinking of Harry Oppenheimer's unexpected liberalism. I liked him very much and liked his noble beliefs. But if the Apartheid problem disturbed me before I came to South Africa, I left even more confused after talking to the country's uncrowned king, in whose good intentions and sincere compassion for the Blacks I found no reason to doubt.

We talked about my book project and I mentioned the difficulties outsiders like me had to be admitted down into a deep mine during operation. The next day I had not only the invitation, but also an escort and a company small plane at my disposal. Descending in the 900-feet-deep platinum mine at Rustenberg presented no problem, and visiting the relatively shallow and clean *Premier Diamond* mine near Pretoria was a real pleasure, especially that it gave me the opportunity of seeing the pretty South-African capital and its magnificent jacaranda trees in full bloom. But the evening when I was told about the next day's arrangements to be taken down to the "working personnel only" areas of the deep goldmine, I confess that I had cold feet. That night I worried a lot about claustrophobia, but could I turn down this exceptional favor, granted by Mr. Oppenheimer personally? So here I am now, perspiring in the darkness of this suffocating sepulcher.

We're advancing painfully; the air gets heavier, the heat is overwhelming. Then suddenly, the tight burrow ends abruptly, barred by a huge vertical rock, the wall of a sort of a vault, where we are able to finally stand up. The subterranean chamber is filled with dust and the strident noise of drilling pierces our eardrums. Sitting on the floor, his naked black torso shining with sweat, his feet planted against the wall and a heavy pneumatic drill between his legs, a powerfully built Bantou bores a hole in the rock. The engineer who serves as our guide directs his searchlight to the wall. I won't forget the thrill I felt at the sight of the ribbon of sparkling paillettes horizontally crossing the somber rock, from side to side: the gold-bearing vein! The layer of gold is very thin, just about one inch wide, and yet Man has managed to locate it precisely, deep in the immensity of the underground, and, mobilizing thousands of people and colossal resources, has dug a whole mile down the hard rock to collect it! What an exploit, I think in admiration as I take off my muddy glove and caress the glittering vein. Then, with the size of the terrestrial globe in mind, I try to imagine the exact point where I'm standing now, right this minute. It's impressive, when I see myself being at a whole one mile underground! But think that there are about 4,000 miles more to the Earth's center! A sense of humility mitigates the pride. I remember that the deepest point any man-made instrument has ever penetrated is 4.8 miles, in a Texas oil well. But what about the rest of those four thousand miles of rock? What do we know about its composition and structure, mile by mile, under our feet? About the behavior of each layer, all the way down the center of the globe? And that center, what is it made of? Some unimaginably compressed hard material, or a liquid, melted by infernal temperatures, or even a super-heated gas? It sounds so elementary, but I've forgotten what they used to teach us in school. However, there obviously must be people who know much more about it, and it would be very interesting to hear where modern science stands on the subject. And on many other Earth-related subjects too.

My present mission was to find some of the most advanced among today's Earth scientists and ask them what they have learned so far about our planet, about its origin and age, its exact shape and measurements, about earthquakes and volcanoes, mountains formation, magnetic poles, glacial epochs, and hundred other mysteries. To penetrate the world of modern researchers, describe them, try to understand their findings and hypotheses (not an easy task for a layman with no formal scientific education, like me), and then come back to *our* readers and tell them, in plain, everyday language, that which I have observed and learned. To me, the task sounded fascinating and I thanked my stars for the luck to have such a job. The research took me about two years, wholeheartedly supported by *Larousse* and *Paris-Match* who were extremely pleased with my first volume, *L'Homme et la Mer*. Raymond Cartier, *Larousse*'s chairman Etienne Gillon, and Pierre Laffont, the *Match* editor in charge of book publishing, couldn't have been more enthusiastic and encouraging.

As I've already said, my previous work on oceanography had put me in touch with the great contemporary discoveries in geophysics and had introduced me to the revolutionary ideas on continental drift, sea-floor expansion, and plate tectonics. I had already met several leaders of the new school, at *Lamont Observatory* in New York, at Princeton, at *Scripps Institute* in La Jolla, at Cambridge, and elsewhere. I used much from these interviews for my book on *The Earth* too, and now tried to keep abreast of the sensational new developments in that field, by subscribing to a few not too esoteric scientific reviews and newsletters and by revisiting scientists I had already spoken to. Extending the research, I went to N.Y. State University in Albany to interview the young geologists John Bird and John Dewey, who had formulated a new hypothesis, linking the origin of the mountains to the movement of tectonic plates. Then I visited at *Lamont* two young seismologists, Bryan Isacks and Lynn Sykes, who, while examining submarine earthquakes, had recently added decisive proofs to the tectonics theory. Sykes' seismographs confirmed that the new crust material, coming from the bowels of the Earth, was "born" at the crest of the oceanic ridges, while Isack's measurements (working with his professor Jack Oliver) established that the rigid plates, after floating away from these ridges, ended by being engulfed into the deep oceanic trenches, where they return back into the globe's interior. It was a rare, stimulating privilege for me to listen about these discoveries directly from the mouth of the two scientists, both barely 30-year old and looking like graduate students. Another young man, their former French colleague from Lamont,

Xavier Le Pichon, calculated the speed and direction of the moving plates, these rigid mosaic fragments that form the Earth's crust. When I met him, Le Pichon showed me his geographic map of the world's tectonic plates, one of the earliest models on which one could see clearly the seams between the slowly moving plates. That's precisely the hot seismic points, where most earthquakes and volcanoes are likely to occur.

Talking about volcanoes, one of the most fascinating characters I had the chance of meeting during my research was Haroun Tazieff, the legendary explorer, part-scientist, part-adventurer, who was spending his life impatiently waiting for the next eruption. As soon as some volcano activity was announced somewhere in the world, no matter where or when, Tazieff jumped on the first available plane and rushed to the scene. There, at the very rim of the crater, and showing a kamikaze-like audacity, the famous volcanologist was in his element, giving free rein to at least three of the colorful personalities who lived in him: first, the aesthete, each time profoundly moved and in awe of the most grandiose spectacle offered by Nature (his poetic descriptions and dramatic photos used to reach millions of readers); second, the daring sportsman (Tazieff was a first-class alpinist, a rock climber, a Mont-Blanc skier, a former semi-professional boxer, and, at the age of 59, when I met him, still a rugby player in one of the best French teams); and third, the scientist, who had examined most of the world's craters, usually during eruption, and whose numerous books and scientific publications had made him the best known publicist of volcanology.

I liked him immediately, from the moment I felt his frank, manly handshake with which he welcomed me in his Paris home. When we met, he was just coming back from Afar, in Ethiopia, the hottest spot on Earth, and I was returning from the South Pole, the coldest. It took us five minutes to discover that we had admired, in our youth, some of the same heroes: Captain Robert Falcon Scott, the martyr of Antarctica, and his victorious rival, Roald Amundsen. Then I discovered that this French explorer was of Russian origin, born in Poland, and educated in Belgium, a refugee like me, who had to learn early to use his fists so his schoolmates would stop making fun of his accent and his funny name. (His mother, he told me, had two heroes: Haroun-al-Rashid, of the *Thousand-and-One Nights*

Arabian tales, and Savonarola. "At least she didn't saddle me with this second name," he chuckled.) We found many things in common to talk about. When I mentioned my skiing vacations in Gstaad, he told me about the revelation which changed his life at age eighteen: traveling in Switzerland on the little train from Thun and Spiez to Adelboden (a train I knew so well), the youth from the Belgian plains saw for the first time in his life a mountain; and not just any mountain, but the breathtaking peaks of the Berner Oberland, some of the most gorgeous sights in the Alps. It was a shock, a love at first sight. Devoting thereafter his life to the mountains, he had a second revelation when, after World War 2 (in which he joined the Resistance and dynamited German trains in Belgium), he took a job at the Geological service in the Congo. It was there, around 1947, when he saw his first volcano in action: the eruption of Virunga, north of the Lake Kivu. He was never the same man after that.

I saw Tazieff a few more times, and he gave me some of his books and many spectacular photographs, which we used later in my book *L'Homme et la Terre*. Good raconteur, he told me about many of his experiences, about Etna, and Niragongo, and other volcanoes where he braved the fury of lava, fire and eruption, practically from the very rim of the inferno. To me, the tales of this extraordinarily daring man were part of the same story, the magnificent venture of brave explorers, inspired scientists, imaginative researchers and assiduous laboratory workers, all burning with curiosity, all trying to understand the mysteries of the planet on which we live. The story, in fact, which I wanted to tell in my book.

I was lucky to be able to add, unexpectedly, a new source of information about the Earth: the space program. As a *Paris-Match* reporter I witnessed, from the beaches of Cape Canaveral, a number of *Apollo* shots, including *Apollo XI*, landing the first man on the Moon, and the last one, *Apollo XVII*. In addition to the thrill of these unforgettable experiences, (some shared with Raymond and Rosie Cartier and other colleagues from *Paris-Match*), and the numerous articles we published in the magazine, I was able, in the last moment, to include in *L'Homme et la Terre* some of the knowledge newly acquired from the moon shots. As the writing of my text and the preparation of the book's lavish illustration took much longer than expected, the analysis of the rock samples, brought in the meantime to Earth by different *Apollo* missions, permitted me to add an entire new chapter. I entitled it "Will Earth's History be explained by the Moon?" and illustrated it by several color photographs coming from the Apollo program and NASA labs studying Moon rocks. (These rocks contained, of course, the same elements as the ones we have on Earth.)

L'Homme et la Terre was finally published in 1974, long after I had finished the last proofreading and written the last caption. Meanwhile, I had almost completed the work on the last book of the *Larousse* series, *L'Homme et le Cosmos*.

*   *   *   *

Man and the Universe

Intellectually, the work for this book turned out to be the most stimulating research I had done yet. To a point that many times during the three years it kept me occupied, I sincerely regretted not having studied astronomy and not having embraced cosmology as a career. I had already tasted some of its fascination more than fifteen years earlier, when doing research for Raymond Cartier's series *The World: Where It Came From, Where It Goes To?*, and had loved it. Indeed, what could be more interesting than asking questions about the universe—its nature, its origin, the reason of its existence? Is it eternal, or was it created, and how, and when? Is it infinite or has it its limits? What is matter and how did it come be? Cartier wrote once that although cosmology and astronomy were in a sense futile sciences, because they could neither explain the "why" of existence, nor served many practical purposes, *"the human spirit's desperate effort to explore the inexplorable and comprehend the non-comprehendible is the most touching testimony of its eminent dignity. Cosmology is more than a science, it's a beau geste, heroism shown for no advantage."*

Since childhood, I've always been deeply interested in those questions, but I considered them the field of philosophy, religion, or metaphysical meditation. Only after my first contacts with astronomers and nuclear physicists did I make the startling discovery that in fact they were also a domain most seriously investigated by what is known as "the exact sciences;" that notions such as "eternity," "infinity," "Genesis" and "nothingness" were being examined with precise instruments, measured with most prosaic laboratory hardware, observed empirically, and even photographed. Most researchers were very "down-to-earth" specialists in their fields, with no particular interest for philosophical or metaphysical questions, and certainly no poetry in their motivation. But that's exactly what excited me most: the fact that the eternal questions of the existence and the universe had become open to experimentalists, to hard science and technology.

First, I had to learn more about the basics of astronomy and cosmology. My initiation had taken place 15 years before, when I first went to the Mt. Wilson, Palomar and Flagstaff telescopes, read extensively about the "Big-Bang" and "Steady-State" theories of the Cosmos origin, visited the late Edwin Hubble's offices and home in Pasadena, and interviewed a few luminaries of contemporary astronomy, such as Humason, Slipher, Ira Bowen, Minkowski and others. But the enormous impression that this made on me at that time turned out to be just a foretaste of the extraordinary experience I was going into now, plunging deep in the subject. Using the name of *Paris-Match* and *Larousse* to open difficult doors, I had the good fortune to hear first hand reports about the latest developments in cosmology and to follow from a front row seat the great debate of the principal schools of thought in the early 1970s.

By then, the Big Bang theory was almost universally accepted. Most cosmologists seemed to agree that the universe, as we know it, had started at a precise date in the remote past, when all existing matter, contracted into an unimaginably dense volume, exploded in a tremendous conflagration. With Hubble's discovery in the 1920s that Andromeda was not just a "nebula" belonging to our Milky Way, as it was then believed, but represented a different galaxy, separated from ours and moving away from us, the entire concept of the cosmos changed radically. The existence of millions other galaxies was established, all flying away from each other, like fragments of an exploded bomb. Hubble and his Pasadena colleagues measured one by one the distances of a great number of galaxies, as well as their velocity of recession from us. With these figures, scientists calculated the time when the original event occurred: about 15 billion years ago. And they concluded that ever since the Big Bang, we are living in an expanding universe. In fact, the American astronomers' observations fitted well with some theoretical models of a non-static universe, proposed by a Belgian, Father Georges Lemaitre and a Russian, Alexander Friedman. Other scientists developed the revolutionary idea of a non-eternal universe, created in a singular event and still in the process of expansion. The theory of Big Bang was born. (The name was coined by a Russian émigré, Georges Gamow, the most successful and imaginative popularizer of the theory, whose accessible, witty writing was among my favorite sources on the subject.)

To reconstruct, step by step, the amazing story of the discovery, I started with the Hubble's observations of Andromeda. Hubble himself had quoted Newton, who said, referring to the great minds who had preceded him: *"If I managed to see further, it was because I could step on the shoulders of giants..."* The same was, of course, true in my case: the tale of today's cosmology could not be understood if the reader didn't know about the previous history of astronomy, the state of Man's knowledge up to the 1920s. Therefore, in the first half of our book, my colleague Jean-Pierre Cartier told the story of astronomy's *giants* of the past. Starting with prehistoric Man's fascination with the starry skies, he went on describing the lives and the discoveries of Copernicus, Ticho Brahe, Kepler and Galileo, Newton and Hershel. Setting thus the stage with six highly entertaining chapters, Jean-Pierre led me to begin my narrative of the birth and evolution of modern cosmology.

I revisited Mt. Wilson and spent a few hours at its giant 2.5-meter telescope, used by Hubble and his colleagues for their first ventures beyond the frontiers of our galaxy. I went again to their offices at 813 Santa-Barbara Street in Pasadena, where they used to analyze the photos and first spectrograms of galaxies. In a pilgrimage mood, I walked along the Shenandoah avenue, which Hubble used to take everyday day, returning home on foot. I read his personal files. I paid a visit to his distinguished widow, Grace Hubble, a charming lady. Inside the house, among his books, his pipes and personal objects, I almost felt his physical presence. This enabled me, or so I thought, to better understand this man, the first of our race to have a peak into the real organization of matter in the cosmos.

Similar feelings brought me to the ancient Belgian town of Louvain, where I tried to recapture the spirit of Abbot Lemaitre in the gothic university buildings where he had taught, and in the old churches where he was saying the Mass. My guide, professor Odon Godart, a former student and assistant of the canon-mathematician, showed me where Lemaitre used to live, walked me to his favorite promenade in Park d'Arenberg, and took me to his working cabinet. The modest old wooden desk, on which he used to fill in his numerous notebooks, was still there. Knowing that he was the first to propose the hypothesis of the Expanding Universe, it was hard for me to remain unmoved when holding in my hands pages filled with the studious handwriting of the Belgian abbot.

By now, ample astronomical observation had confirmed the arcane theoretical predictions. The Big Bang had become the recognized foundation stone of modern cosmology. Or so I read in almost every book and heard from most astronomers. The theory is in itself one of the most fascinating tales ever told, an incredibly imaginative, beautiful tale, as poetic as the finest poetry, as awesome as the biblical story of the Creation. It's a modern-day Book of Genesis, told in terms of most advanced astronomy and physics. Seldom had I been as enthralled as when I had its chapters narrated and patiently explained to me by some of the world's great authorities in the field. What a unique chance for a layman to interrogate Pasadena's Allan Sandage, a disciple of Hubble and one of his most prominent successors, and ask him questions about the flight of galaxies and about the confines of the universe; to discuss the "how" and "why" of Creation with *CalTech*'s Jesse Greenstein; to listen to French physicist Roland Omnes talk about existence of anti-matter; to hear the saga of the surprising discovery directly from the mouth of Milton Humason; to listen to Princeton's John Wheeler, the discoverer of "black holes"! Many of these scientists didn't think of themselves as cosmologists, they called themselves pure, empirical observers, reporting strictly the observed data and leaving it to others to interpret them and construct cosmological hypotheses. Handing me spectrograms of galaxies 3 or 4 billion light-years away, they would matter-of-factedly discuss the red shift shown on the film, without being overly moved by the breath-taking fact that we were looking at events occurring 3 or 4 billion years ago!... Sandage, with whom I had developed closer relationship, showed me one day in his cluttered office spectrograms of quasars 10 billion light years away, which he pulled out of a disorderly pile of photos, papers and transparencies. Their red shift was establishing a record: a 3.5 times displacement of the spectral lines! (In those days, the largest measured red shift of a galaxy was of 0.46.) In other words, this mild man was showing me pictures of events that had happened at the dawn of time, just during the first one-tenth of the time since Creation. "These quasars seem to be at the horizon of the universe," he mumbled modestly. When I couldn't help rhapsodizing about the grandiose philosophical implications of such scientific miracles, he acted almost embarrassed. "I don't know…I'm just an observer. I'm the most un-romantic scientist here." He protested too much, I thought.

The most famous radio astronomer at the time, Sir Bernard Lovell, was no less humble. I met him in England, at his gigantic radio telescope at Jodrell Bank, a wonder of modern technology. "You're asking me to tell you about the creation of the universe, about its nature and structure?" the great man said. "I'm afraid, you came to the wrong person, sir. For what do I know about those things? I'm nothing but a simple radio-astronomer."

Humility was not the most common trait of all astronomers and cosmologists. I found quite a lot of inflated egos, plenty of prima donnas, and enough rivalries, emotional feuds and ill-concealed jealousies, to enable me to write my scientific inquiry in the form of a human, sometimes *very* human, narrative. Cosmology opens the stage for many controversies, but none was as hot and passionate as the celebrated early quarrel between advocates and adversaries of the Expanding universe theory. Because, although recognized by the majority of cosmologists, the Big Bang idea was met with tremendous resistance, and many scientists had the most serious reservations about it.

Not only scientists, of course. To the average layman, the idea of a universe which began at a precise, and identifiable, moment (*"And what was there before that moment?"*), a cosmos whose components are still flying away (*"Where to?"*) after the original explosion (*"Why was all matter packed so tightly into a single place, and where did it come from, anyway?"*), sounded somehow too hard to conceive. Except for the literal believers in the biblical seven-day divine creation, the mind accommodates itself easier to abstract concepts such as an infinite, unchanged and ever-existing universe with no beginning and no end. This had been my own vision too, which amounts in a way to an admission that our mind is unable to ever grasp the mystery of the cosmos. Therefore, the Big Bang theory, when I first heard of it, did not sound entirely convincing to me.

To this inborn resistance, my new contacts with astronomy added an additional, and disturbing, reason for skepticism. Although dazzled by the beauty and imaginativeness of the new cosmology, I couldn't help having certain doubts about the premises on which this intricate edifice had been constructed. How reliable were the assumed numbers and measurements, and how correct the yardsticks for calculating distances, sizes, and velocities? It looked to me that, disappointingly, many figures were arrived at by methods and techniques that non-astronomers would consider frankly as unconvincing, too approximate and imprecise, if not pure guessing. But what disturbed me most was that the entire Big Bang theory seemed to repose on the interpretation of one single measurement, the *red shift* in galaxies' spectra. I could still not reconcile myself with the thought that one of the most uplifting intellectual quests of the human race was based on simple readings of a prosaic instrument. And what if this famous red shift was <u>not</u> the result of receding motion, but had some other cause? In that case the entire Big Bang theory would, of course, collapse, and a new cosmology will have to replace the Expanding universe explanation.

No such danger, I was reassured almost unanimously. Even if our figures weren't absolutely exact, even if the red shift interpretations contained some errors, the Expanding universe is an established, indisputable fact, most scientists told me. The proof is in the pudding: all astronomical evidence arriving from every observatory, all observations and new data, fit in the theory; galaxies and other heavenly bodies behave according to the theoretical predictions.

The major opponent of the Big Bang idea was the school of the Steady-State universe. Founded by 1948 by three irreverent young British men, it refused to accept any idea of a "beginning" of the universe, and especially one in a singular event, the explosion alleged to have happened some 15 billion years ago. Instead, they believed in "continuous creation" of matter everywhere in the infinity of space, an imperceptible process in which new atoms replace the disappearing atoms, thus keeping the universe in a permanently steady state. This theory wouldn't stand a chance against the mainstream trends in modern cosmology had it not been promoted with unusual verve and aggression by its authors, Fred Hoyle, Thomas Gold, and Hermann Bondi, remarkably brilliant iconoclasts, whose mathematical formulation made it extremely difficult to dispute. In fact, Hoyle, *enfant terrible* of the cosmology, had arrogantly dismissed his critics by declaring that there were not ten scientists in the world good enough to understand his superior mathematical equations.

Ever since I had read about Fred Hoyle, I was intrigued by his audacious ideas and his original, impertinent mind, and had a great desire to meet him. After missing him a couple of times in Cambridge, he finally received me at *CalTech* in Pasadena, and the couple of long meetings we had turned out to be even more stimulating and rewarding than anything I had expected. Alone with him in his office or in the Faculty dining room, I had the chance of listening to one of the world's leaders in theoretical astronomy and asking him at will all the questions I wanted. We talked, of course, a lot about his Steady-State theory and he told me about the difficulties it had encountered with the latest discoveries in astronomy. We were in 1974, and much of the self-assurance and intolerance toward the Expanding-Universe hypothesis that he had so combatively displayed during the 1950s and 1960, had mellowed. He had successfully handled many unfavorable arguments, which recent observations had brought up against his "Steady-State," he told me, but when the sensational discovery of a permanent background radio-noise, probably a residue from the primeval heat of the Big Bang, was announced, he felt almost defeated. "Now the theory is in trouble, and I see no way around," he admitted to me.

We talked about the origin of matter and he told me about his quarrel with George Gamow, who thought that all elements were created simultaneously at the moment of the Big Bang, "cooked in less time than it takes to cook a dish of duck and potatoes." Hoyle insisted that all matter in the universe is created as hydrogen, while heavier elements are produced by subsequent evolution in the interior of stars, (which is now the prevalent view). And many other fascinating things, most of them way above my head, in spite of my host's kindness and unusual patience in trying to explain them to me. Anti-matter, for instance.

Hoyle went to the blackboard and drew graphs and formulas, which were showing, said he, that parallel to our universe there was another universe, made of anti-matter, where even time had a minus value, i.e. time ran in opposite direction: coming from the future, going through the present, and headed toward the past...

After these sessions, retiring in my hotel room, my mind was so excited, that I couldn't sleep, obsessed by the things I had just heard and thinking of hundred questions to ask the next day. But also regretting my terrible handicap of not speaking the language of the brilliant people I had given the opportunity to interview: mathematics.

Indeed, Fred Hoyle put it very frankly during one of our conversations: "Excuse me, Mr.Groueff, but I really don't understand how come that an educated person like you didn't care to learn at least some math? Without it, how do you intend to understand the world? You ask me to explain some rather elementary things by using words. But often this is impossible. Words and language are such imprecise, approximate, misleading tools. The same word has different meaning to you, to me, to everybody; it's difficult to describe Nature by using something as subjective as words. Mathematical equations are so clear, and true, and objective!" He said it as friendly advice, not criticism. I think that he felt a little sorry for me.

I met Tom Gold, the other father of the Steady-State theory, at Cornell. Apart from cosmology, we talked about skiing and about Switzerland, where he had gone to boarding school at Zuoz. The lively, Austrian-born, Cambridge-educated astronomer was less prepared to capitulate than Hoyle. He was still not convinced that the universal radio-noise, discovered eight years ago, in 1965, was really coming from the Big Bang. "There is something fishy about this discovery," he said, indicating his willingness to pursue the defense of his "Continuous-Creation." He still believed that atoms of matter are being created all the time and everywhere, although he admitted not knowing where they come from. "From nowhere," he suggested, quite willing to call it just a "miracle." Isn't it illogical, he wondered, that the same people who so readily accept one big, huge miracle—their so-called "Big-Bang"—refuse to admit the possibility of *several* tiny miracles? Talking about the early days of the celebrated controversy, Gold admitted that when they were young, Hoyle and himself (not Bondi, who was a more moderate man) were sometimes too self-confident, brash, occasionally making statements without being fully informed, which used to irritate fellow scientists on whose toes they used to step with no hesitation. But with time they learned to be less aggressive and very careful before they spoke. Now, no more a fanatic believer in the Steady State theory, Gold still thought it, theoretically and mathematically, superior to the Big Bang idea. "But I keep my mind open. Two things cause problems with the Steady State," he confessed. "The background radiation, and the strange red shifts of quasars."

Like Fred Hoyle, Gold was also disturbed by the discovery of that universal background radio noise, known by then as the "3-degree-K radiation." Everybody was talking about it, so I went to the Bell Laboratories in New Jersey to see its discoverers. Their new status of celebrities seemed to have surprised the two obscure radio astronomers, Arno Penzias and Robert Wilson, as much as anybody, especially that they freely admitted their ignorance in cosmology. (Later they received the Nobel Prize in physics.) With my tape-recorder on while having a sandwich with them, I was fascinated to hear their story told with colorful details in the first person. Looking with their radio telescope for noise sources interfering with satellite communications systems, they recorded an inexplicable radio noise corresponding to a thermal radiation of 3 degrees Kelvin. The mysterious radiation was uniform and constant and came from all directions, as if the entire universe were permeated with it. They checked and rechecked many times, taking into consideration all possible sources of such a "static" in the reception, but were unable to identify the source. No matter in what direction they turned their telescope, the 3-degree K radiation was present.

Penzias and Wilson were totally unaware of the theory that if the Big Bang had really occurred, inconceivably high temperatures would have accompanied it. The subsequent explosion should have resulted in gradual reduction of the excessive heat of the "original fireball." Despite of the billions of years of cooling that had elapsed, a residue of the original heat from the Big Bang should still be on hand in the form of thermal radiation, predicted cosmologists, among them a team of theoretical physicists working at Princeton, also in New Jersey. But unfortunately all their attempts to detect such a vestige of Creation had failed. It's a wonderful story how in 1965 the Princeton scientists heard by chance that some radio people, only miles away from them, had been puzzled by an inexplicable "radio noise." Excited beyond words, they rushed to Bell Lab, only to find out that the mysterious "static" corresponded exactly to the residual heat from the Big Bang they were searching for.

To hear such stories told by their heroes was among the best rewards of my inquiry, giving me a thrilling sense of almost participating in the great scientific adventure. This happened to me a number of times. I felt it, for instance, with another breakthrough in modern astronomy, the discovery of the quasars, the mysterious sky objects, looking like individual faint stars, but emitting radio waves, like galaxies. Ever since my new acquaintance Allan Sandage had discovered, at Palomar, the first one, all scientists were puzzled by these radio-sources. But the excitement reached a paroxysm when a Pasadena astronomer, the Dutchman Maarten Schmidt, examining the unusual spectrum of a quasar, came to the daring, almost absurd, conclusion that it showed an impossibly big red shift, indicating a distance never observed before and a power greater than many galaxies put together. How could a single "star" (if it was a star) generate such fantastic luminosity and power, superior to many galaxies with billions of stars? Were we observing some cosmic upheavals, taken place ten billion years ago, or was our interpretation of red shifts and distances wrong? While the dispute about quasars was raging, I had Maarten Schmidt tell me his story personally, in the very room 202 on the second floor of Caltech's Robinson Building, where he decoded the quasars' red shift, and showing me the authentic spectrograms and transparencies he had used. What an exciting time I had! "...That Tuesday, February 5, 1963," he began, "I was looking for the n-th time at my spectra of the 3C 273 and their absurd red shift," he began. "The same six inexplicable spectral, which didn't make any sense and didn't correspond to any known chemical element. Suddenly, I had this crazy thought: what about if the shift was so abnormally big, that many lines, usually observed *inside* the visible spectrum, had quitted its frame and had been displaced *beyond* its red extremity? It sounded impossible, no such deviation had ever been observed before." All of a sudden, he noticed that some of the lines reminded him vaguely of features on hydrogen spectra. But they were positioned at a totally wrong place. The suspense story continued. On the spur of the moment, Schmidt tried something new: plotting hydrogen spectral lines on the sliding piece of a slide rule, representing a spectrum, he started moving it slowly toward the red end. When it was displaced by 16 percent, the lines remaining over the spectrum looked exactly like the ones of the quasars. It was a red shift of a magnitude unheard of for a star. It meant that 3C 273 was located at a distance of two billion light years! Overwhelmed by the revelation, Schmidt rushed to the corridor and called his neighbor, the head of astrophysics department, excitedly: "Jesse, Jesse, come quickly!" It didn't take Jesse Greenstein two minutes to realize that Schmidt had guessed right. "I'm not as calm as Maarten, so I screamed so loud that many colleagues came out of their offices to see what had happened," the urbane Greenstein, who joined the conversation, told me. Rushing to his desk, he applied the new discovery to another quasar, 3C 48, whose spectrum had bothered him for two years. He found an even bigger red shift, 37 percent, or a distance of 4 billion light years. "How stupid of me not to have thought the 'impossible'! The truth was so obvious. But it proves you how conservative the human mind is."

I stayed late at *CalTech* that day. To my delight, Greenstein was in one of his philosophical moods. "I see no contradiction between science and religion," he said. "The essential thing in both is the astonishment and respect the Universe's existence inspires in us. The greatest mystery of all is that it exists. When the biologists tell me that I'm just a geometric and chemical combination of different molecules, I don't feel at all humiliated or diminished; on the contrary, I find it fascinating to be part of Nature. And the Big Bang, with its idea of a catastrophic commencement of the Universe, doesn't it remind you of someone who's supposedly said: 'And let be Light! And there was Light'? But," he smiled, "it doesn't mean that I'm a religious man..."

          *   *   *   *   *

Chapter 32

End of an era

Henri Matisse, whose work I knew no better than any average admirer of his art, played, unwittingly of course, an unexpectedly pleasant role in my life. This he did by painting, among his many works, a charming outdoor scene in light green colors which had enchanted Lil so much in her affluent, "pre-Groueff" days, that she and her first husband had bought it with relish. It represented an artist doing the portrait of a lady seated on the grass, near a brook. After our marriage, this Matisse hung in our New York apartment. A skilled copyist-artist herself, Lil had reproduced it stroke by stroke and the copy went to her parents' home in Long Island.

We were all avid skiers in the family and we especially enjoyed the village of Gstaad. Therefore, we were thrilled and very happy when, thanks to the sale of this precious artwork, Lil and my three Isles stepchildren were able to chip in and buy a lovely chalet in our favorite Swiss resort. As the chalet was rather unimaginatively called *Le Coteau* (French for "little hill"), hard to spell and pronounce in English, our son Paul thought it more fitting to rename it for our Lucas-terrier dog, *Ding-Dong*, a true member of the family. I was simply overjoyed: no dream of material possessions had ever appealed to me more than having a chalet in this charming mountain resort.

It was really a delightful place, the nearest thing to a fairy-tale village with gingerbread chalets and Christmas-cards-like pine-trees covered with snow. It was the most attractive among the winter resorts we knew: less grand and glamorous than St. Moritz, but with much cozier chalet life; less challenging for skiing than Zermatt, Davos, or Chamonix, but with more fun and warmth. Unlike most resorts in the Alps region, a draconian conservation policy had succeeded in preserving the old character of Gstaad, with its obligatory chalet architecture. The presence of a few renowned international schools added to the family atmosphere of the village, where the noisy and garish was frown upon and the ostentatious was kept to a minimum, as much as it's possible in a resort with so many rich (old and nouveau) and famous denizens.

*   *   *   *

Bill and Pat Buckley used to rent every winter *LeChateau* in the neighboring village of Rougemont, an old stone castle bought by an American and run by the Buckleys in quite a seigniorial style.

No one in America reminded me more of a Renaissance Man than William F. Buckley, Jr., the star of the conservative intellectuals. The charismatic founder of the right-wing *National Review*, the erudite author of several books on politics and ideology and a lecturer in hot demand, he was also the host of the provocative weekly TV program *Firing Line* and wrote a controversial newspaper column. One could disagree with his ideas, as most liberals did, but one couldn't help admire his remarkable eloquence, erudition and wit. To understand all polysyllables in his highly elaborate, often esoteric, discourse, one sometimes needed a dictionary and at least a minimum of elementary Latin, and Buckley was regularly criticized and teased about it. But, elitist as he was, he had no intention of changing his ways or making concessions to intellectual plebeians. Bill also happened to be a fervent sailor, crossing the Atlantic once a year on sails with a crew of old schoolmates and close friends, and writing a book about the adventure. As a relaxation between his multiple activities, he skied with passion for about two months and, as a hobby, played the piano and the harpsichord. And yes, he used part of his winter vacations to write, somehow tongue-in-cheek, his yearly action novel, a James-Bond-like series of an agent's incredible adventures.

I never understood how one man could do so many things at the same time, and do them so successfully and with such zest. I envied his extraordinary facility of writing and public speaking. To the average journalist like me, each one of his activities would've required fulltime work for an entire week. After many winters in Gstaad, I understood part of Bill's secret. He was a very disciplined, dedicated man who knew how to organize his time. Thus, in the morning, he was Buckley the columnist, the review's editor, the speechmaker, writing feverishly and conversing by computer. (In the 1970s, he was already a computer enthusiast.) After an early lunch, he became for several hours the fanatic skier, up and down the steep Videmanette runs in his old turtleneck sweater, shapeless ski pants and sea-captain's cap, never stopping to take his breath or to look for his companions. He preferred long, fast "schusses" and cared less for style and new techniques. When we skied together, he liked to lead and, as soon as the lift reached the top, he hurled himself down the run, not waiting for anyone, not even turning to see whether we followed. But his enthusiasm made him a very pleasant skiing pal.

After the time he allowed himself on the slopes, he rushed back to the chateau, where his current thriller's manuscript was waiting on the word-processor. A few hours later, it was the time for Buckley-the-Host, or rather the glamorous hostess Pat's perfect husband—much less of a socialite than her, but nevertheless an attentive and highly entertaining dinner host, delighting the cosmopolitan group of guests. David Niven, a close friend, was one of the regulars, and the Nivens's chalet in Chateau-d'Oex was among the few homes where one used to dine with the Buckleys. At table, the repartee between the two friends ran like fireworks of hilarious stories and witty remarks. Not less brilliant were the mock arguments the ultra-conservative Buckley used to have with the slightly pompous arch-liberal Professor John-Kenneth Galbraith, another Gstaad regular, with whom Bill shared a mutual respect and friendship, despite their diametrically opposite views. It was a true treat to us, the guests, to follow the verbal duels of these superbly articulate men, teasing each other without mercy, one quicker and sharper than the other.

The rivalry of the two friendly adversaries spilt out of the chateau and to Gstaad's bookstore, when it displayed simultaneously both men's latest books. Every day both Ken and Bill inquired with the store which book was selling better, each author demanding that his book be given better window exposure. Then came the surprise: David Niven had just published his first memoirs, a delightfully funny autobiography, which quickly overshadowed the other books and was selling like hot cakes. When the new bestseller took the central place in the bookstore window, both Buckley and Galbraith confronted Niven in mock anger. "Look, David, it's highly unfair! Do <u>we</u> try to be actors? Do <u>we</u> make movies? Instead of writing books, which is our business, not yours, why don't you stay with your films?" But Niven was so ecstatic with his new career, that on his new passport he spelled his profession as "David Niven, author."

Through the years, Lil and I had many happy times at the Rougemont chateau. The after dinner hours revealed another facet of Bill's many-sided personality: the would-be artist. The guests would be led down to the studio in the manor's stony cellar, and brushes, pallets, paint and canvas would be distributed to all amateurs. They would don smocks and start painting in all earnest. Maybe the place didn't exactly evoke the work in some Renaissance Old Master's atelier, but the eagerness was certainly not missing. Lil, having had some experience before, was among the better painters, and some of the others would occasionally turn to her for advice. Most of the amateurs were just beginners, but they all had great fun. David Niven definitely had some talent, and a few canvases Prince Rainier of Monaco had left on the walls from previous seasons, were not too bad for an amateur. The prize for enthusiasm and self-enjoyment, I would give with no hesitation to Bill, our host. As for the guests with no talent whatsoever, we sat around listening to beautiful records, sipping the champaign poured generously by Pat Buckley and enjoying her irresistibly funny asides and witty gossip.

Passionate for music, Bill managed to find time to practice his piano, and the harpsichord he brought to the chateau. Sometimes, an American friend of ours, Connie Anderson, a recital-pianist, came to play along and give him a few tips. It was amusing to watch the schoolboyish diligence of the celebrated intellectual, trying to play some Bach piece: tense, the eyes transfixed by the printed score, the tongue coming out at every difficult passage, mumbling a curse each time he touched the wrong key and beaming after each flawlessly executed phrase. Bill was laboring with a concentration equal only to his touching desire to be a pianist.

A few times, I brought my clarinet to the chateau, but the attempts to play together were a total failure. Bill, a Bach aficionado, was entirely a reader, who wouldn't even play the scale without having the sheet music in front of his eyes. Myself, a Louis Armstrong and Sidney Bechet fan, I was musically illiterate and playing only by ear. Connie, an accomplish classical pianist, was also a reader, capable of playing *prima vista* from most intricate scores, but jazz improvisation was certainly not her forte. Asking her to play jazz was like expecting Nijinsky to tap-dance with Sammy Davis, Jr., on the premise that they're both dancers. However, after I lent her some jazz records, she was so thrilled by the revelation, that she bought a dozen Cole Porter and Gershwin scores and put herself to work. Soon, I started going to play with her at the Harkness Ballets chalet, which Connie was using for the winter. Our repertoire was extremely limited, and often the keys I could play in didn't correspond to the keys on her sheets, but we enjoyed ourselves tremendously. Twice, Connie invited friends and we performed in public in the huge ballet-practice room. To add some jazzy beat and swing, for which Connie's long consorting with Mozart and Chopin had not been the most proper training, we hired the drummer from Olden's nightclub, who somehow managed to save us from embarrassment. Some guests even said that they enjoyed the evening. But then, they were a biased, friendly crowd, and Connie's buffet was really delicious.

*   *   *

The 1970s started as a lucky period for me. Happiness of course, cannot be a permanent commodity, a state that, if once reached, would be enjoyed forever after. Nor does it cover equally each and every aspect of a life. But, being aware of that, I seemed to have enough reasons to be grateful to my lucky star. I was approaching the age of 50 in a pretty good physical shape, still active in sports. At home, I couldn't be happier with Lil and Paul. Having a real home in America gave me a warm, reassuring feeling of stability. By now, we were accustomed to the comforting presence of our house helper Rhoda Chambers, an intelligent and devoted native of the Caribbean island of Montserrat, who had become a part of the family. My profession was also giving me great satisfactions, especially with my three *Larousse* books almost finished and publication dates already in sight; in the same time, our life between Manhattan, Southampton, Gstaad and the frequent visits to Paris, offered us the kind of friendships and excitement that we both loved. Except for worries about my brother, and moments of sadness due to my chronic nostalgia, I could state that I was a truly happy man, and was most gratefully aware of it.

The winter of 1972, for instance, was a particularly pleasant entertaining season. For one thing, Jill came to Gstaad with Polly and Paul joined us later for his spring vacation, so chalet *Ding-Dong* was packed and resounding with young voices, Beetles records and clatter of skis and ski-boots down in the garage. We skied all day and Paul was making good progress, until he had an accident at the Col-des-Mosses, broke a leg and had to spend his last twelve days in Gstaad in a cast. Lil and I were going out almost every night, mostly with our regular Gstaad group. At that time I was writing my book on the Earth sciences, while working intensively on the illustrations for "*L'Homme et la Mer.*" On my way to Gstaad, I managed each time to spend a few days at Larousse's offices in Paris, working closely with an editor and an art director, Mssrs. Boisseau and Cousino, both men luckily quite enthusiastic about the project. And while in Switzerland, I managed to spend a weekend with King Simeon and Queen Margarita in their chalet in Crans-sur-Sierre, visit Jacques and Marie-Claude Piccard in their home outside Lausanne, and see friends in Geneva, where Lil and I, Paul, and even Ding-Dong, enjoyed repeatedly Sadri Khan's princely hospitality at his chateau de Bellerive, on the lake.

It was during one of these wonderfully hectic March weeks in Gstaad that Radka called from Florida to tell me that Mama had been taken to Miami's Baptist hospital. I knew that she hadn't been quite well lately, but I hadn't suspected anything serious. To the contrary, she was, at the age of 79, in a remarkable form, impressing everyone with her perennial cheerfulness, brisk daily walks for a few miles, and taste for sunning herself on the beach for hours in a row, with no hat, no sunglasses, and no protective creams. One thing though she couldn't support was the cold. I teased her that her body thermostat was out of order. Incidentally, this was one of the reasons for her moving to Florida. It started with occasional visits to my sister Radka, who had left Europe for good and lived with her son George in Miami, where she worked in a travel agency in Coral Gables. It was a good solution during my frequent travels and long vacations abroad. Despite Mama's many new and old friends, New York is a lonely city for a widow living by herself, especially a refugee not speaking the language well. She never complained, but I knew it and worried and felt a little guilty. I suppose modern life offers no perfect solutions for aging parents who live alone, no matter how much their children care for them. During my absences, nothing made me happier than knowing her having a good time with people she liked, so I gladly arranged for her to visit Queen Giovanna in Estoril, the Stancioffs in Maryland, the Sarbovs in Washington, or her close friends from Sofia, Ida and Sammy Rosenbaum (now Renel), in Guernavaca, Mexico. Even before Radka came to the States, Mama had already enjoyed the hot Florida beaches twice, staying in small motels with a younger relative, Elena Beneva. Not bad for a septuagenarian widow, her friends commented; "I'd never hoped for such a pleasant old age!" she used to tell me, thus setting me at ease for a while. But the truth is that for a widowed mother there is no real substitute for sharing her children's life, an impossible dream.

For Mama, winter in New York compounded the two things she resented: the cold, and my absences (month-long vacations in Europe, plus a couple of weeks at *Match* in Paris). With Radka in warm Florida and paying high rent out of her small salary, I decided to take a mortgage there, bought a modest home, and moved Mama, Radka and George to Coral Gables. It seemed to be a good solution: It was easy for me to visit them, and for Mama to come to New York during the better months. I would drive her around Miami (Kay Biscayne park was a favorite promenade), or take her for a hamburger at some *Sambo* restaurant, or cross the causeway to Miami Beach to giggle at the garish clientele of the ostentatious hotels. On weekends, to the great joy of young George, we would all go on daylong trips to the Everglades to look at alligators and other wildlife, or to the Sea aquarium, admiring the dolphins jumping in the air. Mama seemed to enjoy sharing her time between her two children and two grandchildren. Then, in that March of 1972, she suddenly became ill.

In the beginning, the symptoms were vague: dizziness, brief losses of coordination, and moments of incoherent speech. When they worsened, Radka brought her to a doctor, who sent her to the hospital. For a few weeks, we believed that it was some temporary ailment. I called Radka every day and talked regularly to the friendly physician, Dr. Rosita Stoik. But the periods of incoherence increased and when Mama became incapable of leaving her bed and taking care of herself, she had to be moved to a Coral Gables convalescence home, where I visited her in April. The diagnosis was insufficient blood irrigation of the brain. Seeing her at the convalescent home upset me very much. Her eyes were vacant, her face drawn and pale. She recognized me and smiled faintly as I kissed her, and even talked a little, albeit incoherently, as I took her out of her room for an hour, pushing her wheelchair around the garden. An odor of sweet tropical flowers, disinfectants and urine permeated the hot, humid air. Around us, feeble, elderly patients in worn-out bathrobes shuffled along and invalids were resting on the benches, some of them talking to themselves. The nurses informed me that most of the time Mama was in a daze, unable to make sense, barely conscious. I made efforts to keep a stiff upper lip, even to smile, as I comforted her, holding her hand, but the sight of her broke my heart. I brought her back to her room and she fell asleep, a restless, disturbed, sleep.

It was dark when I returned to the car I had parked outside. I sat there for a long time before starting the engine. Outside, the shrill sound of cicada filled the hot, sticky night. Now I could realize what Radka was going through in the last weeks, visiting Mama every single day and watching for hours her expressionless, tortured face, before rushing back to work or to take care of George at home. When I recovered a little, I turned the key on and headed for Radka's house. Tears were running down my face, and I made no effort to stop them.

In May, Mama was transferred to the *Merci Hospital,* totally unconscious. The doctors, whom I called from New York every day, told me that the only remaining hope, but with very slim chance of success, was to surgically remove a blockage in a main artery in the neck. After consulting with my doctor, Jay Meltzer, who wasn't optimistic either, I gave my consent and flew to Miami. The operation didn't seem to help much and after a few days in hospital, Mama was moved back to the Coral Gables home.

I returned to New York very saddened and resigned to the tragic evidence. Then, about three weeks later, a miracle seemed to occur in June. Mama suddenly opened her eyes as if awakened from a heavy sleep, lucid and fully aware, speaking perfectly clearly! All tubes were removed from her body and she was feeling quite well. When I called the convalescence home, they put her on the phone and I could hardly believe when I heard her very normal, almost cheerful, voice. I was, of course, greatly relieved and happy, and after several similarly encouraging conversations in the following days, I began to believe that the doctors had been overly pessimistic and that, after all, miracles do happen sometimes...

During the next three months she was improving steadily and we began to talk about her leaving the home, as soon as a bladder infection, and also some pains in a leg, were healed. Combining business and filial devotion, I managed to visit her in July, and then again in August, when Paul Slade and I covered the Democratic convention in Miami. At each visit, she eagerly asked me to tell her what exactly had happened to her and what she was saying in her sleep. She was amused and laughed when told about her incoherent ravings about childhood friends and relatives from Stara-Zagora, whose names I had never heard before, and wanted me to repeat the stories, again and again. The only thing she remembered of her coma was trying to escape from the terrifying darkness into which she had fallen. She had been punished, she felt in her dream, because she had denied God and had turned against Him. The mere memory of the nightmare made her shiver. She had blasphemed, she had renounced God, and was desperately begging Him to forgive her. After an endless torment in the purgatory, He finally gave her forgiveness. She woke up relieved and happy. She had found God again, now everything was all right. Knowing how deeply religious she was, the theme of her nightmare didn't surprise me.

Seeing Mama miraculously healed, I recovered my peace too and could resume my busy life. In July and August, apart from the pleasant Southampton routine, I followed both parties' Conventions, attend an Astronomy conference at the Michigan State University, and even go with Lil to a wild Rolling Stones concert at the marijuana-reeking Madison Square Garden, and the elegant party that followed at St. Regis hotel, given by Ahmet Ertegun, a friend of Mick Jagger's.

Alas, the remission didn't last long. By the end of September, Radka began to notice signs of incoherence in Mama's speech again. Was the doctors' grim prognosis right after all? I hated to abandon the hopes her "miraculous healing" had given me, but I started worrying again. My busy schedule didn't permit me to go to Miami in October. Le Patron arrived in New York for meetings I had arranged with American press leaders. I took him to *Time, Inc.*'s chairman Andy Heiskell, to *CBS* owner Bill Paley, to *Newsday*'s editor Atwood. He dined at our home with *Look Magazine*'s Mike Cowles. We negotiated a French edition of the shocking *Cosmopolitan* with its naughty editor, Helen Gurley-Brown. Then I had appointments in England for my book on cosmology, for the opening of the Cambridge radio-astronomy observatory, followed by a visit to the Jodrell Bank radio telescope near Manchester, to interview its famous director, Bernard Lovell. As Lil was with me, we stopped for five days in Gstaad and three days in London, at our friends Angie and Robin Duke's. On the way back home, I spent a few days in Paris at the *Match* and *Larousse* offices. Meanwhile, I kept in touch with Radka. She reported no changes in Mama's condition, and I kept hoping.

Back in November, I flew to visit her at the Coral Gables convalescent home. I was shocked. She was in bed, asleep most of the time, rambling senselessly when awake. It seemed as if her reason had gone, as if she lived in a dream world. I stayed for three days with Radka, trying to give each other courage, still hoping in a second miracle. Then I had to fly to Pasadena for a long-looked-for interview with Fred Hoyle, the irreverent challenger of Big-Bang theory, and a visit to the widow of Edwin Hubble, the discoverer of the expansion of the Universe. Fascinating meetings, which distracted me for a while from worrying about Mama, before returning to my work and to Lil and Paul in New York. "Call me in case of emergency!" I told Radka. "Anyway, I'll come to Miami soon after Thanksgiving."

I did. But it wasn't the way I had planned. Early on November 30th, Radka called me to tell me that Mama had died at 7 AM that morning, peacefully in her sleep. I flew immediately to Miami. Lil and Paul followed me the next day. Mama was resting in the funeral home, looking beautiful in her calm and serenity. All traces of tension and torment, which upset me so much the last time I saw her alive, had vanished from her face. I saw again the familiar, beloved face, almost smiling. The funeral service took place in a local Greek church, *St. Sophia*, the same name as the old Sofia church facing the house where I was born. With the Orthodox tradition of open coffins, it was the first time that Paul, age 12, was seeing a dead body. He turned a little pale, but was quite brave and recovered quickly. Mama was buried in a sunny Coral Gables' square, the *Graceland Memorial*, a small public garden on the 8th Street open to pedestrian traffic. There are no tombstones, only inscribed slabs laid horizontally on the ground. Hers says "Dafina Groueva, 1893-1972." Who could've thought that a life, which began in remote, provincial Stara-Zagora, would terminate in a most unlikely place across the ocean! That cells and genes from my own family would finally become part of Florida's soil and roots of palm trees!...

*   *   *   *   *

Life went on, of course, not less bursting with events and happenings for me than before. Barely back to New York, I had to return to Florida for *Apollo XVII*, the last moon shot, launched on the 6th of December, just four days after mama's funeral. Raymond and Rosie came from Paris for the historic occasion and I also wanted to share it with Lil and Paul. My stepdaughters Tina, with husband John Barney, and Jill, with boyfriend Terry Middleton, also came and we all spend the night in Cocoa Beach. Watching from the sandy beaches the thunderous, majestic launch—grandiose, Wagnerian fireworks that tore the Florida night,—was a memorable experience, and I was happy to be able to offer it to Paul.

With Paul with us in Florida, I decided to give him another thrill, less "historic" perhaps, but probably equally appreciated: Disney World. It would be a good relief, I thought, from the previous week's funereal mood. For the same reason, I invited my nephew George to join us. The two boys were delighted as we drove from Cocoa Beach to Orlando and entered the fabulous kingdom of Mickey Mouse and Donald Duck. Unfortunately, I had picked an inauspicious day.

We had already visited a couple of fairy-tale castles and the boys were having great fun riding in miniature trains and boats, when I had the unfortunate idea to call my office from a phone booth. Then hell broke loose. Not only the editor Therond was trying to locate me urgently from Paris, but "Le Patron," Jean Prouvost himself, had called several times, each time sounding more impatient and annoyed. *Life Magazine* had just announced its demise, I was told, and "J.P." wanted me to call him immediately. When I reached him, he was in such a vile mood that I didn't dare to admit that this Waterloo for the entire news-magazine business had caught me buying balloons and eating nougat with the kids in Disney World. "I'll inquire with the *Time, Inc.* people and report to you tomorrow, Patron!" was all I could say. We had to leave right away. With a highly disappointed Lil and almost tearful Paul and George in the car, I drove four hours to Miami to drop George, make several phone calls, and fly to New York. The Disney World vacation was a total fiasco.

XXXXXXXX

The reason *Paris-Match* did care so much about *Life's* fate was not only psychological (*Match had, after all, begun as an imitation of the highly successful American magazine.*) In Prouvost's eyes, apart from being a model, *Life* was a weather vane of current trends in the magazine business, a foreteller of things to come, in America first and later, inevitably, in Europe. He followed closely the press experiments in the US, always ready to profit from them and openly copying their better ideas, never disturbed by personal or nationalistic vanity. The person he had chosen to keep him informed about the US press was me. In addition to my journalistic work as bureau chief, my functions also included regular reports on the American media. Indeed, J.P. had said that he expected me to be his correspondent "both in America, geographically, and in the Future, chronologically." Without passing through the editors, I wrote directly to Prouvost, who, by that time, began to know me better. Both JP and Elisabeth liked Lil, were amused by her and had respect for her taste, social *savoir-faire*, and independent character. Contrary to the docile behavior of most of their entourage, and unlike me, who still had difficulties in overcoming my nervousness and tension in the presence of the intimidating "Boss," Lil was totally at ease with him and was one of the very few who called him "Jean" and not "Patron." When we were in Paris, Prouvost and Elisabeth began inviting us to dinner at his beautiful apartment on rue de Rivoli, true gastronomical events with interesting guests, and to weekends at his magnificent country estate in Sologne, a dream-place for pheasant shooting and walks in the woods. During their visits to New York, they treated us more as friends and we spent many relaxed evenings together, usually in the company of Raymond and Rosie Cartier, who were very close to them.

J.P. seemed to appreciate my reports. Insatiable, he asked for more and more information. Periodically, he dispatched to New York our advertising director, my exuberant friend Alain Danet, Elisabeth's son, and together we would go visiting the big US publications. Alain was the gregarious type, a born salesman who thrived among the Martinis-soaked, talk-big, Madison-avenue crowd. We usually managed to combine our "spying" work with a good dose of amusing dinners and parties. Prouvost was particularly interested in the threat the blooming TV industry represented for the magazines. The writing was clearly on the wall: television, our new rival, was not only there to stay, but offered many advantages over the printed press. With no commercial television in France, we were not yet in serious danger. But in the USA, I reported since the 1960s, "...the magazines began to worry since 1953-54, when the volume of TV ads surpassed the volume of magazine ads...The magazines' original reaction was to ignore the TV, to deny its importance and advantages. By now, they admit how wrong this arrogant strategy was and try to change tactics: accept the role of being Number Two..."

I reported also on the titanic but absurd war between the giant-circulation magazines, like *Life* and *Look*, the so-called "numbers game." Spending millions, each was boasting of its ever-increasing circulation. Five million copies, *Life* would proudly announce. Five-and-a-half, *Look* would riposte. Then six, six-and-a-half, seven, eight! The quest for record-circulation became an obsession, the balloon was swelling dangerously. It was foolish, as after reaching an optimum circulation, every additional copy only added to the cost. One day, the balloon burst. Advertisers realized the obvious: they were paying needlessly rates for

8 million or more copies, while their target didn't have to be near that high! Why, for instance, advertise *Rolls-Royce* cars to millions of readers, when no more than a few thousands would ever dream of such luxury? Or advertise skis and golf clubs to non-skiers and non-golfers? For a small fraction of these rates, one could do it much more effectively in smaller, but better targeted publications. Advertising in specialized magazines seemed to be the answer. General-interest magazines were forced to re-think their circulation policies and accept realistically their diminished role in the new, TV-dominated world.

By 1971, *Look* was dead. Then *Life*, in December 1972. Prouvost saw the future of *Paris-Match*, but the absence of private television in France gave him a respite. He used it to redesign his press empire, capitalizing on *Match*'s" fame and glamour. Although well in his 80s, J.P. embarked in a series of new imaginative projects, causing a renewed excitement among his collaborators. My American outpost was of a special interest to him.

In addition to *Match* and *Marie-Claire*, Le Patron owned half of the prestigious daily *Le Figaro*. The other half belonged to the widow of the perfume tycoon Coty, remarried to a Rumanian, Mr. Cotnareanu. Prouvost and M-me Cotnareanu however only had the financial ownership of the newspaper, with no say in editorial matters: at the Liberation, a law had explicitly given all power to *Figaro*'s journalists, led by the director Pierre Brisson. But J.P. wasn't a man to be satisfied with the role of a passive financial backer. He dreamt of running *Le Figaro*, as he had done once with his pre-war *Paris-Soir*. As a first step, he bought M-me Cotnareanu's part, a risky move that worried his heiresses (his only son had died, leaving five daughters), and many associates. Then, when Brisson died, Prouvost took over *Figaro*'s editorial direction, facing the opposition of the editors. A bitter, costly war began between France's most successful press lord and *Figaro*'s" working editors.

In the meantime, J.P. had created, in partnership with *Hachette*, the first French television weekly, *Tele-7 Jours*. Many of us were skeptical: why would anyone buy a magazine covering only two State-owned channels, when every newspaper gives their programs away for free? Once again, Le Patron was proven right. *Tele-7 Jours* was an immediate, huge success, with the largest circulation of all French publications. The idea of specialized magazines seemed to work well in France too. Prouvost's press group started a monthly for parents, unoriginally named *Parents*, attracting a solid readership. For a more frivolous, less family-oriented public, Prouvost bought the French franchise of *Cosmopolitan*, although judging its articles on "How to Seduce your Boss" or "How to marry a Rich Man" rather amoral. "Would anyone explain to me why the Americans are so obsessed by the word 'orgasm'?" he would ask us, with a devilish smile. He rejected, however, any idea of a French *Playboy* magazine. "American men are so sophomoric, acting as if they've never seen a naked woman...It would never work here!" Most of us agreed with the principal reason for his lack of interest: it was unthinkable for a respected press group to get involved in soft-pornography. (Financially, at least, we were proven wrong. Our former colleague Filipacchi, not believing for a minute that French men were different, launched his soft-porn *Lui*, *Oui* and various *Penthouse* editions, and made a killing.)

Other projects were considered, but were never realized. Such was Cartier's idea for an European magazine, *Capitol*, already in the pilot-issue stage. Prouvost's frequent switches between enthusiasm and doubts prevented also the birth of a service magazine on Parisian life, modeled after *New York Magazine*. I had brought to his attention the remarkable success of this type of regional publication, and he became very excited about the new formula, to the point of inviting, through my intermediary, *New York* 's brilliant creators, Clay Felker and Milton Glaser, as his guests in Paris. Both men, whom I had befriended and whose work I followed closely in New York, were as impressed by the grand-seigniorial ways of the old press-baron, as he was by Clay's innovative journalism and Milton's revolutionary artwork. The visit, and a subsequent one, when Lil, Paul and I flew with Milton and Shirley Glaser to the South of France for a 3-day conference of *Match* and *Figaro*'s top editors, resulted in commissioning Glaser to redesign *Paris-Match*'s and other Prouvost publications' logos and layout. For a longtime, Le Patron enjoyed himself like a child with a new toy, yet characteristically changing constantly his mind about the feasibility of a Parisian magazine of the *New York* formula.

Meanwhile, J.P. became increasingly involved with *Radio-Luxembourg*. RTL, one of the few private stations in Europe, had had financial difficulties and had called on him, "the Man with the Golden Touch," for help. He had no radio experience before, but accepted on condition of receiving *carte blanche* to reorganize and run the station, and immediately proceeded to radical transformations. If anybody had worried about "The Old Man" turning *RTL* into a bourgeois, old-fashioned radio, all fears were quickly dissipated when the very "*with it*" octogenarian dispatched long-haired Dee-Jays to the staid studios and wild rock-and-roll shook the bland programs. To the delight of the teen-age listeners, J.P. hired a few notorious characters, such as "Colonel Roscoe," who ran a British "pirate" offshore station. But he installed *Paris-Match*'s Jean Farran and Raymond Castans as director and programs-head. Very soon, *RTL* became the rage of Europe, an immense popular and financial success.

J.P. asked me to inform him on *CBS*'s newly created all-news program, *Radio 880*. It fascinated him and he insisted on hearing it personally, so I spent countless hours recording *880* programs on my home tape-recorder. I sent him 24-hour uninterrupted programs, including adds, jingles, weather reports and the exact hour announcements, plus my own comments and transcripts of my interviews with *CBS* boss Bill Paley. Le Patron was delighted. He played the cassettes at home, listening carefully, taking notes, and, of course, unabashedly stealing all ideas he liked.

At the beginning, I wondered why such an important, busy and busy man like Paley was receiving me so readily in his sumptuous office, answering my sometimes-indiscreet questions so patiently. Then he told me about his own wartime record, and it all became clear. By the end of WW2, *Radio-Luxembourg* played a crucial propaganda role in German-occupied Europe. After the Allied invasion, a special unit, headed by Paley, received the mission to occupy the powerful transmitter and destroy it. Highly impressed by the superb, state-of-the-art station, Paley, a radio man himself, convinced his superiors to use it against the Germans, rather than senselessly demolish it. Thus, he became the first Allied director of *Radio-Luxembourg* and found the job of reorganizing it exceptionally rewarding. Ever since, Paley kept a soft spot in his heart for that station. However, his willingness to tell me all about his *CBS-880* radio was not entirely for sentimental reasons: soon, he asked me to inform Le Patron that he would love to get a piece of *RTL*. With Prouvost telling the price and keeping the majority. For the good old times's sake, he said, but he seemed to be too well informed about *RTL*'s enviable profits. J.P., always especially intrigued by the glamour and the successes of Paley, was flattered, but declined the offer. In the following years, each time the two tycoons talked, the CBS owner renewed the offer. Delighted, almost flirtatiously, Prouvost kept him hoping, and though determined not to sell, he never said a clear "no."

****

The first half of the 1970s was an exciting, if at times disquieting, period of re-thinking *Paris-Match* and searching for new formulas. Prouvost involved me in a few of the projects, but my main activity remained centered on the books we were to co-publish with *Larousse*. The first volume of the series, my *Man and the Sea*, had taken me more than four years of planning, research, travel, and writing. It was finally published in February 1973. *Larousse* took me on a tour of book-signing and press interviews in Lille, Nantes, and Marseilles. Then the lavishly illustrated, coffee-table format volume was presented at a luncheon for the press in Paris, aboard a Seine riverboat anchored at the Alexander III bridge, hosted by Cartier and *Larousse*'s chairman, Etienne Gillon. I was quite tense when I rose to speak without a written text, and not particularly brilliant, but it was a very proud and happy moment for me. The smile was still on my face the next day when I joined Lil, Philip, Tina and Johnny and their sons in Gstaad. Paul arrived one week later and I had a marvelous, month-long vacation of March skiing. On my return, I stopped again in Paris, for radio-interviews on *RTL*, *France-Inter*, and *Radio Suisse Romande*.

It couldn't have been a happier year, with part of the summer spent in Southampton and part in Gstaad, from where I took Lil and Paul for three days to Chamonix. Meanwhile, my next two *Larousse* books were in a very advanced stage and I was writing constantly. But some clouds appeared on the bright sky. In April, Rosie Cartier called to say that Raymond fell sick and went to the

American Hospital in Paris. He recovered soon, but the mere realization that my rock-solid, vigorous mentor was also vulnerable and not immune to human frailty, gave me an odd feeling of insecurity. It coincided with the increasing rumors that not all was going well inside Prouvost's press empire. It appeared that J.P.'s large investments in *Le Figaro* and modernizing the obsolete printing plants had become a heavy financial burden. The word "economies" began to appear more frequently in the inter-office memos. Roger Mauge, the new Editor after Therond's departure, was a partisan of radical cuts in budget and personnel, including the American offices. Anni was in Paris that May and she had learned from Elisabeth Danet that Mauge had proposed the closing of our New York office. The two ladies called me in New York and suggested that I come urgently to talk with the Patron. I left for his St. Jean country estate in Sologne, where we talked until late after midnight, in the presence of Elisabeth and Anni. It was clear that the very future of the New York bureau was at stake.

Prouvost was an autocrat who at times became fascinated with some editor and fell under his influence. His all-time favorite was, of course, Herve Mille, but now the two men didn't even speak to each other, after J.P. accused Herve of siding with a group of reporters who had briefly rebelled against him. A recent favorite was Jean Farran. And now Roger Mauge. It was like having a sort of an intellectual crush on someone.

Mauge was an excellent writer, a reserved, aloof intellectual, almost the opposite of the extrovert, adventurous *Paris-Match* typical reporter. A stranger to the antics and slang of the old gang, he was deep in "serious" subjects and had written a popular book on Freud. The only unorthodox, almost Paris-Matchian touch in his personality was his hobby: Mauge had a farm for raising minks and when he was offered the job of managing editor, he accepted on condition to continue living in the country, near his minks. Typically, J.P. agreed, seeing nothing wrong with the odd arrangement to have the hectic news magazine run by a commuter.

To be honest, Match did need reforms and serious cuts in editorial spending were overdue. But I pleaded with Le Patron that the reorganization plan of Mauge was going against the very spirit and nature of the magazine. Mauge wanted a publication run more rationally, with better discipline and accountability, based more on surveys and organizational charts than on intuition and inspiration. His arguments were logical and in tune with the latest trends in publishing. But I belonged to the opposite, the "romantic" school. To me, *Match's* unique success was largely due to its unusual, individualistic approach to journalism, to its *esprit-de-corps* and taste for risk-taking.

Let's not change "the soul" of *Match*, I pleaded with Prouvost, and with Anni we presented our counter-proposal for a less drastic reduction of the New York bureau's expenses and personnel. He gave us some reassurances, as did Raymond Cartier, whom we saw the next day. But I returned to New York with the feeling that things at *Paris-Match* were going to change soon, to the worse for us.

*   *   *   *

My book on Earth sciences research was published in the spring of 1974. Once more, we had spent March in Gstaad, where, between skiing and partying, I was writing the last volume of the project, *Man and the Cosmos*. On April 1st, I found myself at a book fair in Paris, signing *L'Homme et la Terre* at a table next to Cartier, the initiator and director of the series. He was in a terrible mood that day, suffering from some severe back pain and grumbling how much he hated these "commercial promotions." But he was pleased with the book and had already complimented me warmly. Since I valued no other professional verdict in the world more than Raymond's, his words made me very happy.

Apart from worries about my brother's health problems in Plovdiv and the growing difficulties at Prouvost's press group, 1974 was another happy year for us: a socially active spring in New York, pleasant June and July in Southampton, two delightful weeks in Gstaad in August, followed by a car trip with Lil and Paul through the Grand St. Bernard pass to Tuscany, visiting our New York friend Camilla Pecci-Blunt McGrath at her family's spectacular estate *Marlia*, near Lucca. We felt really spoiled for five days in the opulence of the villa owned once by Pauline Bonaparte, enjoying in private the celebrated gardens, open on certain days to the public, and happy to share it with Paul, then 14, on his first visit to Italy. The fall in New York too had nothing anti-climactic, with Queen Giovanna visiting princess Maria Luisa in New Jersey, Sadri and Katy Aga Khan in town for his annual speech at the United Nations, and many other friends passing through New York. Then suddenly, the big shock.

It was December 14th and we were in Southampton for the weekend. By noon, the telephone rang and I picked it up on the counter, separating the living room from the kitchen. Dimi was calling from Paris and his voice was quivering. "Stefo, our Sava is no more with us," he said and started sobbing. The unexpected news left me stunned, I felt that an irreparable breakage had just occurred inside my own universe. The wishful incredulity, usually a first reaction in such moments, proved no shelter after a minute or so. No, there was no misunderstanding, no dreaming. Dimi's familiar voice was too much part of that Saturday's reality, and so was the plain telephone receiver in my hand, and the music from the College radio station, coming, indifferent, from the corner of the room. It struck me then that Sava had ceased to be part of this reality and will never again be included in it. He was 52.

As if it still mattered, our conversation had to go on: What had happened, how, when? Sava had died in Johannesburg, from a massive heart attack while playing bridge at a friend's house. He seemed to be alright when he stood up from the card table to pick another glass of champagne, then suddenly collapsed, and that was the end. A death very much in character, I couldn't help thinking, typical of the way he liked to live: surrounded by social friends, in dinner-jacket I presume, probably flirting with the attractive ladies at the party, a glass of champagne in hand.

The previous year, he had already suffered a milder heart attack and the doctors had ordered him to lose weight, stop smoking and avoid active sports, which he, formerly a good skier, horseman, and tennis player, had already given up for some time. But when I last saw him, he still looked overweight and at times his morale was low. In March, he joined Pam and the children in Gstaad and we saw each other every day. But he wasn't happy. At the end of my skiing day, we would meet at *Charl's*, the young set's cafe. I would indulge myself in delicious pastries and a cup of hot chocolate, while Sava would order a double vodka. If I made a disapproving remark, he would cut me angrily: "Mind your own business and let me alone!" It was easy for me to lecture him, he would say, when I ski all day, enjoy my family and chalet, and love my job. But what did he have left? Unable to ski, he was bored spending most time in the claustrophobic apartment. By then, his marriage was not without problems. And he was frustrated at his job at Engelhard Co. after his friend and boss Charlie Engelhard had passed him over for a much-hoped-for promotion, and Jane Engelhard had crossed him from her list, suspecting him of having assisted her tycoon husband in a romantic infatuation with another lady. "But think of your health, Sava! You're crazy to ignore the doctors' orders!" I pleaded with him. At that, my closest friend—but a different Sava, apathetic and despondent,—would reply: "You know what? I don't care. I don't give a damn whether I live or not!" Coming from him, an epitome of lust for life, these words worried me.

But after Gstaad, when we spent a week together in Paris where Sava came alone to stay with his parents, no such lack of the will to live was noticeable. Neither in the spark in his eyes while watching the gorgeous nude dancers at *Crazy Horse Saloon* with Dimi and me; nor when teasing me mercilessly about old girlfriends and school day pranks, around Panitzas' table at rue Franklin; nor when we spent a couple of evenings with Heini Thyssen and his pretty Denise dancing until the wee hours *Chez Regine*. And while I was busy that April promoting my *L'Homme et la Terre*, Sava didn't stop calling old friends, going to parties, enjoying thoroughly his beloved Paris, the city which seemed to have given him a shot in the arm.

That was the last time I saw him. Dimi waited one day before telling his mother, but they didn't tell his father, whose heart condition hadn't been good lately. I called Mika several times, some of the most painful conversations I'd ever had. I called also Pam in South Africa—she blamed herself for not being with Sava when he died: she and Nicky had left for Europe just a couple of days before, and Sava and Marina were to join them there. Dimi flew to Johannesburg and Sava's funeral took place there on December 20th.

*   *   *   *

Less than two months later, another blow shook up my universe: Raymond Cartier died in Paris. We had suspected that the mysterious ailment he was fighting for more than one year, was due to cancer, but the word had never been mentioned. Immensely proud, Raymond was not the kind of man one would dare ask questions about his health. Although he had probably found out the truth, and Rosie knew it, they never discussed it between themselves. The New York bureau felt as if it lost a father. Anni, Paul Slade, Gaby and Flora were literally in tears. Cartier had been a combination of a tyrant and a caring protector, a slave driver and a most inspiring and rewarding boss. A difficult man of a towering intellectual authority, it was natural that all his collaborators respected him and feared him, but I had often wished that he knew that most of us also loved him. Of course, even the slightest suggestion of such feelings would embarrass him utterly. Few things he hated more than displays of sentimentality. The next day, deeply saddened, Anni, Paul Slade and I flew to Paris to pay our last respect and to attend the funeral. I think that if he were watching us from above, Raymond would've grumbled that all this was totally useless, a silly waste of time and emotions; but secretly, he would've be very pleased.

For me, Raymond's death was an enormous loss, both personally and professionally. He was among the people who marked most decisively my thinking and my career. He was my mentor, who became also my friend. I was 31 when I met him, and being around him was like going to a great university, only better, because,—awesomely erudite, provocative, opinionated, passionate, as he was,— he awaked new, unsuspected interests in my brain. Thanks to him, I discovered the fascinating world of the sciences. Because of him, I mastered the skills of thorough, responsible research. And, in spite of his suspicious nature, he gave me his total confidence, entrusting me with the bureau's expenses and the books project's budget, letting me use his car and his apartment, even leaving me signed blank checks.

Curious that I would be attracted to a person with a temper, qualities and faults so much unlike mine! But during the 22 years of collaboration with this exceptional mind, a man 15 years my senior, our friendship grew closer and closer. The resolute, blunt, explosive authoritarian, a fiery fighter for his often radical beliefs, never afraid to be unpopular; and me, the pacifier, the indecisive conciliator who cannot ever get really angry because there is always another side of the story…Close as we were, Raymond never talked to me about his own feelings and never asked personal questions. Impatient with any human weakness, he used his immense pride as a shield to hide an unusual bashfulness and purity, almost an innocence. He *thought* he was hiding them, that is…But it was obvious to Rosie, it was obvious to me too. Maybe that's why, beside admiring him, we loved him.

*   *   *   *

I was sad that Raymond didn't live to see the publication in November 1975, nine months after he died, of our last book of the Larousse series. *L'Homme et le Cosmos* was written in half by his son Jean-Pierre Cartier (history of Astronomy) and myself (the story of modern cosmology). I had worked more than two years on that book, whose subject—the origin and nature of the Universe—had become a real passion for me, probably more than anything I had written before. During my research, Raymond acted as excited as I was, barely waiting to hear what the scientists had said and what their latest hypotheses were, and we spent hours in philosophical and metaphysical discussions.

This time, *Larousse* organized a very elaborate promotion campaign, bringing me to conferences with astronomy clubs and local media across France. We started in Lyons in November, continued in Nice and Marseilles, and ended in Lille and Bruxelles. It was a tiring but exhilarating experience. It was wonderfully rewarding to address a public who cares, to describe observatories I had visited and scientists I had met, even to try to answer questions about how the Universe was created and the date of the Big-Bang, as if I were some authority on the subject. To say that I wasn't nervous when facing audiences so much more knowledgeable of astronomy than me, would be a lie. But I had enough sense not to pose as a "scientist," but to approach them as a reporter who brings fresh news from the front of their favorite science, cosmology. And it worked. In most cases, I seemed to catch their attention.

My shaky self-confidence, however, was put to trial when, as a highlight of the promotional tour, I found myself at the lectern of the amphitheatre of the Oceanographic Institute in Paris, as guest speaker to the Societe Astronomique de France, facing a huge and intimidating audience of 550, among them many distinguished French astronomers. Lil came too, and sat with Elisabeth Prouvost, sent by Le Patron, Rosie Cartier and a few colleagues from *Paris-Match*. After being introduced by *Larousse*'s chairman Gillon and Jean-Claude Pecker, the French Astronomy society's president, I spoke for one hour, showed slides of magnificent galaxies and telescopes, and answered questions from the public. Then, the book signing, the shaking of hands, the congratulations...

Under other circumstances, that evening should've been one of the proudest highpoints in my career. Ironically, it was occurring at the very moment when this career was collapsing and my heart was heavy. At 91, Jean Prouvost, hard-pressed by increasing financial difficulties, was on his last legs in his struggle to save *Paris-Match* and his press empire. Lil and I had dined with him and Elisabeth three days before, at rue de Rivoli, and found him tired and upset. Meanwhile, he had finally decided to marry the great love of his life and, to the delight of friends and collaborators, Elisabeth Danet, his companion for 30 years, had become Madame Prouvost. He took me aside after dinner and from the kind of questions he asked about my research ("Do scientists believe that God exists?" "How do they explain life?"), I felt that he was thinking a lot about death. I also understood, that Prouvost's *Paris-Match*, "*our*" *Match*, was doomed.

The agony lasted for several months and we lived in an atmosphere of anxiety and rumors. Being far away from Paris, we couldn't wait to talk to Alain Danet who periodically briefed us on the latest developments. But even Alain began to sound more vague and less comforting. The question was no more "whether," but "when;" "who" will be the new owners; which of us, journalists, will keep their jobs and who will be fired. Only four days after my glorious evening at the Astronomy Society, and briefed by Elisabeth, I called Anni and Paul Slade in New York to tell them that things looked bad: *Match* was being sold and the New York bureau would probably be sacrificed.

1976 began in a depressing way. I was, of course, worried about my future and the jobs of my colleagues in the office. Then we learned that 40percent of *Match* had been sold. A letter from Boubi announced the death in Plovdiv of our beloved aunt, Lemi, which saddened me very much and caused me new worries about my brother, knowing how irreplaceable she was in his lonely life. In February, *Match's*" new Administrator, M. Delort, wrote to me about closing the bureau and I flew to Paris to talk to him and the Patron, leaving my New York collaborators in a state of extreme agitation, not to say panic. I saw Prouvost at his Sologne estate, but he wasn't well and I talked mostly to Elisabeth, still hoping to at least save a few jobs in the bureau. But Le Patron had already lost control of his empire.

As M. Delort's strictly businesslike attitude was "Don't call us, we'll call you when we reach the decisions!" I joined Lil for two weeks in Gstaad. Many of our Gstaad friends were there that month, but the worries were too much for me to fully enjoy the great skiing conditions. Nevertheless, I was having a good time. As good, that is, as one can have while waiting for a verdict...M. Delort did send me a formal letter to Gstaad. He was proposing figures for my *indemnities,* i.e. the amount of my severance pay. This time it was true: I had to think seriously about looking for a new job.

I had not thought about joblessness before. I was 52 and the 26 years with *Match*" had given me some reassuring sense of security, a feeling of belonging. With Prouvost as the king of the group, and Cartier as my mentor and friend, I had nothing to worry for the future. On the contrary, I had often wished to be free from *Match* and devote my entire time to new book projects. Exciting projects were not lacking. Even before finishing *L'Homme et le Cosmos*, Raymond and I were already discussing the next possible subjects. Etienne Gillon, *Larousse's* boss, was so enthusiastic about our series that he couldn't wait for us to propose new titles. Money will be no problem, he assured us, just continue in the same vein! It was an exciting time of dreaming of future books. Pet projects of Raymond were the story of modern knowledge of the brain and its functioning, or the Origin of Man. Myself, I was more interested in exploring the gray area beyond the reach of modern physics, the no-man's land between hard science and metaphysics. In my contacts with physicists and astronomers, many were admitting freely that certain phenomena cannot at present be explained by science, but this didn't mean that they didn't exist. From others, I had heard hypotheses that I would expect from religious believers, extrasensory-perception devotees, or poets, and this fascinated me. I wanted to enter this border zone not through the usual door of mysticism, clairvoyance, and superstition, but through the door of advanced physics, quantum mechanics, and astronomy. I'm very skeptical about things like astrology, flying saucers, ghosts, or occultism, but made a point to read books and articles about it. On the subject of para-psychology, healing, and unexplained phenomena, I found a very knowledgeable guide in the person of my friend Maria Janis, Gary Cooper's daughter. Maria gave me some useful introductions and, as she was herself interested in science, recommended some serious reading. Through her and her husband, concert-pianist Byron Janis, I met the celebrated Uri Geller, the Israeli famous for bending spoons and keys by using mere mental power. I attended a few of his "séances" to his puzzling performance, but he never convinced me of his "supernatural" powers.

With Raymond's death, all these book projects were gravely jeopardized. With the unexpected death, soon after, of Gillon, and the crumbling of Prouvost's empire, they collapsed entirely. Suddenly, I was without job and without my projects. A whole era seemed to be ending for me, and as if another proof was needed, Stati Panitza died too in that February 1976, just days after his 93rd birthday. My dear "Uncle Stati," who for 28 years of my émigré life presided over our "round table" at Rue Franklin and treated me as his own son. The family had never had the heart to tell him about Sava's death, and for over a year we all had to invent pretexts why Sava wasn't coming or writing from South Africa, and at times I had to read him on the telephone passages from fictitious letters.

The closing of the New York office was a traumatic experience, which took the whole spring, involving painful negotiations about each individual's severance pay. In Paris, Le Patron was still bargaining with different potential buyers. Finally, in June, the deals were announced. *Hachette* bought *Tele-7 Jours*; *M. Hersant acquired Le Figaro; Filipacchi, the ex-Match photographer, who had made a fortune promoting rock-and-roll in France and launching soft-porn magazines, bought Paris-Match. Marie-Claire* and *Cosmopolitan* went to one of Prouvost's granddaughters, the supposedly timid Evelyn, who surprised everybody when she suddenly bloomed into a very successful publisher.

The Prouvost press group being dissolved, none of its parts could afford the costly American office and the entire staff received our dismissal letters. Mine was waiting for me on my return from Jean Stralem's fishing camp in Canada, where I had gone with Paul in July to get away from my *Match* problems. I also tried to put them aside in the following week, when Jill married Terry Middleton at a weeding in Southampton. But it was difficult for me not to worry. With no other income outside the promised severance pay, (a more or less decent sum, although way below my expectations), my financial future didn't look bright. I panicked a little and as a first step in cutting expenses, we decided to put our Fifth Avenue apartment for sale. An unfortunate idea, since the real estate market was at its bottom and we really loved our home. In August, our friend Chessy Patcevitch brought a buyer, Hethea Milbank, her son's fiancée. Too worried about my future, we sold in haste. In September 1976 we moved temporarily into Tina's flat on East 66th Street and Lil started looking for a smaller, less expensive home.

****

Chapter 33

Freelancing: refugees in Thailand, Haute Route in the Alps

It is still night, but the moon is bright on the glowing white snow, and the shadows of the towering peaks are etched in inky black. An enchanted silence seems to enfold this desolate yet magnificent landscape. The thin, icy air knifes through our lungs, producing that curious lightheadedness one experiences only in the high mountains. Far ahead, a few points of light are moving slowly in Indian file, like some ritual candlelight procession. A hundred yards to the rear, another caravan is snaking up the slope—spectral figures with flashlights attached to their foreheads. No one speaks. The only sound is the rhythmic squeak of boots, skis and poles advancing on frozen snow.

We've been climbing like this for nearly one hour—ever since we left an overnight alpine refuge high in the Swiss canton of Valais. I am beginning to feel my fatigue. My breathing accelerates, my heart beats faster, and the 25-pound rucksack weighs on my back. My legs obey reluctantly as the slope grows increasingly steep. Then I see something that banishes all thought of fatigue: the first rays of sun emerge from behind a ridge and for an unforgettable moment, half the white landscape glows ghostly in the moonlight, while the other half glitters in the sun. I feel a sudden surge of exhilaration such as I have rarely known before.

The two feelings—fatigue and exhilaration—are curiously and intimately mixed in this world of the high mountain. It was largely the lure of such sights that took me into the high Alps and placed me, panting and spellbound, at six in the morning on an icy glacier at 10,000 feet altitude. Of course, there was more than the promise of scenic beauty that enticed me here. For years I had known about the famous *Haute Route*—the high-level route over glaciers and snow-fields that links Chamonix, in France, to Zermatt or Saas Fe, in Switzerland. The six-day, 100- to 125-kilometer ski traverse over a dozen peaks and passes more than 2,800 meters high is the ambition of every ski-mountaineer in Europe. For although there are more difficult trips, and others that are just as beautiful, there is probably no route across the roof of Europe that packs such a variety of scenery and snow conditions into a traverse of comparable length.

I have been skiing for 30 years and although I'm not an alpinist, I had long been fascinated with the idea of trying the Haute Route—the challenge of testing myself to the limits against the elements and the prospect of skiing amidst breath-taking vistas made it doubly appealing. But I had never found the time to make the trip until this spring. Now I had finally the opportunity. And now I needed badly something of the sort. It had been quite a disturbing year for me, with the end of the old *Paris-Match* and me losing the job I had for 28 years, a depressing period when at times I felt unsettled and confused. With my moorings cut from the only paper I had always worked for and to which I was so attached, I wasn't sure yet whether I'd make it as a freelance journalist. So I was very happy when I sold two story ideas to the *Readers' Digest*: one on the *Haute-Route*, told as a personal experience; the other one, a profile of an exceptional man, the United Nations' High Commissioner on Refugees, Prince Sadruddin Agha Khan, a close friend of mine. Both stories started in Switzerland.

A little worried that at 54 I might be too old for a mountaineering adventure, I telephoned the "Compagnie des Guides de Chamonix-Mont Blanc" for some information. They told me that Haute-Route trips leave Chamonix once a week from late March to mid-May and cost 1,400 francs or $ 280 for the six days, including the guide and food, plus lodging in overnight huts. They also sent me a list of 45 items of equipment I was to bring—including canteen, flashlight, sunglasses, sun cream, knife, matches, aspirin, sleeping pills (altitude makes people restless). Although I had to be a "good skier" in "good condition," there was no physical test required and no age limitation, but skiers must have some experience climbing with seal skins, which are attached to skis to provide traction when climbing. With the termination of my *Paris-Match* job in New York, I was spending longer vacations in Gstaad that winter and had done more skiing than usual. So I signed on for a trip leaving Chamonix two weeks later, rented a set of seal skins and the special kind of bindings that allow the heel to be lifted, and started practicing several 2- or 3-hour runs with a packed rucksack. Later, I would regret not having trained more seriously.

The early pioneers of the *Haute-Route* (some Britishers opened it around 1861) had really to be in superb condition, to be able to scale the heights on foot with their food supplies, heavy canvas tents and camping gear. There was not a single shelter then. Only after World War II did the Swiss build mountain huts along the route, and new cable cars, making the heights more accessible to amateurs like myself. During the 1977 season, the year I went, about 500 people were expected to attempt the famous trek.

On a gloomy April Saturday, I accompanied Lil and Paul down to Geneva, where they took the plane back to New York, while I boarded the bus to Chamonix. There I found that I was one of a group of four, all of them Frenchmen: Claude and Jean-Claude were both 30, both professors and experienced mountaineers; Jean-Louis, a gangling Paris student of 22, was a novice, like me. Our guide, Rene Tournier, 60, was the kind of professional you feel immediately you can trust. Graying, strongly built, with the skin tough as shoe leather, the taciturn Chamoniard had for 30 years climbed and re-climbed countless times every peak and high pass in the Mont Blanc range. His perennial white cap with a huge visor would soon become for me a symbol of security and dependability, a beacon to follow in the moments when my spirits were flagging on the slopes.

We left Chamonix early on a Sunday morning, carrying in our rucksacks bread, bacon, cheese, salami, biscuits and chocolate for snacks en route and for emergencies. Our regular meals, Rene said, would be found in each overnight hut. In addition to his own food, he carried a rope, an ice axe, a folding sleigh, and a first-aid kit. Because of the bad weather, our first leg itinerary had to be changed: the steep Chardonnet pass was closed that day for fear of avalanches. We started the easier way, by a cable-car dropping us above the Argentiere glacier, sunk like a mammoth frozen river in the saw tooth rim of peaks. Our first traverse down the glacier already offered some sobering surprises. I wasn't prepared, for instance, for the wildly out-of-control feeling I got on the first downhill run with the unwieldy rucksack on my back. The variety of snow conditions in high mountain surprised me too. There was powder, of course, but also hard ice, crusty snow, and very mushy spring snow. As we learned to adjust to them all, we found that there was little place for fancy skiing at these altitudes, and a lot of "survival skiing." It took about two hours of careful skiing to reach the hut on the left of the glacier. The guides like to get there not much later than noon, before the sun begins to melt the snow, increasing the danger of avalanches. Therefore, we started each day's traverse before dawn and halted by the end of the morning.

The Argentiere hut, like others on the Haute-Route, was a two-story gray stone and wood affair. Two keepers served the meals at long refectory tables. The dormitories upstairs could accommodate 100 people in double-decker bunks. None of the huts had running water, so one had to get used to the outdoor toilets and to melting snow for washing, no big problems. But most had electric power and all had a telephone to summon emergency aid by helicopter if necessary. I admit that I found the thought reassuring. By 8 o'clock, lights were out at the Argentiere hut and everybody tumbled into bed.

The route next morning took us up to the Chardonnet pass, across the Saleina and Trient glaciers, and then down to the valley of Champex. It was the only time we abandoned the snow-covered peaks. From Champex there were two ways to proceed. We took a bus to the popular Swiss resort of Verbier to ride up again in the cable car.

Ascending from Verbier was like watching a film of the changing seasons—only played in reverse. It was spring as we left the village, and from the cable-car windows we could see a patchwork of green fields and terraced vineyards. Then we gradually mounted into winter. The trees tinned out and turned bare, the sky closed in, snow began to fall. At about 3,000 meters, it seemed a different universe: breathing was more labored, the cold more bitter, the sun bit more ferociously. My ears rang as though pressed against a conch shell. We zipped up our heavy ski jackets, put on our skis and started the traverse to the Montfort hut. It wasn't easy going, with the gray fog giving us an eerie, dizzy sensation and hiding bumps and holes from us until our skis actually hit them. I was having trouble in the tricky light keeping Rene's white cap in view. It was important to follow his tracks closely, because he knew where the old snow-covered crevasses lay and had an uncanny ability to sense the presence of new ones. Next to avalanches, crevasses are the most serious danger on the Haute-Route. It was estimated that some 50 people had lost their lives to crevasses and avalanches on the Haute-Route since World War II. With the visibility worsening, we were relieved to see the silhouette of the Monfort hut looming ahead. There we found a dozen of other skiers—relaxed, unshaven men and a few sturdy young women—and soon sat down with them to a hearty dinner.

It was dark, cold and still snowing when we set out at six on the next morning. Jean-Louis, the Paris student, looked worried. "I got very tired yesterday," he told me. "The altitude bothers me." As we ascended La Chaux glacier, I saw him huffing and puffing, advancing by jerky, irregular steps and occasionally falling. The last time he fell, he didn't get up. "I can't make it," he breathed in the icy air. His pulse was alarmingly fast, his face purple. Rene squatted down next to him and talked to him quietly. Finally he told Jean-Louis to ski back to the hut, luckily still in sight. We watched him moving slowly away, a look of deep dejection on his face. "It often happens on the second or third day," Rene remarked. "The first excitement is over, and you begin to feel the exertion." That the youngest member of our group had to give up was a sobering reminder that the *Haute-Route* should never be under-estimated. I myself was regretting my scanty preparation with each step. The long march with skins across the glacier in gusty winds, and then up the steep, muscle-pulling La Chaux pass seemed endless. At every twist of the route I kept hoping that the crest would appear or that Rene would signal us to take a break. When weather and terrain permitted, we took a short break every hour or two and ate hardened bread and sausage To keep me going those first few days, I played some private games with myself, such as counting 20 steps with my left ski before permitting myself to look ahead.

At the pass we took off the skins and skied down the other side and climbed again for one hour to reach the Momin pass. We were at just over 3,000 meters and I could feel my heart hammering in my throat. I was beginning the think I had reached my limit, when we hit a vast, relatively level plateau ringed with peaks: the Grand Desert glacier. The 60-minute crossing of that glacier was for me one of the delights of the trip. It was late morning, the air was dry and limpid, and the sun blazed off the snow with blinding brilliance. We had taken off our jackets and gloves, the sun cream was running down our faces and we had all but forgotten the fatigue of the three-hour climb. Before us, the immaculate whiteness of the open snow seemed infinite, its immensity marked only by thin, zigzag trail on which ant-like skiers were slowly moving. The blue sky was so near I felt I could reach out and touch it. The Grand Desert is high—above 3,000 meters—so that the surrounding peaks look puny, and one has the odd sensation of being at sea level in a very flat land. At the end of the glacier is the peak of Roseblanche, a 3,336-meter favorite of skiers. From our elevated vantage, it looked like a modest hill. We climbed to its summit and there finally had our bread and sausage, in company with a group of seven young French medical students, who joined us for the rest of the trip. After a short break, we were back on our skis, swooping down through heavy snow to the Prafleuri hut, the only unattended one on the route. While Rene split some of the logs neatly stacked in the kitchen and lit the iron stove, we filled buckets with snow to boil water and sat down to a meal we had carried in our rucksacks. Before going to bed, we cleaned up thoroughly and brought in wood to replace what we had used: the mountaineers' etiquette requires leaving any shelter as you found it.

The following morning we were off at five o'clock to begin long traverse across avalanche country, the arduous climb to the Dix hut, an eagle's nest perched over towering cliffs. It was during that hard ascent that my body began to master what experiences Alpinists call "the rhythm:" skis begin to slide without effort, sticks mark the beat like a metronome, and breathing becomes perfectly coordinated. One feels wonderfully light, as though one could go on forever. When I shared this sensation with my more experienced companion Jean-Claude, he laughed. "Didn't you know it? That's what we're all looking for!" Then I remembered the Monfort hut keeper telling me that there were two obstacles to overcome on the *Haute-Route*: one physical, one mental. I was about to surmount the physical obstacle, I felt. The mental one I had to face the next day.

As we were making the final ascent to the hut, an Alpine ibex with back-curv-ing horns broke from behind a rock on the opposite slope and bounded across the snow field, followed by a second one and then a third. We were wild with excitement: to see even one animal at these altitudes is extremely unusual. This sight somehow gave us the boost we needed to flounder the last precipitous 500 meters to the hut. When I climbed into bed that night, sleep did not come eas-ily: over-tired and hyper-stimulated by the altitude, I understood why sleeping pills are essential on the Haute-Route.

The Serpentine is an impressive wall of bluish ice over 100 feet thick, sur-mounted by a gigantic cornice. We reached it in pre-dawn light and joined a file of 40 or 50 skiers painfully toiling up the Serpentine pass. The steepest part had to be climbed in short zigzags, with 180-degree kick turns at the hairpin corners. It was here, just when I thought I had reached top form that I began to suffer real fatigue. My throat was dry, sweat poured down my face, my heart pounded wildly in my temples and throat. Each step was an agony. "I must rest for a minute!" I called to Rene. He hardly looked back. "Keep going!" I had trouble making the next kick turn, and grumpily he braced my skis from underneath while I wobblingly completed the turn. I was dizzy now, shaking with exhaus-tion. Then a strap of my skins came loose and Rene, himself out of breath, bent to fix it. Lying at an odd angle on the steep wall, I rolled my eyes upward and saw that the pass seemed to mount to the sky. At that point, I lost my courage. It seemed I could climb no further, yet if I stayed here I would die of exposure or slide down the cliff. I'm not sure what got me back on my feet—unless it was Rene's steady words of encouragement and my own bleak realization that the only way out was up. With a supreme effort I got shakily up to my feet, made my next kick turn like a man groping in his sleep and continued the agonizing ascent, leaning desperately against the steep gradient.

When I reached the top at last, I felt an immense elation at having mastered the urge to give up. Rene nodded and told me such crises of discouragement were common. Overcoming them was, in his mind, the real point of the trip. The worst thing a guide can do, he remarked, is show pity or allow too frequent stops. "You'd be surprised," he said dryly, "how much a man can endure before reaching his limit."

The more immediate reward was a view unsurpassed in the Alps. From a peak known as Pigne d'Arolla, most of the giants of the Valais are clearly and splendidly on display. We enjoyed the sight for a few minutes, though. As a storm formed suddenly in the blackening sky, we began the ski descent to the Vignettes hut, where all variants of the Haute-Route converge. We took the run cautiously, skiing between ice blocks and around crevasses, sliding sideways down almost vertical traverses. The air had the visibility of milk, one saw nothing beyond a few inches on either side of the skis. I caught a glimpse of a group of skiers on the far side of a crevasse, roped to each other. They succeeded making it down to Arolla, I later learned, but I didn't envy their descent.

At the Vignettes hut, perched over an apparently bottomless abyss, there was excitement in the air. Everybody was preparing for next day's long run home to Zermatt. That last and longest leg, which takes at least eight hours, is indeed a fitting climax to the trip. I was also looking forward for this run. I had read and heard so much about the run taking you first to the Otemma glacier and across the Eveque pass, then to the marvelous run down to the Arolla glacier and Mont Brule pass, and down the other side. I couldn't wait to climb the majestic Valpelline pass, the threshold to Zermatt, from where, for the first time, one catches sight, far away, of the splendidly solitary Matterhorn. I had heard that the gradual unveiling of that most celebrated peak is so unexpected and dramatic, that it stops even experienced Alpinists in their tracks. And then, the final 18-kilometer descent to Zermatt, and the village I knew and loved, the finish of the *Haute-Route* adventure.

But…Unfortunately, it didn't end this way. In any high mountain undertaking, the weather conditions make all the difference. I was told that the *Haute-Route* could be a paradise, I was also warned that it could be hell. Now I know that both statements are perfectly true. After a few days of sun and no wind, the weather changed dramatically as we arrived at the Vignettes. There, stranded inside the flimsy hut, surrounded by abysses and icy peaks as horrifying as Charles-Adams' cartoons, we were hit by the wildest storm I had ever seen. For two days and two nights the winds howled ferociously and the walls shook as if ready to explode at any moment. The snow from the blizzard had blocked not only the entrance doors, but also all windows on the ground floor. There was no question of leaving the over packed hut, not even for a visit to the outhouse perched atop a slippery ridge, a perilous exercise even in good weather. (We, men, had to use the second floor windows for certain needs; I never found out what the ladies did in the emergency...)

After two frightful nights, the idea of continuing to Zermatt was abandoned and we waited for the storm's rage to subside a little so we could leave Les Vignettes. Early on the third morning we wrapped ourselves solidly and took off in the thick fog. We were lucky that our guide, Rene, knew the way by heart and we followed him blindly, with no accident, down to the village of Arolla, across an area infested with avalanches and crevasses. Finally, the fog lifted and the last descent—about one hour and a half in very deep new snow—was quite enjoyable. It was a tremendous relief to reach peaceful Arolla, in spite of the bitter disappointment of not having completed the classic Haute-Route in the proper way.

"La Haute-Route was much tougher than I had expected," I wrote to Lil a few days later from Geneva. *"And we had no luck with the weather. I did it the hard way. If I have to do it again, now I know how it should be done."* (What I meant was to go with friends and not with strangers, and with a familiar guide; above all, to be better prepared for serious climbing and long distance trekking, not just downhill skiing, like me.) The most important factor, the weather, is, of course, a matter of luck. And the age?... Curious, but I haven't thought of it. Neither of the fact that I had had my double hernia operation only four months before.

After a couple of days rest in Montreux and Gstaad, the time came for my next assignment, the refugee camps. *"Darling, I'm leaving for Bangkok tomorrow, 1:35 P.M. on Swissair,"* I wrote to Lil on April 12 from Geneva.*"...I'm quite excited about Thailand. Just had my gamma globulin shot, plus malaria pills. I miss you very, very much..."*

****

UN HIGH COMMISSIONER FOR REFUGEES.

Bellerive, Sadri Khan's beautiful and impeccably run home, is an impressive 17-th century chateau on Lake Geneva, where Lil and I had stayed many times, on our way to or from Gstaad. On a few occasions we had Paul with us, still a little boy, who was greatly impressed to be served in a princely manner by the Egyptian valets in uniform, yet slightly scared to sleep alone in the imposing guest room in one of the chateau's wings. Sometimes we even traveled with Ding-Dong, our dog, who used to amuse Sadri enormously, although, for some inexplicable reasons, this usually affectionate dog went into a frenzy and attacked him each time he wore a black turtleneck sweater. Sadri knew Paul and Ding-Dong well, from the days of his courtship of Katy, when they spent romantic weekends with us in our house in Southampton. Katy was a friend of mine since my days in Paris, when she used to come with her first husband Cyril on trips from Egypt, where they lived. I had met Sadri in Switzerland, and then in the United States, when he was still studying at Harvard and I had always liked him for his intelligence, culture, and sense of humor.

Later, when he and Katy fell in love, a love that transformed entirely their lives, a new friendship developed between them and Lil and myself. Their love story was very romantic, deep and at times sad and appearing hopeless. I guess that in some moments of doubt, the example of our marriage and happiness must have been reassuring for them. Like Lil, Katy had three children and great affection for her husband. They were facing hard decisions and I suspect that Lil, giving up so much and bravely renouncing her previous life to marry me, had in a way served as an example.

Our visits to Bellerive were always extremely pleasant, thanks to Sadri's and Katy's warm hospitality. They lived in style and great comfort, yet very quietly. Except for a few official lunches and dinners (he had been, since 1965, the UN High Commissioner for Refugees), no lavish parties were given in the several salons filled with precious collections of Islamic art, objets d'art, rare books and family souvenirs. An exceptionally united couple, they jealously protected their privacy and only close friends shared the quiet evenings at the chateau, enjoying a gourmet dinner and fascinating conversation on theater, world affairs or modern art. The evenings usually ended with showing movies, a passion of both of them, in the cozy projection room in the basement, with Sadri, dressed in becoming North-African caftan, expertly running the elaborate professional equipment.

Sadri and Katy used to spend short vacations in Africa or Greece, or sailing on a chartered yacht in the Caribbean. Lil and I were their guests on one of these cruises and had a lovely time around Grenada, the Grenadines, and the neighboring islands. When in New York or Paris, two big cities they loved, they went to the theatre almost every night, visited art galleries and enjoyed seeing numerous artists and writers friends. When in Geneva on Sundays, he sometimes raced in the Lake regattas. The rest of the time, they traveled a lot on UN missions all over the world, frequently visiting refugee camps in Africa, Asia and elsewhere. Then he would return to his headquarters in Geneva and plunge again devoutly into his work.

This time—it was the winter of 1977—I was visiting *Bellerive* alone, on business. Starting the research for my *Reader's Digest* assignment, Sadri's kind invitation to stay at the chateau and to attend a few meetings at his offices at the United Nations in Geneva, gave me a good opportunity to watch him at work. His days began at 7 AM, with thorough reading of the press at home, while having breakfast, followed by one hour devoted to his personal mail, before leaving for his office. To avoid the Pont du Mont-Blanc's traffic-jam, he drove me across the lake in his small motorboat, straight from his dock in *Bellerive*. In five minutes we were on the opposite shore, where he kept a car. Ten more minutes, and we were in his office at the Palais des Nations. His days were packed with staff meetings, appointments with ambassadors and other officials, but also listening to grievances and requests by simple refugees. "But do you, the High Commissioner, have to personally receive individual refugees here?", I asked when an old South American man buttonholed him in front of his office. Sadri was surprised by the question. "What do you think I'm here for?", he sad.

Indeed. What was Sadruddin, the princely scion of one of the world's wealthiest and most illustrious families, doing here, at the center of the refugees' heart-rending universe? His father, the late Aga Khan, a fabulous cosmopolitan figure, was not only the spiritual leader of the world's 20 million Ismaili muslims, but also President of the League of Nations before WWII and the owner of the best stables of thorough-breds. A direct descendent of the Prophet Mohammed, the old Aga was legendary for the ceremony in which his followers weighed him on a huge scale, balanced with the equivalent in gold and precious stones. (Incidentally, he happened to be quite corpulent…) Sadri's elder brother Aly Khan, a jet-set celebrity and international Casanova, had, among many headline-making exploits, married Rita Hayworth. Sadri's nephew Karim, Aly's son, was the present "Aga" or supreme leader of the Ismailis. So, wasn't it surprising that Prince Saddrudin, raised in such incredible luxury and privilege, should devote his time and talents to the service of the world's pariahs? In fact, this contrast was precisely the point of my story, and the Readers' Digest had endorsed it enthusiastically.

I admired Sadri for his zeal and devotion to his noble mission, but knowing him, I wasn't at all surprised. He had always been a serious young man, very intelligent and sincerely interested in public affairs. Unlike his half-brother Aly, 22 years his senior, Sadri had shown no taste for the life of racing stables, nightclubs, polo games and lavish parties. Except for a brief marriage in his early twenties to a glamorous model, Nina Dyer, he was a disappointment to the gossip columnists. After a happy childhood in France (his mother, Princess Andree, the third of Aga Khan's four wives, was French), his parents divorced when he was ten, but the divorce didn't affect the close relationship of the child with his aging father. The Aga, a combination of warmhearted bonvivant and deeply religious man, played a decisive role in the formation of Sadri, for whom he had a special affection. The boy accompanied his father on many visits to Ismaili communities in Africa and Asia. A man of considerable culture and wisdom, the old Aga was actively involved in international affairs and causes, such as India's independence. Sadri was 5-year old when his father was elected President of the League of Nations, which used to convene in the same Palais des Nations in Geneva where the UN High Commissioner of Refugees ("UNHCR") had his offices now. Besides maharajas and socialites, the opulent, jovial Aga entertained friendships with personalities such as Churchill, Stravinsky, Somerset Maugham, Puccini, and Diaghilev, so young Sadri grew up in a milieu where conversation, apart from public affairs and international relations, turned regularly around religion, the arts, anti-colonialism, or ecology. After some exclusive Swiss schools, Sadri took a degree in government and international affairs at Harvard, where the intellectual climate suited his interests well. He spent three more years of advanced studies at Harvard's Center for Middle-Eastern studies.

He first worked for the UN Commissioner for Refugees in 1959 during the World Refugee Year, with missions in Middle and Far Eastern countries, where he had many connections. Then he became consultant to UNESCO and a key figure in saving the archeological treasures in Egypt endangered by the construction of the Aswan dam.

His efficiency and dedication impressed the High Commissioner for Refugees, who appointed the 28-year-old prince his deputy. During the three years as Deputy High Commissioner, Sadri greatly improved the cooperation between that agency and the Third World, starting with the repatriation in 1962 of 180.000 refugees at the end of the Algerian war and visiting ten African and five Latin-American countries to discuss refugee problems with their heads of State, many of whom he knew personally. With his family background, he was trusted by the Third World as one of their own. (By family tradition, Sadri was an Iranian citizen; his father's memory was revered in India, and his brother Aly was Pakistani representative at the UN.) But Sadri also carried a British passport and, of course, his European upbringing and life-style, plus his Harvard education, made him definitely a Westerner. Therefore, there was no surprise when the General Assembly elected him by unanimous vote High Commissioner for Refugees in 1965. At the time of my article, he had already been re-elected twice, by acclamation. My research revealed his rare gift for negotiating and discreet diplomacy in highly sensitive, often secret, missions. I found out that thanks to his unpublicized efforts in Hanoi, the Americans blocked in Vietnam at the end of the war were released; the Biafra children returned from the Ivory Coast and Gabon; Kurdish rebels released kidnapped Polish technicians; 200.000 refugees from Sudan were repatriated; populations were exchanged in Bangladesh. I felt proud to be a friend of such a remarkable and noble achiever. A few years earlier, his name had been mentioned as possible successor of UN Secretary General, U Thant. But at 38, he was judged much too young for the post.

It was a year when 3.500 "boat people" from Vietnam were going through indescribable ordeals and 80.000 refugees from Laos and Cambodia still crowded 14 camps in Thailand; when 170.000 Burundi refugees were accepted in Tanzania and 20.000 Chilean refugees hung on waiting lists in Argentina. And millions more all over the world, alarmingly growing legions of people with no home, country, or passport. Being a "displaced person" myself, I felt better when seeing compassionate and competent people like Sadri and his agency trying to help and protect these outcasts, and caring for them. But the immensity of the problem was often frustrating and Sadri was deeply concerned. "Our time could truly be described as The Age of the Refugee," he said.

To see the problems firsthand, he suggested I visit a few camps in Thailand. I flew to Bangkok, where the UNHCR office gave me a thorough briefing and organized my field trips. One of the officers took me by plane to the Songkhla camp for Vietnamese "Boat people," far in the South of Thailand. Another field officer drove me in his Land Rover to the Laem Sing camp, also for Vietnamese, a 5-hour trip from Bangkok to Eastern Thailand. Then I took the overnight train to Nong Khai in the remote North of Thailand, an unexpectedly comfortable sleeper with excellent, *Wagons-Lits*-type service. There, in view of Communist Laos's capital Vientiane, just across the Mekong river, was a huge camp for Laotian and Montagnard-tribe refugees. All visited camps, despite their very different ethnicities, location and size (from 700 inmates in Songkhla to 16,000 at the Nong Khai, a veritable shantytown), exuded an almost identical pathos: the same stench and sounds and colors of drying laundry, the same misery and squalor in the makeshift huts and dormitories, the same despair in the eyes of frightened grownups. But also the innocent laughter of children playing in the mud. Some spoke French, a leftover of the old Indochina rule, and their tales were enough to break my heart. But nothing matched the horror stories I heard in the camps for Cambodian refugees.

There were 2,400 Cambodians, mostly peasants with their wives and children, in the Kamput camp in the jungle of Eastern Thailand, no more than ten miles from the border. Much too near to the nightmarish Gulag that was Cambodia in those days of Khmer Rouge rule, and everyone in Kamput felt nervous about it. When escaping, on foot through the jungle, the refugees had risked their lives and had abandoned everything they loved and possessed. Even now, in the relative security of this dreary, barracks-like haven, they still shivered at the memories of the genocide, which the Khmer Rouge had started with unprecedented savagery in the spring of 1975.

These events were still relatively recent and almost nothing was known about them in the West. A total, chillingly efficient blackout had been imposed upon a hermetically closed country, where all travel, press, mail and any form of communications had been banned. The first sketchy reports on alleged atrocities of a monstrous scale had begun to appear, but how reliable were they? The quoted figures of people executed or dead from inhuman treatment—800 thousand? 1.2 million? two million?—sounded hardly believable. So were the stories of Phnom Penn's forced evacuation, when the entire, 3-million capital's population, including all old men and women, babies and pregnant mothers, invalids on wheelchairs and sick patients on hospital beds, were ordered to leave for the countryside within hours and herded at gunpoint to the roads out of Phnom Penn. God knows I was familiar with Communist atrocities in other countries, including my own, but the tales I heard in Kamput bordered on the grotesque and initially made me a little skeptical about the eyewitnesses' credibility. "The reality is so horrible anyhow," I thought the first night in the solitude of my bed-bug-stained room at the nearby shanty which passed for a "travel lodge," tossing and turning between the sweaty, filthy sheets, "so why do the poor devils have to embellish and exaggerate?" Indeed, some testimonies sounded wildly excessive, biased by too much emotion. Was it true, that Khmer Rouge systematically executed innocent people by the dozens, by the hundreds, often by smashing their skulls with clubs, to save precious bullets? That everybody wearing eyeglasses, or able to read and write, was automatically branded an enemy of the regime? That an entire nation of slaves was forced into Pharaoh-driven labor at rice fields, dam construction and jungle clearing, brutally beaten and only fed a coffee-cup-full of rice a day? People were dying every day like flies from hunger and malaria, I was told. Private property and money were abolished, books and archives burned, pagodas, statues of Buddha, shops, schools and museums physically destroyed… I didn't have to be reminded of what sadistic excesses a Communist terror was capable of, but in the Khmer Rouge case, the monstrous scale and the cold-blooded premeditation seemed to surpass all tales of Soviet Gulag and Nazi camps. So, nauseated but a little incredulous, I attempted to check the veracity of those tales. I talked to dozens of refugees—in French with the educated, through a translator to the peasants. It was always the same story, different versions of a same nightmare. Alas, it was all true. The UN field officer readily confirmed the facts, a young Scotsman called David Jamieson, liaison between the 11,000 Cambodian refugees in Thailand and Sadri's office. The information wasn't different at the Thai Governor's office in Chantabury, the district capital. A visiting YMCA mission had collected similar testimonies. Back in Bangkok, I talked to the US ambassador, Charles Whitehouse, and the US Consul, Andrew Antipas. By then, they had a clear idea of what was going on in the "People's Republic of Campuchea:" it was even worse than what I had already learned. And when I heard descriptions of Pol Pot's regime by some Jesuits I met in Bangkok—definitely the best informed sources,—there was no doubt left in my mind that Khmer Rouge had indeed brought Dante's Inferno to Earth.

This upset me enormously. I suppose it's one thing to read of horrible things happening to unknown victims, and it's quite different to hear it in person from the mouth of those human wrecks, to face the tears and tragic expressions of desperate mothers, starved children and men who had been tortured. Something else happened to me in Bangkok, adding some guilt feeling to my compassion. Three unknown men surprised me one morning in my hotel's room at the "President" and introduced themselves as "Khmers Serey" (Free Khmers). "My name is Major Dura Narin of the 149th battalion, Seventh infantry division of the old Cambodian army," said their 31-year-old leader, an energetic, ardent looking man with numerous battle scars. Their clandestine group had learned my address through the grapevine and had come to ask me for help. Since he fled Cambodia in 1975, Narin told me, he had returned a dozen times with commandos of refugees engaged in sporadic raids into "Campuchea" and then returning secretly to Thailand to re-supply.

Now I remembered that in the Kamput camp I had visited a makeshift prison, constructed of long bamboo poles, where eleven Cambodian guerrillas were being held. They had crossed the frontier the evening before: having run short of food and ammunition, they had surrendered to the Thais, were put in jail and interrogated by the camp authorities. The other camp inmates looked up with admiration at these "Khmers Serey," but weren't allowed to talk to them.

I spent hours with my visitors, who spoke some French. They gave me horrendous details about present-day life in Cambodia. "It isn't hard to cross the border, despite the mines and the sentries, if you really know this part of the country," Major Narin told me. "Once inside Cambodia, we mingle with the peasants in the rice fields. We stay about a week—watching, listening, and organizing. We avoid skirmishes because we're not strong enough yet. We have only one gun for every two men, and a handful of grenades." But "liberation" was near, he was sure. "Because the world won't tolerate such terror and injustices…" (Sounded familiar. But could I discourage them by saying that in Bulgaria it still lasted, after 33 years, and in Russia, after 60?…)

My visitors implored me, (and all journalists), to tell the world about their country's tragedy. Again and again they asked me how much we knew in the West about the Cambodian genocide, about the premeditated extermination of all vestiges of the past. About the tortures in the rice fields and the evacuees dying on the roads, "with the old people collapsing, fever-ridden children dying in their tracks, the smell everywhere of rotting flesh, with Khmers Rouges, some of them only 13 and 14 years old and only too happy to use their weapons and finish off the stragglers…"

Yes, we had heard accounts of that, I said somehow sheepishly. Then the painful questions: "Tell us, how did the Free World react?" Did the naive Major and his companions imagine that there had been angry mass demonstrations in New York and Paris, thousand indignant editorials written, and emergency meetings called at UN's Security Council? I didn't have the heart to tell them that in the West almost no one spoke about Cambodia…

We met again the next day. I liked the guys' patriotism but couldn't do much to help. They badly needed a photo camera and I gave Dura Narin 100 dollars. (*He wrote me in New York a thank-you letter in schoolboy's French: the camera was bought and was very useful.*) But most important, he made me promise that I would "tell the West about them." I kept my promise. On my return home, I stopped in Paris and managed to publish in June 1977 two articles about the terror in Cambodia and the Free Khmers, in the big-circulation daily "France-Soir." (I was no more with "Paris-Match".) In September, Bill Buckley's *National Review* used this material for a well-displayed cover story, "Cambodian Gore—A Report by Stephane Groueff."

And my article on Prince Sadruddin Aga Khan, the UN High Commissioner for Refugees?—I put a considerable amount of work and time to research and write it. (*Readers' Digest* used to pay well but was most difficult when it came to condensing and editing.) Finally, the definitive version was ready, the editors were pleased, I received my full check, and publication date was scheduled. About two months before printing, Sadri came to New York and asked me to lunch with him. "I have good news," I said cheerfully. "The article is finished, approved, and programmed." "Hmm…We'll talk about all that," he mumbled, rather uneasy. In the restaurant, Sadri gave me the news I expected the least: he had come to New York, he told me confidentially, because he had decided to leave his post and return to family and private life. That day he was going to the Secretary General to offer his resignation. I was stunned. Now, that I had learned a lot about refugee problems, I knew that few people in the world were as qualified for the job as he. I also felt that Sadri had good chances to become soon UN's Secretary General. What a loss for the refugees, for the UN, for all of us! But I also knew that he wasn't a man to make important decisions lightly. Before acting, he and Katy had certainly considered all possible angles. "I'm sorry about your article. But the real subject are the refugees, not me, and the story is still valid and extremely important, no matter who's High Commissioner," he said modestly. "I'm sure the *Digest* will be still interested."

This time, Sadri guessed wrong, and I knew it right away. Journalistically \speaking, the fascinating story was in the person behind the job, not the institution or the tragic statistics of the world's refugees. The striking contrast between the glamour surrounding this most brilliant prince, and the squalor and distress in which lived the miserables, to whom he had devoted eighteen years of his life. But, of course, these are journalistic realities of which "serious" journalists don't boast. Therefore, I dutifully but not very convincingly pleaded Sadri's arguments with the *Readers' Digest* editors. Equally politely, the editors declined the suggestion for a revised emphasis of the article and insisted that I keep the check.

Thus, the article on Prince Saddrudin, "*A Mandate to Protect and Assist Refugees,*" was never published.

*   *   *   *   *

Chapter 34

"New Look" project's failure. Mexico. Oman. Washington

It didn't take me long, after leaving *Paris-Match*, to realize that freelancing, without another regular source of income, wasn't a solution for me. True, I sold articles to the *Readers' Digest* and to *Realites*, and did occasional work for Roger Therond, who was back at *Match*. But this was too irregular and not sufficient to allay my financial worries. They were growing by the week. Indeed, at the age of 55, pension was still a remote mirage, and my savings were rather unimpressive. Worse, it was obvious that salesmanship was not a gift the Creator had spoiled me with. In writing, as in other creative careers, the so-called "talent" is just one ingredient in the formula for success, and not necessarily the major one. Without an aggressive agent, good marketing, and self-promotion, the chances are very slim and the embarrassments too frequent. In my case, this deficiency must be in the genes: if I seemed to be lacking in salesmanship, one should've known my father and my brother! Next to them, I was a pushy hustler.

The precariousness of freelancing pushed me to look for some steady job, preferably in journalism. I was also playing with an old pet idea of mine: starting a magazine devoted to adventure in all its aspects, from exploration and exotic travel, to daredevil sports, commandos missions, and acts of heroism. I had already prepared pilot projects, but the difficulty was to find financing without relinquishing control. It was at that time that I heard that Daniel Filipacchi, after his successes in France, was interested in acquiring some publications in the United States, even in launching an American version of *Paris-Match*. In October 1977, we met for lunch in New York.

I knew Daniel since the first team of *Match*, where he started as a photographer and I as a reporter. He was then a bright, handsome youngster, not yet 20, quite sophisticated for his age and better mannered than most of our colleagues at Rue "Pierre Charron." We had collaborated on a few reportages, without however becoming close friends. In fact, I don't think that Filipacchi, although a full member of the reporters' "gang," was ever really intimate with anyone. Contrary to the typical wild, extrovert *Match* characters, he was somewhat reserved, enjoying the horseplay and pranks of his pals, but remaining rather remote, self-conscious and sometimes slightly ill-at-ease, like a lone wolf at a joyful reunion of the pack. Before long, it became clear that he was aiming much higher than the career of a photo reporter. He left *Match* to become a hugely popular jazz disk jockey and jazz-magazine publisher first, then the major rock-and-roll promoter in France, then the French most successful soft-porn publisher. He became so rich that he finally bought *Paris-Match* and became a partner at *Hachette*.

Spending more and more time in New York, he was now negotiating the purchase of the *Popular Publications,* owners of a half-a-dozen photography and cars magazines. We had lunch at a coffee shop under the Rockefeller Center (despite his new wealth, Daniel had kept his frugal habits and avoided expensive restaurants). He brought with him a future American partner, Bob Gutwillig, a shrewd Californian, one of those hyper-active, fast-talking wheeler-dealers we read about in business pages. Daniel asked me whether I would be interested in helping him if he bought and redesigned these publications. I didn't, of course, know anything about photography or racing cars, but one of the group's titles, *Argozy*, caught my interest. It was a declining monthly with old-fashioned stories about adventures, which could be transformed into a modern magazine of the type I was dreaming about. I told Daniel and Bob that not only was I available, but I already had some ideas about a new magazine and they promised to keep in touch.

Daniel returned to France and called me again one month later, just on the eve of the day Lil and I were leaving on a week vacation to Martinique. He invited me for dinner at a Chinese restaurant in Harlem and, in addition to Gutwillig, he brought his lawyer and two *Hachette* executives, Gerald Rockmortel and Boris Troyan. This time the project of a US Filipacchi company sounded advanced and I left for Martinique with renewed hopes.

However, I didn't hear a word from him during the whole month of December, a month that turned out to be dramatic, almost tragic for us. On our first day after returning from a delightful vacation in Martinique, we had a bad accident while driving to Southampton with Paul. Leaving the city, I had let him drive, with me sitting next to him and Lil in the back seat. We were in a happy mood and Paul was telling some amusing story, when suddenly, in the middle of a sentence, his voice stopped short and his body stiffened. Alarmed, I shouted to him to pay attention to the driving, then shook him by the shoulders. He was not reacting, as the car, on the middle lane of the busy Friday-evening Long Island expressway traffic, kept on speeding.

With Lil leaning forward, almost hysterical at the thought that Paul might be dead and trying to revive him, I grabbed the wheel across his body and attempted to remove his foot from the gas pedal. Impossible, Paul's foot was as rigid as a piece of wood! The car was swaying, Angry motorists right, left, and behind were blowing horns, swearing and cursing, trying to avoid colliding with us. Somehow I managed to slalom my way into the right lane, looking for a near exit from the hectic expressway, and tried to reduce the speed. Unable to reach the brake pedal, I turned off the ignition key and stopped the motor. But I hadn't anticipated that by cutting off the engine, I automatically blocked the steering wheel. We were now at the mercy of fate and a terrifying sense of total helplessness before an imminent disaster overwhelmed me. All I could do was to shout to Lil "Brace yourself! We're going to crash!" For a few seconds, it looked like the whole Groueff family—Lil, Paul, and myself—was about to be wiped out.

But, with the motor off, the speed decelerated and, miraculously, the road exit toward which I had steered the car before loosing control, happened to be an ascending ramp. The slope slowed us down effectively, until it brought us to a halt. One side of the car went into the shallow ditch, but apart from a few scratches, there was no damage.

As Lil and I jumped out and leaned over Paul's inanimate body, trying to revive him, the car was surrounded by concerned motorists, offering advice and help. We were sick with fear and worry: was our son dead? A couple of minutes had barely passed, when we heard police sirens and the flashes of an ambulance lit the scene. As the paramedics pulled Paul out of the car and into a stretcher, his eyes opened and, still stunned, he mumbled a few words. What a relief this was! Crying,—was it for joy or anguish?—Lil joined Paul into the ambulance, while I followed them in my car to the North Shore University Hospital in nearby Manhasset.

That night and the following couple of days and nights were an agony, which we lived between the hospital and the Stralems' home. We were lucky that Lil's former sister-in-law Jean had her country house in the vicinity and that she offered us her warm hospitality. Paul underwent all sorts of medical tests, without however reaching a definite, clear diagnosis. Back to New York, the examinations and treatments continued for months, dominating our life for a long period of time. Paul behaved courageously, but the shock and fears of the disturbing experience were not without affecting profoundly the sensitive 17-year-old boy.

The contacts with Filipacchi resumed in January 1978 and they involved his principal lieutenants Gutwillig, Troyan, and Regis Pagniez, the French art director behind the success of *Lui* magazine, whom Daniel had brought from Paris to repeat this feat with the American *Oui* magazine, in a Filipacchi-Guccione partnership. Regis was a remarkably gifted, independent-minded young Frenchman who not only spoke very little English at that time, but didn't show the slightest interest in making an effort to communicate in any other language but French. He was very close to Daniel who had given him almost full authority in designing his American publications. A totally visual man, Pagniez didn't care much about texts and subject matter and didn't conceal his conviction that in the genre Filipacchi intended to succeed, what counted was brilliant layout and graphics, right selection of shock photographs and a spectacular cover.

I got along well with Regis and found it easier to discuss my ideas about *Argozy* with him, rather than with Daniel, who was most of the time absent and wasn't very communicative anyhow. Early in February I presented a project, which Daniel seemed to like, but he still couldn't make up his mind. Pagniez and Troyan were frankly of the opinion that he should concentrate on his main project, *U.S. Match*, and not disperse his efforts and money before it takes off. Waiting for a decision, I was still without a job and getting more and more depressed. To better organize my freelance writing, I rented a small office on the top floor of the medieval-looking building of the *Explorers Club* on East 70-th street, to which I belonged, a cozy nest, where I found peace and where I started working on some articles for the French *Realites* (the editor covered me with compliments but announced soon his inability to pay. The lavishly printed magazine folded before sending me my check for the published articles...) I had an interview with the *Conde-Nast* press heir Cy Newhose, whose friendly late father I had known. But it took no more than ten minutes of uncomfortable talk with the taciturn new tycoon to realize that his profit-oriented empire had no position to offer to a journalist of my kind. Things didn't look too bright for me, especially that the continuing medical tests had a sad effect on Paul's mood, and even the usually optimistic and cheerful Lil had begun to feel the pressure. Indeed, she worried her children and they offered her one-week rest at the "Golden Door" in San Diego. The luxurious spa worked miracles and Lil returned beautifully refreshed, with fully recharged batteries. And as there was nothing to keep us in gloomy, wintry New York, and with chalet *Ding-Dong* waiting for us, we spent the month of March in Gstaad. Philip was with us for ten days, then Paul joined us, and Emilio and Iris Gioia came for a visit. In spite of my worries, it was another happy vacation among old Gstaad friends—the Angie Dukes and the Heminways, the Toubs, the Nivens and the Woods, Stanley and Lisa Weiss, the Pantzes, Claude and Tigi Barbey, Connie Anderson, and numerous Goulandrises. At the end of the vacation we drove to Rolle for the wedding of Alain Cheneviere and Barbara, a happy reunion of the Panitza clan. When I returned to New York in April, I was in a better shape, sun-tanned, feeling healthy and relaxed after four weeks of skiing. I was arriving at just the right moment: Gutwillig called two days later, offering me work at the future *USA-Match*. On April 24, we signed a contract and I moved to the newly rented offices at 150 East 58th street.

The salary, $ 3,000 a month, wasn't overly generous, but offered me a steady income for a work that promised to be to my taste. My job was not with *USA-Match* proper; I was supposed to create another, smaller magazine, offering to the American public the most noticeable European articles and photo-stories of the month. A sort of topical, "with-it," exciting *Readers' Digest* (if one could imagine such a contradiction in terms), with the accent on the pictures. Such a monthly would cost very little, we thought, because it would use for free some of the best material from *Paris-Match, Hachette* and *Filipacchi Press*, and would only pay minimal reprint rights for the cream of foreign stories and photos. The idea was to take full advantage of the undeniable appeal Europe had to Americans—its history, culture and arts, its taste and sophistication, its savoir-vivre and savoir-faire. I was given a nice, large office (in the beginning Bob Gutwillig used it too during his meteoric appearances from California) and a small budget to get the most important European publications, and plunged into my new assignment. Browsing all day through dozens of magazines was a most pleasant occupation, while selecting the best among the rich material couldn't have been more rewarding. The French and British press presented, of course, no language problem, and as I could read, if not speak, German, Italian and Spanish, the job gave me no difficulties.

In early June I showed Daniel, Bob, and Regis a detailed project for a summary, with selected foreign magazine stories and photos. It contained dramatic coverage of world news, some much talked-about romances and weddings, adventures and crime, a few sports events, enough fashion, celebrities and pretty girls, mixed with science, gossip, and human interest stories. They seemed to like it and asked me to suggest a budget. For title, we chose *Continental* and Regis sketched a few possible logos. Things looked promising. I felt stimulated and was happy enough to treat myself to a present I was craving for a longtime: a nice *Selmer*, the first brand new clarinet I ever owned after years of blowing on the old, beaten relic I had bought third-hand a few decades before in Paris.

But as the weeks passed, I began to doubt in the reliability of the whole venture. Filipacchi's attention had switched to another, more ambitious project. Rather than start from scratch with an American *Match*, he decided to revive the defunct *Look* magazine and bought the legendary title from its owner, Gardner Cowles. Banking on the still vivid prestige of the old *Look* and the "magic touch" reputation of *Paris-Match*, he succeeded in convincing a group of French investors (*Hachette*, billionaire Edmond de Rothschild, *Radio Europe-1*) to supply a capital of $ 10 million. Now Daniel, Gutwillig, and Pagniez were much too busy to spare any time on my *Continental* project. Day after day, I went to my office to work in total isolation, barely able to catch them between two doors. In fact, Daniel was almost never there, and when he came, he never came to talk with me, or asked about my project. I began to feel that I was working in a vacuum, with no one seeming to care about *Continental*. If I asked to talk to Daniel, he was either absent, or "in conference," too busy to see me. The informality of our *Match* camaraderie had gone. This frustrating uncertainty finally ended by end of July, when Daniel announced that the "Continental" project had to be temporarily shelved and everybody, including myself, should give a hand to the creation of a successful *Paris-Match*-modeled *Look* magazine.

I was disappointed, because I really believed that *Continental* had excellent chances to succeed. But having no choice, I agreed to join the new *Look* staff, although my role and functions were totally unclear. What worried me most was the growing feeling that my idea of journalism had very little to do with the general goals and practices of Daniel and his lieutenants. I suspect that they too began to realize that I was not the guy they needed. As it was, we were interested in two different concepts of magazine journalism. My teachers and role models, were dedicated journalists of the type of Raymond Cartier and Gaston Bonheur, gifted professionals working for the great press barons of the epoch—Jean Prouvost, in France, DeWitt Wallace, Henry Luce or Gardner Cowles, in America. These bosses saw themselves as carrying a lofty mission of informing and educating, and were driven by the ambition to influence the public. There was a lot of the preacher-missionary in the approach of Wallace and Luce; as for my "Patron," Prouvost was at heart a frustrated reporter. They were, of course, also eager and delighted to make profits, but money wasn't the main motive. On the other hand, many new press barons were at heart less journalists than astute merchants of media properties. The big tycoons among them—Newhouse, Murdoch, and many others,—would've been equally successful if they sold cars, or shoes, or anything else. Shrewd, aggressive businessmen, realists to the point of cynicism, primarily interested in the bottom line rather than some journalistic "mission," they succeeded much better in the changing world of magazine publishing than the paternalistic old patrons of the pre-television era, who used to spend personal fortunes in the service of their own vocation, ambitions or egos. These were Filipacchi's role models. These, and big market successes of the ilk of *Playboy*'s" Hefner and *Penthouse*'s" Guccione, not old has-beens like Prouvost or Luce. He cared much less about the traditions and legacy of the venerable old "Look" than, for instance, about the efficient news-stand distribution methods of the vulgar *Hustler* magazine.

Personally, Daniel was a man seriously interested in, and knowledgeable of, avant-garde arts and pop culture. But the businessman in him was never too squeamish to discuss any moneymaking project, even ones of a dubious taste. I was appalled once when his entourage brought for his consideration a filthy publication that was making money in France. Called something like *Harakiri*, it thrived on photos of people urinating, soiled women's sanitary napkins, and similar scatological goodies. "What about copying it in English, Daniel?" someone asked. "We'll call it *Trash* and with a good distributor, it'll be gold!" I thought they were kidding and called Daniel's attention on the consequences such a venture would have on the image of *Look*, which hoped to be read by respectable families and influence public opinion. "Oh, we'll publish under some other company's name!" somebody dismissed my arguments. Smiling mischievously, Daniel of course had enough sense to discard the proposal, but not before examining the market studies and the cost-and-profit figures with the same attention he would give to a project for a magazine on surrealist art or food.

The organization of the new *Look*, if one could speak of any organization, was chaotic, even by *Paris-Match* standards. A former *Life* picture editor, John Durniak, was hired as managing editor. He arrived with a small team of *Time-Life* staffers and, bursting with enthusiasm, went straight to work on the first dummies, eagerly searching for story ideas (*"This is dynamite!"* was a favorite word for approval), viewing hundreds of contact sheets, giving assignments right and left, calling frequent editorial conferences. His zeal was soon dampened by the almost insulting indifference shown by the French staffers. Art-director Pagniez would arrive with his team (when he deigned to attend these conferences at all) with a bored, skeptical expression on his face, mumbling a few comments (in <u>French</u>, of course), and would impatiently push aside Durniak's pages to make room on the table for the picture stories <u>he</u> had brought with him. Then Regis would announce (still in French) that *"we'll do this"* or *"we'll give two pages to that."* Usually his choices were visually excellent, but he didn't see any need to ask for Durniak's approval, or at least have his words translated in English. In fact, Regis wasn't *proposing* them, he was *telling* what was going to be published. The staff was puzzled. Who was the deciding authority—Durniak or Pagniez? Filipacchi avoided to get involved. He treated Regis like a difficult but absolutely indispensable favorite child. Lately, Daniel had acted strangely detached, always absent, avoiding clear decisions, using Gutwillig as henchman in unpleasant situations, letting expenses and chaos grow unnecessarily at an alarming pace. In face of accumulating flagrant mistakes and shocking waste of money, he behaved almost as if he couldn't care less whether "Look" was headed toward a disaster and would ever appear at all.

When I finally succeeded to pin him down during a quick snack at the cafeteria of the low-price department store *Alexander's*, Daniel told me that I would be in charge of two sections: research and "Page One," an important regular feature with excerpts from forthcoming best-selling books, sensational documents, or provocative interviews. It sounded interesting, but Daniel was vague and, as usual, in a hurry. For two months I worked establishing contacts with book publishers, science research centers and potential political sources, and exchanging tips with Therond. Alas, I was wasting my time. The confusion at *Look* had taken absurd proportions. Although the magazine's rebirth was announced with fanfare at an October party at Central Park's *Tavern on the Green*, nothing was ready for serious work. While Durniak was readying the weekly format, Daniel decided to switch to bi-weekly frequency, which was, of course, a very different type of magazine. Gutwillig, still commuting from California, was put in charge of the editorial, above Durniak, as if Durniak didn't already have enough problems with Pagniez's mercurial Frenchmen. Then Bob hired former *Village Voice* editor Marianne Partridge as "executive editor," and she came with her own team. Deep into their bitter rivalry, none of these feudal barons was in the slightest interested in my proposals, Daniel and the Frenchmen even less so than the others. Bent on a tabloid-type publication with popular mass appeal, they must have considered me frankly (and not entirely wrongly) as a "square," and my story-ideas (future space colonies, political interviews with Brzezinski or W.F. Buckley, Jr., or a profile of the wheel-chaired genius, crippled physicist Stephen Hawkins)—as too highbrow, maybe boring, surely ill-fitting in the general tone of the magazine. With no clear line of command while Gutwillig, Durniak, Pagniez, and Partridge each assigning stories, and the formula changing each week, I had dialogue with no one. Anyhow, we talked different languages. Isolated, frustrated and neglected, I was told that the "Page One" section had been dropped in the new bi-weekly format. But nobody was telling me what my new role would be, if any. Daniel avoided me even more. By December, between trips to Paris, he held editorial conferences to which I wasn't invited, which hurt me. Then in January Gutwillig informed me that I was fired. Filipacchi had just left for Paris, Bob said, and had asked him to give me the news. Durniak, his team and many others, were fired too. It upset me that Daniel, my old "Paris-Match" colleague, had used a third person to dismiss me. He felt it and called me later in Southampton, where I was licking my wounds, to apologize. *Look* finally came out in February 1979, a big fiasco, folding after ten mediocre issues. It was the first failure in Daniel's long string of successes. I never understood why he allowed, almost deliberately, this ten-million-dollar flop.

MEXICO

After having lunch one day in early spring of 1979 with our friend Georgie Rutherfurd, Lil came home quite thrilled about a place in Mexico that the Rutherfurds had just discovered and fallen in love with. It surprised me a little, because we had never shown any particular interest in Mexico, a country we didn't know, and also because Lil had heard too many people raving about their favorite "divine" and "fabulous" spots, to be really impressed by any new "discovery."

I didn't know what Georgie had said to her, but this time Lil sounded unusually enthusiastic. Same words, same adjectives, can convey different meaning and evoke different images, according to who uses them, and how, and when.

Georgie was an amateur painter whose taste Lil understood and liked and I suppose that the adjectives she had used in describing San Miguel de Allende colors and lights, sounds, flowers and romantic atmosphere, were such that Lil knew exactly, sight unseen, what this picturesque colonial town looked like and felt like. "The Rutherfurds are buying a house there and are going later in the spring for the signing," she told me. "Why don't we go with them, it may be amusing."

Better than just amusing, we thought. It may be therapeutic. My morale had been pretty low lately, after my disappointing experience with the new *Look* magazine. In addition, I was waiting for the results of a competition for grants by the *20th Century Fund* for which I had applied. I had submitted a proposal for a study of Antarctica's international status, a pet subject of mine, and had been told that the jury had selected it as one of the two finalists. Such a grant would've given me full occupation and financial security for two years. But early in April, I heard the verdict: the jury had selected the other proposal. "Let's go and change the scene!" we decided and on April 17th boarded the *Aeromexico* flight, packed to capacity and beyond, with noisy, friendly Latinos with swarms of children and gigantic cartons of extra-luggage, and American tourists with loud voices and even louder shirts. The aircraft could hardly be described as being "state-of-the-art" and the hotel, the very commercial *Alameda*, was certainly no Ritz, but we were thrilled to be in the vibrant heart of the Mexican capital. It's a pity that modern travel (or is it our getting older?) reduces the occasions for experiencing the tingling thrills of exoticism and "*depaysement*" one feels the first visit to a new country or town! But luckily, the magic I thought lost did work at our first discovery of Mexico City, and then San Miguel. As soon as we set foot on Mexican soil, the heat and the sun's glare, the Spanish voices and the smells, awakened exciting sensations of foreignness and we savored again the enchanting taste of the exotic. My vision was, of course, heavily tinted with old clichés, but that's a necessary ingredient of the happy recipe. My eyes had seen too many postcards with mustachioed hombres taking siesta under cactus trees, next to their burros, the large sombrero over the face; or movies about Pancho Villa, banditos and senoritas with fiery eyes dancing flamenco. My mind wasn't virgin of epic tales of Aztecs and Mayas, Conquistadors, and revolutions. For exotic, my first impressions were plenty

exotic. But was that the real Mexico of 1979?—Surely not, yet such a romanticized vision is a delightful privilege of a first visit. It doesn't last long. On consecutive visits, myths and preconceived images gradually dissipate; objective eyes,
facts and better knowledge take over, providing a more sober, truer, perception.
But reality wasn't at all disappointing. The more we saw of Mexico, the more we
grew to appreciate it.

Especially San Miguel de Allende. On our first visit, we stayed at the
Atascadero, a ranch-type hotel atop a steep hill overlooking the town, and from
the first day, we felt that we had found the right place. A year-round paradisiacal
weather, combining subtropical warmth and the freshness of an 8,000-feet-high
plateau. An oasis of blooming bougainvillea, plumbago, oleander and jacaranda
in the middle of a sun-baked landscape of aridity. A historic town, still preserving
its colonial character, with steep, narrow cobblestone streets, terracotta-hued
houses with patios full of geranium, and dozens of old churches. Coming from a
hectic life in New York, I was tempted by some almost forgotten luxuries San
Miguel seemed to offer: the serenity of a resort with none of the obvious touristic attractions—no beach, no casino or spa, no golf or tennis to speak about, no
racetrack. Imagine—to have nothing else to do during the day but walk to the
town square to buy the newspaper and have your shoes shined! The relaxing
unhurriedness of a culture which institutionalized *la siesta* and believed that one
should never leave for tomorrow what could be done the day-after-tomorrow;
and also, bringing back childhood memories from rural Bulgaria, like sights and
sounds of some bucolic film featuring similar bustling open-air markets, beggars,
birds and flies, barefoot children happily playing in the mud next to filthy pigs,
mangy dogs roaming in the streets, donkeys braying—polychrome scenes with a
soundtrack of crowing roosters, church bells and calls of ambulant vendors.

But San Miguel was also a comfortable retreat for expatriates, mostly
American and some Canadians, a favorite spot for foreign art students, and a discreet resort for a cosmopolitan group that enjoyed tranquility, flowers, the arts
and indigenous crafts. There were enough cultured people with sophisticated
tastes for civilized conversation and attractive parties. The lovely houses and gardens were definitely Lil's cup of tea, and once we learned about the prices, the

idea of buying a house became very appealing. We had long ago crossed out Gstaad (my personal first choice, my dream) from the list of desirable places for a future home abroad, when living in the USA would become hard to afford. Switzerland had become more expensive than America, and we were considering selling chalet *Ding-Dong*. But the incomparably cheaper life in Mexico, with almost shockingly low wages for domestic help and attractive houses priced at 30 or 40 thousand dollars, made the old idea sound titillating realizable. Thus, after Day 2, we didn't resist the persuasive real estate ladies who gladly took us on a tour of available houses.

Ten days later, leaving Mexico, which had captured our dreams, we were giving serious consideration to two offers and the thought of both houses made us feel good and happy.

OMAN

But my main problem was still there: I had no job, the erosion of my modest economies was progressing at an alarming pace, and no solution was in sight. Then again, whoever up there in Heaven writes the script of my life intervened again, this time with a really exotic twist. What about trying the Sultanate of Oman, for example? Oman?- never heard of it! But the fact was that three days had hardly passed after we returned to New York and Dimi called me from Paris to tell me that this Arabian-Nights-tales kingdom, which he had recently visited, was looking for a Western journalist to organize its contacts with the American press. Would I be interested in the job, Dimi asked me, adding that the small but oil-rich country was paying well.

The next morning I rushed to the library and started calling people, trying to learn as much as I could about the little-known Persian Gulf nation. Except for Egypt, I didn't know much about the Middle East, but the prospect of working for an Arab state posed a moral problem. In 1979 the passionate hatred between Israelis and Arabs was at its climax and my sympathies, like everybody in America, leaned to the Israeli side. Not that I didn't see that in many ways they were both right. But in the Cold War, which was then my leading criterion, Israel was our ally, while many Arab rulers seemed to be helping Soviet causes. In addition, I abhorred violence, and we were in a period when PLO had become synonymous to terrorism. Thirdly, the anti-Americanism displayed by some Arab countries was frankly annoying. And so were the greed of some OPEC states during the world petrol crisis and the vulgar gaudiness of the new oil millionaires.

I was favorably surprised by what I learned about Oman, an Arab nation that seemed to be "not like the others." The government of young Sultan Qabus was openly pro-Western and strongly anti-communist. It was the only country in the region to refuse to break with Egypt when Sadat, a "traitor" for the Arab extremists, opened talks with Israel. The only one to officially condemn terrorism. No PLO offices were welcome on its territory. Although an oil producer, Oman didn't join OPEC. And if a man can be also judged by his enemies, it was a public secret that there was no love lost between Sultan Quabus and some of the region's bullies, such as Saddam Hussein, colonel Khadaffi, Hafez al-Assad and the pro-Red rulers of South Yemen. It sounded like a country I would like to work for, and Dimi informed his friends in Muscat of my interest in the position, as I sent them my resume.

The next day, May 3, Paul's nineteenth birthday, I drove to Washington D.C. to meet him as he was coming on vacation from Duke University and bring him to New York and Southampton. He was tense and tired and didn't look well when he arrived late in the evening in the nondescript *Holiday Inn* in the capital's periphery, the only room I'd been able to book that day, and renewed worries about his health dampened my joy at seeing him. I was excited and a little nervous myself, waiting for the word from Oman, which could affect all our family's life. During the long drive and the night, I had to face another pending decision: while calling home, Lil had told me that the San Miguel agent had just telephoned, saying that the house we liked the most was available and we had to give a yes-or-no answer. Just when I might start a new job!

The month of May started in a busy tempo, which didn't give me time to agonize over the Omani job. Radka came for one of her rare weekends in New York and we stayed up almost the entire nights in brother-sister reminiscing. Two days later, Queen Giovanna, a very special person to me, who had given me so much warmth during my émigré years in France and with whom I loved to talk, arrived on her yearly month-long visit to daughter Maria Luisa in New Jersey. At the same time, Rosie Cartier was in town, and so was Alain Danet, as exuberant as ever. And also, "Le Patron's" grand-daughter Donatienne de Montmort with her husband, visiting her sister Isabelle—two lovely, shy, exquisitely brought-up girls who had spent time as "interns" in my office and gained my affection. Finally, King Simeon passed through New York, a chance for updating our perennial talk about Bulgaria and, of course, for laughing at old private jokes and newly-found funny words and expressions.

It was as if in that May of 1979, while I waited for an important decision, people I cared about were congregating for 20 days in New York. On the 21st day, the news arrived: Dimi Panitza informed me from Paris that the Omanis were sending me an official invitation to meet me in the Sultanate and were sending me an air ticket.

I left for Muscat, via London, on June 13, just three days after attending the funeral of Paul Slade, who had unexpectedly died from heart attack the previous week. Lil had told me the sad news as I returned from Washington and I had never suspected that Slade's loss would upset me so deeply. Indeed, different as we were in age and in almost everything else, a warm friendship had developed between us and his death was a hard blow to me. Under his disguise of tough, street-smart photo reporter brought up in the Lower East Side, Paul was a soft, sentimental soul, who was totally and touchingly loyal to me as his Bureau chief and older friend. His job was his passion and *Paris-Match* a religion. When our bureau was closed and the new owners didn't keep him, he almost had a nervous breakdown. He couldn't conceive life outside of *Match* and I had repeatedly to give him pep talk and cheer him up.

Oman is not a place to visit in June. On my arrival in Muscat, the temperature was 94 degrees and the water in the hotel's pool felt like hot soup. *The Gulf*, just outside of the capital, was a comfortable place, with good but empty restaurants and even a bar, an exception in Muslim countries. I spent the first two days introducing myself to my hosts at the Information Ministry, the key person there being an efficient but rather aloof Englishman, Anthony Ashworth, an expatriate in his late fifties with the demeanor and accent of the former British military and Colonial Service men who were running the country. Indeed, with the lack of qualified Omanis during the transition period since the very recent modernization of the country, many government jobs, and almost all commanding military posts, were still held by Britishers. "Tony" Ashworth, a veteran Oman specialist, had gained the full confidence of Sultan Qabus and was vigilantly and jealously watching after the monarch's interests. Which was a grateful duty, as the popular sultan happened to be also charming and bright, and a real benefactor to his nation. Ashworth introduced me to the Information minister, Abdul Aziz Rowas, and to the Under-Secretary for Foreign Affairs, Yusuf al-Alawi, an impressively bright young man looking like a college kid. But apart from the official interviews, which all took place in the morning, I was left entirely on my own, having meals by myself and meeting no one "socially." The men were very polite in their offices, but it was not customary for Arabs to invite foreigners to their homes and introduce their families. As Tony and the "Brits" seemed to be always busy, I was quite lonely most of the time. I was though assigned a car with a chauffeur speaking some broken English, who took me as a guide around the city and the vicinity. Then a four-day visit was arranged to Salalah, a picturesque coastal town with superb beaches, palm trees and colorful markets, at an hour-and-a-half flight from Muscat. There finally I could see camels and Bedouins in the desert, and during the hot, starry nights step out from my bungalow directly to the silent beach.

While being shown the country, I was writing a memo on my views of the role of a future press-consultant in America, asked by Ashworth and Rowas. After Salalah, I was driven to the ancient capital of Nizwa, and then flown in an air force plane to the Musandam peninsula and Khassab, a most remote, God-forsaken military base where the temperature that day was 105 degrees. From there a British pilot flew me in his *Defender* over the Straits of Hormuz, in those days the globe's hottest strategic point. As Hormuz belonged to Oman, I knew that most Western journalists' questions would concern this vital bottleneck passage of oil tankers.

The most fascinating thing I learned however was the story of the country's new sultan. Doe-eyed, soft-spoken Quabus had taken over power quite recently, barely nine years ago, in 1970, succeeding—or more precisely, overthrowing— his despotic father, Sultan Said bin Taimur. The plot, except for its happy ending, had many elements of a Shakespearean drama: a xenophobic tyrant who feared any contact with the non-Muslim world and kept the citizens within the cities' walls after dark; a shy, British-educated son, who discovered Western culture and values at Sandhurst military school, dreaming of modernizing his country; plotting, discontented army officers and oppressed intellectuals; a psychological conflict between obeying an autocratic father and doing what the son believed was right for the country; and, of course, a good dose of Middle-Eastern intrigue and British agents' Big-Brotherly advice and help. After 35 years of tyranny, the excesses of Sultan Said had really gone too far. Not only did he forbid travel abroad, but he banned such "frivolities" as singing, dancing, radio, movies, or taking photographs, and anything "artificial," such as sunglasses. More important, he disapproved of education. Although rather well educated himself, he believed that education was not only useless, but was harmful. Everything worth saying, he held, had already been said by the Prophet, 14 centuries ago, and all necessary knowledge and the rules for a meaningful life were already in the Holy Koran, so it would be sacrilegious to try to improve on it. Modern education and foreign contacts meant only moral contamination, sowing the seeds of discontent and rebellion, importing alcohol, pornography, and subversive ideas. As a result of this philosophy, Oman in the 1960s was an anachronistic residue from the Middle Ages, with no roads, no hospitals, with only a dozen of automobiles and a couple of telephones (belonging to the Sultan), with no newspapers and no radio.

But like most despots, Said bin Taimur made one exception, which turned out to be a fatal mistake: he sent his own son to study in England. So, on a hot July day of 1970, the 30-year-old melancholy Prince, kept in sort of internment ever since he had returned home in 1964 with the head full of progressive ideas, deposed his father, in a bloodless palace coup. (In the heat of the action, said the gossip, the irascible old monarch shot himself in the foot.) Quabus took over, while his father, royally allotted, was dispatched to the Dorchester Hotel in London, to sulk in opulent exile to the end of his days.

With the aid of his British friends, Quabus transformed radically the medieval backward nation of illiterate Bedouins and fishermen and in a few years his benevolent, paternalistic rule catapulted it into the twentieth century. It was still an absolute monarchy, but its one million subjects had all the reasons to adore their new Sultan: no taxes, free education, free healthcare, zero-interest loans. When I arrived in 1979, the per-capita income had jumped ten times since the 1970 coup. Instead of only three primary schools for boys, I found already 353 schools with 88,000 boys and girls; roads, airports, hospitals, and railroads were being built everywhere. Of course, the crude oil's higher prices on the world' markets helped, but the spectacular transformation was nothing short of a miracle. I was genuinely impressed.

While my inquiry went on, I was told that the Omanis had liked my ideas on handling the American press for them, and Ashworth made me a concrete offer, with figures and details. The conditions were attractive but there was one that disturbed me: they definitely wanted me in Washington, with a desk in their embassy, and not, as I had hoped, remaining in New York and commuting (most major media were based in New York, I tried to argue, and the shuttle flight took only one hour). But the Omanis were firm on that point. It was a tough decision at this point of my life, with Lil's children, decoration jobs, and most our friends around New York (and just when buying a house in Mexico!) I expected Lil to refuse. And myself, was I ready to change my life so radically and move to a new city? But could I afford turning down an attractive offer and sinking back in the throes of unemployment? It was with great trepidation that I called Lil on the telephone. To my surprise, not only wasn't she upset, but she sounded thrilled at the idea of a change, of a new venture. "I love Washington!" she said, "Let's try it!" How little we know the people we live with, I thought.

So I accepted. In July we went briefly to Washington to look for a home and I rented a lovely, sunny small apartment at the *Watergate*, overlooking the Potomac. Nothing excited Lil more than fixing a new nest, so in the following weeks she was right in her element, moving furniture from Southampton and decorating the new place, which became very attractive and cozy. In September we moved in and for over four years we became Washingtonians. Or almost. For we kept our New York flat and Rhoda, as Lil continued her decorator's work and commuted almost every week, and Paul used it when coming from Duke university. We also kept the Southampton house and as I never felt completely at home in Washington and missed New York, I couldn't wait to take back the shuttle every weekend I could.

Not that I didn't like my new job. I was given a comfortable office, a secretary and all the facilities at the Omani embassy on Massachusetts Avenue, off Sheridan Circle. The ambassador, Sadek Sulaiman, was a warm, wise man, interested in philosophy, geopolitics and ethics, for whom I developed great respect and who became my friend and teacher in things Arab and Muslim. It tickled me that I—the Bulgarian-born, Swiss-educated, French journalist and American citizen, husband and father—suddenly became an Omani "diplomat," speaking on behalf of the exotic Sultanate. It was a thrilling experience, especially during the first couple of years, establishing contacts with American journalists, foreign diplomats and the State Department. To discover the Arab world (I made two more long trips to Oman) and learning what makes Washington tick was greatly satisfying for someone with my curiosity and journalistic background. I was extremely lucky too, when one thinks what a difficult city Washington is for a newcomer. Indeed, without some influential position in government, in the diplomatic corps (but only in major nations' embassies or, for a few exceptional ambassadors with huge expense accounts), or in the major media, the capital city is not much more than a provincial town. For outsiders without political clout, the Washingtonians "who count" would be as inaccessible as would be the top movie stars in Hollywood for those not belonging to the movie community, or in New York if one isn't a celebrity or a multi-millionaire. There is one exception though: the unique institution of Washingtonian *hostesses*, in whose "salons" political stars and influential pundits rub shoulders with the so-called "society." Lil and I had the luck of knowing at least two such hosts who took us under their wing: Gerard and Bernice Smith, from Southampton, and old Senator John Sherman Cooper and his socially prominent wife Loraine, at whose Kentucky home we had spent a weekend a few years earlier. Both husbands had considerable interest and experience in foreign affairs (Smith as chief US negotiator for the SALT and the Disarmament treaties; Cooper as ambassador to East Germany and India); both moderate Republicans, they possessed the gift of wisdom, a rare quality in Washington that I grew to value even above brilliance. Both wives, highly sophisticated ladies and famous hostesses, ran two of the best salons in town. Ever since we arrived, they included us to their parties, where we met many of the capital's celebrities, diplomats, members of the Carter administration, senators, top columnists, and some other hostesses. I loved talking with such well informed (and also pure and likable) men like Gerard and senator Cooper, and enjoyed greatly Bernice's spunk and gossip, and the original elegance of Loraine's peculiar personality. Ironically, it was at their parties and similar social contacts, rather than through my more "serious" professional endeavors, that we met more of the interesting people we saw in Washington. It was during a weekend at the Smiths' country-house, for instance, that I renewed my old acquaintance with Zbignew Brzezinski, then National security adviser to President Carter, after which we often played tennis together. It was also at a New Year's Eve party at the same Chesapeake Bay home that I met a young publisher, Jed Lyons, not suspecting that a few years later he would publish a book of mine. But let's go back to the end of 1979 and the early1980s.

To sum it up, my Washington debuts were quite satisfactory. But after the first year or two, my work became routine and I realized that I had reached the ceiling of my possibilities with the Omanis. The true diplomatic field that could've really interested me, namely contacts with the State Department, the White House, the Pentagon and other embassies, was by definition closed to me. Indeed, the very reason the new Oman needed help from foreigners like me, was to allow time to prepare its own cadres. Myself, I believed that modern Oman had to be represented abroad by Omani citizens; any display of foreign advisers' influence (mostly British, as was the case) wasn't good for the country. But even if I felt differently, it didn't take me long to understand that my direct bosses in Muscat wouldn't permit me to do anything—take initiatives or make contacts—outside of my strict duties as Director of Information, serving only, and exclusively, the

Ministry of Information. This was made very clear on a few occasions when I tried, naively, to be of help to the Ministry of Culture, or even the Foreign Ministry. My boss, Tony Ashworth, and Minister Rowas were particularly, almost jealously, insistent on this point. In a way, it was understandable. They were paying me to do a specific job and were not about to "share" me with others. I was a foreigner and had no business in Omani-American diplomatic relations, they thought. Neither was I in the Sultan's inner circle, like Ashworth. Tony never attempted to introduce me to His Majesty, a major handicap in my job, as the young absolute monarch *was* the New Oman. It was also personally disappointing to me, as Qabus was, with no doubt, the most interesting and humanly attractive personality in the emerging new state.

I had a few successes with major American media running favorable articles and friendly journalists visiting the Sultanate. But my job had also an odd, almost paradoxical, aspect. Apart from explaining and defending their governments' policies, embassies usually pay their press-officers to gain maximum attention and press-coverage for their nations, to promote their countries' qualities and beauty, to encourage tourism. Not the Omanis. I understood early that they expected me to keep the Sultanate's presence in the American media to a minimum, to find friendly ways to delay reporters' travel applications and especially, requests for interviews with His Majesty, to politely discourage any form of tourism. My principal duty was to *prevent* any unfriendly article or visitor. Ashworth was unwilling to take any chances and approved only publications and journalists he already knew or I could recommend as fully trustworthy. Not an easy task because Tony was extremely suspicious and demanded my vouching for the applicant. It wasn't only a question of politically unfriendly journalists. The Omanis abhorred any form of personal questions, indiscretions and discussion of private life. They wouldn't allow any informal photos of the Sultan or description of his homes, family, friends and tastes. This approach, the opposite to the usual Western press curiosity, disappointed many an American reporter. Although I sympathized occasionally with well-meaning journalists intending to write laudatory articles, I had to respect the Omanis' determination to be serious and keep dignity. (I was pretty embarrassed the first time a reporter asked me the simple question what was the name of the Queen. The Queen? I was ashamed to admit to myself that I, the Information officer, didn't even know whether there was a Queen. I asked all my colleagues at the embassy. "There is no Queen, but you mean His Majesty's wife?" they said. No one knew her name or her whereabouts. Some believed the Sultan had been married briefly to his first cousin, a tradition in Oman, but had heard that he had divorced her. Nobody knew for sure, and which was more, they all had the attitude "How would *we* know? This is a strictly private matter, and none of our business.")

The weekdays were quite busy at the embassy, but nothing as the frantic schedule I was used to as a journalist. I would drive myself to work from the Watergate and spent the day at my desk, often having my hamburger lunch there, or lunching frequently at restaurants with journalists and various Washington contacts, or returning home, if Lil was in town. When she was in New York, my evenings were quiet, almost lonely. It was the period I started working on my book *Crown of Thorns*, part of the research being done after office hours at the Library of Congress. Sometimes I played tennis with partners such as my NASA friend Fred Ordway, or Zbig Brzezinski, or a young State Department diplomat, Ralph Bresler. I was seeing Bulgarian compatriots—Emil Karson, the Sarbovs, a few Stancioffs still in town, Peter Orahovats, writer Atanas Slavov, a newcomer. Lil and I went to many parties and to a few concerts at the *Kennedy Center*. We dined frequently at Georgetown restaurants. Our social life intensified particularly in the beginning of 1980, with the inauguration of President Reagan, when his administration was ushered in with a great dose of optimism and glitter, forgotten during the lusterless Carter era. Festive activities awakened the capital's social life and as Lil knew a few of the Reagan's wealthy Californian friends who were taking Washington by assault, we were included in some of the events. Many New York friends pouring into town looked us up and our *Watergate* apartment became a happy meeting place for out-of-town Inauguration visitors.

Most weekends we packed for New York or Southampton. Our calendars from 1980 to 1985 also contain many entries for trips to San Miguel (I would go just for ten days, Lil would stay longer) and Gstaad (meanwhile, we sold our chalet to Louis and Sophie de La Roziere). In between, every month, week, and day of this long period spent away from our New York home seemed to be pretty well filled with happenings, encounters and new impressions for which I can fully account. And yet...

When I think back of Washington, I have a weird feeling that it was another person, not me, who had lived there. Sometimes I find it hard to believe that I have spent four-and-a-half years of my life there. I had read once that in 1572, when Pope Gregory updated the old "Julian" calendar and replaced it by the so-called "Gregorian" calendar, a few days had to be skipped in the readjustment: the 5th of October became automatically October 15th. Thus, the nine days between these two dates had never existed in History. Something similar must have happened with me, a hole in the memory, concerning my Washington years. I clearly remember the events, the places and faces, but not the awareness of having been there. Maybe it was because I had left the major part of my personality in New York and never brought it with me to Washington? Or maybe because part of my stay coincided with a case of mild depression I suffered in 1982 and 1983? It was nothing too serious, but that's when hypertension hit me for the first time and painful memories came back of past depressions, first at the age of 19, and again in Switzerland, after the loss of my father.

Anyhow, I had begun to feel restless. And although my relationship with the new ambassador, Al Hinai, and with all colleagues at the embassy remained excellent, I felt signs of impatience and dissatisfaction in the attitude of my Muscat bosses—Tony Ashworth and the minister, Rowas. I had on my credit a few successes with the American media (the most spectacular coups being a very favorable TV interview of Mike Wallace with the Sultan for the best-selling *60-Minutes* program and a huge coverage in the *National Geographic*; both pleased and impressed Muscat). But in a period of Arab criticism of Oman's pro-Western sympathies, and with the blossoming of the so-called "investigative journalism" in America, Ashworth's jitters and mistrust of the press had reached paranoid proportions. He was particularly nervous about the slightest suspicion that some nosy reporter might ask personal questions about the Sultan, and even worse—inquire about alleged dealings by his entourage. Tony insisted that I find out the precise intentions of any journalist interested in Oman and prevent, at any cost, the publication of unfavorable articles. His fears and worries, often well founded, were understandable. I would also understand if he found me insufficiently enterprising for the task; he was probably right—this part of my job didn't appeal much to me.

So I wasn't overly surprised when in 1984 Tony informed me, in a stiff, formal letter typical for his relationship with me, that "His Excellency the Minister of Information had decided to discontinue your services." In January 1985, we released the *Watergate* apartment, said "goodbye" to our Washington friends, and returned to New York.

Chapter 35

"Crown of Thorns"

In April 1981 I was still working for the Omanis in Washington, when my friend Ivan Tchaprachikoff arrived from Paris on one of his regular visits to New York, bringing a very interesting proposal from "Bulgarian friends," whom at first he didn't want to name. Ivan told me that a few émigrés in London had decided to publish a full biography in English of the late King Boris III, so the free world could at last hear the truth about pre-Communist Bulgaria and learn the story of this remarkable ruler, so viciously distorted by red propaganda. They were ready to fully fund the project and assume all cost necessary for extensive research and a high-quality edition. For authoring such a book, Ivan told me, they had thought of me, because of my close relationship with the Royal family in exile and because I had already published a few books abroad. Would I accept the assignment?

The idea appealed to me. For many years, I was upset by the ignorance about my country in the West, where even with the best intentions no book on Bulgaria could be found except for Communist sources printed after 1944, and I had often thought of doing something about it. My journalistic experience had taught me that subjects are most likely to interest the public when told through personal life stories. Didn't Margaret Mitchell's *Gone With The Wind* do more for making the South known all over the world than hundreds of history books and scholarly articles? But would modern Bulgarian history offer *dramatis personae* fascinating enough to intrigue the Western reader? Yes, I thought: the formidable, majestic King Ferdinand, Boris's irascible but superbly intelligent father, an aristocratic Coburg and Orleans related to all European courts who becomes a Bulgarian ultra-patriot and draws the nation into three wars. What a writer's dream! I had discussed the idea with Queen Giovanna and had asked her to sound out Princess Evdokia, Ferdinand's daughter who lived in exile in Germany.

But the princess, by then deeply hurt by her treatment in Bulgaria and unwilling to see Bulgarians abroad, was quick with her answer: "Tell the young Groueff to leave the Monarch's memory alone!" she told her sister-in-law. To me, it was a command. Evdokia had been very close to my father and I wouldn't even think of doing anything to displease her. Later on, I thought of writing about King Boris; with some hesitation, I must confess: the modest citizen-King, with his dislike of ceremonies and pageantry, seemed a less obvious subject for thrilling copy. Or so I thought. Nevertheless, I had discussed this possibility with his son, King Simeon, and as he had no objection, I had approached a few publishers. But the idea was declined with the usual "it's interesting, but…"

Now Ivan was talking about something concrete, needing no approval by some foreign publisher. I said that I was interested in the project, but for truly serious research and access to the best available sources, I needed to confirm the Royal family's cooperation. And also to know the names of the sponsors. Only then did Ivan reveal them: Dimitar (James) Velkov and Avner ("Struki") Kaleff.

I knew the names, but hadn't met them personally. Velkov, a well-known patriot in exile, had made a fortune as developer of resort communities in the Canary Islands, in Spain. He was an ardent anti-communist, and a generous sponsor to émigré causes and organizations, mostly the right-wing *National Front*, both of whose feuding fractions respected him. His attempt to reconcile the "Dochev Front" and the "Statev Front" had gained him a prestige in émigré circles. Kaleff, a fervent monarchist, was one of those patriotic Jewish-Bulgarians who wouldn't let anyone say anything against Bulgaria and who felt deep gratitude to King Boris for his decisive role in the saving of all Bulgarian Jews from deportation to the Nazi camps.

Back at my job in Washington, I wrote to King Simeon and telephoned his sister, Princess Maria Luisa, who liked the idea immediately. Soon, I received Simeon's approval. He had also talked to his mother, Queen Giovanna. In May, as I was drafting a general outline for the book, Velkov called me from London saying that in two days he would pass through New York on his way to Los Angeles. Our first meeting was very successful. We liked each other and I felt assured that he was serious about the project and ready to finance it personally, as sole sponsor. We agreed to discuss the book and a contract on his way back from Beverly Hills, and I went immediately to the Library of Congress to see what sources were available there.

On June 12, I drove Velkov and my son Paul from New York to Southampton for a long weekend of discussions. Lil was already there, but unfortunately we had already rented out our comfortable house and had moved temporarily to the old Rodgers' carriage-house next door, off South Main Street. It was in the rustic, squeaky-floored rooms of that old barn, with vines climbing through wall cracks and indoor appearances of some field mouse or raccoon, that *Crown of Thorns* was conceived. It was a stimulating weekend. Velkov and I shared the same ideas about the need for such a book and we agreed easily on its spirit, contents and form. The financial arrangements were also agreed upon with no problem. Two days later, Velkov's lawyer drafted a legal agreement and by the end of June a contract was signed. It was a fair arrangement, permitting me to work for a few years without worrying about research and travel expenses or being forced in the meantime to look for another job if and when my Omani contract expired. Neither of us was going to make money out of this project, but we both would feel enormously rewarded if the book materialized. I was very happy and enthusiastic, and grateful to Velkov. Indeed, it was his initiative and without his energetic insistence, *Crown of Thorns* would probably have never been born. My research started at the Library of Congress, where I usually went after work at my Omani offices (diplomats are not an over-worked profession and the embassy, thoughtful of the personnel's worries about the 5 o'clock rush hour, closed at 4:30 PM). The imposing Library soon became one of my favorite places in the capital. In addition to its magnificent architecture, this temple of culture was superbly conducive to concentration and research, and its fabulous wealth of books is unsurpassed in the world. I hardly believed my eyes the first time an attendant handed me a collection of Bulgarian newspapers from the 1920s and 1930s. Holding old copies of "*Zora*" and "*Utro*," dailies from my childhood, which I hadn't seen for forty years, moved me deeply. To find the facts I was looking for didn't take more that 20 minutes, but that night I spent hours, mesmerized, going through unrelated reportages, sports pages, movies ads, even obituaries. Long forgotten memories began to surface from a half-century-deep abyss. *Yes, the wrestler Dan Kolov defeating the black giant Reggie Sicki! Yes, it was in "Kino Evropa" indeed that I saw "The Wizard of Oz"!... The scandal with General Nikolaev's granddaughter eloping with this Jewish fellow Levy!... And Liuben Doytchev winning the Balkan decathlon!* My breathing accelerated when my eyes fell on news photos of my father attending some ceremony or escorting foreign diplomats into the royal palace. In the solitude of the reading room, ghosts from a world vanished fifty years ago were catching up with me, half way across the globe, in Washington, in the solitude of the silent reading room. For a few hours, I indulged myself in a true orgy of nostalgia, fighting back tears of pain and joy. It took several reminders by the librarians to tear myself away from my ephemeral reunion with the past. Luckily, my subsequent visits to the Library, though less sentimental, were far more productive.

I used my 1981 summer vacations for the first round of personal interviews, starting with the Royal family. In July, I spent four days at Queen Giovanna's lovely *Villa Yantra*, her Bulgarian-style home in Estoril, Portugal. After her son Simeon had married, she had moved there from Madrid, to be near her brother, Umberto of Italy. Apart from a small staff, including the loyal Stoyan, who had followed her since Bulgaria, I was the only guest. Filled with hundreds of family portraits, photo-albums, books and all sorts of memorabilia, the quiet villa was a perfect place to talk about and remember King Boris. For the Queen and me, it was the joy of resuming our warm conversations from the days in Madrid and the vacations spent together in Europe—chatting, waxing sentimental about "our country" or giggling over funny memories, she teasing me about old girl-friends, real or imaginary, she had heard of. Meanwhile, when not showing old photographs or pouring tea for me, her hands were never idle, constantly knit-ting sweaters for her charities. I did not learn many new facts about her late hus-band's reign; there were no great surprises, no secrets revealed. The Queen, a rather apolitical person, was brought up in a family who believed that state affairs should be left to the men only. Besides, King Boris was not a man who discussed his work with his wife. But she told me a lot about him as a husband, father, son of a tyrannical father, and mostly about his character, his feelings and worries and sense of humor. Essentially feminine, Queen Giovanna's information was more intuitive than factual, her judgments on people based on instinct rather than well documented evidence. For instance, she believed that King Boris's death was not natural, but cited no concrete reason for her suspicion, other than an "inner feeling" or a dream she had had. What she shared with me, thus providing invaluable guidance for many passages of my book, were personal impressions of people and events, rather than hard facts; only a few descriptions of true archival value, but a treasure trove of perceptive interpretations, direct observations and well-informed guesses.

From Estoril I went to Madrid to see King Simeon and look through his grandfather, King Ferdinand's archives, which Simeon had inherited. King Boris, unfortunately, didn't keep a diary and my father, who we believe destroyed most of the intimate letters and files when the Communists seized power in 1944, kept the King's personal archives in Sofia. Thus Queen Giovanna had carried no documents with her when she and her children were expelled from Bulgaria. But King Ferdinand, who lived in exile in Coburg after WW1, was an entirely different story. The personal archives he had amassed during his long reign, represented a true treasure and were never examined by anyone until King Simeon generously invited me to use them. A methodical, well-organized man, the old monarch had painstakingly saved all sorts of papers: historical state documents and international treaties, as well as routine office memos to and from his chief of cabinet, Dobrovich, very personal correspondence with relatives or close friends, and even trivia, such as dinner menus, tailors' and jewelers' bills, a huge collection of letters, telegrams and notes, arranged by date. The archives were packed in large cardboard boxes, about 110 of them, on shelves in the cellar of King Simeon's home on Avenida del Valle (later, conscious of the fire risks and lack of proper climate control, Simeon entrusted them to the modernly equipped Hoover Institution in California).

During my five-day stay in King Simeon's house, each day I brought up a few boxes to read in my room. Even spending the better part of the night over the files, I managed to go through but a small fraction of these voluminous archives, concentrating mostly on material relating to Ferdinand's son, Boris. To me, both as a would-be biographer and as a Bulgarian, it was a unique, most thrilling experience, and I had to make efforts to keep myself inside the confines of my research's concrete subject and not succumb to the temptation to read every confidential document and intimate note, encompassing some 60 years of Bulgarian history.

This first "working visit" at King Simeon's allowed me to renew my contacts with another major source in Madrid, Didi Draganoff, a close friend. I'll return later to Didi's crucial role in my research, but now I'll continue with my next interview in the Royal family, my visit to Princess Evdokia, and the aging and ailing sister of King Boris.

After being arrested by the Communists, mistreated, humiliated and kept as a prisoner, Princess Evdokia had left Bulgaria in 1946 with her sister-in-law, Queen Giovanna and her children and gone to live in Germany with her sister, Nadezhda, Duchess of Wurttemberg. Deeply disturbed, this highly intelligent Evdokia, known as the most energetic and political minded of all Ferdinand's children, had for years avoided any contacts with Bulgarians in exile, but I saw her a few times in the United States during her visits to Princess Maria Luisa, her niece. In the meantime, Nadezhda and Albrecht Wurttemberg died and the ailing Evdokia went to live with Catholic nuns in Friedrichshafen, on Lake Constance (or Bodensee). It was in this quiet German town across the Swiss border, that I visited her in July 1981.

My lonesome ferryboat crossing in a rented car, the night falling slowly over the burg's dim streets, and the solitary dinner at the *Goldenes Rad Inn*, set the mood for this nostalgic pilgrimage. It was raining, and nothing looks more melancholy than lakes in the rain, especially near the mountains, with phantom-like swans gliding on dark gray water. Besides, old memories haunted me ever since I started the trip: Princess Evdokia had been very close to my father and was also an especially intriguing icon in my childhood imagery.

There was nothing of the intimidating princess of my memories left in the humbly dressed wizened lady who received me the next morning in her room on the third floor of the "St. Antonius Institute." She appeared very shrunken and frail. Only the prominent Coburg nose and the piercing, gray-blue eyes had

remained the same, and—(or was it some imagined residue from my upbringing?)—there was still something regal in her demeanor, which almost made me
stand at attention when she greeted me warmly. "Your Royal Highness..." I
started, in Bulgarian, of course. Somehow, that seemed to startle her. For the next
few minutes, she would interrupt the conversation and, her eyes staring in space,
she would repeat to herself, dreamlike: "*Your Royal Highness...Your Royal
Highness...*"Then, returning to reality: "Do you know how long it has been since
anybody had called me that?" She was eager to talk about Bulgaria and confessed
being nostalgic. "The lake is beautiful, and the people here are very nice to me,"
she said, looking out of the window. The room was monastic, a spartan bed and
a wooden chair the only furniture and a large cross the only ornament on the
bare white walls. On the windowsill, I noticed a jelly jar with a few roots of
zdravetz, the aromatic Bulgarian geranium. "That's the only thing I have from
the old country, somebody brought it to me," she sighed. "Nowhere else in the
world will you find this scent. And you know what I miss the most? A thing I've
been unable to find anywhere else? That Bulgarian air, yes, the air! No place in
the world has our air. In Bulgaria, we didn't know it, we took it for granted. Only
when you're abroad, you realize how different our air is. Have you noticed it?"
She took a deep breath. "Oh, I would give a lot to be transported there and
breathe it again for awhile, even just a few hours, this wonderful, familiar, unique
air..." She was getting sentimental, but trying to control it. For an hour and a
half we reminisced, bringing up names of people and places we both knew, and
she inquiring about my family and my job. It was charming small talk, but the
mood was not for talking "business" and I felt that interviewing her right away
would somehow be indelicate, inappropriate. Later, I regretted my scruples,
because that morning Princess Evdokia was very alert and articulate, which was-
n't always the case in our subsequent conversations. At noon, I drove her to my
inn for a quiet lunch, and then back to her room, for a siesta. At 2 PM I revisited
her and started questioning her about her memories. At the beginning, talking
about her childhood with her brothers "Bo" (Boris) and "Kiki" (Kyril) and her
sister "Mickey" (Nadezhda) and how they feared their severe father, "the

Monarch," Evdokia spoke readily and very clearly. She put me at ease and I ran my tape-recorder, without any objection on her part.

But as soon as I started asking about political personalities and events from her past, her memory suddenly seemed to fail her. "Stamboliiski?...Ah yes, I remember him, he was killed, wasn't he?...Tzankov? The man with the beard?..It was so long ago, I don't remember much." She became more and more vague, adding disappointingly little to what was in the public domain. She came to life when discussing the death of King Boris, volunteering her opinion that "the Germans did it," but giving no new information. As the day advanced, she became less articulate, at times even incoherent. Was the aging lady's memory showing signs of fading? Or was the shrewd Coburg princess simply unwilling to go on the record on controversial political questions? These were questions I pondered that evening during my solitary dinner at the *Goldenes Rad*.

I tried again the next morning. Evdokia was quite cheerful, visibly enjoying this rare change in her monotonous, lonely routine. She gave me many details and anecdotes from King Boris's childhood and family life and helped me better understand his relationship with his father. But again, claiming no recollection, she avoided or sidetracked most political questions. Again we lunched together, two nostalgic refugees talking about the beloved country she hadn't seen for thirty-five years, and I—for thirty-seven. Saying goodbye, I felt very close to this unapproachable princess of my youth and I must admit I was delighted when she embraced me and gave me a kiss on both cheeks.

It would be the last time I saw her. Driving back to Switzerland, I was pleased with my interviews, although my hopes of obtaining unusual inside historical information straight from the mouth of the Royal family's most politically astute living witness and King Boris's first confidante were not fulfilled. I might have tried to interview her a few years earlier, while her memory was entirely lucid. But even after her death, my book profited considerably from her recollections. She had left some personal notes in a sealed envelope addressed to her nephew and niece, King Simeon and Princess Maria-Luisa, "*To be opened after my death,*" which Maria Luisa kindly made available to me.

This is just one of the innumerable examples showing how my research was helped by readily offered contributions by friends and admirers of King Boris. I'm an extremely lucky author: during the six years of my research and writing, there wasn't a single case of someone refusing to assist me, including fervent advocates of a Republic and former Communists. Among the major contributors, I must first mention Didi Draganoff, a child-hood friend, more precisely, daughter of one of my father's closest colleagues, Col. Parvan Draganoff. Ours was a very special friendship: Didi and her mother lived in Madrid during my exile in Paris and New York, and we seldom saw each other. But many things linked the two families. Draganoff and my father served together at the Palace and were among the closest persons to King Boris. During WW2, Draganoff was the Bulgarian envoy to Berlin, then to Madrid, and when the King was traveling, a very private coded correspondence was established between the King, Draganoff, and my father in Sofia. By 1944, as Bulgaria was trying to get out of the war and looking for contacts with the Western Allies, Draganoff accepted the post of Foreign Minister and returned to Sofia, in full knowledge of the risks. With the communist takeover, both my father and Draganoff were sentenced to death by the so-called "People's Tribunal" and executed together. While I lived in Paris, I visited his widow and daughter a few times in Madrid, and Mrs. Draganoff—"Aunt Teska," as I called her—revealed to me that she kept the extremely personal, intimate diaries of her late husband, which she intended to destroy and never let anyone see them. I know that prominent exiles, such as Stefan Popov and Jordan Peyev had asked to read them. Although she liked and trusted them, she thought that the archive was too private to be shown to anyone. Anyone, that is, except for me: she let me read a few pages. Honored by her confidence, I took a few notes, but never mentioned the diary to anyone.

Thirty years later, when I started *Crown of Thorns*, I went to Madrid and talked to Didi." Aunt Teska" had died and Didi lived alone. Although we are very close, it took me an enormous effort to convince her to show me what she still kept from her father. There were not many ladies with her sense of loyalty, discretion, dignity, and duty left in the world. A favorite of Princess Evdokia, whom she used to visit in Germany and who treated her almost as a daughter, for Didi the Royal family, for which her father had lived and died, was like a cult. The very idea of being indiscreet about them was unthinkable and she wasn't quite sure whether writing about the private lives of Their Majesties (even trivia such as Prince Kiril being called "Kiki," or the King referring to Palace officials by nicknames such as "Zuppe" or "Caligula") wasn't something disloyal or in bad taste. Only my insistence that an honest and readable book about King Boris would clear his name of communist lies, and the fact that the Royal family had approved the project, mollified her reluctance to discuss their private life. She agreed to let me read a few confidential pages still in her possession (her intention was to destroy them afterwards), but only in her presence. After 1981 I went several times to Madrid and spent long, fascinating hours with Didi, reading together old letters and reports. Many times when coming across some private detail (a salty expression, a King's weakness or his superstition, or a harsh criticism of someone), my reporter's instincts were excited, while Didi would be made uneasy and highly disturbed. "No, no, you can't use that!" she would say, horrified as if faced with a crime of *lese-majeste*. But, though reluctant at times, Didi ended up trusting, in a sister way, my judgment, taste, and total loyalty to "Their Majesties." And, despite my anecdotal *Paris-Match* style, which she certainly wouldn't favor when writing about revered royalties, I hope that I lived up to that trust. Because if I succeeded in my psychological portrayal of King Boris's complicated personality, I owe it to a great extent to Col. Draganoff and his daughter Didi.

Unexpectedly, another major source of inside information turned out to be the former assistant to my father in the Palace, Stanislav Balan. I hadn't seen or heard of Balan for forty years and only knew that he had been tried at the same "People's Tribunal" as my father but sentenced, as a junior member of the Royal private cabinet, to a few years of prison and released very soon, as being the son of the most eminent Slavistic professor, personally respected by Stalin himself. Balan had accompanied King Boris on most of his visits to Hitler and after the King's death had served as a personal secretary to Queen Giovanna. Through her, I heard that lately he had had the unusual luck to be allowed to travel to France to visit close relatives. His trips were kept secret, but I asked the Queen to notify me if he ever came out of Bulgaria again.

In the summer of 1983 she wrote to me confidentially that Balan was again with his relatives in France, this time vacationing in Corsica, and that she had told him about my book. At that time my research was farther along and I happened to be on vacation in Switzerland. I immediately called him from Gstaad. He had been a great admirer of my father's, his direct boss, and remembered me as the high school boy and then the young soldier, occasionally visiting the Palace office, and agreed to see me. "But we have to be extremely discreet, Stefcho!" he warned me on the telephone.

Without telling anyone, on August 8th I flew from Geneva to Nice and then to Ajaccio, where I booked two rooms at the hotel San Carlu. Balan had given me directions to a remote beach where he was camping with his niece and nephew, but finding it was quite a different story: neither the cab driver, nor anyone in the vicinity had ever heard of the place. After a few hours and tens of miles of fruitless search along interminable string of nondescript beaches, I was getting totally discouraged when on a deserted beach I noticed a solitary old man just coming out of the water and carrying a bunch of freshly caught fish. A suntanned, wiry octogenarian, whose face somehow I recognized. "*Gospodin* (Mister) Balan!" I shouted. "Stefcho! Is that you?" he grinned, baring a set of horribly ravaged teeth, a trademark of many people coming from Eastern Europe. It was a most unlikely sunset encounter of two Bulgarian on a remote Corsican beach. "Get dressed," I said. "The taxi is waiting, I'm taking you to Ajaccio."

During two nights and a whole day at the *San Carlu* we talked and talked and never exhausted the questions and memories. Balan was a wonderful raconteur, eager to talk, and feeling very much at ease, almost sentimental, with "the boy" of his former boss. He told me anecdotes about King Boris's last mountain trek to the Moussalla summit, details of the King's visits with Hitler, that I relate in my book; the commuting of the death sentence of Communist leader Traicho Kostov (a classmate of Balan's); and about my father's last days in prison and other painful details. For my research, he turned out to be a gold mine. But to me, his total trust had a heavy price: "You know that I'm returning to Bulgaria,

Stefcho," he repeated several times, in a touching, fatherly way. "Most of these things cannot be repeated. They're just for your own information."

I left Corsica very excited and moved, but also disturbed. I knew that I couldn't possibly betray Balan's confidence. I knew that if I published details that only Balan could have possibly known, he would be severely punished. And yet, without the corroboration of the notes and recordings of our conversations, much of my story would be meaningless. But my decision was clear: there was no question of abusing Balan's confidences and exposing him to danger. This moral dilemma preoccupied me for a long time. My manuscript was almost ready and I had managed to omit most of the information I had obtained in Ajaccio. Then, a bizarre development took care of the problem, an incredible event similar to many occasions in my life in which "Fate," or "Providence," stepped in. This time, the *Deus ex machina* was so unbelievably grotesque, that no fiction writer could have invented it: Stanislav Balan was visiting Sofia's huge universal store *Zum* and minding his business on the ground floor, when some poor guy decided to commit suicide by jumping from the inside balcony of the top floor. By the weirdest accident, he landed on the unsuspecting Balan, wounding him gravely. Soon after, Balan died, a widower, with no children or immediate family. The tragic event freed me from my obligation not to publish his confidences and permitted me to insert them in time for the first publication in 1987.

****

The writing itself took me about five years, considerably longer than Velkov and I had hoped for. For one thing, I had my day job. And also, I'm a slow writer, working on irregular intervals, rather than on strictly established and observed schedule. Some of the actual writing was done during weekends and free evenings in New York and Southampton. But most of it I did in Washington, after office hours, in the Watergate studio apartment where we lived. Writing in English presented some additional difficulties. A trace of foreign accent is inevitable in the writings of authors like me, who had learned the language only in their twenties. I was lucky to enlist the assistance of a poetess from Washington, Mary Ann Larkin, who not only patiently and expertly took the

"Bulgarisms" out of my rough drafts, but also became fascinated with the story of the book. Later on, she and another poetess, Shirley Cochran, visited Bulgaria, met my brother Simeon, and enjoyed an unusual affinity with him, in spite of his rusty English and the necessary precautions when meeting foreigners.

The launching of *Crown of Thorns* was celebrated in May 1987 with a series of receptions, and honored with the presence of King Simeon. First, my friend and co-director of the *Free Bulgarian Center*, Dr. Peter Orahovats, gave a reception and dinner for the King and Queen Margarita in Washington, at the University Club, where the book was shown for the first time. Then Lil gave a cocktail-party at the then-fashionable New York restaurant *Mortimer's*. King Simeon, with Queen Margarita and their sons Kardam and Kyril visited us in the country for a weekend, where Simeon gave a lecture on the international situation at the Southampton College and, of course, said a few words about my book. By then, the news of a new book on King Boris and pre-Communist Bulgaria began to spread among Bulgarians and in circles interested in Eastern Europe and communism.

Sales started slowly. As expected, the general public largely ignored the book. First among the foreign radio stations transmitting to Bulgaria to mention it was *BBC*, in a long telephone interview with me, conducted by Dimitar Dimitrov. It must have stricken some chord in the Bulgarian public, because other BBC, Free Europe and Voice of America programs soon followed it. At that time, because of our *Free Bulgarian Center*, I was in close touch with the New York correspondent of *Radio Free Europe*, Konstantin Mishev. A very good professional, Mishev was an active young man whose many initiatives (including early telephone contacts with the first dissidents inside Bulgaria) added considerable variety and color to the routine programs. Instantly enthusiastic about *Crown of Thorns*, he interviewed me several times in *RFE's* 8th Avenue studios and as the radio's informers reported an unusual audience interest, he proposed serializing the entire book in hour-long weekly readings, on regular Sunday prime-time program. His London superiors accepted the plan. I was delighted, but there was one big obstacle for the Bulgarian-language radio: *Crown of Thorns* existed in English only. "No problem!" Mishev said. "I'll translate the pages myself as we go, and you'll correct them." He did, and he did it very well. He also added a Beethoven musical intro, repeated for fifty consecutive weeks to identify the program, and many very apt sound illustrations—church-bells, folklore and liturgical music, military marches. The broadcast was a huge success, "the most listened-to radio program in Bulgaria," we were told. Thus, a whole year before the collapse of Communism, the title of my yet-unseen, forbidden book had become a household word in the country I was banned from.

Soon after it was published, I received an unsolicited offer that touched me deeply. An enthusiastic friend from Washington, Slava Orahovats, the wife of Peter, proposed to personally translate the entire book into Bulgarian. For free, of course, expecting no remuneration. Translating 400 pages was an enormous task, I warned her. But convinced that, after being prevented for so long from reading the historical facts, our compatriots were entitled to learn the truth, Slava insisted firmly and, to my grateful delight, started translating. Painstakingly, writing by hand, page after page, in a language she hadn't written except for personal letters for forty years, constantly consulting dictionaries and asking me and other friends about forgotten words and special expressions. For several long months, she put aside all other occupations, totally absorbed in "The Book." "I have no wife anymore," Peter used to joke. "I'm living with a full-time translator." It resulted in a first rough translation of two-thirds of the text, a true "labor of love." I myself translated a dozen of chapters and Evgueni Silianoff enthusiastically volunteered for two others. Meanwhile, Velkov and I were looking for ways to print a Bulgarian version, a sort of *Samizdat* (self-publish) and started negotiations with a Bulgarian refugee-printer in Spain. Our plans were to distribute it, almost manually, among the emigration and maybe smuggle copies to Bulgaria.

Chapter 36

"The Free Bulgarian Center"

As recently as 1987 and 1988 most of us had no more hope of ever seeing our country again. After 44 years of totalitarian regime, the Communists had definitely and, we thought then, irreversibly, consolidated heir dictatorship and none of us had any illusion that things would change in our lifetime. No illusions, yes, but it certainly didn't mean acceptance or resignation. For me personally, there was no other possible attitude than resistance ever since the Red Army installed the repressive Communist rule in my country. I understood that people living in Bulgaria had to deal with the evil regime in all sorts of different ways, and were often forced to accept, compromise, rationalize, even betray. But for any normal, decent person lucky enough to be abroad, I don't think there was any alternative but to be enraged by the terror and try to somehow help the oppressed and defend national honor. It was not a matter of ideology or being heroic; it was simply a natural human reaction. Therefore, ever since I became a refugee at the age of 23, I found myself involved—however naively, and perhaps in vain, if we judge by the results—in émigré "resistance" groups—first with *Le Peuple Bulgare* in Paris, then with *The Free Bulgarians*, then with the *Foyer Bulgare*, and also with *Radio Free Europe* and the *BBC*. At the time of the writing of *Crown of Thorns*, I was active mostly in the recently formed *Free Bulgarian Center*. In fact, it wasn't an entirely new group. It was an offshoot of the *Foyer Bulgare* circle and its magazine, *Bulgarian Review*, founded many years earlier in Rio de Janeiro by exiled diplomat Christo Boyadjieff. Although he was more than ten years my senior, I had always enjoyed a very special relationship with Christo. When I was a boy scout in Sofia, he was a role model to us kids as a charismatic older scoutmaster. Then we saw each other again on Black Sea vacations in my high school years, when more than one many pretty girl of my generation fell enamored of the glamorous young diplomat, just arriving from some foreign capital. He was a tall and handsome, impeccably tailored gentleman, with blondish curly hair and a perennial twinkle in his turquoise-blue eyes, betraying a special sense of humor, but also a warm, romantic nature. In the presence of Christo's charm and elegant manners, Parisian education and sophistication, the aspiring Romeos of my age didn't stand a chance with the girls of our dreams, but in us he inspired more admiration than jealousy. (*Speaking of unfair competition for girlfriends, I'll mention another legendary ladies' conqueror and diplomat, also considerably older than me, who similarly became my personal and ideological close friend in exile, Evgueni Silianoff.*) Yet they were two very different, if not opposite, charmers. While Christo, the very image of moral purity, was a slightly shy romantic eager to fall in love, an idealist who would appeal sentimentally to a girl's dreams of eternal Love with a capital "L," Evgueni was the enterprising, highly experienced, seducer whose reputation for sexual exploits and prowess could inspire the naughtiest female fantasies. Both men were brilliant, witty, and highly cultured, juggling with literature and history. But their charm affected parents of the Sofia belles differently: when Silianoff used to return on a leave, fathers locked up their excited daughters; when Boyadjieff's visits were announced, many mothers wished that their daughters would meet him.)

We met again shortly before I left to study in Switzerland. Sava Panitza and I visited Bucharest (my first trip abroad), where Christo was serving as secretary at the Bulgarian Royal embassy and he received us warmly. Apart from the great time we had, (he introduced us to interesting friends and Rumanian girls we found fabulous), Christo fascinated me with his political knowledge and the serious approach to his diplomatic duties. I had always known of his ardent patriotism, but now, with the war going on, I realized how deeply he cared for Bulgaria's future. Although very cosmopolitan, he was first and mostly a deeply devoted Bulgarian.

When the communists took over, Boyadjieff was offered a post at the embassy in Budapest, but he defected to Argentina and Brazil, where he spent several difficult years in financial hardship, working as a truck driver and other menial jobs, but refusing to compromise his ideals. We reestablished contact while I lived in Geneva and Paris, discussing Bulgarian affairs and looking for ways to fight communism.

Christo gave me his enthusiastic support in all of my émigré activities in Paris and Munich. And when he started his initiatives in Brazil, I was among his first and devoted collaborators. As the years passed, Christo solved his financial problems (he became the representative of a Scandinavian importer of paper), bought himself a nice apartment over Copacabana and, as a good bridge player and delightful conversationalist, earned a respected position in Rio society. He continued writing poetry, on old hobby, published a few poetry books, still philosophical and melancholy, this time in Portuguese. But his absolute priority remained the same: his concern for the old, traditional values of his beloved Bulgaria, and the suffering of its people. When I visited Brazil in the late 1970s and he showed me around Rio, we spent wonderful moments of reminiscences and nostalgia. His touching love for Bulgaria hadn't changed. Neither were his charm and good looks. Nor his youthfully romantic heart: he had never forgotten the great love of his life, an Argentinean ambassador's daughter, whom he met while serving in Rumania, more than 30 years before. They were separated during the war, when her father was transferred, but he never stopped thinking of her. After the war, when Christo emigrated to Argentina, he learned that she had married. Heartbroken, he never saw her again, and he never married. *(A few years later, when we met in Washington, Christo poured his heart to me: having learned that her husband had died in Spain, where they lived, Christo took all his courage and called her on the telephone. She was very happy and overwhelmed to hear from him, and insisted that he come and see her. They spoke a few more times and he felt the old feelings revived, but was very disturbed and hesitant: "after all, I'm an old man now," he told me. "After so many years, disappointment is almost inevitable. We may destroy something which was so beautiful!" Maybe because I had just read a similar love story in Garcia Marquez' "Love in the Time of Cholera," I advised him strongly to take the risk. But Christo wasn't convinced and never dared to try.)*

Meanwhile, Boyadjieff's reputation for absolute integrity and political wisdom had increased enormously among Bulgarians abroad and had vested him with uncontested moral authority. But things had changed during our long years of exile. By the early 1980s, the focus in Rio was still on ideological and cultural matters, while many collaborators, including Christo himself, felt that the new developments behind the Iron Curtain and the first signs of dissidence in Bulgaria called for more combative anti-communism abroad. Our centrist organization of *The Free Bulgarians* had ceased its activities and outside of the right-wing *National Front* and the leftish *National Committee* of Dr.G.M. Dimitrov, no centrist exiles were systematically briefing Western governments and media about the situation in Bulgaria, or were in touch with dissidents. As we kept collaborating with *Bulgarian Review*, and as the unanimously trusted Boyadjieff was planning its reorganization, the idea of transforming the intellectual circle into an activist center matured progressively, first, in increased correspondence among us; then with a few trips to Europe and New York, made possible by complimentary air tickets supplied to Christo by his friend Boubi Petroff, a director of Lufthansa.. A major factor in the activization of "Foyer Bulgare" in the last several years was Boyadjieff's increasing closeness with another former diplomat, Dr.Panayot Panayotof, an enterprising refugee, who had succeeded in business in Venezuela and was now Christo's principal collaborator, constantly proposing new initiatives and contributing his own money. Panayot, a fervent patriot, had lived for a couple of years in communist Bulgaria after being fired from the Foreign ministry. Joining the opposition, he tried to make a living as a lawyer, until he felt that his freedom, and maybe his very life, were in danger. Then he made the agonizing decision to leave his wife and little daughter behind and escape, crossing the Rhodope mountains on foot to the Greek border. Unlike me and most of my fellow-exiles, he had personally suffered through the ordeal of the refugee camps and the misery of a newly arrived "sateteless person" in the West. It was much later, after years of hard work, that he made some money in Venezuela and succeeded in bringing his wife and daughter to him. Maybe these experiences explained parts of his earnestness and his total lack of frivolity. A short, erect man with little time or taste for social life and pleasures, Panayot always seemed serious, sober, and disciplined, at times even a little cranky. If he had a hobby, it was reading political history (he felt particularly strongly about the persistent attempts of Russia, both Soviet and tsarist, to dominate Bulgaria). He was very outspoken and often blunt, but all émigrés respected his reliability, working capacity and absolute dedication to the dream of national liberation.

In Europe, the promoter of the new Center project became Dimi Panitza. Traveling extensively for *The Readers Digest*, the world's largest publication, in which his position was increasing rapidly, Dimi kept in touch with compatriots and interested foreigners in many Western countries and especially in the United States, where he established impressive professional and personal contacts in American political circles.

In Washington, the most important capital to us, a natural choice was Dr. Peter Orahovats, recently retired senior vice-president of the pharmacological giant *Bristol-Myers*, a huge position he had reached starting from scratch. He enjoyed the respect of the local Bulgarian colony and shared our political ideas. "Petio" Orahovats and I had grown up on the same "Moskovska" street in Sofia and attended the same public high school, he being two classes ahead of me. His father, a prominent professor of medicine with good connections with the royal family, was the president of the Bulgarian Red Cross. Shortly after the communist takeover, Petio managed to get permission to continue his medical studies in the United States. He had already married his high school sweetheart Slava and had a baby girl. They never returned to Bulgaria. Our roads crossed again in exile. We exchanged letters between New Jersey, where he lived, and Paris, where I was active in the *Free Bulgarians* organization, and saw each other from 1953 on, when I started going to New York. Peter helped me organize an American chapter of the *Free Bulgarians*. He led a quiet family life, totally dedicated to his wife and daughter and to his work, his only hobby being hunting (an excellent shot, Petio's collection of guns was impressive even to non-shooters like me). I saw him more during the following years, mostly because the Orahovatses became close to Princess Maria Luisa, with whom I was in almost daily contact, and also because they bought a vacation house in Shelter Island, not far from Southampton.

In addition to his ideological orientation, excellent professional connections and, by then, good financial situation, Petio's value as a political exile resided also in his strong personality. His allegiance to USA, his adoptive country, was unconditional; he was proud of his American citizenship and well connected in the Republican party; yet his heart had remained as Bulgarian as his accent. A blunt man of strong conservative opinions who didn't mince his words and a declared monarchist, Orahovats had established himself as a leading figure in Washington's Bulgarian colony, with a reputation for zero tolerance of left-wingers, "pinko liberals" and fellow-travelers, present or past (in that category he put several followers of Dr. G.M. Dimitrov's *National Committee*). He had proven himself efficient in the colony's cultural, charity, or Orthodox-Church initiatives, and couldn't care less when criticized for his somewhat autocratic style. "Results are what counts; I'm not interested in popularity contests," he used to say. I introduced Petio to Christo, Panayot, and Dimi, and he accepted to be the new Bulgarian Center's point man in Washington.

By the 1980s, Panayot had left Venezuela and lived with his wife between Canada and Florida. In May 1985 Christo Boyadjieff was visiting them in Singer Island, a sunny resort near Palm Beach, and that's where the *Free Bulgarian Center* was formally founded. On Sunday, May 5th, I checked into a nearby motel and Petio Orahovats arrived the same day from Washington. Dimi. retained by his job, was unable to attend. So was Alex Alexiev, another Bulgarian exile whom we had also invited. Alex, the son of a well-known cartoonist and humorist killed by the communists, had good connections with US military and intelligence circles. He worked for the Rand think tank and occasionally appeared on American television as an expert on Afghanistan and the Muslim Soviet republics.

I was in a particularly good spirits, because I had just received very happy news about my book.. Indeed, the manuscript of *Crown of Thorns* had been finally completed (yes, it was two years <u>before</u> I found someone to print it!) and I had sent copies to my partner James Velkov, to King Simeon, Princess Maria Luisa, Dimi Panitza and Evgueni Silianoff. Nobody had seen the text before, except for Lil, who used to read first drafts of separate chapters as I was writing them, but had not read the entire finished product. The opinion of these people counted enormously to me and I anxiously awaited their reactions.. First to call from Paris was Velkov, the book's sponsor, his voice trembling with emotion. "You've written a very, very good book!" he said and I felt a tremendous relief. Then Dimi called, and so did Silianoff, both from Paris. The Bulgarian adjective Evgueni used delighted me: "Your book is *prekrassna* (splendid), I couldn't put it down the whole week-end." Coming from a friend versed equally well in history and literature, I couldn't feel more reassured. I didn't wait long for the other two reactions I considered crucial: from King Simeon and from Princess Maria Luisa, both extremely encouraging. So I entered our meeting at Panayot's with a great feeling of fulfillment.

During three days and evenings, the four of us practically didn't leave the comfortable apartment with gorgeous view over the ocean, comparing information, reviewing the situation in Bulgaria, commenting on the latest developments in the Communist world. The marathon session, held in an atmosphere of warm friendship and almost total identity of views, produced some concrete decisions, something usually rare in meetings of exiles. We agreed to make both *Foyer Bulgare* and *Bulgarian Review* more combative and rename them the *Free Bulgarian Center*." Christo announced his project for a authoritative book on the saving of the Bulgarian Jews during WWII. We gave him our enthusiastic support and Orahovats took the commitment to find the financing for it. Panayot gave a report on the publication of Georgi Markov's book (the dissident writer assassinated with a poisonous umbrella in London). On behalf of our Center, he had advanced $ 13,500, of which the widow, Annabel Markov, had already returned $ 2,900. He also reported a $ 2,500 contribution to the book by another physically attacked dissident, Vladimir Kostov, and rallied our commitment to sponsor a novel by dissident Atanas Slavov. Panayotof had supplied all these sums personally, with a $ 2,000 help from Orahovats, and we thanked them for their generosity. Concerned about the crucial need for a regular budget, while determined not to seek or accept any foreign financing, such news was encouraging, as was Boyadjieff's report of a $1,000 donation by the family Christo Popov from Caracas.

We devoted considerable time to discussing the unexpected and puzzling political changes in the communist world, including Bulgaria, and the reported transformations in the closed societies there, especially since Gorbachev. Like everyone in the West, we wondered whether these were genuine, or just wishful thinking, or another Communist propaganda tactic? Although still skeptical and distrustful of anything coming from behind the Iron Curtain, the four of us voiced for the first time certain intimate doubts we had recently begun to feel, some second thoughts about the nature of our anti-communism and the adequacy of our strategy. Wasn't our refusal to recognize some signs of evolution in Sofia's regime wrong? Had our old approach become obsolete? Acknowledging the gradual relaxation of the physical police terror and certain improved civility in the manners, appearance and language of the ruling *apparatchiks*, we concluded that the enemy's new image only made him more dangerous and difficult to combat and, while we should adapt our tactics to the new conditions, we shouldn't lower our vigilance. We agreed that now the gravest danger was not the communist ideology, obviously no longer taken very seriously, but the threat of 'Sovietization' of Bulgaria. And we agreed that we should encourage and help any resistance against this denationalization menace, even when coming from people connected with the official state or cultural structures. Panayot was elected as Board-of-Directors' coordinator and he mailed minutes of our deliberations to Dimi, Alex, and close collaborators such as Silianoff, Johnny Stancioff, and Dianko Sotirov. This was the formal birth of the *Free Bulgarian Center*.

Because of the geographical distances between us directors, most of our contacts continued by letters and telephone. Meanwhile, each one of us tried to approach influential foreign politicians and opinion-makers, to open doors at the State Department, Foreign Office and Quai-d'Orsay, to get in touch with Human Rights groups and Bulgarian dissidents.

The next visit of Boyadjieff to Washington was in September 1988. It was a very busy period for me, with radio interviews about my book on the *RFE* and *BBC* Bulgarian-language programs, in addition to the project of a Bulgarian edition of *Crown of Thorns,* on which I worked by mail with an amateur-publisher, a refugee in Malaga, Spain, Emile Illiev. I also made more frequent broadcasts, acting as a sort of *BBC* correspondent in New York, a position the Bulgarian desk chief, Valery Tchoukov, came in March from London to offer to me. It was an election year, and among my weekly choice of subjects, I wrote and read several scripts on George Bush, Dukakis, and their campaigns. Meanwhile, other Bulgaria-connected activities kept me occupied. In April, for instance, we were shocked to hear that some phony Sofia-produced "documentary" film, giving the credit for saving the Bulgarian Jews during WW2 to the Communist party and to dictator Zhivkov, was about to be shown in Washington. So Dimi Panitza, who happened to be in the States, Nicholas Pentcheff, Boyan Choukanoff and myself took the train in New York. With friends of the Free Bulgarian Center in the capital, we organized an advance screening of the absurd propaganda piece at the American Film Institute, and sent invitations and commentaries to journalists and people we hoped to interest. A letter about the gross distortion of historical truth was sent to Congressman Tom Lantos; a friendly journalist, Georgie-Ann Geyer, wrote a strong column in the *Washington Times*, and I read a script on the *BBC*. That same May, King Simeon arrived incognito in New York and I met him at the hotel *Barbizon*. He was very generous in his praise of my book and surprised me with making me a Grand-Officer of the Royal Order of Saint-Alexander. In June, the magnificent decoration arrived—star, cross, and impressive wide red cordon. It looked poignantly familiar: in my childhood, my father proudly wore the Saint-Alexander star, his highest Bulgarian decoration. No outsider or foreigner would be able to understand the emotions that overwhelmed me that day.

When Boyadjieff arrived, Panayot, Petio, and I spent three days with him at *Murna Manor*, Orahovats's Maryland house on Chesapeake Bay and we set up a telephone conference with Dimi Panitza and Evgueni Silianoff in Paris. It was a very productive meeting and among other things, we decided to start an information bulletin in English. On September 13th, we returned to Washington for a round-table with Mishev at the *Radio Free Europe*'s studio. Alexiev joined us at a press conference and a dinner we hosted at the *University Club*, attended by two representatives from the State Department and American scholars on Bulgaria, such as Paul Henze, John Bell and Charles Moser. The next day, we paid a visit to the State Department's Bulgarian desk and gave a reception for the Bulgarian colony, with speakers Christo, Panayot, Petio and myself, as well as Steven Ashley, a well-informed *Free Europe*, European analyst.

Our first Newsletter was published in January 1989, a do-it-yourself job of five tightly printed pages (soon increased to seven) of news about Bulgaria. All material came to me in New York, where I edited the issues (except for one, done by Panayot) and had it type-set and printed in a few hundred copies at a *CopyCat* shop on Lexington avenue. Then I addressed them and carried them to the post office. Petio took care of distributing the newsletter to congressmen, government officials and journalists in Washington; Dimi and Johnny Stancioff did the same in Europe, and Christo in Latin America. The first reactions were encouraging. Thanks to an increasing number of travelers from Bulgaria—relatives of emigrants, scientists attending international conferences, businessmen, foreign diplomats, etc.—as well as private calls and letters to compatriots living abroad, we managed to obtain fresh and reliable information and offer it to the readers of our Newsletter. Of special help were sources such as RFE's Konstantin Mishev, who had found ways of receiving calls by dissidents from anonymous telephones inside the country and who called me when something interesting was communicated; and a young idealist, Ted Zang, who had abandoned a promising lawyer's career to work for *Helsinki Watch*, a Human Rights activists group in New York. There were also unexpected opportunities. Dimi Panitza contacted Bulgarian dissidents expelled to France and others coming through Paris on internationally sponsored meetings. In the fall of 1988, a former high school mate of mine, Marin Pundeff, by then a professor in California, attended academic festivities in Sofia and brought back very confidential messages to us from Bulgarian dissident-minded academics. By that time, *RFE* had begun the serialization of *Crown of Thorns* and in various broadcasts to Bulgaria I had spoken about the *Free Bulgarian Center*. On Pundeff's passage through New York, Panayot and I met him discreetly, almost conspiratorially, at *PANAM's* airport terminal (by looking for collaboration with people like us, the academics were indeed taking a serious risk) and we learned some very interesting facts about the mood of certain Bulgarian intellectuals. In 1989, after a few issues of our *Newsletter*, it seemed that we had established a good reputation for reliability and we began to receive signals from journalists and interested agencies that the existence of the *Free Bulgarian Center* had not gone unnoticed.

We faced an important test at the time when the Bulgarian Communist regime launched a campaign against the ethnic Turkish and Muslim minorities, a really senseless, cruel and revolting persecution. From both a humanitarian point of view and as members of the traditionally tolerant Bulgarian nation, we were absolutely shocked and reacted with anger and disgust. After a few violent incidents were reported and hundred of thousands Bulgarian Turks fled to Turkey, the scandal took international proportions and a special hearing of a US Senate committee was called to investigate. Publicly and privately, our group took a firm stand against the Communist regime's police measures of forcefully changing minorities' names, religion, language and customs, and declared ourselves in favor of the minorities's rights ("Shame on you!" some ultra-nationalist compatriots, even anti-Communists, attacked us. "Siding with foreigners against your own people! Have you forgotten what the Turks have done to us in the past?") Ignoring this kind of criticism, our Center prepared a detailed Memo to the intention of the U.S. Congress, which Peter Orahovats, appearing in our behalf, presented in person to the Committee. Our testimony became official part of the Congressional hearings and was incorporated into their printed Proceedings.

While I was publishing *Crown of Thorns* and was increasingly involved with the *Free Bulgarian Center*, I met an unusual man, who impressed me greatly and influenced the nature of my anticommunism. George Soros was already a fabulously successful financier when he started spending his summers in Southampton, but I was quite ignorant about Wall Street and not particularly interested in the world of finance, so I didn't know anything about him. The first time I heard his name was when Lil was asked whether she would be interested in decorating his new house in Southampton. Soros's fiancée, Susan Weber, an attractive blonde New Yorker considerably younger than the fifty-ish, divorced financial wizard, had seen the recent Southampton Decorators' Show and had loved Lil's exhibit. Lil met her and Soros, liked them, and accepted the job. It was obvious that while Susan was very interested in the project of her future house, and quite knowledgeable (an Arts graduate working on her Ph.D., she had studied styles and furniture and had her own strong opinions about decoration), George couldn't care less about the details. He just wanted a pleasant, comfortable home and was delighted to leave the decoration to Susan.

He was a likable man, Lil told me, an intelligent, alert Hungarian exile educated in England, remarkably *au courant* and with many diverse interests outside of business, including philosophy, politics, philanthropy, tennis and skiing. After meeting him, I couldn't agree more with Lil. In addition, I realized that Soros was deeply involved in East-European affairs and anti-communism. Right away, I was intrigued and wanted to know him better. As we saw George and Susan occasionally, I began to learn fascinating details about his unique politico-philanthropic activity. In the meantime, the nature of our relationship had changed. In a period when the rebellious-minded Susan had temporarily left her fiancé, calling their wedding plans off, George abandoned the decoration project and regretfully informed Lil that he was canceling her job. But the sincerity of their final "business" meeting made it the beginning of a lasting personal friendship. Susan, of course, came back, the happy wedding took place, and we started seeing them more often.

They certainly had nothing of the stereotype Hamptonite socialites. While George, in his detached manner, simply stayed aloof from the local *smart set,* Susan, true to the non-conformism of her campus radical days, didn't resist showing her impatience with characters one reads about in the gossip columns, and her often caustic and sarcastic remarks didn't always make her very popular with local society matrons. The Soroses' luncheons and dinner parties—generous, motley gatherings held every week-end in total informality,—had a family air of *Mittel-Europa* about them, with touches of Wall Street, émigrés's Russia, and Oxford-Cambridge academia. No protocol and no black ties. Important bankers sat next to refugee intellectuals with heavy accents, chic Hamptonites rubbed elbows with bearded physicists, sentimental Jewish relatives, politicians, and tennis pros. Sweaters and open collars outnumbered the blazers and high-heeled pumps went toe-to-toe with Adidas sneakers. George, as host, would often arrive after the first guests, still in tennis shorts, and would behave as a guest, leaving it entirely to the waiters to offer drinks, and to the guests to introduce themselves, if they so decided. Which was often a pity, as occasionally one would learn only the next morning that last night's quiet dinner companion was a prominent political figure, or the unassuming gentleman in sneakers was in fact a Nobel laureate.

Nevertheless, at the Soroses' we met some very interesting people, intellectually and humanly. When *Crown of Thorns* was first printed in 1987, I signed a copy for George and we discussed it at length. He also came to the book party Lil gave me at *Mortimer's*" and he talked to King Simeon, whom he already knew. Simultaneously, George offered me, "from one author to another," his newly-published *The Alchemy of Finance.* Some passages on economy I might have found not easy, but his dedication to Susan enchanted me: "*To my wife,*" it said, "*without whom this book would have been finished much earlier.*" I wished I had written that before him. Anyhow, we were two lucky husbands...

Meanwhile, George's portrait was appearing more frequently on the covers of *Fortune, Business Week* and other business magazines and in headlines of *Wall Street Journal* and *Financial Times* articles. No doubt, our new Southampton acquaintance and the fabulous returns of his *Quantum* investment fund were the talk of the financial world. But it wasn't this that fascinated me. I was thrilled to hear about Soros's unprecedented, imaginative venture in Eastern Europe, a veritable one-man crusade against communism. Starting with his native Hungary, he had managed to establish philanthropic foundations in communist countries that found ways to efficiently encourage and overtly help local dissidents. First, he offered to donate large quantities of badly needed copying machines and similar equipment to public libraries, which these countries had no hard currency to afford. Then he offered to pay all expenses for native scientists and intellectuals willing to attend international conferences. The government was strongly tempted, but on condition to keep control over the Foundation's composition and activities. "No deal!" replied Soros. "You may have 49 percent, but I must have the majority 51 percent." As the communists balked at such arrangements, Soros declared the deal off. But each time he headed for the exit, the officials, loath to miss the windfall, stopped him and resumed bargaining. "I call it 'my doorknob tactics,'" Soros told me. "The moment I reach the handle of the door, they would call me back: 'Wait, let's negotiate!' But I would remain firm about having the final say in my Foundation. And it usually works!" Thus, Soros succeeded in appointing dissidents tot his Foundation's board. Spending his own money, and taking advantage of the increasing relaxation during Gorbachev's era, he sponsored several liberal scientific, publishing, and artistic projects, generously providing fax and Xerox machines, printers, and all sorts of means for communications and publishing. The authorities weren't happy, but Soros's large cultural and philanthropic contributions were too tempting to turn down.. And the times were different. Brezhnev was dead, not to mention the other ruthless successors of Stalin. The present rulers themselves were torn by insecurity and doubts, thinking about their own and their Party's future. A fertile ground for dissidence. As his Hungarian experiment showed signs of success, Soros repeated it in Poland, in Czechoslovakia, in the Soviet Union itself. Surprisingly, his crusade for an "Open Society" (a term dear to his favorite philosopher, Karl Popper), was bearing results.

I was fascinated. To me, Soros's approach was something new and original. His personality intrigued me genuinely, for he was markedly different from most anti-Communist refugees I knew. Unlike their(or should I say "our"?) anger, emotional rhetoric and patriotic ardor, and especially our categorical refusal to even consider talking with the enemy, George seemed calm and cerebral, an undemonstrative pragmatist ready to put aside his own indignation and aversions when he deemed that businesslike bargaining was more likely to achieve the desired results. No Quixotic visions, no pathos, no grandiloquence. Just a cool, competitive chess player in a difficult game, as if he held no personal grudge against the adversary across the table. (And yet, as a youth, he had witnessed first-hand considerable Nazi and communist persecution.)

The old philosophical questions about the right ways of reacting to evil have always disturbed and preoccupied me enormously. Of course, I haven't found any more answers than anyone else. So wide and nuance-filled is the spectrum between the two extremes of abject collaboration and suicidal opposition, and so innumerable the possible forms of resistance, that we're all left to decide according to our individual beliefs and conscience. De Gaulle or Petain? Do we remain true to principles and honor at any price, or try by compromise, to save what's still savable and limit human suffering ? And just how far should the honorable compromise go? Inside Bulgaria, as in all totalitarian states, the citizens didn't have much choice; they all were forced to make compromises on a daily basis, albeit to very different degrees. But as refugees, we had a few options. Myself and most my friends opted for intransigence, never set foot in a red embassy or consulate, never shook hands with communists, never recognized any of their achievements and closed our eyes to the reality that they were holding the trump cards. We never sought to negotiate. Alas, I don't think our kind of resistance helped our compatriots much in their plight or seriously sapped the foundations of communism. Now, I was observing the radically different Soros strategy at work, more rationalism and realism than emotion. Rather than bitterly denouncing them with slogans, he switched the accent from ideology to economics, bombarding the evil fortress with barrages of money and new communications technology. He was well able to afford it, and it worked. One single individual was able to make a difference in a number of enslaved countries, putting his imprint on their political and cultural lives, efficiently undermining their police regimes and sowing the seeds of a free, open society!

In these East-European countries, Soros single-handedly did probably more for destabilizing totalitarianism than most Western governments, including the US administration. Yet his action was still largely unknown to the general public; people were more interested in whether his fortune had reached one or three billion dollars. In Southampton, George had a rather unassuming presence, known as just one among the resort's many new millionaires and mostly noticed for his good, competitive tennis game. I gladly helped him to join our beautiful Meadow Club, where his good sportsmanship and simple, unpretentious manner made him a popular member. We played a few times together, but by then his regular, all-year-round game was greatly improving, while my sporadic tennis was going downhill, and he switched to younger and stronger partners. He was happier on the tennis court than at any Hamptons' social events. The so-called "society" didn't interest him at all.

Apart from his political action, I was intrigued by his rather relativistic personal philosophy, in which I detected similarities with the way I was seeing the world. Skeptical about the existence of absolute truth and convinced that perfection could never be reached, Soros was fearful of teachings and ideologies which claim to possess the ultimate truth and considered them as the greatest threat to any open society. He was a very unusual, almost paradoxical mixture of self-confidence (some critics even talked of "Messianic arrogance"), combined with sincere intellectual humility. Not the humility of the shy, weak, and insecure, but rather a well-substantiated awareness of our inherent incapacity of ever really understanding the world in which we live. Not only did he have the intelligence of knowing his limitations, but he considered human "fallibility" an essential and even useful element of the human condition. He claimed that admission of one's own fallibility, a cornerstone in his life philosophy, guided him in his personal life and also as a moneymaker and philanthropist and contributed greatly to his success. Recognizing the truth that in the financial markets erratic human actions and false perceptions often count more than logical theories and actual facts, helped him make his huge fortune.

Impressed by the results of Soros's actions in other communist countries, I hoped that he would start a similar foundation in Bulgaria too. But his answer was that Bulgaria didn't seem ready yet. And indeed, there had been no Budapest-like uprisings in my country, no "Solidarity" rebellion, no "Prague Spring." There were of course signs of nascent ferment, but no one knew for sure how strong it was and whether it would emerge on the surface, or when..

Soros was responsible for my first visit ever to a communist country. Exactly 45 years after I had left the Kingdom of Bulgaria, never to return to the so-called "People's republic," he and Susan invited Lil and me, along with a group of friends, to join them in Budapest for the board meeting of his *Quantum* money fund. On May 11, the day of our wedding anniversary, we arrived in the Hungarian capital and joined the Soros cosmopolitan group in the *Ramada*, the refurbished old *Grand Hotel* on Margaret Island on the Danube. I was thrilled, but I would lie if I said that I wasn't a little nervous: During the decades of my exile, I had heard, read and dreamt about too many horror stories of arrests, abduction, and worse. But my fears evaporated overnight at the sight of Soros's welcome in his native country. If anyone believed that communists were not impressed by big money power, they should have watched the obsequiousness of Hungarian officials, nominally still a communist state in 1989. George was treated like a king, not only by waiters in restaurants where he entertained us lavishly for four days, or museum attendants, mostly supported by his foundation or gypsy dancers, violinists, artists and intellectuals he sponsored, but also by local economists, attending his conferences and by all sorts of red bureaucrats, hanging on his every word. There was a sea change in the air and one could almost physically the weight of "capitalist" Soros's impact on Hungarian life. I left Budapest somewhat envious. Could rigidly communist Bulgaria one day also become if not more democratic—an impossible dream!—at least more flexible, like Hungary?

Leaving the group in Budapest, Lil and I boarded a hovercraft for a lovely, 6-hour trip up the Danube river, to Vienna, a city Lil had never visited and always wanted to see. We spent six charming days at the cozy *Kaiserin-Elizabeth* hotel, unabashedly enjoying the rewards of simply being typical tourists on a first-time visit.

Soon after returning to New York, a new development threw me back into the inescapable Bulgarian-related realities of my personal life. In June, my brother Simeon informed us that, unexpectedly, he had finally been granted a passport and an exit visa to visit us in America! In the past few years, at my urging, he had repeatedly applied for a passport and, in a frustrating routine, the authorities had regularly refused to issue him one. And now suddenly he was allowed to travel! I started organizing his trip, but because of some health problems of his, he preferred to postpone it until September. This allowed me to take advantage of the July departure for Bulgaria of our friends Chandler Cowles and his girlfriend, Bulgarian concert pianist Pavlina Dokovska (by then we suspected that they have been discreetly and unofficially married...), who kindly offered to make all travel arrangements for my totally helpless brother. The delay also allowed Lil and me to spend a week in August with Paul, his wife Jane, and baby Alexa in Bozeman, together with Philip and Philip Junior, and to go to Yellowstone Park with them.

Boubi arrived on September 9, 1989, one day after Paul, Jane and Alexa, and also Tina, had come to Southampton to stay with us. That week I had bought a new car, an *Oldsmobile-Ciera*, and I drove to Kennedy airport to meet him. It was quite an emotional reunion, of course, after our painful, 27-year-long separation.

So many things had happened to both of us since his last visit in 1962! Mama had died, the two-year-old Paul he knew had become a father, I had written the book about King Boris's reign and was no longer a *Paris-Match* journalist, and Boubi had gone through such ordeals in bleak Bulgarian labor camps and psychiatric clinics. We could only touch briefly upon these subjects that night as I brought him to our New York apartment, before he surrendered to fatigue and jet lag. We continued the next morning while driving to Southampton, where the entire family, including Philip, was waiting around the pool. Simeon was the same as they remembered him: a mild, polite man, rather shy and not very talkative, especially with his rusty French and limited English.

From time to time he went through moments of depression, remaining silent and absorbed in his thoughts, barely answering a question. Sadly, this state lasted during all of his stay in America, worrying me a lot and spoiling my joy of being together. But in between he had, I hoped, some very good and interesting time. He stayed in the States for 50 days, mostly in New York and Southampton, when I was continuously with him (in Manhattan, Tina kindly lent him her apartment on Gramercy Park, while she was away), and he visited Radka for one week in Miami, including a visit to Orlando's Disneyland. Boubi and I had plenty of time to talk, for me to hear details from his difficult life in Bulgaria (sometimes I took notes or recordings), for him to listen to my interviews and broadcasts on tape and to read *Crown of Thorns*, of which he only had heard a few chapters from the Bulgarian-language programs of *Radio Free Europe*. In New York he saw old friends. We dined with the Tchaprachikoffs and Mara Palmer, and Bobby Daskaloff showed him his studio and Soho. Dim was passing through New York, and so was Panayot, so we held a *Free Bulgarian Center* meeting and Boubi met Panayot. Lil and I even brought him one Sunday for lunch at George and Susan Soros's, where he met Miklos Vasahrelyi, one of the 1957 Hungarian Revolution heroes. In Southampton, as Lil's beautiful granddaughter Pauline was charmingly attentive to him, I was amused to watch "depressed" Simeon suddenly waking up: the old flirtatious spark in his eyes hadn't been completely extinguished...In October I drove him to Washington D.C. where Boubi was very happy to sty with childhood friends, Milo Karson first, then Petio Orahovats, and see the people with whom he had kept in touch—the Sarbovs, Kosta Tchipev, poetesses Mary Ann Larkin and Shirley Cochran, who had traveled through Bulgaria. Few things made me feel so happy as seeing Boubi enjoying himself, smiling, interested in people, places and conversations. He looked very well that fall, neatly-dressed in the new clothes I had bought him, and well rested after the first week of fatigue. But pleased as he seemed to be with us in America and having at last a normal, comfortable life, we never brought up the subject of his remaining permanently in the West. Not this time. God knows how I tried frantically, desperately, in 1962, on his first trip here, and so did Mama, Radka, and every friend! But no begging, warning, cajoling, threats, shouting or crying had succeeded then against his stubborn determination to return to what we all saw as a bleak, miserable existence. Now it was too late. At the age of 68, one doesn't start a radically new life. Especially not with his biography, health record and beliefs. All I tried this time was to keep him as long as I could out of the hell in which he lived and to provide some medical care, physical comfort, and brotherly warmth. So when he began talking about returning, we didn't fight and, regretfully, I made his Air France reservations. On October 27, I drove him to Kennedy airport and the next morning Dimi Panitza met him at Charles-de-Gaulle. After two days in Paris, Simeon returned to Bulgaria. On the 1st of November, I called him on the telephone in Plovdiv. He was OK, he said, and thanked me for the "marvelous time" he had had.

Only ten days later, ironically, dictator Todor Zhivkov resigned and the disintegration of Communism began.

****

Chapter 37

Return to Bulgaria

I learned the sensational news that Friday at 11 A.M., when a refugee friend, the artist Christo Popov, called me from out of town.. Then Dimi telephoned from Paris, as excited as I was. Lil and I were on our way to attend a luncheon at the *Knickerbocker Club* honoring Dr. Jonas Salk, discoverer of the polio serum. Although the famous Nobel-prize laureate's talk couldn't have been more fascinating, I could barely concentrate and listen, my thoughts totally absorbed by the announcement of the Zhivkov regime's end. After lunch, I rushed home and started frantically calling all my Bulgarian friends, congratulating each other, exchanging newly learned details, commenting on the news. Then Lil and I drove to Alpine, New Jersey, for a dinner with Edie and Nicholas Stancioff, the son of my close friend and *Free Bulgarian Center* member Johnny Stancioff. Johnny, still unaware, arrived soon after us and when I told him the news, we fell in each others' arms, overcome by emotion.

For us, exiles from Eastern Europe, these were days of unprecedented euphoria. In a crescendo, the stunning reports of the rapid unraveling of the "Evil Empire" dominated world news and, of course, all our conversations. We hardly could wait for the morning papers, and stayed glued to the TV evening bulletins. Among many people I called, I talked to Soros and reminded him of his words that "Bulgaria wasn't ready yet." What about the new developments? On November 17, only one week after Zhivkov's fall, George invited me to discuss the Bulgarian situation. I brought Panayot with me, who had arrived in New York especially for this meeting, and *RFE*'s Konstantin Mishev, my best source of information. George received us in his office with spectacular view over Central Park, on the 33rd floor at 888 Seventh avenue. He was accompanied by his wife Susan, her friend Jeri Laber, executive director of "Helsinki Watch," and Arieh Neier, a trusted Soros collaborator and *Helsinki Watch* president. We commented on the latest events in Sofia and when we exposed the arguments in favor of the creation of a Bulgaria *Open Society* branch, George smiled somewhat mysteriously, pulling a letter out of his pocket. "We are thinking of it," he said happily. "I just received this letter from Bulgaria, from a most competent person whom I trust. He advises me to do it as soon as possible." The letter was from John Menzies, a young diplomat at the American embassy in Sofia. Panayot, Mishev, and I were delighted. Soros then told us to keep in touch through Susan, whom he designated as liaison for Bulgaria, and through Jeri Laber, who would manage the assistance to the dissidents.

We didn't waste any time to taking advantage of Soros's generosity. The dissident groups, opposed to the post-Zhivkov Communist government, urgently needed computers, printers and fax-machines, and Mishev put us in touch with some of these as-yet totally unknown new political figures. One speaker, whose fiery speeches we liked, was a young doctor, Boyko Proychev, who had caused a huge stir at a mass street demonstration simply by beginning his speech with the words "Ladies and Gentlemen," instead of the usual, hated "Comrades." My first application for computers and printers (the bill amounted to $7,486) was readily approved by Susan and I bought the equipment. But as the shippers required personal, and not office, recipients in Sofia, I gave the names of Dr. Proychev and somebody called Yanko Yankov, whose address Mishev happened to have.

Events were unfolding rapidly. More dissidents started traveling to the West. An inspiring addition to our New York anti-Communist scene was very young Koyana Trencheva, bravely fighting for the liberation of her imprisoned husband, Dr. Konstantin Trenchev, one of the prominent new pro-democracy leaders. I intensified the exchange of information with Mishev of *RFE*, Ted Zang and Jeri Laber of *Helsinki Watch*, Alex Alexiev, and some newly arrived dissidents, and at the *Free Bulgarian Center* we increased the frequency of our *Newsletter*.

In January and February 1990, we were thrilled to watch King Simeon on the popular TV program *Good Morning, America*, then read interviews with him in Madrid by the official Bulgarian news agency *BTA* and the pro- communist daily *Otechestven Front*, heard on *Radio Sofia*—all these being new, hard to believe, milestones. But the biggest sensation was the television interview by Kevork

Kevorkian, the controversial host of the most popular program *Every Sunday*. A Bulgarian audience had never before seen King Simeon and his appearance was a true revelation. He became an overnight national hero and the show, to the great annoyance of the "reformed Communist" government, one of the most discussed topics for several weeks. Accustomed to half-a-century of cheap, venomous propaganda by vulgar, hateful politicians, the unprepared viewers were almost shocked to hear the gentlemanly King's appeal for moderation, tolerance, and civility in the political life.

The same month, Dimi Panitza and his friend, American financier John Train, started a new initiative, the "Free Elections Project," aiming at involving foreign personalities in the forthcoming first free elections in Bulgaria (former French President Giscard d'Estaing was among them). Together with Anni Tchaprachikoff and Mishev, I attended several meetings at Train's offices. In February, Jeri Laber and Ted Zang left for Bulgaria and at their return they gave a fascinating report on their somewhat risky experiences in villages of Muslim minorities at the Fifth Avenue offices of *Helsinki Watch*. George and Susan Soros also went to Bulgaria, where they met the directors and trustees of the newly created *Open Society-Sofia*. I couldn't wait for them to return and hear their impressions from my native country. (Typically, Susan almost scolded me: "What are you still doing here? Your place is there!" They had loved Bulgaria and especially Tsarska-Bistritza, the Rila mountain royal lodge I knew in my childhood.)

Meanwhile, two of my closest friends and colleagues in our *Free Bulgarian Center*, Ivan ("Johnny") Stancioff and Dimi Panitza, had returned on short visits to Bulgaria, for the first time in more than 40 years. Apart from moving and disturbing me deeply, their impressions from the country of our birth provided me with a much clearer image of the rapidly evolving situation. As an editor of the *Readers' Digest*, Dimi was received by the new President, Mladenov, and had extensive and frank conversations both with top officials of the regime and with leaders of the Democratic opposition. As for Johnny, he delivered to the opposition an important load of computers, printers, fax machines, copiers, and other donations he had collected in Great Britain and Western Europe. Attending opposition rallies, Johnny, although a foreign citizen but typically impulsive by nature, found it difficult to restrain himself and not address the crowds himself.

Meanwhile, Velkov and I were trying hard to have *Crown of Thorns* translated and published in Bulgaria. The translation needed some more work and Velkov, who was then mostly in Paris and London, enlisted the services of an excellent professional, Nikola Botzev, whose corrected galley proofs were regularly mailed to New York for my approval and promptly returned to Paris. At the same time, Velkov was actively searching for a Bulgarian publisher. But, although every Sofia publishing house was eager to get our book, already famous from the *Radio Free Europe's* broadcasts, it wasn't an easy task. Velkov, as an émigré, didn't really know the new people in Bulgaria, and it took him only a couple of "business" talks to realize, in a shock, that none of the Western practices concerning contracts, copyrights and royalties had any relevance whatsoever in a country just emerging from 45-years of communism. That's why I was enormously relieved when he finally called me in February to say that a leading literary review, *Septemvri*, was willing to publish *Crown of Thorns*, first in monthly installments and then in a book form. I felt even better after receiving samples of back issues of *Septemvri*: the editorial quality was on a high level. After talking with the editor, Toncho Zhechev, a highly respected literary critic and historian, Velkov was left with a very favorable impression.

For me, it was a springtime of incredible excitement. After 45 years of exile, with all hope already abandoned, the oppressive pall that had chronically stifled major parts of my otherwise normalized, happy life, had begun miraculously to crack and tear to pieces. Long-unseen sunrays appeared through rifts in the black cloud, carrying forgotten joys and thrills, and some suppressed tears too. The previous month, for instance, it was the first totally free, un-censored conversations with Boubi in Plovdiv; then, came echoes of half-a-million voices deliriously shouting "Freedom!" and "Down with Dictatorship!" in the streets of Sofia; one week later, on the telephone from Sofia, I heard for the first time since 1944 the voice of my closest schoolmate, Zhivko Krapchev (our sophomoric jokes hadn't changed much); then, this new, unknown experience of receiving in New York freshly arrived, officially published, Bulgarian anti-communist newspapers.

People could travel, parcels could be sent with no restrictions, Bulgarians could openly criticize, denounce, and damn the government. I doubt that any of my foreign friends could really understand what this meant to us!

Not before long, we saw some of the new actors of the ongoing Bulgarian drama in the flesh. By the end of March, at the invitation of the American organizations, eight representatives of dissident groups visited the United States. I had dinner with them and a few émigrés at the Manhattan apartment of Dr. Liubo Kanev, a psychiatrist who also wrote "absurd" fiction stories. That's where I first met promising, newly hatched leader Philip Dimitrov, and also Stefan Stoyanov, a young Democrat, who brought me messages from my childhood friend Stefan Savov, emerging leader of the restored Democratic Party. Fascinated to meet compatriots "coming from the old country," we spent most of the night discussing the pre-election situation in Bulgaria.

A few days later, we were delighted to welcome famous poetess Blaga Dimitrova, a warm, cultured lady with a considerable following in the country and now a prominent dissident. Having recently read some of her beautifully sensitive, romantic poems, I was very curious to meet this master of Bulgarian verse. In New York she was honored at the *Helsinki Watch* headquarters and then gave a reading at the N.Y.C. Public Library across Fifth Avenue, which moved us, Bulgarians in the audience, and made us feel proud, a refreshing experience for refugees from a country with not a particularly good reputation. Blaga Dimitrova continued to Washington and as Christo Boyadjieff and Panayot Panayotof had just arrived there, the *Free Bulgarian Center* invited the poetess in for a discreet meeting. There were four of us directors—Christo, Panayot, Petio Orahovats, and myself—to welcome her in the privacy of a Watergate apartment a friend of Petio's had put at our disposal for the occasion. We spent the better part of the after-noon in a warm, friendly exchange of confidences, some of which a real eye-opener for us, so starved for first hand, reliable information after 45 years away from home. Then Petio took us to the *University Club* and a sincere friendship was born that night in the cozy private dining room.

The June elections in Bulgaria, the first after Zhivkov, were approaching, raising enormous hopes and causing unprecedented excitement. In May, when two top leaders of the anti-Communist coalition *CDC*, or Union of the Democratic Forces, Dr. Zheliu Zhelev and Dr. Petar Beron, made their first visit to the United States, we at the "Free Bulgarian Center" received them with open arms. Orahovats and I had dinner with them on their first evening in Washington, along with Radi Slavov and Alex Alexiev. Panayot arrived the next day and, after a reception at a Human Rights Law group, the Free Bulgarian Center gave a dinner for the delegation, to which we invited columnist Georgie Ann Geyer and a State Department official. Zhelev and Beron were traveling with two *CDC* advisers, economist Ognian Pishev, and foreign policy specialist Stefan Tafrov, a young man barely thirty, looking like a college student, but obviously well versed in international affairs and speaking excellent English, French, and other languages. Tafrov was also one of the directors of the new *Open Society-Sofia* selected by Soros.

We were favorably impressed by the *CDC* delegation and encouraged by their determination to win the elections and get rid of Communism altogether, rather to try to reform it, as many believers in *"perestroyka"* still preached. I felt reassured by Zhelev angrily refuting the fears of many commentators that, regardless of their sins, only the Communists could provide efficient cadres capable to run the State machine, while the non-Communists, having been deprived of opportunities and proper education, supposedly lacked the necessary experience. "A malevolent myth, spread intentionally!" he declared indignantly. Listening to Pishev on free-market economics and Tafrov on foreign relations, seemed to justify some of Zhelev's optimism. The delegation was well received by the State Department and influential politicians, such as Senators Bob Dole and Claiborne Pell, all expressed warm encouragement and wishes for a victory of the opposition in the forthcoming elections.

The long-awaited democratic elections, the first in Bulgaria for several decades, were held on June 10th. I spent that Sunday in Southampton in a state of rare excitement, glued to the radio and the television set, anxiously waiting for the results, repeatedly calling Jivko Krapchev, Stefan Savov, and other friends in Sofia. My sister Radka and most compatriots in America were frantically trying the same, and we eagerly exchanged any scarce bits of information. As the evening advanced and results began to arrive, our fears turned to a shock, and then tremendous disappointment. The opposition had lost! I was stunned. There were, of course, many explanations, some of them quite plausible, of <u>why</u> this had happened, but they couldn't soften the blow. Added to the disappointment, I also felt enormously disturbed intellectually, almost betrayed. For 45 years I had passionately preached that the Bulgarian people were not only not responsible for the horrors of the imposed totalitarian regime, but had been its innocent and long-suffering victims. And now, offered a long-awaited opportunity to express its will in free elections, a majority had voted for the thinly disguised "reform" Communists! Had I been so wrong all this time? Had I, and my ideological friends, been misinforming all these who listened to us? Cruel doubts tore at me, and even some guilt, mixed with shame for my compatriots.

By chance, during the same week I put my back out badly and was forced to spend eight days in pain, doing stretching exercises and getting shots in the hips. Paul and I had intended to leave for Bulgaria in the summer, but because of my bad back, and also because he and Jane were about to move from Bozeman into a new house in the nearby Montana town of Livingston, I postponed the trip for September. However, the elections upset was another, and probably the main, factor for this decision.

Some Bulgarians friends reacted more violently. Peter Orahovats was so upset and disgusted, that he swore never to care for Bulgarian politics again. "Don't bother telling me news from Bulgaria anymore!" he told me each time I called him. "I don't want to hear about that country again! If you want us to talk about other things, as old friends, please do! But don't waste your long-distance coins to tell me what happens there, I'm not interested!" Thus, he resisted for a few months, but being the patriot he was, he returned to our *Free Bulgarian Center* activities as soon as his anger subsided.

The election results notwithstanding, "reform Communist" President Mladenov resigned in early July and, in early August, opposition leader Zheliu Zhelev was elected President of the republic, an encouraging sign. Late in August, during anti-government demonstrations, crowds tried to burn down the Communist Party headquarters in Sofia. It was a period when the Bulgarian public showed great interest in us exiles, and I was among those approached by various media, especially after *Radio Free Europe* and the literary review *Septemvri* (later renamed *Letopissi* serialized *Crown of Thorns*. Christo Kurteff was the first to come to New York and do an extensive interview with me for *Horizont*, the same program where Kevorkian had recently interviewed King Simeon. Then came Jordan Lozanov from the *National Radio*, Ivan Nikolchev from *Orbita*, and many others, all good professionals and not any less anti-Communists than me.

Meanwhile, I continued working on the *Free Bulgarian Center Bulletin* and kept in touch with Bulgaria by calls to my brother, my friends Zhivko Krapchev and Stefan Savov, and also Stefan Tafrov of the Opposition. I was in close contact with James Velkov about our book and telephoned its future publisher, Toncho Zhechev in Sofia. And I kept King Simeon informed about my travel plans. From recent visitors to Bulgaria, such as Dimi Panitza, Johnny Stancioff, and Konstantin Mishev, I was getting pretty detailed information about the latest developments in the country, but I still wanted to see it with my own eyes.

Was Bulgaria really free? Was the Communist nightmare really over? We all knew that with the ascent of Gorbachev, Bulgarian dictator Zhivkov, who had ruled for over thirty years, became a burden to his own party and his colleagues had gotten rid of him in November 1989. The "reform Communists," renamed "Bulgarian Socialist Party," proclaimed *glasnost and perestroika,* and the end of totalitarianism. It all sounded terrific, but the same people—yesterday's *nomenclatura*—remained in power. I was anxious to find out for myself how free Bulgaria was now. And with travel finally possible for exiles like me, I finally set off for Sofia in September 1990.

It wasn't an easy decision. I confess to a lot of apprehension and doubts. Nostalgia, of course, was strongly pulling me in the direction of my country of birth. So few people really know what nostalgia for a forbidden homeland is! In the beginning, it's so painful as to be almost unbearable. It's like the first day of a little child away from his family, crying "I want to go home!" To make things worse, in my case the news from home was always tragic, and I was unable to help. With time, the acute pain becomes a chronic ache, and one has to live with it. Forty-six years is a terribly long time! And I was never cured. There hadn't been a single week that I haven't had at least one night-dream connected with Bulgaria. Memories recur at the most unexpected moments. Just a sound, a word, a scent—and off it goes, as if you had inadvertently touched an old wound you thought had healed. A whiff of a familiar wind, and for a few seconds you're transported, almost physically, into some place from your youth, and you again become the youngster who vanished so long ago. A painful feeling, yet one of great beauty. I knew I could cure my nostalgia. Other exiles had told me, "Just go back, see it, and all nostalgia will evaporate!" But I hesitated. Did I, honestly, want to be cured? Because, painful as it was, this longing had become a depository for so many memories, dreams, and illusions, a part of the best in me. Does a person in love really want to be cured, even when it hurts? Until now, I had excuses: no way of getting entry visa, a serious risk to be arrested. With the political changes, these raisons were no longer valid. So now I simply had to return.

But I worried a lot about my emotions. To better collect my thoughts, I started jotting down some notes. "I toss and turn in my bed, worrying about the forthcoming trip," I wrote, several weeks before I left. "How disturbed will I be at the moment of the arrival, when I'll first breathe the long-forgotten native air, and hear Bulgarian voices all around me at the airport? Will I be able to take it? And, entering Sofia, will I recognize the streets? Might I be embarrassingly moved when I see the familiar Alexander-Nevsky cathedral, the old Parliament, the equestrian monument of Alexander II, the royal palace? Especially my father's offices on the ground floor of the palace? As a child, it was such a thrill to visit him there! Of course, I'd visit my birthplace, on Moskovska Street, where I'd spent my early childhood. I know that a new building stands in its place, but at least I would see the wall of the old Saint-Sophia church, facing our windows. I wonder how I would feel visiting my old schools? I'll also go to the Boulevard Tsar-Osvoboditel apartment, where we moved to when I was a teenager. Wouldn't it be fun to take the elevator to the fourth floor and ask the present occupants to take a look inside? Then, I can retrace the route from there to school, exactly as I walked it every morning carrying my school bag!

"It would be hard to see a Bulgaria without my parents. I've never known it without Tatko and Mama. Will the place feel the same? Will I constantly be looking for them? I can't even visit my father's grave: nobody knows for sure where he was buried after his execution in 1945. The disappointment could be terrible, and I fear it. I may find the country so deteriorated, run down, and vulgarized as to have become foreign to me. Wouldn't I be deeply distressed if I discover that I can no longer love it?"

In spite of my apprehension, I went. My son Paul volunteered to accompany me, in what turned out to be one of the most gratifying experiences I ever had as a father. The very first hours, the first night, everything was so unreal, as though I were in a dream. At the airport, I went though the motions of shaking hands, hugging friends and relatives, trying to joke and appear composed. I found myself in a curious state of elation, which kept recurring during my entire stay. Sofia had grown enormously and I couldn't recognize the outskirts. But once the taxi entered familiar streets, I was moved and my jaw started trembling. I had many similar moments during the following days. It was, on the whole, a pleasant feeling, and greatly rewarding. Paul's presence prevented me from overindulging in sentimentality: he served as my point of reference to real life.

Most of Sofia's center was unchanged—unpainted for fifty years, shabby, unkempt,—but still a pretty city and I felt happy to stroll in its streets. The nostalgic pilgrimage part was bittersweet. I was thrilled to stare again at the familiar church opposite the house of my birth; as a child I used to spend hours looking at it from our windows. But the house itself wasn't there, nor was the yard where we used to play. I visited the royal palace (now the National Art gallery), but the wing where my father used to work was closed. In Plovdiv, my grandfather's house was intact, but squeezed between new cement buildings, obliterating all trace of the sweet, overgrown garden I yearned to see again. In Koprivshtitza, the small town of my father's ancestors, I located the century-old wooden gate, but beyond it there was a new house of strangers. Still, revisiting the old places was wonderful and I was thrilled to show my son some of the country he had heard about all of his life.

An unexpected problem turned out to be a shortage of time. People had already heard parts of *Crown of Thorns* on the Bulgarian programs of the foreign stations, my name was recognized from my radio scripts, and returning émigrés were still newsworthy novelty at that time, so I was received with a red carpet and besieged by the press, the television and the radio, and even autograph seekers. With my *Free Bulgarian Center* co-directors Boyadjieff and Panayotof in Sofia at the same time, we were continuously solicited for interviews, lectures, and press conferences. And most rewarding but time-consuming, relatives, old friends, and all sorts of acquaintances filled my hotel's lobby all day long, insisting to see me. It was a new and heart—warming experience, but with the scores of people to see, I had to skip many places I had planned to revisit, and even to hide. After a particularly crowded day, Paul summed up this treatment by one of his generation's superlatives: "Gee, Dad, you're like a rock star!"

My reunion with my brother Simeon in Plovdiv was less of a shock, as we had seen each other the previous year in America. Still, I was pained to see, at last, the miserable, unkempt room from which he had written me so many letters and which I had tried so often to imagine, a room whose poverty he didn't seem to mind a bit and had grown attached to.

Now and then, I had the uncanny feeling that I had dreamt this past, that the Bulgarian boy I was searching for—"Stefcho," as they called me—had never lived there. Then I would come across some piece of evidence, some material proof, corroborating the memories. Such as my father's gold fountain pen, which a nephew handed me; I remember it so well! Or a portrait a cousin had saved— Dad, Mom, and three of us children in the old living room. So I didn't invent this room! And, most disturbing of all, a green school notebook (God only knows how it survived the scattering of our belongings!), sixty-four pages in my handwriting, of a play I wrote as a youngster. It was no Shakespeare, but it contained so many of my private thoughts that I felt that the reunion of the white-haired Mr.Groueff and the teenager Stefcho had, at that moment, been achieved.

Did the people disappoint me? The man of the street, yes! I discovered a new kind of citizens, uncivil—unpleasant, arrogant—with whom I felt a total strangers. But I liked the young: bright, admiring the West, and resenting communism. My old friends, the ones still there, were all very poor and aged, but most had kept their principles and dignity. They had been the victims. I didn't recognize some of them immediately—people do change in 46 years!—but after a minute or two, the eyes and the smile gave them away and everything was almost as it had been before. Some of those cute, sexy little girls we used to date introduced me to their teenage grandchildren, while we reassured each other: "Oh, you haven't changed at all!" A little hypocritical, but both sides liked it.

I took Paul to a party at a friend's young brother's apartment with several childhood friends. Lots of laughs, and reminiscing, and drinking. To my son it all probably looked not much different from any noisy class reunion. Then suddenly a disturbing thought struck me and I pulled Paul aside. "Let me tell you about those guys," I said. "Starting from the left: Here is Vlado (Stanishev), his father was sentenced to death; Zhivko (Krapchev), his father was assassinated in the street; your uncle Simeon, whose father was executed; Stefan (Savov),his father died in a camp." And so on and on...Except for the tragic cast, the party looked much like any class reunion in America and elsewhere: the slivovitz flowed freely, and the banter never stopped.

Could these people be like us? After a lecture I gave at Sofia's University, students asked me whether I found them different from U.S. students. Looking at their blue jeans and T-shirts, and having heard nothing but rock-and-roll and Western music for days, my first impulse was to say no. But then I thought of a less obvious, but tragic difference: they were all children of parents who, in order to protect them, had had to muzzle their real thoughts. They have been thought always to watch what they say, never to trust anyone. They grew up in homes where conversations stop abruptly when a child entered the room. They saw their parents acting differently in front of strangers—lying, pretending, bootlicking. Every child has, at some point, feared for his parents, seen them humiliated, or felt ashamed for them. "I ceased to be my daughter's hero when she saw me— me, the anti-communist—carrying a red banner at a parade," a friend confessed tearfully. "How could I explain to the child that I had to do it, for her sake?"

In the few weeks of my first return from exile, I had to reach many other disturbing conclusions. One was that the ravages caused by the totalitarian regime were not only in human lives, suffering and material losses. The entire moral fiber of society had been affected. Secondly, I realized how much we, the ones from the "old" country, had grown in one direction, while they, in "new"

Bulgaria,—even relatives and schoolmates—had been marching on a different course. We disagreed even on our assessment of the post-Communist "transition" period: To me, their expectations to see a prospering democracy in one or two years seemed unreasonably optimistic; considering myself more realistic, I disappointed everybody there by "wisely" predicting a much longer period, "say five years, maybe more…" (How foolish and wrong we all turned out to be!…)

Fulfillment of my exile's dreams didn't end with that first return visit. Other dreams came true when I repeated the trip the following summer. A particularly cherished one was showing the country to my wife, who accompanied me for the launching of the Bulgarian edition of *Crown of Thorns*. The elaborate affair, quite lavish by Sofia standards, was organized by monarchist leader Christo Kurteff in the restaurant on the roof of hotel *Sofia* and, in spite of the boiling heat that July day, assembled the political and cultural elite of the capital, plus a crowd of old friends, relatives, and new acquaintances. Toncho Zhechev, the publisher, introduced me and the book, and a few other speakers made extremely complimentary comments. Then Kurteff, who was also president of the "International Art Academy," awarded me its annual prize. Almost overwhelmed by emotion and overheated by the record temperature and the cameramen's flashes, I had to improvise a short speech, while Lil, standing next to me, was busy wiping the sweat running down my drenched face. It was a moment of glory such as I had never expected. Indeed, *Crown of Thorns*, printed in 207,000 copies, a record for small Bulgaria, was already selling tremendously well and the reviews were extremely favorable.

Proud and elated, I showed Lil the places where I used to live, go to school, and play in Sofia. After seeing the Rila monastery and Borovets in the Rila mountains, I took her on a brief trip, which my voluble reminiscing transformed into a sort of guided tour back in time into my childhood. Instead of the "time machines" of science fiction, I simply rented a red *Mercedes* driven by a strong, likable former bicycle champion in his fifties, Assen, who served as our chauffeur, bodyguard, and nanny. We visited old houses and Roman ruins in Plovdiv, crossed the Southern plains along miles of orchards and sunflowers in bloom and drove all the way to Bourgas and Sozopol to swim in the Black Sea. On the way back, Assen took us through the Valley of the Roses (disappointingly out of season) and to the restored Koprivshtitza, the town of my Groueff ancestors.

Back in Sofia, more thrills were in store for me. The President of the Republic, Zheliu Zhelev, after publicly and generously praising the activities in exile of our *Free Bulgarian Center*, invited Lil and me for tea in his offices, where I seized the opportunity to air some critical remarks about the new Constitution which was just being voted in the Parliament.

By that time, many people had asked me what I thought of "The Play." "Which play?" I had to ask. Then to my great surprise and no smaller concern, I learned that a theater play, based on the last chapters of my *Crown of Thorns*, was currently enjoying a considerable success on a Sofia stage. A leading Bulgarian movie star, Nevena Kokanova, and a young actor, Nikolay Kaltchev, had personally selected passages from my book and, using also lines from Queen Giovanna's Memoirs, had produced and acted in a show entitled *The Last 13 Days of the Life of King Boris.* My name figured on the posters, but not only had no one ever asked for my permission or bothered about copyright formalities, but I hadn't even been informed about the play. Not having the slightest idea how faithfully it followed my text or adulterated it, or even massacred it, I became very nervous, even after meeting the actors, whom I found extremely attractive and well-meaning. They simply considered their initiative as a gesture of high appreciation of my work, a sincere compliment that would only delight me.

On my last day in Sofia, curious and still worried, I anonymously bought three tickets and took my wife and my brother to the small *Theatre-199* on Rakovski street. Lil doesn't speak Bulgarian, but was familiar enough with my *Crown of Thorns* to be able to follow the scenes of the illness and death of King Boris. In the dark, it took me not more than five minutes as a spectator to forget all my fears as an author. The drama was staged masterfully with liturgical chants, patriotic songs, church bells, candles and other sound and visual effects, and the words—my words!—were flowing effortlessly. A few more soliloquies and dialogues, and I realized that Kokanova and Kaltchev had achieved a dramatization much better than any script I could ever had prepared for the stage.

Listening to my own prose was a thrilling experience and when I felt the public's reaction in the dark, I was overwhelmed.

The curtain fell. The lights came back. Around me, the audience was applauding, some people had tears in the eyes. The actors were taking their bows. Then Kokanova made a sign to silence the public and to my surprise (I didn't know that she had noticed my presence), she announced: "I'm happy to welcome tonight among us the author of this play." Pointing at me, she left the proscenium, walked down the alley toward my seat, took me by the hand, and led me back to the stage, while the public clapped and shouted *Author! Author!*

Lil told me later that at this moment the color of my face switched rapidly from crimson red to such white pallor, and back to blush, that she feared that I was about to suffer a stroke. Indeed, I was going through an unprecedented, most glorious apotheosis. And yet, somehow it rang a familiar bell, a vague *deja vu*, emerging from the depths of some remote past. Slowly, I recognized it. But the scene was not the *Theatre-199*, it was the festively lit stage of the Sofia National Theater; the lionized author wasn't me, it was young, timid Stefcho, the teenager hoping to be one day a successful playwright; actually, this whole glorious scene never took place in reality, it was just a fantasy, my childhood secret dream. But I recognized the sound of the clamor: *Author! Author!*, and this time it was real.

In the plane taking us back to New York, I couldn't help but muse over my homecoming's grand finale. A bittersweet exercise. What a turn in my story's plot! The orphaned refugee welcomed back with a red carpet...The former "enemy of the people" received at the Presidency of the Republic...The would-be chronicler of a forgotten nation celebrated in his liberated country...Why couldn't some of this happen earlier, before I was 69? Anyhow, for the better or for the worse, the full circle was closed. In Toncho Zhechev's metaphor, the uneven, eventful 46-year-long Odyssey was over. Ulysses was back in Ithaca.

About the Author

Stephane Groueff, a former US correspondent of *Paris-Match* magazine, was born in Sofia and graduated from the U. of Geneva. A refugee with a "Displaced Person" status, he became involved in exile activities since the Communist takeover in 1944 and didn't return to Bulgaria until 1990. He's the author of eight books in English, French, and Bulgarian. Groueff lives with his American-born wife in New York and Southampton (Long Island).

0-595-25709-7